Nikolay Andreevich Rimsky-Korsakov

ROUTLEDGE MUSIC BIBLIOGRAPHIES

RECENT TITLES

COMPOSERS

Isaac Albéniz (1998)
Walter A. Clark

William Alwyn (2012)
John C. Dressler

C. P. E. Bach (2002)
Doris Bosworth Powers

Samuel Barber, Second edition (2010) Wayne C. Wentzel

Béla Bartók, Third edition (2011)
Elliott Antokoletz and
Paolo Susanni

Vincenzo Bellini, Second edition (2009) Stephen A. Willier

Alban Berg, Second edition (2009)
Bryan R. Simms

Leonard Bernstein (2001)
Paul F. Laird

Johannes Brahms, Second edition (2011) Heather Platt

Benjamin Britten (1996)
Peter J. Hodgson

William Byrd, Third edition (2012) Richard Turbet

Elliott Carter (2000)
John L. Link

Carlos Chávez (1998)
Robert Parker

Frédéric Chopin (1999)
William Smialek

Aaron Copland (2001)
Marta Robertson and
Robin Armstrong

Frederick Delius, Second edition (2009) Mary Christison
Huismann

Gaetano Donizetti, Second edition (2009) James P. Cassaro

Edward Elgar, Second edition (2013) Christopher Kent

Gabriel Fauré, Second edition (2011) Edward R. Phillips

Alberto Ginastera (2011)
Deborah Schwartz-Kates

Christoph Willibald Gluck, Second edition (2003)
Patricia Howard

Charles François Gounod (2009)
Timothy S. Flynn

G. F. Handel, Second edition (2004) Mary Ann Parker

Paul Hindemith, Second edition (2009) Stephen Luttmann

Gustav Holst (2011)
Mary Christison Huismann

Charles Ives, Second edition (2010)
Gayle Sherwood Magee

Quincy Jones (2014)
Clarence Bernard Henry

Scott Joplin (1998)
Nancy R. Ping-Robbins

Zoltán Kodály (1998)
Mícheál Houlahan and
Philip Tacka

Franz Liszt, Third edition (2009)
Michael Saffle

Guillaume de Machaut (1995)
Lawrence Earp

Gustav and Alma Mahler (2008)
Susan M. Filler

Bohuslav Martinů (2014)
Robert Simon

Felix Mendelssohn Bartholdy, Second edition (2011)
John Michael Cooper with
Angela R. Mace

Olivier Messiaen (2008)
Vincent P. Benitez

Giovanni Pierluigi da Palestrina (2001) Clara Marvin

Giacomo Puccini (1999)
Linda B. Fairtile

Maurice Ravel (2004)
Stephen Zank

Nikolay Andreevich Rimsky-Korsakov, Second edition (2015)
Gerald Seaman

Gioachino Rossini, Second edition (2010) Denise P. Gallo

Camille Saint-Saëns (2003)
Timothy S. Flynn

Alessandro and Domenico Scarlatti (1993) Carole F. Vidali

Heinrich Schenker (2003)
Benjamin Ayotte

Alexander Scriabin (2004)
Ellon D. Carpenter

Jean Sibelius (1998)
Glenda D. Goss

Giuseppe Verdi, Second edition (2012) Gregory W. Harwood

Tomás Luis de Victoria (1998)
Eugene Casjen Cramer

Richard Wagner, Second edition (2010) Michael Saffle

Anton Webern (2016)
Darin Hoskisson

Adrian Willaert (2004)
David Michael Kidger

GENRES

American Music Librarianship
(2005) Carol June Bradley

Blues, Funk, R&B, Soul, Hip
Hop, and Rap (2010) Eddie S.
Meadows

Chamber Music, Third edition
(2010) John H. Baron

Choral Music, Second edition
(2011) Avery T. Sharp
and James Michael Floyd

Church and Worship Music
(2005) Avery T. Sharp and
James Michael Floyd

The Concerto (2006)
Stephen D. Lindeman

Ethnomusicology, Second edition
(2011) Jennifer C. Post

Jazz Scholarship and Pedagogy,
Third edition (2005)
Eddie S. Meadows

The Madrigal (2011)
Susan Lewis Hammond

The Musical, Second edition
(2011) William A. Everett

North American Fiddle Music
(2011) Drew Beisswenger

Opera, Second edition (2000)
Guy A. Marco

Piano Pedagogy (2009)
Gilles Comeau

The Recorder, Third edition
(2012)
Richard Griscom and
David Lasocki

Serial Music and Serialism (2001)
John D. Vander Weg

String Quartets, Second edition
(2011) Mara E. Parker

The Violin (2006)
Mark Katz

Women in Music, Second edition
(2011)
Karin Pendle and Melinda Boyd

NIKOLAY ANDREEVICH RIMSKY-KORSAKOV

A Research and Information Guide

Second Edition

GERALD R. SEAMAN

ROUTLEDGE MUSIC BIBLIOGRAPHIES

Routledge
Taylor & Francis Group

NEW YORK AND LONDON

Second edition published 2015
by Routledge
711 Third Avenue, New York, NY 10017

and by Routledge
2 Park Square, Milton Park, Abingdon, Oxon, OX14 4RN

First issued in paperback 2018

Routledge is an imprint of the Taylor & Francis Group, an informa business

© 2015 Taylor & Francis

The right of Gerald Seaman to be identified as author of this work has been asserted by him in accordance with sections 77 and 78 of the Copyright, Designs and Patents Act 1988.

All rights reserved. No part of this book may be reprinted or reproduced or utilized in any form or by any electronic, mechanical, or other means, now known or hereafter invented, including photocopying and recording, or in any information storage or retrieval system, without permission in writing from the publishers.

Trademark notice: Product or corporate names may be trademarks or registered trademarks, and are used only for identification and explanation without intent to infringe.

First edition published by Garland Publishing 1988

Library of Congress Cataloging-in-Publication Data
Seaman Gerald R, compiler.
 Nikolay Andreevich Rimsky-Korsakov: a research and information guide/Gerald Seaman.
  pages cm -- (Routledge music bibliographies)
 Includes bibliographical references and index.
  1. Rimsky-Korsakov, Nikolay, 1844-1908--Bibliography. I. Title. II. Series: Routledge music bibliographies.
 ML134.R57S4 2015
 016.78092--dc23
       2014025947

ISBN 13: 978-1-138-33974-3 (pbk)
ISBN 13: 978-0-415-81011-1 (hbk)

Typeset in Minion
by Exeter Premedia Services Private Ltd., Chennai, India

Contents

Preface	ix
Acknowledgments	xi
Introduction	xiii
Acronyms	xvii
Institutions named after N. A. Rimsky-Korsakov	xxi
Frequently Cited Works	xxiii
Transliteration of Russian Names	xxv
List of Abbreviations	xxvii
Rimsky-Korsakov: Genealogy	xxviii
Rimsky-Korsakov: Chronology	xxix
Rimsky-Korsakov: Sonnet by Henri Allorge	xxxv

1. Rimsky-Korsakov's Musical Works — 1

Operas	1
Other Operatic Projects	5
Works for Orchestra	5
Solo Instrument and Orchestra	15
Solo Instrument and Wind Orchestra	16
Chamber Music	17
Piano Music	20
Choral Music: Sacred	27
Choral Music: Secular	29
Vocal Works	34
Folk Song Collections	46
Arrangements, Orchestrations, and Revisions	46
Arrangements for Military Band (1873–83)	48

2. Rimsky-Korsakov's Literary Works — 49

Literary Works, Articles, Reviews, Forewords	49
Correspondence (Chronological)	54
Other References	62
Complete Collection of Compositions, Literary Works, and Correspondence	62

3. Bibliography: Musical Works — 70

Operas: General	70
Operas: Individual	91

vii

viii   Contents

Other Operatic Projects   144
Libretti   145
Performers: General   147
Performers: Individual   147
Orchestral Works: General   155
Orchestral Works: Individual   158
Solo Instrument with Orchestra   166
Chamber Works   167
Piano Works   169
Choral Works: Sacred   169
Choral Works: Secular   172
Vocal Works   173
Rimsky-Korsakov: Editor   175

4. Bibliography: General   **184**
Esthetic Credo, Ideological Interpretations   184
Archives and Museums: Resources   192
Personal Relationships   200
Biography   214
Conducting   231
Rimsky-Korsakov's Family   232
Rimsky-Korsakov and Film   234
Folk Song   235
General   239
Literary Works   255
Memoirs   261
Military Bands   273
Music Education   273
Musical Style   280
Portraits   288
Resource Materials   288
Revolution of 1905   295
Rimsky-Korsakov and the Soviet Republics   298

Index of Rimsky-Korsakov's Musical Works   **299**

Index of Rimsky-Korsakov's Literary Works   **306**

Index of Authors, Editors, Compilers, Translators, and Librettists **309**

Index of Composers and Conductors   **320**

Index of Names   **323**

Index of N. A. Rimsky-Korsakov, Life and Creativity   **325**

Subject Index   **330**

Preface

The second edition of this work, originally published in 1988, has been considerably revised and updated. Since that time many new publications about Rimsky-Korsakov have appeared, these amounting to several thousand, a number far exceeding the parameters of this volume. Each entry included, however, has been carefully selected with the aim of revealing a particular facet of the composer's work and personality. Regarding the problem of translation of Russian names, with a few minor exceptions, I have followed the system of transliteration of modern Russian as employed by the British Library. Wherever possible, Russian spellings of composers' or performers' names have been used, these being followed by the name more commonly encountered in English enclosed in square brackets. Imperial Russia adhered to the Old Style (Julian) calendar, which in the nineteenth century was 12 days behind that of the New Style (Gregorian) calendar, 13 days behind in the twentieth century, and 14 days behind in the twenty-first century. These differences are indicated by []. Cross references are provided throughout the book, these being indicated by [see No....]. A new development since the publication of the first edition has been the widespread adoption of the International Standard Book Number (ISBN) and the International Standard Serial Number (ISSN), in consequence of which more recent publications of Russian books and periodicals can be easily identified. The materials contained in this volume are drawn from many sources worldwide, including the United Kingdom, the USA, Estonia, the Russian Federation, and New Zealand.

ix

Acknowledgments

Special thanks for assistance in the writing of this book must go to the staff of the Bodleian Library, together with the Oxford University Libraries of the Faculty of Music, the Department for Continuing Education, and the Taylor Bodleian Slavonic and Modern Greek Library. I am particularly grateful to John Wagstaff, Head of the Music & Performing Arts Library, University of Illinois, Joe Lenkart of the Slavic Reference Service of the University of Illinois at Urbana-Champaign, and Professor Robert Oldani of the Arizona State University. I am also indebted to the library staff of the St. Petersburg Conservatory, the Glinka State Central Museum of Musical Culture, Moscow, the National Library of Estonia, and the library of the University of Auckland. Kind assistance has also been provided by Nick Hearn, subject consultant for French Language, Literature and Culture in the Central Bodleian and Taylor Institution. I am also thankful to Ms Susan Halstead, Curator of the Czech, Slovak and Lusatian Studies at the British Library, Dr. Stephen Muir at the University of Leeds, and Professor Michael Talbot of Liverpool University. Thanks, too, must be expressed to my Russian colleagues Professor Alexander Fiseisky of the Gnesin Institute, Professor Natalia Savkina of the Moscow Conservatory, and my editors Constance Ditzel and Denny Tek of Routledge/Taylor & Francis, New York. Most of all I must thank my remarkably patient wife, Katherine, for her meticulous and assiduous work in researching, editing, and preparing the manuscript for publication.

xi

Introduction

As was stated in the first edition of the present work, Rimsky-Korsakov was a man of many parts. Apart from his work as a prolific composer of 16 operas, and a substantial body of compositions in many other genres, he was also active as a teacher, music inspector, conductor, editor and writer, as well as leading a full and busy life within the bosom of his family. Apart from his voluminous correspondence, his *Chronicle of My Musical Life* provides a unique insight into Russian musical life in the second half of the nineteenth century and the work of the *Moguchaya Kuchka* [Mighty Handful]. His unselfish efforts in completing and arranging his colleagues' works, for which he refused any remuneration, were instrumental in bringing about their performance, thus enriching the musical world. All these manifold aspects of his work have been examined extensively by Russian and Western scholars. The current study presents a selection of these materials, originally published in 10 European languages.

Important as a starting point for any research into Rimsky-Korsakov are the substantial bibliographies by Zinaida Savelova and Tamara Livanova appearing in the journal *Sovetskaya muzyka* [Soviet Music], 3 (1933), which include numerous materials published before the Revolution, and that of Sof'ya Vil'sker published in the volume *Rimsky-Korsakov and Musical Education*, Leningrad, 1959, which contains over 800 items covering the period 1917–57. O. B. Stepanov's bibliography in Vol. 4 of the *Musical Encyclopedia*, edited by Yury Keldysh, Moscow, 1978, includes publications up to 1977, while of importance, too, are the various bibliographies of Bernandt and Yampol'sky, Startsev, Uspenskaya, Koltypina, Yagolim, and others, whose works are listed under "Resource Materials" in Part 4 of the present volume.

Statistical materials relating to the performance of Rimsky-Korsakov's operas are to be found in the *Yearbooks of the Imperial Theaters*, while further references to the composer and his work are contained in the *Bibliography of the Russian Nineteenth Century Periodical Press*, edited by Tamara Livanova. An important chronology of the composer's life is to be found in Aleksandra Orlova's and Vladimir Nikolaevich Rimsky-Korsakov's 4-volume *Pages from Rimsky-Korsakov's Life*, Leningrad, 1969–73. The publication of an abridged version of Yastrebtsëv's *Reminiscences*, translated by Florence Jonas, New York, 1985, has added a further dimension to Rimsky-Korsakov's research, while other bibliographies are to be found in standard reference works such as *Die Musik in Geschichte und Gegenwart, The New Grove Dictionary of Music and Musicians, The New Grove Dictionary of Opera*, and other international dictionaries and encyclopedias.

In the period preceding the Revolution, Vol. 39–40 of the journal *Russkaya Muzykal'naya Gazeta* [Russian Musical Gazette] (1908) was devoted entirely to the composer, while a similar task was fulfilled by Vol. 22–23 of the same journal in 1909. Other important anniversaries have been commemorated in volumes of the periodical *Sovetskaya muzyka*, in particular No. 6 (1958), marking the 50th anniversary of his death. In more recent times, many articles on Rimsky-Korsakov, often containing new

xiii

xiv   *Introduction*

and hitherto unpublished materials, have been published in the 2004 numbers of the journal *Muzykal'naya Akademiya* [Musical Academy], the continuation of *Sovetskaya muzyka*, Vol. 2 (2004), being a special issue to mark the 150th anniversary of the composer's birth.

Although the composer's voluminous correspondence has never been recorded in its entirety, the entries in the present volume provide one of the most comprehensive surveys yet made. Many of the composer's letters and other bibliographical materials are still unpublished, preserved in various archives in St. Petersburg and Moscow, although scholars are now able to investigate materials which were often previously inaccessible. Details of Rimsky-Korsakov's liturgical works are taken from Vasily Yastrebtsëv's list of compositions, from materials from the Vladimir Morosan collection of Russian sacred music in the University of Illinois and the more recent publication of *The Complete Sacred Choral Works* in 1999.

The purpose of the present volume is to list and categorize all these varying aspects of Rimsky-Korsakov's many-faceted activities. Commencing with a genealogy and brief chronology of his life, the work falls into four major sections, of which the first deals with the composer's musical compositions, including details of the time and place of composition and publication, location of principal autograph materials and the number of the work as it appears in the Soviet edition of the Complete Works: Rimsky-Korsakov, Nikolay Andreevich. *Polnoe sobranie sochineniy.* [Complete Collection of Compositions.] Moscow: Muzgiz, 1955–82. Works in the Complete Edition appearing in full score are indicated by Roman numerals, while those written in piano score are signified by Arabic numbers. The first four letters of the Russian alphabet employed in some numbers of the Complete Edition have been replaced by the English letters A, B, C, and D. It may be noted that a reprint of the 50 volumes of Rimsky-Korsakov's Complete Works, with Russian and English translations of introductions and some texts, was made by Belwin-Mills, New York, commencing in 1979, amounting, in all, to 103 volumes.

Part 2 of the work is devoted to the composer's literary works and correspondence, the letters being set out in order of publication. Letters appearing in their entirety are included in the Correspondence Section, while those consisting of extracts are listed elsewhere.

Part 3 takes the form of a bibliography of literature on the musical works, including Rimsky-Korsakov's role as an editor. In the materials relating to opera, a number of accounts of performances in the 1920s have been included, many of them taken from the journal *Zhizn' iskusstva* [Life of Art], which are interesting for the insight they provide into the style of production and performance of the period.

Part 4 is a general bibliography, covering Rimsky-Korsakov's esthetic credo, archival, and biographical materials, his part in the 1905 Revolution, memoir literature, resource materials, and other matters. The work is concluded with author and subject indexes. No attempt has been made to list the many recordings of Rimsky-Korsakov's music.

What information, therefore, can be gleaned from consulting this volume? Firstly, it can be seen that Rimsky-Korsakov's significance as an opera composer outweighs his importance in any other creative field. Secondly, he was more active as a composer of liturgical music than is generally realized and in his own time his religious musical

Introduction xv

compositions were regarded as breaking new ground in the treatment of Russian sacred chant. Thirdly, apart from his well-known work in editing and arranging the compositions of Dargomyzhsky, Borodin, and Musorgsky, it may be seen that he was responsible for the publication of a considerable amount of other music as well, and that, as advisor to the publisher Belyaev, his work as a propagandist of Russian music was of immense significance. Fourthly, despite his apparent reserve, Rimsky-Korsakov was extremely fluent with the pen. Although he rarely seems to have used the intimate 'ty' [thou] form of address outside members of his family, his writings on education and esthetics, to say nothing of his huge correspondence, bear witness to his unceasing desire for communication. Rimsky-Korsakov's significance as a teacher and professor of composition at Russia's leading conservatory was unequalled, while the importance of his influence on the young Stravinsky and countless others cannot be overestimated. Of particular interest are the various autobiographical accounts and reminiscences of the composer, a number of which are not referred to in Russian biographies.

Since the publication of the first edition of the present work in 1988, a great deal has happened, not the least being the demise of the former Soviet Union, as a result of which archival materials often inaccessible during the Soviet period are now open to scholars. Further opportunities for research have been made available through the appearance of many new Russian music periodicals, while access to international publications has been facilitated through valuable research tools such as RILM. One of the most remarkable developments in Russian research has been the increase in the investigation of sacred musical elements in Rimsky-Korsakov's work, a factor which was largely ignored during the atheistic Soviet period. Recent performances of Rimsky-Korsakov's operas have highlighted religious elements underlying specific works, of which *The Legend of the Invisible City of Kitezh and the Maiden Fevroniya* is an outstanding example. New articles on Rimsky-Korsakov have provided many details highlighting the composer's personality, such as his love of punctuality, the fact that his French was not very good and that he liked nature and astronomy. More information, too, has been revealed about the various opera projects which were contemplated but never realised, such as the operas on Russian themes *Sten'ka Razin, Dobrynya Nikitich, Il'ya Muromets*, and *The Tale of the Fisherman and the Fish* (after Pushkin), together with works based on Western-European sources including *Nausicaä* (from Homer's *Odyssey*), *The Tempest, Earth and Sky* (after Byron), and *Saul and David* (from the Bible). How these subjects might have been set can only be imagined.

Despite the abundance of materials already existing, there is no doubt, however, that research relating to Rimsky-Korsakov is far from exhausted. As stated in 1988, much uninvestigated material still lies in Russian archives, including untranslated letters, a plethora of memoirs written by his pupils, to say nothing of the many materials contained in Russian pre-revolutionary newspapers and journals. Examination of many facets of his compositional and literary work, his employment of new scales, in particular the octatonic, are only some of the aspects that offer fertile ground to the research scholar and lover of Russian music.

Gerald R. Seaman, DPhil, MA
University of Oxford, 2014.

Acronyms

RUSSIAN STATE INSTITUTIONS

GTTMB
Gosudarstvenny Tsentral'ny Teatral'ny Muzey imeni Bakhrushina, Moskva [State Central Theater Museum named after A. A. Bakhrushina, Moscow].

IRLI
Institut russkoy literatury (Pushinsky Dom) Rossiyskoy Akademii Nauk [Institute of Russian Literature (Pushkin House) of the Russian Academy of Sciences].
Formerly: *Institut russkoy literatury (Pushkinsky Dom) Akademii nauk SSR, Leningrad* [IRLI] [Institute of Russian Literature (Pushkin House) of the Academy of Sciences of the USSR, Leningrad].

KKG
Khorovaya kapella imeni M. I. Glinki [Choral Capella named after M. I. Glinka].
Formerly: *Leningradskaya gosudarstvennaya akademicheskaya kapella* [LGAK] [Leningrad State Academic Cappella].

MGK
Moskovskaya gosudarstvennaya konservatoriya imeni P. I. Chaykovskogo [Moscow State Conservatory named after P. I. Tchaikovsky].
Formerly: *Moskovskaya gosudarstvennaya konservatoriya imeni P. I. Chaykovskogo* [MGK] [Moscow State Conservatory named after P. I. Chaykovsky].

MMKG
Muzey muzykal'noy kul'tury imeni M. I. Glinki, Moskva [Museum of Musical Culture named after M. I. Glinka, Moscow]. Also known as *Vserossiyskoe muzeynoe ob'edinenie muzykal'noy kul'tury imeni M. I. Glinki* [All-Russian Museum Association of Musical Culture named after M. I. Glinka].
Formerly: *Gosudarstvenny tsentral'ny muzey muzykal'noy kul'tury imeni M. I. Glinka, Moskva* [GTSMMK] [State Central Museum of Musical Culture named after Glinka, Moscow].

RGALI
Rossiysky gosudarstvenny arkhiv literatury i iskusstva [Russian State Archive of Literature and Art].
Formerly: *Tsentral'ny gosudarstvenny arkhiv literatury i iskusstva SSSR, Moskva* [TSGALI] [Central State Archive of Literature and Art of the USSR, Moscow].

xvii

xviii *Acronyms*

RGB *Rossiyskaya gosudarstvennaya biblioteka, Moskva* [Russian State Library, Moscow].
Formerly: *Gosudarstvennaya biblioteka SSSR imeni V. I. Lenina, Moskva* [GBL] [State Library of the USSR named after V. I. Lenin, Moscow].

RNB *Rossiyskaya natsional'naya biblioteka* [Russian National Library].
Formerly: *Gosudarstvennaya publichnaya biblioteka imeni Saltykova-Shchedrina, Leningrad* [GPB] [State Public Library named after Saltykov-Shchedrin, Leningrad].

SOSPF *Zasluzhenny kollektiv Rossii Akademichesky simfonichesky orkestr Sankt-Peterburgskoy filarmonii* [Honored Collective of Russia, the Academic Symphony Orchestra of the St. Petersburg Philharmonic].
Formerly: *Leningradskaya gosudarstvennyia filarmoniya* [LGF] [Leningrad State Philharmonic].

SPBGATI *Teatral'nogo iskusstva akademiya S.-Peterburgskaya gosudarstvennaya* [St. Petersburg State Academy of Theater Art].
Formerly: *Gosudarstvenny nauchno-issledovatel'sky institut teatra, muzyki i kinematografii, Leningrad* [ITMK] [State Scientific Research Institute of Theater, Music and Cinematography, Leningrad].

SPGK *Sanktpeterburgskaya gosudarstvennaya Konservatoriya imeni N. A. Rimskogo-Korsakova* [St. Petersburg State Conservatory named after N. A. Rimsky-Korsakov].
Formerly: *Leningradskaya gosudarstvennaya Konservatoriya imeni N. A. Rimskogo-Korsakova* [LGK] [Leningrad State Conservatory named after N. A. Rimsky-Korsakov].

SPGTB *Sankt-Peterburgskaya Gosudarstvennaya Teatral'naya Biblioteka* [St. Petersburg State Theater Library].
Formerly: *Tsentral'naya muzykal'naya biblioteka pri Gosudarstvennom akademicheskom teatre opery i baleta imeni S. M. Kirova, Leningrad* [TSMB] [State Musical Library attached to the Academic Theater of Opera and Ballet named after S. M. Kirov, Leningrad].

TSGIA SPB *Tsentral'ny gosudarstvenny istorichesky arkhiv Sankt-Peterburga* [Central State Historical Archive of St. Petersburg].
Formerly: *Gosudarstvenny tsentral'ny istorichesky arkhiv Leningradskoy oblasti* [GTIALO] [State Historical Archive of the Leningrad Province].

TSNB *Tsentral'naya notnaya biblioteka gosudarstvennogo akademicheskogo Mariinskogo teatra* [Central Music Library of the State Academic Mariinsky Theater].
Formerly: *Tsentral'naya notnaya biblioteka gosudarstvennykh akademicheskikh teatrov, Leningrad* [TSNBGAT] [Central Music Library of the State Academic Theaters, Leningrad].

ADDITIONAL ACRONYMS

BL   British Library.

EIT   Ezhegodnik Imperatorskikh Teatrov [Yearbook of the Imperial Theaters].

JALS   Journal of the American Liszt Society.

JAMS   Journal of the American Musicological Society.

MA   Muzykal'naya akade miya [Musical Academy].

MGG   Die Musik in Geschichte und Gegenwart.

ML   Music & Letters.

MQ   Musical Quarterly.

MT   Musical Times.

MZ   Muzykal'naya zhizn' [Musical Life].

RILM   Répertoire International de Littérature Musicale.

RMG   Russkaya muzykal'naya Gazeta [Russian Musical Gazette].

SM   Sovetskaya muzyka [Soviet Music].

Institutions Named After N. A. Rimsky-Korsakov

ARCHIVES AND MUSEUMS

Gosudarstvenny memorial'ny dom-myzey N. A. Rimskogo-Korsakova. [State Memorial House Museum of N. A. Rimsky-Korsakov.]
Formerly: *Dom-muzey N. A. Rimskogo-Korsakova v Tikhvine.* [N. A. Rimsky-Korsakov House Museum in Tikhvin.]

Memorial'ny muzey-kvartira N. A. Rimskogo-Korsakova. [Rimsky-Korsakov Memorial Apartment Museum, St. Petersburg.]

In 1995 museums were established in Vechasha and Lyubensk, these being in the two restored dachas where Rimsky-Korsakov occasionally resided.

EDUCATIONAL INSTITUTIONS

Detskaya shkola iskusstv imeni N. A. Rimskogo-Korsakova. [Children's School of Arts named after N. A. Rimsky-Korsakov.]
Formerly: *Detsky dom muzykal'no-khudozhestvennogo vospitaniya imeni N. A. Rimskogo-Korsakova.* [Children's Home of Esthetic Education named after N. A. Rimsky-Korsakov.]

Muzykal'naya shkola imeni N. A. Rimskogo-Korsakova. [Music School named after N. A. Rimsky-Korsakov.]
Formerly: *Muzykal'naya shkola dlya vzroslykh imeni N. A. Rimskogo-Korsakova.* [Music School for Adults named after N. A. Rimsky-Korsakov.]

Sanktpeterburgskaya gosudarstvennaya Konservatoriya imeni N. A. Rimskogo-Korsakova. [St. Petersburg State Conservatory named after N. A. Rimsky-Korsakov.] [SPGK]

Srednyaya spetsial'naya muzykal'naya shkola Sankt-Peterburgskoy konservatorii imeni N. A. Rimskogo-Korsakova. [Intermediate Special School of the St. Petersburg Conservatory named after N. A. Rimsky-Korsakov.]
Formerly: *Shkola-desyatiletka pri ordena Lenina Konservatoriya imeni N. A. Rimskogo-Korsakova.* [Ten-Year School of the Order of Lenin Conservatory named after N. A. Rimsky-Korsakov.]

xxi

Frequently Cited Works

210   Rimsky-Korsakov, Nikolay Andreevich. *Letopis' moey muzykal'noy zhizni.* [Chronicle of My Musical Life.] Ed. N. N. Rimskaya-Korsakova, St. Petersburg, 1909.

211   ——. *Muzykal'nye stat'i i zametki (1869–1907). So vstupitel'noy stat'ey M. F. Gnesina. Pod redaktsiey N. Rimskoy-Korsakovoy.* [Articles and Notes on Music (1869–1907). With an introductory article by M. F. Gnesin. Edited by N. Rimskaya-Korsakova.] St. Petersburg: M. Stasyulevich, 1911. xlvi, 223 pp.

212   ——. *Osnovy orkestrovki. S partiturnymi obraztsami iz sobstvennykh sochineniy.* [Principles of Orchestration. With Examples in Score from his Own Works.] Ed. M. O. Shteynberg. Vols. I and II. Berlin, Moscow, St. Petersburg: Ros. Muz. Izd., 1913. Second edition, 1946. In No. 282: *Literary Works* III. French trans. 1914. German trans. 1922. English trans. 1922. English trans. Rimsky-Korsakov, N., *Principles of Orchestration with Music Examples Drawn from his Own Works.* Ed. M. Steinberg. Trans. E. Agate. 2 Vols. New York: Dover, London: Constable, 1964. Vol. I: 152 pp., Vol. II: 333 pp. Reprinted: 2005. ISBN-10: 0486212661. ISBN-13: 978-0486212661. Italian trans. Rimsky-Korsakov, N. A. *Principi de orchestrazione.* Trans. L. Ripanti. Milan: Rugginenti editore, 1992. 180 pp. ISBN: 8876650733.

282   ——. *Polnoe sobranie sochineniy. Literaturnye proizvedeniya i perepiska.* [Complete Collection of Compositions. Literary Works and Correspondence.] Vols. I–VIII. Moscow: Muzgiz, 1955–82.

283   Abraham, Gerald. *Studies in Russian Music: Critical Essays on the Most Important of Rimsky-Korsakov's Operas, Borodin's "Prince Igor'," Dargomizhsky's "Stone Guest," Etc.; With Chapters on Glinka, Mussorgsky, Balakirev and Tchaikovsky.* London: William Reeves, n.d. [1935]. 355 pp. Reprint: *Studies in Russian Music. Rimsky-Korsakov and His Contemporaries.* London: William Reeves, 1965. Reprint: [1935] edition. London: William Reeves, 1969. Reprint: *Studies in Russian Music. Rimsky-Korsakov and His Contemporaries.* Scholarly Press, 1976. Reprint: Reprint Services Corp., 1988. Reprint: London: Faber & Faber, 2011; 2014. ISBN-10: 0571277861. ISBN-13: 978-0571277865.

284   ——. *On Russian Music: Critical and Historical Studies of Glinka's Operas, Balakirev's Works, etc., With Chapters Dealing With Compositions by Borodin, Rimsky-Korsakov, Tchaikovsky, Mussorgsky, Glazunov, and Various Other Aspects of Russian Music.* London: William Reeves, 1939. 279 pp. Reprint: New York: Books for Libraries Press, 1970. Reprint: Native Amer Books, 1976. Reprint: Scholarly Press, 1976. Reprint: Books for Libraries, Arno Press, 1980. Reprint: Irvington Publishers, May 1982. Reprint: Reprint Services Corp., March 2013.

xxiii

xxiv   *Frequently Cited Works*

Reprint: Faber Finds, November 2013. 290 pp. ISBN-10: 0571307272. ISBN-13: 978-0571307272.

296   Asaf'ev, Boris Vladimirovich [pseud. Glebov, Igor']. *Simfonicheskie etyudy.* [Symphonic Studies.] Petrograd, 1922. Reprinted: Leningrad: Muzyka, 1970. 264 pp. Reprint of first edition, Kompozitor, 2008. English trans. David Haas, ed. *Symphonic Etudes: Portraits of Russian Operas and Ballets.* Lanbam, MD: Scarecrow Press, 2007. xxviii, 319 pp. ISBN-10: 0810860309. ISBN-13: 978-0810860308.

313   Engel', Yuly Dmitrievich. *Glazami sovremennika. Izbrannye stat'i o russkoy muzyke,1898–1918.* [In the Eyes of a Contemporary. Selected Articles on Russian Music, 1898–1918.] Ed. and comp. I. Kunin. Moscow: Sovetsky Kompozitor, 1971. 524 pp.

1180 Rimsky-Korsakov, Andrey Nikolaevich. *N. A. Rimsky-Korsakov. Zhizn' i tvorchestvo.* [N. A. Rimsky-Korsakov. Life and Work.] Vols. I–V. Moscow: Ogiz-Muzgiz, 1933–46.

1204 Yankovsky, Moisey Osipovich, ed. *Muzykal'noe nasledstvo. Rimsky-Korsakov. Issledovaniya. Materialy. Pis'ma. (V dvukh tomakh).* [Musical Legacy. Rimsky-Korsakov. Research. Materials. Letters. (In Two Volumes).] Vol. I. Moscow: Izd. Akad. Nauk SSSR, 1953. 416 pp. Vol. II. *Publikatsii i vospominaniya.* [Publications and Reminiscences.] Moscow: Izd. Akad. Nauk. SSSR, 1954. 368 pp.

1256 Asaf'ev, Boris Vladimirovich [pseud. Glebov, Igor']. *Izbrannye trudy.* [Selected Works.] 5 Vols. Moscow: Izd. Akad. Nauk SSSR, 1952–57.

1294 Kyui, Tsezar' Antonovich [Cui, César]. *Izbrannye stat'i.* [Selected Articles.] Ed. and comp. I. L. Gusin. Leningrad: Muzgiz, 1952. lxviii, 692 pp.

1435 Ginzburg, Semën L'vovich, ed. *N. A. Rimsky-Korsakov i muzykal'noe obrazovanie. Stat'i i materialy.* [N. A. Rimsky-Korsakov and Music Education. Articles and Materials.] Leningrad: Muzgiz. 1959. 327 pp.

Transliteration of Russian Names

Belyaev, Mitrofan Petrovich [Belaieff, Mitrofan].

Chaykovsky, Pëtr Il'ich [Tchaikovsky, Pyotr Ilyich].

Dyagilev, Sergey Pavlovich [Diaghilev, Serge; Diaghileff, Serge].

Kyui, Tsezar' Antonovich [Cui, César].

Musorgsky, Modest Petrovich [Mussorgsky, Modest].

Rakhmaninov, Sergey Vasil'evich [Rachmaninov, Sergey].

Shalyapin, Fëdor Ivanovich [Chaliapin, Fyodor].

Skryabin, Aleksandr Nikolaevich [Scriabin, Alexander].

Yurgenson, Pëtr Ivanovich [Jürgenson, Peter Ivanovich].

List of Abbreviations

arr.	arranged, arrangement
cols.	columns
comp(s).	compiled, compiler(s)
cond.	conductor, conducted
corr.	corrected
ed(s).	edited, editor(s)
enl.	enlarged
fs	full score
intro.	introduction
izd.	izdatel'stvo [publishing house]
orch.	orchestrated
n.d.	no date
pf	pianoforte
pseud.	pseudonym
re-orch.	re-orchestrated
rev.	revised
suppl.	supplement, supplemented
trans.	translated, translator(s)
vol(s).	volume(s)
vs	vocal score

Rimsky-Korsakov: Genealogy

Yakov Nikitich Rimsky-Korsakov, landrikhter [a country court judge] of the Ingermanland Province and Vice-Governor of St. Petersburg (exiled in 1715); married Praskov'ya Ageevna (surname unknown).

- Vladimir Yakovlevich.
- Voin Yakovlevich, Admiral, god-child of Peter the Great and favorite of Elisaveta Petrovna; married Mariya Ivanovna Neplyueva (daughter of Iv. Neplyuev, Acting Privy Councillor).

Pëtr Voinovich, Marshal of the Nobility of the Province of Novgorod; married a priest's daughter from Pskov, Avdotya Yakovlevna (surname unknown).

- Pëtr Petrovich.
- Nikolay Petrovich.
- Andrey Petrovich (1784–1862), Civil Governor of the Province of Volynsk; married Sof'ya Vasil'evna (1802–1890), daughter of Vasily Fëdorovich Skaryatin (brother of the sybarite Yakov Fëdorovich Skaryatin, who owned almost all of the Maloarkhangel'sk District of the Province of Orlov) and a domestic serf-girl (name and surname unknown) from the village of Troitsky, Maloarkhangel'sk District.
- Pavel Petrovich.

- Voin Andreevich (1822–1871), Director of the St. Petersburg Naval College from 1861.
- Nikolay Andreevich (1844–1908), married Nadezhda Nikolaevna Purgol'd (1848–1919) in 1872.

  - Mikhail [Misha] (1873–?)
  - Sof'ya [Sonya] (1875–?)
  - Andrey (1878–1940)
  - Vladimir [Volodya] (1882–1970)
  - Nadezhda [Nadya] (1884–?), married M. Shteynberg
  - Mariya [Masha] (1888–1893)
  - Slava [Slavchik] (1889–1890)

Georgy Mikhaylovich (1901–65). Andrey Vladimirovich (1910–2002).

Rimsky-Korsakov: Chronology

1844　Born 6 [18] March, Tikhvin, Province of Novgorod, son of Andrey Petrovich Rimsky-Korsakov, retired Civil Governor of Volhynia and his wife Sof'ya Vasil'evna.

1850　The beginning of an interest in music; took piano lessons with local teachers Ekaterina Unkovskaya, Olga Nikitishna, and her pupil Ol'ga Fel'.

1854–55　First attempts at composition, namely an overture and a duet "Babochka" [Butterfly] (not preserved); showed a fondness for church music and the sound of bells.

1856　Left Tikhvin for St. Petersburg with his father; entered Naval College; took piano lessons with Ulikh, a cellist.

1857–58　First visits to the opera in St. Petersburg.

1858　Heard Glinka's *A Life for the Tsar*; went to sea on a training cruise on the ship *Prokhor*, commanded by his brother Voin.

1858–59　First attempts at composition; started to make piano arrangements of orchestral and operatic fragments and songs.

1859　Began attending orchestral concerts; another voyage on the *Prokhor*; took piano lessons with Fëdor Kanille [Théodor Canillé]; founding of the Russian Music Society.

1859–60　Composed various piano pieces and commenced the writing of a Symphony in E-flat Minor.

1860　Undertook a training cruise on the ship *Vola*; ended lessons with Kanille [Canillé].

1861　Heard Glinka's *Ruslan and Lyudmila*; worked with an amateur choir in the Naval College; another cruise on the *Vola*; introduced to Balakirev by Kanille; met Cui, Musorgsky, and V. V. Stasov; continuation of the composition of the Symphony in E-flat Minor under Balakirev's aegis; brother Voin appointed Director of the St. Petersburg Naval College.

1862　Death of his father; founding of the St. Petersburg Conservatory; establishment of the Free School of Music.

1862–65　Graduated from the Naval College; took a round-the-world voyage on the clipper ship *Almaz*, visiting England, the United States, Brazil, Spain, France, and Norway; further work on the First Symphony; made sketches for others; appointed Midshipman; active letter-writer.

xxix

1865	Returned to Kronshtadt; visited the Balakirev Circle; made the acquaintance of Borodin; composition of his first song "Schchekoyu k shcheke" [Cheek to Cheek]; the First Symphony given under Balakirev at a Free Music School concert 19 [31] December; start of his career as a composer.
1866	Introduced to Lyudmila Shestakova (Glinka's sister); attended her musical gatherings; first performance of the *Overture on Themes of Three Russian Songs* at the Free Music School concert, cond. Balakirev.
1867	First performance of the *Serbian Fantasy* under Balakirev; the *Musical Picture "Sadko"* given at a Russian Music Society concert under Balakirev; in his review of the *Serbian Fantasy* Stasov coined the phrase "Moguchaya Kuchka" [the Mighty Handful].
1867–68	Visit to Russia by Berlioz; performance of the *Symphonie fantastique* and *Harold en Italie.*
1868	Appointed Lieutenant; attended Dargomyzhsky's musical gatherings; made the acquaintance of the Purgol'd sisters; met Tchaikovsky at Balakirev's apartment; commenced composition of *The Maid of Pskov*; Musorgsky began work on *Boris Godunov.*
1869	Death of Dargomyzhsky; published his first article (on Nápravník's opera *Nizhegorodtsy* in the *Sanktpeterburgskie Vedomosti*); première of *Antar*, Russian Music Society concert under Balakirev.
1870	Orchestrated Dargomyzhsky's opera *The Stone Guest.*
1871	Accepted an invitation to teach practical composition and instrumentation at the St. Petersburg Conservatory; shared an apartment with Musorgsky until 1872.
1872	*The Stone Guest* given in St. Petersburg; collective composition of the Opera-Ballet *Mlada* with Borodin, Cui, and Musorgsky; marriage to Nadezhda Purgol'd; honeymoon in Switzerland, Italy, Austria, and Poland; completed *The Maid of Pskov.*
1873	Première of *The Maid of Pskov*, Mariinsky Theater, cond. Nápravník; resigned naval commission; appointed Inspector of Naval Bands; birth of son, Mikhail; completed Third Symphony.
1874	Made his début as conductor in the première of the Third Symphony; invited to become director and conductor of the Free Music School.
1874–75	Undertook a systematic study of harmony and counterpoint, writing over 60 fugues.
1875	Composed the String Quartet in F Major; birth of his daughter, Sof'ya; gave excerpts from Bach's *St. Matthew Passion* at a Free Music School concert.

1876	Compiled the Collection *100 Russian Folksongs*, Op. 24; composed the String Sextet and Choruses Op. 16 and 18; began initial work on his *Chronicle of My Musical Life*.
1877	Completed the second version of *The Maid of Pskov*; wrote incidental music to Mey's drama of the same name.
1877–78	Commenced the editing of Glinka's operas together with Balakirev and Lyadov.
1878	Birth of his son, Andrey.
1879	Assisted Borodin in work on *Prince Igor* and in re-orchestrating the former's Second Symphony; orchestrated Musorgsky's *Persian Dances* from *Khovanshchina*; Glazunov became a pupil.
1880	Première of *May Night*, Mariinsky Theater, cond. Nápravník; composed *Skazka*; resigned from the Free Music School; began taking an increased interest in Russian folklore.
1881	Death of Musorgsky.
1882	Birth of his son, Vladimir; première of *The Snow Maiden*, Mariinsky Theater, cond. Nápravník; completed Musorgsky's *Khovanshchina*, *Songs and Dances of Death*, and other works.
1882–83	Composition of the Piano Concerto and Songs, Op. 26 and 27.
1883	Appointed Assistant Director of the Imperial Chapel under Balakirev; resigned from the Mariinsky Theater Operatic Committee due to their refusing to stage *Khovanshchina*; formation of the Belyaev Circle with regular "Friday" meetings.
1883–84	Composed sacred music.
1884	Post of Inspector of Naval Bands dissolved; birth of his daughter, Nadezhda; completed work on his *Manual of Harmony*; composed the *Simfonietta*; revised the First Symphony.
1885	Completed the editing of the Prologue and Act I of *Prince Igor*; Belyaev's Russian Symphony Concerts founded with Rimsky-Korsakov as advisor.
1886	Taught a full course in composition at the Conservatory; appeared frequently as conductor of the Russian Symphony Concerts; completed the final version of Musorgsky's *Night on Bald Mountain*; revised the Third Symphony; composed the *Fantasia on Two Russian Themes*.
1887	*Capriccio espagnol* given under the composer's baton; death of Borodin.
1888	Birth of his daughter, Mariya; premières of *Scheherazade* and the *Russian Easter Festival Overture* given at the Russian Symphony Concerts, conducted by the composer; completed *Prince Igor* with Glazunov.

xxxii   *Rimsky-Korsakov: Chronology*

1889   Wagner's *Der Ring der Nibelungen* given by Neumann's Opera Company
        in St. Petersburg; conducted concerts of Russian music with the Colonne
        Orchestra at the Paris Exposition Universelle; birth of his son, Slava [died
        1890].

1890   Conducted concerts of Russian music in Brussels; death of his mother;
        25th jubilee of his work as a composer; the beginning of a psychological
        crisis.

1892   Worked on music esthetics; articles on music education, conducting,
        and on Wagner; première of the opera *Mlada*, Mariinsky Theater, cond.
        Nápravník; composed the third versions of the *Musical Picture "Sadko"* and
        The Maid of Pskov.

1893   A substantial part of his *Chronicle* completed; death of Tchaikovsky.

1894   Resigned from the Imperial Chapel; met Bel'sky, a future librettist; moved
        to a new summer residence at Vechasha.

1895   A return of creative activity; première of *Christmas Eve*, Mariinsky Theater,
        cond. Nápravník; began work on an opera *The Barber of Baghdad* [not
        completed].

1896   Commenced work on the *Principles of Orchestration*; première of the arr.
        of Musorgsky's *Boris Godunov*, Bol'shoy Zal [Great Hall], St. Petersburg
        Conservatory, cond. Rimsky-Korsakov.

1897   Cantata *Svitezyanka* written; composed the String Quartet in G Major and
        Piano Trio in C Minor; further revision of *Antar*.

1898   Premières of the operas *Sadko*, *Mozart and Salieri* with Shalyapin [Chaliapin]
        and *Boyarynya Vera Sheloga*, Mamontov's Private Russian Opera, Moscow.

1899   Première of *The Tsar's Bride*, Mamontov's Private Opera, Moscow, cond.
        Ippolitov-Ivanov.

1900   Conducted concerts of Russian music in Brussels; resigned as conductor
        of the Russian Symphony Concerts, but continued as manager; première
        of *The Tale of Tsar Saltan*, Association of Russian Private Opera, Moscow,
        cond. Ippolitov-Ivanov; 35th jubilee of his work as a composer.

1901   Composed the Prelude-cantata *From Homer*.

1902   Premières of the operas *Servilia*, Mariinsky Theater, cond. Blumenfel'd,
        and *Kashchey the Immortal*, Association of Russian Private Opera, Moscow,
        cond. Ippolitov-Ivanov; final revision of Dargomyzhsky's *The Stone Guest*;
        contemplated setting *Nausicaä* from *The Odyssey*.

1904   Première of the opera *Pan Voevoda*, Bol'shoy Zal [Great Hall], St. Petersburg
        Conservatory, Prince Tseretelli's Private Opera, cond. Suk; made chief
        trustee of Belyaev's estate regarding concerts and publishing.

Rimsky-Korsakov: Chronology

1905   Rimsky-Korsakov's support for striking students caused his dismissal from the Conservatory, with widespread protests and resignations; performance of *Kashchey the Immortal* in the St. Petersburg Conservatory ended in a political demonstration; the Conservatory given autonomy; Glazunov appointed as Director; Rimsky-Korsakov reinstated; contemplated setting Byron's *Heaven and Earth* (taken from the Book of *Genesis*) and *Sten'ka Razin*; composed *Dubinushka*; published an article on *The Snow Maiden*; continued working on the *Principles of Orchestration*.

1906   New chapters of his *Chronicle* written; orchestrated works by Musorgsky and Borodin; made a new version of *Boris Godunov*.

1907   Première of *The Tale of the Invisible City of Kitezh*, Mariinsky Theater, cond. Blumenfel'd; conducted the Concerts Historiques Russes organized by Dyagilev [Diaghilev] in Paris; the *Manual of Harmony* published in France; a "Project for the Reorganisation of a Program of Music History and Practical Composition" drawn up by Rimsky-Korsakov and published in the journal *Russkaya Muzykal'naya Gazeta*.

1908   Problems with censorship over the opera *The Golden Cockerel* (performed posthumously on 24 September [7 October] 1909, Zimin's Opera Theater, Moscow); deterioration of his health; instrumentation of Musorgsky's vocal works, including "Night" and "Serenade" from *Songs and Dances of Death*; *The Snow Maiden* given at Opéra Comique, Paris; further work on the *Principles of Orchestration*; died 8 [21] June; buried in the Novodevich'y Cemetery, St. Petersburg.

1937   His remains transferred to the Necropolis of Masters of the Arts in the Alexander Nevsky Monastery.

Rimsky-Korsakov

Sonnet by Henri Allorge

Magicien, roi des splendeurs orientales,
Qui fais surgir d'un coup de sa baguette d'or
Des palais merveilleux, plus beaux que ceux d'Anghor,
Et d'innombrables fleurs aux milliers de pétales,
Tes rhythmes font revivre, au son clair de crotales,
Des sistres, tympanon, harpe, flûte ou kinnor,
La Perse et ses parfums, l'Inde et son Koh-i-Nor,
L'Arabe à l'oeil altier, le Turc aux mains brutales.

Tu regnes sur la Rêve et les enchantements;
Ton orchestre fait ruisseler les diamants
Sur l'éclat somptueux des brocards et des soies;
Tu ne prends pas mon coeur, mais mon oeil ébloui
De ce prestigieux mirage où tu me noies,
Pleure après cet Eden trop vite évanoui!

Magician, of the Orient's splendours you are king;
With one stroke of your golden wand you cause to soar
Such wondrous palaces as might surpass Angkor,
And countless flowers with myriad petals blossoming.
Your rhythms bring to life, to crotalum's clear ring
And sistrum, tympanum, harp, flute, and the kinnor,
Persia and its perfumes, India, its Koh-i-Noor,
The Arab, haughty-eyed; Turk, rough hands threatening.

Your orchestra sends streams of diamonds to cascade
On sumptuous luxury of silks, and of brocade;
Of dreams and all their magic spells you bear the crown.
You do not steal my heart, but my eye sheds a tear;
Dazed with the bright mirage in which you make me drown,
It mourns this Eden's loss, too swift to disappear.

Translated Susan Reynolds

This French sonnet by Henri Allorge (1878–1938) appears in a collection of verse entitled *Le Clavier des harmonies, transpositions poétiques*. Dedicated to Rimsky-Korsakov, its vivid imagery was no doubt inspired by the exotic colors of such works as *Antar* and *Sheherazade*. It was published in the journal *Russkaya muzykal'naya gazeta* [Russian Musical Gazette] No. 7 (1907) cols. 215–16.

1

Rimsky-Korsakov's Musical Works

OPERAS

1   *Pskovityanka* [The Maid of Pskov], Op. 4.

Opera in 4 acts. Libretto by the composer assisted by Stasov, Musorgsky, and Nikol'sky, based on the eponymous drama by L. Mey. Dedicated "To my dear Musical Circle."

Version 1: Date of composition: 1868–72. Première: 1 [13] January 1873, Mariinsky Theater, St. Petersburg, cond. Nápravník. Published: St. Petersburg: Bessel', 1872 (vs); *Works*: Ia, b, 1966 (fs); 29a (reduction for piano solo and duet). Autograph: RNB, TSNB, MMKG.

Version 2: Date of composition: 1868–77. Not performed.

Version 3: Date of composition: 1891–92. Final chorus revised 1898. New aria, Act III, 1898. Première: 6 [18] April 1895, Members of the Society of Musical Gatherings, Panaevsky Theater, St. Petersburg, cond. Davidov. Published: St. Petersburg: Bessel', 1894 (vs); 1895 (fs?); *Works*: Ic, d, 29b. Autograph: RNB, MMKG.

2   *Mlada*.

Ballet-opera in 4 acts. Collective work by Cui, Musorgsky, Borodin, Rimsky-Korsakov, and Minkus. Libretto by Krylov. Rimsky-Korsakov contributed mainly choruses. Date of composition: 1872. Work not performed in its entirety. Concert performance of Act I (by Cui), February 1917, Petrograd. Published: Leipzig: Belaieff, 1911 (vs).

1

3   *Mayskaya noch'. Opera v trëkh deystviyakh po povesti Gogolya* [May Night. An opera in three acts after the story by Gogol].

Libretto by the composer. Dedicated to Nadezhda Ivanovna Rimskaya-Korsakova. Date of composition: 1878–79. Première: 9 [21] January 1880, Mariinsky Theater, St. Petersburg, cond. Nápravník. Published: Hamburg: D. Rahter, 1882 (vs in German trans.); Leipzig: Belaieff, 1890 (vs); Leipzig: Belaieff, 1893 (fs); St. Petersburg: E. Goppe, 1879 (libretto); *Works*: IIa, b; 30. Autograph: SPGK (fs), RNB (vs), TSNB (other materials).

4   *Snegurochka (Vesennyaya skazka). Syuzhet zaimstvovan iz odnoimennoy p'esy A. N. Ostrovskogo. Opera v 4-kh deystviyakh s prologom* [The Snow Maiden (Spring Fairy Tale). Subject borrowed from Ostrovsky's eponymous play. Opera in 4 acts with a prologue].

Libretto by the composer.

Version 1: Date of composition: 1880–81. Première: 29 January [10 February] 1882, Mariinsky Theater, St. Petersburg, cond. Nápravník, rôle of Ded-Moroz: F. I. Stravinsky (father of Igor Stravinsky). Published: St. Petersburg: Bessel', 1881 (fs, vs). *Works*: not included. Autograph: TSNB (fs), RNB (Rimsky-Korsakov Archive No. 33a) (vs).

Version 2: Date of composition: c.1895. Première: not known. Published: St. Petersburg: Bessel', 1898 (fs, vs?); *Works*: IIIa, b; 31a, b. Autograph: location unknown.

5   *Mlada. Volshebnaya opera-balet v 4-kh deystviyakh* [Mlada. A magical opera-ballet in 4 acts].

Libretto by the composer based on materials by Gedeonov and Krylov. Date of composition: 1889–90. Première: 20 October [1 November] 1892, Mariinsky Theater, St. Petersburg, cond. Nápravník, rôle of Mstivoy: F. I. Stravinsky (father of Igor Stravinsky). Published: Leipzig: Belaieff, 1891 (fs, vs, libretto); *Works*: IVa, b; 32. Autograph: RNB, SPBGATI (Rimsky-Korsakov Archive).

6   *Noch' pered Rozhdestvom. Byl'-kolyadka iz povesti N.V. Gogolya. Opera v 4-kh deystviyakh* [The Night Before Christmas. A Christmas tale after the story by N. V. Gogol. Opera in 4 acts].

Date of composition: 1894–95. Première: 28 November [10 December] 1895, Mariinsky Theater, St. Petersburg, cond. Nápravník, rôle of Panas: F. I. Stravinsky (father of Igor Stravinsky). Published: Leipzig: Belaieff, 1895 (fs, vs, libretto); *Works*: Va, b; 33. Autograph: RNB (Rimsky-Korsakov Archive and Yastrebtsëv Archive); other materials: MMKG, RGALI, SPBGATI.

7   *Bagdadsky borodobrey* [The Barber of Baghdad].

Opera in 1 Act. Libretto by the composer. Music exists only in sketches. Date of composition: 1895. Autograph: RNB.

8   *Sadko. Opera-bylina v semi kartinakh* [Sadko. Opera-bylina in seven scenes].

Libretto by the composer and Bel'sky, with assistance from Stasov, Yastrebtsëv, Shtrup, and Findeyzen, based on the epic ballad *Sadko the Rich Merchant* and other materials. Date of composition: 1895–96. Première: 26 December 1897 [7 January 1898], Artists of the Russian Private Opera, Solodovnikov's Theater, Moscow, cond. Esposito. Published: Leipzig: Belaieff, 1897 (fs, vs); *Works*: VIa, b, c; 34. Autograph: RNB, SPBGATI (other materials). *Bylina*: a traditional Russian heroic poem.

9   *Motsart i Sal'eri. Dramaticheskie stseny A. S. Pushkina* [Mozart and Salieri. Dramatic scenes from A. S. Pushkin], Op. 48.

Opera in 1 act, 2 scenes, based almost verbatim on the eponymous play by Pushkin. The scenes were to have been connected by a fugal intermezzo, left uncompleted. Date of composition: 1897. Première: 25 November [7 December] 1898, Artists of the Private Russian Opera, Solodovnikov's Theater, Moscow, cond. Iosif Truffi, rôle of Salieri: Shalyapin. Published: Leipzig: Belaieff, 1898 (fs, vs); *Works*: VII and 35 (incl. surviving 57 bars of the intermezzo). Autograph: RNB.

10   *Boyarynya Vera Sheloga. Muzykal'no-dramatichesky prolog k drame L. Meya "Pskovityanka"* [Boyarynya Vera Sheloga. A Musical-dramatic prologue to L. Mey's drama "The Maid of Pskov"], Op. 54.

Originally composed as a prologue to the second version of *The Maid of Pskov*. Libretto by the composer after Mey. Date of composition: 1898. Première: 15 [27] December 1898, Solodovnikov's Theater, Moscow, cond. Al'tani. Published: St. Petersburg-Moscow: Bessel', 1898 (vs, libretto); *Works*: VIII, 36. Autograph: Formerly in Moscow. M. Shteynberg's possession; present location unknown.

11   *Tsarskaya nevesta. Opera v 4-kh deystviyakh. Soderzhanie zaimstvovano iz dramy L. Meya. Dopolnitel'nye stseny napisany I. Tyumenevym* [The Tsar's Bride. Opera in 4 acts. Content borrowed from the drama by L. Mey. Extra scenes written by I. Tyumenev].

Libretto by Rimsky-Korsakov and Tyumenev. Date of composition: 1898; new aria for Act III, 1899. Première: 22 October [3 November] 1899, Artists of the Russian Private Opera, Solodovnikov's Theater, Moscow, cond. Ippolitov-Ivanov. Published: Leipzig: Belaieff, 1899 (fs, vs, libretto); *Works*: IXa, b; 37. Autograph: RNB (Sobr. M. P. Belyaeva No. i/23); other materials: SPGK, RNB (Rimsky-Korsakov Archive, No. 8.g).

12   *Skazka o Tsare Saltane, o syne ego slavnom i moguchem bogatyre knyaze Gvidone Saltanoviche i o prekrasnoy Tsarevne Lebedi* [The Tale of Tsar Saltan, of his son the renowned and mighty Bogatyr Prince Gvidon Saltanovich and the beautiful Swan Princess].

Opera in 4 acts with a prologue. Libretto by Bel'sky, based on the eponymous poem by Pushkin. Date of composition: 1899–90. Première: 21 October [3 November] 1900, Artists of the Russian Private Opera, Solodovnikov's Theater, Moscow, cond. Ippolitov-Ivanov. Published: St. Petersburg: Bessel', 1900 (vs); 1901 (fs); *Works*: Xa, b; 38. Autograph: RNB, SPBGATI.

13   *Serviliya. Opera v 5 deystviyakh* [Servilia. Opera in 5 acts].

Libretto by the composer, based on the drama by Mey, to whom the work is dedicated. Date of composition: 1900–01. Première: 1 [14] October 1902, Mariinsky Theater, St. Petersburg, cond. Blumenfel'd. Published: St. Petersburg: Bessel', 1901 (vs); 1902 (fs); *Works*: XIa, b; 39. Autograph: Only partly preserved; Acts I, II, and first 4 scenes of Act V missing; other materials: RNB, SPBGATI.

14   *Kashchey bessmertny. Osennyaya skazochka. Opera v 1 deystvii (v trëkh kartinakh, bez pereryva muzyki)* [Kashchey the Immortal. An Autumn Fairy Tale. Opera in 1 act (in three scenes, without a break in the music)].

Libretto by the composer, assisted by Sofiya Nikolaevna Rimskaya-Korsakova, based on a plan by Petrovsky. Date of composition: 1901–02; conclusion rewritten 1906 (included in *Works* XII and 40). Première: 12 [25] December 1902, Association of Russian Private Opera (formerly Solodovnikov's Theater, Moscow), cond. Ippolitov-Ivanov. Published: St. Petersburg: Bessel', 1902 (fs, vs); *Works*: XII; 40. Autograph: RNB; SPBGATI.

15   *Pan Voevoda. Opera v 4-kh deystviyakh* [Pan Voevoda. Opera in 4 acts].

Libretto by Tyumenev "In memory of Frederic Chopin." Date of composition: 1902–03. Première: 3 [16] October 1904, Prince Tseretelli's Private Opera, St. Petersburg Conservatory, cond. Suk. Published: St. Petersburg: Bessel', 1904 (fs, vs); *Works*: XIIIa, b; 41. Autograph: RNB.

16   *Skazanie o nevidimom grade Kitezhe i deve Fevronii. Opera v 4-kh deystviyakh (v 6-ti kartinakh)* [The Legend of the Invisible City of Kitezh and the Maiden Fevroniya. Opera in 4 acts (in 6 scenes)].

Libretto by Bel'sky, based on old Russian legends. Date of composition: 1903–05. Première: 7 [20] February 1907, Mariinsky Theater, St. Petersburg, cond. Blumenfel'd. Published: Leipzig: Belaieff, 1906 (fs, vs); *Works*: XIVa, b, supp.; 42. [Supplementary Vol. contains a number of variants, the first group consisting of notes and appendices to the final version of the score, the second composed of miscellaneous materials.] Autograph: RNB (Rimsky-Korsakov Archive, No. 10); other materials: RGALI, SPGK, SPBGATI, MMKG.

17   *Sten'ka Razin.*

Projected opera. Libretto by Bel'sky. Music in sketches only. Date of composition: 1906. Autograph: RNB.

18   *Zemlya i nebo* [**Earth and Sky**].

Projected opera. Libretto based on Byron's Mystery "Heaven and Earth" (Genesis, Chapter VI). Music in sketches only. Date of composition: 1906. Autograph: RNB. A work of this title by M. Steinberg [Shteynberg], partly based on Rimsky-Korsakov's sketches, can be found in BL.

19   *Zolotoy petushok. Nebylitsa v litsakh. Opera v trëkh deystviyakh po skazke A. S. Pushkina* [**The Golden Cockerel. A Dramatised Fairy Tale. Opera in 3 acts based on the fairy tale by A. S. Pushkin**].

Libretto by Bel'sky. Date of composition: 1906–07. Première: 24 September [7 October] 1909, Zimin's Opera Company, Solodovnikov's Theater, Moscow, cond. Emil Cooper. Published: Moscow: Yurgenson, 1908 (fs, vs, libretto); *Works*: XVa, b, c; 43. Autograph: RNB (Rimsky-Korsakov Archive); MMKG (other materials).

OTHER OPERATIC PROJECTS

20   *Dobrynya Nitkitich.* Autograph: RNB.

21   *Navzikaya* [**Nausicaä**]. Based on Homer. Autograph: RNB.

22   *Il'ya Muromets.* Autograph: RNB.

23   *Burya* [**The Tempest**]. Scenario only.

24   *Saul i David* [**Saul and David**]. Based on the Bible; scenario only.

WORKS FOR ORCHESTRA

25   *Pervaya simfoniya* [**Symphony No. 1**], **Op. 1**.

Dedicated to Fëdor Andreevich Kanille. Exists in two versions, of which the second differs in key, order of movements, and treatment of thematic material.

Version 1: E-flat minor. Date of composition: 1861–65. Première: 19 [31] December 1865, Free Music School, St. Petersburg, cond. Balakirev. Published: Moscow: Muzgiz, 1953; *Works*: XVI. Autograph: SPGK; RNB (other materials). The *Andante* (B major) has the caption: "Na temu russkoy pesni pro 'tatarsky polon'" [On the theme of the Russian song about the "Tatar captivity"].

Version 2: E minor. Date of composition: 1884. Première: 4 [16] December 1885, Student Orchestra, University, St. Petersburg, cond. Dyutsh. Published: St. Petersburg-Moscow: Bessel', 1885; *Works*: XVI. Autograph: RNB (Rimsky-Korsakov Archive No. 42e). The *Andante tranquillo* (C major) has a slight change of caption: "Na temu pesni pro 'tatarsky polon'" [On the theme of the song about the "Tatar captivity"].

26 *Uvertura na Russkie temy* [**Overture on Russian Themes**], **Op. 28.**

Employs the folk songs "Slava" [Glory], "U vorot, vorot" [At the gates, the gates], and "Na Ivanushke chapan" [Ivan has a big coat on].

Version 1: D major. Date of composition: 1866. Première: 11 [23] December 1866, Free School of Music, St. Petersburg, cond. Balakirev. Published: Moscow: Muzgiz, 1954; *Works*: XX. Autograph: RNB, MMKG (other materials).

Version 2: *Ouverture sur des thèmes russes – Ré Majeur – pour grand orchèstre.* Dedicated "À M-r Anatole Liadow." Date of composition: 1879–80. Première: 26 April [8 May] 1880, Bol'shoy Theater, Moscow, cond. Rimsky-Korsakov. Published: Leipzig: Belaieff, 1886 (fs, also piano duet); *Works*: XX; 49b. Autograph: RNB.

27 *Fantaziya na serbskie temy* [**Fantasia on Serbian Themes**], **Op. 6.**

Dedicated to Aleksandr Porfir'evich Borodin.

Version 1: B minor. Date of composition: 1867. Première: 12 [24] May 1867, Free School of Music, St. Petersburg, cond. Balakirev. Published: St. Petersburg: Iogansen, 1870; *Works*: XIXb. Autograph: Location unknown.

Version 2: Date of composition: 1886–87. Première: Unknown. Published: Leipzig: Belaieff, 1895 (with Russian and French title: *Fantaisie sur des thèmes serbes pour orchèstre*); *Works*: XIXb. Autograph: RNB (Rimsky-Korsakov Archive).

28 *"Sadko." Muzykal'naya kartinka. Epizod iz byliny o Sadko, Novgorodskom goste* [**"Sadko." A Musical Picture. Episode from the bylina about Sadko, the Novgorod merchant**], **Op. 5.**

Dedicated to Mily Alekseevich Balakirev.

Version 1: Date of composition: 1867. Première: 9 [12] December 1867, Russian Music Society, St. Petersburg, cond. Balakirev. Published: Moscow: Muzgiz, 1951; *Works*: XIXa. Autograph: RNB (Rimsky-Korsakov Archive, No. 40).

Version 2: *Sadko, tableau musical pour orchèstre.* Date of composition: 1869. Première: 16 [28] November 1869, Free School of Music, St. Petersburg, cond. Balakirev. Published: Moscow: Yurgenson, 1870 (fs); *Works*: XIXa. Autograph: Location unknown.

Rimsky-Korsakov's Musical Works 7

Version 3: *Sadko, tableau musical pour orchèstre*. Date of composition: 1891–92. Première: 16 [28] January 1893, Second Russian Symphony Concert, St. Petersburg, cond. Glazunov. Published: Moscow: Yurgenson, 1892 (fs); 1893 (arr. for 2 pianos, 8 hands); *Works*: XIXa. Autograph: MMKG.

29   *Simfoniya h-moll* [**Symphony in B minor**].

Exists only in two variants of the first movement, together with two fragments from the *Andante* and Finale. Part of the second subject of the first movement was subsequently employed as Mizgir's aria "O lyubi menya" [O love me] in the opera *Snegurochka* [The Snow Maiden].

Date of composition: 1866–69. Published: Moscow: Muzgiz, 1970; *Works*: 50. Autograph: RNB.

30   *"Antar." Simfonicheskaya syuita (Vtoraya simfoniya)* [**"Antar." Symphonic Suite (Symphony No. 2)**], **Op. 9**.

Written at the suggestion of Balakirev and Musorgsky, and based on an Arabian tale by Senkovsky, the work employs Arab melodies taken from the collections of Salvador-Daniel and Khristianovich. Dedicated to Tsezar' Antonovich Kyui [Cui].

Version 1: Date of composition: 1868. The score is preceded by a program covering the four movements:

I. Beautiful was the desert of Sham; beautiful were the ruins of Pal'mira, a town built by evil spirits, but Antar, pride of the desert, did not fear them and proudly stood amidst the ruined city. Antar has left people for ever and has sworn to hate them, since they rewarded his good with evil... All at once a gazelle appeared, light-footed and beautiful. Antar was about to catch it, when suddenly a terrible storm arose high above and the air was darkened by a black shadow; a monstrous bird was pursuing the gazelle. In a moment Antar changed his mind. He plunged his lance into the monster, which flew away with a shriek. Almost immediately the gazelle disappeared too. Antar, left alone among the ruins, thinking about what had happened, soon fell asleep... He saw himself in a palace, where a crowd of slave girls attended him and delighted his ear. It was the abode of Princess Pal'mira, the peri Gyul' Nazar. The peri was that very gazelle whom he had saved from the pursuit of the evil spirit. In gratitude the peri promised Antar the three great delights of life, and when Antar decided to experience them, the vision disappeared and he found himself again among the ruins.

II. The first delight given to Antar by the Princess Pal'mira was the joy of vengeance.

III. The second delight was the joy of power.

IV. Again Antar found himself in the ruins of Pal'mira. The third and final delight was the joy of love. Antar begged the peri to take his life away as soon as she noticed in him the slightest sign of cooling and she swore to do this. When one day, after long mutual happiness, the peri noticed that he was absent-minded and was gazing thoughtfully into the distance, she straightaway guessed the reason. Then she passionately embraced Antar, her ardour flew like a spark to his heart... and the peri with a final kiss joined Antar's soul with her own and he fell asleep forever on her bosom.

Version 2: *"Antar." Ilya simfoniya dlya orkestra... (Syuzhet iz arabskoy skazki Senkovskogo)* ["Antar." Second Symphony for Orchestra... (Subject from the Arabian tale by Senkovsky)]. Date of composition: 1875. Première: 10 [22] January 1876, Russian Music Society, St. Petersburg, cond. Rimsky-Korsakov. Published: St. Petersburg: Bessel', 1880 (fs, also piano duet), first publication of "Antar" during the composer's lifetime. *Works*: Not included. Autograph: RNB.

Version 3: Definitive and most authoritative version. Frequently performed during the composer's lifetime, but not published until 1913. 1913 edition: *"Antar." Simfonicheskaya syuita (Vtoraya simfoniya)* ["Antar." Symphonic Suite (Second Symphony)]. Date of composition: 1897. Published: St. Petersburg: Bessel', 1913 (fs); 1921 (arr. piano solo); *Works*: XVIIa. Autograph: RNB.

Version 4: A variant of the Second Version of 1875. Date of composition: 1903. Published: St. Petersburg: Bessel', 1903; *Works*: XVIIb. Autograph: RNB.

31   ***Tret'ya simfoniya*** [**Symphony No. 3**], **Op. 32**.

Version 1: C major. Date of composition: 1866–73. Première: 18 February [2 March] 1876, Salle de la Noblesse [Hall of the Nobility], St. Petersburg, cond. Rimsky-Korsakov. Published: Moscow: Muzgiz, 1959; *Works*: XVIII. Autograph: RNB (Rimsky-Korsakov Archive, No. 35a).

Version 2: *3me Symphonie en Ut majeur pour Orchèstre* [3rd Symphony in C major for Orchestra]. Date of composition: 1886. Première: 29 October [10 November] 1886, Third Russian Symphony Concert, St. Petersburg, cond. Rimsky-Korsakov. Published: Leipzig: Belaieff, 1888; *Works*: XVIII. Autograph: RNB.

32   ***Uvertyura i antrakty k drame L. Meya "Pskovityanka" (na temu opery "Pskovityanka")*** [**Overture and Entr'actes to L. Mey's Drama "The Maid of Pskov" (on the theme of the opera "The Maid of Pskov")**].

Suite consisting of an Overture and four Entr'actes, reworked by Rimsky-Korsakov using some of the materials from the revision of his opera *The Maid of Pskov* (second version), with which he was dissatisfied. Dedicated to Anatoly Konstantinovich Lyadov.

Version 1: Date of composition: 1877. Published: Moscow-Leningrad: Muzgiz, 1951; *Works*: XIXb. Autograph: RNB (Rimsky-Korsakov Archive).

Version 2: Date of composition: 1881–82. Further changes introduced. Première: 5 [17] February 1883, in its definitive form. Published: St. Petersburg: Bessel', [no date]. Score of the Suite published by Bessel', and also that published by Breitkopf & Härtel, differs from that printed in *Works* XIXb, primarily in the Overture, which is almost identical with that of the Overture to the opera *Boyarynya Vera Sheloga* [see *Works* VIII]. In the score published by Bessel', contents are given as *Ouverture du prologue*, Entr'acte 1: "Olga," Entr'acte 2: "Vetsche. On attend l'arrivée d'Ivan le Terrible," and Entr'acte 4: "Le couvent de Petschera. Le Saint Nicolas." Reduction for piano duet published: St. Petersburg: Bessel', c.1911.

33 *Skazka* [A Fairy Tale], Op. 29.

Originally entitled "Baba-Yaga," the work is preceded by the opening lines of the Prologue to Pushkin's poem *Ruslan and Lyudmila*, although, as the composer has observed, there is no specific musical representation of particular events. The dedication to Aleksandr Konstantinovich Glazunov appears only in the published score, the autograph being dedicated to Semën Nikolaevich Kruglikov.

Key: D minor–D major. Date of composition: 1879–80. Première: 10 [22] January 1881, Russian Music Society, St. Petersburg, cond. Rimsky-Korsakov. Published: Leipzig: Belaieff, 1886 (with Russian and French title: *Conte féerique pour grand orchèstre*) (fs, also piano duet arr. by the composer); *Works*: XX; 49b. Autograph: MMKG.

34 *Simfonietta* [Sinfonietta], Op. 31.

Dedicated to Georgy Ottonovich Dyutsh. A reworking of the first three movements of an unpublished string quartet of 1878–79 [see No. 64].

Key: A minor. Date of composition: 1879–84. Première: 17 [29] November 1884, Russian Music Society, St. Petersburg, cond. Rimsky-Korsakov. Published: Leipzig: Belaieff, 1887 (fs, Russian and French title: *Symphoniette (en la mineur) sur des thèmes russes pour orchèstre*); 1888 (arr. for piano duet by Artsybushev).

35 *Eskiz skertso dlya chetvërtoy simfonii* [Sketch of a Scherzo for a Fourth Symphony] (*Rondo Scherzando*).

Rimsky-Korsakov's proposed Fourth Symphony survives only in the form of a sketch in piano score of a single Scherzo movement, containing details of orchestration, structure, and dynamics. On the first page of the autograph are written the words "4th Symphony, Rondo Scherzando," followed by the phrase "Rondo 2oy formy" [Rondo 2nd form].

Key: D minor. Date of composition: 15–19 [27–31] August 1884 at Taitsy. Published: Moscow: Muzgiz, 1970; *Works*: 50. Autograph: RNB.

36 *Capriccio espagnol. Kaprichchio na ispanskie temy* [Spanish Caprice. Capriccio on Spanish Themes], Op. 34.

Intended originally as a virtuoso fantasia on Spanish themes for violin, instead the *Capriccio espagnol* became a sparkling work for orchestra, abounding in brilliant colors, vital rhythms, and scintillating orchestral effects. At its first rehearsal, so great was the applause from members of the St. Petersburg Russian Opera Orchestra that Rimsky-Korsakov dedicated the work to them.

Key: A major. Date of composition: 1887. Première: 31 October [12 November] 1887, Russian Symphony Concert, St. Petersburg, cond. Rimsky-Korsakov. Published: Leipzig: Belaieff, 1887 (reduction for piano duet); 1888 (fs, French title: *Capriccio espagnol pour grand orchèstre*); *Works*: XXI; 49b. Autograph: RNB.

37 *Malorossiyskaya fantaziya* [Little-Russian Fantasia].

Intended as an orchestral work utilizing Little-Russian [Ukrainian] folk themes, this exists only in the form of piano sketches and 129 bars of orchestral score.

Date of composition: 1887. Published: Moscow: Muzgiz, 1970; *Works*: 50. Autograph: RNB.

38 *Shekherazada. Simfonicheskaya syuita po 1001 nochi* [Scheherazade. Symphonic Suite after the 1001 Nights], Op. 35.

One of the most successful of all Rimsky-Korsakov's works, the title page of the autograph reads: "À monsieur Wladimir Stassoff. 'Chehérazade'. Suite symphonique (d'après 1001 nuits) pour grande orchèstre par N. Rimsky-Korsakow. 'Shekherazada'. Simfonicheskaya syuita (po 1001 nochi) dlya orkestra N. Rimskogo-Korsakova, soch. 35 (ork. partitura) I Prelude, II Ballade, III Nocturne, IV Finale et Postludium." The names of the movements are struck out.

On the following page is set out the program of *Scheherazade*, which differs from that printed in the published score: "Sultan Shakhriar, convinced of the perfidy and faithlessness of women, has vowed to execute each of his wives after the first night [the words 'On the next day after the wedding' are crossed out in the autograph]; but the Sultana Shekherazada saved her life by the fact that she was able to occupy him with her stories, which she told him over 1001 nights, so that, roused by curiosity Shakhriar continually put off her execution and finally completely abandoned his intention. Many wonders Shekherazada told him of Sinbad's voyages at sea, of the wandering Kalender princes, of the knights turned into stone, of the great bird Rul, of the evil genii, of the pleasures and amusements of the eastern rulers, of the ship dashed to pieces on the magnetic rock with the bronze horseman and much else, quoting the verses of poets and the words of songs, weaving story into story and tale into tale." Following the account of the program are written

Rimsky-Korsakov's Musical Works

the words: "N. B. The composer has not kept to a line by line reproduction of any one tale in particular, recommending the listener to find out those pictures to which the program refers."

In a letter to Glazunov dated 7 July 1888, the composer reiterated that the work had no specific program ["osoboy programmy ne budet"], that the first movement was a Prélude (E major), the second a narrative ("Rasskaz") (B minor), the third a Rêverie (G major) and the fourth "an Eastern festival, a dance, in a word a kind of Baghdad carnival (!) (E minor–E major)."

Scheherazade's international success stems from its performance in Brussels under the composer's baton on 18 March 1900 when it was given at the Fifth Russian Symphony Concert at the Théâtre de la Monnaie. It was staged as a ballet in Paris in 1910 at the Grande Opéra as part of Dyagilev's [Diaghilev's] celebrated season.

Key: E minor–E major. Date of composition: 1888. Première: 28 October [9 November] 1888, First Russian Symphony Concert, St. Petersburg, cond. Rimsky-Korakov. Published: Leipzig: Belaieff, 1889 (fs, with Russian and French title: *Schéhérazade d'après "Mille et une nuits." Suite symphonique pour orchèstre*); *Works*: XXII; 49b (arr. for piano duet by the composer). Autograph: RNB.

39   **Svetly prazdnik. Voskresnaya uvertyura na temy iz Obikhoda** [Joyous Festival. Easter Overture on Themes from the Obikhod], **Op. 36**.

Dedicated to the memory of Borodin and Musorgsky. The score is prefaced with the following lines: "Let God arise, let his enemies be scattered: let them also that hate him flee before him. As smoke is driven away, so drive them away: as wax melteth before the fire, so let the wicked perish at the presence of God." Psalm of David 67 [Protestant numeration: Psalm 68].

"And when the sabbath was past, Mary Magdalene, the mother of James, and Salome, had brought sweet spices, that they might come and anoint him. And very early in the morning the very first day of the week, they came unto the sepulchre at the rising of the sun. And they said among themselves, Who shall roll us away the stone from the door of the sepulchre? And when they looked, they saw that the stone was rolled away: for it was very great. And entering into the sepulchre, they saw a young man sitting on the right side, clothed in a long white garment; and they were affrighted. And he saith unto them, Be not affrighted: Ye seek Jesus of Nazareth, which was crucified: he is risen." Gospel according to St. Mark, Chapter 16.

"And the joyous tidings flew round the whole world; and those that hated him ran from his face, vanishing as smoke vanishes."

"Christ is risen from the dead!" sing the angelic hosts in heaven with cherubims and seraphims.

"Christ is risen from the dead!" sing the priests in the smoke of incense, in the glitter of innumerable candles and the sound of bells.

Key: B minor. Date of composition: 1888. Première: 3 [15] December 1888, Third Russian Symphony Concert, St. Petersburg, cond. Rimsky-Korsakov. Published: Leipzig: Belaieff, 1890 (fs, with Russian and French title: *La Grande pâque russe. Ouverture sur des thèmes de l'église russe pour grand orchèstre*, Op. 36); *Works*: XXI; 49b (arr. for piano duet by the composer). Autograph: RNB, SPBGATI (other materials).

40   *Snegurochka. Syuita iz opery* [**The Snow Maiden. Suite from the Opera**].

Introduction.
Dance of the Birds.
Procession of Tsar Berendey.
Dance of the Skomorokhi [Dance of the Tumblers].
Date of composition: c.1890. Published: St. Petersburg: Bessel', c.1895.

41   *Noch' na gore Triglave (tret'ye deystvie opery-baleta). Kontsertnoe perelozhenie dlya odnogo orkestra* [**Night on Mount Triglav (Third Act of the Opera-ballet** [*Mlada*]**). Concert arrangement for orchestra alone**].

The second of two versions of Act III of the opera *Mlada*, arranged for conventional symphony orchestra, omitting the exotic instruments demanded in the earlier version (two panpipes, alto flute, E-flat and D clarinets, twelve "corni o tube non cromatici" with crooks of different lengths to be played by "military musicians" onstage, as well as six French horns in the orchestra, three harps, eight to ten lyres, and a backstage organ). The autograph consists of two manuscripts, one written by Rimsky-Korsakov, the other by V. Kalafati, although with Rimsky's editorial comments. The score differs in a number of respects from that published by Belyaev [Belaieff] in 1902: *Nuit sur le Mont Triglav. Troisième acte de l'Opera-Ballet de N. Rimsky-Korsakow. Arrangement pour execution de concert, orchèstre seul, par l'auteur. Partition d'orchèstre.* Preceded by a program, the work is divided into five scenes. Not performed during the composer's lifetime.

Key: B major. Date of composition: 1899–1901. Published: Moscow: Muzgiz, 1959; *Works*: V, Suppl. Autograph: SPBGATI; other materials: RNB.

42   *Tema i 4-ya variatsiya iz "Variatsii na russkuyu temu"* [**Theme and Fourth Variation from "Variations on a Russian Theme"**].

Part of a collective work on the Russian folk song "Uzh ty pole moë" [O my Field], suggested by Rimsky-Korsakov's wife, Nadezhda. Written, together with Artsybushev, Vitols, Lyadov, Sokolov, and Glazunov, in 1901 to mark Galkin's tenth anniversary as a conductor at the Pavlovsk Vauxhall, a popular concert venue near St. Petersburg, at which he frequently played the Nationalists' compositions. Dedicated to N. V. Galkin.

Key: F major. Date of composition: 1901. Première: 4 [17] July 1901, Pavlovsk, cond. N. V. Galkin. Published: Leipzig: Belaieff, 1903; *Works*: XXIII. Autograph: MMKG.

43   *Muzykal'nye kartinki k Skazke o Tsare Saltane. Syuita dlya orkestra* [**Musical Pictures from the Tale of Tsar Saltan. Suite for Orchestra**], **Op. 57.**

The Tsar's Farewell and Departure (Introduction to Act I of the opera).
The Tsarina in a Barrel at Sea (Introduction to Act II).
The Three Wonders (Introduction to Act IV, Scene 2).

Date of composition: c.1901. Published: St. Petersburg: Bessel', 1901? (fs, with Russian and German title: *Musikalische Bilder zum Märchen von dem Zaren Saltan. Suite für Orchester, Op. 57. Partitur*); c.1905 (arr. for piano solo, piano duet).

44   *Mlada, Syuita iz opera* [**Mlada. Suite from the Opera**].

Introduction.
Redowa: A Bohemian Dance.
Lithuanian Dance.
Indian Dance.
Cortège: Procession of the Nobles [Procession of the Princes].

Date of composition: 1903. Published: Leipzig: Belaieff, 1895 (with Russian and French title: *Suite pour orchèstre tirée de l'opera-ballet Mlada. Partition*). Autograph: RNB [?].

45   *Noch' pered Rozhdestvom. Syuita iz opery* [**The Night Before Christmas. Suite from the Opera**].

Introduction.
Tableaux VI and VII.
Polonaise.
Tableau VIII.

Date of composition: 1903. Published: Leipzig: Belaieff, 1904 (with Russian and French title: *Suite de l'opéra "La Nuit de Noël" d'après Gogol'. Tableaux musicaux mouvants pour orchèstre (avec choeur ad libitum). Partition d'orchèstre* [Suite from the opera "The Night before Christmas" after Gogol. Moving Musical Pictures for Orchestra (with chorus ad libitum). Score for Orchestra]).

46   *Pan Voevoda: Syuita iz opery* [**Pan Voevoda. Suite from the Opera**], **Op. 59.**

Introduction.
Krakowiak.
Nocturne "Moonlight."

Mazurka.
Polonaise.
Date of composition: 1903–04. Published: Bessel' [?], Belaieff [?], c.1904.

47 **Nad mogiloy. Prelyudiya [On the Tomb. Prelude], Op. 61.**

Written in memory of the publisher Mitrofan Petrovich Belyaev. In his *Chronicle* Rimsky-Korsakov states that in this work he used *panikhida* themes [themes from the Mass for the Dead], taken from the *Obikhod* [the collection of chants used in the Russian liturgical year], together with an imitation of the monastery funeral knell, which he recalled from his childhood days in Tikhvin.

Key: B-flat minor. Date of composition: 1904. Première: 19 February [2 March] 1904, Russian Symphony Concert, St. Petersburg, cond. Rimsky-Korsakov. Published: Leipzig: Belaieff, 1905 (fs); *Works*: XXIII; 49b (arr. for piano duet by the composer). Autograph: Location unknown.

48 **Dubinushka. Russkaya pesnya [Dubinushka (The Little Oak Stick). A Russian Song], Op. 62.**

Version 1: *Dubinushka. Russkaya pesnya* [Dubinushka. A Russian Song] (67 bars). B-flat minor. Date of composition: 1905. Première: 5 [14] November 1905, Symphony Concert, St. Petersburg, cond. Ziloti. Published: Moscow: Muzgiz, 1966; *Works*: XXII. Autograph: SPBGATI.

Version 2: *Dubinushka. Russkaya pesnya* [Dubinushka. A Russian Song] for Orchestra and Chorus *ad libitum* (189 bars). A-flat major. Date of composition: 1906. Première: Unknown. Published: Leipzig: Belaieff, 1907 (fs, with Russian and French title: *Chanson russe pour orchèstre avec choeur ad libitum. Partition d'orchèstre*); *Works*: XXIII; 49b (arr. for piano duet). Autograph: RNB.

49 **Zdravitsa A. K. Glazunovu [Toast to A. K. Glazunov].**

Written to mark Glazunov's 25th anniversary as a composer, 1907.

Key: E-flat major. Date of composition: 1906. Première: 27 January [8 February] 1907, Jubilee Concert, St. Petersburg, cond. Rimsky-Korsakov. Published: Moscow: Muzgiz, 1966; *Works*: XXIII. Autograph: RNB; SPGK.

50 **Neapolitanskaya pesenka [Neapolitan Song], Op. 63.**

Orchestral arrangement of Denza's "Funiculi, funicula." On hearing it performed, the composer was dissatisfied. It was never published. Two variants of the score survive.

Key: C major. Date of composition: 1907. Première: At a rehearsal in 1907. Published: Moscow: Muzgiz, 1966; *Works*: XXIII; 49b. Autograph: RNB.

51 **Zolotoy petushok. Vvedenie i Svadebnoe shestvie** [The Golden Cockerel. Introduction and Wedding Procession].

Concert arrangement of two numbers from the opera. Following a suggestion made by Rimsky-Korsakov in a letter to B. P. Yurgenson in 1908, the frequently performed 4-movement concert suite was arranged by A. Glazunov and M. Shteynberg after the composer's death.

Date of composition: 1907. Published: Moscow: Yurgenson, c.1908 (fs); Moscow-Leipzig: P. Yurgenson, 1908 (arr. for piano solo entitled: *Introduction et Cortège de noces. Edition de concert...Pour piano seul*).

52 **Skazka o rybake i o rybke** [The Tale of the Fisherman and the Fish].

Projected symphonic poem, based on Pushkin's story. The music exists only in sketches.

Date of composition: 1907. Autograph: Unknown.

53 **Skazanie o nevidimom grade Kitezhe i deve Fevronii. Syuita iz opery** [The Legend of the Invisible City of Kitezh and the Maiden Fevroniya. Suite from the Opera].

Prelude: A Hymn to Nature.
Wedding Procession – Tatar Invasion.
Battle of Kerzhenets.
Apotheosis of Fevroniya.

Date of composition: c.1907. Published: Leipzig: Belaieff, c.1909.

SOLO INSTRUMENT AND ORCHESTRA

54 **Kontsert dlya fortepiano s orkestrom** [Concerto for piano and orchestra], **Op. 30**.

Autograph bears the inscription: "À François Liszt. Hommage respectueux de l'auteur. Concerto (cis moll) pour le piano avec accompagnement d'orchèstre. Composé par Nicolas Rimsky-Korsakov."

Key: C-sharp minor. Date of composition: 1882–83. Première: 27 February [10 March] 1884, Free Music School, St. Petersburg, soloist N. Lavrov, cond. Balakirev. Published: Leipzig: Belaieff, 1886 (fs); *Works*: XXVI; 48 (arr. for 2 pianos). Autograph: RNB; SPBGATI.

55 **Kontsertnaya fantaziya na russkie temy dlya skripki s orkestrom** [Concert Fantasia on Russian Themes for violin and orchestra], **Op. 33**.

Utilizes the Russian folk song "Nadoeli nochi, da nadoskuchili" [I am tired of the nights, so tired] in the *Lento* section, while bars 5–6 of the melody are used in the Introduction. The fast sections and cadences are based on the folk song "Khodila mladëshen'ka po borochku" [A young girl was walking in the forest]. Dedicated to P. A. Krasnokutsky.

Key: B minor. Date of composition: 1886–87. Première: 5 [17] December 1887, Fifth Russian Symphony Concert, St. Petersburg, soloist Krasnokutsky, cond. Rimsky-Korsakov. Published: Leipzig: Belaieff, 1887 (fs, with French title: *Fantaisie de concert, Si mineur, pour violon et orchèstre sur des thèmes russes, Op. 33*); *Works*: XXV; 48 (arr. for violin and piano). Autograph: Missing.

56   *Mazurka na polskie narodnye temy dlya skripki s orkestrom* [Mazurka on Polish Folk Themes for violin and orchestra].

Based on Polish themes sung to Rimsky-Korsakov by his mother and used later in the opera *Pan Voevoda*. The inscription on the title page of the score reads: "Souvenir des trois thèmes de masurka par N. Rimsky-Korsakow pour violon solo et orchèstre. Partition." Title of the autograph of the composer's arrangement for violin and piano reads: "Souvenir des trois chants polonais. Mazurka pour violon et orchèstre. N. Rimsky-Korsakow, 1889." The score differs from the piano arrangement in a number of details.

Date of composition: 1888. Not performed during the composer's lifetime. Published: *SM* 11, 1949 (Music Suppl.); Moscow: Muzyka, 1964 (fs); *Works*: XXVI: 48 (arr. for violin and piano). Autograph: SPBGATI.

57   *Serenada dlya violoncheli s orkestrom* [Serenade for cello and orchestra], Op. 37.

Orchestral arrangement of the original Serenade for cello and piano, written in 1893 [see No. 71]. Orchestrated in 1903. Autograph of title page reads: "À mon fils André. Sérénade pour Violoncelle avec accompagnement d'orchèstre par Nicolas Rimsky-Korsakov, Op. 37."

Key: B-flat major. Date of composition: 1903. Première: Unknown. Published: Moscow: Muzgiz, 1964 (fs); *Works*: XXVI; 48 (arr. for cello and piano). Autograph: RNB, SPBGATI (other materials).

SOLO INSTRUMENT AND WIND ORCHESTRA

58   *Konsert dlya trombona s dukhovym orkestrom* [Concerto for trombone with wind orchestra].

Key: B-flat major. Date of composition: 1877. Première: 16 [29] March 1878, Kronshtadt, St. Petersburg, soloist Warrant-officer Leonov, cond. Rimsky-Korsakov. Published: Moscow-Leningrad: Muzgiz, 1950; *Works*: XXV. Autograph: Missing.

Rimsky-Korsakov's Musical Works   *17*

59   *Variatsii dlya goboya s dukhovym orkestrom* [Variations for oboe with wind orchestra].

Variations on the theme of Glinka's song "Chto krasotka molodaya" [Wherefore doth the beauteous maiden], consisting of the theme, 12 variations and finale.

Key: G minor. Date of composition: 1878. First performed: 16 [28] March 1878, Kronshtadt, St. Petersburg, soloist Warrant-officer Ranishevsky, cond. Rimsky-Korsakov. Published: Moscow-Leningrad: Muzgiz, 1950. Autograph: Formerly in the possession of M. Shteynberg.

60   *Kontsert dlya klarneta s dukhovym orkestrom* [Concerto for clarinet with wind orchestra].

When heard in rehearsal, Rimsky-Korsakov was dissatisfied. Never publicly performed.

Key: E-flat major. Date of composition: 1878. Published: Moscow-Leningrad: Muzgiz, 1950; *Works*: XXV. Autograph: SOSPF.

CHAMBER MUSIC

61   *Strunny kvartet. F-dur* [String Quartet in F major], Op. 12.

Date of composition: 1875. Première: 11 [23] November 1875, Moscow, L. Auer, I. Pikkel', I. Veykman, K. Davydov. Published: Moscow: Yurgenson, c.1875; *Works*: 27. Autograph: Missing.

62   *Sekstet dlya dvukh skripok, dvukh al'tov i dvukh violoncheley* [Sextet for two violins, two violas and two cellos].

Key: A major. Date of composition: 1876. Première: 14 [26] January 1878, St. Petersburg, L. Auer, I. Pikkel', I. Veykman, K. Davydov, A. Egorov, A. Kuznetsov. Published: Moscow: Rossiyskoe Muz. Izd., 1912; *Works*: 27. Autograph: Missing.

63   *Kvintet dlya fortepiano i dukhovykh instrumentov* [Quintet for piano and wind instruments].

For flute, clarinet, horn, bassoon, and piano. Key: B-flat major. Date of composition: 1876. Première: 1876. Published: Leipzig: Belaieff, 1911; *Works*: 28a. Autograph: Missing.

64   *Strunny kvartet na russkie temy. Fuga "V monastyre"* [String Quartet on Russian Themes. Fugue "In the Monastery"].

As Rimsky-Korsakov states in his *Chronicle*, the work originally consisted of four movements, the first three subsequently being reworked to become the *Sinfonietta*, Op. 31. Although it was previously thought that the first three movements were lost, an autograph manuscript in short score entitled

"Sinfonietta" [see No. 34], bearing Rimsky-Korsakov's initials, and previously in the possession of Aaron Rubinstein, cousin of Anton and Nikolay Rubinstein, was auctioned in 2008 by Christie's. At the end is the inscription "Dedicated to G. O. Diutsh," Taitsy, 30 May 1884. The last movement, a fugue based on the church chant "Prepodobny otche, imya rek, moli boga za nas" [Reverend father, (name of the person in question), pray to God for us], was arranged as the piano duet "In Church" (1879). The chant was also used as part of the sixth scene of the opera *Sadko* at the entrance of the "Apparition" [St. Nicolas].

Key: B minor. Date of composition: 1878–79. Not performed. Published: Moscow: Muzgiz, 1955; Works: 27 (4th mvt. only); 49b. Autograph: SPGK (Finale).

65   *Chetyre variatsii na khoral dlya strunnogo kvarteta* [**Four Variations on a Chorale for string quartet**].

Written during Rimsky-Korsakov's time as a teacher at the Imperial Chapel, 1883–94.

Key: G minor. Date of composition: 1885. Published: Moscow: Muzgiz, 1955; *Works*: 27. Autograph: KKG.

66   *Strunny kvartet na temu B-la-F. Pervaya chast'* [**String Quartet on the Theme B-la-F. First movement**].

Written as a tribute to the publisher and philanthropist Mitrofan Petrovich Belyaev on the occasion of his Name-day (the Saint's day after which one was named, considered in pre-revolutionary Russia to be more important than one's birthday). A collective work, in which Rimsky-Korsakov contributed the first movement, *Sostenuto assai et Allegro*, each occurrence of the notes bearing Belyaev's name being marked in the score. Other movements by Lyadov [*Scherzo*], Borodin [*Serenade*], and Glazunov [*Finale*].

Key: B-flat major. Date of composition: 1886. Première: 2 [14] December 1887, St. Petersburg Chamber Music Society, St. Petersburg, performers E. K. Al'brekht (violin), Khille (violin), Gil'debrandt (viola), Verzhbilovich (cello). Published: Leipzig: Belaieff, 1887; *Works*: 27; 49b (arr. for piano duet). Autograph: RNB.

67   *Khorovod iz strunnogo kvarteta "Imeniny"* [**Khorovod from the String Quartet "Name-day" ("Jour de Fête")**].

Rimsky-Korsakov composed only the finale of this collaborative 3-movement work, dedicated to M. P. Belyaev. Other contributors were Glazunov: "Slavil'shchiki" [Carol-singers], and Lyadov: "Velichan'e" [Songs of Praise].

Key: D major. Date of composition: 1887. Published: Leipzig: Belaieff, 1889; *Works*: 27. Autograph: RNB.

Rimsky-Korsakov's Musical Works

68   *Notturno dlya chetyrëkh valtorn* [Nocturne for four horns].

Published in three forms, corresponding to the surviving materials.

Key: F major. Date of composition: c.1888. Published: Moscow: Muzgiz, 1955; *Works*: 27. Autograph: RNB (Rimsky-Korsakov Archive, No. 121e); other materials formerly in the possession of M.F. Gnesin.

69   *Dva dueta dlya dvukh valtorn* [Two Duets for two horns].

Written during Rimsky-Korsakov's time as a teacher at the Imperial Chapel, 1883–94.

Key: F major. Date of composition: c.1883–94. Published: Moscow: Muzgiz, 1955; *Works*: 27. Autograph: RNB (Glazunov Archive).

70   *Canzonetta e tarantella dlya dvukh klarnetov* [Canzonetta and Tarantella for two clarinets].

Written during Rimsky-Korsakov's time as a teacher at the Imperial Chapel, 1883–94.

Key: A minor-A-flat major. Date of composition: c.1883–94. Published: Moscow: Muzgiz, 1955; *Works*: 27. Autograph: RNB (Glazunov Archive).

71   *Serenada dlya violoncheli i fortepiano* [Serenade for cello and piano], Op. 37.

Key: B-flat major. Date of composition: 1893. Published: Leipzig: Belaieff, 1895; *Works*: 48. Autograph: SPBGATI. Arr. for cello and orchestra, 1903 [see No. 57].

72   *Trio dlya fortepiano, skripki i violoncheli* [Trio for piano, violin and cello].

Only the outer movements were finished by Rimsky-Korsakov, other movements being completed by M. Shteynberg, the composer's son-in-law, 1936–39.

Key: C minor. Date of composition: 1897. Première: 19 April 1939, Rimsky-Korsakov's flat, St. Petersburg, M. Shteynberg (piano), V. Rimsky-Korsakov (violin), B. Burlakov (cello). Published: Moscow: Muzyka, 1970; *Works*: 28b. Autograph: RNB.

73   *Strunny kvartet. G-dur* [String Quartet in G major].

Having completed this work, Rimsky-Korsakov became dissatisfied with it, deciding that chamber music was not his métier.

Date of composition: 1897. Not performed. Published: Moscow: Muzgiz, 1955; *Works*: 27. Autograph: RNB (Rimsky-Korsakov Archive, Nos. 29 and 30b).

20   *Nikolay Andreevich Rimsky-Korsakov: A Research and Information Guide*

74   ***Tema i 4-ya variatsiya iz "Variatsii na russkuyu temu" dlya strunnogo kvarteta*** [**Theme and Fourth Variation from "Variations on a Russian Theme" for string quartet**].

Dedicated to Mitrofan Petrovich Belyaev. Part of a collective composition by Rimsky-Korsakov, Artsybushev, Skryabin [Scriabin], Glazunov, Lyadov, Vitols, Blumenfel'd, Eval'd, Vinkler, and Sokolov on the Russian theme "Nadoeli nochi, nadoskuchili" [I am tired of the nights, so tired].

Key: G major. Date of composition: 1898. Published: Leipzig: Belaieff, 1899; *Works*: 27. Autograph: RNB.

75   ***Allegro iz sbornika "Pyatnitsy" dlya strunnogo kvarteta*** [**Allegro from the Collection "The Frídays" ("Les Vendredis") for string quartet**].

A collective work, the first movement written by Rimsky-Korsakov, other contributors being Lyadov, Borodin, Sokolov, Glazunov, and Kopylov.

Key: B-flat major. Date of composition: 1899. Published: Leipzig: Belaieff, 1899; *Works*: 27. Autograph: Missing.

PIANO MUSIC

76   ***Overture.***

Incomplete, mentioned in the *Chronicle of My Musical Life* [see No. 210], date of composition: c.1855.

77   ***Allegro in D minor.***

Mentioned in the *Chronicle*, date of composition: 1859–60.

78   ***Variations on a Russian Theme.***

Mentioned in the *Chronicle*, date of composition: 1859–60.

79   ***Nocturne in B-flat minor.***

Mentioned in the *Chronicle*, date of composition: c.1860.

80   ***Funeral March in D minor.***

Mentioned in the *Chronicle*, date of composition: c.1860.

81   ***Scherzo in C minor for Piano Duet.***

Mentioned in the *Chronicle*, date of composition: c.1860.

82   ***Fantaziya na serbskie temy*** [**Fantasia on Serbian Themes**], **Op. 6**.

Arrangement for piano duet of the first version of the orchestral work [see No. 27].

Key: B minor. Date of composition: c.1870 [?]. Published: St. Petersburg: Iogansen, date [?]; Leipzig: Belaieff, 1895; *Works*: 49b. Autograph: Missing.

Rimsky-Korsakov's Musical Works 21

83   *Chetyrëkhgolosnaya fuga* [Four-Part Fugue].

Piano solo; preserved in a notebook entitled "Contrapuntal Exercises."

Key: C major. Date of composition: 1875. Published: Moscow: Muzgiz, 1959; *Works*: 49a. Autograph: RNB (Rimsky-Korsakov Archive, No. 31).

84   *Dve trëkhgolosnye fugi* [Two Three-Part Fugues].

Fugue 1: G major. Date in autograph: "10 May 1875. Peterburg." Date of composition: 1875. Published: Moscow: Muzgiz, 1959; *Works*: 49a. Autograph: RNB.

Fugue 2: F major. Date in autograph: "19 June." Date of composition: 1875. Published: St. Petersburg: Bessel', c.1875; *Works*: 49a; also in Op. 17 [No. 2]. Autograph: RNB.

85   *Tri trëkhgolosnye fugi* [Three Three-Part Fugues].

Fugue 1: E major. Date in autograph: "9 August 1875. On the steamer." Date of composition: 1875. Published: St. Petersburg: Bessel', c.1875; *Works*: 49a; also in Op. 17 [No. 4]. Autograph: RNB.

Fugue 2: A major. Date in autograph: "11 August 1875. On the steamer." Date of composition: 1875. Published: St. Petersburg: Bessel', c.1875; *Works*: 49a; also in Op. 17 [No. 5]. Autograph: RNB.

Fugue 3: D minor. Date in autograph: "14 August 1875. Ostrovki." Date of composition: 1875. Published: St. Petersburg: Bessel', c.1875; *Works*: 49a; also in Op. 17 [No. 1]. Autograph: RNB; other materials in MMKG.

86   *Trëkhgolosnaya fuga* [Three-Part Fugue].

A note in the autograph reads: "Three-part fugue, written on a single theme with Lyadov."

Key: D major. Date in autograph: "17-27 August." Date of composition: 1875. Published: Moscow: Muzgiz, 1959; *Works*: 49a. Autograph: RNB.

87   *Trëkhgolosnaya fuga. Variant predydushchey fugi* [**Three-Part Fugue. Variant of the preceding fugue**].

A note in the autograph states: "Fugue (the same, shortened to 45 bars)" [actually 44 bars].

Key: D major. Date in autograph: "10 September." Date of composition: 1875. Published: Moscow: Muzgiz, 1959; *Works*: 49a. Autograph: RNB.

88   *Tri fugetty na russkie temy* [**Three Fughettas on Russian Themes**].

Date of composition: 1875. Published: Moscow: Muzgiz, 1959; *Works*: 49a. Autograph: RNB.

Chetyrëkhgolosnaya [4-part]: G minor. Written on the theme: "Matushka chto vo pole pyl'no" [Mother, it's dusty in the field], printed in the Appendix of *Works* 49a [p. 176]. Also included in Rimsky-Korsakov's *Sbornik russkikh narodnykh pesen* [Collection of Russian Folk Songs], No. 91. Date in autograph: "23 August."

Chetyrëkhgolosnaya [4-part]: D minor. Written on the theme: "Ne bylo vetru" [There was no wind], printed in the Appendix of *Works* 49a [p. 176]. Also included in Balakirev's *Sbornik russkikh narodnykh pesen* [Collection of Russian Folk Songs], No. 1. Date in autograph: "23-27 August."

Trëkhgolosnaya [3-part]: G minor. Written on the theme "Kak po sadu, sadu sadiku" [How in the garden, the garden], printed in the Appendix of *Works* 49a [p. 176]. Also included in the Collection: *40 narodnykh pesen, sobrannykh T. I. Filippovym i garmonizovannykh N. A. Rimskim-Korsakovym* [40 Folk Songs collected by T. I. Filippov and harmonised by N. A. Rimsky-Korsakov], No. 28. Date in autograph: "28 August."

89 **Tri chetyrëkhgolosnye fugi [Three Four-Part Fugues].**

Fuga [Fugue]: C major. Date in autograph: "29 August 1875. Ostrovki." Date of composition: 1875. Published: St. Petersburg: Bessel', c.1875; *Works*: 49a; also in Op. 17 [No. 4]. Autograph: RNB, MMKG (other materials).

Dvoynaya fuga [Double fugue]: E minor. Date in autograph: "1 October 1875. Ostrovki." Date of composition: 1875. Published: St. Petersburg: Bessel', c.1875; *Works*: 49a; also in Op. 17 [No. 6]. Autograph: RNB, MMKG (other materials).

Dvoynaya (BACH) [Double (fugue) (BACH)]: G minor. Date in autograph: "8 October 1875. Peterburg," on the notes B-A-C-H. Date of composition: 1875. Published: Moscow: Muzgiz, 1959; *Works*: 49a. Autograph: RNB.

90 **Shest' fug [Six Fugues], Op. 17.**

Only individual numbers are published in *Works* 49a, not the complete set.

Nos. 1 in D minor, 2 in F major, 3 in C major, and 6 in E minor: Date of composition: 1875. Published: St. Petersburg: Bessel', c.1875; Autograph: RNB, MMKG (other materials).

Nos. 4 in E major and 5 in A major: Date of composition: 1875. Published: St. Petersburg: Bessel', c.1875; Autograph: RNB.

91 **Val's, Romans i Fuga [Waltz, Song and Fugue], Op. 15.**

Dedicated to Nadezhda Nikolaevna Rimskaya-Korsakova.

Val's [Waltz]: C-sharp major. Date of composition: 1875–76. Published: St. Petersburg: Bessel', c.1880; *Works*: 49a. Autograph: Missing.

Romans [Song]: A-flat major. Date of composition: 1875–76. Published: St. Petersburg: Bessel', c.1880; *Works*: 49a. Autograph: Missing.

Fuga [Fugue]: C-sharp minor. Date in autograph: "27 June 1875. Ostrovki." Date of composition: 1875. Published: St. Petersburg: Bessel', c.1880; *Works*: 49a. Autograph: RNB (Rimsky-Korsakov Archive, No. 31).

Rimsky-Korsakov's Musical Works

92   *Trëkhgolosnaya fuga* [Three-Part Fugue].

Key: G minor. Date in autograph: "8 January 1876. Peterburg." Published: Moscow: Muzgiz, 1959; *Works*: 49a. Autograph: RNB.

93   *Ekspromt, Noveletta, Skertsino, Etyud* [Impromptu, Novelette, Scherzino, Etude], Op. 11.

Dedicated to Pëtr Adamovich Shostakovsky. Date of composition: 1876–77. Published: St. Petersburg: Büttner, 1878; *Works*: 49a. Autograph: Missing.

94   *Shest' variatsii na temu B-A-C-H dlya fortepiano* [Six Variations on the Theme B-A-C-H for Piano], Op. 10.

Dedicated to Anatoly Konstantinovich Lyadov. Consists of five movements and a fugue.

Val's [Waltz]: B-flat major.
Intermetstso [Intermezzo]: B-flat major.
Skertso [Scherzo]: F major.
Noktyurn [Nocturne]: B-flat major.
Prelyudiya [Prelude]: B minor, Attacca.
Fuga na temu I. S. Bakha [Fugue on the theme of J. S. Bach]: G minor.

Date of composition: 1878. Published: St. Petersburg: Büttner, 1880; Leipzig: Belaieff, 1890; *Works*: 49a. Autograph: Missing.

95   *Parafrazy. 24 variatsii i 15 p'es na neizmenyaemuyu izvestnuyu temu... posvyashchayutsya malen'kimi pianistam, sposobym igrat' temu odnim pal'tsem kazhdoy ruki* [Paraphrases. 24 variations and 15 pieces on an unchanged well-known theme... dedicated to young pianists able to play the theme with one finger of each hand].

The idea of writing variations on the theme of "Tati-tati" or "Chopsticks" greatly appealed to Rimsky-Korsakov and his friends. Rimsky-Korsakov himself wrote variations 1, 2, 6, 11, 12, 13, 16, and 19, and the pieces *Cradle Song, Little Fugue on B-A-C-H, Tarantella, Menuet, Carillon,* and *Comic Fugue,* other contributions being by Borodin, Cui, and Lyadov. The second edition, published by Belaieff in 1893, differs from the first, containing additional pieces by Liszt, Borodin, Shcherbachëv, and Rimsky-Korsakov. Some sketches written by Cui and Lyadov for *Paraphrases,* but not published in it, are preserved in the Rimsky-Korsakov and Cui Archives in RNB, and also included in *Works*: 49a Appendix. The *Cradle Song* is based on the children's folk song "Idët koza rogataya" [There goes a goat with horns].

Kolybel'naya [Cradle Song]: C major.
Malen'kaya fuga B-A-C-H [Little Fugue on B-A-C-H]: C major.
Tarantella: C major.
Menuet: C major.
Trezvon [Carillon]: C major.

Komicheskaya fuga [Comic Fugue]: C major.

Date of composition: 1878. Published: St. Petersburg: Büttner, 1880; Leipzig: Belaieff, 1893; *Works*: 49a. Autograph: Missing.

96   *Muzykal'noe pis'mo* [**Musical Letter**].

A musical letter written by Rimsky-Korsakov on a postcard sent to Lyadov in 1878, consisting of an exotic harmonization of the *Paraphrases* theme. The harmonization was later used by the composer in Variation XVI of *Paraphrases*.

Date of composition: 1878. Published: *Muzykal'ny sovremennik*, 7 (1916): 37; *Works*: 49a. Autograph: RNB (Rimsky-Korsakov Archive, No. 223a).

97   *Fuga: "V monastyre"* [**Fugue: "In the Monastery"**].

Rimsky-Korsakov's arrangement for piano duet of the last movement of his *String Quartet on Russian Themes* [see No. 64]. On the first page of the manuscript of the arrangement the title "In the Monastery" has been crossed out and replaced with the words "In Church."

Date of composition: 1879 [?]. Published: Moscow: Muzgiz, 1966; *Works*: 49b. Autograph: RNB.

98   *Variatsii na temu Mishi* [**Variations on a Theme by Misha**].

Written for piano, 3 hands, on a theme provided by Rimsky-Korsakov's eldest son, Mikhail [Misha].

Key: C major. Date of composition: 1879. Published: Moscow: Muzgiz, 1959; *Works*: 49a. Autograph: SPBGATI.

99   *Skazka* [**A Fairy Tale**], **Op. 29**.

Rimsky-Korsakov's arrangement for piano duet of the orchestral work *Skazka* [see No. 33].

Key: D minor–D major. Date of composition: c.1880. Published: Leipzig: Belaieff, 1886; *Works*: 49b. Autograph: RNB.

100   *Uvertura na Russkie temy* [**Overture on Russian Themes**], **Op. 28**.

Rimsky-Korsakov's arrangement for piano duet of the second version of the orchestral work *Uvertura na Russkie temy* [see No. 26].

Key: D major. Date of composition: 1882. Published: Leipzig: Belaieff, 1886; *Works*: 49b. Autograph: RNB.

101   *Strunny kvartet na temu B-la-f. Pervaya chast'* [**String Quartet on the Theme B-la-F. First movement**].

Rimsky-Korsakov's arrangement for piano duet of the last movement of the collective quartet on the theme B-la-F [see No. 66].

Key: B-flat major. Date of composition: 1887. Published: Leipzig: Belaieff, 1887; *Works*: 49b. Autograph: RNB.

102 **Capriccio espagnol. Kaprichchio na ispanskie temy [Spanish Caprice. Capriccio on Spanish Themes], Op. 34.**

Rimsky-Korsakov's arrangement for piano duet of the orchestral work *Capriccio espagnol* [see No. 36].

Key: A major. Date of composition: 1887. Published: Leipzig, Belaieff, 1887; *Works*: 49b. Autograph: RNB.

103 **Shekherazada. Simfonicheskaya syuita po 1001 nochi [Scheherazade. Symphonic Suite after the 1001 nights], Op. 35.**

Rimsky-Korsakov's arrangement for piano duet of the orchestral work *Shekherazada* [see No. 38].

Key: E minor–E major. Date of composition: 1888–89. Published: Leipzig, Belaieff, 1889; *Works*: 49b. Autograph: Missing.

104 **Shutka, kadril'. Finale [Finale from Joke-quadrille].**

A collective composition for piano duet consisting of five movements by Artsybushëv ("Pantalon"), Vitols ("Eté"), Lyadov ("Poule"), Sokolov ("Trénis"), and Glazunov ("Pastourelle"), together with a Finale by Rimsky-Korsakov.

Key: C major. Date of composition: 1890. Published: Leipzig, Belaieff, 1891; *Works*: 49a. Autograph: RNB.

105 **Allegretto.**

Key: C major. Date of composition: 1895. Published: Moscow: Muzgiz, 1959; *Works*: 49a. Autograph: RNB (N. I. Abramychev Archive, No. 103).

106 **Prelyudiya [Prelude].**

Key: G major. Date of composition: 1896. Published: Moscow: Muzgiz, 1959; *Works*: 49a. Autograph: RNB (Rimsky-Korsakov Archive, No. 21).

107 **Prelyudiya-ekspromt, Mazurka [Prelude-Impromptu, Mazurka], Op. 38.**

Prelyudiya-ekspromt [Prelude-Impromptu], Op. 38, No. 1: A-flat major. Date of composition: 1896. Published: St. Petersburg: Bessel', 1896; *Works*: 49a. Autograph: Missing.

Mazurka, Op. 38, No. 2: F-sharp minor. Date of composition: 1896–97. Published: St. Petersburg: Bessel', 1897 [?]; *Works*: 49a. Autograph: Missing.

The Prelude-Impromptu was written in 1896 to mark the 25th anniversary of the firm of Bessel'. As part of the celebrations, Bessel' published a collection of pieces entitled: "À la mémoire de Jubilé 1869-1894. Album russe. Recueil de pièces pour piano. 1. Artcibouscheff N. Mazurka. 2. Cui César.

Impromptu-caprice. 3. Glasounow A. Barcarolle. 4. Liadow A. Prélude-Pastorale. 5. Rimsky-Korsakow, N. Prélude-Impromptu. 6. Sokolow N. Prélude." Rimsky-Korsakov's *Mazurka* was added in a later edition (1897?) as No. 5a.

108   *Intermetststo-fugetta* [**Intermezzo-fughetta**].

Rimsky-Korsakov's arrangement for piano duet of the uncompleted fugal intermezzo linking the two scenes of the opera *Mozart and Salieri* [see No. 9].

Key: G minor. Date of composition: c.1897. Published: Moscow-Leningrad: Muzgiz, 1950. *Works*: 35. Autograph: RNB.

109   *Variations sur un thème russe tiré du recueil populaire d'Abramitscheff* [**Variations on a Russian Theme taken from Abramychev's Folk Song Collection**], **Theme and First Variation**.

Dedicated to Nikolay Ivanovich Abramychev. A collective work written by Rimsky-Korsakov, Vinkler, Blumenfel'd, Sokolov, Vitols, Lyadov, and Glazunov based on the theme "Malen'ky mal'chishechko" [Little Boy], taken from Abramychev's folk song collection. Rimsky-Korsakov provided the theme and first variation.

Key: A major. Date of composition: 1899. Published: Leipzig: Belaieff, 1900; *Works*: 49a. Autograph: RNB.

110   *Pesenka (v doriyskom ladu)* [**Little Song (in the Dorian Mode)**].

Composed in 1901 for a volume in memory of I. K. Ayvazovsky. Subsequently reprinted in a literary-musical album "Artsunker" [Tears], published in the Armenian language [St. Petersburg, 1907], and issued in aid of the Armenian famine.

Key: E minor. Date of composition: 1901. Published: St. Petersburg: Bessel', 1903; *Works*: 49a. Autograph: Missing.

111   *Nad mogiloy. Prelyudiya* [**At the Grave. Prelude**], **Op. 61**.

Rimsky-Korsakov's arrangement for piano duet of the orchestral work *Nad mogiloy* [see No. 47]. On the first page of the autograph is written: "'Nad mogiloy'. Sur la tombe. Am Grabe. Praeludium. N. Rimsky-Korsakov, Op. 58, 1904." The opus number, it seems, was changed by the composer on publication.

Key: B-flat minor. Date of composition: c.1904. Published: Leipzig: Belaieff, 1905; *Works*: 49b. Autograph: RNB.

112   *Dubinushka. Russkaya pesnya* [**Dubinushka (The Little Oak Stick). Russian Song**].

Rimsky-Korsakov's arrangement for piano duet of the second version of the orchestral work *Dubinushka* [see No. 48].

Date of composition: 1906–07. Published: Leipzig: Belaieff, 1907; *Works*: 49b. Autograph: RNB.

113   ***Neapolitanskaya pesenka* [Neapolitan Song], Op. 63**.

Rimsky-Korsakov's arrangement for piano duet of the orchestral work *Neapolitanskaya pesenka* [see No. 50].

Key: C major. Date of composition: c.1907. Published: Moscow: Muzgiz, 1966. *Works*: 49b. Autograph: RNB.

CHORAL MUSIC: SACRED

114   ***Tebe Boga khvalim* [We Praise Thee, O God]**.

For double chorus; arranged by Rimsky-Korsakov from the "Greek chant" Tone [Glas] III.

Date of composition: 1883. Published: St. Petersburg: Bessel', 1883; Imperial Chapel, 1893.

115   ***Sobranie dukhovno-muzykal'nykh sochineniy, zaklyuchayushchee v sebe 8 numerov iz "Liturgii sv. Ioana Zlatousta"* [Collection of Sacred-Musical Works, including 8 numbers from the "Liturgy of St. John Chrysostom"], Op. 22**.

For four-part mixed chorus *a cappella*.

Kheruvimskaya [Cherubic Hymn No. 1].
Kheruvimskaya [Cherubic Hymn No. 2].
Veruyu [I Believe].
Milost' mira [A Mercy of Peace].
Tebe poëm [We Praise Thee].
Dostoyno est' [It is Truly Fitting].
Otche nash [Our Father].
Voskresny prichastny stikh ("Khvalite Gospoda s nebes") [Sunday Communion hymn ("Praise the Lord from the Heavens")].

Date of composition: 1883. Published: St. Petersburg: Imperial Chapel, 1884.

116   ***Sobranie dukhovno-muzykal'nykh perelozheniy* [Collection of Sacred-Musical Arrangements], Op. 22b**.

For 4-part mixed chorus *a cappella*.
Kheruvimskaya pesnya [Cherubic Hymn].
Da molchit vsyakaya plot' chelovecha [Let All Mortal Flesh Keep Silent].
Voskresny prichastny stikh [Sunday Communion hymn].
Se zhenikh gryadet [Behold the Bridegroom Comes].
Chertog tvoy vizhdu, Spase Moy [I Enter Thy Mansion, My Saviour].
Psalma: "Na rekakh Vavilonskikh" [Psalm: By the Waters of Babylon].

28   *Nikolay Andreevich Rimsky-Korsakov: A Research and Information Guide*

Date of composition: 1884. Published: St. Petersburg: S. Shmidt, 1885.

117   ***Sobranie dukhovno-muzykal'nykh sochineniy i perelozheniy N. A. Rimskogo-Korsakova. Dlya smeshannogo khora. Izdanie pod redaktsiey E. S. Azeev* [Collection of Sacred-Musical Compositions and Arrangements by N. A. Rimsky-Korsakov. For mixed chorus. Ed. E. S. Azeev].**

A collection of works and arrangements written during Rimsky-Korsakov's time at the Imperial Chapel, found after his death.

    i.   *Kto est' sey Tsar' slavy?* [Who Is This King of Glory?]. First performed at the Consecration of the Temple of Christ the Saviour in Moscow, 1883.

    ii.   *Krestu Tvoemu* [Before Thy Cross]. Kiev chant arrangement.

    iii.   *Kheruvimskaya pesn', No. 4* [Cherubic Hymn, No. 4].

    iv.   *Kheruvimskaya pesn', No. 5* [Cherubic Hymn, No. 5].

    v.   *Kheruvimskaya pesn', No. 6* [Cherubic Hymn, No. 6].

    vi.   *Tebe poëm, No. 2* [We Praise Thee, No. 2].

    vii.   *Tebe poëm, No. 3* [We Praise Thee, No. 3].

    viii.   *Tebe poëm, No. 4* [We Praise Thee, No. 4].

    ix.   *Tebe poëm, No. 5 (Perelozh. s Kievsk. rospeva)* [We Praise Thee, No. 5 (Arrangement from the Kiev chant)].

    x.   *Tebe poëm, No. 6 (Perelozh. s. Kievsk. rospeva)* [We Praise Thee, No. 6 (Arrangement from the Kiev chant)].

    xi.   *Dostoyno est, No. 2* [It is Truly Fitting, No. 2].

    xii.   *Khvalite Gospoda s nebes* [Praise the Lord from the Heavens]. For double chorus.

    xiiia.   *Khvalite Gospoda s nebes, No. 1 (Prichastny stikh No. 1 v Voskresen'e. Perelozhenie)* [Praise the Lord from the Heavens, No. 1 (Communion Hymn No. 1 for Sunday. Arrangement)].

    xiiib.   *Khvalite Gospoda s nebes, No. 2 (Prichastny stikh No. 1 v Voskresen'e. Perelozhenie)* [Praise the Lord from the Heavens, No. 2 (Communion Hymn No. 1 for Sunday. Arrangement)].

    xiv.   *Tvoryay Angely svoya dukha (Prichastny stikh No. 2 v ponedel'nik. Perelozhenie)* [Thou Makest Thine Angels Spirits (Communion Hymn No. 2 for Monday. Arrangement)].

    xv.   *V pamyat' vechnuyu (Prichastny stikh No. 3 vo vtornik. Perelozhenie)* [The Memory of the Righteous (Communion hymn No. 3 for Tuesday. Arrangement)].

    xvi.   *Chashu spaseniya (Prichastny stikh No. 4 v sredu. Perelozhenie)* [The Chalice of Salvation (Communion Hymn No. 4 for Wednesday. Arrangement)].

    xvii.   *Vo vsyu zemlyu (Prichastny stikh No. 5. V chetverg. Perelozhenie)* [To all the Earth Gone Out (Communion Hymn No. 5 for Thursday. Arrangement)].

Rimsky-Korsakov's Musical Works 29

xviii. *Spasenie sodelal esi (Prichastny stikh No. 6 v pyatok. Perelozhenie)* [You Have Created Salvation (Communion hymn No. 6 for Friday. Arrangement)].

xixa. *Raduytesya pravednii, No. 1 (Prichastny stikh No. 7 v subbotu. Perelozhenie)* [Rejoice in the Lord, O You Righteous, No. 1 (Communion Hymn No. 7 for Saturday. Arrangement)].

xixb. *Raduytesya pravednii, No. 2 (Prichastny stikh No. 7 v subbotu. Perelozhenie)* [Rejoice in the Lord, O You Righteous, No. 2 (Communion Hymn No. 7 for Saturday. Arrangement)].

xx. *Znamenasya na nas svet litsa (Prichasten na Vozdvizhenie kresta. Perelozhenie)* [Bestow on Us the Light of Your Countenance (Communion for the Exaltation of the Cross. Arrangement)].

xxi. *Vzyde Bog (Prichasten na Voznesenie Gospodne. Sochinenie)* [Arise O God (Communion for the Ascension of Our Lord. Composition)].

xxii. *Dogmatik 1-go Glasa. Vsemirnuyu slavu. Perelozh. demestvenno, s bol'sh. Znamennogo Rosp.* [Dogmatik of the First Mode. Glory to the Whole World. Arrangement of a Demestvenny Chant from the Great Znamenny].

xxiii. *Irmosy Kanona na Utreni v Velikuyu Subbotu (Volnoyu morskoyu). Znamennogo rospeva* [Irmos of the Canon for Matins on Easter Saturday (Beneath the Waves of the Sea). Znamenny Chant].

Date of composition: 1883–84. Published: St. Petersburg: Akkord, not earlier than 1913.

CHORAL MUSIC: SECULAR

118 **Dva trëkh-golosnykh zhenskikh khora na slova M. Yu. Lermontova [Two Three-Part Women's Choruses to Words by M. Yu. Lermontov], Op. 13.**

Tuchki nebesnye [Heavenly storm clouds]. Key: D major. Date of composition: 1874. Published: St. Petersburg: Büttner, 1875; Reprinted: Belaieff; *Works*: 46b. Autograph: Missing.

Nochevala tuchka zolotaya [The golden cloud had gone to rest]. Key: E minor. Date of composition: 1874. Published: St. Petersburg: Büttner, 1875; Reprinted: Belaieff; *Works*: 46b. Autograph: Missing.

119 **Chetyre variatsii i fugetta na temu russkoy pesni "Nadoeli nochi" dlya chetyrëkh-golosnogo zhenskogo khora [Four Variations and Fughetta on the theme of the Russian song "Nadoeli nochi" (I am tired of the nights) for four-part women's chorus], Op. 14.**

Melody borrowed from Balakirev's *Collection of Russian Folk Songs*.

Key: B-flat major. Date of composition: 1875. Published: St. Petersburg: Büttner, 1875; Reprinted: Belaieff; *Works*: 46b. Autograph: Missing.

30   *Nikolay Andreevich Rimsky-Korsakov: A Research and Information Guide*

120   *Shest' khorov* [**Six Choruses**], **Op. 16**.

For unaccompanied voices. The autograph has the caption: "Piano [Harmonium] ad libitum." Dedicated to Nadezhda Nikolaevna Rimskaya-Korsakova.

Set I:

Na severe dikom [In the wild north], for 4-part mixed choir, text by Lermontov. Key: A minor. Date of composition: 1875. Published: St. Petersburg: Bessel', 1876; *Works*: 46b. Autograph: MMKG.

Vakhicheskaya pesnya [Bacchic song], for 4-part male voice choir, text by Pushkin. Key: F major. Date of composition: 1875. Published: St. Petersburg: Bessel', 1876; *Works*: 46b. Autograph: MMKG.

Staraya pesnya: Iz lesov dremuchikh severnykh [An old song: From the dense northern forests], for 8-part mixed choir, text by Kol'tsov. Key: F minor. Date of composition: 1876. Published: St. Petersburg: Bessel', 1876; *Works*: 46b. Autograph: MMKG.

Set II:

Mesyats plivët i tikh i spokoen [The moon sails quietly and peacefully], for 4-part mixed choir, text by Lermontov. Key: G minor. Date of composition: 1876. Published: St. Petersburg: Bessel', 1876; *Works*: 46b. Autograph: MMKG.

Poslednyaya tucha razseyannoy buri [The last cloud of the scattered storm], for 4-part women's choir, text by Pushkin. Key: E major. Date of composition: 1876. Published: St. Petersburg: Bessel', 1876; *Works*: 46b. Autograph: MMKG.

Molitva: Vladyko dney moikh [A prayer: Rule my days], for multi-voice mixed chorus, text by Pushkin. Key: D minor. Date of composition: 1875. Published: St. Petersburg: Bessel', 1876; *Works*: 46b. Autograph: MMKG.

121   *Dva khora* [**Two Choruses**], **Op. 18**.

Published by Bessel' in 1877 as "Op. 22," with the caption: "Six choruses, which gained a prize at a Competition held by the St. Petersburg Branch of the Russian Music Society." When reprinted by Bessel' in 1887, they were designated as Op. 18.

Pred raspyat'em [Before the Cross], for 5-part mixed choir, subtitled: "Fuga v miksolidiyskom lade" [Fugue in the Mixolydian mode], text by A. Kol'tsov. Date of composition: 1876. Published: St. Petersburg: Bessel', 1876; Reprinted: Bessel', 1887; *Works*: 46b. Autograph: Missing.

Tatarsky polon [The Tatar captivity]. For multi-voice mixed choir, subtitled: "Variatsii na russkuyu temu. V miksolidiyskom lade" [Variations on a Russian theme. In the Mixolydian mode], written to folk words. Date of composition: 1876. Published: St. Petersburg: Bessel', 1877; Reprinted: Bessel', 1887; *Works*: 46b. Autograph: Missing.

122 **Stikh ob Aleksee bozh'em cheloveke. Dlya khora i orkestra. Slova i napev narodnoy pesni [Poem about Aleksey, Man of God. For chorus and orchestra. Words and melody from folk song], Op. 20.**

For alto, tenor and bass chorus and orchestra.

Key: B minor. Date of composition: 1878. Première: 22 January [3 February] 1894, Third Russian Symphony Concert, St. Petersburg, cond. Rimsky-Korsakov. Published: Leipzig: Belaieff, c.1878 (fs, vs); *Works*: XXIV; 44. Autograph: Missing.

123 **Pyatnadtsat' russkikh narodnykh pesen perelozhennykh na narodny lad, dlya zhenskogo, muzhskogo i smeshannogo khora – bez soprovozhdeniya [Fifteen Russian Folk Songs, set in folk style for women's, men's and mixed chorus – unaccompanied], Op. 19.**

Date of composition: 1879. Published: Moscow: Yurgenson, 1879; *Works*: 46b. Autograph: MMKG.

Set I, Women's Chorus:

Svadebnaya: "Iz za lesu, lesu tëmnogo" [Wedding song: "From the forest, the dark forest"]. Melody taken from Rimsky-Korsakov's *Collection of Russian Folk Songs*, Op. 24 [No. 81].

Svadebnaya: "Kak pri vechere" [Wedding song: "At evening"]. Melody taken from Rimsky-Korsakov's *Collection of Russian Folk Songs*, Op. 24 [No. 74].

Troitskaya: "A i gusto na berëze list'e" [Trinity song: "The leaves are thick on the birch tree"]. Melody taken from Rimsky-Korsakov's *Collection of Russian Folk Songs*, Op. 24 [No. 51].

Svadebnaya: "Zelená grusha vo sadu" [Wedding song: "Green is the pear-tree in the garden"]. Melody taken from Rimsky-Korsakov's *Collection of Russian Folk Songs*, Op. 24 [No. 75].

Velichal'naya: "Kak za rechkoyu" [Ceremonial: "Beyond the river"]. Melody taken from Rimsky-Korsakov's *Collection of Russian Folk Songs*, Op. 24 [No. 100].

Set II, Men's Chorus:

Khorovodnaya: "Vo luzyakh" [Khorovod: "In the meadows"]. Melody taken from Balakirev's *Collection of Russian Folk Songs* (1866) [No. 20].

Protyazhnaya: "Chto vilis'-to moi rusy kudri" [Drawling song: "When you waved my light brown curls"]. Melody taken from *40 Folk Songs Collected by T. I. Filippov and harmonised by N. A. Rimsky-Korsakov* (1882) [No. 10].

Protyazhnaya: "Poduy, poduy nepogodushka" [Drawling song: "Begone, begone bad weather"]. Melody taken from Balakirev's *Collection of Russian Folk Songs* (1866) [No. 21].

Protyazhnaya: "Akh, talan moy" [Drawling song: "Oh, my good fortune"]. Melody taken from Rimsky-Korsakov's *Collection of Russian Folk Songs*, Op. 24 [No. 13].

Razboynich'ya: "Ty vzoydi, vzoydi solntse krasnoe" [Robbers' song: "Rise, rise, thou red sun"]. Melody taken from *40 Folk Songs Collected by T. I. Filippov and harmonised by N. A. Rimsky-Korsakov* (1882) [No. 13].

Set III, Mixed Chorus:

Khorovodnaya: "Vzoydi ty, vzoydi ty, solntse ne nizko, vysoko" [Khorovod: "Rise, rise, O sun, not low, but high"]. Melody taken from *40 Folk Songs Collected by T. I. Filippov and harmonised by N. A. Rimsky-Korsakov* (1882) [No. 30].

Troitskaya khorovodnaya: "Ay vo pole lipen'ka" [Trinity khorovod: "In the field is a lime tree"]. Melody taken from Rimsky-Korsakov's *Collection of Russian Folk Songs*, Op. 24 [No. 54].

Vesennyaya khorovodnaya: "Zapletisya pleten'" [Spring khorovod: "Plait the wattle fencing"]. Autograph states: "Given to me by Konstantin Nikolaevich Solov'ëv."

Khorovodnaya: "Posmotrite-ka, dobrye lyudi" [Khorovod: "Look, good people"]. Melody taken from Rimsky-Korsakov's *Collection of Russian Folk Songs*, Op. 24 [No. 64].

Khorovodnaya: "So v'yunom ya khozhu" [Khorovod: "With a youth I go"]. Melody taken from Rimsky-Korsakov's *Collection of Russian Folk Songs*, Op. 24 [No. 56].

124 ***Chetyre trëkhgolosnykh khora dlya muzhskikh golosov bez soprovozhdeniya* [Four Three-Part Choruses for unaccompanied men's voices], Op. 23.**

The first and third choruses were entered in a competition sponsored by the St. Petersburg Branch of the Russian Music Society under the heading: "Music is the art of expressing feeling by means of sounds," the third being given an honorable mention.

Krest'yanskaya pirushka [The peasant feast], text by Kol'tsov.
Voron k voronu letit [Raven flies to raven], text by Pushkin.
Plenivshis' rozoy solovey (Vostochnaya pesnya) [Enslaved by the rose, the nightingale (Eastern song)], text by Kol'tsov.

Dayte bokaly [Pass the goblets], text by Kol'tsov.

Date of composition: 1876. Published: St. Petersburg: Büttner, 1876; Reprinted: Belaieff; *Works*: 46b. Autograph: Missing.

125 **Slava. Podblyudnaya pesnya. Dlya khora i orkestra. Slova i napev narodnoy pesni [Glory. "Under the Dish" Song. For chorus and orchestra. Words and melody from folk song], Op. 21.**

Written to mark the 25th anniversary of the reign of Tsar Alexander II. Based on the "Slava" theme taken from Práč's *Collection of Russian Folk Songs*, utilized by Beethoven in his Razumovsky Quartet, Op. 59, No. 2, and in the Prologue to Musorgsky's opera *Boris Godunov. Podblyudnaya pesnya* ["podblyudnaya" song]: a peasant song used in folk divination ceremonies. Rings, combs, or trinkets were placed in a covered dish and, while the songs were being sung, the articles would be withdrawn at appropriate points. The correspondence of the words of the song at the time of withdrawal provided a key as to the owner's future fortune. From the Russian words "pod" [under] and "blyudo" [dish]. [See Simon Karlinsky, "Stravinsky and Russian Pre-Literate Theater." *Nineteenth Century Music* 6 (3) (1983)].

Dedicated to Evstafy Stepanovich Azeev. Key: A-flat major. Date of composition: 1879–80. Première: 22 January [3 February] 1894, Third Russian Symphony Concert, St. Petersburg, cond. Rimsky-Korsakov. Published: St. Petersburg: Büttner, 1895; Belaieff, 1896; *Works*: XXIV. Autograph: RNB.

126 **Dva khora dlya detskikh golosov [Two Choruses for children's voices].**

Written to folk words. Autograph of *Repka* [The Turnip] incomplete. Date of composition: 1884. Published: Moscow: Muzgiz, 1954; *Works*: 46b. Autograph: SPBGATI.

Repka [The Turnip].
Kotik [The Kitten].

127 **Razboynich'ya Pesnya. "Ty vzoydi, vzoydi, solntse krasnoe" [Robbers' Song. "Rise, rise, thou red sun"].**

For male voice choir, written to folk words. Date of composition: c.1884. Published: Moscow: Yurgenson, 1884, in *Dumsky kruzhok. Repertuar lyubiteley khorovogo peniya*, Vyp. II [Dumsky Circle. Lovers of Choral Singing Repertoire, Issue II]; Reprinted: Yurgenson, 1889; *Works*: 46b. Autograph: Missing.

128 **Svitezyanka (Iz Mitskevicha). Kantata dlya soprano i tenora solo, smeshannogo khora i orkestra [Switezianka (From Mickiewicz). Cantata for soprano and tenor solo, mixed chorus and orchestra], Op. 44.**

Text by L. Mey after Mickiewicz. Dedicated to Sergey Ivanovich Taneev. Key: E major. Date of composition: 1897. Première: 21 March [2 April] 1898, Russian Symphony Concert, St. Petersburg, cond. Glazunov. Published:

Leipzig: Belaieff, 1898 (fs and vs, title in Russian and French: *Switezianka. Cantate pour Soprano et Ténor Solo, Choeur et Orchèstre,* Op. 44); *Works:* XXIV; 44. Autograph: RNB.

129 ***Pesn' o Veshchem Olege. Dlya muzhskikh golosov i orkestra*** [**Song of the Prophet Oleg. For male voices and orchestra**], **Op. 58.**

For tenor and bass soloists and male chorus, text by Pushkin. Dedicated to Pushkin's memory. Key: G minor. Date of composition: 1899. Première: 18 [30] December 1899, Russian Music Society, St. Petersburg, cond. Rimsky-Korsakov. Published: St. Petersburg: Bessel', 1901; Breitkopf, 1909; *Works:* XXIV; 44. Autograph: RNB (V. Bel'sky Archive).

130 ***Iz Gomera. Prelyudiya-kantata. Dlya orkestra i zhenskikh golosov*** [**From Homer. Prelude-cantata for orchestra and women's voices**], **Op. 60.**

For soprano, mezzo-soprano, contralto, and tenor soloists, and women's chorus, text taken from *The Odyssey.* Key: G minor. Date of composition: 1901. Première: 15 [28] November 1903, Celebrity Concert, St. Petersburg, cond. Ziloti. Published: Leipzig: Belaieff, 1905; *Works:* XXIV; 44. Autograph: RNB (Rimsky-Korsakov Archive No. 58a).

VOCAL WORKS

All the songs published in *Works* 45 are printed in the original key. From Op. 39 onwards, with the exception of two songs for bass (Op. 49), four for tenor (Op. 55), and two for soprano (Op. 56), all exist in two forms: (i) in the original key and (ii) as arranged by the composer for a voice of a different tessitura [see note in *Works*: 45, 498].

131 ***Babochka*** [**Butterfly**].

A duet written in 1855 to children's words. Referred to in Rimsky-Korsakov's *Chronicle,* but apparently not performed.

132 ***Vykhodi ko mne Sinyora*** [**Come Out to Me, Signora**].

Only 15 bars in length, sent to V. Yastrebstsëv. Date of composition: 1861. Published: *RMG* 1 (1909) cols. 7–9.

133 ***V krovi gorit ogon' zhelan'ya*** [**In the Blood Burns the Fire of Desire**].

Words by Pushkin. Date of composition: 1865. Apparently not preserved.

134 ***Chetyre romansa*** [**Four Songs**], **Op. 2.**

Shchekoyu k shcheke ty moey prilozhis' [Lean thy cheek to mine], for medium voice, text by Heine, trans. by Mikhaylov, piano part written by Balakirev. Key: G-sharp minor. Dedicated to Modest Petrovich Musorgsky. Date of composition: 1865. Published: St. Petersburg: Bernard, 1866; *Works*: 45 (1). Autograph: Missing.

Rimsky-Korsakov's Musical Works 35

Vostochny romans. Plenivshis' rozoy, solovey [Eastern song. Enslaved by the rose, the nightingale], for medium voice, text by Kol'tsov. Key: F-sharp minor. Dedicated to Malvina Rafailovna Kyui [Cui]. Date of composition: 1865–66. Published: St. Petersburg: Bernard, 1866; *Works*: 45 (2). Autograph: Missing.

Kolybel'naya pesnya iz dramy "Pskovityanka" [Cradle song from the drama *The Maid of Pskov*], for medium voice, text by Mey. Key: D-flat major. Included in the second version of *The Maid of Pskov* and in *Boyarinya Vera Sheloga*. Dedicated to Sofiya Ivanovna Belenitsyna. Date of composition: 1866. Published: St. Petersburg: Bernard, 1866; *Works*: 45 (3). Autograph: Missing.

Is slëz moikh [From my tears], for medium voice, a setting of Heine's "Aus meinen Tränen," trans. by Mikhaylov. Key: D major. Dedicated to Lyudmila Ivanovna Shestakova. Date of composition: 1866. Published: St. Petersburg: Bernard, 1866; *Works*: 45 (4). Autograph: Missing.

135   **Ty skoro menya pozabudesh'** [**You Will Soon Forget Me**].

Composed 1866; apparently not preserved.

136   **Chetyre romansa** [**Four Songs**], **Op. 3**.

El' i pal'ma [The pine tree and the palm], for medium voice, a setting of Heine's "Ein Fichtenbaum steht einsam," trans. by Mikhaylov. Key: E-flat minor. Dedicated to Aleksandr Porfir'evich Borodin.

Version 1: *Na severnom golom utëse* [On the northern bare cliff]. Date of composition: 1866. Published: St. Petersburg: Iogansen, 1866; *Works*: 45 (5). Autograph: Missing.

Version 2: *El' i pal'ma. Muzykal'naya kartinka* [The pine tree and the palm. A musical picture]. Based on the preceding, but arranged for orchestra, transposed from the original E-flat minor to E minor, the time signature changed from 3/2 to 3/4, and with some alterations to the harmony. Date of composition: 1889. Published: Leipzig: Belaieff, 1891; *Works*: XXIII. Autograph: RNB.

Version 3: The second version arr. for piano and voice. Date of composition: Not known. Published: Moscow: Muzgiz, 1946; *Works*: 45 (5a). Autograph: Missing.

Yuzhnaya noch' [Southern night], for medium voice, text by N. Shcherbina. Key: B minor. Dedicated to Mily Alekseevich Balakirev. Date of composition: 1866. Published: St. Petersburg: Iogansen, 1866; *Works*: 45 (6). Autograph: Missing.

Nochevala tuchka zolotaya [The golden cloud had slept], for medium voice, text by Lermontov. Key: G-sharp minor. No dedication. Date of composition:

1866. Published: St. Petersburg: Iogansen, 1866; *Works*: 45 (7). Autograph: Missing.

Na kholmakh Gruzii [On the hills of Georgia], for medium voice, text by Pushkin. Key: C-sharp minor. Dedicated to Sofiya Ivanovna Belenitsyna. Date of composition: 1866. Published: St. Petersburg: Iogansen, 1866; *Works*: 45 (8). Autograph: Missing.

137   *Chetyre romansa* [**Four Songs**], **Op. 4.**

Chto v imeni tebe moëm? [What is my name to thee?], for medium voice, text by Pushkin. Key: G-flat major. No dedication. Date of composition: 1866. Published: St. Petersburg: Iogansen, 1866; *Works*: 45 (9). Autograph: Missing.

Gonets [The messenger], for low voice, a setting of Heine's "Die Botschaft," trans. by Mikhaylov. Key: G-sharp minor. Dedicated to A. D. Myshetsky. Date of composition: 1866. Published: St. Petersburg: Iogansen, 1866; *Works*: 45 (10). Autograph: Missing.

V tëmnoy roshche zamolk solovey [In the dark grove the nightingale is silent], for medium voice, text by I. Nikitin. Key: D-flat major. Dedicated to Tsezar' Antonovich Kyui [Cui].

Version 1 (with piano accompaniment): Date of composition: 1866. Published: St. Petersburg: Iogansen, 1866; *Works*: 45 (11). Autograph: Missing.

Version 2 (with orchestral accompaniment): Date of composition: 1891. Published: Moscow: Muzgiz, 1922; *Works*: XXIII. Autograph: RNB.

Tikho vecher dogoraet [Quietly evening falls], for medium voice, text by Fet. Key: A major. Dedicated to A.P. Arsen'ev.

Version 1 (with piano accompaniment): Date of composition: 1866. Published: St. Petersburg: Iogansen, 1866; *Works*: 45 (12). Autograph: Missing.

Version 2 (with orchestral accompaniment): Date of composition: 1891. Published: Moscow: Muzgiz, 1922; *Works*: XXIII. Autograph: RNB.

138   *Chetyre romansa* [**Four Songs**], **Op. 7.** [Originally designated as Op. 5.]

Moy golos dlya tebya i laskovy, i tomny [My voice for thee is both sweet and languid], for medium voice, text by Pushkin. Key: D-flat major. Dedicated to Mariya Fëdorovna Rimskaya-Korsakova. Date of composition: 1867. Published: St. Petersburg: Iogansen, 1867; *Works*: 45 (13). Autograph: Missing.

Evreyskaya pesnya [Hebrew song], for medium voice, text by Mey. Key: B minor. Dedicated to Modest Petrovich Musorgsky. Date of composition: 1867. Published: St. Petersburg: Iogansen, 1867; *Works*: 45 (14). Autograph: Missing.

Rimsky-Korsakov's Musical Works   37

Svitezyanka [Switezianka], for high voice, text by Mickiewicz, trans. by Mey. Key: D-flat major. Dedicated to Sofiya Ivanovna Belenitsyna. Later used in a choral setting, Op. 44 [see *Works* XXIV]. Date of composition: 1867. Published: St. Petersburg: Iogansen, 1867; *Works*: 45 (15). Autograph: Missing.

Kak nebesa, tvoy vzor blistaet [Thy glance is radiant as the heavens], for low voice, text by Lermontov. Key: F-sharp major. Dedicated to Nikolay Nikolaevich Lodyzhensky. Date of composition: 1867. Published: St. Petersburg: Iogansen, 1867; *Works*: 45 (16). Autograph: Missing.

139   ***Shest' romansov*** [**Six Songs**], **Op. 8.**

Gde ty, tam mysl' moya letaet [Where art thou, my thought flies there], for medium voice, author of text unknown. Key: G-flat major. Dedicated to Pëtr Il'ich Chaykovsky [Tchaikovsky]. Date of composition: 1870. Published: Moscow: Yurgenson, 1870; *Works*: 45 (17). Autograph: MGK.

Noch' [Night], for medium voice, text by Pleshcheev. Key: D major.

Version 1 (with piano accompaniment): Dedicated to Nadezhda Nikolaevna Purgol'd. Date of composition: 1868. Published: Moscow: Yurgenson, 1870; *Works*: 45 (18). Autograph: MGK.

Version 2 (with orchestral accompaniment): No dedication. Date of composition: 1891. Published: Moscow: Muzgiz, 1922; *Works*: XXIII. Autograph: RNB.

Tayna [The Secret], for high voice, text after Chamisso. Key: C major. Dedicated to Aleksandra Nikolaevna Purgol'd. Date of composition: 1868. Published: Moscow: Yurgenson, 1870; *Works*: 45 (19). Autograph: MGK, RNB.

Vstan' soydi! Davno dennitsa [Arise, come down! Long the dawn], for medium voice, text by Mey. Key: F-sharp minor. Dedicated to Fëdor Andreevich Kanille. Date of composition: 1870. Published: Moscow: Yurgenson, 1870; *Works*: 45 (20). Autograph: MGK.

V tsarstvo rozy i vina – pridi! [Into the kingdom of roses and wine – come!], for medium voice, text by Fet. Key: F-sharp major. Dedicated to Ekaterina Sergeevna Borodina. Date of composition: 1870. Published: Moscow: Yurgenson, 1870; *Works*: 45 (21). Autograph: MGK.

Ya veryu: ya lyubim [I believe: I love], for medium voice, text by Pushkin. Key: D-flat major. Dedicated to Mily Alekseevich Balakirev. Date of composition: 1870. Published: Moscow: Yurgenson, 1870; *Works*: 45 (22). Autograph: MGK.

140   ***Dva romansa*** [**Two Songs**], **Op. 25.**

K moey pesne [To my song], for low voice, setting of Heine's "Mir träumte einst von wildem Liebesglühn" from *Traumbilder*, trans. by

Mikhaylov. Key: D major. Dedicated to Vladimir Vasil'evich Stasov. Date of composition: 1870. Published: St. Petersburg: Büttner, 1877; *Works*: 45 (23). Autograph: RNB.

Kogda glyazhu tebe v glaza [When I gaze into thine eyes], for high voice, setting of Heine's "Wenn ich in deine Augen seh," trans. by Mikhaylov. Key: D major. Dedicated to Fëdor Nikolaevich Purgol'd. Date of composition: 1876 [1877?]. Published: St. Petersburg: Büttner, 1877; *Works*: 45 (24). Autograph: Missing.

141   *Chetyre romansa* [**Four Songs**], **Op. 26.**

V poryvke nezhnosti serdechnoy [In a moment of heartfelt tenderness], for high voice, setting of Byron's "In moments to delight devoted," trans. by Kozlov. Key: D-flat major. Dedicated to Sëmen Nikolaevich Kruglikov. Date of composition: 1882. Published: St. Petersburg: Büttner, 1882; *Works*: 45 (25). Autograph: Missing.

Zaklikanie [Evocation], for medium voice, text by Pushkin. Key: E-flat major. Dedicated to Vladimir Nikanorovich Il'insky. Date of composition: 1882. Published: St. Petersburg: Büttner, 1882; *Works*: 45 (26). Autograph: Missing.

Dlya beregov otchizny dal'noy [For the shores of thy far native land], for medium voice, text by Pushkin. Key: E major. No dedication. Date of composition: 1882. Published: St. Petersburg: Büttner, 1882; *Works*: 45 (27). Autograph: Missing.

Pesnya Zuleyki [Zuleika's song], for medium voice, setting of verses from Byron's "The Bride of Abydos," trans. by Kozlov [Precise identification of specific verses has proved impossible]. Key: F-sharp minor. Dedicated to Nadezhda Nikolaevna Rimskaya-Korsakova. Date of composition: 1882. Published: St. Petersburg: Büttner, 1882; *Works*: 45 (28). Autograph: Missing.

142   *Chetyre romansa* [**Four Songs**], **Op. 27.**

Gornimi tikho letela dusha nebesami [Softly the spirit flew up to Heaven], for medium voice, text by Count A. K. Tolstoy. Key: D-flat major. Dedicated to Aleksandr Konstantinovich Glazunov. BL gives this as Op. 24 No. 1. Date of composition: 1883. Published: St. Petersburg: Büttner, 1883, with orchestral accompaniment by M. O. Shteynberg; Belaieff, 1915; *Works*: 45 (29). Autograph: Missing.

Ekho [Echo], for medium voice, text by F. Coppée, trans. by A. Andreevsky. Key: F-sharp minor. Dedicated to Vladimir Nikanorovich Il'insky. Date of composition: 1883. Published: St. Petersburg: Büttner, 1883; *Works*: 45 (30). Autograph: Missing.

Ty i vy [Thou and you], for high voice, text by Pushkin. Key: A-flat major. Dedicated to Nadezhda Nikolaevna Rimskaya-Korsakova. Date of

Rimsky-Korsakov's Musical Works   39

composition: 1883. Published: St. Petersburg: Büttner, 1883; *Works*: 45 (31). Autograph: Missing.

Prosti! Ne pomni dney paden'ya [Forgive! Remember not these tearful days], for high voice, text by Nekrasov. Key: E-flat major. No dedication. Date of composition: 1883. Published: St. Petersburg: Büttner, 1883; *Works*: 45 (32). Autograph: Missing.

143   ***Chetyre romansa*** [**Four Songs**], **Op. 39**.

All four songs dedicated to Nadezhda Nikolaevna Rimskaya-Korsakova.

O, esli by ty mogla [Oh, if thou couldst for one moment], for medium voice, text by Count Aleksey Tolstoy. Key: C minor. Also arr. for high voice, E-flat minor. Date of composition: 1897. Published: Leipzig: Belaieff, 1897; *Works*: 45 (33). Autograph: RNB.

Zapad gasnet v dali bledno-rozovoy [The west dies out in pallid rose], for medium voice, text by Count Aleksey Tolstoy. Key: E minor. Also arr. for high voice, G minor. Date of composition: 1897. Published: Leipzig: Belaieff, 1897; *Works*: 45 (34). Autograph: RNB.

Na nivy zhëltye niskhodit tishina [Silence descends on the golden cornfields], for medium voice, text by Count Aleksey Tolstoy. Key: D minor. Also arr. for high voice, F minor. Date of composition: 1897. Published: Leipzig: Belaieff, 1897; *Works*: 45 (35). Autograph: RNB.

Usni, pechal'ny drug [Sleep, my poor friend], for medium voice, text by Count Aleksey Tolstoy. Key: E-flat major. Also arr. for high voice, F-sharp major. Date of composition: 1897. Published: Leipzig: Belaieff, 1897; *Works*: 45 (36). Autograph: RNB.

144   ***Chetyre romansa*** [**Four Songs**], **Op. 40**.

Kogda volnuetsya zhëlteyushchaya niva [When the golden cornfield waves], for medium voice, text by Lermontov. Key: D major. Also arr. for high voice, F major. Dedicated to Rimsky-Korsakov's daughter, Sonya. Date of composition: 1897. Published: Leipzig: Belaieff, 1897; *Works*: 45 (37). Autograph: RNB.

Po nebu polunochi angel letel [Across the midnight sky the angel flew], for medium voice, text by Lermontov. Key: A-flat major. Also arr. for high voice, B major. Dedicated to Anna Grigor'evna Zherebtsova-Evreinova. Date of composition: 1897. Published: Leipzig: Belaieff, 1897; *Works*: 45 (38). Autograph: RNB.

O chëm v tishi nochey (Elegiya) [Of what I dream in the quiet night (Elegy)], for medium voice, text by Maykov. Key: B-flat major. Also arr. for high voice, D-flat major. Dedicated to Anatoly Konstantinovich Lyadov. Date of composition: 1897. Published: Leipzig: Belaieff, 1897; *Works*: 45 (39). Autograph: RNB.

Ya v grote zhdal tebya v urochny chas [I waited for thee in the grotto at the appointed hour], for medium voice, text by Maykov. Key: E major. Also arr. for high voice, G major. Dedicated to Feliks Mikhaylovich Blumenfel'd. Date of composition: 1897. Published: Leipzig: Belaieff, 1897; *Works*: 45 (40). Autograph: RNB.

145   **Chetyre romansa [Four Songs], Op. 41.**

Nespyashchikh solntse, grustnaya zvezda [Sun of the sleepless, melancholy star], for medium voice, setting of Byron's "Sun of the Sleepless, Melancholy Star!" trans. by Count Aleksey Tolstoy. Key: B major. Also arr. for high voice, D-flat major. Dedicated to Nikolay Martynovich Shtrup. Date of composition: 1897. Published: Leipzig: Belaieff, 1897; *Works*: 45 (41). Autograph: RNB.

Mne grustno [I am sad], for medium voice, text by Lermontov. Key: D minor. Also arr. for high voice, F minor. Dedicated to Nikolay Aleksandrovich Sokolov. Date of composition: 1897. Published: Leipzig: Belaieff, 1897; *Works*: 45 (42). Autograph: RNB.

Lyublyu tebya, mesyats (Melodiya s beregov Ganga) [I love thee, moon (Melody from the banks of the Ganges)], for medium voice, text by A. Maykov. Key: E major. Also arr. for high voice, F-sharp major. Dedicated to Vladimir Ivanovich Bel'sky. Date of composition: 1897. Published: Leipzig: Belaieff, 1897; *Works*: 45 (43). Autograph: RNB.

Posmotri v svoy vertograd (Iz vostochnogo mira) [Look in thy garden (From the eastern world)], for medium voice, text by Maykov. Key: D-flat major. Also arr. for high voice, E-flat major. Dedicated to Nina Aleksandrovna Frid. Date of composition: 1897. Published: Leipzig: Belaieff, 1897; *Works*: 45 (44). Autograph: RNB.

146   ***Chetyre romansa* [Four Songs], Op. 42.**

Shopot, robkoe dykhan'e [A whisper, a gentle breath], for high voice, text by Fet. Key: G major. Also arr. for medium voice, E major. Dedicated "To my Son, Mikhail." Date of composition: 1897. Published: Leipzig: Belaieff, 1897 [?]; *Works*: 45 (45). Autograph: RNB.

Ya prishël k tebe s privetom [I have come to greet thee], for high voice, text by Fet. Key: C major. Also arr. for medium voice, A major. Dedicated to Nikolay Stepanovich Lavrov. Date of composition: 1897. Published: Leipzig: Belaieff, 1897; *Works*: 45 (46). Autograph: RNB.

Redeet oblakov letuchaya grada (Elegiya) [The clouds begin to scatter (Elegy)], for high voice, text by Pushkin. Key: B minor. Also arr. for medium voice, G-sharp minor. Dedicated to Vasily Vasil'evich Yastrebtsëv. Date of composition: 1897. Published: Leipzig: Belaieff, 1897 [?]. *Works*: 45 (47). Autograph: RNB.

Moya balovnitsa [My spoiled darling], for high voice, setting of a poem by Mickiewicz, trans. by Mey. Key: G major. Also arr. for medium voice, F major. Dedicated to Sigizmund Mikhaylovich Blumenfel'd. Date of composition: 1897. Published: Leipzig: Belaieff, 1897 [?]; *Works*: 45 (48). Autograph: RNB.

147 **Vesnoy** [In Spring], **Op. 43.**

Zvonche zhavoronka pen'e [The lark sings louder], for high voice, text by Count Aleksey Tolstoy. Key: E major. Also arr. for medium voice, D major. Dedicated to Varvara Dmitrievna Komarova. Date of composition: 1897. Published: Leipzig: Belaieff, 1898; *Works*: 45 (49). Autograph: RNB.

Ne veter, veya s vysoty [Not the wind, blowing from the heights], for high voice, text by Count Aleksey Tolstoy. Key: F major. Also arr. for medium voice, E-flat major. Dedicated to Aleksandra Karlovna Runge. Date of composition: 1897. Published: Leipzig: Belaieff, 1898; *Works*: 45 (50). Autograph: RNB.

Svezh i dushist tvoy roskoshny venok [Cool and fragrant is thy splendid garland], for high voice, text by Fet. Key: G major. Also arr. for medium voice, E major. Dedicated to Ippolit Petrovich Pryanishnikov. Date of composition: 1897. Published: Leipzig: Belaieff, 1898; *Works*: 45 (51). Autograph: RNB.

To bylo ranneyu vesnoy [It was in early spring], for high voice, text by Count Aleksey Tolstoy. Key: A major. Also arr. for medium voice, F-sharp major. Dedicated to Mariya Danilovna Kamenskaya. Date of composition: 1897. Published: Leipzig: Belaieff, 1898. *Works*: 45 (52). Autograph: RNB.

148 **Poetu** [To the Poet], **Op. 45.**

Ekho [Echo], for high voice, text by Pushkin. Key: D minor. Also arr. for medium voice, C minor. Dedicated to Stanislav Ivanovich Gabel'. Date of composition: 1897. Published: Leipzig: Belaieff, 1898; *Works*: 45 (53). Autograph: RNB.

Iskusstvo [Art], for high voice, text by Maykov. Key: E-flat major. Also arr. for medium voice, D-flat major. Dedicated to Vasily Maksimovich Samus'. Date of composition: 1897. Published: Leipzig: Belaieff, 1898; *Works*: 45 (54). Autograph: RNB.

Oktava [The Octave], for high voice, text by Maykov. Key: F major. Also arr. for medium voice, D major. Dedicated to Lyudmila Ivanovna Shestakova. Date of composition: 1897. Published: Leipzig: Belaieff, 1898; *Works*: 45 (55). Autograph: RNB.

Somnenie [Doubt], for high voice, text by Maykov. Key: E minor. Also arr. for medium voice, C-sharp minor. Dedicated to Aleksandr Pavlovich Dianin. Date of composition: 1897. Published: Leipzig: Belaieff, 1898; *Works*: 45 (56). Autograph: RNB.

42 Nikolay Andreevich Rimsky-Korsakov: A Research and Information Guide

149 *Poet* [The Poet].

For high voice, text by Pushkin. Key: B-flat major. Also arr. for medium voice, G major. No dedication; not part of the preceding group of songs, Op. 45. Date of composition: 1899. Published: Leipzig: Belaieff, 1899; *Works*: 45 (57). Autograph: RNB.

150 *U morya* [By the Sea], Op. 46.

Drobitsya, i pleshchet, i bryzzhet volna [The wave breaks, and foams, and splashes], for medium voice, text by Count Aleksey Tolstoy. Key: D-flat major. Also arr. for high voice, E-flat major. Dedicated "To my Son, Andrey." Date of composition: 1897. Published: Leipzig: Belaieff, 1898; *Works*: 45 (58). Autograph: RNB.

Ne penitsya more; ne pleshchet volna [The sea does not foam, the wave does not splash], for medium voice, text by Count Aleksey Tolstoy. Key: F major. Also arr. for high voice, G major. Originally dedicated to Natal'ya Aleksandrovna Iretskaya, subsequently to Feliks Mikhaylovich Blumenfel'd. Date of composition: 1897. Published: Leipzig: Belaieff, 1898; *Works*: 45 (59). Autograph: RNB.

Kolishetsya more; volna za volnoy [The sea is tossing; wave after wave], for medium voice, text by Count Aleksey Tolstoy. Key: G-sharp minor. Also arr. for high voice, B minor. Dedicated to Sigizmund Mikhaylovich Blumenfel'd. Date of composition: 1897. Published: Leipzig: Belaieff, 1898; *Works*: 45 (60). Autograph: RNB.

Ne ver' mne, drug [Do not believe me, friend], for medium voice, text by Count Aleksey Tolstoy. Key: E-flat major. Also arr. for high voice, F major. Originally dedicated to Mariya Ivanovna Polina, subsequently to Sigizmund Mikhaylovich Blumenfel'd. Date of composition: 1897. Published: Leipzig: Belaieff, 1898; *Works*: 45 (61). Autograph: RNB.

Vzdumayutsya volny [The waves rise up], for medium voice, text by Count Aleksey Tolstoy. Key: B-flat minor. Also arr. for high voice, C-sharp minor. Dedicated to Feliks Mikhaylovich Blumenfel'd. Date of composition: 1897. Published: Leipzig: Belaieff, 1898; *Works*: 45 (62). Autograph: RNB.

151 *Dva Dueta* [Two Duets], Op. 47.

Both songs are published in three forms: for mezzo-soprano and baritone, for soprano and tenor, and for soprano and tenor with orchestral accompaniment.

Pan. Text by Maykov. Dedicated to Anatoly Konstantinovich Lyadov.

Version 1: For (i) mezzo-soprano and baritone, A major, (ii) soprano and tenor, C major, both with piano accompaniment. Date of composition: 1897. Published: Leipzig: Belaieff, 1898; *Works*: 46a. Autograph: RNB and/or SPBGATI. [Soprano and tenor manuscript missing.]

Version 2: For soprano and tenor, with orchestral accompaniment. Date of composition: 1897–1905. Published: Leipzig: Belaieff, 1906; *Works*: 46a. Autograph: RNB and/or SPBGATI.

Pesnya pesen [Song of Songs]. Text by Mey after the Bible. Dedicated to Anatoly Konstantinovich Lyadov.

Version 1: For (i) mezzo-soprano and baritone, B minor, (ii) soprano and tenor, D minor, both with piano accompaniment. Date of composition: 1897. Published: Leipzig: Belaieff, 1898; *Works*: 46a. Autograph: RNB and/or SPBGATI.

Version 2: For soprano and tenor, with orchestral accompaniment. Date of composition: 1897–1905. Published: Leipzig: Belaieff, 1906; *Works*: 46a. Autograph: Missing.

152 *Dva romansa* [Two Songs], Op. 49.

Anchar – drevo smerti [The upas tree, tree of death], for bass voice, text by Pushkin. Key: C minor. Second and third versions dedicated to Fëdor Ignat'evich Stravinsky.

Version 1: Date of composition: 1882. Not published. Autograph: Missing.

Version 2: Date of composition: 1897; orchestrated 1906. Published: Leipzig: Belaieff, 1898; Leipzig: Belaieff, 1907 (orchestral version); *Works*: XXIII. Autograph: Missing.

Version 3: Vocal score of Second Version. Date of composition: 1906 [?]. Published: Moscow: Muzgiz, 1946; *Works*: 45 (63). Autograph: [?].

Prorok [The Prophet], for bass voice, text by Pushkin. Key: C major. Dedicated to Vladimir Vasil'evich Stasov.

Version 1: Date of composition: 1897. Published: Leipzig: Belaieff, 1898; *Works*: Not included. Autograph: [?].

Version 2: Entitled: *The Prophet. Arioso for bass and chorus ad libitum*; orchestrated. Date of composition: 1899. Published: Leipzig: Belaieff, 1899; *Works*: XXIII. Autzograph: RNB.

Version 3: Second Version arr. for voice and piano. Date of composition: 1899. Published: Moscow: Muzgiz, 1946; *Works*: 45 (64). Autograph: RNB.

153 *Chetyre romansa* [Four Songs], Op. 50.

Maykov's texts are all based on modern Greek poems.

Deva i solntse [The maiden and the sun], for high voice, text by Maykov. Key: A major. Also for medium voice, F-sharp major. Dedicated to Evgeniya Konstantinovna Mravina. Date of composition: 1897. Published: Leipzig: Belaieff, 1898; *Works*: 45 (65). Autograph: RNB.

Pevets [The singer], for high voice, text by Maykov. Key: B-flat major. Also for medium voice, G-sharp major. Dedicated to Gavriil Alekseevich Morskoy. Date of composition: 1897. Published: Leipzig: Belaieff, 1898; *Works*: 45 (66). Autograph: RNB.

Tikho more goluboe! [Quiet is the blue sea!], for high voice, text by Maykov. Key: A-flat major. Also for medium voice, F major. Dedicated to Mitrofan Mikhaylovich Chuprynnikov. Date of composition: 1897. Published: Leipzig: Belaieff, 1898; *Works*: 45 (67). Autograph: RNB.

Eshchë ya poln, o drug moy mily [I am still full, O my dear friend], for high voice, text by Maykov. Key: A major. Also for medium voice, F-sharp major. Dedicated to Nadezhda Ivanovna Zabela. Date of composition: 1898. Published: Leipzig: Belaieff, 1898; *Works*: 45 (68). Autograph: RNB.

154 **Pyat' romansov [Five Songs], Op. 51.**

Medlitel'no vlekutsya dni moi [Slowly drag my days], for high voice, text by Pushkin. Key: A minor. Also for medium voice, G minor. Dedicated to Mikhail Vasil'evich Lunacharsky. Date of composition: 1897. Published: Leipzig: Belaieff, 1898; *Works*: 45 (69). Autograph: RNB.

Ne poy, krasavitsa, pri mne [Do not sing to me, O lovely one], for high voice, text by Pushkin. Key: G major. Also for medium voice, F major. Dedicated to Anton Vladislavovich Sekar-Rozhansky. Date of composition: 1897. Published: Leipzig: Belaieff, 1898; *Works*: 45 (70). Autograph: RNB.

Tsvetok zasokshy [Withered flower], for high voice, text by Pushkin. Key: A minor. Also for medium voice, G minor. Dedicated to Nikolay Dimitrievich Kashkin. Date of composition: 1897. Published: Leipzig: Belaieff, 1898; *Works*: 45 (71). Autograph: RNB.

Krasavitsa [The Beauty], for high voice, text by Pushkin. Key: A-flat major. Also for medium voice, F-sharp major. Dedicated to Semën Nikolaevich Kruglikov. Date of composition: 1897. Published: Leipzig: Belaieff, 1898; *Works*: 45 (72). Autograph: RNB.

Nenastny den' potukh [A rainy day has waned], for high voice, text by Pushkin. Key: C-sharp minor. Also for medium voice, B minor. Dedicated to Nadezhda Nikolaevna Rimskaya-Korsakova. Date of composition: 1897. Published: Leipzig: Belaieff, 1898; *Works*: 45 (73). Autograph: RNB.

155 **Dva dueta [Two Duets], Op. 52.**

Gorny klyuch [The mountain spring], text by Maykov. Key: F major. Dedicated to Aleksandr Konstantinovich Glazunov.

Version 1: For (i) soprano and mezzo-soprano, (ii) tenor and baritone. Date of composition: 1897. Published: Leipzig: Belaieff, 1898; *Works*: 46a. Autograph: RNB and/or SPBGATI.

Version 2: Trio for soprano, mezzo-soprano, and contralto, with orchestral accompaniment, Op. 52b. Date of composition: 1905. Published: Leipzig: Belaieff, 1906; *Works*: 46a. Autograph: RNB and/or SPBGATI.

Angel i demon [Angel and demon], for (i) soprano and baritone, (ii) tenor and mezzo-soprano, text by A. Maykov. Key: F minor. Dedicated to Aleksandr Konstantinovich Glazunov. Date of composition: 1898. Published: Leipzig: Belaieff, 1898. Works: 46a. Autograph: RNB and/or SPBGATI.

156 **Strekozy. Trio dlya zhenskikh golosov** [Dragonflies. Trio for women's voices], Op. 53.

Text by Count Aleksey Tolstoy. Key: D major. Dedicated to August Rudol'fovich Berngard.

Version 1: For two sopranos and mezzo-soprano. Date of composition: 1897. Published: Leipzig: Belaieff, 1898; *Works*: 46a. Autograph: RNB and/or SPBGATI.

Version 2: For two sopranos and mezzo-soprano *ad libitum*, with orchestral accompaniment. Date of composition: 1897. Published: Leipzig: Belaieff, 1898; *Works*: 46a. Autograph: RNB and/or SPBGATI.

157 **Chetyre romansa** [Four Songs], Op. 55.

Probuzhden'e [Awakening], for tenor voice, text by Pushkin. Key: A major. Dedicated to Il'ya Fëdorovich Tyumenev. Date of composition: 1897. Published: Leipzig: Belaieff, 1898; *Works*: 45 (74). Autograph: RNB.

Grechanke [To a Grecian girl], for tenor voice, text by Pushkin. Key: F-sharp major. Dedicated to Il'ya Fëdorovich Tyumenev. Date of composition: 1898. Published: Leipzig: Belaieff, 1898; *Works*: 45 (75). Autograph: RNB.

Snovidenie [The Dream], for tenor voice, text by Pushkin. Key: F major. Dedicated to Vladimir Ivanovich Bel'sky. Date of composition: 1898. Published: Leipzig: Belaieff, 1898; *Works*: 45 (76). Autograph: RNB.

Ya umer ot schast'ya [I died from happiness], for tenor voice, setting of poem by Uhland, trans. Zhukovsky. Key: A major. Dedicated to Vladimir Ivanovich Bel'sky. Date of composition: 1898. Published: Leipzig: Belaieff, 1898; *Works*: 45 (77). Autograph: RNB.

158 **Dva romansa** [Two Songs], Op. 56.

Nimfa [The Nymph], for soprano voice, text by Maykov. Key: E major. Dedicated to Nadezhda Zabela-Vrubel'.

Version 1: Date of composition: 1898. Published: Leipzig: Belaieff, 1899; *Works*: 45 (78). Autograph: RNB.

Version 2: With orchestral accompaniment. Date of composition: 1905. Published: Leipzig: Belaieff, 1908; *Works*: XXIII. Autograph: Missing.

Son v letnyuyu noch' [Summer night's dream], for soprano voice, text by Maykov. Key: B major. Dedicated to Mikhail Aleksandrovich Vrubel'.

Version 1: Date of composition: 1898. Published: Leipzig: Belaieff, 1899; *Works*: 45 (79). Autograph: RNB.

Version 2: With orchestral accompaniment. Date of composition: 1906. Published: Leipzig: Belaieff, 1908; *Works*: Not included. Autograph: Missing.

FOLK SONG COLLECTIONS

159   *Sbornik russkikh narodnykh pesen* [Collection of Russian Folk Songs], Op. 24.

Consists of 100 songs divided into five genres: Byliny and Narrative Songs, Lyrical Songs, Dance Songs, Game Songs, and Ritual Songs. Set out in two main parts: Songs 1–40; 41–100.

Dedicated to Vladimir Vasil'evich Stasov. Date of composition: 1875–76. Published: St. Petersburg: Bessel', 1877; *Works*: 47. Autograph: MMKG [Songs 1–40 only].

160   *40 narodnykh pesen, sobrannykh T. I. Filippovym i garmonizovannykh N. A. Rimskim-Korsakovym* [40 Folk Songs, collected by T. I. Filippov and harmonised by N. A. Rimsky-Korsakov].

Includes six *Dukhovnye Stikhi* [Spiritual Verses], Nos. 1–6.

Date of composition: 1875–82. Published: Moscow: Yurgenson, 1882; *Works*: 47. Autograph: Missing; MMKG (some materials).

ARRANGEMENTS, ORCHESTRATIONS, AND REVISIONS

Borodin

161   *Knyaz' Igor'* [Prince Igor], Opera. Final chorus orch. 1879. Prologue and Act I, Scene 1 rev. 1885. Entire opera completed and orch. by Rimsky-Korsakov and Glazunov 1887–88. Published: 1896.

162   String Quartet No. 2. *Nocturne* arr. for violin and orchestra 1887.

163   Symphonies Nos. 1 and 2. Revised by Rimsky-Korsakov and Glazunov.

164   *Mlada* [collective work]. *Finale* to Act IV orch. 1890. Published: 1891.

165   Songs: "The Sleeping Princess," orch. 1897. "The Sea," orch. 1906.

Cui

166   *William Ratcliff,* Opera. First number orch. 1868. Introduction to Act I and Entr'acte to Act III re-orch. 1894.

Rimsky-Korsakov's Musical Works

Dargomyzhsky

167   *Kamenny Gost'* [**The Stone Guest**], **Opera**. Orch. 1869–70. First scene re-orch. c.1899. Entire opera re-orch. and rev. 1902.

168   *Rogdana,* **Opera**. "Chorus of Maidens" orch. 1873.

Glinka

169   *Ruslan and Lyudmila,* **Opera**. Music for stage band orch. 1876. Entire opera arr. and ed. by Balakirev, Rimsky-Korsakov, and Lyadov. Published: 1878.

170   *A Life for the Tsar,* **Opera**. Arr. and ed. by Balakirev, Rimsky-Korsakov, and Lyadov, published: 1881. New edition by Rimsky-Korsakov and Glazunov, published: 1907.

171   **Works arr. and ed. by Rimsky-Korsakov:** *Jota aragonesa, Finsky zaliv* [Gulf of Finland], *Kamarinskaya, Prince Kholmsky, Souvenir d'une Nuit d'Eté à Madrid, Valse-Fantaisie,* and others.

Handel

172   *Samson,* **Oratorio**. Seven numbers orch. by Rimsky-Korsakov and students of the Conservatory, 1875–76.

Musorgsky

173   *The Destruction of Sennacherib,* **Opera**. Version 2 of the Trio orch. 1874. Entire opera later orch. Published: 1894.

174   *Khovanshchina,* **Opera**. "Persian Dances" completed and orch., 1881–83. Published: 1883.

175   Various orchestral and choral works, songs, etc., ed. and orch. 1881–83.

176   *Sorochintsy Fair,* **Opera**. "Dream Intermezzo" rewritten and re-orch. as *Night on Bald Mountain,* 1886.

177   *Boris Godunov,* **Opera**. *Polonaise* re-orch. 1892–96. "Coronation Scene" re-orch. 1892. Entire opera shortened, rev., and re-orch. 1892–96. Opera again rewritten and re-orch., with restoration of cuts, 1906. "Coronation Scene": two short passages arr. for Dyagilev's [Diaghilev's] Paris production, 1907.

178   *The Marriage,* **Opera**. Revised and partly orch. 1906.

179   **Songs**: "Hopak," "Gathering Mushrooms" and "Peasant Lullaby" orch. 1906. "With Nurse" freely arr. 1908. "Night" (with restoration of Pushkin's words) and "The Field-Marshall" orch. 1908.

180 **Songs and Dances of Death**. Song cycle, re-harmonized; orch. 1908.

Schubert

181 **Grand March in A Minor**. Orch. 1869.

Schumann

182 *Carnaval*, **Op. 9**. Orch. by Rimsky-Korsakov and others. Score in BL.

ARRANGEMENTS FOR MILITARY BAND (1873–83)

183 **Beethoven: Overture to *Egmont*.**

184 **Glinka: *A Life for the Tsar*: Finale.**

185 **L. de Meyer: *Marche marocaine*: Berlioz's version.**

186 **Mendelssohn: *Incidental Music to A Midsummer Night's Dream*:** Nocturne and Wedding March.

187 **Meyerbeer: *Robert le Diable*:** Isabela's Aria, arr. for clarinet solo and military band.

188 **Meyerbeer: *Les Huguenots*:** Conspiracy Scene.

189 **Meyerbeer: *Le Prophète*:** Coronation March.

190 **Schubert: March in B-Flat Minor.**

191 **Wagner: Prelude to *Lohengrin*.**

2

Rimsky-Korsakov's Literary Works

LITERARY WORKS, ARTICLES, REVIEWS, FOREWORDS

192   "'Nizhegorodtsy'. Opera Napravnika." [*The People of Nizhny-Novgorod*. Opera by Nápravník.] *Sanktpeterburgskie Vedomosti* (3 January 1869). Reprinted: No. 211: 3–46; No. 282: 13–30.

193   "'Vil'yam Ratklif', opera v 3kh deystviyakh g. Kyui." [*William Ratcliff*, Opera in 3 Acts by Mr. Cui.] *Sanktpeterburgskie Vedomosti* (21 February 1869). Reprinted: No. 211: 3–46; No. 282: 13–30.

194   Foreword to the vocal score of Musorgsky's *Khovanshchina*. St. Petersburg: Bessel', 1883.

195   "Moya pervaya simfoniya." [My First Symphony.] (1884). In No. 282: *Literary Works* II, 61–62.

196   *Uchebnik garmonii* [Manual of Harmony], Parts 1–2. St. Petersburg, 1884–85. Second edition entitled: *Praktichesky uchebnik garmonii.* [Practical Manual of Harmony.] St. Petersburg, 1886. German trans. Leipzig, 1895. French trans. Paris, 1910. Italian trans. Milan, 1913. English trans. New York, 1930. 19th edition, corr. and suppl. M. O. Shteynberg, Moscow, 1956. Reprint of 1886 edition: Moscow: LIBROKOM, URSS, 2009. In No. 282: *Literary Works* IV, 3–327; No. 1341.

197   Foreword to the orchestral score of Musorgsky's *Ivanova noch' na Lysoy gore*. [St. John's Night on Bald Mountain.] St. Petersburg: Bessel', 1886.

50   *Nikolay Andreevich Rimsky-Korsakov: A Research and Information Guide*

198 "O muzykal'nom obrazovanii." [On Music Education.] (1892). In No. 211: 49–119; No. 282: *Literary Works* II, 175–211.

In the form of two articles:

i. "Obyazatel'noe i dobrovol'noe obuchenie v muzykal'nom iskusstve." [Compulsory and Voluntary Instruction in the Art of Music].

ii. "Teoriya i praktika i obyazatel'naya teoriya muzyki v russkoy konservatorii" [Theory and Practice and Compulsory Theory of Music in the Russian Conservatory].

199 "Vagner i Dargomyzhsky." [Wagner and Dargomyzhsky.] (1892). In No. 211: 143–65; *SM* 3 (1933): 136–43; No. 282: *Literary Works* II, 47–60.

200 "Epidemiya dirizhërstva." [The Epidemic of Conducting.] (1892). In *Orkestr* 12, 13, 15, 17 (1911). Reprinted: No. 211: 123–39; No. 282: *Literary Works* II, 31–38. For a German trans. see No. 1343.

201 "Izvlechenie iz plana sochineniya o muzykal'nom iskusstve." [Excerpt from a Planned Work on the Art of Music.] (1892–93). In No. 211: 214–21; No. 282: *Literary Works* II, 65–69.

202 "Otryvok iz vvedeniya k 'Estetike Muzykal'nogo Iskusstva'." [Excerpt from the Introduction to "Esthetics of the Art of Music."] (1893). In No. 211: 209–12; No. 282: *Literary Works* II, 63–64.

203 Foreword to Musorgsky's *Boris Godunov*. St. Petersburg: Bessel', 1896.

204 "K slushatelyam i tsenitelyam opery kak khudozhestvenno-muzykal'nogo proizvedeniya i posetitelyam Mariinskogo teatra." [To Listeners and Connoisseurs of Opera as a Musical Art-Work and to Visitors to the Mariinsky Theater.] In No. 211: 169–77; No. 282: *Literary Works* II, 39–44.

205 "O slukhovykh zabluzhdeniyakh." [On Auditory Delusions.] (1901). In No. 211: 212–14; No. 282: *Literary Works* II, 70–72.

206 "Raznye mysli dlya pamyati." [Various Thoughts to Remember.] (1902). In No. 282: *Literary Works* II, 70.

207 "Tri stikhotvornykh ekspromta Rimskogo-Korsakova." [Three Verse Impromptus by Rimsky-Korsakov.] *RMG* 1 (1909): cols. 8–9.

Consists of three short humorous poems addressed to Lyadov, of which the first, in imitation of Lermontov, written on a postcard in 1903, discusses the correcting of proofs of the opera *Pan Voevoda*, the second is dated 1904, and the third, a whimsical invitation, is dated 1905.

208 "*Snegurochka* – Vesennyaya skazka (tematichesky razbor)." [*The Snow Maiden* – A Spring Fairy Tale (Thematic Analysis).] (1905). Published: *RMG* 39–40 (1908): cols. 804–16. Reprinted: No. 211: 182–200; No. 282: *Literary Works* IV, 391–426; No. 468.

Rimsky-Korsakov's Literary Works 51

209 "Iz dnevnika." [From a Diary.] (1904–07). In No. 211: 222–23; No. 282: *Literary Works* I, 237–42.

210 *Letopis' moey muzykal'noy zhizni.* [Chronicle of My Musical Life.] N. N. Rimskaya-Korsakova, ed. St. Petersburg, 1909.

Principal Russian Editions:

Second edition, corr. and enl., St. Petersburg, 1910.
Third edition, corr. and enl., with intro. and notes, Moscow: Muzsektor, 1928.
Fifth edition, A. N. Rimsky-Korsakov, ed. Corr. and suppl. with intro., notes, appendices, chronology, and illustrations, Moscow: Muzgiz, 1935.
Seventh edition, V. N. Rimsky-Korsakov and A. V. Ossovsky, eds., with the addition of a Diary, Moscow, 1955.
Ninth edition, Moscow, 1982. Also published in *Polnoe sobranie sochineniy. Literaturnye proizvedeniya i perepiska.* [Complete Collection of Compositions. Literary Works and Correspondence.] Vol. I [see No. 282].
Russian Federation edition. Foreword by M. L. Rostropovich. Moscow, 2004. ISBN-10: 5868841107. ISBN-13: 978-5868841101.

French Translations:

N. A. Rimsky-Korsakov. Ma vie musicale. Intro. and adaptation by E. Halpérine-Kaminsky. Paris: Pierre Lafitte, 1914. xviii, 263 pp.

N. A. Rimsky-Korsakov. Journal de ma vie musicale. Trans. Georges Blumberg. Preface by Boris de Schloezer. Paris: Gallimard, 1938. 318 pp.

N. A. Rimsky-Korsakov. Ma vie musicale. Trans. E. Halpérine-Kaminsky, preface and notes by Guy Erismann. Paris: Stock, 1981. 324 pp. ISBN-10: 2234014697. ISBN-13: 978-2234014695.

Nikolaï Rimski-Korsakov. Chronique de ma vie musicale. Trans. and annotated by André Lischke. Paris: Fayard, 2008. 454 pp. ISBN-10: 2213635463. ISBN-13: 978-2213635460.

English Translations:

N. A. Rimsky-Korsakov. My Musical Life. Trans. of rev. second Russian edition by Judah A. Joffe. New York, 1924.

N. A. Rimsky-Korsakov. My Musical Life. Trans. of fifth Russian edition by Judah A. Joffe. New York: Knopf, 1942. Reprinted: London: Ernst Eulenburg, New York: Vienna House, 1974.

N. A. Rimsky-Korsakov. My Musical Life. Ed. with intro. Carl van Vechten. Trans. Judah A. Joffe. London and Boston: Faber & Faber, 1989. 536 pp. Reprint of a translation originally published New York: Knopf, 1942. 478 pp. ISBN-10: 0571142451. ISBN-13: 978-0571142453.

German Translations:

Nikolai Rimski-Korsakow. Chronik meines musikalischen Lebens 1844-1906. Trans. Dr. Oskar von Riesemann. Stuttgart, Berlin, and Leipzig, 1928.

Nikolai Rimski-Korsakow. Chronik meines musikalischen Lebens. Trans. Lothar Fahlbusch. Leipzig: Reclam, 1968. 524 pp.

Spanish Translations:

N. A. Rimski-Korssakow. Mi vida musical 1844-1906. Ed. Bruno del Amo. Madrid, 1934. 278 pp.

N. Rimsky-Korsakov. Diario de Mi Vida Musical. Ed. José Janés. Barcelona, 1947. 337 pp.

Rimsky-Korsakov's *Chronicle of My Musical Life* is one of the most important musical documents concerning the history of Russian music in the second half of the nineteenth century and the first years of the twentieth century. Originally published in 1909, the ninth Russian edition was published in 1982. A new edition was published in the series *Dostoyanie Rossii* [Heritage of Russia] in 2004 [ISBN-10: 5868841107, ISBN-13: 978-5868841101]. The *Chronicle* has been translated into many languages.

Of the various Russian publications, the contents of the fifth edition, continuing the innovations introduced into the third Russian (first Soviet) edition, fall into 10 sections:

Introduction to the fifth edition: 3.
Introduction to the first section: 4–5.
Introduction: 6–19.
N. A. Rimsky-Korsakov. *Chronicle of My Musical Life*: 20–331.
Chronology of Rimsky-Korsakov's life over the period not covered by the *Chronicle* (September 1906–June 1908): 332–59.

Appendices:

i.   Three letters by L. I. Shestakova: 360–61.
ii.   Programs of five concerts, Free Music School (1869–70): 361–63.
iii–iv. Programs of concerts of the Free Music School (1876): 363.
v.   Programs of concerts, Paris All-World Exposition (1889): 364–66.
vi.a.   Open letter to the Editor of the paper *Rus'*: 366.
vi.b.   Open letter to the Director, St. Petersburg Conservatory: 366–67.
vii.   Open letter to the Administration, St. Petersburg Branch of the Russian Music Society: 368.
viii.   Letter to the Arts Council, St. Petersburg Conservatory: 369–70.

List of Contents: 371–75.
List of important publications and articles cited in the Notes: 375–76.
List of names and titles of musical works cited in the *Chronicle*: 377–92.

Rimsky-Korsakov's Literary Works 53

List of Rimsky-Korsakov's works cited in the *Chronicle*: 393–97.
Twenty-six pages of photographs and portraits.

The sixth edition, published as Vol. I of Rimsky-Korsakov's *Literary Works and Correspondence* (1955), also contains new materials, including fragments from a diary (1904–07) [see No. 1366].

211 *Muzykal'nye stat'i i zametki (1869–1907). So vstupitel'noy stat'ey M. F. Gnesina. Pod redaktsiey N. Rimskoy-Korsakovoy.* [Musical Articles and Notes (1869–1907). With an introductory article by M. F. Gnesin. Edited by N. Rimskaya-Korsakova.] St. Petersburg: M. Stasyulevich, 1911. xlvi, 223 pp. [For German trans. of the introductory article, see No. 1340.]

Preceded by a 46-page introductory article on Rimsky-Korsakov's literary works, this collection of writings by the composer comprises:

Two newspaper reviews published 1869: 3–46.

Monograph: *O muzykal'nom obrazovanii.* [On Music Education.] (1892): 49–119, comprising two articles:

i. "Obyazatel'noe i dobrovol'noe obuchenie v muzykal'nom iskusstve." [Compulsory and Voluntary Instruction in the Art of Music.]

ii. "Teoriya i praktika i obyazatel'naya teoriya muzyki v russkoy konservatorii." [Theory and Practice and Compulsory Theory of Music in the Russian Conservatory.]

"Epidemiya dirizhërstva." [Epidemic of Conducting.] (1892): 123–39.

"Vagner i Dargomyzhsky." [Wagner and Dargomyzhsky.] (1892): 43–165.

"K slushatelyam i tsenitelyam opery kak khudozhestvenno-muzykal'nogo proizvedeniya i posetitelyam Mariinskogo teatra." [To Listeners and Connoisseurs of Opera as a Musical Art-Work and to Visitors to the Mariinsky Theater.]: 169–77.

"Snegurochka – Vesennyaya skazka (tematichesky razbor)." [*The Snow Maiden* – A Spring Fairy Tale (Thematic Analysis).] (1905): 181–200. [For German trans. see No. 463.]

Miscellaneous notes and excerpts: 201–23

i.   Excerpt from the foreword to the *Principles of Orchestration.*
ii. Excerpt from introduction to the "Esthetics of the Art of Music."
iii. On Auditory Delusions. [For German trans. see No. 1345.]
iv. Excerpt from a Planned Work on the Art of Music.
v.   From a Diary.

There is no bibliography.

212 *Osnovy orkestrovki. S partiturnymi obraztsami iz sobstvennykh sochineniy.* [Principles of Orchestration. With Examples in Score from his Own Works.] M. O. Shteynberg, ed. Vols. I and II. Berlin, Moscow, St. Petersburg: Ros. Muz. Izd., 1913. Second edition, 1946. In No. 282: *Literary Works* III. French trans. 1914. German trans. 1922. English trans. 1922. English trans. Rimsky-Korsakov, N., *Principles of Orchestration with Music Examples Drawn from his Own Works.* M. Steinberg, ed. Trans. E. Agate. 2 Vols. New York: Dover, London: Constable, 1964. Vol. I: 152 pp., Vol. II: 333 pp. Reprinted: 2005. ISBN-10: 0486212661. ISBN-13: 978-0486212661. Italian trans. Rimsky-Korsakov, N. A. *Principi de orchestrazione.* Trans. L. Ripanti. Milan: Rugginenti editore, 1992. 180 pp. ISBN: 8876650733.

Since first appearing in 1913, this work has been regarded as outstanding. Constantly reprinted, it has been translated into many languages and continues to hold its place. A listing of its contents is given in *Literary Works* III. For reviews of the 1964 English edition, Rimsky-Korsakov, N., *Principles of Orchestration with Music Examples Drawn from his Own Works,* see:

Music and Musicians 13 (May 1965): 52.
Musical Opinion 88 (August 1965): 673.
Music Teacher 44 (May 1965): 223.
Music in Education 29 (1965): 140–41.
Neue Zeitschrift für Musik 128 (1967): 167.

213 "N. A. Rimsky-Korsakov o svoikh sochineniyakh ('Antar,' Fortepianny kontsert, 'Ispanskoe kaprichchio,' 'Pesn' o veshchem Olege')." [N. A. Rimsky-Korsakov on his Own Works ("Antar," Piano Concerto, "Spanish Caprice," "Song of Oleg the Wise").] *Muzyka* 133 (1913).

CORRESPONDENCE (Chronological)

214 "Pis'mo N. A. Rimskogo-Korsakova k redaktsiyu 'Russkoy Muzykal'noy Gazety'." [A Letter of N. A. Rimsky-Korsakov to the Editorial Board of the *Russian Musical Gazette.*] *RMG* 35 (1899): cols. 819–20.

215 "Ob uproshchennoy partiture." [On the Simplified Score.] *RMG* 45 (1907): cols. 1021–23.

216 "Dva pis'ma k A. P. Borodinu (1879g.)." [Two Letters to A. P. Borodin (1879).] *RMG* (1909) cols. 562–64.

Relating to *Prince Igor,* this forms part of the special edition of the *RMG* published on the first anniversary of his death.

217 "Pis'ma k A. P. Borodinu i V. V. Yastrebtsëvu." [Letters to A. P. Borodin and V. V. Yastrebtsëv.] *RMG* 22–23 (1909).

218 "Tri pis'ma k V. V. Yastrebtsëvu (1906g.)." [Three Letters to V. V. Yastrebtsëv (1906).] *RMG* (1909) cols. 564–67.

Rimsky-Korsakov's Literary Works 55

In the first letter the composer asks Yastrebtsëv for information on the date and year on which various parts of the first version of *The Maid of Pskov* were completed. He also expresses his bewilderment over current political and artistic events. The second letter acknowledges receipt of the materials and then goes on to a lyrical description of the beauties of the Italian lakes and the wild life. The last letter opens with a quotation from *Il Trovatore* (musical letters were in vogue at the time), and then discusses the furore around *Dubinushka*. Forms part of the special edition of the *RMG* published on the first anniversary of his death.

219   "Pis'ma N. A. Rimskogo-Korsakova i V. S. Kalinnikova S. N. Kruglikovu." [Letters of N. A. Rimsky-Korsakov and V. S. Kalinnikov to S. N. Kruglikov.] *Muzyka* 2–3 (1910).

220   "Perepiska V. V. Stasovym." [Correspondence with V. V. Stasov.] *Russkaya Mysl'* 6–9 (1910).

221   "Perepiska N. A. Rimskogo-Korsakova i V. V. Stasova." [Correspondence of N. A. Rimsky-Korsakov and V. V. Stasov.] *RMG* 49–51/52 (1910).

222   "Perepiska s V. V. Stasovym po povodu opery-byliny 'Sadko'." [Correspondence with V. V. Stasov a propos of the Opera-bylina 'Sadko'.] *Muzyka* 4–5, 7, 8 (1910–11).

223   "Pis'ma k Ts. A. Kyui." [Letters to C. A. Cui.] *Muzyka* 28 (1911).

224   "(Pis'mo) k A. N. Rimskomu-Korsakovu." [(Letter) to A. N. Rimsky-Korsakov.] *Russkaya Molva* 110 (9 May 1913). Reprinted: *Muzyka* 113 (1913); *SM* 6 (1958): with corr. date.

225   "Neizdannoe pis'mo N. A. Rimskogo-Korsakova k V. V. Yastrebtsëvu." [An Unpublished Letter of N. A. Rimsky-Korsakov to V. V. Yastrebtsëv.] *Muzyka* 133 (1913).

226   "Perepiska s M. P. Musorgskim." [Correspondence with M. P. Musorgsky.] *Muzyka* (1913): 457–60.

227   "Iz neizdannykh pisem N. A. Rimskogo-Korsakova (k N. F. Findeyzenu)." [From Unpublished Letters of N. A. Rimsky-Korsakov (to N. F. Findeyzen).] *EIT* 5 (1913).

228   "Iz neizdannoy perepiski N. A. Rimskogo-Korsakova i Musorgskogo." [From Unpublished Correspondence of N. A. Rimsky-Korsakov with Musorgsky.] *Russkaya Molva* 174 (1913).

229   Lyapunov, S. M., ed. "Perepiska s M. A. Balakirevym." [Correspondence with M. A. Balakirev.] *Muzykal'ny Sovremennik* 1–3 (1913); 1–7 (1916); 7–8 (1917).

230   "Iz pisem k V. V. Yastrebtsëvu." [From Letters to V. V. Yastrebtsëv.] *Muzyka* 185, 187 (1914).

231 "Perepiska N. A. Rimskogo-Korsakova s An. K. Lyadovym." [Correspondence of N. A. Rimsky-Korsakov with An. K. Lyadov.] *Muzykal'ny Sovremennik* 7 (1916): 37–58.

232 "Pis'ma k L. I. Shestakovoy." [Letters to L. I. Shestakova.] *Muzykal'ny sovremennik*, kniga 2 [Book 2] (October, 1916).

233 Lyapunov, S. M., ed. "Perepiska M. A. Balakireva i N. A. Rimskogo-Korsakova." [Correspondence of M. A. Balakirev with N. A. Rimsky-Korsakov.] *Muzykal'ny Sovremennik* 1–3 (1915); 1–7 (1916); 7–8 (1917).

234 "Pis'ma k V. I. Suku." [Letters to V. I. Suk.] *Teatr* 5 (1922).

235 "Pis'ma N. A. Rimskogo-Korsakova k Findeyzenu." [Letters of N. A. Rimsky-Korsakov to Findeyzen.] *Muzykal'naya nov'* 4 (1) (1924).

236 "Pis'ma k V. I. Suku." [Letters to V. I. Suk.] *Programmy Gosudarstvennykh Akademicheskikh Teatrov* [Programs of the State Academic Theaters] 37. Moscow, 1926.

237 "Perepiska s M. P. Musorgskim." [Correspondence with M. P. Musorgsky.] In M. P. Musorgsky. *Pis'ma i dokumenty.* [Letters and Documents.] Moscow-Leningrad, 1932.

238 Van'kovich, G., ed. "Iz perepiski N. A. Rimskogo-Korsakova s M. P. Belyaevym." [From the Correspondence of N. A. Rimsky-Korsakov with M. P. Belyaev.] *SM* 5 (1933): 126–28.

These seven letters from Rimsky-Korsakov to Belyaev written between 1890 and 1897 are part of the 57 letters to him preserved in the library of the Moscow State Conservatory. Preceded by an introductory note by Van'kovich, the correspondence deals with the problems of concert organization, Rimsky-Korsakov's relations with Belyaev, and especially with Balakirev to whom he refers in uncomplimentary terms.

239 "(Pis'mo) k V. I. Suku." [(Letter) to V. I. Suk.] In I. I. Remezov. *V. I. Suk. Materialy k biografii.* [V. I. Suk. Materials for a Biography.] Moscow: Muzgiz, 1933.

240 "Iz perepiski N. A. Rimskogo-Korsakova i M. M. Ippolitova-Ivanova." [From the Correspondence of N. A. Rimsky-Korsakov with M. M. Ippolitov-Ivanov.] *SM* 3 (1933): 143–46.

Consists of six letters by Rimsky-Korsakov to Ippolitov-Ivanov written 1878–1902, including discussion of the operas *The Tale of Tsar Saltan* and *Kashchey the Immortal.*

241 "A. N. Ostrovsky i N. A. Rimsky-Korsakov. (Pis'ma)." [A. N. Ostrovsky and N. A. Rimsky-Korsakov. (Letters).] In E. Kolosova and V. Filippov, eds. *A. N. Ostrovsky i russkie kompozitory. Pis'ma.* [A. N. Ostrovsky and Russian Composers. Letters.] Moscow-Leningrad: Iskusstvo, 1937: 172–85.

Rimsky-Korsakov's Literary Works 57

Consists of three letters exchanged between the composer and Ostrovsky between October and November 1880 relating to work on the opera *The Snow Maiden*, accompanied by detailed commentaries by Kiselëv.

242 "Neizdannye pis'ma k S. I. Taneevu." [Unpublished Letters to S. I. Taneev.] *SM* 6 (1937): 75–80.

This collection of letters to Taneev includes one from Rimsky-Korsakov written on 24 January 1894, pp. 77–78. Clearly a response to a query from Taneev, it explains the St Petersburg Conservatory's policy on the teaching of harmony, counterpoint, and fugue. It is preceded by an explanatory note by Kiselëv.

243 "Pis'ma k V. V. Vasil'evu." [Letters to V. V. Vasil'ev.] *SM* 4 (1939): 95–100.

244 "Pis'mo k A. V. Ossovskomu." [A Letter to A. V. Ossovsky.] *Literatura i iskusstvo* 12 (116) (1944).

245 "Perepiska P. I. Chaykovskogo i N. A. Rimskogo-Korsakova." [Correspondence of P. I. Tchaikovsky with N. A. Rimsky-Korsakov.] *SM*, sbornik [Collective Vol.] 3 (1945): 121–48.

Consists of 32 letters, attesting to the good relations between Tchaikovsky and Rimsky-Korsakov during the period 1868–91.

246 "Dva neopublikovannykh pis'ma k S. I. Taneevu." [Two Unpublished Letters to S. I. Taneev.] In *Pamyati S. I. Taneeva. Sbornik statey i materialov.* [In Memory of S. I. Taneev. Collection of Articles and Materials.] Moscow-Leningrad, 1947.

247 Kunin, I. and Shteynberg, A. eds. "Iz perepiski N. A. Rimskogo-Korsakova." [From the Correspondence of N. A. Rimsky-Korsakov.] *SM* 4 (1948): 52–55.

Consists of six letters by Rimsky-Korsakov, of which the first two, dated 31 August 1907 and 9 March 1908, are to Kruglikov. The second of the letters, giving an account of his poor health, includes the statement that he is "the prime enemy of coarse realism and naturalism." The remaining letters (to Belanovsky), dated 22 October and 15 December 1905 and 19 February and 19 May 1908, likewise reflect his mood of depression in the last months of his life when he was no longer a well man. The composer's comments on modernism are of particular interest.

248 Pashkalov, V. *V. S. Kalannikov.* Moscow-Leningrad: Muzgiz, 1951: 228.

A revision of an earlier study by Pashkalov, published in 1938. For correspondence between Rimsky-Korsakov and Kruglikov, see pp. 86–95 of the 1951 edition.

249 "N. Rimsky-Korsakov. Pis'ma k E. Petrovskomu." [N. Rimsky-Korsakov. Letters to E. Petrovsky.] *SM* 12 (1952): 68–72.

Consists of 11 letters from Rimsky-Korsakov to Petrovsky, a music critic with *RMG*, written between 1902 and 1906. The letters concern *Kashchey the Immortal* in particular, but also discuss the liturgical aspects of *The Legend of the Invisible City of Kitezh*, Rimsky-Korsakov's aims in editing *Boris Godunov* and other works. The letter dated 6 January 1906 contains the comment: "... and in the second place, I avoid speaking about myself too much in public. I know that this deprives others and myself of the possibility of saying a great deal; but so be it."

250   "Perepiska S. I. Taneeva s N. A. Rimskim-Korsakovym." [The Correspondence of S. I. Taneev with N. A. Rimsky-Korsakov.] In S. I. Taneev. *Materialy i dokumenty.* [Materials and Documents.] Vol. I. Moscow: Izd. Akademii Nauk SSSR (1952): 28–50.

251   "Neizvestnye pis'ma V. A. Telyakovskogo i N. A. Rimskogo-Korsakova." [Unknown Letters of V. A. Telyakovsky and N. A. Rimsky-Korsakov.] *SM* 10 (1953): 47–49.

Rimsky-Korsakov's letter, p. 49, is written to Telyakovsky, Director of the Moscow Branch of the Imperial Theaters, 1901–17, requesting the forthcoming production of *The Legend of the Invisible City of Kitezh* in 1907 to be temporarily postponed.

252   "Izbrannye pis'ma N. A. Rimskogo-Korsakova k N. N. Rimskoy-Korsakovoy." [Selected Letters of N. A. Rimsky-Korsakov to N. N. Rimskaya-Korsakova.] In M. O. Yankovsky, ed. *Muzykal'noe nasledstvo. Rimsky-Korsakov. Issledovaniya. Materialy. Pis'ma. (V dvukh tomakh).* [Musical Legacy. Rimsky-Korsakov. Research. Materials. Letters. (In Two Volumes).] Vol. II, 1954: 19–112. [See No. 1204.]

A selection of 89 of the 491 letters of Rimsky-Korsakov to his wife, taken from the Rimsky-Korsakov family archive, and covering the period 1879–1906. The letters are diverse in content and include materials on his attitude to Russian sacred music, his reactions to performances of some of his operas, including *The Snow Maiden, The Tsar's Bride,* and *The Tale of Tsar Saltan*, together with comments on the political scene. Extracts from Rimsky-Korsakov's letters to his wife are also published in: A. N. Rimsky-Korsakov. *N. A. Rimsky-Korsakov. Life and Work* [see No. 1180].

253   Gusin, I. "Iz istorii russkoy opery." [From the History of Russian Opera.] *SM* 9 (1954): 75–77.

Rimsky-Korsakov was a member of the committee appointed to assess the suitability of Cui's just completed opera *Andzhelo* for performance on the Imperial Stage, each member being required to submit a written evaluation. Rimsky-Korsakov's letter is published on p. 77.

254   Lifar, Serge and Korabel'nikova, Lyudmila Zinov'evna. "Rimsky-Korsakov v Parizhe: Pyat' neopublikovannykh pisem kompozitora." [Rimsky-Korsakov

Rimsky-Korsakov's Literary Works 59

in Paris: Five Unpublished Letters of the Composer.] *Vozrozhdenie* [Revival] 48 (1955). Reprinted: *MA* (2) (1994): 133–38. ISSN: 0869-4516.

This consists of five letters written by Rimsky-Korsakov to the French critic Michel Delin, when visiting Paris in 1907 and 1908.

255 "Perepiska s B. Kalenskim." [Correspondence with B. Kalensky.] In I. Belza, ed. *Iz istorii russko-cheshkikh muzykal'nykh svyazey.* [From the History of Russo-Czech Musical Links.] Vol. I. Moscow: Muzgiz, 1955.

256 "Pis'mo k Yanu Batke." [A Letter to Yan Batka.] In I. Belza, ed. *Iz istorii russko-cheshkikh muzykal'nykh svyazey.* [From the History of Russo-Czech Musical Links.] Vol. I. Moscow, 1955.

257 Kyui, Tsezar' Antonovich [Cui, César]. *Izbrannye pis'ma.* [Selected Letters.] I. L. Gusin, ed. Leningrad: Muzgiz, 1955. 754 pp.

Consisting almost entirely of letters by Cui, six letters by Rimsky-Korsakov to Cui are included in the Appendix, all written in 1863 except the last which belongs to 1890. The early letters contain good-natured humour, one of them having a whimsical drawing [see pp. 484–87, 489–90, 492–93, 515].

258 "Iz neopublikovannykh dokumentov: Pis'ma k synu Andreyu, Dva pis'ma k H. fon Bulow, Pis'ma k P. Sheynu, k A. Ossovskomu." [From Unpublished Documents: Letters to his Son Andrey, Two Letters to H. von Bülow, Letters to Sheyn, to Ossovsky.] *SM* 6 (1958): 66–80.

A compilation of materials, including several letters published for the first time. Part of a series of articles in a volume of *SM* marking the 50th anniversary of the composer's death.

259 Dianin, Sergey Aleksandrovich. *Borodin. Zhizneopisanie. Materialy i dokumenty.* [Borodin. Account of his Life. Materials and Documents.] Second edition. Moscow: Muzgiz, 1960. 404 pp.

Includes six of Rimsky-Korsakov's letters to Borodin in the period 1877–79 [see pp. 207, 211, 213, 215, 216–28, 231–32]. The last two letters are concerned with numbers from *Prince Igor* [see pp. 216–28 and 231–32].

260 "Perepiska s A. K. Glazunovym." [Correspondence with A. K. Glazunov.] In *Glazunov. Issledovaniya. Materialy. Publikatsii. Pis'ma.* [Glazunov. Research. Materials. Publications. Letters.] Vol. II. Leningrad: Muzgiz, 1960.

261 "Pis'mo k N. N. Ikonnikovu." [A Letter to N. N. Ikonnikov.] *MZ* 10 (1961).

262 Letter to A. N. Vinogradsky, dated 1 November 1891. In A. Bykov, ed. *Iz arkhivov russkikh muzykantov.* [From Russian Musicians' Archives.] Moscow: Muzgiz (1962): 162–63.

263 Velimirović, M. "An Unpublished Letter from Rimsky-Korsakov." *JAMS* XV, 3 (1962): 352–53.

60   *Nikolay Andreevich Rimsky-Korsakov: A Research and Information Guide*

Description of a letter sent by the composer on 10 October 1905 to a pupil, identified by Velimirović as Berka Leibovich Levenson. The letter is preserved in the Houghton Library, Harvard University.

264   Raaben, Lev Nikolaevich, ed. *Aleksandr Il'ich Ziloti. 1863-1945. Vospominaniya i pis'ma.* [Aleksandr Il'ich Ziloti. 1863-1945. Reminiscences and Letters.] Leningrad: Muzgiz, 1963.

For an exchange of letters between the pianist Aleksandr Ziloti and Rimsky-Korsakov over the period 1901–07, see pp. 203–17.

265   "Pis'ma k M. A. Vrubelyu." [Letters to M. A. Vrubel.] In *Vrubel'. Perepiska. Vospominaniya o khudozhnike.* [Vrubel'. Correspondence. Reminiscences of the Artist.] Leningrad-Moscow, 1963.

266   "Iz pisem N. A. Rimskogo-Korsakova k synu (Andreyu)." [From the Letters of N. A. Rimsky-Korsakov to his Son (Andrey).] *SM* 2 (1964).

267   "Pis'mo k A. G. Chesnokovu." [A Letter to A. G. Chesnokov.] *MZ* 10 (1964).

268   Nikulin, L. ed. "Rimsky-Korsakov, Nikolay Andreevich. 'O Vagnere i russkoy muzyke'." [Rimsky-Korsakov, Nikolay Andreevich. "On Wagner and Russian Music."] Commentary by B. Yarustovsky. *Moskva* 9 (1965): 218–19.

A letter from the composer to M. I. Delin (Ashkenazi).

269   Kharkeevich, Irina. "Po sledam neizvestnogo pis'ma N. A. Rimskogo-Korsakova." [In the Tracks of an Unknown Letter by N. A. Rimsky-Korsakov.] *SM* 6 (1971): 79–83.

Describes the contents of a letter, written by Rimsky-Korsakov, found in the holdings of the East Siberian Branch of the Imperial Russian Geographical Society, containing materials relating to the work of Nikolay Protasov, an avid folk song collector and ethnologist.

270   Kutateladze, L., ed. and comp. *F. Stravinsky, stat'i, pis'ma, vospominaniya.* [F. Stravinsky, Articles, Letters, Reminiscences.] Leningrad: Muzyka (1972). 207 pp.

Fëdor Stravinsky was well-known as a performer of several Rimsky-Korsakov roles. The correspondence section includes three letters to Fëdor Stravinsky from the composer [see pp. 144, 167–68].

271   Orlova, A., ed. "Iz perepiski N. A. Rimskogo-Korsakova s V. I. Bel'skim." [From the Correspondence of N. A. Rimsky-Korsakov with V. I. Bel'sky.] *SM* 2 (1976): 95–115; 3 (1976): 99–112; 6 (1976): 86–103.

A series of articles concerned with Rimsky-Korsakov's artistic collaborations with Bel'sky. Preceded by an introductory commentary, they include a total of ninety-two letters, exchanged between composer and librettist, which discuss *The Tale of Tsar Saltan* [letters 1–24], *The Legend of the*

Invisible City of Kitezh [letters 24(sic)–52], *The Golden Cockerel* [letters 53–92], as well as other projected works: *Navzikaya* [Nausicaä], *Odissey u Tsarya Alkinoya* [Odysseus and King Alcinous], *Nebo i zemlya* [Earth and Sky], *Gero i Leandr* [Hero and Leander], *Tsar' Saul* [King Saul], *Evridika* [Eurydice], *Konchina mira* [End of the World], *Edip* [Oedipus], *Rusalka, Bylina o Solov'e Budimiroviche* [Bylina about Solovey Budimirovich], and *Sten'ka Razin*. Provides insight into the composer's esthetic beliefs and personality.

272   Vakhromeev, V., ed. "Neizvestnoe pis'mo N. A. Rimskogo-Korsakova." [An Unknown Letter of N. A. Rimsky-Korsakov.] *SM* 4 (1977): 141–42.

A letter written by Rimsky-Korsakov to the conductor, palaeographer, and sacred music composer Stepan Vasil'evich Smolensky, dated St. Petersburg, 26 November 1901.

273   Bogdany, Wanda. "Archiwum wilenskie Emila Mlynarskiego w mikrofilmach Biblioteki Narodowej." [The Vilna Archives of Emil Mlynarski in the Microfilm Collections of the Biblioteka Narodowa (in Warsaw).] *Ruch muzyczny* 11 (June 1980): 17–18.

Includes letters from Rimsky-Korsakov.

274   Kopytova, Galina Viktorovna. "Iz pisem." [From the Letters.] *MA* (4) (1992): 140. ISSN: 0869-4516.

Letters written by Igor Stravinsky to Rimsky-Korsakov's widow and son, Nadezhda Rimskaya-Korsakova and A. Rimsky-Korsakov, and to the composer's son-in-law, composer Maksimilian Shteynberg.

275   Anonymous. "Pis'ma V. I. i A. K. Bel'skikh." [Letters of V. I. and A. K. Bel'sky.] *MA* (2) (1994): 147. ISSN: 0869-4516.

Consists of two letters, one from Vladimir Ivanovich Bel'sky to Rimsky-Korsakov and another from Bel'sky's widow, Agrippina K. Bel'skaya, to Mikhail Rimsky-Korsakov, the composer's son.

276   Kopytova, Galina Viktorovna. "'Brat Voin, mne ochen' khochetsya znat'..." ["Brother Voin, I would very much like to know..."] *MA* (2) (1994): 106–14. ISSN: 0869-4516.

Rimsky-Korsakov was much influenced in his early years by his elder brother, Voin Andreevich, with whom he conducted an extensive correspondence, excerpts from which are reproduced in this article, together with competent drawings by the composer of sailing ships.

277   Rakhmanova, Marina Pavlovna. "Iz pisem N. M. Shtrupa." [From the Letters of N. M. Shtrup.] *MA* (2) (1994): 149. ISSN: 0869-4516.

Consists of letters by Nikolay M. Shtrup, organizer of the Obshchestvo Muzykal'nykh Sobraniy [Society of Music Assemblies] in St. Petersburg

62   *Nikolay Andreevich Rimsky-Korsakov: A Research and Information Guide*

and one of the assistant librettists for Rimsky-Korsakov's opera *Sadko.* The letters written to Rimsky-Korsakov cover the period 1895–98.

278   Somov, Vladimir Aleksandrovich. "Materialy N. A. Rimskogo-Korsakova v Belyaevskom arkhive Peterburgskoy konservatorii." [Materials Relating to N. A. Rimsky-Korsakov in the Belyaev Archive of the St. Petersburg Conservatory.] In V. M. Vasil'eva, comp. *N. A. Rimsky-Korsakov i russkaya khudozhestvennaya kul'tura. Materialy nauchnoy konferentsii. Vechasha-Lyubensk.* [N. A. Rimsky-Korsakov and Russian Artistic Culture. Materials from a Scientific Conference. Vechasha-Lyubensk.] Pskov, 2008.

Discusses excerpts from the unpublished correspondence of Rimsky-Korsakov preserved in the M. P. Belyaev Archive of the St. Petersburg Conservatory, providing information on the publishing of some of his works and their distribution outside of Russia.

279   Alekseevsky, N. "Chredu vekov pitaet novost'." [Novelty Feeds the Turn of the Ages.] *MZ* (3) (2009): 36. ISSN: 0131-2383.

Includes letters written by Rimsky-Korsakov to Glinka's sister, Lyudmila Shestakova, concerning Musorgsky's progress in endeavouring to complete his opera *Sorochinskaya yarmarka* [Sorochintsy Fair].

OTHER REFERENCES

280   Rimsky-Korsakov, Andrey Nikolaevich. *N. A. Rimsky-Korsakov. Zhizn' i tvorchestvo.* [N. A. Rimsky-Korsakov. Life and Work.] Vols. I–V. Moscow: Ogiz-Muzgiz, 1933–46. [See No. 1180.]

Contains letters to his family and friends.

281   Yankovsky, Moisey Osipovich, ed. *Muzykal'noe nasledstvo. Rimsky-Korsakov. Issledovaniya. Materialy. Pis'ma. (V dvukh tomakh).* [Musical Legacy. Rimsky-Korsakov. Research. Materials. Letters. (In Two Volumes).] Vol. I. Moscow: Izd. Akad. Nauk SSSR, 1953. 416 pp. Illustrations, music examples. Vol. II. *Publikatsii i vospominaniya.* [Publications and Memoirs.] Moscow: Izd. Akad. Nauk. SSSR, 1954. 368 pp. Illustrations, music examples, index. [See No. 1204.]

Contains letters of Rimsky-Korsakov to Al'brekht, Andreev, Bessel', Veynberg, Gubert, Dulova, Zimin, Klementova-Muromtseva, Kyui, Lipaev, Mamontov, Popov, Safonov, Suvorin, Khudekov, Cheshikhin, Espozito, P. I., B. P. and A. I. Yurgenson, and Yanovsky.

COMPLETE COLLECTION OF COMPOSITIONS, LITERARY WORKS, AND CORRESPONDENCE

282   Rimsky-Korsakov, Nikolay Andreevich. *Polnoe sobranie sochineniy. Literaturnye proizvedeniya i perepiska.* [Complete Collection of Compositions. Literary Works and Correspondence.] Vols. I–VIII. Moscow: Muzgiz, 1955–82.

Rimsky-Korsakov's Literary Works

List of Contents:

I (1955):	Chronicle; Diary; Documents.
II (1963):	Critical writings, Esthetics, Education, Professional Life.
III (1959):	Principles of Orchestration.
IV (1960):	Practical Harmony Manual (1884–85); Analysis of The Snow Maiden; Miscellaneous materials.
V (1963):	Correspondence with M. A. Balakirev, A. P. Borodin, C. A. Kyui, M. P. Musorgsky, V. V. and D. V. Stasov, L. I. Shestakova, V. V. Vasil'ev.
VI (1965):	Correspondence with A. K. Glazunov and A. K. Lyadov.
VII (1970):	Correspondence with P. I. Chaykovsky, S. I. Taneev, I. F. Tyumenev, A. S. Arensky, A. V. Ossovsky, A. A. Spendiarov, A. T. Grechaninov, F. S. Akimenko, I. E. Molchanov, K. N. Chernov, A. R. Berngard, V. P. Kalafati, M. N. Barinova, N. N. Cherepnin, O. Ya. Levenson, Ya. V. Prokhorov, M. O. Shteynberg, M. M. Ippolitov-Ivanov, A. S. Arensky.
VIIIa, b (1981–82):	Correspondence with S. N. Kruglikov.

Description of Contents:

Vol. I: *Letopis' moey muzykal'noy zhizni.* [**Chronicle of My Musical Life.**] A. V. Ossovsky and V. N. Rimsky-Korsakov, eds. Moscow: Muzgiz, 1955. xi. 399 pp. Autograph: Leningrad State Conservatory.

This consists of Rimsky-Korsakov's *Chronicle*, a diary relating to 1904–07, and a number of documents, some previously unpublished. According to the editorial introduction, Rimsky-Korsakov's complete text is printed here for the first time, the editors having adhered closely to the first edition and subsequent volumes, and making any necessary restorations or emendations in the matter of cuts or inaccuracies of dates.

List of Contents:

Editorial Foreword: vii–x.
N. N. Rimsky-Korsakov's Introduction to the first edition: xi–xii.
Chronicle of My Musical Life: 3–236.
"Diary": 237–42.
Notes: 243–86.
Chronology of Rimsky-Korsakov's Life, September 1906 to June 1908: 287–328.

Appendices:

Plan of the *Chronicle*: 329–38.
Rimsky-Korsakov. Autobiography: 339.
Rimsky-Korsakov. Autobiography: 340.
Rimsky-Korsakov. Materials for a biographical sketch: 340–41.

Rimsky-Korsakov's enrolment as a naval cadet from a Naval Cadet Corps entry book: 341.

Two notes by L. I. Shestakova: 342.

Rimsky-Korsakov's application for permission to conduct concerts of his own works: 343.

Programs of five subscription concerts of the Free Music School conducted by Balakirev: 343–44.

Program of a Free Music School concert conducted by Rimsky-Korsakov on 3 February 1876: 345.

Program of a Free Music School concert conducted by Rimsky-Korsakov on 23 March 1876: 345.

Open letter by Rimsky-Korsakov to the Editor of the paper *Rus'*: 346.

Open letter to the Director of the St. Petersburg Conservatory: 346.

Open letter to the Management of the St. Petersburg Branch of the Russian Music Society: 347.

Rimsky-Korsakov's letter to the Art Council of the St. Petersburg Conservatory: 348.

Chronological table of the writing of parts of the *Chronicle*: 349.

Chronological table of writing the *Chronicle* by chapters: 350.

List of names: 352–80.

List of Rimsky-Korsakov's works referred to in the present vol.: 381–84.

List of works by other composers referred to in the present vol.: 385–92.

List of 48 illustrations: 393–95.

Vol. II: *Kriticheskie stat'i, estetika, obrazovanie, professional'naya zhizn'*. [**Critical writings, Esthetics, Education, Professional Life**.] N. V. Shelkov, ed. Moscow: Muzgiz. 1963: 280 pp.

This volume, concerned with Rimsky-Korsakov's critical writings, works on esthetics, education and professional life, is divided into seven sections.

List of Contents:

Musical-critical articles: 11–44.

Articles and materials on questions of music history and esthetics: 45–72.

Documents and materials pertaining to Naval-Military Bands: 73–127.

Materials pertaining to the Imperial Chapel: 129–68.

Materials pertaining to the St. Petersburg Conservatory: 169–222.

Materials pertaining to the Russian Music Society and Rimsky-Korsakov's role as founder of Higher Education Courses in Music: 223–33.

Articles to the Press: 235–58.

The volume is preceded by an introductory article and concludes with a list of names, pp. 259–72, a list of Rimsky-Korsakov's works mentioned in the text, p. 273, a list of works by other composers referred to in the text, pp. 274–76, a list of illustrations, p. 277, and a list of contents, pp. 278–80.

Vol. III: *Osnovy orkestrovki*. [Principles of Orchestration.] A. N. Dmitriev, ed. Moscow: Muzgiz, 1959. xvi. 805 pp. Autograph: SPGK.

This volume is the third edition of Rimsky-Korsakov's *Principles of Orchestration*. Following Shteynberg's edition, though differing from it in a number of respects, it contains new materials relating to the work, which are published for the first time. The whole of this volume, however, should be examined in the light of a review by A. I. Kandinsky, *SM* 5 (1960): 186–88, who considers that some of the editing is inappropriate to an academic edition and is unsystematic.

List of Contents:
Editorial Foreword: vii–x.
Editor's Foreword to the first edition: xi–xv.
Editor's Foreword to the second edition: xvi.
Editor's Foreword to the 1891 edition: 3–7.
From the Author's Foreword to the last edition: 8.
Principles of Orchestration: 9–568.

Appendices:

i.   Use of orchestral devices in polyphonic music: 569–780.
ii. Introduction to instrumentation: 781–83.
iii. Questions of esthetics: 784–91.
iv. Examples of orchestration of separate tutti chords: 792–97.

List of examples of orchestral devices: 798–800.
List of Rimsky-Korsakov's works employed: 801.
List of musical contents: 802–05.

Vol. IV: *Praktichesky uchebnik garmonii (1884-1885)*. [Practical Harmony Manual (1884-1885).] Vl. V. Protopopov, ed. Moscow: Muzgiz, 1960. xvi, 454 pp.

This volume is concerned with Rimsky-Korsakov's musical-theoretical works. Of prime interest is the publication of the two editions of his *Practical Harmony Manual*, the first of which was published in St. Petersburg, 1884, under the title: *Uchebnik garmonii. Kurs Pridvornoy kapelly, vypusk pervy. Garmonizatsiya akkordami v predelakh lady* [Harmony Manual. A Course for the Imperial Chapel, First Issue. Harmonization with Chords within the Limits of a Mode]. This was followed in 1885 by a complete revision of the 1884 edition, together with new material, this being published under the title: *Uchebnik garmonii, sostavil N. Rimsky-Korsakov* [Harmony Manual, Compiled by N. Rimsky-Korsakov]. The idea of writing the work originally arose as a result of his teaching a course of harmony at the Imperial Chapel for which, he felt, a new approach was required. Between 1885 and 1956, the *Harmony Manual* was issued 19 times, of which seven editions appeared during the composer's lifetime. The editor of Vol. IV of the *Complete Works*, while utilizing the 1884 edition, chose not to reprint the 1885 volume, but to use the ninth edition of 1909, together with modifications appearing in subsequent editions. This volume is entitled *Praktichesky uchebnik garmonii* [Practical Harmony Manual], the name given to the work when published in 1886. Other materials in Vol. IV include an unfinished analysis of his opera *The Snow Maiden*, while in the Appendix are published miscellaneous works, including an analysis of the content of his own operas divided into three periods, concluding with the opera *Servilia* (1901).

List of Contents:
Editorial Foreword: vii–xvi.
Harmony Manual: 3–227.
Commentaries: 228–36.
Practical Harmony Manual: 237–387.
Commentaries: 388–92.
Analysis of *The Snow Maiden*: 393–428.

Appendices:

i.   Melodies for harmonization: 429.
ii. Classification of harmonic sequences in the natural modes: 430–34.
iii. Notes on Glinka's *Ruslan and Lyudmila*: 435.
iv. Rimsky-Korsakov's observations in the margins of text books on music theory [all based on Russian translations of works of the German L. Bussler]: 436–44.
v.   Thoughts on my own operas: 445–48.

List of contents: 449–54.

Vol. IV, Supplement: *Notnye zapisnye knizhki*. [**Music Notebooks**.] Vl. V. Protopopov, ed. Moscow: Muzgiz, 1970. 325 pp. Autographs: SPGK, SPBGATI.

This contains twelve music notebooks covering the period 1884–1906, including themes and sketches for works subsequently completed or projected, many of which are published for the first time. The introductory article, pp. 7–10, is informative.

Vol. V: *Perepiska*. [**Correspondence**.] A.S. Lyapunova, ed. Moscow: Muzgiz, 1963. xi, 591 pp.

This volume is concerned with Rimsky-Korsakov's correspondence with M. A. Balakirev, A. P. Borodin, Ts. A. Kyui, M. P. Musorgsky, V. V. and D. V. Stasov, L. I. Shestakova [Glinka's sister], and V. V. Vasil'ev, while in the Appendix are published an exchange of letters between Rimsky-Korsakov's wife and V. V. Stasov, together with letters to her from Borodin. The correspondence covers a period from autumn 1861, when Rimsky-Korsakov first met Balakirev, to the last months of his life in 1908, and includes a number of letters not previously published.

Rimsky-Korsakov's Literary Works

List of Contents:
Editorial Foreword: vii–viii.
Abbreviations of names of institutions holding materials: ix.
Location of MS Sources: ix.
Abbreviations of published sources: x–xi.
Correspondence between Rimsky-Korsakov and Balakirev (1862–98) [249 letters]: 17–210.
Correspondence with Borodin (1871–86) [19 letters]: 217–31.
Correspondence with Kyui (1862–1908) [54 letters]: 240–79.
Correspondence with Musorgsky (1867–80) [18 letters]: 289–319.
Correspondence with V. V. Stasov (1866–1906) [113 letters]: 330–455.
Correspondence with D. V. Stasov (1866–1907) [14 letters]: 460–69.
Letters to V. V. Vasil'ev (1870–72) [2 letters]: 474.
Letters to L. I. Shestakova (1878–89) [2 letters]: 479–80.

Appendices:

i.   N. N. Rimskaya-Korsakova's correspondence with V. V. Stasov (1870–1905): 486–520. [36 letters.]

ii. Borodin's letters to N. N. Rimskaya-Korsakova (1871–81): 521–22. [3 letters.]

Addendum: Two letters of Rimsky-Korsakov to Balakirev (1890, 1892): 525.

List of names: 526–64.

List of Rimsky-Korsakov's works mentioned in the text: 565–68.
List of works by other composers mentioned in the text: 569–79.
List of illustrations: 580–81.
List of contents: 582–91.

Vol. VI: *Perepiska N. A. Rimskogo-Korsakova i A. K. Glazunova.* [**The Correspondence of N. A. Rimsky-Korsakov with A. K. Glazunov.**] E. E. Yazovitskaya, ed. Moscow: Muzgiz, 1965. x, 234 pp.

This volume includes the correspondence between Rimsky-Korsakov and his favorite pupils and close friends, Glazunov and Lyadov, covering the period 1878–1908. The correspondence with A. K. Lyadov consists of 51 letters of which 25 are by Rimsky-Korsakov, while that with Glazunov is considerably larger, comprising 163 letters, with 61 letters belonging to Rimsky-Korsakov himself. Of the Lyadov correspondence, five letters were published earlier in the journal *Muzykal'ny sovremennik*. Of the Glazunov correspondence, 29 letters are published for the first time, another 134 having been published in the years 1958–60. For a detailed criticism of this volume, see G. Yudin. "N. Rimsky-Korsakov. *Polnoe sobranie sochineniy. Literaturnye proizvedeniya i perepiska.* T. VI." *SM* 11 (1966): 143–44.

List of Contents:
Editorial Foreword: vii.
Abbreviations of names of institutions holding materials: ix.
Location of MS sources: ix.
Abbreviations of published sources: x.
Correspondence with Lyadov (1878–1908) [51 letters]: 10–45.
Correspondence with Glazunov (1882–1908) [163 letters]: 59–200.
List of names: 201–19.
List of Rimsky-Korsakov's works mentioned in the text: 220–21.
List of works by other composers mentioned in the text: 222–28.
List of illustrations: 229.
List of contents: 230–34.

Vol. VII: *Perepiska.* [**Correspondence.**] A. S. Lyapunova and E. E. Yazovitskaya, ed. Moscow: Muzyka, 1970. 472 pp.

Correspondence with Tchaikovsky, Taneev, and his pupils, I. Tyumenev, A. Ossovsky, M. Shteynberg, M. Ippolitov-Ivanov, N. Artsybushev, and others. In his review of this volume [*SM* 1, 1972: 139–42] A. Kunin points out that, whereas Tchaikovsky's letters in the Complete Edition of his *Literary Works* are arranged chronologically, Rimsky-Korsakov's letters are a collected correspondence with one person, which has the advantage that it can be preceded by an introductory article. Kunin notes that although a number of Rimsky-Korsakov–Tchaikovsky letters were published in the third volume of articles of *SM* (1945), the new edition contains some letters from 1875, which are published for the first time. Vol. VII also contains material illuminating Rimsky-Korsakov's attitude towards the work of Skryabin.

Vols. VIIIa, VIIIb: *Perepiska N. A. Rimskogo-Korsakova i S. N. Kruglikova.* [**The Correspondence of N. A. Rimsky-Korsakov with S. N. Kruglikov.**] A. P. Zorina and I. A. Konopleva, eds. Moscow: Muzyka, 1981–1982: Vol. VIIIa: 353 pp.; Vol. VIIIb: 252 pp. Review: *SM* 7 (1983): 108–09.

List of Contents:
Rimsky-Korsakov's correspondence with Kruglikov, containing a total of 503 letters covering the periods 1879–95 and 1896–1908.
Index of names.
List of works mentioned.
List of musical compositions by different authors.
List of contents.

In her review of these volumes, M. Rakhmanova notes that it is one of the most substantial collections of the composer's letters. The friendship with Kruglikov was long-lasting and one untroubled by the conflicts that occurred between Rimsky-Korsakov and Stasov, Balakirev, and even Glazunov and Lyadov. The letters cover the last 30 years of Rimsky-Korsakov's life, including the period from the composition of *May Night* to *The Golden Cockerel.*

Among the many subjects touched upon are questions of musical education, his work at the Free School of Music, his own music, and his role as an editor of the compositions of Borodin and Musorgsky. The letters are notable for their frankness and highlight his sense of insecurity and self-doubt. Also included is a group of letters, which speak of his work in the harmonization of ancient Russian melodies and chants from the *Obikhod*.

3

Bibliography: Musical Works

OPERAS: GENERAL

283   Abraham, Gerald. *Studies in Russian Music: Critical Essays on the Most Important of Rimsky-Korsakov's Operas, Borodin's "Prince Igor'," Dargomizhsky's "Stone Guest," Etc.; With Chapters on Glinka, Mussorgsky, Balakirev and Tchaikovsky.* London: William Reeves, n.d. [1935]. 355 pp. Reprint: *Studies in Russian Music. Rimsky-Korsakov and His Contemporaries.* London: William Reeves, 1965. Reprint: [1935] edition. London: William Reeves, 1969. Reprint: *Studies in Russian Music. Rimsky-Korsakov and His Contemporaries.* Scholarly Press, 1976. Reprint: Reprint Services Corp., 1988. Reprint: London: Faber & Faber, 2011; 2014. ISBN-10: 0571277861. ISBN-13: 978-0571277865.

Though references to Rimsky-Korsakov are scattered liberally throughout the 16 chapters of Abraham's book [see first edition (1935)], Chapters VIII–XIV are directly concerned with Rimsky-Korsakov's operas, being entitled:

Rimsky-Korsakov's first opera [*The Maid of Pskov*]: 142–66.
Rimsky-Korsakov's Gogol Operas [*May Night, Christmas Eve*]: 167–92.
Snegurochka [*The Snow Maiden*]: 193–220.
Sadko: 221–45.
The Tsar's Bride: 246–60.
Kitezh: 261–89.
The Golden Cockerel: 290–310.

Despite the absence of footnotes enabling one to identify the precise sources of the quotations, this and its companion studies are a useful starting point for any investigation of Rimsky-Korsakov in the English language.

Bibliography: Musical Works 71

284 ——. *On Russian Music: Critical and Historical Studies of Glinka's operas, Balakirev's Works, etc., with Chapters Dealing with Compositions by Borodin, Rimsky-Korsakov, Tchaikovsky, Mussorgsky, Glazunov, and Various Other Aspects of Russian Music.* London: William Reeves, 1939. 279 pp. Reprint: New York: Books for Libraries Press, 1970. Reprint: Native Amer Books, 1976. Reprint: Scholarly Press, 1976. Reprint: Books for Libraries, Arno Press, 1980. Reprint: Irvington Publishers, May 1982. Reprint: Reprint Services Corp., March 2013. Reprint: Faber Finds, November 2013. 290 pp. ISBN-10: 0571307272. ISBN-13: 978-0571307272.

As in Abraham's preceding volume *Studies in Russian Music,* there are many references to Rimsky-Korsakov and his work throughout the pages of this survey. The chapters specifically concerned with the composer are:

Chapter VIII, The Collective *Mlada*: 91–112.
Chapter IX, Rimsky-Korsakov's *Mlada*: 113–21.
Chapter X, *Tsar Saltan*: 122–37.

Other chapters contain observations on harmonic and melodic aspects of Rimsky-Korsakov's style, together with remarks on his psychological make-up.

285 ——. "Rimsky-Korsakov's letters to a publisher." *Monthly Musical Record* 75 (1945): 105–08, 152–55, 182–85.

Consisting of 15 letters written by Rimsky-Korsakov to the publisher Bessel' between 1898 and 1905, translated by Gerald Abraham, these are concerned primarily with the composer's work on *The Snow Maiden, The Stone Guest,* and *Kashchey the Immortal.* The personal nature of the letters provides an insight into his psychology and working habits, as well as revealing his increasing recognition as a composer outside of Russia.

286 Anonymous. "Novosibirsky teatr opery i baleta." [The Novosibirsk Opera and Ballet Theater.] *SM* 1 (1980): 138.

Brief mention of a cycle of seven operas by the composer given by the Novosibirsk Company in a single season: *Sadko, Pan Voevoda, May Night, The Tale of Tsar Saltan, The Tsar's Bride, Christmas Eve,* and *Kashchey the Immortal*; probably the largest number of his operas given in any one place at any one time. With a dramatic photograph of Kashchey.

287 Anonymous. *Opery N. A. Rimskogo-Korsakova. Putevoditel'.* [The Operas of N. A. Rimsky-Korsakov. A Guidebook.] Moscow: Muzyka, 1976. 476 pp.

A collection of 11 articles on 10 operas by Rimsky-Korsakov, of which the first is a general survey of his operatic works by V. Tsendrovsky. Several of the articles are based on published guides to the opera (e.g., V. Berkov and Vl. Protopopov on *The Golden Cockerel*).

288 Arenzon, Evgenij. *Savva Mamontov.* In the series *Rossii slavnye imena.* [Famous Names of Russia.] Russkaya kniga, 1995. 236 pp. ISBN-10: 5268014455. ISBN-13: 978-5268014457.

An illustrated biography of Savva Ivanovich Mamontov (1841–1918), a prominent Russian entrepreneur and patron of the arts, founder of the Moskovskaya Chastnaya Russkaya Opera [Moscow Private Russian Opera], which staged a number of operas by Rimsky-Korsakov.

289 ——. *Savva Mamontov: iskusstvo i zheleznye dorogi.* [Savva Mamontov: Art and Railways.] Moscow: Bizneskom, 2011. 237 pp. ISBN-10: 5916631197. ISBN-13: 978-5916631197.

Mamontov was an industrialist who made a fortune from constructing railways, particularly the Severnaya Zheleznaya Doroga [Northern Railway], which linked Moscow with the North. One of his most notable charitable undertakings was the founding of the Artists' Colony in Abramtsevo.

290 Asaf'ev, Boris Vladimirovich [pseud. Glebov, Igor']. *Rimsky-Korsakov. Opyt kharakteristiki.* [Rimsky-Korsakov. A Character Sketch.] Petrograd: Svetozar, 1922. 56 pp.

This modest volume is useful in its observations about Rimsky-Korsakov's operas, which are examined under a series of evocative titles:

Winter Vespers [*Christmas Eve*].
The Incantation of Spring and Summer [*The Snow Maiden*].
The Spring Vespers [*May Night*].
The Cult of Fire [*Mlada*].
Lyric Poetry of a Woman's Soul [a general discussion of some of the heroines in Rimsky-Korsakov's operas].
The Problem of the Holy Town [*The Legend of the Invisible City of Kitezh*].

A novel feature is Asaf'ev's interpretation of *Mozart and Salieri* in which he identifies Mozart with Rimsky-Korsakov's doomed heroines (Snegurochka, Kashcheevna, Servilia, Volkhova, Ol'ga, Marfa), pp. 50–51. "Rimsky-Korsakov's Fairy Tales" is an examination of some of the orchestral works.

291 ——. "Rimsky-Korsakov." *Teatr* 1 (1923): 9–11.

A general article on the composer and his operas, stressing the need for them to be extensively performed.

292 ——. "Rimsky-Korsakov (k 20-letiyu so dnya konchiny)." [Rimsky-Korsakov (on the 20th Anniversary of His Death).] *Muzyka i Revolyutsiya* 5–6 (May–June, 1928): 3–9.

Asaf'ev examines some of the recurring ideas and symbols in the composer's operas, particularly those of suffering womanhood, the folk element, his love of nature and his powers of musical description.

293 ——. "Opery Chaykovskogo i Rimskogo-Korsakova." [The Operas of Tchaikovsky and Rimsky-Korsakov.] In E. M. Orlova, ed. *Russkaya muzyka (XIX i nachalo XX veka).* [Russian Music (XIX and Early XX Century).] Leningrad: Muzyka, 1968: 27–37.

Bibliography: Musical Works

First published in Moscow in 1930 under the pen name Igor' Glebov by the Publishing House of the Soviet Academy of Sciences, Asaf'ev's survey of nineteenth-century Russian music, considered genre by genre, was translated into English by Alfred J. Swan: *Russian Music from the Beginning of the Nineteenth Century* (Ann Arbor: J. W. Edwards, 1953): 329 pp., this being No. 22 in the Russian Translation Project series of the American Council of Learned Studies. Like all Asaf'ev's work, each of the seven main sections of the book contains many references to Rimsky-Korsakov and his compositions. A systematic examination of Tchaikovsky's and Rimsky-Korsakov's operas, and discussion of their historical, cultural, and artistic musical context are found on pp. 27–37.

294 ——. "Bol'shoy teatr." [The Bol'shoy Theater.] In *Gosudarstvenny ordena Lenina akademichesky Bol'shoy teatr Soyuza SSR.* [The State Order of Lenin Academic Bol'shoy Theater of the Union of Soviet Socialist Republics.] Moscow: Izd. GABT., 1947. Reprinted: No. 1256, Vol. IV: 161–81.

Discusses performances of several of Rimsky-Korsakov's operas, including *The Snow Maiden, Pan Voevoda,* and the more frequent staging of his works in the years 1906–09. With comments on notable singers (e.g., Nezhdanova, Sobinov) and conductors (e.g., Suk, Rakhmaninov), and extracts from the composer's *Chronicle of My Musical Life.*

295 ——. "Russky narod, russkie lyudi." [Russian Folk, Russian People.] *SM* (1 January 1949): 59–70. Reprinted: No. 1256, Vol. IV: 109–22.

A broad survey of the part played by mass scenes in Russian opera, including Rimsky-Korsakov's *Sadko, The Maid of Pskov, The Legend of the Invisible City of Kitezh,* and other works highlighting various composers' methods of approach.

296 ——. *Simfonicheskie etyudy.* [Symphonic Studies.] Petrograd, 1922. Reprinted: Leningrad: Muzyka, 1970. 264 pp. Reprint of first edition, Kompozitor, 2008. English trans. David Haas, ed. *Symphonic Etudes: Portraits of Russian Operas and Ballets.* Lanbam, MD: Scarecrow Press, 2007. xxviii, 319 pp. ISBN-10: 0810860309. ISBN-13: 978-0810860308.

Asaf'ev's *Symphonic Studies* [references are to 1970 edition] is a collection of monographs written in the period 1917–21, of which more than half are concerned with Rimsky-Korsakov. Commencing with the article "N. A. Rimsky-Korsakov (1844-1908)," first published as a supplement to a program of a concert given by the Petrograd Philharmonic in 1919, pp. 40–48, Asaf'ev discusses the composer's outstanding attributes, namely his self-discipline, unremitting labor, determination, pedagogical work, and esthetic attitudes, together with a brief outline of his life. This is succeeded by nine articles regarding his operas, these being entitled:

Pskovityanka [The Maid of Pskov]: 49–53.
Mayskaya noch' [May Night]: 53–62.

Snegurochka [The Snow Maiden]: 62–66.
Zaklyatiya [The Oath], a discussion of *Mlada* and *Kashchey the Immortal*: 66–73.
Noch' pered Rozhdestvom [Christmas Eve]: 74–86.
Problema grada vidimogo [The Problem of the Visible City], a discussion of *Sadko*: 86–95.
Skazka [A Fairy Tale, i.e., *The Tale of Tsar Saltan*]: 95–101.
Skazanie o nevidimom grade [The Legend of the Invisible City (*Kitezh*)]: 101–18.
Skomorosh'e tsarstvo [The Kingdom of Clowns (*The Golden Cockerel*)]: 119–25.

Asaf'ev's articles are full of observations, comparisons, and psychological insights, written in a complex, sophisticated, literary language.

297   Bagirova, Liana Mashallaevna. "K probleme muzykal'noj sinopsii: Na primere oper Rimskogo-Korsakova." [On the Question of Musical Synopsis: Using the Example of Rimsky-Korsakov's Operas.] In *Vzaimodeystvie iskusstv: Metodologiya, teoriya, gumanitarnoe obrazovanie.* [Interaction of the Arts: Methodology, Theory, Humanitarian Education.] Russian Federation, 1997.

A discussion as to how a synthesis of color and sound [synesthesia] is achieved in Rimsky-Korsakov's operas.

298   ——. "Tonal'naya dramaturgiya oper N. A. Rimskogo-Korsakova v aspekte logiki i poetiki solyarnykh mifov." [The Tonal Dramaturgy of N. A. Rimsky-Korsakov's Operas from the Perspective of Logic and Poetics of Solar Myths.] In Larissa Danko, ed. *Peterburgskaya konservatoriya v mirovom muzykal'nom protsesse, 1862-2002: Materialy mezhdunarodnoy muzykal'noy nauchnoy sessii, posvyashchënnoy 140-letiyu Konservatorii.* [The St. Petersburg Conservatory in the World Musical Process, 1862-2002: Materials of the International Musical Scientific Session, Dedicated to the 140th Anniversary of the Conservatory.] St. Petersburg Conservatory, 2002.

An examination of the tonal symbolism used by Rimsky-Korsakov in his mythological and fairy tale operas.

299   Balakirev, Mily Alekseevich. *Perepiska s N. G. Rubinshteynom i s M. P. Belyaevym.* [Correspondence with N. G. Rubinstein and M. P. Belyaev.] V. A. Kiselëv, ed. Moscow: Muzgiz, 1956. 103 pp.

Contains a number of references to Rimsky-Korsakov and his works, including *The Maid of Pskov, Antar,* and the Musical Picture "Sadko."

300   Berkov, V. and Protopopov, Vl. "Putevoditeli po operam N. Rimskogo-Korsakova." [Handbooks on the Operas of N. Rimsky-Korsakov.] *SM* 10 (1936): 105–10.

Bibliography: Musical Works

A critical review of three handbooks on Rimsky-Korsakov's operas, highlighting Gorodetskaya's work for its weakness:

i. Gorodetskaya, Z. *"Pskovityanka"* – *opera Rimskogo-Korsakova*. ["The Maid of Pskov" – Opera by Rimsky-Korsakov.] Moscow: Muzgiz, 1936.

ii. Kulakovsky, L. *"Snegurochka"* – *opera Rimskogo-Korsakova*. ["The Snow Maiden" – Opera by Rimsky-Korsakov.] Moscow: Muzgiz, 1935.

iii. Tsukkerman, V. *"Sadko"* – *opera bylina Rimskogo-Korsakova*. ["Sadko" – Opera Bylina by Rimsky-Korsakov.] Moscow: Muzgiz, 1935.

301 Calvocoressi, Michael Dimitri. "Rimsky-Korsakov's Operas Reconsidered." *MT* 72 (1931): 886–88.

In this review of Gilse Van der Pals' *N. A. Rimsky-Korssakow Opernschaffen nebst Skizze über Leben und Wirken*, Calvocoressi regrets that he cannot share the author's enthusiasm for the composer's music, which, in Calvocoressi's opinion, "even at its most delightful, consists of colour, rather than of expression." Van der Pals' book, he considers, is far too supportive of the composer and his aims and thus lacks a critical element. This applies particularly to the question of Rimsky-Korsakov's associations of color with key, the implications of which Van der Pals accepts without question.

302 *Central Opera Service Bulletin* 6 (December 1960).

This includes a directory of opera sets and costumes for hire or rent within the United States, including four locations for *The Golden Cockerel*. To this list should also be added the name of Indiana University.

303 *Central Opera Service Bulletin. Part Two of the Directory of Operas and Publishers*. 18 (3) (1977): 67–68.

Two pages of information on scores and materials available within the United States with regard to twelve operas by Rimsky-Korsakov.

304 Cheshikhin, Vsevolod Evgrafovich. *Istoriya russkoy opery (s 1674 po 1903 g.)*. [History of Russian Opera (from 1674 to 1903).] First edition. St. Petersburg: Yurgenson, 1902. Second edition, corr. and enl. St. Petersburg: Yurgenson, 1905. 638 pp.

The first edition of Cheshikhin's *History of Russian Opera* is a bibliographical rarity, the work being better known through the second edition of 1905, a monumental volume and a milestone in Russian music historiography. Cheshikhin's *History* is unique, in that no other histories of Russian Opera were written in the nineteenth century by Russian scholars. Despite inaccuracies in his review of the early period of Russian opera, his chapter on late nineteenth-century opera is written from his acquaintance with the scores and sometimes with personal knowledge of the composers in question. His views are expressed in a forthright manner and, though some of his opinions were questioned by Soviet scholars, they still merit attention.

The high regard in which he held Rimsky-Korsakov is confirmed by the fact that a substantial section of Chapter V, pp. 410–49, is devoted to him. Cheshikhin's work is full of factual information, often supplemented by extracts from contemporary criticisms and, although there are few music examples, each opera is described in a perceptive manner. The section on Rimsky-Korsakov concludes with a discussion of *Pan Voevoda*.

305   Cooper, Martin. *Russian Opera*. London: Max Parrish, 1951. 66 pp. Reprinted: Michigan: Scholarly Press, 1977. ISBN-10: 0403015286. ISBN-13: 978-0403015283.

A discussion of Rimsky-Korsakov's operas is to be found on pp. 48–57, special attention being given to *The Legend of the Invisible City of Kitezh*. Unique in Rimsky-Korsakov's work, the opera is seen as essentially a product of the "mysticism and apocalyptic religion," together with the moral ideas of Lev Tolstoy current during the period.

306   Cooper, Martin, ed. *The New Oxford History of Music*, Vol. 10: *The Modern Age. 1890-1960*. Oxford and New York: Oxford University Press, 1974. 784 pp. ISBN-10: 0193163101. ISBN-13: 978-0193163102.

For a discussion of the late operas of Rimsky-Korsakov, see pp. 174–77.

307   Danilevich, Lev Vasil'evich. *Poslednye opery N. A. Rimskogo-Korsakova*. [The Last Operas of N. A. Rimsky-Korsakov.] Moscow: Muzgiz, 1961. 279 pp.

Consists of an Introduction, together with eight chapters entitled:

The Start of an Age.
The Thinker.
Some Questions of Style.
Servilia.
Pan Voevoda.
Kashchey the Immortal.
The Legend of the Invisible City of Kitezh and the Maiden Fevroniya.
The Golden Cockerel.

In the author's opinion, Rimsky-Korsakov's last operas all present moral themes, including the struggle of good and evil, and the use and misuse of autocratic power, issues which are also reflected in the works of contemporary Russian writers. Danilevich's examinations of the various operas are wide-ranging and illustrated with 68 music examples.

308   Druskin, Mikhail Semënovich. *Voprosy muzykal'noy dramaturgii opery. O materiale klassicheskogo naslediya*. [Questions of Musical Operatic Dramaturgy. On Material from the Classical Heritage.] Leningrad: Muzgiz, 1952. 344 pp. Review: E. Grosheva. "Kniga ob opernoy dramaturgii." [A Book about Operatic Dramaturgy.] *SM* 4 (1953): 110–11.

Essentially an ideological interpretation of Russian "classical" opera, Druskin's study consists of eight chapters and an Introduction, covering such themes as "The Ideological Bases of Russian Classical Opera," "Realism and Russian Operatic Esthetics," "Recitative," "Aria, Arioso and Song," "The Chorus," and "The Orchestra," in which Rimsky-Korsakov is referred to frequently. Illustrated with nearly 100 music examples, and taking the form of comparative studies, the undoubted value of the book is somewhat lessened by the absence of an index.

309 ——, ed. *50 Oper. Istoriya sozdaniya. Syuzhet. Muzyka.* [50 Operas. History of Composition. Subject. Music.] Second edition. Leningrad: Sovetsky Kompozitor, 1960. 328 pp.

This includes a discussion of six of Rimsky-Korsakov's operas, pp. 174–205, preceded by a short account of the composer and his achievements. The operas described are *May Night, The Snow Maiden, Sadko, The Tsar's Bride, The Tale of Tsar Saltan,* and *The Legend of the Invisible City of Kitezh.*

310 ——, ed. *100 Oper. Istoriya sozdaniya. Syuzhet. Muzyka.* [100 Operas. History of Composition. Subject. Music.] Leningrad: Muzyka, 1968. 624 pp.

An expanded version of the preceding volume, this discusses 11 operas of Rimsky-Korsakov, the additional ones being *The Maid of Pskov, Christmas Eve, Mozart and Salieri, Kashchey the Immortal,* and *The Golden Cockerel.* No music examples, illustrations, or index.

311 Earl of Harewood, George Henry Hubert Lascelles, Peattie, Antony, and Kobbé, Gustav, eds. *The New Kobbé's Opera Book.* 11th edition. New York: G. P. Putnam's Sons, 1997. xviii, 1012 pp. ISBN-10: 0399143327. ISBN-13: 978-0399143328.

Comprising an account of nine operas by Rimsky-Korsakov (see pp. 636–52), each opera is accompanied by valuable information written in an approachable literary style.

312 Engel', Yuly Dmitrievich. "Bol'shoy operny teatr v 1909-1910 gg." [The Bol'shoy Opera Theater 1909-1910.] *EIT* IV (1910): 189–93.

Typical of the wealth of information to be found in the *Yearbooks of the Imperial Theaters,* one learns from this article that during the 1909–10 season Rimsky-Korsakov's *Sadko* was given eight times, and *May Night* and *The Golden Cockerel* twelve times. All yielded in popularity, however, to Tchaikovsky's *Evgeny Onegin,* given 13 times.

313 ——. *Glazami sovremennika. Izbrannye stat'i o russkoy muzyke,1898-1918.* [In the Eyes of a Contemporary. Selected Articles on Russian Music, 1898-1918.] Ed. and comp. I. Kunin. Moscow: Sovetsky Kompozitor, 1971. 524 pp.

Engel's activity as a music critic lasted for some 25 years (1893–1918), during the last 17 of which he wrote almost exclusively for the Moscow journal

Russkie Vedomosti. An enthusiastic, cultivated and colorful writer, Engel' was a strong partisan of the Russian National School and his articles on Rimsky-Korsakov and his work are of musical and historical interest. The period 1900–18 was a rich one for Russian opera, thanks to conductors such as Suk and Emil Cooper, and the singers Shalyapin, Sobinov, Nezhdanova, and Ershov. The editor singles out Engel's articles on "The Golden Cockerel" (1909) and "Kashchey the Immortal" (1902) for special mention. Engel' was also responsible for reviewing Rimsky-Korsakov's *Chronicle* on its appearance in 1909. [See "Rimsky-Korsakov on His Contemporaries" and "Rimsky-Korsakov on Himself." In *Russkie Vedomosti* 114 (21 May 1909), 130 (9 June 1909) and 135 (14 June 1909).]

314   Ferman, Valentin Eduardovich. "Nekotorye osobennosti muzykal'noy dramaturgii russkoy opernoy shkoly." [Some Peculiarities of the Musical Dramaturgy of the Russian Operatic School.] *SM* 10 (1946): 100–06.

A discussion of some of the notable qualities of Russian opera, for example, mass scenes, use of reminiscence motives, "Leitmotive" distinctive structural devices, as manifest in the operas of Rimsky-Korsakov, Glinka, Dargomyzhsky, Musorgsky, and Tchaikovsky.

315   Frelikh, O. "Tsarevna-Lebed'. (Iz vospominaniy)." [Swan Princess. (From Reminiscences).] In No. 1204, Vol. II: 348–50.

A short account by O. Frelikh of the impression the singing of Nadezhda Ivanovna Zabela-Vrubel' produced upon him, especially her performance of the part of the Swan Princess in Rimsky-Korsakov's *The Tale of Tsar Saltan*.

316   Geylig, M. "Nekotorye osobennosti krupnoy formy v skazochnykh operakh N. A. Rimskogo-Korsakova." [Some Peculiarities of Large-scale Form in Rimsky-Korsakov's Fairy Tale Operas.] In *Nauchno-metodicheskie zapiski Saratovskoy Konservatorii*. [Scientific-methodical Transactions of the Saratov Conservatory.] Saratov, 1959.

317   Gilse van der Pals, N. van. "N. A. Rimsky-Kors[s]akow: Opernschaffen nebst Skizze über Leben und Wirken." Inaugural-Dissertation zur Erlangung der Doktorwürde vorgelegt der hohen philosophischen Fakultät der Universität Leipzig. Leipzig: Breitkopf und Härtel, 1914: 120 pp. Reprinted, enl.: Paris-Leipzig: W. Bessel, 1929. vii, 691 pp. Reprinted: Hildesheim: G. Olms, 1977. ISBN-10: 3487064278. ISBN-13: 978-3487064277.

A detailed examination of the composer's 15 operas, each of which is discussed systematically from the point of view of genesis and meaning, content of libretto, and music. Copiously illustrated with music examples, this is an important reference work. A short account of the composer's life and other compositions is included.

318   Gilyarovskaya, N. "Rimsky-Korsakov i khudozhniki. (Materialy k stsenicheskoy istorii oper Rimskogo-Korsakova)." [Rimsky-Korsakov and

Artists. (Materials for a Stage History of Rimsky-Korsakov's Operas).] In No. 1204, Vol. II: 261–318.

A discussion of the costumes and décors of various operas by Rimsky-Korsakov, with numerous illustrations of sketches by Shishkov, Bocharov, Golovin, Vrubel', Vasnetsov, Matorin, Bilibin, and others. Includes information on some Soviet productions.

319 Gozenpud, Abram Akimovich. *N. A. Rimsky-Korsakov. Temy i idei ego opernogo tvorchestva.* [N. A. Rimsky-Korsakov. Themes and Ideas of His Operatic Works.] Moscow: Muzgiz, 1957. 187 pp.

This is concerned with the ideological content of Rimsky-Korsakov's operas, their links with folk poetry, literature, and the related arts, in the writing of which the author has utilized new materials and manuscript sources. It does not pretend to be a specialized musicological analysis. Divided into 12 chapters, special attention is paid to a re-evaluation of the significance of the works of Rimsky-Korsakov's last period, many of which he considers to have been misunderstood.

320 ——. *Operny slovar'.* [Operatic Dictionary.] Moscow-Leningrad: Muzyka, 1965. 480 pp.

A reference volume listing 15 operas by Rimsky-Korsakov, with factual information about each work, its première, principal performers, subsequent history, and its social and musical significance for Russian audiences.

321 ——. *Izbrannye stat'i.* [Selected articles.] Leningrad-Moscow: Sovetsky Kompozitor, 1971. 240 pp.

Among this collection of articles by Gozenpud are two important ones on Rimsky-Korsakov, the first being entitled "Rimsky-Korsakov's work on an opera libretto," pp. 128–73, the second "Rimsky-Korsakov's notebooks," pp. 174–239. The first article discusses the composer's choice of subjects, his reasons for their selection and, using archival and other materials, examines the manner in which various libretti evolved. The second article discusses the content of some of the composer's notebooks, which contain sketches for both completed and projected works, including numerous musical drafts.

322 ——. "Dostoevsky i muzykal'noe teatral'noe iskusstvo." [Dostoevsky and Musical Theatrical Art.] Leningrad: Muzyka, 1971. Second edition, 1981. 175 pp.

Includes a discussion of some of the possible influences of Dostoevsky on the composer's music, as seen in *The Maid of Pskov* and *The Legend of the Invisible City of Kitezh* [see pp. 147–48].

323 ——. *Russky operny teatr mezhdu dvukh revolyutsiy. 1905-1917.* [The Russian Opera Theater between Two Revolutions. 1905-1917.] Leningrad: Muzyka, 1975. 367 pp.

Rimsky-Korsakov is referred to frequently in this study. Of chief interest are Chapter IV, devoted to an examination of *The Legend of the Invisible City of Kitezh*, pp. 155–94, and Chapter VI, a survey of *The Golden Cockerel*, pp. 233–74. Gozenpud is an erudite scholar and his sources of information are diverse, drawing on contemporary accounts and personal memoirs.

324   Grachev, Panteleymon Vladimirovich. "Leytmotiv v operakh Rimskogo-Korsakova." [The Leitmotiv in Rimsky-Korsakov's Operas.] In *De Musica: Vremennik Otdela Teorii i Istorii Muzyki Gosudarstvennogo Instituta Istorii Iskusstv.* [De Musica: Chronicle of the Department of History and Music Theory of the State Institute of the History of the Arts.] Vol. III. Leningrad, 1927: 76–96.

A short discussion of the role of the Leitmotiv in the history of music and its employment in the Romantic period, its use by Glinka, and some of the ways it is employed by Rimsky-Korsakov in *The Snow Maiden, Mlada, Christmas Eve, Sadko, The Tale of Tsar Saltan*, and *The Golden Cockerel*. With comparative music examples.

325   Griffiths, Steven. "A Critical Study of the Music of Rimsky-Korsakov, 1844-1890." PhD dissertation, Sheffield University, 1982. 314 pp. In *Outstanding Dissertations from British Universities*. New York: Garland, 1989. ISBN-10: 0824001974. ISBN-13: 978-0824001971.

Includes discussion of the four Rimsky-Korsakov operas written prior to 1890, namely *The Maid of Pskov, May Night, The Snow Maiden*, and *Mlada*.

326   Grosheva, Elena Andreeva. *Iz zala Bol'shogo teatra. Stat'i. Retsenzii. Ocherki.* [From the Hall of the Bol'shoy Theater. Articles. Reviews. Essays.] Moscow: Sovetsky Kompozitor, 1969. 510 pp.

Among the many references to Rimsky-Korsakov, mention should be made of the articles "The Tale of Tsar Saltan," pp. 125–30, and "The Snow Maiden," pp. 221–26, together with the accompanying critical observations.

327   ——. "Obnovlennaya klassika." [Renewed Classics.] *SM* 3-4 (1976): 35–48.

Includes a discussion of Rimsky-Korsakov's operas at the Bol'shoy Theater in the 1920s.

328   Gurevich L. Ya., ed. *O Stanislavskom. Sbornik vospominaniy.* [About Stanislavsky. A Collection of Reminiscences.] Moscow: Vserossiyskoe teatral'noe obshchestvo, 1948. 659 pp., 47 pp. of illustrations.

Stanislavsky was one of the greatest Russian stage directors of his time. Information relating to his interpretation of a number of Rimsky-Korsakov's operas is to be found on pp. 396, 419, 423, 451, and 468.

329   Hofmann, Rostislav-Michel. *Un Siècle d'Opéra Russe (de Glinka à Stravinsky).* Paris: Corrêa et Cie, 1946. 254 pp.

Chapter VIII discusses Rimsky-Korsakov's operas and the circumstances of their composition. Written in an approachable, intimate style, incorporating a number of quotations from critics and the composer himself. No documentation, bibliography, or index.

330 Kabalevsky, Dmitry Borisovich. "Rimsky-Korsakov i modernizm." [Rimsky-Korsakov and Modernism.] *SM* 6 (1953): 58–69; 7 (1953): 45–57; 8 (1953): 32–40. Reprinted: No. 1204, Vol. l: 17–78.

Kabalevsky's three articles are concerned with Rimsky-Korsakov's last operas *Kashchey the Immortal*, *The Legend of the Invisible City of Kitezh*, and *The Golden Cockerel*. Through a discussion of their ideological content, together with harmonic, contrapuntal, and "modernistic" elements, Rimsky-Korsakov's music is shown to be fully in keeping with Russian "classical" music. Copiously illustrated with music examples, sketches, and photographs.

331 Kandinsky, Aleksey Ivanovich. "O muzykal'nykh kharakteristikakh v tvorchestve Rimskogo-Korsakova 90kh godov." [On the Musical Characteristics of Rimsky-Korsakov's Work of the 1890s.] Reprinted in No. 1204, Vol. I: 79–144. Music examples.

An article concerned with the composer's increasing interest in psychological opera in the 1890s, as manifest in *Mozart and Salieri*, *Boyarynya Vera Sheloga*, and *The Tsar's Bride*, together with the musical means employed to obtain development and unity.

332 ——. "Rimsky-Korsakov v 1890-1900-e gody." [Rimsky-Korsakov in the 1890-1900s.] In D. V. Zhitomirsky, ed. *Muzyka XX veka. Ocherki.* [Twentieth Century Music. Essays.] Chast' pervaya [Part I] 1890–1917. Kniga vtoraya [Book 2], Moscow: Muzyka, 1977: 5–44; 491–94.

Divided into six sections, this article is concerned with Rimsky-Korsakov's work in the period 1890–1908. Following a general introduction to the composer, the ensuing chapters are concerned with his last operas, commencing with *Sadko* and *Mlada*. The bibliography, pp. 491–94, contains more detail than is customary.

333 ——, ed. *Istoriya russkoy muzyki. Tom II. Vtoraya polovina XIX veka. Kniga vtoraya. N. A. Rimsky-Korsakov. Dopushcheno Upravleniem uchebnykh zavedeniy i nauchnykh uchrezhdeniy Ministerstva Kul'tury SSSR v kachestve uchebnika dlya studentov muzykal'nykh vuzov.* [History of Russian Music. Vol. II. Second Half of the 19th Century. Book 2. N. A. Rimsky-Korsakov. Approved by the Governing Board of Academic Establishments and Scientific Organisations of the USSR Ministry of Culture as a Manual for Students of Musical Tertiary Institutions.] Moscow: Muzyka, 1979. 279 pp. Second edition, corr. and enl., 1984. 310 pp.

An assessment of the composer from the ideological point of view prevailing at the time, this consists of the following sections:

Introduction: 3–8.

Problematics of his creative genius. Esthetic principles. Evolution and questions of style: 9–30.

Operatic esthetic. The initial step: *The Maid of Pskov*: 31–47.

Operas on the fringe of the 1870s–80s: *May Night, The Snow Maiden*: 48–74.

The fantastic operas of the 1890s: *Mlada, Christmas Eve*: 75–94.

The opera-bylina *Sadko*: 95–114.

The lyrico-psychological operas of the 1890s: *Mozart and Salieri, Boyarnynya Vera Sheloga, The Tsar's Bride*: 115–34.

Operas of the 1900s. Operatic intermezzo: *Servilia, Pan Voevoda*. The fairy tale operas: *The Tale of Tsar Saltan, Kashchey the Immortal*: 135–68.

The Golden Cockerel: 169–88.

The Legend of the Invisible City of Kitezh: 189–222.

Symphonic composition. Works of the 1860s–70s: 223–34.

Instrumental music of the 1860s. Concertos, cantatas: 235–51.

Vocal lyric: 252–64.

Conclusions. Short chronology of life and work. List of principal compositions. List of recommended literature.

334 ——. "Klassika na opernoy stsene. K voprosu o tvorcheskoy interpretatsii." [Classics on the Operatic Stage. On the Question of Creative Interpretation.] *SM* 11 (1986): 42–55.

A discussion of contemporary performances in the Soviet Union of Russian "Classical" operas, by Glinka, Musorgsky, Tchaikovsky, Rimsky-Korsakov, and others, noting positive and negative features of their interpretations.

335 Kenigsberg, A., ed. and comp. *111 Oper. Spravochnik-putevoditel'*. [111 Operas. Handbook-Guide.] St. Petersburg: Kul't Inform Press, 2001. 686 pp. ISBN-10: 5839201510. ISBN-13: 978-5839201514.

Apart from discussing operas in Austria, England, Hungary, Germany, Italy, France, Bohemia, and the United States, the Russian section includes articles on nine operas by Rimsky-Korsakov. Each monograph falls into three divisions comprising a list of characters and history of composition, subject, and music. Although of limited length, the comments regarding the opera subject and the music are full of perceptive observations.

336 Khoprova, Tat'yana Aleksandrovna. "Russkaya skazka v tvorchestve N. A. Rimskogo-Korsakova." [The Russian Fairy Tale in the Work of N. A. Rimsky-Korsakov.] In T. A. Khoprova, et al., eds. *Ocherki po istorii russkoy muzyki kontsa XIX – nachala XX veka*. [Essays on the History of Russian Music from the End of the 19th to the Beginning of the 20th Century.] Leningrad: Gos. Uchebno-pedagogicheskoe izdatel'stvo Ministerstva prosveshcheniya RSFSR, 1960: 207–47.

A general examination of some of the fantastic elements in Rimsky-Korsakov's operas, in particular *May Night, The Snow Maiden, Sadko*, and *The Tale of Tsar Saltan*.

Bibliography: Musical Works 83

337 Komarnitskaya, Ol'ga Vissarionovna. "Poetika skazki i opery N. A. Rimskogo-Korsakova." [The Poetics of the Fairy Tales and Operas of N. A. Rimsky-Korsakov.] *Muzyka v shkole* [Music in School] (3) (2008): 41. ISSN: 2072-0440.

A general discussion of Rimsky-Korsakov's fairy tale operas *The Snow Maiden*, *The Golden Cockerel*, and *Kashchey the Immortal*, including their philosophical concept and principles of poetics.

338 Kristi, G. *Rabota Stanislavskogo v opernom teatre.* [Stanislavsky's Work in the Opera Theater.] Moscow: Iskusstvo, 1952. 383 pp.

In this general examination of Stanislavsky's work in the opera theater, pp. 131–43 discuss Rimsky-Korsakov's *The Tsar's Bride*, the opera chosen to mark the opening of the Gosudarstvennaya Studiya-teatr im. Stanislavskogo [The Stanislavsky State Studio Theater] on 28 November 1926, an opera, which, on account of its diverse characterization, lent itself well to Stanislavsky's approach ("artistic-psychological realism"). Pages 146–51 discuss his performance of *May Night* (January 1928) and pp. 165–68 *The Golden Cockerel* (May 1932). Music examples, 27 illustrations.

339 Livanova, Tamara Nikolaevna. "Rimsky-Korsakov i khudozhestvennaya Moskva." [Rimsky-Korsakov and Artistic Moscow.] In No. 1204, Vol. I: 285–336.

Concerned with Rimsky-Korsakov's links with Moscow, this article falls into four sections:

i.   Rimsky-Korsakov and Tchaikovsky.
ii. Rimsky-Korsakov and the 1880s: Accounts of performances of his compositions in Moscow and his work on the opera *The Snow Maiden*.
iii. Correspondence with Kruglikov.
iv. Rimsky-Korsakov and the Moscow Private Opera: Accounts of performances of his works, especially *The Snow Maiden*, *The Maid of Pskov*, and *Sadko*, and of the singer Nadezhda Zabela-Vrubel'.

340 ——. *Opernaya kritika v Rossii.* [Opera Criticism in Russia.] Issue 4, Moscow: 1973.

The initial volume in this series was first published in Moscow, 1966, this being succeeded by three further volumes, of which Issue 4 was published in Moscow, 1973. Only Issue 4, covering the period of the 1860s–70s, which is also cataloged as Tome 2, Issue 4, contains a few references to the composer.

341 Malkov, Nikolay Petrovich. "Puti russkoy opery. (K 20-letiya so dnya smerti Rimskogo-Korsakova)." [Paths of Russian Opera. (A propos of the 20th Anniversary of Rimsky-Korsakov's Death).] *Zhizn' iskusstva* 26 (1928): 6.

342 Muir, Stephen. "The Operas of N. A. Rimsky-Korsakov from 1897 to 1904." PhD dissertation, University of Birmingham. Unpublished, 2000.

Noting that while Rimsky-Korsakov's operas are generally regarded as among the most important in Russian music, his later operas written between 1897 and 1904 have tended to receive less attention from scholars because they do not conform to a traditional view of Rimsky-Korsakov as a composer. The thesis provides a historical, critico-analytical examination of the operas from the final period of the composer's life up to *Pan Voevoda*. [A copy of the thesis is available freely from the author.]

343   Neef, Sigrid. *Handbuch der russischen und sowjetischen Oper*. Kassel-Basel: Bärenreiter, 1989. 760 pp. ISBN-10: 3761809255. ISBN-13: 978-3761809259.

Preceded by a 10-page analysis of the basic principles underlying Rimsky-Korsakov's operatic creativity, the remaining 102 pages are devoted to a description of 15 of his operas, each of which is accompanied by a commentary systematically examining the plot, content of each act, operatic genesis, structure, brief history of outstanding performers, international performances, details of the autograph, versions, editions, and bibliography.

344   Neff, Lyle Kevin. "Close to Prose or Worse than Verse? Rimsky-Korsakov's Intermediate Type of Opera Text." *Opera Quarterly* 15 (2) (1999): 238-50. ISSN: 0736-0053.

A detailed examination of the language employed in the libretti of Rimsky-Korsakov's operas *May Night, Christmas Eve,* and *The Tsar's Bride.*

345   ——. *Story, Style, and Structure in the Operas of Cesar Cui*. PhD dissertation, Musicology. Bloomington: Indiana University Press, 2002. 1371 pp. Publication No. AAT 3054368. ISBN-13: 978-0493694139.

Though primarily concerned with examination of the operas of César Cui, reference is also made to his personal relations with Rimsky-Korsakov.

346   Newmarch, Rosa. "The Development of National Opera in Russia, Rimsky-Korsakov." *Proceedings of Music Association* 31 (1904–05): 111–29.

An outline of the composer and his work. Includes the information that Rimsky-Korsakov's sister-in-law was married to Admiral Molas, p. 127.

347   ——. *The Russian Opera*. New York: Dutton, London: Herbert Jenkins, 1914. 403 pp. Reprinted: Westport, CT: Greenwood Press, 1972. Reprinted: Charleston, Carolina: BiblioBazaar, 2010. 452 pp. [See No. 1266.] ISBN-10: 117174448X. ISBN-13: 978-1171744481.

Rosa Newmarch was a pioneer in the study of Russian music. Born in Leamington Spa, England, in 1857, she visited Russia frequently in the period 1897–1915, studying under Stasov and meeting the surviving members of the Balakirev circle. Apart from her writings on Russian and Slavonic music, she translated the libretto of *The Maid of Pskov,* a work given during the Sir Joseph Beecham season of Russian Opera at Drury Lane in 1913, in which Shalyapin [Chaliapin] took the part of Ivan the Terrible. In the period

Bibliography: Musical Works   85

1900–05, Rosa Newmarch delivered several lectures on Russian opera before the Musical Association of London, which served as the foundation of her later book. Chapter XII is devoted entirely to the life of Rimsky-Korsakov and his operatic composition, pp. 281–333, and contains personal details and fragments of unusual information.

348   Pokrovsky, Boris. *Opernoe proizvedenie.* [Opera production.] Moscow: Vserossiyskoe teatral'noe obshchestvo, 1973. 308 pp.

Includes a discussion of the musical dramaturgy of *The Legend of the Invisible City of Kitezh* and the work of Fëdor Shalyapin.

349   Popov, Sergey Sergeevich, ed. *Russkaya khorovaya literatura. Ocherki* [Russian Choral Literature. Essays], Vyp. 2 [Issue 2]. Moscow: Muzyka, 1969. 167 pp.

A manual for music schools, containing discussion of choruses from the operas *May Night, The Snow Maiden, Christmas Eve, Sadko,* and *The Tsar's Bride,* together with the large choruses and choral arrangements.

350   Pougin, Arthur. "Rimsky-Korsakow." *Music* 14 (1898): 17–26.

An early short biographical article on Rimsky-Korsakov in English in the form of an examination of his operas up to *Christmas Eve,* and a discussion of orchestral and other works. While acknowledging his skills as an operatic composer, Pougin considers Korsakov to be primarily a symphonist and recalls with pleasure the performance of the symphonic picture "Sadko," conducted by Nicolas Rubinstein at the Exposition Universelle, Paris, in 1878.

351   Protopopov, Vladimir Vasil'evich. "Nekotorye osobennosti opernoy formy Rimskogo-Korsakova." [Some Peculiarities of Rimsky-Korsakov's Use of Form in Opera.] In *Sovetskaya Muzyka. Trety sbornik statey* [Third Volume of Articles], Moscow: Muzgiz, 1945: 87–104.

An informative discussion of some of Rimsky-Korsakov's attempts to give formal unity to his operas, especially through the use of reminiscence motives.

352   ——. *Variatsii v russkoy klassicheskoy opere.* [Variations in Russian Classical Opera.] Moscow: Muzgiz, 1957. 128 pp.

Observations on Rimsky-Korsakov's operatic style, with music examples illustrating the manner in which he develops his material by means of variation. No index.

353   ——. *Istoriya polifonii v eë vazhneyshikh yavleniyakh. Russkaya klassicheskaya i sovetskaya muzyka.* [History of Polyphony in its Most Important Aspects. Russian Classical and Soviet Music.] Moscow: Muzgiz, 1962.

Chapter IV, entitled "Rimsky-Korsakov's Polyphony," pp. 82–101, contains examples of contrapuntal elements in his operas.

354 Rabeneck, Nicolai. "The Magic of Rimsky-Korsakov." *Opera News* 16 March (1959): 31–33.

A brief account of Rimsky-Korsakov's operas, stressing the manner in which he pursued two lines of creative development, one leaning towards realism and historical subjects, the other towards fantasy and folklore. Highlighting the composer's pantheistic outlook and his preoccupation with the forces of nature, Rabeneck notes the presence of Christian elements, pointing out that it is St. Nicholas who intervenes in *Sadko* at the height of the storm. The article is illustrated with photographs of performances of *The Golden Cockerel* at the Metropolitan (1945) and Covent Garden, and a sketch by Benois for *The Tale of Tsar Saltan* at La Scala, Milan.

355 Rakhmaninov, Sergey Vasil'evich. *Pis'ma.* [Letters.] Z. Apetyants, ed., with introduction and commentary. Moscow: Muzgiz, 1955. 603 pp.

Rakhmaninov, conductor of the first Moscow performances of Rimsky-Korsakov's operas *May Night* and *Pan Voevoda*, was a frequent performer of his orchestral music and made the first transcription of the "Flight of the Bumble Bee" from *The Tale of Tsar Saltan* for piano. A year after Rakhmaninov's opera *Aleko* was given in Moscow, Rimsky-Korsakov performed the dances from the work in St. Petersburg. In gratitude, Rakhmaninov dedicated to him his Orchestral Fantasia *Utës* [The Cliff]. Letter No. 232, dated 17 September 1905, is from Rakhmaninov to Rimsky-Korsakov and discusses the proposed performance of *Pan Voevoda*. For the letter and a general discussion of their relationship, see pp. 254–56.

356 Ratser, Evgeny. "Rabota s pevtsami nad muzykal'nymi obraztsami Grigoriya Gryaznogo, Lyubashi i Marfy v opere Rimskogo-Korsakova 'Tsarskaya nevesta'." [Working with Singers on the Musical Roles of Grigory Gryaznoy, Lyubasha and Marfa in Rimsky-Korsakov's Opera *The Tsar's Bride*.] In O. Agarkov and L. Yaroslavtsev, eds. *Muzykal'no-tvorcheskoe vospriyatoe artistov opernoy stseny.* [The Musical and Creative Reception of Operatic Artists.] Moscow: Gos. muzykal'-pedagogichesky inst. Gnesinykh, 1981.

A discussion of practical issues arising from the training of opera singers in specific roles.

357 Redepenning, Dorothea. "Nikolai Andrejewitsch Rimski-Korsakow." In Carl Dahlhaus, ed. *Pipers Enzyklopädie des Musiktheaters.* Vol. 5. München: R. Piper, 1994: 254–87. ISBN-10: 3492024157. ISBN-13: 978-3492024150.

A perceptive examination of the operas *The Maid of Pskov, May Night, The Snow Maiden, Mlada, Sadko, Mozart and Salieri, The Tsar's Bride, The Tale of Tsar Saltan, Servilia, Kashchey the Immortal, The Legend of the Invisible City of Kitezh,* and *The Golden Cockerel,* with attractive illustrations.

358 Remezov, Ivan Ivanovich. "V bor'be za realizm. (Iz proshlogo russkoy opernoy stseny)." [In the Struggle for Realism. (From the Past of the Russian Opera Stage).] *SM* 6 (1937): 55–74.

Bibliography: Musical Works   87

An article concerned with the difficulties Russian nineteenth-century opera composers experienced in having their works performed, together with an analysis of some of the problems. Includes details of Rimsky-Korsakov's battles with double censorship as affecting *The Maid of Pskov*, *Christmas Eve* (in which the part of Catherine the Great had to be replaced by a male voice, representing Potëmkin), and *The Golden Cockerel*.

359   ——. *Vyacheslav Suk*. Moscow-Leningrad: Muzgiz, 1951. 62 pp.

Suk conducted a number of Rimsky-Korsakov's operas, including *Sadko*, in Khar'kov in December 1898, *The Tsar's Bride* in the 1899–1900 season, and the first performances of *Sadko*, *The Legend of the Invisible City of Kitezh*, and *The Golden Cockerel* at the Moscow Bol'shoy. He also gave *Pan Voevoda*. See pp. 4–5, 20–22, 25–27, 29–31. Contains correspondence.

360   Ruch'evskaya, Ekaterina Aleksandrovna. *"Ruslan" Glinki, "Tristan" Vagnera i "Snegurochka" Rimskogo-Korsakova: Stil', dramaturgiya, slovo i muzyka.* [Glinka's *Ruslan*, Wagner's *Tristan* and Rimsky-Korsakov's *The Snow Maiden*: Style, Dramaturgy, Text and Music.] St. Petersburg: Kompozitor, 2002.

A comparison of three different types of operatic musical dramaturgy as represented by Glinka's *Ruslan and Lyudmila*, Wagner's *Tristan und Isolde*, and Rimsky-Korsakov's *The Snow Maiden*.

361   Rumyantsev, Pavel Ivanovich. "Sistema K. S. Stanislavskogo v opernom teatre." [K. S. Stanislavsky's System in the Opera Theater.] *Ezhegodnik Moskovskogo Khudozhestvennogo teatra 1947.* Moscow: MKHAT, 1949: 375–522.

An account of Stanislavsky, his exceptional knowledge of music, and his performances in the Opera Studio. For a discussion of Rimsky-Korsakov's songs and the opera *Boyarynya Vera Sheloga*, see pp. 384–86, *The Tsar's Bride*, pp. 418–35, *May Night*, pp. 442–50, and *The Golden Cockerel*, pp. 496–502, together with sketches for costumes. No index.

362   ——. *Stanislavsky i opera*. [Stanislavsky and Opera.] Moscow: Iskusstvo, 1969. 493 pp., 47 pp. illustrations.

Among the many references to Rimsky-Korsakov in this work on the Russian producer and director, three chapters are concerned with the operas *The Tsar's Bride*, pp. 202–71, *May Night*, pp. 342–78, and *The Golden Cockerel*, pp. 447–60. The performance of *The Tsar's Bride* by the fledgling Opera Studio company on 28 November 1926 was an important event in the history of Soviet opera and Rumyantsev gives a detailed description of Stanislavsky's interpretation and production. A list of reviews of each of the operas appearing in contemporary periodicals is to be found in the Commentaries Section, pp. 469, 471, 477–78.

363   Sabaneev, Leonid Leonidovich. "Rimsky-Korsakov." Trans. S. W. Pring. *MT* 69 (May, 1928): 403–05.

A discussion of pantheistic elements in Rimsky-Korsakov's operas.

364 Shkafer, Vasily Petrovich. "N. A. Rimsky-Korsakov v moskovskoy chastnoy opere Mamontova." [N. A. Rimsky-Korsakov in Mamontov's Moscow Private Opera.] In *Komitet po chestvovaniyu pamyati N. A. Rimskogo-Korsakova. N. A. Rimsky-Korsakov i ego epokha. Kratky putevoditel' po vystavke v Russkom Muzee. Zëleny zal.* [Committee Honouring Rimsky-Korsakov's Memory. N. A. Rimsky-Korsakov and his Epoch. Short Guide to the Exhibition in the Russian Museum. Green Hall.] Leningrad: Russky Muzey, 1933. 20 pp.

Article on the Moscow Private Opera, formerly known as the Solodovnikov Theater, which became the State Experimental Theater in 1933. Founded by the philanthropist Savva Mamontov, the Private Opera gave a number of performances of Rimsky-Korsakov's operas, when the Imperial Theaters refused to sponsor them. Mamontov gathered round him a group of gifted artists, including Vasnetsov, Valentin Serov, Vrubel', and Korovin, and the musicians S. N. Kruglikov, Kashkin, Ippolitov-Ivanov, and Rakhmaninov, among the works performed being *The Snow Maiden, Sadko, Mozart and Salieri, The Tale of Tsar Saltan, The Tsar's Bride, May Night* (under Rakhmaninov), and *Kashchey the Immortal* (under Ippolitov-Ivanov). Following Mamontov's bankruptcy in 1899, the company, under the direction of Ippolitov-Ivanov, was called the Association of Russian Private Opera.

365 Solovtsov, Anatoly Aleksandrovich. "Pozdnie opery Rimskogo-Korsakova." [Rimsky-Korsakov's Late Operas.] In A. A. Solovtsov. *Kniga o russkoy opere.* [A Book about Russian Opera.] Moscow: Molodaya Gvardiya, 1960: 190–216.

Chapter VII of this book is a study of Rimsky-Korsakov's last six operas, commencing with *Sadko.* Written in simple, non-technical language, the work is intended for young people, with emphasis on the various operas' socio-political significance. Thus, Kashchey, in the opera of the same name, is seen as the personification of oppression. No footnotes, music examples, bibliography, or index.

366 Stanislavski, C. and Rumyantsev, P. *Stanislavski on Opera.* Elizabeth Reynolds Hapgood, trans. and ed. New York: Theater Arts Books, 1975. ISBN-10: 0878305521. ISBN-13: 978-0878305520.

An informative book on the Russian theater and a *sine qua non* for any student of Russian opera. Pages 152–210 are concerned specifically with *The Tsar's Bride* and pp. 269–303 with *May Night.*

367 Taruskin, Richard. "The Case for Rimsky-Korsakov." Part I. *Opera News* 56 (16) (May 1992): 12–14, 16, 60. Part II. *Opera News* 56 (17) (June 1992): 24–26, 28, 57. ISSN: 0030-3607. Reprinted: *On Russian Music.* University of California Press, 2009. ISBN-10: 0520249798. ISBN-13: 978-0520249790.

A survey of the life and work of Rimsky-Korsakov, with special attention being paid to his operas, their role in the Russian operatic repertoire, and the relationship between Russian operatic realism and folk allegory.

Bibliography: Musical Works

368 ——. "Rimsky-Korsakov, Nikolay Andreyevich." In Stanley Sadie, ed. *The New Grove Dictionary of Opera*. Vol. III. London and New York: Macmillan Press, 1992: 1331–41. ISBN-10: 0935859926. ISBN-13: 978-0935859928.

A comprehensive article on Rimsky-Korsakov's operas, showing their relationship to specific events in the composer's life. The extensive bibliography, found on pp. 1338–41, falls into two parts, the first dealing with books on the operas in general, the second being concerned with individual operas.

369 Tsendrovsky, Vladimir Mikhaylovich. "Uvertyury i vstupleniya k operam Rimskogo-Korsakova." [The Overtures and Introductions to Rimsky-Korsakov's Operas.] In S. Skrebkov, ed. *Voprosy teorii muzyki. Sbornik statey.* [Questions of Music Theory. A Collection of Articles.] Moscow: Muzyka, 1968: 103–20.

Noting that Rimsky-Korsakov's overtures and introductions fall into two basic types, that connected with a dramatic opera on a Russian subject (e.g., *The Maid of Pskov, The Tsar's Bride*), and the fairy-tale or fantastic opera (e.g., *The Snow Maiden, The Golden Cockerel*), Tsendrovsky examines various overtures from a structural point of view, noting their dramaturgical relevance. Later expanded into a book [see No. 371].

370 ——. "Opernoe tvorchestvo N. A. Rimskogo-Korsakova." [Rimsky-Korsakov's Operatic Compositions.] In I. Uvarova, ed. *Opery N. A. Rimskogo-Korsakova. Putevoditel'.* [The Operas of N. A. Rimsky-Korsakov. A Handbook.] Moscow: Muzyka, 1976. [See No. 373: 3–23.]

A general article preceding discussion of 11 of the composer's operas, placing them in their historical ideological context, and noting the manner in which elements of realism and fantasy are often intermingled.

371 ——. *Uvertyury i vstupleniya k operam Rimskogo-Korsakova.* [Overtures and Introductions to Rimsky-Korsakov's Operas.] Moscow: Muzyka, 1974. 147 pp.

An expanded edition of Tsendrovsky's article appearing in 1968, this falls into four main chapters, framed by a Foreword and Conclusion, the chapter titles as follows:

i. Types of overtures and introductions. Their role in the musical dramaturgy of the opera.
ii. Musical connection with the opera.
iii. The overtures to the dramatic operas.
iv. The introductions to the fairy-tale-epic operas.

Tsendrovsky's main contention is that to Rimsky-Korsakov, the orchestra was the all important factor, and is therefore the fundamental component of the dramaturgical structure.

372 Tsukkerman, Viktor Abramovich. "Interesnoe issledovanie." [An Interesting Investigation.] *SM* 4 (1962): 138–40.

A generally favorable review of L. Danil'evich's *Poslednye opery N. A. Rimskogo-Korsakova* [N. A. Rimsky-Korsakov's Last Operas], Moscow: Muzgiz, 1961, although the critic expresses some reservations about Danil'evich's ideological interpretation of *The Legend of the Invisible City of Kitezh* [see No. 307].

373 Uvarova, I., ed. *Opery N. A. Rimskogo-Korsakova. Putevoditel'.* [The Operas of N. A. Rimsky-Korsakov. A Handbook.] Moscow: Muzyka, 1976. 477 pp.

Though intended for the non-specialist, the 11 articles in this volume contain information arising from recent research. The contents of each chapter are listed under the respective author. No index.

374 Yakovlev, Vasily Vasil'evich. "N. A. Rimsky-Korsakov i operny teatr S. I. Mamontova." [Rimsky-Korsakov and Mamontov's Opera Theater.] *Teatral'ny al'manakh*, kniga 2 [Book 2] (4) (1946): 300–26.

A discussion of the composer's links with Mamontov and the productions given at his private theater with unusual information.

375 ——. *Izbrannye trudy o muzyke. Russkie kompozitory.* [Selected Works on Music. Russian Composers.] E. Gordeeva and T. Sokolova, eds. Vol. 2, Moscow: Sovetsky Kompozitor, 1971. 458 pp.

Apart from the many references to Rimsky-Korsakov in this collection of Yakovlev's works, of interest are the chapters "Russian Musicians," pp. 168–229, and "Rimsky-Korsakov and Mamontov's Opera Theater," pp. 230–74. The first article is an examination of the composer's esthetic opinions towards operatic composition as revealed by his writings and operas up to and including *The Snow Maiden*. The second examines the part played by Mamontov's Private Opera Company in Russian musical life and the Rimsky-Korsakov operas performed there.

376 Yarustovsky, Boris Mikhaylovich. *Dramaturgiya russkoy opernoy klassiki. Rabota russkikh kompozitorov-klassikov nad operoy.* [The Dramatic Art of Russian Classical Opera. Russian Classical Composers' Work on Opera.] Second edition. Moscow: Muzgiz, 1953. 404 pp. Review: D. Kabalevsky. *SM* 4 (1953): 104–09. German trans. Berlin: Henschelverlag, 1957.

This lengthy volume is an ideological examination of Russian nineteenth-century opera, in which the author makes systematic use of operatic comparisons. The location of specific items is difficult due to the absence of an index, and usually no single opera is discussed for more than two pages. Divided into 10 chapters, there are frequent references to Rimsky-Korsakov.

377 ——. *Ocherki po dramaturgii opery XX veka* [Essays on the Dramaturgy of 20th Century Opera.] Book I. Moscow: Muzyka, 1971. 355 pp.

Yarustovsky is well known in Russia for his work on operatic dramaturgy. The present volume discusses *Kashchey the Immortal* and *The Legend of the Invisible City of Kitezh*, and their significance in the Soviet period.

Bibliography: Musical Works

OPERAS: INDIVIDUAL

Pskovityanka [The Maid of Pskov]

378   Abraham, Gerald. "Rimsky-Korsakov's First Opera." In No. 283: 142–66.

A discussion of the first version of *The Maid of Pskov*.

379   ——. "Pskovityanka: The Original Version of Rimsky-Korsakov's first Opera." *MQ* 54 (January 1968): 58–73.

An examination of the original version of the composer's first opera, which the author sees as a work of great talent, and whose originality was to be whittled away in subsequent revisions.

380   Anonymous. "Khronika. S.-Peterburg. Mariinsky teatr. 'Pskovityanka'." [Chronicle. St. Petersburg. Mariinsky Theater. *The Maid of Pskov*.] *RMG* 45 (1903): cols. 1095–98; 46 (1903): cols. 1127–28.

A critical account of the opera and its performance.

381   Asaf'ev, Boris Vladimirovich [pseud. Glebov, Igor']. "Pskovityanka." [*The Maid of Pskov*.] In Nos. 296: 49–53; 1256: Vol. III, 281–83.

First published in 1921 as a supplement to the program of a performance of the Petrograd Academic Theater of Opera and Ballet (26 February), this discusses the opera and the ideas running through it. Asaf'ev equates the tragic content of the work with the myth of Iphigenia.

382   ——. "Pskovityanka." [*The Maid of Pskov*.] *Rabochy i teatr.* 40 (1925): 26–27.

Asaf'ev was particularly interested in Rimsky-Korsakov's opera *The Maid of Pskov*, discussion of which occurred several times in his literary writings.

383   Ashkinazi, Mikhail Osipovich. *Nicolas Rimsky-Korsakov. La pskovitaine; résumé du livret et guide thématique musical, par Michel Delines* [pseud.]. St. Petersburg: W. Bessel et Cie, 1909. 20 pp.

A musical thematic guide to *The Maid of Pskov*, illustrated with many music examples set out primarily in short score.

384   C. M. "London Notes." *I.M.G. Zeitschrift* 15 (Leipzig, 1913): 72–73.

Brief notes on the London performances of *Boris Godunov* and *The Maid of Pskov*, given on 1 July 1913.

385   Churova, Marina Abramovna, ed. *Bol'shoy Teatr SSSR (Sezony 195-196).* [The Bol'shoy Theater of the USSR (Seasons 195-196).] Moscow: Sovetsky Kompozitor, 1976. 472 pp.

Of principal interest in this book devoted to a description of the various productions at the Bol'shoy Theater 1971–72, is the section by Yury Simonov entitled "On the production of the opera *The Maid of Pskov*," pp. 76–88. Performed in a new guise on Saturday 20 February 1971, full details of the production are given, including the number of different types of rehearsals

92 Nikolay Andreevich Rimsky-Korsakov: A Research and Information Guide

(i.e., orchestra alone, with piano, with orchestra, etc.), together with an article on the performance, and two reviews from *Pravda* and *Vechernyaya Moskva*. A further nine reviews listed include details of articles in *SM* and *MZ*.

386   Engel', Yuly Dmitrievich. "'Pskovityanka' N. A. Rimskogo-Korsakova." [N. A. Rimsky-Korsakov's *The Maid of Pskov*.] Reprinted: No. 313: 78–95.

Published originally in *Russkie Vedomosti* 283 (13 October 1901), this discusses the Prologue to *The Maid of Pskov* entitled *Boyarynya Vera Sheloga*.

387   F. "Moskovskaya russkaya chastnaya opera. Gl. II, 'Pskovityanka'." [The Moscow Russian Private Opera. Chapter II, *The Maid of Pskov*.] *RMG* 3 (1908): 291–92.

388   Findeyzen, Nikolay Fëdorovich. "'Pskovityanka', opera Rimskogo-Korsakova. Postanovka v novoy redaktsii na stsene Panaevskogo teatra obshchestvom muzykal'nykh sobraniy." [*The Maid of Pskov*, Opera by Rimsky-Korsakov. Performed in a New Version on the Stage of the Panaevsky Theater by the Society of Musical Gatherings.] *RMG* 5–6 (1895): cols. 297–314.

A review of a performance of *The Maid of Pskov*, with comments on structure, orchestration, and staging.

389   Fukac, J. "Brmenska Pskovitanka a problemy dramatismu." *Hudebni Rozhledy* 34 (4) (1981): 156–57.

Divided into two main sections, the first part consists of details of the work's inception, the subject of the opera, and the work's musical language. The second part contains a detailed description of the content of the opera, act by act, illustrated with numerous musical examples.

390   Gorodetskaya, Zinaida Izrailevna. *"Pskovityanka"* – *opera Rimskogo-Korsakova*. [*Pskovityanka* – Opera by Rimsky-Korsakov.] Moscow: Muzgiz, 1936. 94 pp. Review: *SM* 10 (1936).

A detailed examination of Rimsky-Korsakov's *The Maid of Pskov*.

391   Gozenpud, Abram Akimovich. *Russky operny teatr XIX veka. 1873-1889.* [The Russian Opera Theater of the 19th Century. 1873-1889.] Leningrad: Muzyka, 1973. 328 pp.

In this series of studies of the history of Russian opera, Gozenpud discusses the effect of censorship on Rimsky-Korsakov's work. Attention is focussed on *The Maid of Pskov*, the personalia and content of which are examined from a variety of viewpoints. The censor's comments are given, along with extracts from critical writings. Contains new materials on the first performances of the opera.

392   Kandinsky, Aleksey Ivanovich. "Obrashchenie k russkoy klassike." [A Return to the Russian Classics.] *SM* 7 (1971): 49–55.

Bibliography: Musical Works 93

A discussion of *The Maid of Pskov*, its ideological significance, and its performance at the Bol'shoy Theater, in which Kandinsky criticizes the theater for its production, seeing in it a lack of understanding of many of the opera's chief qualities.

393 Kandinsky, A. I. "Istoriya i legenda: Obraz Pskovityanki v opere Rimskogo-Korsakova." [History and Legend: the Image of the Maid of Pskov in the Opera by Rimsky-Korsakov.] In *Nauchnye trudy*. [Scientific Works.] 30: *Nikolay Andreevich Rimsky-Korsakov. K 150-letiyu so dnya rozhdeniya i 90-letiyu so dnya smerti*. [Nikolay Andreevich Rimsky-Korsakov. On the 150th Year of the Day of his Birth and the 90th Anniversary of the Day of his Death.] Moscow Conservatory, 2000: 9–36. Reprinted: A. I. Kandinsky. *Stat'i o russkoy muzyke*. [Articles on Russian Music.] Moscow Conservatory, 2010: 409–34.

A well-researched and informative study by a leading Russian scholar.

394 Kashkin, Nikolay Dmitrievich. "'Pskovityanka' i 'Vera Sheloga'." [*The Maid of Pskov* and *Vera Sheloga*.] *Moskovskie Vedomosti* 33 (2 February 1905).

Nikolay Kashkin (1839–1920) was active in many fields of music as a professor at Moscow Conservatory, translator, and critic, writing many informative articles for newspapers and journals.

395 Kruglikov, Semën Nikolaevich. "'Pskovityanka'." [*The Maid of Pskov*.] *Novosti Dnya* (22 October 1901).

Semën Kruglikov (1851–1910) was by profession an educationalist. A pupil of Rimsky-Korsakov, he was a prolific writer, contributing to leading journals and newspapers.

396 Kyui, Ts. A. [Cui, César]. "'Pskovityanka'." [*The Maid of Pskov*.] *Sanktpeterburgskie Vedomosti* 9 (9 January 1873). Reprinted: No. 1294: 215–24, 590.

Cui's critique contains observations on Rimsky-Korsakov's employment of Russian folk song, which he sees as justified in specific instances.

397 Larosh, German Avgustovich. "Muzykal'nye ocherki. 'Pskovityanka', opera N. A. Rimskogo-Korsakova." [Musical Sketches. *The Maid of Pskov*, Opera by N. A. Rimsky-Korsakov.] *Golos* (10 January 1873).

German [Herman] Larosh (1845–1904), a professor at the St. Petersburg Conservatory, was an active writer and music critic for many newspapers and journals. His seemingly countless articles, often concerned with the music of Rimsky-Korsakov, provide a panoramic insight into the musical activity of the period.

398 ——. "Muzykal'nye pis'ma iz Peterburga. Russkaya opera v pervoy polovine sezona 1872-1873 god." [Musical Letters from Petersburg. Russian

Opera in the First Half of the 1872-1873 Season.] *Moskovskie Vedomosti* (29 January–1 February 1873).

Includes an account of the opera *The Maid of Pskov*.

399 Martin Bermúdez, Santiago. "Rimski, sobre todo operista: Cien años de la muerte de Nikolai Rimski-Korsakov." *Scherzo: Revista de música* 23 (234) (October 2008): 152. ISSN: 0213-4802.

A discussion of Rimsky-Korsakov's operas and their place within the Russian operatic tradition published on the centenary of the composer's death.

400 Newman, Ernest. "Ivan the Terrible." *The New Witness* 10 (256) (1917): 518–19.

A short critical article written in connection with Sir Thomas Beecham's London production of *Ivan the Terrible* (i.e., *The Maid of Pskov*), in which Newman comments on Rimsky-Korsakov's heterogeneous style and the tendency of Russian composers to think in terms of loosely connected frescoes, rather than being bound by a central dramatic idea. In only a few works, Newman considers, did the composer display a real musical logic, outstanding in this respect being *The Golden Cockerel*.

401 Polyakova, Lyudmila Viktorovna. "'Pskovityanka' v filiale Bol'shogo Teatra." [*The Maid of Pskov* at a Branch of the Bol'shoy Theater.] *SM* 5 (1953): 88–92.

A review, with some reservations expressed, of a new production of *The Maid of Pskov*, with some introductory remarks about Rimsky-Korsakov and the composition of the opera.

402 ——. "'Pskovityanka' i 'Vera Sheloga'." [*The Maid of Pskov* and *Vera Sheloga*.] In No. 373: 24–64.

Discusses *The Maid of Pskov* and *Vera Sheloga*, with information on their manner of composition, observations on structural details, Rimsky-Korsakov's method of musical characterization, and synopses of the operatic content.

403 S. "Pskovityanka." [*The Maid of Pskov*.] *Zhizn' iskusstva* 41 (1925): 11.

404 Shlifshteyn, Semën Isaakovich. "Ot Gogolya k Pushkinu." [From Gogol to Pushkin.] *SM* 3 (1971): 109–22.

Primarily a discussion of Musorgsky's *Boris Godunov*, this includes a number of references to *The Maid of Pskov*, both of which are seen as products of the Russian intellectual movement of the 1860s.

405 Sokolov, O. "Leytmotivy opery 'Pskovityanka'." [Leitmotifs in the Opera *The Maid of Pskov*.] In *Trudy kafedry teorii muzyki Moskovskoy konservatorii* [Transactions of the Department of Music Theory of Moscow Conservatory], Vyp. 1 [Issue 1]. Moscow: Muzgiz, 1960: 219–56.

Bibliography: Musical Works 95

A discussion of the employment of leitmotifs in the opera as symbols, musical portraits, and formal components.

406 Taruskin, Richard. "'The Present in the Past': Russian Opera and Russian Historiography, *ca.* 1870." In Malcolm Hamrick Brown, ed. *Russian and Soviet Music. Essays for Boris Schwarz.* Ann Arbor, Michigan: UMI Research Press, 1984: 77–146. ISBN-10: 0835715450. ISBN-13: 978-0835715454.

Together with many references to Rimsky-Korsakov, Richard Taruskin's article discusses ideological questions of the period, including an examination of *The Maid of Pskov,* which the author sees as a truly "realist" manifestation. Copiously documented.

407 ——. "The Maid of Pskov." In Stanley Sadie, ed. *The New Grove Dictionary of Opera,* III. London and New York: Macmillan Press, 1992: 154-56. ISBN-10: 0935859926. ISBN-13: 978-0935859928.

A detailed examination of the opera.

408 Vikhanskaya, A. "Neopublikovannaya redaktsiya opery 'Pskovityanka' Rimskogo-Korsakova." [The Unpublished Version of Rimsky-Korsakov's Opera *The Maid of Pskov.*] In *Russkaya i zarubezhnaya muzykal'naya klassika. Voprosy teorii muzyki i ispolnitel'stva.* [Russian and Foreign Musical Classics. Problems of Music Theory and Performance Practice.] Leningrad: Muzyka, 1974.

409 Weaver, W. "Palermo." *Opera* 10, 7 (1959): 460.

An account of a performance of *Ivan the Terrible* (i.e., *The Maid of Pskov*) given at the Teatro Massimo, Palermo in 1959.

410 Yastrebtsëv, Vasily Vasil'evich. "Neskol'ko slov o IIy i IIIy redaktsiyakh Pskovityanki i narodnykh temakh, vzyatykh Rimskim-Korsakovym v etu opery." [A Few Words about the Second and Third Versions of *The Maid of Pskov* and the Folk Themes employed by Rimsky-Korsakov in the Opera.] *RMG* 5–6 (1895): cols. 314–22.

Discusses the three versions of *The Maid of Pskov* and the Incidental Music to Mey's drama.

The Collective "Mlada"

411 Abraham, Gerald. "The Collective 'Mlada'." In No. 284: 91–112.

Discusses the collective "Mlada" of 1872, including Rimsky-Korsakov's contribution.

412 Gaub, Albrecht. "Die kollektive Ballett-Oper *Mlada*: Ein Werk von Kjui, Mussorgskij, Rimskij-Korsakov, Borodin, und Minkus." PhD dissertation, Universität Hamburg. In *Studia slavica musicologica* 12. Berlin: Ernst Kuhn, 1998. 624 pp.

A detailed study of the opera-ballet *Mlada*, a collective work with contributions by Cui, Musorgsky, Rimsky-Korsakov, Borodin, and Minkus. Commissioned in 1872 by Stepan Aleksandrovich Gedeonov, director of the St. Petersburg Mariinsky Teatr Opery i Baleta [St. Petersburg Mariinsky Theater of Opera and Ballet], the work was left unfinished.

413 ——. "Muzyka N. A. Rimskogo-Korsakova dlya gedeonovskoy *Mlady*." [N. A. Rimsky-Korsakov's Music to Gedeonov's *Mlada*.] In V. M. Vasil'eva, comp. *N. A. Rimsky-Korsakov i russkaya khudozhestvennaya kul'tura. Materialy nauchnoy konferentsii. Vechasha-Lyubensk*. [N. A. Rimsky-Korsakov and Russian Artistic Culture. Materials from a Scientific Conference. Vechasha-Lyubensk.] Pskov, 2008.

Discusses the part played by Rimsky-Korsakov in contributing to the collective opera-ballet *Mlada*, an unfinished work based on a libretto by Viktor Krylov, commissioned in 1872 by Stepan Aleksandrovich Gedeonov, director of the St. Petersburg Mariinsky Teatr Opery i Baleta [St. Petersburg Mariinsky Theater of Opera and Ballet].

414 Taruskin, Richard. "*Mlada*. Opera-ballet in four acts." In Stanley Sadie, ed. *The New Grove Dictionary of Opera*, III. London and New York: Macmillan Press, 1992: 416–17. ISBN-10: 0935859926. ISBN-13: 978-0935859928.

A short account of the opera, describing the circumstances pertaining to the composition of the work, including Rimsky-Korsakov's contribution in the form of Acts 2 and 3.

Mayskaya noch' [May Night]

415 Abraham, Gerald. "Rimsky-Korsakov's Gogol Operas." In No. 283: 167–92.

A discussion of the operas *May Night* and *Christmas Eve*, copiously illustrated with music examples, noting the composer's transition from a "simple lyrical musical idiom" to one of "artificiality, picquancy and technical sophistication."

416 Alekseevsky, N. "Noch' grusti i vesel'ya." [Night of Sadness and Joy.] *MZ* (2) (2009): 35. ISSN: 0131-2383.

A discussion of the history of the creation and première of Rimsky-Korsakov's opera *May Night*, based on Nikolay Gogol's novel *Mayskaya noch', ili Utoplennitsa* [May Night, or the Drowned Girl], including an account of the part played by the conductor Eduard Nápravník and the critical writings of M. A. Balakirev, V. V. Stasov, and Ts. Kyui.

417 Anonymous. "Postanovka 'Mayskoy nochi' Rimskogo-Korsakova." [A Performance of Rimsky-Korsakov's *May Night*.] *RMG* 13–14 (1909): cols. 372–77.

Bibliography: Musical Works 97

An account of a performance at the St. Petersburg Conservatory.

418 Asaf'ev Boris Vladimirovich [pseud. Glebov, Igor']. "Mayskaya noch'." [*May Night.*] *Zhizn' iskusstva* 473 (1920).

419 ———. "Mayskaya noch'." [*May Night.*] In Nos. 296: 53–62; 1256: Vol. III, 283–87.

First published in 1921 as a supplement to the program of a performance of the Petrograd Academic Theater of Opera and Ballet (1 October). A discussion of the opera, raising the question as to why Russian opera differs stylistically from that of other countries.

420 Engel', Yuly Dmitrievich. "Mayskaya noch'." [*May Night.*] Reprinted: No. 313: 263–64.

First published in *Russkie Vedomosti* 99 (1 May 1909), this is a brief account of a performance of the opera at the Bol'shoy Theater.

421 Finkel'shteyn, Z. "Mayskaya noch'." [*May Night.*] In No. 373: 65–109.

Consisting of a chapter in I. Uvarova's handbook to the operas of Rimsky-Korsakov, this falls into four sections, including excerpts from the libretto:

i.   The Path from *The Maid of Pskov* to *May Night.*
ii. Gogol and Rimsky-Korsakov.
iii. The Opera's Dramaturgy and Music.
iv. Content of the Opera.

422 Kyui, Ts. A. [Cui, César]. "'Mayskaya noch',' volshebno-komicheskaya opera g. Rimskogo-Korsakova. Pogreshnosti protiv deklamatsii." [*May Night,* a Magic Comic Opera by Mr. Rimsky-Korsakov. Errors against Declamation.] *Golos* 19 (November 1880).

423 ———. "'Mayskaya noch',' volshebno-komicheskaya opera N. A. Rimskogo-Korsakova." [*May Night,* a Magic Comic Opera by N. A. Rimsky-Korsakov.] *Artist* 42 (October 1894). Reprinted: No. 1294: 425–35, 613.

Cui was a self-opinionated critic, of which this article is a typical example.

424 Larosh, German Avgustovich. "Dva pervye kontserta 'besplatnoy shkoly'." [The First Two Concerts of the "Free School."] *Golos* (3 February 1879).

Includes an account of the opera *May Night.*

425 Lyutsh, Vs. "Mayskaya noch'. (Studiya im. nar. artistka K. S. Stanislavskogo)." [*May Night.* (Studio Named after People's Artist K. S. Stanislavsky).] *Muzyka i revolyutsiya* 4 (1928): 33.

A short, generally favorable account of the opera, as given at the Stanislavsky Opera Studio. Lyutsh comments on the work's expressive qualities.

426 Malkov, Nikolay Petrovich. "Pochemu Shtraus predpochten Korsakovu. (Dva pokazatel'nykh spektaklya v ak-opere)." [Why Strauss is Preferable to Korsakov. (Two Instructive Shows at the Academic-Opera).] *Zhizn' iskusstva* 42 (1015) (1924): 9–11.

An unusual review comparing a poor performance of *May Night* with one of Richard Strauss's *Salome*.

427 Shtrup, N. "'Mayskaya noch'" v Prage." [*May Night* in Prague.] *RMG* 12 (1896): cols. 1579–96.

A compilation of Czech reviews of the opera *May Night* following its performance in Prague, quoting excerpts from *Národni Listy*, *Národni Politika*, *Politik*, *Svêtozor*, and *Hlas Národa*.

428 Slonimsky, Nicholas. "The May Night." *MQ* 41 (3) (1955): 409–10.

A review of the first complete recording of the opera *May Night*, performed by artists of the Moscow Bol'shoy Theater, with comments on the work's history.

429 Taruskin, Richard. "May Night." In Stanley Sadie, ed. *The New Grove Dictionary of Opera*, III. London and New York: Macmillan Press, 1992: 281-83. ISBN-10: 0935859926. ISBN-13: 978-0935859928.

A perceptive analysis of the opera.

430 Velichko, A. *"Mayskaya Noch'" N. A. Rimskogo-Korsakova.* [*May Night* by N. A. Rimsky-Korsakov.] Moscow: Muzgiz, 1959. 85 pp. Second edition. Moscow: Muzyka, 1980. 64 pp.

A volume in the series "Opera Libretti," this comprises a short introduction by Velichko, pp. 3–7, giving details of the composition of the work, its extensive use of folk ritual, the manner in which he adhered closely to Gogol's original text, and information on the opera's first performances. The remainder of the booklet consists of the libretto.

Snegurochka (Vesennyaya skazka) [The Snow Maiden (Spring Fairy Tale)]

431 Abraham, Gerald. "Snegurochka." [*The Snow Maiden.*] In No. 283: 193–220.

A discussion of the opera, noting its symbolic elements.

432 Anonymous. "Opera v Narodnom Dome: postanovka 'Snegurochki.'" [Opera in the Narodny Dom: A Performance of *The Snow Maiden.*] *RMG* 6 (1905): 170–72.

An account of a performance of the opera in the Narodny Dom.

433 Anonymous. "Russkaya opera za granitsey. K istorii postanovki 'Borisa Godunova' i 'Snegurochki' v Parizhe." [Russian Opera Abroad. On the History of the Production of *Boris Godunov* and *The Snow Maiden* in Paris.] *RMG* 32–33 (1908): cols. 664–68.

Concerns the part played by the French translator of the text of the opera, Madame P. Halpérine, and her relations with Sergey Dyagilev [Serge Diaghilev], the producer.

434 Anonymous. "'Snegurochka'. (K postanovke opery Rimskogo-Korsakova v Malom opernom Ak-teatre)." [*The Snow Maiden*. (On the Staging of Rimsky-Korsakov's Opera in the Maly Opera Academic-Theater).] *Zhizn' iskusstva* 14 (1928): 21.

435 Asaf'ev Boris Vladimirovich [pseud. Glebov, Igor']. "'Snegurochka' Rimskogo-Korsakova v Bol'shom teatre." [Rimsky-Korsakov's *The Snow Maiden* in the Bol'shoy Theater.] *Muzyka* 251 (1916).

An informative account of a performance of Rimsky-Korsakov's *The Snow Maiden* in the Bol'shoy Theater.

436 ——. "Vpechatleniya i mysli." [Impressions and Thoughts.] *Melos*, kniga 2 [Book 2] [Petrograd] (1918): 142–59.

437 ——. "'Snegurochka'. (Akademichesky teatr opery i baleta)." [*The Snow Maiden*. (Academic Theater of Opera and Ballet).] *Zhizn' iskusstva* 675–676 (1921).

A critical account of a performance of *The Snow Maiden*, highlighting some of the technical problems presented by the work.

438 ——. "'Snegurochka'. Vesennyaya skazka." [*The Snow Maiden*. A Spring Fairy Tale.] In No. 296: 62–66.

First published in 1921 as a supplement to the program of a performance of the Petrograd Academic Theater of Opera and Ballet (30 January), the article highlights some of the symbolism of the opera and its underlying philosophies.

439 ——. "Nakanune postanovki 'Snegurochki'." [On the Eve of the Production of *The Snow Maiden*.] *Zhizn' iskusstva* 12 (1928): 6.

440 Bakanova, Lyudmila. "Gimn Apollonu Aleksandra Sanina." [Sanin's Hymn to Apollo.] *MZ* (4) (2013): 76. ISSN: 0131-2383.

A discussion of the 1910 production of Rimsky-Korsakov's opera *The Snow Maiden* by Aleksandr Sanin, given at the St. Petersburg Narodny Dom.

441 Bellaigue, Camille. "De la musique russe et d'un opéra de M. Rimsky-Korsakow." *Impressions musicales et littéraires*. Paris: C. Delagrave, 1900: 97–140.

Consisting of two major sections, the first is a general examination of some of the characteristics of Russian music, the second an article on *The Snow Maiden*, which Bellaigue sees as an essentially Russian phenomenon.

442 Bely, P. "'Snegurochka' – nadezhdy i somneniya." [*The Snow Maiden* – Hopes and Doubts.] *SM* 3 (1979): 45–49.

Preceded by a discussion of the ideological significance of the opera, this is a critical account of a recent production at the Moscow Bol'shoy Theater.

443 E. P. "'Snegourotschka, Fleur de neige'. Conte de printemps. Opéra en 4 actes et un prologue. Musique de N. Rimsky-Korsakow. (Le livret est tiré de la pièce d'A. Ostrovsky). Traduction français de M-me P. Halpérine et M-r P. Lalo. Nouvelle édition revue et retouchée par l'auteur. W. Bessel et C-ie, Editeurs." *RMG* 39–40 (1908): cols. 856–57.

A short review of the French publication of the opera, following its performance at the Opéra Comique, commenting on the difficulties of translation.

444 Es. "'Snegurochka'. (Akadem. Teatr Opery)." [*The Snow Maiden.* (Academic Theater of Opera.)] *Zhizn' iskusstva* 12 (887) (1923): 9–10.

An account of a performance of the opera, criticizing the production though praising some of the voices.

445 Engel', Yuly Dmitrievich. "'Snegurochka'." [*The Snow Maiden.*] *Russkie Vedomosti* 260 (11 November 1911). Reprinted: No. 313: 326–30.

This contrasts the performances of Wagner's *Götterdämmerung* with Rimsky-Korsakov's opera, both works being given at the Moscow Bol'shoy Theater. An amplification of this article entitled "'Gibel' bogov' Vagnera i 'Snegurochka' Rimskogo-Korsakova" [Wagner's *Götterdämmerung* and Rimsky-Korsakov's *The Snow Maiden*] was published in *EIT*, Vyp. 1 [Issue 1] (1912).

446 Findeyzen, Nikolay Fëdorovich. "Tematizm opery 'Snegurochka' N. A. Rimskogo-Korsakova." [The Thematic Structure of Rimsky-Korsakov's *The Snow Maiden.*] *RMG* (1894): 121–24, 139–45, 157–59, 179–84, 197–200, 219–22.

Findeyzen's detailed thematic analysis of the opera anticipates Rimsky-Korsakov's own thematic outline first published in *RMG* in 1908 and in a more modern edition in 1978 [see No. 282]. Employing 50 music examples, Findeyzen underlines the element of theme transformation, the first time such a concept had been used so extensively in Russian opera.

447 Getteman, H. "'Sniegourotchka' opéra de M. Rimsky-Korsakoff." *Revue musicale* 8 (1908): 137–43, 179–87, 213–16.

Commencing with a discussion of the manner in which Rimsky-Korsakov's *The Snow Maiden* differs from contemporary German music in its avoidance of continuous music and complete dependence on Leitmotiv, the author examines the folk song sources of the opera, noting the composer's ingenious harmonizations, and comments on the work's reception from contemporary critics. Also includes discussion of the libretto, the significance of the characters in the context of Russian folklore, and a biographical note on the composer.

448   Halbe, Gregory A. "Music, Drama, and Folklore in Rimsky-Korsakov's Opera 'Snegurochka'." PhD dissertation, Musicology. Ohio State University, 2004.

A detailed examination of Rimsky-Korsakov's third and extremely successful opera *The Snow Maiden*, approached from a historical and analytical perspective, including the manner in which the composer transformed the nature of the musical play by A. N. Ostrovsky on which the opera is based, and the extent to which the opera reveals Rimsky-Korsakov's awareness of Wagner.

449   Kandinsky, Aleksey Ivanovich. "Rozhdenie vesenney skazki." [Birth of a Spring Tale.] *SM* 3 (1969): 52–63.

A general survey of the opera, paying particular attention to the use of leitmotifs and the composer's creative aims, while also showing the manner in which various episodes developed from the composer's sketches. Includes a discussion of the manuscript sources of the work.

450   Karatygin, Vyacheslav Gavrilovich. "Obzor sezona 1909-1910 gg. Opera." [Survey of the 1909-1910 Opera Season.] *EIT*, Vyp. 4 [Issue 4] (1910): 94–128.

A survey of the Imperial Opera, including details of *The Snow Maiden*, the 59th performance of which had just taken place. Includes information on the cast and other factual materials, pp.116–17.

451   Kazansky, Sergey Pavlovich. "'Snegurochka'." [*The Snow Maiden.*] *Teatr i Iskusstvo* 190 (22 October 1885).

An article by Sergey Kazansky (1857–1901), a teacher and music critic, whose many articles were supportive of the Russian Nationalist composers.

452   Kiselëv, Vasily Aleksandrovich. "A. N. Ostrovsky i N. A. Rimsky-Korsakov (K istorii sozdaniya opery 'Snegurochka')." [A. N. Ostrovsky and N. A. Rimsky-Korsakov (On the History of the Writing of the Opera *The Snow Maiden*).] In No. 453: 172–85.

Preceded by a short introductory article, this consists of three letters exchanged between Ostrovsky and Rimsky-Korsakov in the period October–November 1880 concerning aspects of the libretto.

453   Kolosova, E. and Filippov, V., eds. *A. N. Ostrovsky i russkie kompozitory. Pis'ma.* [Ostrovsky and Russian composers. Letters.] Moscow-Leningrad: Iskusstvo, 1937. 251 pp.

Preceded by a long introductory article [pp. 31–37] by V. Yakovlev: "A. N. Ostrovsky v perepiske s russkimi kompozitorami" [Ostrovsky's Correspondence with Russian Composers], concerned with Rimsky-Korsakov's *The Snow Maiden*, a discussion of the correspondence between

Rimsky-Korsakov and Ostrovsky, with a commentary by Kiselëv is to be found on pp. 172–85. There are many plates, photographs of actors, actresses, costumes, and sets of various productions of the opera in St. Petersburg and Moscow. No index.

454 Kruglikov, Simën Nikolaevich. "'Snegurochka', opera N. Rimskogo-Korsakova." [*The Snow Maiden*, Opera by N. Rimsky-Korsakov.] *Muzykal'noe Obozrenie* 8 (1885): 10.

An informative article, written by a former pupil of Rimsky-Korsakov.

455 Kulakovsky, Lev Vladimirovich. "'Snegurochka'." [*The Snow Maiden.*] In No. 373: 110–44.

Containing extracts from the libretto, this consists of four sections:

i. History of the Opera's Composition.
ii. Musical Language of *The Snow Maiden*.
iii. On the Artistic Idea of the Opera.
iv. Content of the Opera.

456 Kyui, Ts. A. [Cui, César]. "'Snegurochka', vesennyaya skazka Rimskogo-Korsakova." [*The Snow Maiden*, a Spring Fairy Tale by Rimsky-Korsakov.] *Novosti i Birzhevaya Gazeta* 79 (19 March 1898). In No. 1294: 479–82, 617.

An account of the opera.

457 Mokul'sky, Stefan Stefanovich. "'Snegurochka' v Leningradskom Gosudarstvennom akademicheskom malom opernom teatre." [*The Snow Maiden* in the Leningrad State Academic Maly Opera Theater.] *Zhizn' iskusstva* 19 (1928): 7.

A short account of the performance in a novel interpretation.

458 Nápravník, Eduard Franzevich. "'Snegurochka'. Otzyz na operu, predstavlennuyu na rassmotrenie v direktsiyu peterburgskikh imperatorskikh teatrov." [*The Snow Maiden*. Review of the Opera, Inspected by the Administration of the Petersburg Imperial Theaters.] In E. F. Nápravník. *Avtobiograficheskie, tvorcheskie materialy, dokumenty, pis'ma.* [Autobiographical, Creative Materials, Documents, Letters.] L. M. Kutateladze, ed. Leningrad: Muzgiz, 1959: 63, 66–67, 89–90.

A review by the conductor Nápravník of Rimsky-Korsakov's opera, in which he notes a number of defects in melody and harmony. A brief report on the opera *May Night* is also given on p. 63.

459 O'Riordan, C. L. "Aspects of the Inter-Relationship Between Russian Folk- and Composed-Music." PhD dissertation, Musicology, Cambridge University, 1970.

Includes a discussion of the opera.

Bibliography: Musical Works 103

460 Ostrovsky, Aleksandr Nikolaevich. "Pis'mo k A. D. Mysovskoy." [Letter to A. D. Mysovskaya.] In A. N. Ostrovsky. *Polnoe sobranie sochineniy. Tom. 16. Pis'ma. 1881-1886.* [Complete Collection of Works. Vol. 16. Letters. 1881-1886.] Moscow: Goslitizdat, 1953.

Letter 1021, dated 21 May 1885, written from Shchelikovo, addressed to Anna Dmitrievna Mysovskaya, pp. 171–72, discusses the two "Snegurochkas" – the incidental music by Tchaikovsky and the opera by Rimsky-Korsakov. Mysovskaya wished to write a work on the subject herself, but was dissuaded by Ostrovsky. He also points out that operettas are not given on the Imperial stages.

461 Prokhorova, I. *"Snegurochka" N. Rimskogo-Korsakova.* [N. Rimsky-Korsakov's *The Snow Maiden.*] Moscow-Leningrad: Muzgiz, 1952. 48 pp.

One of the "Guides to Russian Music" series, this is an illustrated analytical account of the opera with 32 music examples. Sections include "On the history of the composition of *The Snow Maiden*," and "Some features of the opera's musical dramaturgy."

462 Rimsky-Korsakov, Nikolay Andreevich. *"Snegurochka" – vesennyaya skazka (tematichesky razbor).* [*The Snow Maiden* – A Spring Fairy Tale. (Thematic Analysis).] (1905). Published in the special memorial issue of *RMG* 39–40 (1908): cols. 804–16. In Nos. 211: 182–200; 282: Vol. IV, 391–426; No. 468: 32 pp.

Rimsky-Korsakov's article on *The Snow Maiden* is preceded by an introductory commentary by A. Solovtsov. The composer divides the themes of the opera into three categories, though the detailed thematic analysis which he hoped to write was never completed. No bibliography or index.

463 Rimsky-Korsakow, Nikolai. "Snegurotschka: Ein Frühlingsmärch. Fragment." In *Studia slavica musicologica* 16: *Nikolai Rimsky-Korsakow. Kleinere musiktheoretische Schriften und Fragmente. Texte zur Musikgeschichte, Musikpädagogik und Musikästhetik.* Berlin: Ernst Kuhn, 2004. ISBN-10: 392886467X. ISBN-13: 978-3928864671.

A German translation of Rimsky-Korsakov's analysis of *Snegurochka* [see No. 208].

464 ——. "Die Bürger von Nishni-Nowgorod: Eine Oper von Eduard Napravnik." In *Studia slavica musicologica* 16: *Nikolai Rimsky-Korsakow. Kleinere musiktheoretische Schriften und Fragmente. Texte zur Musikgeschichte, Musikpädagogik und Musikästhetik.* Berlin: Ernst Kuhn, 2004. ISBN-10: 392886467X. ISBN-13: 978-3928864671.

German translation of a review by Rimsky-Korsakov of Eduard Nápravník's opera *Nizhegorodtsy* [The Nizhny Novgorodites], originally published in the *Sanktpeterburgskie vedomosti* (3 January 1869) [see No. 211].

104   Nikolay Andreevich Rimsky-Korsakov: A Research and Information Guide

465 ——. "Skizzen und Fragmente zu einer Ästhetik der Musik." In *Studia slavica musicologica* 16: *Nikolai Rimsky-Korsakow. Kleinere musiktheoretische Schriften und Fragmente. Texte zur Musikgeschichte, Musikpädagogik und Musikästhetik*. Berlin: Ernst Kuhn, 2004. ISBN-10: 392886467X. ISBN-13: 978-3928864671.

A German translation of Rimsky-Korsakov's analysis of *Snegurochka*, written in St. Petersburg in 1892–93, this is a subjective introduction to the esthetics of music, including the perception of sounds, parallels between the arts, and the role of associations [see No. 211].

466 Ritter, William. "Un opéra russe: 'Sniégourotchka' de M. Nikolai Andrejevitch Rimskij Korsakof." In *Études d'art étranger*. Paris: Soc. du Mercure de France, 1906. 471 pp.

Ritter's account, which is to be found on pp. 182–96, is enthusiastic but somewhat romanticized.

467 Sabinina, Marina Dmitrievna. "'Snegurochka' v Bol'shom teatre." [*The Snow Maiden* at the Bol'shoy Theater.] *SM* 3 (1955): 82–88.

A somewhat tentative review of a performance at the Bol'shoy Theater in which Galina Vishnevskaya is praised for her singing of the part of Kupava.

468 Solovtsov, A., ed. *N. A. Rimsky-Korsakov. "'Snegurochka' – Vesennyaya skazka (tematichesky razbor)."* [N. A. Rimsky-Korsakov. *"The Snow Maiden – A Spring Fairy Tale* (Thematic Analysis)."] Moscow: Muzyka, 1978. [See Nos. 208, 462.]

One of a series of publications by a prominent specialist on Rimsky-Korsakov.

469 Taruskin, Richard. "The Snow Maiden." In Stanley Sadie, ed. *The New Grove Dictionary of Opera*, IV. London and New York: Macmillan Press, 1992: 428–30. ISBN-10: 0935859926. ISBN-13: 978-0935859928.

A substantial and informative account of the opera.

470 Tideböhl, Ellen von. "Rimsky-Korsakov and His Opera *The Snow Maiden*." *The Musician* (1911): 156.

A brief account of the opera given at the Private Opera, Moscow.

Mlada

471 Abraham, Gerald. "Rimsky-Korsakov's *Mlada*." In No. 284: 113–21.

A concise discussion of the opera.

472 Aleksandrov, A. "'Mlada' Rimskogo-Korsakova i eë problemy." [Rimsky-Korsakov's *Mlada* and its Problems.] *SM* 3 (1982): 73–78.

A discussion of the opera, reassessing its value and stressing its novelty, noting the manner in which Rimsky-Korsakov was influenced in its composition by such diverse figures as Schopenhauer and Wagner, and the world of fantasy.

Bibliography: Musical Works

473 Asaf'ev, Boris Vladimirovich [pseud. Glebov, Igor']. "Zaklyatiya." [*The Oath*.] In No. 296: 66–73.

Published as a supplement to a program of concerts given by the Petrograd Philharmonic (7 and 10 September, 1921), Asaf'ev discusses Rimsky-Korsakov's intellectual approach towards musical composition as seen especially in the operas *Mlada* and *Kashchey the Immortal*.

474 ——. "Nezasluzhenno zabytaya opera. (K vozobnovleniyu 'Mlady')." [An Undeservedly Forgotten Opera. (On the Renewal of *Mlada*).] *Teatr* 2 (1923): 9–11.

475 ——. "Petrogradskie vpechatleniya." [Petrograd Impressions.] *Muzykal'naya nov'* 1 (1923): 39–40.

Discusses productions of the operas *Mlada* and *The Golden Cockerel*.

476 Findeyzen, Nikolay Fëdorovich. "Vydayushcheesya sobytie. (O postanovke 'Mlady')." [An Outstanding Event. (On the Performance of *Mlada*).] *Teatr* 1 (1923): 19–20.

An enthusiastic account of a performance of the opera, noting the composer's skills as an orchestral innovator.

477 Prokof'ev, Grigory Petrovich. "'Mlada' Rimskogo-Korsakova." [Rimsky-Korsakov's *Mlada*.] *RMG* 41 (1913): cols. 896–900.

An account of a performance in Moscow.

478 Rakhmanova, Marina Pavlovna. "Vokrug *Mlady*." [On *Mlada*.] *SM* 54 (3) (1990): 12. ISSN: 0131-6818.

A discussion of Rimsky-Korsakov's opera *Mlada*, in which Rimsky-Korsakov is seen to share a common philosophical outlook with Wagner in regarding the opera as "a carrier of mythological consciousness."

479 Rimsky-Korsakov, Vladimir Nikolaevich. "Otkrytoe pis'mo." [An Open Letter.] *SM* 9 (1965): 52–54.

An examination of the opera, its strengths and weaknesses, and the feasibility of making changes primarily to the libretto. With a request that it be performed by the Bol'shoy Theater.

480 Serova, Valentina Semënovna. "'Mlada', opera g. Rimskogo-Korsakova." [*Mlada*, an Opera by Mr. Rimsky-Korsakov.] *Artist* 1, 26 (1893): 179–85.

An article on Rimsky-Korsakov and the opera *Mlada*, written in a romantic vein.

481 Taruskin, Richard. "Mlada." In Stanley Sadie, ed. *The New Grove Dictionary of Opera*, III. London and New York: Macmillan Press, 1992: 417-18. ISBN-10: 0935859926. ISBN-13: 978-0935859928.

An informative article containing commentary, details of plot, and musical analysis.

Noch' pered Rozhdestvom [Christmas Eve]

482   Asaf'ev, Boris Vladimirovich [pseud. Glebov, Igor']. "'Noch' pered Rozhdestvom'. Byl'-kolyadka." [*Christmas Eve. A Christmas Tale.*] In No. 296: 74–86.

Written in 1921, this is a discussion of the opera, noting its mythological bases, rhythmic, harmonic, and melodic structure, dramatic characterization, and specific national musical features.

483   Engel', Yuly Dmitrievich. "Noch' pered Rozhdestvom." [*Christmas Eve.*] *Novosti Dnya* 5541 (1 November 1898). Reprinted: No. 313: 31–35.

A critical account of the opera, in which Engel' sees a number of defects, considering the action to be overloaded with too many incongruous elements.

484   Ferman, Valentin Eduardovich. "'Cherevichki' ('Kuznets Vakula') Chaykovskogo i 'Noch' pered Rozhdestvom' Rimskogo-Korsakova (opyt sravneniya opernoy dramaturgii i muzykal'nogo stilya)." [Tchaikovsky's *The Little Shoes* (*Vakula the Smith*) and Rimsky-Korsakov's *Christmas Eve* (an Attempt at a Comparison of the Operatic Dramaturgy and Musical Style).] In *Voprosy muzykoznaniya. Ezhegodnik.* [Questions of Musicology. Yearbook.] A. S. Ogolevets, ed., Vol. I. 1953–1954. Moscow: Muzgiz, 1954: 205–38.

A comparison of Rimsky-Korsakov's opera with Tchaikovsky's *The Little Shoes* (*Vakula the Smith*), noting the different musical, textual and esthetic approaches. Rimsky-Korsakov is seen as favoring contrast of reality and fantasy, which often results in scenic pictures rather than continuous development.

485   Ivanov, Mikhail Mikhaylovich. "'Noch' pered Rozhdestvom'. Muzykal'nye zametki." [*Christmas Eve.* Musical Notes.] *Novoe Vremya* 4 (16 December 1895). English trans.: No. 493: 256–60.

This article criticizes the libretto, the composer's departures from Gogol, and the colorlessness of the music, although the performance as a whole is praised.

486   Kashkin, Nikolay Dmitrievich. "Dve novye russkie opery." [Two New Russian Operas.] *Russkoe Obozrenie* 37 (January 1896): 426–34.

On the opera première in St. Petersburg.

487   L. "Yubiley O. O. Palecheka. – 1-e predstavlenie opery 'Noch' pered Rozhdestvom' N. A. Rimskogo-Korsakova." [O. O. Palechek's Jubilee. First Performance of Rimsky-Korsakov's Opera *Christmas Eve.*] *RMG* 12 (1895): cols. 817–19.

A short account of the bass Palechek and the first performance of the opera.

Bibliography: Musical Works

488 Larosh, German Avgustovich. "Novaya opera N. A. Rimskogo-Korsakova." [A New Opera by N. A. Rimsky-Korsakov.] *Novosti i Birzhevaya Gazeta* (10 [22] December 1895): 878–90. English trans.: No. 493: 247–250.

An account of the opera, noting the manner in which Rimsky-Korsakov has assimilated Lisztian influences and allied them with Russian melodies, together with a description of its content and staging at the Mariinsky Theater.

489 Mörchen, Roland. "Noël! Noël! Die Weihnacht in Werken des Musiktheaters: Mehr als bloss Kolorit." *Das Orchester: Zeitschrift für Orchesterkultur und Rundfunk-Chorwesen* 50 (12) (2002): 27. ISSN: 0030-4468.

Entitled "Noel! Noel! Christmas in Works for Music Theater: More than just Atmosphere," this article takes the form of an examination of the manner in which the theme of Christmas has been depicted by composers in operas, including Rimsky-Korsakov's opera *Christmas Eve.*

490 Myers, Gregory. "The Collision of the Pagan and Christian in a Rimsky-Korsakov Fantasy Opera, or How Nikolai Andreevich Spent His Christmas Holidays." *Bălgarsko muzikoznanie* 27 (1) (2003): 87. ISSN: 0204-823X.

An exploration of the way in which Christian and pagan elements are fused in Rimsky-Korsakov's opera *Christmas Eve* and expressed in musical terms.

491 P-sky, E. "Noch' pered Rozhdestvom." [*Christmas Eve.*] *RMG* 1 (1896): cols. 53–76.

An examination of the opera, assessing its strengths and weaknesses and suggesting reasons for its poor public reception.

492 Taruskin, Richard. "Christmas Eve." In Stanley Sadie, ed. *The New Grove Dictionary of Opera*, I. London and New York: Macmillan Press, 1992: 854–55. ISBN-10: 0935859926. ISBN-13: 978-0935859928.

An account of the opera, outlining its essential characteristics.

493 Taylor, Philip. *Gogolian Interludes. Gogol's Story "Christmas Eve" as the Subject of the Operas by Tchaikovsky and Rimsky-Korsakov.* London and Wellingborough: Collets, 1984. iv, 264 pp. Reprinted: Pro Am Music Resources, 1987. ISBN-10: 0912483229. ISBN-13: 978-0912483221.

Divided into three parts, this study is concerned with a comparative examination of the two settings of Gogol's story *Christmas Eve,* by Tchaikovsky and Rimsky-Korsakov. Both libretti are translated, the history of each opera's composition given, and the works analyzed. The pagan elements in Rimsky-Korsakov's work are also discussed. In the appendices are translations of several articles by Larosh on Tchaikovsky's opera *Cherevichki* [*The Little Shoes*], and Rimsky-Korsakov's *Noch' pered Rozhdestvom* [*Christmas Eve*]. Appendix 5, entitled: "A few Observations Concerning the Staging of the

Fantastic Part of the Opera," is a translation of Korsakov's own instructions. Appendix 6 consists of the composer's Preface. Appendix 8 is a translation by Philip Taylor of an excerpt from Boris Andriyanov's *Na velikoy russkoy ravnine* [On the Great Russian Plain] (1981), this being an account of the *kolyada*, the festival of the winter solstice and the customs associated with it. Appendix 10 is a translation of a long article by Mikhail Ivanov, published in the journal *Novoe Vremya* in 1895, in which he takes Rimsky-Korsakov severely to task [see Nos. 485 and 488].

494   V-va, O. "Tematizm opery N. A. Rimskogo-Korsakova 'Noch' pered Rozhdestvom'." [The Thematic Structure of Rimsky-Korsakov's Opera *Christmas Eve*.] *RMG* 11 (1895): cols. 666–701.

A structural examination of the opera, with 54 music examples.

Sadko

495   Abraham, Gerald. "The Music of Sadko." *Musical Standard* 37 (1931): 183–84, 197–98.

A short factual account of the opera.

496   ——. "Sadko and The Tsar's Bride." *Monthly Musical Record* 6 (June 1931): 168–69.

A discussion primarily of the opera *Sadko* and its evolution, together with the composer's varying reaction to his librettists.

497   ——. "Sadko." In No. 283: 221–45.

A discussion of the opera and its music, noting that its structure is symphonic in outline but not in growth and texture. Abraham tends to detect more weaknesses in the work than strengths.

498   Anonymous. "Khronika. S.-Peterburg. Mariinsky teatr. XLI. 'Sadko'." [Chronicle. St. Petersburg. Mariinsky Theater. XLI. *Sadko*.] *RMG* 5 (1901): cols.145–48.

An account of a performance, with the composer enthusiastically feted.

499   Anonymous. "'Sadko' v Narodnom dome." [*Sadko* in the Narodny Dom.] *RMG* 39 (1906): cols. 855–57.

A short, witty account of its performance.

500   Anonymous. "K istorii opery-byliny 'Sadko' (iz perepiski N. A. Rimskogo-Korsakova i V. V. Stasova)." [On the History of the Opera-bylina *Sadko* (from N. A. Rimsky-Korsakov's Correspondence with V. V. Stasov).] *Muzyka* 4–5 (1910): 110–12; 7 (1910): 150–56; 8 (1910): 178–83.

501   Asaf'ev, Boris Vladimirovich [pseud. Glebov, Igor']. "'Sadko.' (Gosudarstvenny Bol'shoy operny teatr)." [*Sadko*. (State Bol'shoy Opera Theater).] *Zhizn' iskusstva* 399–400 (1920).

Bibliography: Musical Works

502 ——. "'Sadko.' (Mariinsky teatr)." [*Sadko*. (Mariinsky Theater).] *Zhizn' iskusstva* 566–567 (1920).

A critical account of a performance of the opera, with observations on the work's structure.

503 ——. "Problema grada vidimogo." [The Problem of the Visible City.] In No. 296: 86–95.

Written in 1921, this discusses the problems faced by the composer in utilizing folk material.

504 Chemodanov, Sergey. "'Sadko' v Bol'shom teatre." [*Sadko* in the Bol'shoy Theater.] *Novy mir* 7 (1935): 278–85.

Sergey Mikhaylovich Chemodanov (1888–1942) was active in revolutionary circles from an early age, his writings being colored by his political sympathies.

505 Engel', Yuly Dmitrievich. "'Sadko' Nikolaya Rimskogo-Korsakova. (Bol'shoy teatr)." [Rimsky-Korsakov's *Sadko*. (Bol'shoy Theater).] *Russkie Vedomosti* 268 (2 November 1906). Reprinted: No. 313: 172–77. Reprinted: *MA* (2) (1994): 86. ISSN: 0869-4516.

An article by the prominent pre-revolutionary writer, Yuly Engel', who, from 1898, was music editor of *Russkie Vedomosti*, containing remarks on dramatic theory and the predominance of symmetry in the musical conception of the opera as staged at the Bol'shoy Theater. Reference is also made to the novel décor by Korovin.

506 Farizova, N. *'Sadko' N. A. Rimskogo-Korsakova.* [N. A. Rimsky-Korsakov's *Sadko*.] Moscow: Muzgiz, 1958. 101 pp.

This volume, in the series "Opera Libretti," comprises a short introduction by N. Farizova, pp. 3–8, including several quotations from Serov and Stasov, followed by a general discussion of the opera. With observations on the use of folk elements and details of some notable performers of the opera. The remainder of the booklet consists of the opera libretto.

507 Il'in, Igor' Pavlovich. "'Sadko' na stsene Bol'shogo teatra." [*Sadko* on the Stage of the Bol'shoy Theater.] *SM* 9 (1949): 90–94.

A discussion of Rimsky-Korsakov's opera and its production at the Bol'shoy Theater. With one portrait and two engravings.

508 Kandinsky, Aleksey Ivanovich. "Kogda molchat klassiki." [When the Classics are Silent.] *SM* 6 (1969): 32–38.

An article examining the history and musical significance of the opera, criticizing K. Simeonov's production at the Leningrad Kirov Theater, which included cuts and changes to the libretto. With some observations on the role of the Starchishche (St. Nicolas), which was omitted in the performance.

509　——. "Russkaya klassika v Bol'shom teatre SSSR." [Russian Classics at the Bol'shoy Theater of the USSR.] *SM* 7 (1977): 63–79.

Includes a discussion of *Sadko* and *Mozart and Salieri*, their significance and the method of their staging.

510　Kashkin, Nikolay Dmitrievich. "Muzykal'noe obozrenie 'Sadko'. Opera-bylina v semi kartinakh N. A. Rimskogo-Korsakova." [A Music Review of *Sadko*. Opera-bylina in Seven Scenes by N. A. Rimsky-Korsakov.] *Russkoe Obozrenie* 49 (1 January 1898): 563–77.

An article discussing the evolution of Russian nineteenth-century opera, the relationship between the recitative employed by Dargomyzhsky, Wagner, and that of Rimsky-Korsakov in the opera *Sadko*, and the structure of the work in general.

511　——. "'Sadko' na stsene chastnoy opery." [*Sadko* on the Stage of the Private Opera.] *Russkie Vedomosti* 7 (7 January 1898).

An informative account of a performance of the opera *Sadko*.

512　Khessin, Aleksandr Borisovich. "Dva 'Sadko' (1901-1949)." [Two *Sadko*s (1901-1949).] *SM* 9 (1949): 95.

A comparison between the première of Rimsky-Korsakov's opera at the Imperial Mariinsky Theater in 1901 and the Bol'shoy Theater production in 1949, depicting the pre-revolutionary one in an unfavorable light.

513　Khubov, Georgy Nikitich. "'Sadko.' Opera Rimskogo-Korsakova v Bol'shom teatre (*Pravda*, 24 iyunya 1949)." [*Sadko*. Rimsky-Korsakov's Opera in the Bol'shoy Theater (*Pravda*, 24 June 1949).] In G. N. Khubov. *O muzyke i muzykantakh*. [On Music and Musicians.] Moscow: *Sovetsky Kompozitor*, 1959: 141–46.

An ideologically orientated article, appearing originally in *Pravda*, reviewing a performance of the opera at the Bol'shoy Theater, with special praise for G. Nelepp in the title role.

514　Kiselëv, Vasily Aleksandrovich. "O pervoy postanovke 'Sadko' v Bol'shom teatre. Neizdannoe pis'mo N. A. Rimskogo-Korsakova." [On the First Performance of *Sadko* in the Bol'shoy Theater. An Unpublished Letter of N. A. Rimsky-Korsakov.] *SM* 6 (1938): 57–59.

Concerns the first performance of the opera on 24 October 1906 at the Moscow Bol'shoy Theater, conducted by Suk. The original conductor was to have been Rakhmaninov. However, before Suk's arrival, and unknown to Rimsky-Korsakov, the administration appointed a young and inexperienced conductor, N. A. Fëdorov, to whom Rimsky-Korsakov objected. The situation became confused and was seized upon by the press. The present letter is a reply by Rimsky-Korsakov to Serafima Andreevna Sinitsina, the performer of

Nezhata, in which he explains the whole situation and at the same time makes several observations on what he considers to be the role of the composer (e.g., "...as for a composer, he should compose and write, but not interfere in the performance.").

515   Kyui, Ts. A. [Cui, César]. "'Sadko,' opera-bylina Rimskogo-Korsakova." [*Sadko*, Opera-bylina by Rimsky-Korsakov.] *Novosti i Birzhevaya Gazeta* 64 (6 March 1898). Reprinted: No. 1294: 472, 617.

A discussion of the opera.

516   Lipaev, Ivan Vasil'evich. "'Sadko.' Opera-bylina N. Rimskogo-Korsakova na Moskovskoy stsene." [*Sadko*. Rimsky-Korsakov's Opera-bylina on the Moscow Stage.] *RMG* 1 (1898): 69–77.

An informative discussion of the opera and its performance.

517   Marchenkov, Vladimir Leonidovich. *The Orpheus Myth on Musical Thought of Antiquity, the Renaissance, and Modern Times.* PhD dissertation, Ohio State University: UMI, 1998. Published in the series *Interplay: Music in Interdisciplinary Dialogue*, No. 7: *The Orpheus Myth and the Powers of Music.* Hillsdale, NY: Pendragon Press, 2009. 205 pp. ISBN-10: 1576471764. ISBN-13: 978-1576471760.

A historical examination of the myth of Orpheus as recounted in the esthetics of Plato, Marsilio Ficino, and Vyacheslav Ivanovich Ivanov, including discussion of Rimsky-Korsakov's opera *Sadko*.

518   Martynov, Ivan Ivanovich. "Sadko." In I. I. Abramsky, ed. *Al'bom. Bol'shoy Teatr SSSR. Opera. Balet.* [Album. Bol'shoy Theater of the USSR. Opera. Ballet.] Moscow: Muzgiz, 1958: 84–93.

The main value of this book lies in its lavish photographs and illustrations, in some cases double-paged, which give a good idea of the grandiosity of the Russian stage productions of the period. Though most are in sepia, a few are in color.

519   Muir, Stephen. "Rimsky-Korsakov, *Sadko*, and the *Byliny*." *British Postgraduate Musicology* 1 (1) (October 1997): 5–13. ISSN: 1460-9231.

Although Rimsky-Korsakov considered his opera *Sadko* to be imbued with the spirit of the *byliny* [epic ballads], the author raises the question as to whether *Sadko* can be regarded as a true folk opera.

520   Nest'ev, Izrail Vladimirovich. "Novoe prochtenie klassiki." [A New Reading of a Classic.] *Teatr* 5 (1951): 52–66.

Refers to the opera *Sadko*.

521   P. "Moskovskaya Russkaya Chastnaya Opera. 'Sadko'." [The Moscow Russian Private Opera. *Sadko.*] *RMG* 3 (1898): 285–90.

A sympathetic, though critical, review of the opera at its première in Moscow.

522 P-sky, E. "Tematichesky analiz opery 'Sadko'." [Thematic Analysis of the Opera *Sadko*.] *RMG* 9 (1898): 790–800.

A detailed musical analysis of the opera, illustrated with 35 music examples.

523 Rappaport, Viktor Romanovich. "Stsenichesky syuzhet opery 'Sadko'. (Iz rechi proiznesennoy na pervoy repetitsii)." [The Stage Subject of the Opera *Sadko*. (From a Speech Delivered at the First Rehearsal).] *Zhizn' iskusstva* 610–612 (1920): 1.

The context of a speech delivered at the first rehearsal of the opera, giving Rappaport's own philosophical-ideological interpretation of the work, which he sees as a transition from negation to acceptance of the world, from loneliness to communal fraternization.

524 Roberge, Marc-André. "The Busoni Network and the Art of Creative Transcription." *Canadian University Music Review/Revue de musique des universités canadiennes* 11 (1) (1991): 68. ISSN: 0710-0353.

Includes discussion of Kaikhosru Shapurji Sorabji's *Pastiche on the Hindu Merchant's Song from "Sadko" by Rimsky-Korsakov* (1922), including excerpts from the music.

525 *Sadko*. Program of *Sadko* as given at the Bol'shoy Theater, Moscow, 1951. Moscow: Gosudarstvennoe izdatel'stvo Iskusstvo, 1951. 23 pp.

An official program, the sepia illustrations being of artistic and historical interest.

526 Shaverdyan, Aleksandr Isaakovich. *Bol'shoy teatr Soyuza SSR*. [The Bol'shoy Theater of the Union of the SSR.] Moscow: Muzgiz, 1952. 229 pp. Review: *SM* 4 (1953): 113–14.

References to the composer, his operas, and notable performers are scattered throughout the volume, the different historical productions of *Sadko* being discussed on pp. 151–56. No index.

527 Shpiller, Natal'ya Dmitrievna. "Radost' nezabyvaemykh vstrech." [The Joy of Unforgettable Meetings.] *SM* 3 (1976): 58–64.

A discussion of the Soviet conductor Nikolay Golovanov and his interpretation of the opera.

528 Shumskaya, N. 'Sadko' Rimskogo-Korsakova. [Rimsky-Korsakov's *Sadko*.] Moscow: Muzgiz, 1956. 77 pp. Second edition. Moscow: Muzgiz, 1969. Third edition. Moscow: Muzyka, 1982 (with short bibliography).

A volume in the series "Guide-books on Russian Music," this consists of an enthusiastic preface, followed by an examination of the introduction to the opera and the following seven scenes. Described as "one of the Soviet

Bibliography: Musical Works

audiences' favorite works," p. 40, Shumskaya provides an analysis, some details of the history of the opera's composition as well as its place in the composer's work.

529   Sollertinsky, Ivan Ivanovich. "'Sadko' (Otkrytie opernogo teatra v Nardome)." [*Sadko* (Opening of the Opera Theater in the Narodny Dom).] *Zhizn' iskusstva* 42 (1929): 6.

An article written by Ivan Sollertinsky (1902–44) early in his career.

530   Taruskin, Richard. "Sadko." In Stanley Sadie, ed. *The New Grove Dictionary of Opera*, IV. London and New York: Macmillan Press, 1992: 120–22. ISBN-10: 0935859926. ISBN-13: 978-0935859928.

A well-informed discussion of the opera.

531   Toorn, Pieter van den. *The Music of Igor Stravinsky*. New Haven and London: Yale University Press, 1983. 514 pp. ISBN-10: 0300038844. ISBN-13: 978-0300038842.

Among the many references to Rimsky-Korsakov, the harmonic structure of the opening 10 bars of the second tableau of the opera is discussed, pp. 35–39, noting octatonic elements.

532   Tsukkerman, Viktor Abramovich. "O syuzhete i muzykal'nom yazke opery-byliny 'Sadko'." [On the Subject and Musical Language of the Opera-bylina *Sadko*.] *SM* 3 (1933): 46–73. Reprinted: V. A. Tsukkerman. *Muzykal'no-teoreticheskie ocherki i etyudy*. [Musical-theoretical Essays and Studies.] Vol. I. Moscow: Sovetsky Kompozitor, 1970: 441–504.

Divided into 11 main sections and a conclusion, this is a major survey of the opera, examined from different viewpoints, including its origins, history of composition, subject matter, musical content, musical style, ideology, and its links with art (e.g., Repin's *Sadko* of 1876, and works by Vasnetsov). Of interest is Tsukkerman's discussion of the religious elements both in the opera and in the earlier orchestral "musical picture."

533   ——. "'Sadko'." In No. 373: 145–218.

A chapter in I. Uvarova's handbook on the operas of Rimsky-Korsakov, this consists of four sections, including excerpts from the libretto:

i.   History of the composition of *Sadko*; place of the opera in Rimsky-Korsakov's work.
ii.   The opera's musical language.
iii.   Subject of the opera.
iv.   Content of the opera.

534   V. M-y. "'Sadko' v Gosnardome." [*Sadko* in the Gosnardom.] *Zhizn' iskusstva* 10 (1926): 10.

A description of a performance of *Sadko* in the Narodny Dom.

Motsart i Sal'eri [Mozart and Salieri]

535 Anonymous. "'Motsart i Sal'eri,' 'Torzhestvo Vakha' v Gosudarstvennom Bol'shom opernom teatre." [*Mozart and Salieri, The Triumph of Bacchus* in the State Bol'shoy Opera Theater.] *Zhizn' iskusstva* 663–665 (1921).

Consists of several articles dealing with the performance of Rimsky-Korsakov's *Mozart and Salieri* and Dargomyzhsky's opera-ballet *The Triumph of Bacchus* given as a double bill at the Moscow Bol'shoy Theater. The article "Utverzhdenie zhizni" [Affirmation of Life] contains observations about characterization, form, and structure in Rimsky-Korsakov's opera.

536 Asaf'ev, Boris Vladimirovich [pseud. Glebov, Igor']. "Torzhestva Vakkha' i 'Motsart i Sal'eri.' (Bol'shoy operny teatr)." [*The Triumph of Bacchus* and *Mozart and Salieri*. (Bol'shoy Opera Theater).] *Zhizn' iskusstva* 666–668 (1921).

A short descriptive account of the two works given at the Bol'shoy Opera Theater, Moscow.

537 Belza, Igor' Fëdorovich. *Motsart i Sal'eri. Tragediya Pushkina. Dramaticheskie stseny Rimskogo-Korsakova.* [*Mozart and Salieri*. Tragedy by Pushkin. Dramatic Scenes by Rimsky-Korsakov.] Moscow, 1953: 134. Review: *SM* 11 (1954): 141–44.

Divided into two parts, the first is a general account of the literary aspects of the work, Pushkin's interpretation of the characters of *Mozart and Salieri*, and the circumstances surrounding Mozart's death. The second part is concerned with Rimsky-Korsakov's treatment of the theme, together with a musical analysis and some comments from the point of view of Marxist-Leninist ideology.

538 Braudo, Evgeny Maksimovich. "Motsart i Sal'eri." [*Mozart and Salieri*.] In V. Ossovsky, ed. *Orfey* [Orpheus] Book I. Petrograd: Gosudarstvennaya Filarmoniya, 1922: 102–07.

First published in the program of a symphony concert "In Memory of Pushkin," given in the Petrograd Philharmonic on 12 February 1922, this is an informative discussion of Pushkin's *Mozart and Salieri*, providing background for any study of Rimsky-Korsakov's opera.

539 Durylin, S. N. *Pushkin na stsene.* [Pushkin on the Stage.] Moscow: Izd. Akad. Nauk SSSR, 1951. 287 pp.

A discussion of Pushkin's *Mozart and Salieri* and its relationship to his other "Little Tragedies" of 1830 can be found on pp. 93–103. Provides a useful literary background, describing the poet's creative intentions and some of

Bibliography: Musical Works   115

the first performers of the dramatic and operatic work, particularly Fëdor Ivanovich Shalyapin [Chaliapin]. No index.

540   Engel', Yuly Dmitrievich. "Motsart i Sal'eri." [*Mozart and Salieri.*] *Russkie Vedomosti*, 267 (27 November 1898). Reprinted: No. 313: 38–41.

An account of the opera, in which Engel' praises the singing of Shalyapin [Chaliapin] in the role of Salieri, as well as noting a number of defects in the work's structure and performance.

541   ——. "'Motsart i Sal'eri' i 'Payatsy'." [*Mozart and Salieri* and *I Pagliacci.*] *Russkie Vedomosti* 60 (15 March 1911). Reprinted: No. 313: 322–24.

Engel' draws comparisons between *Mozart and Salieri* and *I Pagliacci*, presented as a double bill at Solodovnikov's Private Theater.

542   Guseynova, Zivar Mahmudovna. "Glyuk i Pichchini, zacherknutye Rimskim-Korsakovym." [Gluck and Piccini, Crossed Out by Rimsky-Korsakov.] In *Zadumannoe, zabytoe, vozvrashchënnoe – Sbornik nauchnykh statey. K 150-letiyu Sankt-Peterburgskoy konservatorii.* [Considered, Forgotten, Retrieved – A Volume of Scientific Articles. To Mark the 150th Anniversary of the St. Petersburg Conservatory.] St. Petersburg, 2012.

An examination of the manuscript of the piano score of Rimsky-Korsakov's opera *Mozart and Salieri*, which contains numerous corrections in the composer's hand, including an analysis of three episodes that Rimsky-Korsakov deleted.

543   Hadland, F. A. "Mozart and Salieri." *Monthly Musical Record* 57 (October 1927): 292.

A note written to precede the English première of the opera, in which the choral parts were performed by a choir of 1,000 voices and the orchestral accompaniment provided by the London Symphony Orchestra.

544   Kharissov, Ildar. "Zitate und Quasi-Zitate in der Oper Mozart und Salieri von Rimski-Korsakow." In *The Past in the Present: Papers read at the IMS Intercongressional Symposium and the 10th Meeting of the Cantus Planus.* Budapest and Visegrád, 2000. Hungary, 2003.

Entitled "Quotation and quasi-quotation in Rimsky-Korsakov's opera *Motsart i Sal'eri* [Mozart and Salieri]," the article comments on the work's unusual format.

545   Kudryumov, Yu. V. "'Motsart i Sal'eri' Rimskogo-Korsakova." [Rimsky-Korsakov's *Mozart and Salieri.*] *RMG* 12 (1898): 1113–16.

An examination of the opera.

546   Kyui, Ts. A. [Cui, César]. "Moskovskaya chastnaya russkaya opera. 'Motsart i Sal'eri'." [Moscow Private Russian Opera. *Mozart and Salieri.*] *Novosti i Birzhevaya Gazeta* 70 (12 March 1899). Reprinted: No. 1294: 494–97, 618.

A general discussion of the opera.

547 Larosh, German Avgustovich. "Po povodu odnogo muzykal'nogo spektaklya. 'Orfey' Gluka i 'Motsart i Sal'eri' Rimskogo-Korsakova." [On the Occasion of a Musical Performance. Gluck's *Orfée* and Rimsky-Korsakov's *Mozart and Salieri.*] *Mir Iskusstva* 6 (1899).

An interesting discussion of two disparate operas by a well-informed writer.

548 Levik, Boris Veniaminovich. "'Motsart i Sal'eri'." [*Mozart and Salieri.*] In No. 373: 219–38.

A short discussion of the opera and the circumstances of its composition, followed by a synopsis of its content.

549 Lipaev, Ivan Vasil'evich. "'Motsart i Sal'eri,' opera N. Rimskogo-Korsakova, v Moskve." [*Mozart and Salieri*, N. Rimsky-Korsakov's Opera in Moscow.] *RMG* 1 (1899): cols. 12–13.

On a performance of the opera.

550 Lunacharsky, Anatoly Vasil'evich. "Iz moskovskikh vpechatleniy." [Moscow Impressions.] *Zhizn' iskusstva* 53 (1919).

Apart from his role as People's Commissar for Education (1917–29), Anatoly Lunacharsky (1875–1933) was active as a writer and music critic, many of his critiques being devoted to the work of Rimsky-Korsakov. The article discusses the opera *Mozart and Salieri*.

551 Montagu-Nathan, Montagu. "The Russian Operatic Gospel: According to Dargomijsky, Moussorgsky and Rimsky-Korsakoff. IV. Mozart and Salieri." *Musical Opinion and Music Trade Review* 454 (July 1915): 661–62.

A stimulating discussion of the opera.

552 Pekelis, Mikhail Samoylovich. "Dramaturgiya Pushkina i russkaya opera." [Pushkin's Dramaturgy and Russian Opera.] *SM* 5 (1937): 45–60.

Includes a discussion of Rimsky-Korsakov's *Mozart and Salieri*, Cui's *Feast in Time of Plague*, and Rakhmaninov's *The Miserly Knight*, all of which draw their inspiration from Pushkin. *Mozart and Salieri* is seen as being closely connected with Dargomyzhsky's *The Stone Guest* [see pp. 55–57].

553 Shteynberg, A. "'Motsart i Sal'eri' N. Rimskogo-Korsakova." [N. Rimsky-Korsakov's *Mozart and Salieri.*] *SM* 8 (1937): 93.

A criticism of a booklet on Rimsky-Korsakov's *Mozart and Salieri*, ed. I. Shishov, published in 1937, with some additional information on the intermezzo separating the two scenes of the opera.

554 Taruskin, Richard. *Opera and Drama as Practiced and Preached in the 1860s*. Ann Arbor: UMI Research Press, 1981. xvii, 560 pp. ISBN-10: 1878822322. ISBN-13: 978-1878822321.

Primarily concerned with the 1860s, this book is essential reading for its insight into the contemporary Russian musical ethos, as well as containing a

Bibliography: Musical Works

number of Rimsky-Korsakov's comments on operas of the period. Includes a useful discussion of Dargomyzhsky's *Stone Guest* and *Mozart and Salieri.*

555 ——. "Mozart and Salieri." In Stanley Sadie, ed. *The New Grove Dictionary of Opera*, III. London and New York: Macmillan Press, 1992: 503. ISBN-10: 0935859926. ISBN-13: 978-0935859928.

A short account of the opera, highlighting its essential features.

556 Tsuker, Anatoly Moiseevich. "Muzyka o muzyke." [Music about Music.] *MA* (2) (2010): 35. ISSN: 0869-4516.

An examination of Rimsky-Korsakov's one-act opera *Mozart and Salieri*, based on the poem by Aleksandr Pushkin, including questions of dramaturgy and psychology, together with the composer's reworking of the literary source.

Boyarynya Vera Sheloga

557 "Efgro." "'Vera Sheloga.' (Maly letny Operny teatr)." [*Vera Sheloga.* (Maly Summer Opera Theater).] *Zhizn' iskusstva* 798–803 (1921).

A short account of the opera, stressing its tenderness and femininity.

558 Kyui, Ts. A. [Cui, César]. "Moskovskaya chastnaya russkaya opera. 'Boyarynya Vera Sheloga' Rimskogo-Korsakova." [The Moscow Private Russian Opera. *Boyarynya Vera Sheloga* by Rimsky-Korsakov.] *Novosti i Birzhevaya Gazeta*. 82 (24 March 1899). In No. 1294: 497–99, 619.

An account of the opera.

559 Lipaev, Ivan Vasil'evich. "'Boyarynya Vera Sheloga.' Muzykal'no-ramaticchesky prolog N. Rimskogo-Korsakova v Moskve." [*Boyarynya Vera Sheloga.* A Musical-Dramatic Prologue by Rimsky-Korsakov in Moscow.] *RMG* 2 (1899): cols. 48–49.

A short description of the opera and its musical content.

560 Vikhanskaya, Anna Moiseevna. "K istorii 'Very Shelogi'." [Something about the History of *Vera Sheloga.*] *SM* 6 (1958): 42–47.

A discussion of the opera, with numerous illustrations. Part of a series of articles in a volume of *SM* marking the 50th anniversary of Rimsky-Korsakov's death.

Tsarskaya nevesta [The Tsar's Bride]

561 Abraham, Gerald. "The Tsar's Bride." In No. 283: 246–60.

An examination of the opera, highlighting the composer's difficulties in expressing emotion, together with a lack of psychological insight. For much

118   *Nikolay Andreevich Rimsky-Korsakov: A Research and Information Guide*

of the time Abraham sees Rimsky-Korsakov as being confronted by the Voltairean dilemma: "the necessity of saying something and the perplexity of having nothing to say."

562   Anonymous. "Khronika. S.-Peterburg. Opera i kontserty. 'Tsarskaya nevesta' v Narodnom dome." [Chronicle. St. Petersburg. Opera and Concerts. *The Tsar's Bride* in the Narodny Dom.] *RMG* 25–26 (1903): cols. 607–09.

A critical account of the work's performance.

563   Asaf'ev, Boris Vladimirovich [pseud. Glebov, Igor']. "Rimsky-Korsakov. 'Tsarskaya nevesta'." [Rimsky-Korsakov's *The Tsar's Bride*.] *Muzyka* 246 (1916).

A perceptive article underlining essential elements of the opera *The Tsar's Bride*.

564   ——. "Kommunal'nye opernye teatry. B. Narodny dom." [Communal Opera Theaters. B. Narodny Dom.] *Zhizn' iskusstva* 17 (1918).

A discussion of *The Tsar's Bride*.

565   ——. "Novoe delo." [A New Affair.] *Zhizn' iskusstva* 518–519 (1920).

A discussion of *The Tsar's Bride*.

566   ——. "'Tsarskaya nevesta.' (Gosudarstvenny Bol'shoy operny teatr)." [*The Tsar's Bride*. (State Bol'shoy Opera Theater).] *Zhizn' iskusstva* 568 (1920).

A long, general article on Rimsky-Korsakov's operas and the sources of his inspiration, with particular reference to *The Tsar's Bride*.

567   Bakulin, V. "Leytmotivnaya i intonatsionnaya dramaturgiya v opere Rimskogo-Korsakova 'Tsarskaya nevesta'." [Leitmotiv and Intonation Dramaturgy in Rimsky-Korsakov's Opera *The Tsar's Bride*.] In Yu. N. Tyulin, ed. and comp. *Voprosy opernoy dramaturgii*. [Problems of Operatic Dramaturgy.] Moscow, 1975.

568   Belyaev, Viktor Mikhaylovich. *Gosudarstvennaya opernaya studiya-teatr imeni narodnogo artista respubliki K. S. Stanislavskogo.* [State Opera Studio Theater Named after People's Artist of the Republic K. S. Stanislavsky.] Moscow: Izd. Obshchestva Druzey Opernoy Studii-Teatra imeni K. S. Stanislavskogo, 1928. 60 pp.

Of interest on account of its photographs of productions of *The Tsar's Bride*, pp. 38–43, and *May Night*, pp. 48–54, together with portraits of some of the leading singers.

569   Bemol'. "'Tsarskaya nevesta' v Nardome." [*The Tsar's Bride* in the Narodny Dom.] *Zhizn' iskusstva* 8 (1926): 10.

570   Cunningham, Thomas Thurston. *Terrible Visions: The Sublime Image of Ivan the Terrible in Russian Opera.* PhD dissertation, New Jersey: Princeton University Press: UMI, 1999.

Bibliography: Musical Works 119

A historical picture of Tsar Ivan the Terrible [Ivan IV], using materials contained in Volumes 8 and 9 of Nikolay Mikhaylovich Karamzin's *Istoriya gosudarstva rossiyskogo* [History of the Russian State], including the representation of Ivan Grozny, better translated as "Ivan the Dread," in Rimsky-Korsakov's opera *The Tsar's Bride*.

571 Durylin, S. N., ed. *K. S. Stanislavsky. Materialy. Pis'ma. Issledovaniya.* [K. S. Stanislavsky. Materials. Letters. Research.] Moscow: Akademiya Nauk SSSR, 1955. 699 pp.

For a discussion of *The Tsar's Bride* see pp. 445–51.

572 Engel', Yuly Dmitrievich. "'Tsarskaya nevesta' v Chastnoy Opere." [*The Tsar's Bride* in the Private Opera.] *Russkie Vedomosti* 296 (26 October 1899). Reprinted: No. 313: 56–59.

A review of the production, highlighting its novel features and praising its orchestration. Contains information on the quality of the performers.

573 ——. "'Tsarskaya nevesta' v opere Zimina." [*The Tsar's Bride* at Zimin's Opera Theater.] *Russkie Vedomosti* 16 (19 January 1913). Reprinted: No. 313: 368–70.

A brief account of a performance of the opera *The Tsar's Bride*.

574 Kashkin, Nikolay Dmitrievich. "'Tsarskaya nevesta' Rimskogo-Korsakova." [Rimsky-Korsakov's *The Tsar's Bride*.] *Moskovskie Vedomosti* 291 (22 October 1899).

An examination of the opera scene by scene.

575 ——. "'Troyantsy v Karfagene' Berlioza." [Berlioz's *Les Troyens à Carthage*.] *EIT, Sezon* 1899–1900. Prilozhenie [Suppl.] 1. St. Petersburg (1900): 40–48.

A discussion of Berlioz's *Les Troyens à Carthage*, in the course of which Kashkin compares the French manner of approach with that of Rimsky-Korsakov in *The Tsar's Bride*.

576 Kustodiev, B. "Zadumannoe i osushchestvlennoe." [Conceived and Accomplished.] *Zhizn' iskusstva* 564–565 (1920).

A factual account of the opera at the Bol'shoy Theater, giving details of the scenery and lighting.

577 Lipaev, Ivan Vasil'evich. "'Tsarskaya nevesta'. Novaya opera N. Rimskogo-Korsakova. (Pervoe predstavlenie 22-go oktyabrya na stsene Chastnoy opery v Moskve)." [*The Tsar's Bride*. A New Opera by Rimsky-Korsakov. (First Performance on 22 October at the Private Opera in Moscow).] *RMG* 44 (1899): cols. 1104–07; 45 (1899): cols. 1125–29.

An account of the opera and its presentation, with a facsimile of the composer's handwriting.

120   *Nikolay Andreevich Rimsky-Korsakov: A Research and Information Guide*

578   Lyutsh, V. "'Tsarskaya nevesta.' (Opernaya studiya im. K. S. Stanislavskogo, 26 XI 1926)." [*The Tsar's Bride*. (Stanislavsky Opera Studio, 26 XI 1926).] *Muzyka i revolyutsiya* 12 (1926): 32.

An account of a production by Stanislavsky of the opera in which the critic accuses the producer of over-emphasizing the dramatic aspects of the work at the expense of the musical aspects. Comments on the weakness of the orchestra.

579   Muzalevsky, Vladimir Il'ich. "'Tsarskaya nevesta.' Opernaya studiya konservatorii." [*The Tsar's Bride*. Conservatory Opera Studio.] *Zhizn' iskusstva* 9 (1928): 10.

Although Vladimir Il'ich Muzalevsky [real name Bunimovich] (1894–1964) was primarily concerned with piano studies, he wrote prolifically on many different aspects of music, including reviews and critiques.

580   P. "'Tsarskaya nevesta' v Mariinskom teatre." [*The Tsar's Bride* in the Mariinsky Theater.] *RMG* 44 (1901): cols. 1092–94.

An account of the first performance of the opera at the Mariinsky Theater, noting some of the work's characteristic features.

581   Palmer, Christopher. "Prokofiev, Eisenstein and *Ivan*." *MT* 132 (1778) (April 1991): 179–81. ISSN: 0027-4666.

A discussion of Prokofiev's work as a composer of incidental music to Eisenstein's films *Alexander Nevsky* and *Ivan grozny* [Ivan the Terrible], Parts I and II, noting the influence of Rimsky-Korsakov's opera *Pskovityanka* [The Maid of Pskov] on his music.

582   Sobolevskaya, Ol'ga. "Kak stavilas' 'Tsarskaya nevesta'?" [How was *The Tsar's Bride* Performed?] *SM* 8 (1968): 80–86.

An account of Stanislavsky's staging of the opera at the Bol'shoy Theater in 1926.

583   Solovtsov, Anatoly Aleksandrovich. "'Tsarskaya nevesta'." [*The Tsar's Bride*] In No. 373: 239–302.

Consists of quotations from the libretto, together with musical examples, and two sections entitled: "The Tsar's Bride of Mey and Rimsky-Korsakov" and "Content of the Opera."

584   Strel'nikov, Nikolay Mikhaylovich. "'Tsarskaya nevesta'." [*The Tsar's Bride*.] *Zhizn' iskusstva* 16 (839) (1922).

A short critical account of the opera and its performance.

585   Taruskin, Richard. "The Tsar's Bride." In Stanley Sadie, ed. *The New Grove Dictionary of Opera*, IV. London and New York: Macmillan Press, 1992: 832–33. ISBN-10: 0935859926. ISBN-13: 978-0935859928.

A perceptive article outlining the opera's essential features.

Bibliography: Musical Works 121

586 ——. "Rimsky's Whodunnit. Richard Taruskin on *The Tsar's Bride*." *Opera* 62 (4) (April 2011): 382–87. ISSN: 0030-3526.

A concise discussion of the part played by Lev Aleksandrovich Mey, whose play *Tsarskaya nevesta* [The Tsar's Bride] (1849) was the source of Rimsky-Korsakov's opera of the same name, including information about the historical circumstances surrounding Ivan the Terrible, together with a brief analysis of the opera.

587 Teroganyan, M. I. "'Tsarskaya nevesta' N. A. Rimskogo-Korsakova." [Rimsky-Korsakov's *The Tsar's Bride*.] Second edition. Moscow: Muzgiz, 1959: 86.

Forming one of the series "Opera Libretti," this comprises a short introduction by M. Teroganyan, pp. 3–9, giving details of the circumstances of the work's composition, together with information on some of the notable performers of the opera. The remainder of the booklet consists of the libretto.

588 ——. "'Tsarskaya nevesta'." [*The Tsar's Bride*.] In I. I. Abramsky, ed. *Al'bom. Bol'shoy Teatr SSSR. Opera. Balet.* [Album. The Bol'shoy Theater of the USSR. Opera. Ballet.] Moscow: Muzgiz, 1958: 94–101.

A description of the Bol'shoy Theater production of the opera, lavishly illustrated with large, sometimes double-page photographs, some in color, with a commentary.

589 Uglov, Anton [real name: Kashintsev, Dmitry Aleksandrovich]. "'Tsarskaya nevesta' u Stanislavskogo." [Stanislavsky's *The Tsar's Bride*.] *Zhizn' iskusstva* 51 (1926): 9.

590 Vitols, Yazep [Vītols, Jāzeps]. "'Tsarskaya nevesta', opera v trëkh deystviyakh N. A. Rimskogo-Korsakova." [*The Tsar's Bride*, an Opera in Three Acts by N. A. Rimsky-Korsakov.] In A. Darkevich, ed. *Vitols. Vospominaniya, stat'i, pis'ma.* [Vitols. Reminiscences, Articles, Letters.] Leningrad: Muzyka, 1969: 154–57.

Yazep Vitols [Vītols] was music critic of the St. Petersburg German language journal *St. Petersburger Zeitung* over the period 1897–1914, in the course of which he wrote nearly a thousand reviews. The present article was published in the period 1901–02 (no date is given) and gives a generally positive assessment of the opera, noting in Marfa's second aria in particular "a psychology, no less subtle, than in Dostoevsky."

Skazka o Tsare Saltane [The Tale of Tsar Saltan]

591 Abraham, Gerald. "Tsar Saltan." In No. 284: 122–37.

A general discussion of the opera, illustrated with numerous music examples.

592 Anonymous. "Opera i kontserty. 'Skazka o tsare Saltane' Rimskogo-Korsakova v chastnoy opere." [Opera and Concerts. Rimsky-Korsakov's *The Tale of Tsar Saltan* at the Private Opera.] *RMG* 1 (1903): cols. 14–15.

An enthusiastic account of the opera and its distinctive features.

593   Anonymous. "Mariinsky teatr. CLIX 'Skazka o tsare Saltane'." [Mariinsky Theater. CLIX *The Tale of Tsar Saltan.*] *RMG* 14 (1915): cols. 255–56.

A brief, witty account of a performance of the opera at the Mariinsky Theater.

594   Asaf'ev, Boris Vladimirovich [pseud. Glebov, Igor']. "Mysli i razmyshleniya po povodu postanovki 'Skazka o tsare Saltane' v Mariinskom teatre." [Thoughts and Reflections on the Production of *The Tale of Tsar Saltan* in the Mariinsky Theater.] *Muzyka* 214 (1915): 172–77.

Boris Asaf'ev (1884–1949) was a student of Rimsky-Korsakov from 1904. One of the most erudite Russian musicologists, the work of Rimsky-Korsakov occurs frequently in his numerous publications.

595   ——. "'Skazka o tsare Saltane'." [*The Tale of Tsar Saltan.*] *Zhizn' iskusstva* 815 (1921).

A short account of the opera and its ideological interpretation.

596   ——. "Skazka." [*A Fairy Tale.*] (25 October 1921). In Nos. 296: 95–101; 1256: Vol. III, 288–90.

First published as a supplement to a program of a performance of the opera by the Petrograd Academic Theater of Opera and Ballet (25 October 1921), in which Asaf'ev states what he considers to be the essential qualities of the opera and the manner in which the composer realizes his intentions.

597   ——. "Muzykal'nye zametki." [Musical Notes.] *Teatr* 5 (1923): 3–4.

A short account of *The Tale of Tsar Saltan.*

598   Engel', Yuly Dmitrievich. "Prem'era opery 'Skazka o Tsare Saltane'." [Première of the Opera *The Tale of Tsar Saltan.*] *Russkie Vedomosti* 294 (22 October 1900). Reprinted: No. 313: 63–64.

A short lyrical description of the warm reception afforded the composer at the première of the work given by the Private Opera Company.

599   ——. "Novaya opera N. A. Rimskogo-Korsakova 'Skazka o tsare Saltane'." [Rimsky-Korsakov's New Opera *The Tale of Tsar Saltan.*] *Russkie Vedomosti* 297 (25 October 1900). Reprinted: No. 313: 64–71.

A descriptive account of the opera given by the Private Opera Company, a performance which Engel' found somewhat overlong.

600   ——. "Prem'era 'Skazki o tsare Saltane' v Bol'shom teatre." [The Première of *The Tale of Tsar Saltan* in the Bol'shoy Theater.] *Russkie Vedomosti* 230 (6 October 1913). Reprinted: No. 313: 377–78.

Describes a performance at the Bol'shoy Theater.

Bibliography: Musical Works 123

601 ——. "'Skazka o tsare Saltane' v Bol'shom teatre." [*The Tale of Tsar Saltan* in the Bol'shoy Theater.] *Russkie Vedomosti* 232 (9 October 1913). Reprinted: No. 313: 378–85.

A eulogistic account of a performance of the opera given at the Bol'shoy Theater.

602 G. N-ov. "Skazka o tsare Saltane." [*The Tale of Tsar Saltan.*] *Zhizn' iskusstva* 44, 917 (1923): 23.

A short review by an unidentified author, praising A. Kobzareva's singing in the role of Militrisa, and Emil Cooper's conducting.

603 Grosheva, Elena Andreevna. "Pushkin v opere." [Pushkin in Opera.] In *Pushkin na stsene Bol'shogo teatra.* [Pushkin on the Stage of the Bol'shoy Theater.] Moscow, 1949: 3–73.

A general discussion of "Pushkin and Russian Composers," pp. 3–21, with comment on the chief Pushkin works and notable performers. No index.

604 Gulyants, E. I. *N. A. Rimsky-Korsakov i ego "Skazka o tsare Saltane."* [N. A. Rimsky-Korsakov and his *Tale of Tsar Saltan.*] Moscow: Sovetsky Kompozitor, 1971. 53 pp.

A volume in the "For the Young Music Lover" series.

605 Lipaev, Ivan Vasil'evich. "'Skazka o tsare Saltane'. Novaya opera N. A. Rimskogo Korsakova. (1-e predstavlenie 21 oktyabrya, v Moskve)." [*The Tale of Tsar Saltan.* A New Opera by Rimsky-Korsakov. (First Performance 21 October, Moscow).] *RMG* 45 (1900): cols. 1066–70.

Of interest as a first-hand account of the opera's première.

606 Lunacharsky, Anatoly Vasil'evich. "Skazka o tsare Saltane." [*The Tale of Tsar Saltan.*] In No. 1162: 279–81.

607 Montagu-Nathan, Montagu. "The Tale of Tsar Saltan." *Musical Opinion* June (1917).

A description of the opera with quotations from Gilse van der Pals' analysis of the work [see No. 317].

608 Okser, S. and Vladimirov, V. *Muzykal'naya literatura.* [Music Literature.] Vol. I. Third edition. Moscow: Muzgiz, 1961. 399 pp.

Contains a piano arrangement of three numbers from the opera: Introduction to Act I, pp. 359–70, Introduction to Act II, pp. 371–81, and Introduction to Scene VII, pp. 382–97.

609 Ozeretskovskaya. I. "Skazka o tsare Saltane." [*The Tale of Tsar Saltan.*] In No. 373: 303–38.

Consists of excerpts from the libretto, together with two sections entitled "Rimsky-Korsakov and his Opera *The Tale of Tsar Saltan*" and "Content of the Opera."

610   Prokof'ev, Grigory Petrovich. "'Tsar Saltan' v Bol'shom Teatre." [*Tsar Saltan* in the Bol'shoy Theater.] *RMG* 44 (1913): cols. 988–90.

An account of a performance of the opera in Moscow.

611   Taruskin, Richard. "The Tale of Tsar Saltan." In Stanley Sadie, ed. *The New Grove Dictionary of Opera*, IV. London and New York: Macmillan Press, 1992: 635–37. ISBN-10: 0935859926. ISBN-13: 978-0935859928.

A comprehensive survey of the opera and its essential features.

612   Walker, Robert Matthew. "The Flight of the Bumblebee." *Musical Opinion* 132 (1469) (March–April 2009): 22. ISSN: 0027-4623.

An article describing the history of the orchestral interlude *Polët shmelya* [Flight of the Bumblebee] from Rimsky-Korsakov's opera *The Tale of Tsar Saltan*.

613   Yastrebtsëv, Vasily Vasil'evich. "O vremeni instrumentovki 'Skazki o tsare Saltane' i o narodnykh temakh, vzyatykh v etu operu." [Concerning the Date of Orchestration of *The Tale of Tsar Saltan*, and the Folk Themes Introduced into this Opera.] *Muzyka* 150 (5 October 1913): 623–27.

Gives dates of the opera's composition, details of the folk sources, and an unpublished page in the composer's handwriting.

Serviliya [Servilia]

614   Dietz, Max. "Die neueste russische Oper." *Neue Musik-Zeitung* 25, Stuttgart (1904): 442–45.

An analytical description of the opera, illustrated with music examples, in which Dietz, noting Wagnerian influences, stresses Rimsky-Korsakov's strong creative personality.

615   Findeyzen, Nikolay Fëdorovich. "'Serviliya' – novaya opera Rimskogo-Korsakova." [*Servilia* – Rimsky-Korsakov's New Opera.] *RMG* 40 (1902): cols. 949–54.

Nikolay Findeyzen was one of the most active music critics of the period. As editor of *RMG*, his critiques provide an unparalleled chronicle of the progress of Russian opera. The present article is a first-hand account of the première of *Servilia*.

616   Frolova-Walker, Marina. "Grand Opera in Russia: Fragments of an Unwritten History." In *The Cambridge Companion to Grand Opera*. Cambridge University Press, 2003. ISBN-10: 0521641187. ISBN-13: 978-0521641180.

An examination of the Russian grand opera tradition, with special reference to Rimsky-Korsakov's opera *Servilia*.

617 Grushke, N. "Serviliya." *Stsena i Muzyka* [Odessa] 3 (1905): 10–12.

Details of the Moscow première.

618 Lipaev, Ivan Vasil'evich. "Serviliya." *RMG* 46 (1904): cols. 1095–96.

Details of the première at Solodovnikov's Theater, Moscow.

619 Muir, Stephen and Katonova, Natal'ya Yur'evna. "*Serviliya* N. A. Rimskogo-Korsakova." [N. A. Rimsky-Korsakov's Opera *Servilia*.] In Larissa Danko, ed. *Peterburgskaya konservatoriya v mirovom muzykal'nom protsesse, 1862–2002: Materialy mezhnarodnoy muzykal'noy nauchnoy sessii, posvyashchënnoy 140-letiyu Konservatorii.* [The St. Petersburg Conservatory in the World Musical Process, 1862-2002: Materials of an International Musical Scientific Session, Dedicated to the 140th Anniversary of the Conservatory.] St. Petersburg: St. Petersburg Conservatory, 2002.

An account of the Russian reception of Rimsky-Korsakov's opera *Servilia*, one of three operas by the composer based on Russian traditional tales, including a discussion of the role of the librettist, Lev Aleksandrovich Mey.

620 Taruskin, Richard. "Servilia." In Stanley Sadie, ed. *The New Grove Dictionary of Opera*, IV. London and New York: Macmillan Press, 1992: 331. ISBN-10: 0935859926. ISBN-13: 978-0935859928.

A short account of the opera *Servilia* and its place in Rimsky-Korsakov's oeuvre.

621 Zataevich, Aleksandr Viktorovich. "Inostranets o russkoy opere." [A Foreigner on Russian Opera.] *Varshavsky dnevnik* 278 (4 October 1904).

An article on the opera by the Viennese music critic, M. Dietz.

Kashchey bessmertny. Osennyaya skazochka [Kashchey the Immortal. An Autumn Fairy Tale]

622 Anonymous. "Periodicheskaya pechat' o muzyke." [The Periodical Press on Music.] *RMG* 5 (1903): cols. 145–47.

Consists of reviews of the opera appearing in Moscow papers: N. Kochetov (*Moskovsky Listok*), "Yu. E." (*Russkie Vedomosti*), N. Kashkin (*Moskovskie Vedomosti*), and Semën Kruglikov (*Novosti Dnya*).

623 Anonymous. "Khronika. S. Peterburg. Opera i kontserty. 1-e predstavlenie 'Kashcheya Bessmertnogo'." [Chronicle. St. Petersburg. Opera and Concerts. First Performance of *Kashchey the Immortal.*] *RMG* 14 (1905): cols. 421–22.

A short account of the opera, the events leading to the demonstration and the curtailment of the performance.

624 Asaf'ev, Boris Vladimirovich [pseud. Glebov, Igor']. "Novinka." [A Novelty.] *Zhizn' iskusstva* 64 (1919).

A description of the opera, with observations on its content.

625 ——. "Mariinsky teatr." [The Mariinsky Theater.] *Zhizn' iskusstva* 71 (1919).

An article on the opera.

626 B.-B. "'Kashchey bessmertny' (v Opernoy studii)." [*Kashchey the Immortal* (in the Opera Studio).] *Zhizn' iskusstva* 9 (1926): 9.

A monograph on the opera *Kashchey the Immortal* by an unidentified author.

627 B. M-g. "Otvlechennaya traktovka." [An Abstract Treatment.] *Rabochy i teatr* 9 (1926): 12.

An account of the opera by an unidentified author.

628 Bozina, Ol'ga Arkad'evna. "Semanticheskie vozmozhnosti ladovogo sinteza." [Semantic Possibilities of Modal Synthesis.] In *Nauka, iskusstvo, obrazovanie v III tysyacheletii.* [Science, Art, Education in the Third Millenium.] Russian Federation, 2006.

An analysis of Rimsky-Korsakov's opera *Kashchey the Immortal*, including a discussion of modal elements.

629 Engel', Yuly Dmitrievich. "*Kashchey Bessmertny* – novaya opera N. A. Rimskogo-Korsakova." [*Kashchey the Immortal* – a New Opera by Rimsky-Korsakov.] *Russkie Vedomosti* 354 (23 December 1902). Reprinted: *MA* (2) (1994): 82–83. ISSN: 0869-4516.

Engel' stresses the opera's unusual structure and the novelty of its harmonic and melodic language. The editorial commentary, pp. 111–12, is informative.

630 Gnesin, Mikhail Fabianovich. "O muzykal'noy dramaturgii Rimskogo-Korsakova v opere 'Kashchey Bessmertny'." [On Rimsky-Korsakov's Musical Dramaturgy in the Opera *Kashchey the Immortal*.] In *Sovetskaya Muzyka. Trety sbornik statey* [Soviet Music. Third Volume of Articles.] Moscow: Muzgiz, 1945: 105–20. Reprinted: No. 1381: 128–60.

A discussion of the opera's musical structure, noting Rimsky-Korsakov's use of thematic metamorphosis.

631 Kruglikov, Semën Nikolaevich. "'Kashchey bessmertny.' Osennyaya skazochka." [*Kashchey the Immortal*. An Autumn Fairy Tale.] *Stsena i Muzyka* 21–22 (1904): 2–5.

A brief account of the opera *Kashchey the Immortal* and its salient characteristics.

632 Lyutsh, V. "Opera 'Kashchey Bessmertny' N. A. Rimskogo-Korsakova (v kontsertnom ispolnenii operno-simfonicheskogo kollektiva pod

Bibliography: Musical Works

rukovodstvom V. I. Sadovnikova, 22.IV.1926, Maly zal MGK.)" [Rimsky-Korsakov's Opera *Kashchey the Immortal* in a Concert Performance by an Operatic-Symphonic Collective under the Direction of V. I. Sadovnikov, 22.IV.1926, in the Small Hall of the Moscow State Conservatory.] *Muzyka i revolyutsiya* 6 (1926): 32.

A description of a concert performance of the opera in which Lyutsh notes that Rimsky-Korsakov seemed to be much better at portraying the forces of evil than the powers of good, since the chromatic harmonies of Kashcheevna are much more interesting than the pallid diatonicism of the Tsarevna and Ivan-Korolevich.

633 Malecka, Teresa. "Muzyczne obrazy wolności w operach Rimskiego-Korsakowa." [Musical Images of Freedom in the Operas of Rimsky-Korsakov.] In *Muzykolog wobec dzieła muzycznego: Zbiór prac dedykowanych doktor Elżbiecie Dziębowskiej w siedemdziesiątą rocznicę urodzin*, 1999.

An examination of the representation of the idea of freedom in Rimsky-Korsakov's operas, with particular reference to the fairy tale opera *Kashchey bessmertny* [Kashchey the Immortal] and the religious opera *Skazanie o nevidimom grade Kitezhe* [The Legend of the Invisible City of Kitezh].

634 Prokop'eva, Ekaterina. "'Moë dekadenstvo': *Kashchey Bessmertny* Rimskogo-Korsakova." ["My Decadence": *Kashchey the Immortal* by Rimsky-Korsakov.] *MA* (1) (2009): 92. ISSN: 0869-4516.

An examination of modernistic elements in Rimsky-Korsakov's late works, having special reference to the imagery and musical language contained in the opera *Kashchey the Immortal*, noting their relationship to similar trends in other Russian artistic movements of the time.

635 Rakhmanova, Marina Pavlovna. "'Pevets vechnoy, neuvyadaemoy vesny': Iz perepiski s E. M. Petrovskim." ["Eternal Singer, of Everlasting Spring": From the Correspondence with E. M. Petrovsky.] *MA* (2) (1994): 154. ISSN: 0869-4516.

A discussion of the correspondence, embracing the years 1900–02 and 1904–06, between Rimsky-Korsakov and the critic Evgeny M. Petrovsky, the source of the libretto of Rimsky-Korsakov's *Kashchey the Immortal*.

636 Senilov, Vladimir Alekseevich. "Kashchey bessmertny." [*Kashchey the Immortal.*] *Teatral'naya Rossiya. Muzykal'ny Mir* 14 (1905): 201–02.

On the work's première in St. Petersburg.

637 Taruskin, Richard. "Kashchey the Deathless." In Stanley Sadie, ed. *The New Grove Dictionary of Opera*, II. London and New York: Macmillan Press, 1992: 954–55. ISBN-10: 0935859926. ISBN-13: 978-0935859928.

An informative article pointing out the opera's essential characteristics.

638 Tsendrovsky, Vladimir Mikhaylovich. "'Kashchey bessmertny'." [*Kashchey the Immortal.*] In No. 373: 339–60.

Consists of an Introduction and two sections entitled "Musical Language of the Opera," and "Content of the Opera." Includes musical examples and excerpts from the libretto.

639 Yastrebtsëv, Vasily Vasil'evich. "'Kashchey bessmertny' (osennyaya skazochka)." [*Kashchey the Immortal* (an Autumn Fairy Tale).] *Muzyka* 253 (1916): 230–34.

A detailed discussion of the opera *Kashchey the Immortal*.

Pan Voevoda

640 An. Kup. "Opera 'Pan Voevoda' N. A. Rimskogo-Korsakova v Bol'shom teatre." [N. A. Rimsky-Korsakov's Opera *Pan Voevoda* in the Bol'shoy Theater.] *RMG* 41 (1905): cols. 990–91.

An account of a performance of the opera *Pan Voevoda*.

641 Engel', Yuly Dmitrievich. "'Pan Voevoda' Rimskogo-Korsakova. (Bol'shoy teatr, 27 sentyabrya)." [Rimsky-Korsakov's *Pan Voevoda*. (Bol'shoy Theater, 27 September).] *Russkie Vedomosti* 264 (9 October 1905). Reprinted: No. 313: 153–57.

Describes the opera in relation to *The Tsar's Bride, Servilia,* and other works.

642 Findeyzen, Nikolay Fëdorovich. "Pan Voevoda." *RMG* 41 (1904): cols. 897–904.

A substantial account of the première of the opera at Prince Tseretelli's Theater.

643 Grosheva, Elena Andreevna. "Novosibirsky operny teatr v Moskve." [The Novosibirsk Opera Theater in Moscow.] *SM* 9 (1955): 81–88.

The Novosibirsk Opera Company's visit to Moscow, including a description of a performance of *Pan Voevoda*, a rarely heard opera.

644 Muir, Stephen. "Rimsky-Korsakov. *Pan Voevoda* and the Polish Question: Exposing the 'Occidentalist Irony'." In Rachel Cowgill, David Cooper, and Clive Brown, eds. *Art and Ideology in European Opera: Essays in Honour of Julian Rushton.* Woodbridge: Boydell & Brewer, 2010: 237–50. ISBN-13: 978-1843835677.

Pan Voevoda, one of the least known of Rimsky-Korsakov's operas, is exceptional in that, unlike the subject matter of many of his operas, it is based on a Polish theme. The article reveals Rimsky-Korsakov's personal feelings towards Poland, its people, and the Polish Question. Pro-Polish sympathies were not always widespread in Russia at the time.

Bibliography: Musical Works 129

645 Solov'ëv, Nikolay Feopemptovich. "'Pan Voevoda'. Novaya opera Rimskogo-Korsakova." [*Pan Voevoda*. A New Opera by Rimsky-Korsakov.] *Stsena i Muzyka* [Odessa] 23–24 (1904): 4–6.

On the work's première in St. Petersburg.

646 Taruskin, Richard. "Pan Voevoda." In Stanley Sadie, ed. *The New Grove Dictionary of Opera*, III. London and New York: Macmillan Press, 1992: 847. ISBN-10: 0935859926. ISBN-13: 978-0935859928.

A brief account of the opera *Pan Voevoda* and its significant features.

647 Zataevich, Aleksandr Viktorovich. "N. A. Rimsky-Korsakov i ego noveyshaya opera 'Pan Voevoda'." [Rimsky-Korsakov and his Latest Opera *Pan Voevoda*.] *Varshavsky Dnevnik* 11 (11 January 1905).

Although Aleksandr Zataevich (1869–1936) first studied at a military academy, he was also a prolific writer about music, his publications including accounts of operas by Rimsky-Korsakov.

Skazanie o nevidimom grade Kitezhe i deve Fevronii [**The Legend of the Invisible City of Kitezh and the Maiden Fevroniya**]

648 Abraham, Gerald. "Kitezh." In No. 283: 261–89.

Discusses the opera, its characters, music, and symbolic significance.

649 Anonymous. "Diskussiya v Bol'shom teatre." [Discussion in the Bol'shoy Theater.] *SM* 4 (1954): 144–46.

Arising from a number of articles published previously in *SM*, this discusses the question as to whether changes in the libretti of Russian "classical" works are permissible or desirable. With special reference to *The Legend of the Invisible City of Kitezh*.

650 Asaf'ev, Boris Vladimirovich [pseud. Glebov, Igor']. "Skazanie o nevidimom grade." [The Legend of the Invisible City.] In No. 296: 101–18.

First published as a supplement to the program of a performance of the opera given by the Petrograd Academic Theater of Opera and Ballet (14 April 1921), Asaf'ev analyzes the work from a variety of angles, including the psychological and esthetic.

651 ——. "'Skazanie o nevidimom grade Kitezhe'. Pis'ma o russkoy opere i balete." [*The Legend of the Invisible City of Kitezh*. Letters about Russian Opera and Ballet.] *Ezhenedel'nik Petrogradskikh Gosudarstvennykh Akademicheskikh teatrov* 10, 12. (1922).

An account of the opera, interesting in that it was written by Asaf'ev in the 1920s.

652 ——. "Narodno-patrioticheskie idei v russkoy muzyke." [Folk-patriotic Ideas in Russian Music.] *SM* 1 (1954): 16–25.

Although the first part of this article consists of a discussion of patriotic elements in the music of Glinka, Tchaikovsky, and Borodin, pp. 21–23 are concerned with *The Legend of the Invisible City of Kitezh*, especially the role in the opera of the symphonic picture *Sech' pri Kerzhentse*.

653 Bernstein, N. D. "Un opéra nouveau de Rimski-Korsakof." Trans. Louis Laloy. *Mercure musical* 3 (15 June 1907): 282–84.

Bernstein discusses the opera as an art form, concluding that the European work it most closely resembles in spirit is Liszt's *Die Legende von der heiligen Elisabeth*, with which it shares a number of common features.

654 Bugoslavsky, Sergey Alekseevich. "Skazanie o nevidimom grade Kitezhe." [*The Legend of the Invisible City of Kitezh*.] *Rabochy i teatr* 24 (1926): 4.

655 E. P-sky. "Skazanie o nevidimom grade Kitezhe i deve Fevronii." [*The Legend of the Invisible City of Kitezh and the Maiden Fevroniya*.] *RMG* 7 (1907): cols. 193–200; 8 (1907): 240–46; 11 (1907): 297–308.

Discusses the opera's religious significance and its relationship with contemporary works.

656 Engel', Yuly Dmitrievich. "'Skazanie o nevidimom grade Kitezhe i deve Fevronii'." [*The Legend of the Invisible City of Kitezh and the Maiden Fevroniya*.] *Russkie Vedomosti* 52 (2 March 1908). Reprinted: *MA* (2) (1994): 92–94. ISSN: 0869-4516.

This account is full of details, highlighting the opera's mystical qualities and symbolism. The characterization of Fevroniya, for example, shows similarity to that of St. Evfrosinya, the whole concept being a new element in Russian opera.

657 Gippius, Evgeny Vladimirovich [signed Evg. G-s.]. "'Skazanie o nevidimom grade Kitezhe'. (Akademichesky Teatr Opery i Baleta)." [*The Legend of the Invisible City of Kitezh*. (Academic Theater of Opera and Ballet).] *Zhizn' iskusstva* 14 (1923): 23.

An article giving details of the performance, and praising the interpretation of the conductor Emil Cooper.

658 Gribble, Lyubomira Parpulobova. "The *Life of Peter and Fevroniia*: Transformations and Interpretations in Modern Russian Literature and Music." *Russian Review* 52 (2) (April 1993): 184. ISSN: 0036-0341.

Describing how the fairy tale about Peter and Fevroniya is one of the most popular works of old Russian literature, the author examines its employment

Bibliography: Musical Works   131

in modern literary works, including, among other things, Rimsky-Korsakov's opera *The Legend of the Invisible City of Kitezh.*

659   Gryunfel'd, Nil's Edgarovich. "'Kitezh' v Latviyskom teatre." [*Kitezh* in the Latvian Theater.] *SM* 10 (1955): 120–25.

An account of a performance by the Latvian Theater of Opera and Ballet.

660   Islamey. "'Kitezh' v Ak-opere." ["Kitezh" at the Ak-Opera.] *Zhizn' iskusstva* 19 (1926): 15–16.

An account of a performance of the opera at the Academic Theater as performed at this historical period.

661   Karasev, Pavel Alekseevich. "'Skazanie o nevidimom grade Kitezhe i deve Fevronii' N. A. Rimskogo-Korsakova." [*The Legend of the Invisible City of Kitezh and the Maiden Fevroniya* by N. A. Rimsky-Korsakov.] *RMG* 39–40 (1908): cols. 845–52.

A sympathetic discussion of the opera and its relationship to the composer's other works, printed in the special memorial issue of *RMG.*

662   Kashkin, Nikolay Dmitrievich. "Skazanie o nevidimom grade Kitezhe i deve Fevronii." [*The Legend of the Invisible City of Kitezh and the Maiden Fevroniya.*] *Russkoe Slovo* 38 (15 February 1908).

An introductory article, explaining the opera's content and its musical significance.

663   Keldysh, Yury Vsevolodovich. "Za glubokoe izuchenie naslediya." [A Detailed Study of our Heritage.] *SM* 10 (1953); 11 (1953).

Following the publication of Kabalevsky's articles on "Rimsky-Korsakov and Modernism" in the June, July, and August 1953 numbers of *SM* [see No. 330], Keldysh further elaborates on the question of realism in music, as seen in Rimsky-Korsakov's last works, in particular *The Legend of the Invisible City of Kitezh.*

664   Kenigsberg, Alla Konstantinovna. "Rimsky-Korsakov i Vagner." [Rimsky-Korsakov and Wagner.] In *Muzykal'naya kul'tura Evropy v mezhnatsional'nykh kontaktakh.* [The Musical Culture of Europe in International Contacts.] Russian Federation, 1995.

A comparative study of operas by Rimsky-Korsakov and Wagner, comparing *Sadko* and *Tannhäuser, Skazanie o nevidimom grade Kitezhe* [The Legend of the Invisible City of Kitezh] and *Parsifal,* noting similarities and differences in principles of epic dramaturgy and the manner in which certain works by Rimsky-Korsakov reveal Wagnerian influence. A comparison is also made of the differences between Rimsky-Korsakov's *Letopis' moey muzykal'noy zhizni* [Chronicle of My Musical Life] and Wagner's *Mein Leben.*

665 Kershner, L. "Skazanie o nevidimom grade Kitezhe i deve Fevroniya." [*The Legend of the Invisible City of Kitezh and the Maiden Fevroniya.*] In No. 373: 361–431.

Contains detailed analyses of the various scenes.

666 Komarnitskaya, Ol'ga Vissarionovna. "Khristianskie aspekty opery N. A. Rimskogo-Korsakova *Skazanie o nevidimom grade Kitezhe i deve Fevronii.*" [Christian Aspects in N. A. Rimsky-Korsakov's Opera *The Legend of the Invisible City of Kitezh and the Maiden Fevroniya.*] *Muzykovedenie* [Musicology] (3) (2006): 2. ISSN: 2072-9979.

A discussion of the part played by the librettist Vladimir Ivanovich Bel'sky in writing the libretto of Rimsky-Korsakov's opera *The Legend of the Invisible City of Kitezh,* together with the composer's own remarks concerning the Christian subject matter of the work. Special attention is paid to the employment in the opera of Eastern Orthodox Church rituals.

667 ——. "Otrazhenie zhitiya svyatykh blagovernykh knyazya Pëtra i knyagini Fevronii – muromskikh chudotvortsev v libretto i syuzhetno-stsenicheskikh situatsiyakh opery Rimskogo-Korsakova *Skazanie nevidimoy grade Kitezhe i deve Fevronii.*" [The Reflection of the Lives of the Holy Prince Pëtr and Princess Fevroniya – the Miracle Workers from Murom in the Libretto and Plot Situations of Rimsky-Korsakov's Opera *The Legend of the Invisible City of Kitezh and the Maiden Fevroniya.*] *Iskusstvo i obrazovanie* [Art and Education] 3 (77) 2012: 6. ISSN: 2072-0432.

An exploration of the lives of the miracle workers Pëtr and Fevroniya and the manner in which their real lives were adapted by Rimsky-Korsakov's librettist, Vladimir Ivanovich Bel'sky, to suit the demands of the opera *The Legend of the Invisible City of Kitezh.*

668 Korableva, A. "Rol' drevnerusskoy pesennosti v opere N. Rimskogo-Korsakova 'Skazanie o nevidimom grade Kitezhe i deve Fevronii'." [The Role of Ancient Russian Chant in Rimsky-Korsakov's Opera *The Legend of the Invisible City of Kitezh and the Maiden Fevroniya.*] In M. Pekelis and I. Givental, comps. *Iz istorii russkoy i sovetskoy muzyki* [From the History of Russian and Soviet Music], Vyp. 3 [Issue 3]. Moscow: Muzyka, 1978: 75–95.

An article showing links between musical themes in Rimsky-Korsakov's opera and Russian sacred chant.

669 Kukharsky, Vasily Fedos'evich. "K sporam o nasledstve." [On the Arguments about Heritage.] *SM* 4 (1954): 78–85.

Arising from previous articles published in *SM* by Dmitry Kabalevsky and Yury Keldysh [see Nos. 330 and 663], this sheds further light on the ideological interpretation of the opera, showing conflicting interpretations of the work's significance.

Bibliography: Musical Works 133

670 ——. "Postizhenie klassiki." [Grasping the Classics.] *SM* 6 (1984): 34–43. ISSN: 0131-6818.

A review of a recent production of the opera at the Bol'shoy Theater, accompanied by discussion of the work's historical sources and ideological significance and the various ways in which the work may be interpreted.

671 Lapin, V. "'Skazanie o nevidimom grade Kitezhe' i russkaya svad'ba." [*The Legend of the Invisible City of Kitezh* and the Russian Wedding.] In A. I. Klimovitsky, ed. *Voprosy teorii i estetiki muzyki.* [Questions of Musical Theory and Esthetics.] Vol. 14. Leningrad: Muzyka, 1975: 31–38.

An examination of some of the folk sources of the opera, noting the manner in which the composer has reproduced faithfully elements of the traditional folk wedding.

672 Lunacharsky, Anatoly Vasil'evich. "Mysli o grade Kitezhe." [Thoughts about the City of Kitezh.] *Zhizn' iskusstva* 29 (1918).

A perceptive article by a well-informed critic.

673 Lyubimov, A. "Beregite opernuyu klassiku. (O libretto opery 'Kitezh')." [Guard Our Opera Classics. (About the Libretto of the Opera *Kitezh*).] *SM* 5 (1954): 154.

A continuation of a discussion of the opera published in *SM* during the period 1953–54, defending Keldysh, while pointing out the undesirability of making changes to the libretto. [See Nos. 330, 663, 669.]

674 Molzinsky, Vladimir Vladimirovich. "I snova o grade Kitezhe (k probleme voploshcheniya tendentsiy staroobryadchestva v opere Rimskogo-Korsakova)." [And Once Again about the Town of Kitezh (On the Problem of the Embodiment of the Old Believer Tendencies in Rimsky-Korsakov's Opera).] In Georgy Grigor'evich Tigranov. *K 100-letiyu so dnya rozhdeniya – Stat'i, materialy, vospominaniya.* [On the 100th Anniversary of a Birthday – Articles, Materials, Recollections.] Russian Federation, 2008.

An examination of the Old Believers' beliefs and traditions in Russian literature and the arts, having special reference to Rimsky-Korsakov's opera *The Legend of the Invisible City of Kitezh.*

675 Morrison, Simon Alexander. *Russian Opera and Symbolist Poetics.* PhD dissertation, Princeton University, 1997. 277 pp. In *California Studies in 20th-Century Music* (2): *Russian Opera and the Symbolist Movement.* University of California Press, 2002. 392 pp. ISBN-10: 0520229436. ISBN-13: 978-0520229433.

Using source materials taken from Russian archives, the dissertation examines Symbolist elements in four operas written during Russia's so-called "Silver Age," including Rimsky-Korsakov's opera *The Legend of the Invisible*

City of Kitezh. The discussion covers such subjects as "literary and musical decadence, pagan-Christian syncretism, theurgy, and life creation, or the portrayal of art in life."

676   Orlov, Genrikh Aleksandrovich. "K sporam o 'Kitezhe'." [On the Disputes over *Kitezh.*] *SM* 1 (1954): 75–80.

This highlights the ideological significance of the opera, in which the author claims that the work has still not been presented on the Soviet stage in a manner sufficient to show its true worth. He also rejects the idea that the libretto should be rewritten in any way, believing that the opera should be presented as the composer envisaged it. [See Nos. 330, 663, 669, 673.]

677   ——. "Tvorcheskaya evolyutsiya Rimskogo-Korsakova v 90-e i 900-e gody i 'Skazanie o nevidimom grade Kitezhe'." [Rimsky-Korsakov's Creative Evolution in the 1890s and 1900s and *The Legend of the Invisible City of Kitezh.*] In Yu. V. Keldysh, ed. *Voprosy muzykoznaniya. Sbornik statey.* [Questions of Musicology. A Collection of Articles.] Tom [Vol.] III. Moscow: Muzgiz, 1960: 499–538.

Divided into five sections, this substantial article includes a discussion of some of the many interpretations of Rimsky-Korsakov's opera on the Russian stage, ranging from the pre-revolutionary performances, stressing the religious mystical aspects, to the completely atheistic ones of the late 1940s. Also considered are the circumstances of the work's composition, the composer's state of mind at the time, examination of other projects contemplated during this period, its relationship with his other operas, and the prevailing philosophical trends.

678   Pashenko, Mikhail V. "Sistema leytmotivov v libretto *Grada Kitezha.*" [The System of Leitmotives in the Libretto of *The Town of Kitezh.*] In *Nasledie N. A. Rimskogo-Korsakova v russkoy kul'ture: K 100-letiyu so dnya smerti kompozitora – Po materialam konferentsii "Keldyshevskie chteniya – 2008."* [The Legacy of N. A. Rimsky-Korsakov in Russian Culture: To Mark the 100th Anniversary of the Day of the Composer's Death – Based on Materials from the Conference "Keldysh Readings – 2008."] Russian Federation, 2009.

A discussion of the the leitmotifs employed in the libretto of Rimsky-Korsakov's opera *The Legend of the Invisible City of Kitezh.*

679   Petrovsky, Evgeny M. "Skazanie o nevidimom grade Kitezhe i deve Fevronii." [The Legend of the Invisible City of Kitezh and the Maiden Fevroniya.] *RMG* 7, 8, 11 (1907). Reprinted: *MA* (2) (1997): 96–98. ISSN: 0869-4516.

Discussion of a contemporary review of a performance of Rimsky-Korsakov's opera *The Legend of the Invisible City of Kitezh.*

680   Pokrovsky, Boris Aleksandrovich. "S mechtoyu o prekrasnom." [With a Dream of the Beautiful.] *SM* 3 (1969): 89–92.

Bibliography: Musical Works

135

A discussion between the producer Boris Pokrovsky and an interviewer, in which Pokrovsky expresses his views on the opera, which he was about to produce at the Sofia Theater of Opera and Ballet.

681   Quraishi, Ibrahim. "Kitezh and the Russian Notion of Oriental Despotism." *The Opera Quarterly* 13 (2) (Winter 1996): 69. ISSN: 0736-0053.

A discussion of symbolic elements in Rimsky-Korsakov's opera *The Legend of the Invisible City of Kitezh.*

682   Rakhmanova, M. "K byloy polemike vokrug 'Kitezha'." [On the Former Controversy Surrounding *Kitezh.*] *SM* 10 (1984): 82–90. ISSN: 0131-6818.

Discussion of the significance of the opera, following on from that published in No. 670, including excerpts from contemporary accounts, refuting the work as a mere copy of Wagner's *Parsifal.*

683   Schloezer, Boris de. "Le dit de la ville invisible de Kitej'. Essai de psychologie musicale." *Revue musicale Année* 4 (1 December 1922): 155–63.

Draws comparisons with Wagner's *Parsifal* and Vincent d'Indy's *Légende de Saint Christophe*. Schloezer sees Rimsky-Korsakov's work as a manifestation of "un culture semi-oriental....le sentiment religieux russe...le mysticisme russo-byzantin."

684   Serebryakova, Lyubov' Alekseevna. "Kitezh: Otkrovenie 'Otkroveniya'." [*Kitezh*: A Revelation of the "Revelation" Scene.] *MA* (2) (1994): 90–106. ISSN: 0869-4516.

An extended discussion, forming part of an increasing interest in religious elements in Russian opera, this is a discussion of the images and concept of revelation and other sacred elements as manifest in Rimsky-Korsakov's opera *The Legend of the Invisible City of Kitezh.*

685   ——. "Mif nevidimogo grada v russkoy kul'ture." [The Myth of the Invisible City in Russian Culture.] In T. A. Khoprova, ed. and comp. *Bibleyskie obrazy v muzyke.* [Biblical Images in Music.] St. Petersburg Conservatory, 2004. ISBN-10: 5887180374. ISBN-13: 978-5887180373.

An examination of the symbolism of the myth of the invisible city and its musical role in Russian culture of the nineteenth and twentieth centuries, with special reference to Rimsky-Korsakov's opera *The Legend of the Invisible City of Kitezh.*

686   ——. "Tema Apokalipsisa v russkoy muzyke XX veka." [The Theme of Apocalypse in Russian Music of the 20th Century.] In T. A. Khoprova, ed. and comp. *Bibleyskie obrazy v muzyke.* [Biblical Images in Music.] St. Petersburg Conservatory, 2004. ISBN-10: 5887180374. ISBN-13: 978-5887180373.

Contained in a collection of articles published by the St. Petersburg Conservatory, this takes the form of an examination of various

136 Nikolay Andreevich Rimsky-Korsakov: A Research and Information Guide

twentieth-century Russian musical works reflecting on the theme of Apocalypse, including Rimsky-Korsakov's opera *The Legend of the Invisible City of Kitezh*.

687 Taruskin, Richard. "Legend of the Invisible City of Kitezh and the Maiden Fevroniya." In Stanley Sadie, ed. *The New Grove Dictionary of Opera*, II. London and New York: Macmillan Press, 1992: 1123–26. ISBN-10: 0935859926. ISBN-13: 978-0935859928.

A substantial article discussing the history of the opera's composition, its essential stylistic elements, and its religious symbolism.

688 Taruskin, Richard. "*Kitezh*: Religious Art of an Atheist." *New York Times*, 26 February 1995. Reprinted: R. Taruskin. *On Russian Music*. University of California Press, 2009: 179–83. ISBN-10: 0520249798. ISBN-13: 978-0520249790.

An article written to preview the Kirov Opera Company's performance of Rimsky-Korsakov's opera *The Legend of the Invisible City of Kitezh* at the Brooklyn Academy of Music.

689 Tideböhl, Ellen von. "A new opera of M. Rimsky-Korsakoff: The Legend of the Vanished Town of Kitage and the Maiden Theuronia." *Monthly Musical Record London* 38, 449 (1908): 103–04.

A "Letter from Moscow," written by Ellen von Tideböhl to the *Monthly Musical Record*, this is a first-hand account of the opera, with a contemporary interpretation of the events.

690 V. and M. "'Skazanie o grade Kitezhe' i nasha kritika." [*The Legend of the City of Kitezh* and Our Criticism.] *Muzyka i revolyutsiya* 6 (1926): 6–12.

A discussion of the ideological relevance of such a composition in the early years of the Revolution, in which the basic idea of the opera is interpreted as the overcoming of evil by means of the achievements of personal individual perfection and not as a work of religious content. The necessity of having a brochure at each operatic performance explaining the work's ideological significance is also stressed.

691 Val'ter, Viktor Grigor'evich. "Rytsar' Parsifal i deva Fevroniya." [The Knight Parsifal and the Maiden Fevroniya.] *Biryuch Petrogradskikh gos. teatrov.* [Herald of the Petrograd State Theaters.] Petrograd: June–August 1919: 10–43.

692 Velichko, Artem Tagievich. "Pis'ma N. A. Rimskogo-Korsakova k F. I. Grusu: K istorii izdaniya *Kitezha*." [Letters of N. A. Rimsky-Korsakov to F. I. Grus: On the History of Publishing *Kitezh*.] *Musicus* 3 (31) (July–September 2012). ISSN: 2072-0262.

An article published in *Musicus*, journal of the St. Petersburg Conservatory, investigating details of the publishing of Rimsky-Korsakov's opera *The Legend*

Bibliography: Musical Works 137

of the Invisible City of Kitezh, using letters from the composer addressed to Fëdor Ivanovich Grus.

693 Vitols, Yazep [Vītols, Jāzeps]. "'Legenda o nevidimom grade Kitezhe i deve Fevronii', opera N. A. Rimskogo-Korsakova. Prem'era v Mariinskom Teatre, v sredu, 7 Fevralya." [*The Legend of the Invisible City of Kitezh and the Maiden Fevroniya,* an Opera by N. A. Rimsky-Korsakov. Première in the Mariinsky Theater, Wednesday, 7 February.] In No. 1418: 198–201.

Published originally in the *St. Petersburger Zeitung* on 11 February 1907, this article about the première of the opera, praises its composition and performance, written by an "unsurpassed master of musical illustration."

694 Wittig, Peter. "Die Stadt der selbsternannten Heiligen: Das *Unsichtbare Große Kitesh* bei Nikolaj Rimskij-Korssakow." In P. Csobadi, et al., eds. *Mahagonny: Die Stadt als Sujet und Herausforderung des (Musik-Theaters: Vorträge und Materialen des Salzburger Symposions 1998).* Anif/Salzburg (2000).

Entitled "The City of the Self-proclaimed Saints: *The Legend of the Invisible City of Kitezh and the Maiden Fevroniya,*" Rimsky-Korsakov's opera is seen here as a religious play combining two independent legends.

695 Zetel, I. "Skazanie o grade Kitezhe." [*The Legend of the City of Kitezh.*] SM 3 (1975): 53–55.

A review of a performance at the Bol'shoy Theater, notable for its massive cuts.

696 Zataevich, Aleksandr Viktorovich. "'Skazanie o nevidimom grade Kitezhe i deve Fevronii.' Novaya opera N. A. Rimskogo-Korsakova." [*The Legend of the Invisible City of Kitezh and the Maiden Fevroniya. A New Opera by N. A. Rimsky-Korsakov.*] *Varshavsky Dnevnik* 55 (24 February 1907); 59 (28 February 1907).

Zolotoy petushok. Nebylitsa v litsakh [The Golden Cockerel. A Dramatised Fairy Tale]

697 Abraham, Gerald. "The Golden Cockerel." In No. 283: 290–310.

Discussion of the composer's last opera, which Abraham sees as being "perhaps ... the most elaborately fabricated of all Rimsky-Korsakov's scores," characterized by an "unsurpassed intellectual brilliance."

698 ——. "Satire and Symbolism in 'The Golden Cockerel'." *ML* 52 (1) (1971): 46–54.

A close examination of the opera and its significance, noting Pushkin's indebtedness to two chapters from a French translation of Washington Irving's novel *The Alhambra.* Besides discussing the changes to the libretti necessitated by censorship, and the alterations made by Bel'sky, the librettist,

Abraham examines each of the operatic characters in turn and comes to the conclusion that although political satire may be found in the opera, "to look for deeper symbolism is useless: there is none."

699 Anonymous. "Russkaya muzyka za granitsey." [Russian Music Abroad.] *RMG* 22–23 (1914): cols. 539–41.

An account of the opera as given by Sergey Dyagilev [Serge Diaghilev] in Paris in the form of a ballet.

700 Asaf'ev, Boris Vladimirovich (pseud. Glebov, Igor'). "Rimsky-Korsakov. 'Zolotoy petushok' – nebylitsa v litsakh." [Rimsky-Korsakov's *The Golden Cockerel* – a Dramatised Fairy Tale.] *Muzykal'ny Sovremennik. Khronika* 5–6 (1916).

A perceptive article highlighting the opera's outstanding features.

701 ——. "Mariinsky teatr. ('Zolotoy petushok')." [The Mariinsky Theater. (*The Golden Cockerel*).] *Zhizn' iskusstva* 83 (1919).

A review of a performance of *The Golden Cockerel* at the Mariinsky Theater in 1919.

702 ——. "Skomorosh'e tsarstvo." [*The Kingdom of Clowns.*] In No. 296: 119–25.

Written in 1921, this is an examination of the work and its place in the cycle of Rimsky-Korsakov's operas, having special regard to the composer's method of characterization. Contains observations on his portrayal of women.

703 ——. "'Zolotoy petushok'." [*The Golden Cockerel.*] *Teatr* 1 (1923): 14–16.

An account of the opera and its performance at the Maly Theater, with a photograph of one of the sets.

704 Benua, A. "O 'Zolotom petushke'." [On *The Golden Cockerel.*] *Rech'* 325 (25 November 1916).

Discusses the performance of the opera at the Narodny Dom and the various ways in which it may be interpreted, written by the distinguished artist and historian Aleksandr Benua [Alexander Benois].

705 Berkov, V. and Protopopov, Vl. "'Zolotoy petushok'." [*The Golden Cockerel.*] In No. 373: 432–76.

Consists of three sections:

i.   Rimsky-Korsakov and his Opera *The Golden Cockerel.*
ii. Musical Characteristics of the Personalia.
iii. Content of the Opera.

Use is made of comparative examples, showing the differences between the original literary text and the manner in which it was changed by the censor.

Bibliography: Musical Works   *139*

706   Beskin, Em. "O chëm pel Ak-petushok." [What the Ak-Cockerel Sang About.] *Zhizn' iskusstva* 39 (1924): 4–6.

A whimsical discussion of the opera at the Academic Theater, together with a damning account of its performance.

707   Borovsky, Victor. "Private Opera Companies in Russia." *Opera* 31 (7) (1980): 648.

An account of a performance of the opera by Zimin's Private Opera Company.

708   Dobrynina, E. "Klassika v Saratovskoy opere ('Zolotoy petushok')." [A Classic at the Saratov Opera (*The Golden Cockerel*).] *SM* 12 (1956): 83–88.

Includes a discussion of a spectacular production of the opera in Saratov by the Saratov State Theater. With an attractive color photograph.

709   Dolinskaya, Elena Borisovna. "Nebylitsa v litsakh." [Fable in People.] In *MZ* (5) (2013): 22. ISSN: 0131-2383.

Pushkin himself called his poem "Zolotoy petushok" [The Golden Cockerel] a "Nebylitsa v litsakh," an ambiguous title capable of many translations and one often associated with woodcuts. Dolinskaya's article discusses the revival of Rimsky-Korsakov's opera *The Golden Cockerel*, based on Sergey Dyagilev's opera-ballet interpretation staged in 1914, as performed in 2013 by the Moskovsky Gosudarstvenny Akademichesky Detsky Muzykal'ny Teatr [Moscow State Academic Children's Music Theater].

710   Dorati, Antal. "The Golden Cockerel: Political Satire and Fairy Tale." *Opera* 13 (11) (1962): 713–15.

A discussion of the opera's significance, prior to its performance at Covent Garden in English.

711   Durylin, S.N., ed. *K. S. Stanislavsky. Materialy. Pis'ma. Issledovaniya.* [Stanislavsky. Materials. Letters. Research.] Moscow: Akademiya Nauk SSSR, 1955. 699 pp.

For a discussion of Stanislavsky's staging of *The Golden Cockerel*, together with a facsimile of his original production plan, see pp. 326–30.

712   Es. "Zolotoy petushok." [*The Golden Cockerel.*] *Zhizn' iskusstva* 9 (1925): 10.

An account of a performance in the former Mikhaylov Theater, praising the orchestra and some of the performers, but criticizing the unconvincing mise-en-scène, the stereotyped movements of the crowds, and the poor décor.

713   Engel', Yuly Dmitrievich. "Prem'era 'Zolotogo petushka' u Zimina." [Première of *The Golden Cockerel* at Zimin's (Theater).] *Russkie Vedomosti* 219 (25 September 1909). Reprinted: No. 313: 264–65.

A brief account of the Moscow première of the opera.

714 ——. "'Zolotoy petushok'. (Operny teatr Zimina)." [*The Golden Cockerel*. (Zimin's Opera Theater).] *Russkie Vedomosti* 221 (27 September 1909). Reprinted: *MA* 2 (1994) 87–88.

Describes the opera's musical and dramatic structure. For a review of a performance of the same opera at the Bol'shoy Theater on 6 November, see *Russkie Vedomosti* 257 (8 November 1909): 276–80.

715 ——. "'Zolotoy petushok' Rimskogo-Korsakova." [Rimsky-Korsakov's *The Golden Cockerel*.] *Ezhenedel'nik Imperatorskikh Teatrov* Part II (1910).

A thought-provoking article written in an authoritative publication.

716 Engel', Yuly Dmitrievich. "*Zolotoy petushok*: Operny Teatr Zimina." [*The Golden Cockerel*: Zimin's Opera Theater.] *MA* (2) (1994): 87–88. ISSN: 0869-4516.

A searching article by Yury Engel', first appearing in the influential pre-revolutionary paper *Russkie Vedomosti*, of which he was music editor, concerning different aspects of the structure of Rimsky-Korsakov's opera *The Golden Cockerel*.

717 Everett, William A. "Chernomor, the Astrologer, and Associates: Aspects of Shadow and Evil in *Ruslan and Lyudmila* and *The Golden Cockerel*." *The Opera Quarterly* 12 (2) (Winter 1995): 23. ISSN: 0736-0053.

An article amplifying a statement by the Swiss Jungian psychologist and scholar Marie-Louise von Franz (1915–98) that characters in both Glinka's *Ruslan and Ludmila* and Rimsky-Korsakov's *The Golden Cockerel* represent "shadows".

718 Findeyzen, Nikolay [signed N. F.]. "N. Rimsky-Korsakov. 'Zolotoy petushok'." [N. Rimsky-Korsakov. *The Golden Cockerel*.] *RMG* 39–40 (1908): cols. 853–56.

A discussion of the opera, following the publication of Yurgenson's vocal score, pointing out that the composer never succeeded in setting Byron's *Heaven and Earth*, which he wished to entitle *Tragediya synov chelovecheskikh* [*A Tragedy of Human Sons*]. With brief allusions to Weber's *Oberon*, Humperdinck's *Hänsel und Gretel*, and Strauss' *Salome*.

719 Gippius, Evgeny Vladimirovich. "'Zolotoy petushok'. (Bol'shoy operny teatr)." [*The Golden Cockerel*. (Bol'shoy Opera Theater).] *Zhizn' iskusstva* 749–751 (1921).

An enthusiastic account of the opera and its performance.

720 Humiston, William H. *Rimsky-Korsakoff*. New York: Breitkopf Publications, 1922. 27 pp.

Bibliography: Musical Works 141

A survey of the composer and his aims, utilizing Rimsky-Korsakov's *Chronicle* and writings by Montagu-Nathan, Rosa Newmarch, and others, with observations on his operas, particularly the fact that *The Golden Cockerel* was given in Paris and New York as a ballet, with singers on each side of the stage, and with pantomimic actions provided by the dancers.

721   Kandinsky, Aleksey Ivanovich. "Zametki o 'Zolotom petushke'." [Notes on *The Golden Cockerel.*] *SM* 6 (1958): 24–32.

A general discussion of the opera accompanied by a number of illustrations, one in color. Part of a series of articles in a volume of *SM* marking the 50th anniversary of the composer's death.

722   Karatygin, Vyacheslav Gavrilovich. "'Zolotoy petushok'. (Poslednyaya opera Rimskogo-Korsakova)." [*The Golden Cockerel.* (Rimsky-Korsakov's Last Opera).] *Biblioteka Teatra i Iskusstva*, Tom [Vol.] 9 (1908).

A stimulating article by Vyacheslav Karatygin (1875–1925), a discerning forward-looking critic who advocated modernistic trends at a time when many considered these to be undesirable.

723   Keldysh, Yury Vsevolodovich. "'Zolotoy petushok' v teatre Kovent-Garden." [*The Golden Cockerel* at Covent Garden.] *SM* 12 (1954): 124–26.

One of the rare accounts in the Soviet press of a performance of a Russian opera in England, in this case *The Golden Cockerel* given at Covent Garden on 7 January 1954, together with some previous performances of Russian operas in England.

724   L. "Postanovka 'Zolotogo petushka'." [A Performance of *The Golden Cockerel.*] *RMG* 2 (1910): cols. 44–45.

An account of a performance of the opera in the Great Hall of the St. Petersburg Conservatory.

725   Lunacharsky, Anatoly Vasil'evich. *V mire muzyki. Stat'i i rechi.* [In the World of Music. Articles and Speeches.] G. B. Bernandt and I. A. Sats, eds. Second edition enl. Moscow: Sovetsky Kompozitor, 1971. 540 pp.

Apart from his political activities, Lunacharsky was a prolific writer on music. Among the many references to Rimsky-Korsakov and his work, of special interest in this volume are the articles on *The Golden Cockerel*, pp. 274–78, *The Tale of Tsar Saltan*, pp. 279–81, and an imaginary conversation with the composer à la Hoffman-Van Loon, who obligingly returns from beyond the grave 25 years later and even mentions the word "Marxism" ("Rimsky-Korsakov. A Musical-Critical Fantasy on the 25th Year of his Death."), pp. 413–23.

726   L'vov, Pavel Rubimovich. "Poslednee proizvedenie N. A. Rimskogo-Korsakova. ('Skazka o Zolotom Petushke')." [N. A. Rimsky-Korsakov's Last Work (*The*

Tale of the Golden Cockerel).] *Moskovsky Ezhenedel'nik* 7 (13 February 1910): 46–54.

A sympathetic discussion of the opera, noting its departures from Pushkin's text and its place in the composer's work.

727   Martens, Frederick H. "Rimsky-Korsakoff's *The Golden Cockerel* (Le coq d'or) as produced at the Metropolitan Opera House." *Musical Observer* 17 (4) (1918): 14–16.

An account of a performance at the New York Metropolitan Opera House on 6 March 1918, performed as a simultaneous opera and ballet. Whereas in the performances of the work given in Petrograd under Rakhmaninov the singers were invisible to the audience, in the Metropolitan production they were in full view. Martens writes enthusiastically of Pierre Monteux, conductor of previous performances in Paris and London (1914), and of the superb choreography of maître de ballet Adolf Bolm. To refute the critics of the dual art form of opera-ballet, he cites the example of the Cambodian royal theater, Phnom-penh, where at the performance of the *Rung-ram* the story is enacted by the dancers, accompanied by a vocal chorus.

728   Montagu-Nathan, Montagu. "The origin of The Golden Cockerel." *Music Review* 15 (February 1954): 33–38.

An account of the composition of the opera, its political implications, problems with censorship, and Diaghilev's presentation as a ballet in Paris, London, and New York.

729   ——. "The Golden Cockerel at Covent Garden." *MT* 95 (February 1954): 93.

A short account of the performance of the opera at Covent Garden, and thoughts about the opera itself. Montagu-Nathan suggests that the model for King Dodon could well have been the jittery Admiral Rozhdestvensky, who, during the Russo-Japanese war, fired on some English fishing vessels, mistaking them for part of the Japanese fleet.

730   ——. "King Dodon's Love-song." *Monthly Musical Record* 84 (October 1954): 210–12.

A witty discussion of the children's song "Chizhik, chizhik, gde ty byl?" [Chaffinch, chaffinch, where've you bin?] as sung in the opera by King Dodon.

731   Prokof'ev, Grigory Petrovich. "'Loengrin' i 'Zolotoy petushok' v Bol'sh. teatre." [*Lohengrin* and *The Golden Cockerel* in the Bol'shoy Theater.] *RMG* 46 (1909): cols. 1073–78.

A eulogistic account of a performance of the opera in Moscow.

732   ——. "'Zolotoy petushok' Rimskogo-Korsakova." [Rimsky-Korsakov's *The Golden Cockerel*.] *RMG* 40 (1909): cols. 860–64; 41 (1909): cols. 899–906.

An account of the spectacular première of the opera at the Solodovnikov Theater, given a year after the composer's death.

733 Protopopov, Vladimir Vasil'evich. "O muzykal'nom yazyke 'Zolotogo Petushka'." [The Musical Language of *The Golden Cockerel*.] *SM* 6 (1938): 20–31.

A harmonic and melodic analysis with 15 music examples. The opera is seen both as a political, satirical work and as a reflection of the Symbolist philosophy of the period. Pays special attention to the role of leitmotifs.

734 Rappaport, Viktor Romanovich. "Neponyatny namëk (Pushkin, Rimsky-Korsakov, Bel'sky, Lunacharsky)." [An Unintelligible Allusion. (Pushkin, Rimsky-Korsakov, Bel'sky, Lunacharsky).] *Zhizn' iskusstva* 730–732 (1921).

Written in reply to Lunacharsky's article on the opera [see No. 725], the author warns of the dangers of adopting a purely political approach in endeavoring to grasp the work's significance.

735 Reilly, Edward R. "Rimsky-Korsakov's *The Golden Cockerel*: A Very Modern Fairy Tale." *Musical Newsletter* VI (1) (Winter 1976): 9–16.

A speculative interpretation of the symbolism underlying the opera.

736 Rimsky-Korsakov, Andrey Nikolaevich. "'Zolotoy petushok' na Parizhskoy i Londonskoy stsenakh." [*The Golden Cockerel* on the Paris and London stages.] *Apollon* 6/7 (1914): 46–54.

On the performance of the opera given in the form of a ballet.

737 Schuster-Craig, John. "'Bizarre Harmony and the so-called Newest Style': The Harmonic Language of Rimsky-Korsakov's *Le Coq D'or*." *JALS* 43 (January–July 1998): 45. ISSN: 0147-4413.

Describes how, in his final years, the musical language of Rimsky-Korsakov's operas became increasingly complex, the composer utilizing in such works as *The Golden Cockerel* symmetrical pitch collections, including a mode of limited transposition (as used by Liszt), together with whole-tone and octatonic scales.

738 Skrynnikova, Ol'ga Anatol'evna. "*Zolotoy petushok* – zagadki mifa." [*The Golden Cockerel* – the Mystery of the Myth.] *MA* (1) (1998): 134. ISSN: 0869-4516.

An examination of the mythological motifs in Rimsky-Korsakov's opera *The Golden Cockerel*, written to a libretto by Vladimir Ivanovich Bel'sky, based on the eponymous poem by Aleksandr Pushkin. Attention is drawn to parallels with ancient Slavic mythology.

739 Strel'nikov, Nikolay Mikhaylovich. "Zolotoy petushok ili Sinyaya ptitsa? (Otkrytie b. Mikhaylovskogo teatra)." [*The Golden Cockerel* or *Blue Bird*?

(Opening of the Former Mikhaylov Theater).] *Zhizn' iskusstva* 39 (912) (1923): 15–17.

A generally negative account of a performance, attacking the singing, staging, and production, written in a singularly witty manner.

740   Taruskin, Richard. "The Golden Cockerel." In Stanley Sadie, ed. *The New Grove Dictionary of Opera*, II. London and New York: Macmillan Press, 1992: 474–76. ISBN-10: 0935859926. ISBN-13: 978-0935859928.

An extensive article discussing the opera and its various interpretations.

741   Tideböhl, Ellen von. "Rimsky-Korsakov's last opera 'Zolotoi petouschok' ('The Golden Cock')." *Monthly Musical Record* 38 (456) (1908): 275–76.

A descriptive account of the opera, prior to its première by Zimin's Private Opera Company.

742   ——. "The Performance of Rimsky-Korsakov's opera 'The Golden Cock'." *The Musical Courier* 59 (2) (1909):18.

A first-hand account of the performance of the opera sent by the writer to *The Musical Courier* from Moscow on 10 November 1909, with a number of unusual photographs.

743   Weir, Justin. "*The Golden Cockerel* between Realism and Modernism." In Andrew Baruch Wachtel, ed., with an intro. *Intersections and Transpositions: Russian Music, Literature, and Society.* Evanston, Il.: Northwestern University Press: 1998. ISBN-10: 0810115808. ISBN-13: 978-0810115804.

A discussion of the conflicting interpretations of Rimsky-Korsakov's opera *The Golden Cockerel.*

744   Zhilyaev, Nikolay Sergeevich. "Ob opere voobshche (po povodu postanovki 'Zolotogo petushka')." [On the Opera in General (A propos of a Performance of *The Golden Cockerel*).] *Zolotoe Runo* 10 (1909): 59–64.

OTHER OPERATIC PROJECTS

745   Gozenpud, Abram Akimovich. "Neosushchestvlenny operny zamysel." [An Unaccomplished Operatic Project.] In No. 1204, Vol. II: 253–60.

A discussion of Rimsky-Korsakov's projected opera *Bagdadsky borodobrey* [*The Barber of Baghdad*], based on *The Arabian Nights*. Relating to the period 1895, it was intended to be a comic opera in one act. The libretto reproduced by Gozenpud is taken from materials preserved in the Rimsky-Korsakov archives in RNB and the Institute of Theater and Music.

746   Tsvetkova, Anastasiya Nikolaevna. "*Zemlya i nebo*: Neosushchestvlenny zamysel N. A. Rimskogo-Korsakova." [*Earth and Sky*: An Unrealized Project of N.

Bibliography: Musical Works 145

A. Rimsky-Korsakov.] *Musicus* 4 (13) (October–December 2008): 19. ISSN: 2072-0262.

An investigation published in *Musicus*, the journal of the St. Petersburg Conservatory, into Rimsky-Korsakov's work in 1905 on the unfinished opera *Earth and Sky*. The libretto, prepared by Vladimir Ivanovich Bel'sky, was based on Lord Byron's play *Heaven and Earth*.

747 ——. "Istoriya zamysla opery-misterii N. A. Rimskogo-Korsakova *Nebo i zemlya*." [The History of N. A. Rimsky-Korsakov's Project for an Opera-Mystery *Sky and Earth*.] In T. A. Khoprova, comp. *Zhizn' religii v muzyke. Sbornik Statei*. [Life of Religion in Music. Collection of Articles.] IV. St. Petersburg: Severnaya Zvezda, 2010. ISBN-13: 978-5874990143.

Part of a series published by the St. Petersburg Conservatory, this is an examination of the 1905 project of Rimsky-Korsakov's unfinished opera using a libretto by Vladimir Ivanovich Bel'sky, based on Lord Byron's play *Heaven and Earth*, the subject matter being taken from the book of *Genesis*.

LIBRETTI

748 Angert, G. A. *100 oper. Libretto oper, kharakteristika i biografii kompozitorov*. [100 Operas. Libretti of Operas, Character Sketch and Biographies of Composers.] L. Sabeenev, ed. Moscow: Russkoe Teatral'noe Obshchestvo, 1927. 281 pp.

Comprising a total of 45 composers (including 16 Russians), each section is made up of a biographical-critical sketch of the composer, with a portrait, followed by a resumé of his chief operatic compositions. Synopses of 10 operas (*The Maid of Pskov, Christmas Eve, The Snow Maiden, Sadko, The Tale of Tsar Saltan, The Tsar's Bride, The Golden Cockerel, The Legend of the Invisible City of Kitezh, Kashchey the Immortal*, and *Pan Voevoda*) are found on pp. 206–28. In his introduction Angert stresses the composer's indebtedness to Russian folk song and his use of legend and fantasy, which are employed more extensively than by any other Russian composer. The synopses of the operas are factual.

749 Bel'sky, Rafail. "Kratkaya biografiya V. I. Bel'skogo." [Brief Biography of V. I. Bel'sky.] *MA* (2) (1994): 145. ISSN: 0869-4516.

Vladimir Ivanovich Bel'sky was one of Rimsky-Korsakov's most gifted librettists, his works including *The Golden Cockerel, Sadko, The Legend of the Invisible City of Kitezh*, and *The Tale of Tsar Saltan*.

750 Bronsky, P. *Nikolay Andreevich Rimsky-Korsakov. Biografichesky ocherk. Kratkiya libretto oper. Spisok proizvedeniy*. [Nikolay Andreevich Rimsky-Korsakov. Biographical Sketch. Short Operatic Libretti. List of

146 *Nikolay Andreevich Rimsky-Korsakov: A Research and Information Guide*

Works.] St. Petersburg: Akts. Obshchestva Tipografsk. Dela v Spb. (c.1912). 88 pp.

Preceded by a note on the composer and his works, together with a list of compositions, the main part of the book is made up of synopses of the libretti of the 15 operas. Includes details of the librettist, date of composition, première, location, first performers, and later history.

751   Cheshikhin, Vsevolod Evgrafovich. *Kratkiya libretto. Soderzhashchie 132 oper sovremennago repertuara, s prilozheniem ocherkov vseobshchey istorii opery i istorii russkoy opery, kritiko-biograficheskikh zametok o kompozitorakh i operakh, i ukazateley.* [Short Libretti. Containing 132 Operas from the Contemporary Repertoire, with an Appendix of Essays on the General History of Opera and the History of Russian Opera, Critical-Biographical Notes on the Composers and the Operas, and Indexes.] Second edition, corr. and enl. Riga: Kal'nin and Deychman, 1904. xxix, 213 pp.

For a discussion of the composer and his aims, see pp. 42–56. Cheshikhin notes that Rimsky-Korsakov is the first Russian Wagnerian, then summarizes the content of eight of the operas, commencing with *The Maid of Pskov* and concluding with *Kashchey the Immortal.*

752   Edmunds, Catherine J. "Pushkin and Gogol' as Sources for the Librettos of the Fantastic Fairy Tale Operas of Rimskij-Korsakov." *Dissertation Abstracts International* 46 (8): 2314A (February 1986).

753   Frangopulo, M. Kh. and Entelis, L. A. *75 baletnykh libretto.* [75 Ballet Libretti.] Leningrad: Sovetsky Kompozitor, 1960. 303 pp. Reprinted: L. A. Entelis. *100 baletnykh libretto.* [100 Ballet Libretti.] Moscow-Leningrad: Muzyka, 1966: 202–04.

For a short description of Rimsky-Korsakov's *Scheherazade* arranged as a ballet and performed in this form at the Maly Opera Theater, Leningrad, on 17 June 1950, see pp. 210–12. Glossary of Russian ballet terms.

754   Gozenpud, Abram Akimovich. "Iz nabludeniy nad tvorcheskim protsessom Rimskogo-Korsakova." [Some Observations on Rimsky-Korsakov's Creative Process.] In No. 1204, Vol. I: 145–251.

Consisting of two articles, the first, entitled "Zapisnye knizhki kompozitora" [The Composer's Notebooks], pp. 145–207, examines the content of 10 notebooks, preserved in the RNB. The notebooks, which provide an insight into the composer's creative process, contain musical sketches both for completed operas and ideas for projects which were never realized, including the proposed opera *Sten'ka Razin.* The second article, entitled "N. Rimsky-Korsakov v rabote nad opernym libretto" [Rimsky-Korsakov's Work on an Opera Libretto], pp. 208–51, discusses the sources of some of his operas, noting the relationship with his librettists and his treatment of operatic libretti.

Bibliography: Musical Works   147

755   Pankratova, V. A., Polyakova, L. V., and Tsypin, G. M. *Opernye libretto.*
       Kratkoe izlozhenie soderzhaniya oper. [Operatic Libretti. A Short Description
       of the Content of the Operas.] Moscow: Muzgiz, 1962. 800 pp. Second enl.
       edition. Moscow: 1970.

       For a discussion of Rimsky-Korsakov's 15 operas, see pp. 68–101. Preceded
       by a short general article, each opera is described separately, together with
       details of place and date of first performance.

PERFORMERS: GENERAL

756   Anonymous. "Znamenitye ispolniteli roley v operakh Rimskogo-Korsakova."
       [Famous Performers in Rimsky-Korsakov's Operas.] *MZ* 5 (1969): 2–3.

       Photographs of notable performers in famous roles: Shalyapin, Zabela-
       Vrubel', Nezhdanova, Sobinov, Obukhova, Ershov, Derzhinskaya, Savransky,
       Pirogov, Kozlovsky, and Nelepp.

757   Stark, E. A. *Peterburgskaya opera i eë mastera. 1890-1910.* [The Petersburg
       Opera and its Masters. 1890-1910.] Moscow-Leningrad: Iskusstvo, 1940. 272
       pp.

       Memoirs about performers and performances at the Imperial Mariinsky
       Theater, describing such singers as Mikhail Vasilev (the third), Aleksandr
       Antonovsky, Sof'ya Gladkaya, Mitrofan Chuprynnikov, Fëdor Stravinsky,
       Ivan Ershov, Leonid Sobinov, and others.

PERFORMERS: INDIVIDUAL

Barsova, Valeriya Vladimirovna

758   Polyanovsky, Georgy Alexsandrovich. *Barsova.* Moscow-Leningrad: Isskustvo,
       1941. 222 pp.

       A description of the soprano Valeriya Vladimirovna Barsova, a Soviet
       performer renowned for the roles of Princess Shemakhan in *The Golden*
       Cockerel, Snegurochka, Volkhova, the Swan Princess, and Marfa, and who
       was noted for the "silvery bell-like quality" of her voice and her psychological
       insight into the part in question [see pp. 91–103, 132–45].

Derzhinskaya, Kseniya Georgievna

759   Grosheva, Elena Andreevna. *K. G. Derzhinskaya.* Moscow: Muzgiz, 1952. 122
       pp.

       Contains 12 sheets of photographs and a portrait of Kseniya Georgievna
       Derzhinskaya, a noted performer of Kupava (*The Snow Maiden*), Fevroniya

(The Legend of the Invisible City of Kitezh), Militrisa *(The Tale of Tsar Saltan)*, and Vera Sheloga. She sang 25 roles in 1044 performances. Commencing her career in 1913 in the Sergievsky Narodny Dom, from 1915 she performed regularly with the Bol'shoy Theater. For a detailed study of her interpretation of Rimsky-Korsakov roles, see pp. 77–86.

Ershov, Ivan Vasil'evich

760   Asaf'ev, Boris Vladimirovich [pseud. Glebov, Igor']. "Divny dar." [A Wonderful Gift.] *Zhizn' iskusstva* 15 (1918).

An account of Ershov's interpretation of the role of Grishka Kuter'ma in the opera *The Legend of the Invisible City of Kitezh*.

761   ——. "Ershov." *Zhizn' iskusstva* 715–717 (1921).

Describes the singer Ershov, praising his performance in the role of Grishka Kuter'ma in *The Legend of the Invisible City of Kitezh*.

762   Bogdanov-Berezovsky, Valerian Mikhaylovich. *Ivan Ershov.* Moscow-Leningrad: Muzgiz, 1951. 74 pp.

The singer Ivan Vasil'evich Ershov (1867–1943) was renowned in Russia for his performance of the parts of Mikhaylo Tucha (*The Maid of Pskov*), Tsar Berendey (*The Snow Maiden*), Vakula (*Christmas Eve*), Valery Rustik (*Servilia*), Sadko, Gvidon, Kashchey, and Grishka Kuter'ma. He was associated with the Leningrad Conservatory vocal faculty and its Opera Studio, enjoying a distinguished position with notable pre-revolutionary performers such as Fëdor Stravinsky and Shalyapin as well as Sobinov and Nezhdanova. For an account of his interpretations of various Rimsky-Korsakov roles as vocalist and actor, see pp. 43–54.

763   Mazing, Boris Vladimirovich. *Ershov. (Materialy k kharakteristike).* [Ershov. (Materials for a Character Sketch).] Moscow-Leningrad: Kinopechat', 1928. 40 pp.

Ivan Vasil'evich Ershov performed Wagnerian roles (Lohengrin, Tannhäuser, Tristan, Siegmund, Siegfried) and Rimsky-Korsakov parts (Sadko, Mikhaylo Tucha, Kashchey, Grishka Kuter'ma). His dramatic and vocal skills, as well as his ability to portray a wide range of emotions, are discussed. Pages 30–33 are concerned with his interpretation of Grishka Kuter'ma in the opera *The Legend of the Invisible City of Kitezh*. Ershov also played the part of Vakula in the première of *Christmas Eve* at the Mariinsky Theater in 1895, he was in the première of *Servilia* in 1902, and also played Kashchey, Sadko, Mikhaylo Tucha, and Berendey. His interpretation of Grishka Kuter'ma is considered his masterpiece.

Bibliography: Musical Works 149

Eykhenval'd, Margarita Aleksandrovna [Eichenwald, Margaret]

764   Favia-Artsay, Aida. "Margaret Eichenwald: A Remembrance of the Bolshoi's Unforgettable *Snegurochka.*" *The Opera Quarterly* 8 (4) (Winter 1991): 65. ISSN: 0736-0053.

An account of the opera singer Margaret Eichenwald [Margarita Aleksandrovna Eykhenval'd] (1866–1957), who, on graduating from the Moscow Conservatory, joined the Bol'shoy Theater, Moscow, in 1889. In the course of 12 years at the Bol'shoy Theater, she sang at least 23 different roles, including the role of Snegurochka in the eponymous opera by Rimsky-Korsakov, a part for which she is particularly remembered.

Levik, Sergey Yur'evich

765   Levik, Sergey Yur'evich. *Zapiski opernogo pevtsa. Iz istorii russkoy opernoy stseny.* [Memoirs of an Opera Singer. From the History of the Russian Opera Stage.] Moscow: Iskusstvo, 1955. 473 pp. Second edition, 1962. English trans. of second edition: Edward Morgan. *The Levik Memoirs: An Opera Singer's Notes.* Foreword by the Earl of Harewood. London: Symposium Records, 1995. xi, 538. ISBN-10: 0952436116. ISBN-13: 978-0952436119.

The memoirs of Levik, who made his St. Petersburg début in 1909, contain a wealth of material drawn from his first-hand experiences, presenting a portrayal of the Russian operatic world at the time of one of its greatest periods. Frequent references are made in his *Memoirs* to Rimsky-Korsakov's operas, their staging and the personal qualities of the performers. Of the various singers, he considered the performances of Nezhdanova and Ershov to be outstanding.

Maksakova, Mariya Petrovna

766   L'vov, Mikhail L'vovich. *M. P. Maksakova.* Moscow: Muzgiz, 1953. 52 pp.

A biographical account of the Russian mezzo-soprano Mariya Petrovna Maksakova, noted for her performance in the role of Lyubasha in *The Tsar's Bride.* For personal observations on performing Rimsky-Korsakov's songs, which she saw as following the subtleties of the text, see p. 31. Maksakova considered that the melodies of the songs were composed first and the accompaniments later. Her interpretation of Lyubasha can be found on pp. 31–34.

Maslennikova, Irina Ivanovna

767   Maslennikova, Irina Ivanovna. "Moya Snegurochka." [My *Snow Maiden.*] *SM* 3 (1969): 98–100.

An autobiography by the Soviet coloratura soprano, Irina Maslennikova, giving her interpretation of the role of *The Snow Maiden.*

Nezhdanova, Antonina Vasil'evna

768   L'vov, Mikhail L'vovich. *A. V. Nezhdanova.* Moscow: Muzgiz, 1952. 224 pp.

Antonina Vasil'evna Nezhdanova, a Ukrainian, performed many of Rimsky-Korsakov's operatic roles, including Volkhova (*Sadko*), the Shemakhan Princess (*The Golden Cockerel*), Kashcheevna (*Kashchey the Immortal*), Marfa (*The Tsar's Bride*), and the Swan-Princess (*The Tale of Tsar Saltan*). She was also well known as a performer of his songs. Includes six photographs of Nezhdanova in various operatic parts.

769   Polyanovsky, Georgy Aleksandrovich. *A. V. Nezhdanova.* Moscow: Muzyka, 1970. 144 pp.

Antonina Nezhdanova (1873–1950), coloratura soprano, performed a number of women's roles in Rimsky-Korsakov's operas, including Volkhova, Snegurochka, Maria, and the Shemakhan Princess. Polyanovsky's biography discusses her life and work and the qualities of her performances. Included are a number of photographs of her in these roles.

Obukhova, Nadezhda Andreevna

770   Obukhova, Nadezhda Andreevna. *Vospominaniya. Stat'i. Materialy.* [Reminiscences. Articles. Materials.] I. Belza, ed. Moscow: Vserossiyskoe Teatral'noe Obshchestvo, 1970. 319 pp.

Nadezhda Obukhova (1886–1961) performed six roles in Rimsky-Korsakov's operas, including Lyubava (*Sadko*), Lyubasha (*The Tsar's Bride*), and Kashcheevna (*Kashchey the Immortal*). For her performances at the Bol'shoy Theater, see pp. 70–72, 74–77, and 80–85. Chapter VI, pp. 86–93, describes her interpretation of Lyubasha. The illustrations are well-chosen and informative.

Olenina-d'Alheim, Maria

771   Tumanov, Alexander. *The Life and Artistry of Maria Olenina-d'Alheim.* Christopher Barnes, trans. University of Alberta Press, 2000. xix, 359 pp. ISBN-10: 0888643284. ISBN-13: 978-0888643285.

A translation of A. Tumanov's book *Ona i muzyka, i slovo* [She is the Music, and the Word], the title of which is taken from a poem by Osip Mandelstam, this account of the Russian singer Maria Olenina-d'Alheim (1869–1970) provides an informative insight into the musical world surrounding Rimsky-Korsakov and the personalities of the *Moguchaya Kuchka* [Mighty Handful].

Bibliography: Musical Works

Ozerov, Nikolay Nikolaevich

772   Sletov, V. *N. N. Ozerov.* Moscow-Leningrad: Muzgiz, 1951. 63 pp.

Nikolay Nikolaevich Ozerov, a lyric dramatic tenor, was renowned for his performance of the roles of Sadko, Kuter'ma, Levko, Vakula, and Lykov. From 1920 to 1946 he was a soloist with the Bol'shoy Theater. For his interpretation of the part of Grishka Kuter'ma, see pp. 32–36.

Panteleev, Maksim Petrovich

773   Kurkov, Nikolay Vasil'evich. "Artist russkoy opery M. I. Panteleev v Amerike: Po materialam arkhivnogo fonda Muzeya russkoy kul'tury v San-Frantsisko SSHA." [The Artist of the Russian Opera M. I. Panteleev in America. Based on Materials in the Archival Section of the Museum of Russian Culture in San Francisco, USA.] In *Russkie muzykal'nye arkhivy za rubezhom. Zarubezhnye muzykal'nye arkhivy v Rossii. VI: Materialy mezhdunarodnykh konferentsiy.* [Russian Music Archives Abroad. Foreign Music Archives in Russia. VI: Materials of International Conferences.] Russian Federation, 2013.

A discussion of the activities of the Russian opera singer Maksim Petrovich Panteleev and his opera company Russkaya Grand-Opera in the United States, including details of the performance of Rimsky-Korsakov's opera *The Golden Cockerel.*

Reyzen, Mark Osipovich

774   Reyzen, Mark Osipovich. "Iz vospominaniy." [From Reminiscences.] *SM* 5 (6) (1980): 78–83.

Fragments from the memoirs of the Soviet singer, Mark Reyzen, including discussion of his performance of the role of Ivan Grozny in *The Maid of Pskov.*

Rozhdestvenskaya, Natal'ya Petrovna

775   Rozhdestvenskaya, Natal'ya Petrovna. "Ot Kupavy do devy Fevronii." [From Kupava to the Maiden Fevroniya.] *SM* 3 (1969): 92–97.

The singer Rozhdestvenskaya describes her acquaintance with Rimsky-Korsakov's operas and their performance.

Shalyapin, Fëdor Ivanovich [Chaliapin, Fyodor]

776   Borovsky, Victor. *Chaliapin. A Critical Biography.* London: Hamish Hamilton, New York: Alfred A. Knopf, 1988. xv, 630 pp. ISBN-10: 0394560965. ISBN-13: 978-0394560960.

152   *Nikolay Andreevich Rimsky-Korsakov: A Research and Information Guide*

This vivid and detailed account of the life and work of Fëdor Shalyapin [Chaliapin] (1873–1938), one of the greatest and best known Russian singers of all time, contains many references to Rimsky-Korsakov's operas, particularly Shalyapin's distinctive interpretation of the roles of Salieri and Ivan the Terrible. The Notes and Discography are extensive.

777   Gozenpud, Abram Akimovich. *Russky operny teatr na rubezhe xix i xx vekov i F. I. Shalyapin. 1890-1904.* [The Russian Opera Theater at the Turn of the 19th and 20th Centuries and F. I. Chaliapin. 1890-1904.] Leningrad, 1974.

Includes discussion of Shalyapin's roles in various Rimsky-Korsakov operas.

778   Grosheva, E. A., et al., eds. *Fëdor Ivanovich Shalyapin.* Vol. I: "Literaturnoe nasledstvo. Pis'ma." [Literary Legacy. Letters.] Third edition, corr. and enl. Moscow: Iskusstvo, 1976. 760 pp. Vol. II: "Vospominaniya o F. I. Shalyapine." [Recollections of Shalyapin.] Moscow: Iskusstvo, 1977. 600 pp. Vol. III: "Vskazyvaniya. Prilozheniya." [Opinions. Supplements.] Moscow: Iskusstvo, 1979. 392 pp.

These three volumes contain many references to Rimsky-Korsakov and his work, together with Chaliapin's role as a celebrated performer of Salieri, Ivan Grozny, and other parts.

779   Stasov, Vladimir Vasil'evich. "Shalyapin v Peterburge." [Chaliapin in Petersburg.] *Novosti i Birzhevaya Gazeta* 314 (16 November 1903). Reprinted: V. V. Stasov. *Stat'i o Shalyapine.* [Articles on Chaliapin.] Moscow: Muzgiz, 1952. 22 pp.

Consists of two articles:

i.   "Shalyapin v Peterburge" [Chaliapin in Petersburg]: 3–16.
ii.   "Radost' bezmernaya" [An Immense Joy]: 17–21.

Both are panegyrical in style and include references to the operas *The Maid of Pskov* and *Sadko.*

780   Steane, John. "English Opera Criticism in the Interwar Years. 8. Hussey of 'The Spectator'." *Opera* 38 (2) (1987): 143–48.

For a description of Chaliapin as Ivan the Terrible, see p. 145.

781   Yankovsky, Moisey Osipovich. *Shalyapin i russkaya opernaya kul'tura.* [Chaliapin and Russian Operatic Culture.] Moscow-Leningrad: Muzgiz, 1947. 223 pp.

Contains references to Chaliapin and his work with Rimsky-Korsakov. For photos of Chaliapin in various roles, including three as Ivan Grozny (*The Maid of Pskov*) and three as Salieri (*Mozart and Salieri*), see pp. 177–216.

782   ——. *F. I. Shalyapin.* Moscow-Leningrad: Muzgiz, 1951. 128 pp.

Renowned for his roles as Ivan Grozny in *The Maid of Pskov*, Eremka in *The Legend of the Invisible City of Kitezh*, the Varangian Merchant in *Sadko*, and the Mayor in *May Night*, Chaliapin also sang a number of Rimsky-Korsakov's songs. For an account of the opera *Mozart and Salieri* and Chaliapin's performance of the role of Salieri, considered to be one of his masterpieces, see pp. 75–78.

Shkafer, Vasily Petrovich

783   Shkafer, Vasily Petrovich. *Sorok let na stsene russkoy opery: Vospominaniya. 1890-1930 gg.* [Forty Years on the Russian Opera Stage: Reminiscences. 1890-1930.] Leningrad: Izd. Teatra Opery i Baleta im. S. M. Kirova, 1936.

Vasily Shkafer was both a singer and an opera director [régisseur]. His memoirs describe his performances as an opera singer at Solodovnikov's Private Theater, the Mariinsky Theater, and the Bol'shoy Theater. Also includes an account of his visit to Italy.

Shpiller, Natal'ya Dmitrievna

784   Shpiller, Natal'ya Dmitrievna. "Osobennosti i trudnosti partiy Marfy, Tsarevny-Lebed', Oksany, i Volkhovy iz oper Rimskogo-Korsakova." [Characteristics and Difficulties of the Parts of Maria, the Swan Princess, Oksana and Volkhova in Rimsky-Korsakov's Operas.] In O. Agarkov and L. Yaroslavtseva, eds. *Muzykal'no-tvorcheskoe vospriyatie artistov opernoy stseny.* [The Musical and Creative Reception of Operatic Artists.] Moscow: Gos. Muzykal'-pedagogichesky inst. Gnesinykh, 1981.

A discussion by the Soviet operatic soprano and teacher, Natal'ya Shpiller, a soloist at the Bol'shoy Theater from 1935 to 1958.

Sobinov, Leonid Vital'evich

785   L'vov, Mikhail L. *L. V. Sobinov.* Moscow-Leningrad: Muzgiz, 1951. 103 pp.

Leonid Sobinov (1872–1934) sang some of Rimsky-Korsakov's best known songs and performed the lyric tenor roles of Tsar Berendey in *The Snow Maiden* (1900, Bol'shoy Theater) and Levko in *May Night* (1909, Bol'shoy Theater). For details of his performances, see pp. 58–59.

786   Migay, Sergey Ivanovich. "Leonid Vital'evich Sobinov (Iz vospominaniy o druge)." [Leonid Vital'evich Sobinov (From Recollections of a Friend).] *SM* 6 (1952): 68–72.

Observations on Sobinov's interpretation of various Rimsky-Korsakov roles, especially that of Tsar Berendey in *The Snow Maiden*, on which he worked under the composer's personal supervision. Two portraits of Sobinov.

154 Nikolay Andreevich Rimsky-Korsakov: A Research and Information Guide

787 Vladykina-Bachinskaya, Nina Mikhaylovna. *Leonid Vital'evich Sobinov.* Yaroslavl': Yaroslavsk. oblizd., 1951. 107 pp. Second edition. Moscow, 1958. 302 pp.

Sobinov is renowned for his performances of Tsar Berendey in *The Snow Maiden* and Levko in *May Night.* He also sang 11 songs of Rimsky-Korsakov, and many by Tchaikovsky and Rubinstein. This volume, No. 9 in the series "Lives of Famous People" (founded in 1933 by Gorky), is a popular biography in 15 chapters. For a discussion of Sobinov's performance in *May Night* and *The Snow Maiden,* see the 1958 edition, pp. 182–91. Included is a bibliography of 54 entries, 3 obituaries, and a list of contents, but no index.

Stravinsky, Fëdor Ignat'evich

788 Bogdanov-Berezovsky, Valerian Mikhaylovich. *Fëdor Stravinsky.* Moscow-Leningrad: Muzgiz, 1951. 52 pp.

Fëdor Stravinsky, father of Igor, was a soloist with the Imperial Mariinsky Theater, noted for his comic bass roles, including Golova (the Mayor) in *May Night,* Ded Moroz (Uncle Frost) in *The Snow Maiden,* Panas in *Christmas Eve,* and others. Bogdanov-Berezovsky discusses briefly Fëdor Stravinsky's interpretation of some of these parts and also includes a photograph of him in the role of the Mayor. Includes a list of the 66 parts played by Stravinsky in the course of his career.

789 Stark, E. A. "Fëdor Ignat'evich Stravinsky, 1843-1902. (Opyt kharakteristiki)." [Fëdor Ignat'evich Stravinsky, 1843-1902. (A Character Sketch).] *EIT,* Sezon 1903–04: Suppl. I: 116–79.

A valuable source of information on the singer and his roles.

Zabela [Zabela-Vrubel'], Nadezhda Ivanovna

790 Barsova, Lyudmila Grigor'evna. "Vrubel' i Zabela." [Vrubel' and Zabela.] *SM* 3 (1982): 79–86.

A discussion of the artist Vrubel' and the singer Nadezhda Zabela, whom he married. Zabela performed many of the leading women's roles in the composer's operas, the part of the Princess in *Kashchey the Immortal* being written to suit her voice and personality.

791 ——. *N. I. Zabela-Vryubel' glazami sovremennikov.* [Zabela-Vryubel' As Seen by Contemporaries.] Leningrad: Muzyka, 1982.

An amplification of the preceding entry.

792 ——. *N. A. Rimsky-Korsakov: Perepiska s N. I. Zabeloy-Vrubel'.* [N. A. Rimsky-Korsakov: Correspondence with N. I. Zabela-Vryubel'.] *Rossiyskie muzykal'nye arhivy.* [Russian Music Archives.] Kompozitor, 2008.

Includes correspondence between Rimsky-Korsakov and the opera singer Nadezhda Ivanovna Zabela-Vryubel'.

793   Koposova-Derzhanovskaya, Ekaterina Vasil'evna. "Zamechatel'naya russkaya pevitsa (Iz vospominaniy o N. I. Zabele-Vrubel')." [A Remarkable Russian Singer (From Recollections about N. I. Zabela-Vrubel').] *SM* 4 (1948): 57–58.

An article giving personal details of Nadezhda Ivanovna Zabela's life, stressing her talents as a coloratura soprano at the Imperial Mariinsky Theater and the Moscow Private Opera Theater. Emphasis is placed on her relationship with the composer.

794   Osipova, Liya. "Zabela i Vrubel'." [Zabela and Vrubel'.] *MZ* 7 (2006): 40. ISSN: 0131-2383.

A discussion of the relationship of the singer Nadezhda Zabela and her husband, the artist Mikhail Vrubel', with Rimsky-Korsakov and Mikhail Fabianovich Gnesin.

795   Yankovsky, Moisey Osipovich. *N. I. Zabela-Vrubel'*. Moscow: Muzgiz, 1953. 141 pp.

Describes Zabela-Vrubel', noted for her roles as Volkhova in *Sadko*, Snegurochka in *The Snow Maiden*, Marfa in *The Tsar's Bride*, and the Swan Princess in *The Tale of Tsar Saltan*.

796   ———. "B. K. Yanovksy. Vospominaniya o N. I. Zabele-Vrubel'." [B. K. Yanovsky. Recollections of N. I. Zabela-Vrubel'.] In No. 1204, Vol. II: 334–47.

Yanovsky's reminiscences of the Russian singer, preserved in the N. A. Rimsky-Korsakov Archive of RNB, describe the period 1892–1913, including reference to *May Night*, *The Tsar's Bride*, and *The Tale of Tsar Saltan*.

Zlatogorova, Bronislava Yakovlevna

797   Zlatogorova, Bronislava Yakovlevna. "Nash prazdnik." [Our Holiday.] *SM* 3 (1976): 64–67.

The Soviet singer Zlatogorova discusses her time at the Bol'shoy Theater and her performances in Rimsky-Korsakov's operas under Golovanov.

ORCHESTRAL WORKS: GENERAL

798   Abel, Jörg Michael. *Die Entstehung der sinfonischen Musik in Russland.* PhD dissertation, Johann Wolfgang Goethe-Universität, Frankfurt am Main. In *Studia slavica musicologica* 7. Berlin: Ernst Kuhn, 1996. 384 pp. ISBN-10: 3928864416. ISBN-13: 978-3928864411.

A discussion of the historical development of the symphony and symphonic poem in Russia, including the symphonies of Rimsky-Korsakov.

799   Abraham, Gerald. "Rimsky-Korsakov as Self-critic." In Anna Amalie Abert and Wilhelm Pfannkuch, eds. *Festschrift Friedrich Blume zum 70 Geburtstag.* Kassel: Bärenreiter, 1963: 16–21. Reprinted: *Slavonic and Romantic Music. Essays and Studies.* London: Faber & Faber, 1968: 195–201. Reprinted: 2013. ISBN-10: 0571302807. ISBN-13: 978-0571302802.

Discusses Rimsky-Korsakov's powers of self-criticism and his indebtedness to works of other composers (including Liszt, David, Glinka, Serov, Cui, and Dargomyzhsky), and gives a survey of some of the composer's revisions. These comprise the youthful First Symphony in E-flat minor, the *Overture on Russian Themes,* and the so-called "Second Symphony" *Antar.* While noting that in his revisions Rimsky-Korsakov tended to favor a lightening of the orchestration, Abraham observes that the generally known version of *Antar* is, in his opinion, neither the best nor the most representative. Includes comparative music examples.

800   Chernov, Konstantin Nikolaevich. "Programnye simfonicheskie proizvedeniya Rimskogo-Korsakova." [Rimsky-Korsakov's Symphonic Program Works.] *RMG* (1905): cols. 1027–32, 1073–82, 1105–13.

This article serves as the basis for a number of subsequent Soviet publications and is a critical-analytical examination of the Musical Picture "Sadko," Op. 5, *Antar,* Op. 9, and *Skazka,* Op. 29. While noting the indebtedness of these works to foreign models, the author stresses their novelty and importance in the history of Russian Music.

801   Eeckhout, Antoon. Muzikale exploraties. *Tweede Reeks: Ouverturen en symfonische gedichtey.* Mechelen-Leuven: Uitgeverij de Monte, 1970. 106 pp.

Includes a discussion of some orchestral works.

802   Eyges, Iosif. "O predrassudkakh programnosti v muzyke. (Rimsky-Korsakov.)" [About Prejudices Concerning the Program Element in Music. (Rimsky-Korsakov).] *Muzykal'naya nov', zhurnal muzykal'nogo iskusstva* 9 (1924): 11–12.

A discussion of program music, having special regard to Rimsky-Korsakov's programmatic compositions and his thoughts on that question.

803   Gnesin, Mikhail Fabianovich. "O russkom simfonizme. (Epichesky simfonizm i epicheskaya muzykal'no-stsenicheskaya dramaturgiya)." [On Russian Symphonism. (Epic Symphonism and Epic Musical-Stage Dramaturgy).] *SM* 6 (1948); 3 (1949); 1 (1950). In No. 1381 in abbreviated form.

804   Gordeeva, Evgeniya Mikhaylovna, ed. and comp. *Kompozitory Moguchey Kuchki o programnoy muzyke. Izbrannye otryvki iz pisem, vospominaniy i kriticheskikh statey.* [The Composers of the Mighty Handful on Program Music. Selected Excerpts from Letters, Reminiscences and Critical Articles.] Moscow: Muzgiz, 1956. 187 pp. List of sources.

Bibliography: Musical Works 157

Preceded by a short essay on the development of program music in Russia, the section on Rimsky-Korsakov consists of extracts from his writings on program music, especially *Antar, Skazka*, and *Scheherazade*.

805 Greenwalt, Terence Lee. "A Study of the Symphony in Russia from Glinka to the early 20th Century." PhD dissertation, University of Rochester, Eastman School of Music, 1972. 239 pp.

Includes a discussion of the composer's symphonies.

806 Kandinsky, Aleksey Ivanovich. "Simfonicheskie skazki Rimskogo-Korsakova 60kh godov." [Rimsky-Korsakov's Symphonic Fairy Tales of the 60s.] In *Ot Lyulli do nashikh dney.* [From Lully to Our Era.] Konen, V., comp. Moscow: Muzyka, 1967.

Includes a discussion of Rimsky-Korsakov's musical picture "Sadko" and the orchestral *Skazka* [A Fairy Tale].

807 Kloiber, Rudolf. *Handbuch der Symphonischen Dichtung.* Wiesbaden: Breitkopf und Härtel, 1967. 228 pp. ISBN-10: 3765100188; ISBN-13: 978-3765100185.

Includes a discussion of Rimsky-Korsakov's symphonic poems.

808 "Loge." "Tvorchestvo Rimskogo-Korsakova. (Kontsert Filarmonii)." [Rimsky-Korsakov's Creative Work. (Philharmonia Concert).] *Zhizn' iskusstva* 808 (1921).

Discusses three works given at a Philharmonic concert, *Night on Mount Triglav, Capriccio espagnol*, and *Scheherazade*, together with specific characteristics of Rimsky-Korsakov's musical style.

809 Riesemann, Oskar von. "Russische Symphonien." *Die Musik.* Sechster Jahrgang. Dritten Quartalsband. XXIII (1906–07): 12–27.

For a discussion of the composer's symphonies, see pp. 16–19.

810 Solovtsov, Anatoly Aleksandrovich. *Simfonicheskie proizvedeniya Rimskogo-Korsakova.* [Rimsky-Korsakov's Symphonic Works.] Moscow: Muzgiz, 1953. 202 pp. Second edition, Moscow, 1960.

An annotated musical guide to Rimsky-Korsakov's symphonic compositions in four sections, with introduction:

i. Symphonic Program Works: Sadko, Antar, Skazka, Scheherazade, Russian Easter Overture.
ii. Works Not Having a Published Program: Symphony No. 1, Fantasia on Serbian Themes.
iii. Works for Solo Instruments With Orch. Accompaniment: Piano Concerto.
iv. Overtures, Orchestral Suites from Operas and Transcriptions of Operatic Scenes for Symphony Orchestra.

158   Nikolay Andreevich Rimsky-Korsakov: A Research and Information Guide

The link between Rimsky-Korsakov and the music of "eastern" (i.e., Near-Eastern and Central Asian) peoples is stressed. No bibliography. A volume in the series *Guide Books on Russian Music*.

ORCHESTRAL WORKS: INDIVIDUAL

Pervaya simfoniya [Symphony No. 1], Op. 1

811   Kyui, Ts. [Cui, César]. "Pervy kontsert v pol'zu Besplatnoy muzykal'noy shkoly." [The First Benefit Concert for the Free Music School.] *Sanktpeterburgskie Vedomosti* 340 (24 December 1865). Reprinted: No. 1294: 66–71, 571.

Discusses Rimsky-Korsakov's First Symphony.

812   ——. "Muzykal'nye zametki. Poslednye kontserty Russkogo muzykal'nogo obshchestva. Simfoniya g. Rimskogo-Korsakova v rukakh Lyadova." [Music Notes. The Last Concerts of the Russian Music Society. Mr. Rimsky-Korsakov's Symphony in the Hands of Lyadov.] *Sanktpeterburgskie Vedomosti* (24 March 1866).

An account of Rimsky-Korsakov's First Symphony, conducted by Lyadov.

813   Rimsky-Korsakow, Nikolai. "Meine erste Symphonie (zwischen 1884 und 1890)." In *Studia slavica musicologica* 16: *Nikolai Rimsky-Korsakow. Kleinere musiktheoretische Schriften und Fragmente. Texte zur Musikgeschichte, Musikpädagogik und Musikästhetik*. Berlin: Ernst Kuhn, 2004. ISBN-10: 392886467X. ISBN-13: 978-3928864671.

A description by Rimsky-Korsakov of his Symphony No. 1, which he places stylistically between Schumann and Glinka. Originally written in E-flat major, he later transposed the work to E minor for ease of performance [see No. 211].

814   Shakhov, Vadim Viktorovich. "Pervaya simfoniya." [First Symphony.] *MA* (2) (1994): 44–50. ISSN: 0869-4516.

An informative discussion of the evolution of Rimsky-Korsakov's First Symphony and the changes he included in the second printing of the symphony, together with observations on the work made by his contemporaries.

Fantaziya na serbskie temy [Fantasia on Serbian Themes], Op. 6

815   Chaykovsky, Pëtr Il'ich. "Po povodu 'Serbskoy fantazii' g. Rimskogo-Korsakova." [A Propos of Mr. Rimsky-Korsakov's "Serbian Fantasy."] In Yakovlev, V. V., ed. *P. I. Chaykovsky. Muzykal'no-kriticheskie stat'i.* [P. I. Tchaikovsky. Musical-Critical Articles.] Moscow: Muzgiz, 1953: 25–27, 383–85.

Bibliography: Musical Works 159

In this article Tchaikovsky defends Rimsky-Korsakov's work from a hostile attack appearing in the journal *Antrakt* 8 (25 February 1868), and praises the Fantasy's harmonic and melodic structure, development, and orchestration. Pointing out that Rimsky-Korsakov is still a young man, Tchaikovsky foresees him as "one of the best adornments of our art."

816   Koren, Marija. "Serbian Themes in Russian Music of the Second Half of the 19th Century." *Muzikol Zbornik* IV (1968): 78–87.

Includes a discussion of the *Fantasy on Serbian Themes.*

817   Kyui, Ts. A. [Cui, César]. "Russkaya opera. Konservatoriya. Nekrologicheskie kontserty. Bibliografiya." [Russian Opera. The Conservatory. Obituary Concerts. Bibliography.] *Sanktpeterburgskie Vedomosti* 319 (19 November 1871). Reprinted: No. 1294: 189, 588.

Discusses the *Fantasia on Serbian Themes.*

818   Serov, Aleksandr Nikolaevich. "'Serbskaya fantaziya' N. Rimskogo-Korsakova." [Rimsky-Korsakov's *Serbian Fantasy*.] In Khubov, G., ed. *A. N. Serov. Izbrannye stat'i* [A. N. Serov. Selected Articles.] Vol. II. Moscow: Muzgiz, 1957: 617. Full text: Serov, A. N. *Kriticheskie stat'i* [Critical Articles], Vol. IV. (St. Petersburg, 1895): 1834–36. Reprinted: Ogolevets, A. S. *Materialy i dokumenty* [Materials and documents], Vol. I. Moscow, 1954.

A eulogistic account of the work as described in Serov's review "The Second and Third Concerts of the Russian Music Society" and published in the Chronicle of his journal *Muzyka i Teatr* 14 (1867).

819   Stasov, Vladimir Vasil'evich. "Slavyansky kontsert g-na Balakireva." [Mr. Balakirev's Slavonic Concert.] *Sanktpeterburgskie Vedomosti* 130 (13 May 1867). Reprinted: Stasov, V. V. *Sobrannye sochineniya* [Collected Works], Vol. 3. St. Petersburg, 1894: cols. 217–19; Stasov, V. V. *Izbrannye sochineniya* [Selected Works], Vol. 1. Moscow, 1952: 171–73; *Materialy i dokumenty po istorii russkoy realisticheskoy muzykal'noy estetiki* [Materials and Documents on the History of Russian Realist Musical Esthetics], Vol. 2. Moscow, 1956: 100–02; Stasov, V. V. *Stat'i o muzyke* [Articles on Music], Vol. 2. Moscow, 1976: 110–12.

A review of a concert given on 12 [24] May 1867, including the première of the *Serbian Fantasy*, notable in the history of Russian music in that it includes the first known use of the expression "moguchaya kuchka" [Mighty Handful]: "Let us end our comments with a wish: God grant that they will always remember how much poetry, feeling, talent and skill is to be found in our small yet already mighty handful of Russian musicians."

Uvertura na Russkie temy [Overture on Russian Themes], Op. 28

820   Kyui, Ts. A. [Cui, César]. "Pervy kontsert Besplatnoy shkoly." [First Concert of the Free School.] *Sanktpeterburgskie Vedomosti* (20 December 1866).

A discussion of a performance of the *Overture on Russian Themes*.

"Sadko." Muzykal'naya kartinka. Epizod iz byliny o Sadko, Novgorodskom goste ["Sadko." A Musical Picture. Episode from the Bylina about Sadko, the Novgorod Merchant], Op. 5

821   Kyui, Ts. A. [Cui, César]. "Muzykal'nye zametki. Novoe proizvedenie Rimskogo-Korsakova." [Music Notes. A New Work by Rimsky-Korsakov.] *Sanktpeterburgskie Vedomosti* 355 (24 December 1867). Reprinted: No. 1294: 126–28, 581.

A discussion of the first version of the orchestral work "Sadko."

822   Levenson, Osip Yakovlevich. *V kontsertnom zale. (Muzykal'nye fel'etony). 1878-1880.* [In the Concert Hall. (Musical Articles). 1878-1880.] Moscow, 1880: Article XVII, 113–20.

Discusses a performance of the musical picture "Sadko" at a concert given by the Society of Lovers of Music and Dramatic Art. Levenson gives a detailed description of the work, comparing it with Mendelssohn's *The Hebrides* and Rubinstein's *Ocean Symphony*, though regrets that there was no harp available for the performance, a piano having to be used instead.

823   Odoevsky, Vladimir Fëdorovich. *Muzykal'no-literaturnoe nasledstvo.* [Musical-Literary Legacy.] G. Bernandt, ed. Moscow, 1956.

Although Odoevsky, Russian writer and critic, died before Rimsky-Korsakov's music became well-known, less than two months before his death, he noted in his diary on the day of the performance of the symphonic picture "Sadko" (4 January 1869): "At a Musical Society concert 'Sadko' by Korsakov – a wonderful thing, full of fantasy, original orchestration. If Korsakov doesn't stop on the way, he'll be a man of great talent".

824   Serov, Aleksandr Nikolaevich. "'Sadko' – bylina N. Rimskogo-Korsakova." [*Sadko* – a Bylina by N. Rimsky-Korsakov.] In Khubov, G., ed. *A. N. Serov. Izbrannye stat'i* [A. N. Serov. Selected Articles] Vol. II. Moscow: Muzgiz, 1957: 618–20. Full text: Serov, A. N. *Kriticheskie stat'i* [Critical Articles], Vol. IV. St. Petersburg: 1895: 1841.

A laudatory account of Rimsky-Korsakov's early orchestral picture "Sadko" as described in Serov's review "Seventh Concert of the Russian Music Society" (9 December 1867), published in the Chronicle section of the journal *Muzyka i Teatr* (15).

825   ——. "Simfonicheskaya kartina Rimskogo-Korsakova." [Rimsky-Korsakov's Symphonic Picture.] In Khubov, G., ed. *A. N. Serov. Izbrannye stat'i* [A. N. Serov. Selected Articles] Vol. II. Moscow: Muzgiz, 1957: 627–28.

A eulogistic article on Rimsky-Korsakov's musical picture "Sadko," originally written in French and published in the *Journal de St.-Pétersbourg*, 279

Bibliography: Musical Works 161

(12 December 1869), subsequently appearing in translation in his *Kriticheskie stat'i* [Critical Articles], Vol. IV. (St. Petersburg, 1895).

"Antar." Simfonicheskaya syuita (Vtoraya simfoniya) ["Antar." Symphonic Suite (Symphony No. 2)], Op. 9

826   Abraham, Gerald. "Arab Melodies in Rimsky-Korsakov and Borodin." *ML* 56 (3) (1975): 313–18.

An examination of the authentic Arab melodies employed in the Symphony *Antar*, and their sources in Francesco Salvador-Daniel's *Album de Chansons arabes, mauresques et kabyles* and Alexandre Christianowitsch's *Esquisse historique de la musique arabe aux temps anciens*.

827   Borodin, A. P. "Kontsert Besplatnoy muzykal'noy shkoly. Kontserty Russkogo Muzykal'nogo Obshchestva (7-y i 8-y)." [Concert of the Free Music School. Concerts of the Russian Music Society (7th and 8th).] *S.-Peterburgskie Vedomosti* 78 (20 March, 1869). Reprinted: A. P. Borodin. *Muzykal'no-kriticheskie stat'i*. [Musical-Critical Articles.] Moscow-Leningrad: Muzgiz, 1951.

Although Borodin wrote comparatively little as a music critic, what he did write was of interest. The present article contains a report of the Eighth Concert of the Russian Music Society, pp. 57–61 of the 1951 reprint, which included a performance of Rimsky-Korsakov's new Second Symphony *Antar*. Borodin comments on the harmonic and formal structure, its exotic coloring, and fine orchestration, although finds weaknesses in the last movement.

828   Dukas, Paul. "Musiciens russes: Antar de Rimsky-Korsakoff." In *Les Écrits de Paul Dukas sur la musique*. Paris: Société d'éditions Françaises et Internationales, 1948: 145–48.

An informal account of *Antar* and some comments about program music.

829   Kyui, Ts. A. [Cui, César]. "Vtoroy kontsert Besplatnoy shkoly." [Second Concert of the Free School.] *Sanktpeterburgskie Vedomosti*. (11 January 1872). Reprinted: No. 1294: 191–93, 588.

An account of the Second Symphony *Antar*.

830   Larosh, German Avgustovich. "O programmnoy muzyke i 'Antare' Rimskogo-Korsakova v osobennosti." [On Program Music and Rimsky-Korsakov's *Antar* in Particular.] *Golos*, 29 December 1871. Reprinted: G. A. Larosh. *Izbrannye stat'i* [Selected articles], Vol. 4. Leningrad: Muzyka, 1977: 73–79, 289.

A substantial discussion of program music in general and the relationship of Rimsky-Korsakov's *Antar* to comparable works of other composers (e.g., Beethoven, Berlioz, Liszt).

162 Nikolay Andreevich Rimsky-Korsakov: A Research and Information Guide

831 ——. "Muzykal'nye pis'ma iz Peterburga. Pis'mo tret'e." [Musical Letters from St. Petersburg. Letter Three.] *Moskovskie Vedomosti* 66 (15 March 1872).

An article on the St. Petersburg musical scene in general, with an account of Rimsky-Korsakov's *Antar*. Larosh stresses the composer's strengths and predicts that his talents will continue to develop.

832 Tolstoy, Feofil Matveevich [pseud. "Rostislav"]. "Peterburgskie pis'ma. 'Antar', dve simfonii g. Rimskogo-Korsakova." [Letters from St. Petersburg. *Antar*, Two Symphonies by Mr. Rimsky-Korsakov.] *Moskovskie Vedomosti* (18 January 1876).

Includes a discussion of the Second Symphony.

833 Vanovskaya, Irina Nikolaevna. "K istorii analiza muzykal'nykh proizvedeniy: Nasledie N. A. Rimskogo-Korsakova." [On the History of Music Analysis: The Legacy of N. A. Rimsky-Korsakov.] *MZ* (8) (2012): 64. ISSN: 0131-2383.

An exploration of Rimsky-Korsakov's legacy in the context of the history of music, including an analysis of the symphonic suite "Antar".

Tret'ya simfoniya [Symphony No. 3], Op. 32

834 Chaykovsky, Pëtr Il'ich. "Pyatoe simfonicheskoe sobranie." [Fifth Symphonic Meeting.] In Yakovlev, V. V., ed. *P. I. Chaykovsky. Muzykal'no-kriticheskie stat'i.* [P. I. Tchaikovsky. Musical-Critical Articles.] Moscow: Muzgiz, 1953: 227–29, 413.

A discussion of Rimsky-Korsakov's Third Symphony, which Tchaikovsky sees as suffering from an excess of technique over quality of ideas, though he praises the orchestration and harmonic combinations.

835 Kyui, Ts. A. [Cui, César]. "Kontsert Samarskogo komiteta v pol'zu golodayushchikh. Novaya simfoniya g. Korsakova i ego kapel'meystersky debyut." [Concert of the Samarian Committee to Help the Starving. A New Symphony by Mr. Korsakov and his Debut as a Conductor.] *Sanktpeterburgskie Vedomosti* 52 (22 February 1874). Reprinted: No. 1294: 242–46, 593.

Discusses the Third Symphony.

836 ——. "'Verter', liricheskaya opera Massne. Pervy Russky simfonichesky kontsert." [*Werther*, Lyrical Opera by Massenet. First Russian Symphony Concert.] *Novosti i Birzhevaya Gazeta* 22 (22 January 1896). Reprinted: No. 1294: 443–52, 615–16.

Includes a discussion of the Third Symphony.

837 Longyear, Rey M. "Communication." *JAMS* 39 (1) (Spring 1986): 216. ISSN: 0003-0139.

Bibliography: Musical Works 163

An amplification of Richard Taruskin's description of Rimsky-Korsakov's *Tret'ya simfoniya* [Symphony No. 3], Op. 32, which exists in two versions, a conventional one written in 1866–73 and a more adventurous one belonging to 1886.

Skazka [A Fairy Tale], Op. 29

838   Tovey, Sir Donald Francis. "Rimsky-Korsakov. CLXXXII. Conte Féerique, Op. 29." In D. F. Tovey. *Essays in Musical Analysis* Vol. IV: *Illustrative Music.* London: OUP, 1946: 140–43. Reprinted: London: OUP, 1969; 1972. ISBN-10: 0193151405. ISBN-13: 978-0193151406.

A short analysis of *Skazka* [Fairy Tale].

Capriccio espagnol. Kaprichchio na ispanskie temy [Spanish Caprice. Capriccio on Spanish Themes], Op. 34

839   Hale, Philip. "Rimsky-Korsakov viewed by Tschaikowsky and others." *Boston Symphony Orchestra Programmes,* Season 27. Boston, 1907–08: 1159–83.

A general discussion of the composer and his works, with special attention paid to the *Capriccio espagnol.* Has a wealth of peripheral information, and includes a number of references to contemporary critical articles.

840   Kyui, Tsezar' A. [Cui, César]. "Vtoroy Russky simfonichesky kontsert." [The Second Russian Symphony Concert.] *Grazhdanin* 42 (11 November 1887). Reprinted: No. 1294: 376–78, 608.

Includes a discussion of the *Capriccio espagnol.*

841   Sánchez, Ramón Sobrino. "José Inzenga: ¿Un zarzuelista fracasado?" [José Inzenga: An unsuccessful zarzuela composer?] In *Actualidad y futuro de la zarzuela: Actualidad y futuro de la zarzuela: Actas de las jornadas celebradas en Madrid del 7 al 9 de noviembre de 1991.* [Current and Future Zarzuela: Proceedings of the conference held in Madrid from 7-9 November 1991.] Madrid: Editorial Alpuerto, Fundación Caja de Madrid, 1994: 215–34. ISBN-10: 8438102085. ISBN-13: 978-8438102084.

Entitled "José Inzenga: An Unsuccessful *Zarzuela* Composer?," this article, written in Spanish, notes that although Inzenga was not successful as a *zarzuela* composer, themes from his collection of traditional Spanish melodies were used by Rimsky-Korsakov in his *Capriccio espagnol. Kaprichchio na ispanskie temy* [Spanish Caprice. Capriccio on Spanish Themes], Op. 34.

842   Stahl, Erik. "Lo hispánico en la música rusa." In Relaciones musicales entre España y Rusia/Muzykal'nye svyazy Rosii i Ispanii. Spain: Ministerio de

Educación y Cultura, 1999: 13–24. ISBN-10: 8487583296. ISBN-13: 978-8487583292.

An article in Spanish given at a seminar to mark the 150th anniversary of Glinka's visit to Spain, describing the musical relations between Spain and Russia from the seventeenth century. It includes discussion of Rimsky-Korsakov's *Capriccio espagnol. Kaprichchio na ispanskie temy* [Spanish Caprice. Capriccio on Spanish Themes], Op. 34.

Malorossiyskaya fantaziya [Little-Russian Fantasia]

843 Obram, V. "'Malorossiyskaya fantaziya' N. A. Rimskogo-Korsakova." [N. A. Rimsky-Korsakov's *Little-Russian Fantasy.*] In No. 1204, Vol. II: 248–52.

Discusses Rimsky-Korsakov's indebtedness to Ukrainian folk music and the employment of Ukrainian motives in the unfinished *Little-Russian Fantasy,* which exists in the form of 10 pages of penciled sketches and 14 pages of score.

Shekherazada. Simfonicheskaya syuita po 1001 nochi [Scheherazade. Symphonic Suite after the 1001 Nights], Op. 35

844 Abraham, Gerald. "The programme of 'Scheherazade'." *Monthly Musical Record* 63 (September 1933): 154–55.

A brief survey of the work's programmatic content and the composer's ambivalent attitude towards it.

845 ——. "New light on Old Friends. (a) The Programme of 'Scheherazade'." In No. 284: 138–43.

A discussion of the work's programmatic evolution.

846 Chernov, Konstantin Nikolaevich. "Programnye simfonicheskie proizvedeniya N. A. Rimskogo-Korsakova. V. 'Shekherazada', simfonicheskaya syuita (Op. 35)." [N. A. Rimsky-Korsakov's Symphonic Program Works. V. *Scheherazade,* Symphonic Suite (Op. 35).] *RMG* 50 (1905): cols. 1217–20; 51–52 (1905): cols. 1261–67.

An analysis of the Symphonic Suite, *Scheherazade,* with numerous music examples.

847 Donald, Paul. "Great Orchestra Works by Modern Composers. A Series of Papers of Important Symphonic Orchestra Works by Modern Composers, Describing Their Style, History, Characteristic Meaning and Illustrated with Thematic Extracts." 5. *Scheherazade,* Symphonic Suite, after "The Thousand Nights and a Night" for Orchestra, Op. 35, by Nicolas A. Rimsky-Korsakoff." In *Metronome* 32 (8) New York (1916): 46–47.

A description of *Scheherazade* with 14 music examples and a short note by the composer.

Bibliography: Musical Works   165

848   Kyui, Ts. A. [Cui, César]. "Russkie simfonicheskie kontserty." [The Russian
        Symphony Concerts.] *Muzykal'noe Obozrenie.* (27 October 1888).

        Discusses the Symphonic Suite, *Scheherazade.*

849   Lepel, Felix von. *Nikolai Andrejewitsch Rimsky-Korssakow. Bildnis eines
        grossen russischen Opernkomponisten und Sinfonikers.* Berlin-Charlottenburg:
        Privatsdruck, 1955. 16 pp.

        A sympathetic account of the composer and his work, referring several times
        to performances of *Scheherazade* as a ballet-pantomime in the former Dresden
        Hof- und Staatsoper and in Berlin, seeing Rimsky-Korsakov as a "genialer
        Meister des tonmalerischen Ausdrucks und ein glänzender Beherrscher des
        Orchesters," in which are combined the sophisticated harmonic resources
        of contemporary European harmony with the simplicity of the old Russian
        church chants. Mention is also made of his distinguished pupils.

850   Mason, Daniel Gregory. "Short Studies of Great Masterpieces. IV. Symphonic
        Suite, 'Scheherazade,' by Nicolas Rimsky-Korsakoff, Opus 35." *The New
        Music Review* 16 (182) (1917): 426–30.

        A descriptive account of *Scheherazade*, with numerous music examples,
        preceded by a short historical note. Observations on the characters in the
        work as recounted in the *Arabian Nights' Entertainments.*

851   Nectoux, Jean-Michel. "Shéhérazade, danse, musiques." *Romantisme: Revue
        de la Société des Études Romantiques* (78) (October–December 1992): 35.
        ISSN: 0048-8593.

        An article discussing different settings of *Sheherazade* both as an orchestral
        work and as a ballet, including an account of the first perfomance in Paris
        of Rimsky-Korsakov's *Sheherazade.* A French translation of the *Book of the
        Thousand Nights and One Night*, entitled *Mille et une nuits*, was made by J.
        C. Mardrus in 1903.

852   Vuillermoz, E. "A propos de Schéhérazade de Rimsky-Korsakoff." *Le Courrier
        Musical* 8 (15 February 1905): 104–06.

        A witty discussion of the New Russian School and its significance, with
        special reference to *Scheherazade.*

**Svetly prazdnik. Voskresnaya uvertyura na temy iz Obikhoda [Joyous Festival.
Easter Overture on Themes from the Obikhod], Op. 36**

853   Kyui, Ts. A. [Cui, César]. "Trety Russky simfonichesky kontsert." [Third
        Russian Symphony Concert.] *Muzykal'noe Obozrenie* (8 December 1888).

        A discussion of the Russian Easter Festival Overture.

854   Werck, Isabelle. "L'ouverture de la Grande Pâque russe de Nicolaï Rimsky-
        Korsakov." *Revue musicale de Suisse romande* 58 (3) (2005): 38–44. ISSN: 0035-
        3744.

Takes the form of a formal analysis of Rimsky-Korsakov's Overture *Svetly prazdnik* [Russian Easter Festival], composed in July–August 1888, noting that, structurally, the work consists of a slow introduction followed by an *Allegro* in sonata form.

Zolotoy petushok [The Golden Cockerel], Suite

855 Feinberg, Saul. "Rimsky-Korsakov's Suite from Le Coq d'Or." *Music Review* 30 (February 1969): 47–64.

A discussion of the influence of the "Korsakovian tradition and heritage" on composers associated with the St. Petersburg Conservatory, particularly Stravinsky, Prokofiev, and Shostakovich, together with a detailed examination of the Suite from *The Golden Cockerel* and its relationship to the opera as a whole.

SOLO INSTRUMENT WITH ORCHESTRA

Kontsert dlya fortepiano s orkestrom [Concerto for piano and orchestra], Op. 30

856 Garden, Edward. "Three Russian Piano Concertos." *ML* 60 (1) (1979): 166–79.

A comparative examination of three piano concertos by Balakirev, Rimsky-Korsakov, and Tchaikovsky, discussing their evolution and structure. A discussion of Rimsky-Korsakov's Piano Concerto in C-sharp minor, a one-movement work outstanding in its homogeneity and brevity of statement, based on transformations of a Russian folk song, can be found on pp. 172–73.

857 Kyui, Ts. A. [Cui, César]. "Obshchedostupny Russky simfonichesky kontsert." [A Popular Russian Symphony Concert.] *Muzykal'noe Obozrenie* 11 (5 December 1885). Reprinted: No. 1294: 335–40, 605.

Includes a discussion of Rimsky-Korsakov's Piano Concerto.

858 Norris, Jeremy P. "A Note on Balakirev's Piano Concerto." *MT* 131 (1769) (July 1990): 361–62. ISSN: 0027-4666.

A discussion of the employment of the Russian folk song *Sobiraytes'-ka, brattsy-rebyatushki* [Gather Round, Fellow Brothers] by several composers, in particular Rimsky-Korsakov in his *Kontsert dlya fortepiano s orkestrom* [Concerto for piano and orchestra], Op. 30.

859 ——. "The Development of the Russian Piano Concerto in the 19th Century." PhD dissertation, University of Sheffield, 1989. Published under the title: *The Russian Piano Concerto*. Vol. 1: *The Nineteenth Century*. In *Russian Music Studies*. Bloomington: Indiana University Press, 1994. xii, 228 pp. ISBN-10: 0253341124. ISBN-13: 9780253341129.

Bibliography: Musical Works   *167*

A discussion of the evolution of the piano concerto in Russia, including Rimsky-Korsakov's *Kontsert dlya fortepiano s orkestrom* [Concerto for piano and orchestra], Op. 30.

860   Orlov, Genrikh Aleksandrovich. *Sovetsky fortep'yanny kontsert.* [The Soviet Piano Concerto.] Moscow: Muzgiz, 1954. 211 pp.

For references to Rimsky-Korsakov, see pp. 6, 9, 34, 36, 38, 49–50.

861   Smirnov, Mstislav Anatol'evich. *Fortepiannye proizvedeniya kompozitorov "Moguchey kuchki".* [The Piano Works of the Composers of the "Mighty Handful".] Moscow: Muzyka, 1971. 114 pp.

For an examination of Rimsky-Korsakov's Piano Concerto, paying special attention to folk elements, which are considered to be of particular importance, see pp. 47–56. The work is seen as playing a significant part in the development of the Russian piano concerto. No index or bibliography.

862   ——. *Russkaya fortepiannaya muzyka. Cherty svoeobraziya.* [Russian Piano Music. Features of Originality.] Moscow: Muzyka, 1983. 335 pp.

For a discussion of Rimsky-Korsakov's Piano Concerto, see pp. 297–301, although, unlike Smirnov's 1971 volume [see No. 861], there are no music examples. Emphasis is placed on the concerto's novel features, both structural and harmonic.

863   Strel'nikov, Nikolay Mikhaylovich. "Umnoe delanie." [A Clever Piece of Artifice.] *Zhizn' iskusstva* 246 (1919).

A discussion of the Piano Concerto, noting its ingenious monothematic structure.

Kontsertnaya fantaziya na russkie temy dlya skripki s orkestrom [Concert Fantasia on Russian Themes for violin and orchestra], Op. 33

864   Kyui, Ts. A. [Cui, César]. "Posledny Russky simfonichesky kontsert." [The last Russian Symphony Concert.] *Grazhdanin* (16 December 1887).

Concerns the Fantasy for violin and orchestra.

CHAMBER WORKS

Strunny kvartet. F-dur [String Quartet in F major], Op. 12

865   Larosh, German Avgustovich. "Muzykal'nye ocherki… kvartetnye sobraniya muzykal'nogo obshchestva i novoe proizvedenie g. Rimskogo-Korsakova." [Musical Sketches…Quartet Meetings of the Musical Society and a New Work by Mr. Rimsky-Korsakov.] *Golos* (13 November 1875).

Concerns the String Quartet in F major, Op. 12.

168   *Nikolay Andreevich Rimsky-Korsakov: A Research and Information Guide*

Sekstet dlya dvukh skripok, dvukh al'tov i dvukh violoncheley [Sextet for two violins, two violas and two cellos]

866   Myaskovsky, Nikolay Yakovlevich. "N. Rimsky-Korsakov. Sekstet dlya 2-kh skripok, 2-kh al'tov i 2-kh violoncheley (A-dur), posmertnoe izdanie, partitura. Ts. 70k. Izd. Rossiysk. Muzyk. Izdat." [N. Rimsky-Korsakov. Sextet for 2 Violins, 2 Violas and 2 Cellos (A Major), Posthumous Edition, Score. Price 70k. Pub. Russian Music Publishing House.] *Muzyka* 80 (6 June 1912): 514. Reprinted: S. Shlifshteyn, ed. *N. Ya. Myaskovsky. Sobranie materialov v dvukh tomakh. Tom vtoroy. Literaturnoe nasledie. Pis'ma.* [Myaskovsky. Collection of Materials in Two Volumes. Volume II. Literary legacy. Letters.] Moscow: Muzyka, 1964: 73–74.

       A short account of Rimsky-Korsakov's String Sextet, edited by M. Shteynberg, which Myaskovsky finds complete, cheerful, and interesting, the second, third, and fourth movements having a beautiful sonority.

867   Raaben, Lev Nikolaevich. "Kompozitory 'Novoy russkoy shkoly'." [The Composers of the "New Russian School".] In L. N. Raaben. *Instrumental'ny ansambl' v russkoy muzyke.* [The Instrumental Ensemble in Russian Music.] Moscow: Muzgiz, 1961: 287–328.

       Includes a discussion of Rimsky-Korsakov's chamber works, together with the circumstances of composition, place in the composer's output, and a short structural analysis.

868   Sabaneiev, L. "Rimsky-Korsakov." In Walter W. Cobbett, ed. *Cyclopedic Survey of Chamber Music.* Second edition, Vol. II. London: OUP, 1963: 297–98. Reprinted: OUP, 1987. ISBN-10: 0193183064. ISBN-13: 978-0193183063.

       An essay on Rimsky-Korsakov's chamber music, with special reference to the works written for the Belyaev Circle [see Nos. 66 and 67].

Trio dlya fortepiano, skripki i violoncheli [Trio for piano, violin and cello]

869   Gaydamovich, Tat'yana Alekseevna. *Russkoe fortepiannoe trio: Istoriya zhanra. Voprosy interpretatsii.* [The Russian Piano Trio: History of the Genre. Problems of Interpretation.] PhD dissertation, Gosudarstvennaya Konservatoriya imeni P. I. Chaykovskogo. Moskva. [State Conservatory named after P. I. Tchaikovsky. Moscow.] Moscow, 1993. Published: Moscow: Muzyka, 2005. 263 pp. ISBN-10: 506158922X. ISBN-13: 978-5061589220.

       A discussion of the history of the piano trio in Russia, including Rimsky-Korsakov's *Trio dlya fortepiano, skripki i violoncheli* [Trio for piano, violin and cello], composed in 1897 and completed by his son-in-law Maksimilian Shteynberg in 1939.

Bibliography: Musical Works

PIANO WORKS

870 Alekseev, Aleksandr Dmitrievich. "Fortepiannoe tvorchestvo Rimskogo-Korsakova." [Rimsky-Korsakov's Piano Works.] In *Russkaya fortepiannaya muzyka. Ot istokov do vershin tvorchestva.* [Russian Piano Music. From its Origins to the Heights of its Achievement.] Moscow: Izd. Akad. Nauk, 1963: 219–47.

A substantial discussion of Rimsky-Korsakov's keyboard works, including the Piano Concerto, describing mode of composition and place in the composer's output, with a structural analysis. Numerous music examples.

871 Belyaev. V. "Fugi Rimskogo-Korsakova, Op. 17." [Rimsky-Korsakov's Fugues, Op. 17.] *Muzyka* 176, 177 (1914).

One of the earliest analytical articles by the ethnomusicologist Viktor Belyaev (1888–1968).

872 Maksimov, Evgeny Ivanovich. "Fenomen kollektivnykh variatsiy v *Parafrazakh* russkikh kompozitorov." [The Phenomenon of Collective Variations in *Paraphrases* by Russian Composers.] In *Nasledie: Russkaya muzyka – mirovaya kul'tura.* [Legacy: Russian Music – World Culture.] Russian Federation, 2009.

An examination of the circumstances surrounding the composition of the collective work *Parafrazy na neizmenyaemuyu izvestnuyu temu* [Paraphrases on an Unchanging Well Known Theme], composed in 1878 by Borodin, Cui, Lyadov, Rimsky-Korsakov, and Franz Liszt.

873 Smirnov, Mstislav Anatol'evich. *Fortepiannye proizvedeniya kompozitorov moguchey kuchki.* [The Piano Works of the Composers of the Mighty Handful.] Moscow: Muzyka, 1971.

CHORAL WORKS: SACRED

874 Brill, Nicholas P. *History of Russian Church Music.* Bloomington, Il.: Nicholas P. Brill, 1980: 112–13.

A discussion of Rimsky-Korsakov's work at the Imperial Chapel and a brief examination of some of his sacred compositions and his significance as a writer of liturgical music.

875 Gardner, I. A. [Johann von]. *Bogosluzhebnoe penie russkoy pravoslavnoy tserkvi. Sushchnost', sistema i istoriya. Izdaëtsya pri sodeystvii russkago pravoslavnago bogoslovskago fonda v N'yu Iorke.* [The Divine Chant of the Russian Orthodox Church. Essence, System and History. Published with the Help of the Russian Orthodox Theological Fund in New York.] Vol. l. Jordanville, NY: Holy Trinity Russian Orthodox Monastery, 1978; Vol. II, NY, 1982. ISBN-10: 0884650081. ISBN-13: 978-0884650089.

For Rimsky-Korsakov's sacred music, the nature of his compositions and his work in the Imperial Chapel, see pp. 433–35, 437–38, 454, and 550.

876 Kandinsky, Aleksey Ivanovich. "*Vsenoshchnoe bdenie* Rakhmaninova i russkoe iskusstvo rubezha vekov." [Rachmaninov's *All-Night Vigil* and Russian Art at the Crossroads of the Centuries.] *SM* 55 (5) (1991): 4. ISSN: 0131-6818.

An account of Rachmaninov's *Vsenoshchnoe bdenie* [All-night Vigil] and its place in Russian liturgical music alongside the sacred music of composers such as Rimsky-Korsakov.

877 Klimenko, Tat'yana Valer'evna. "Dukhovnye sochineniya russkikh kompozitorov XIX veka: Garmonichesky aspekt." [Sacred Compositions of Russian Composers of the 19th Century: Aspects of Harmony.] *MA* (3) (2008): 50-55. ISSN: 0869-4516.

An examination of the harmonization of church hymns in the sacred works of Glinka, Tchaikovsky, and Rimsky-Korsakov, including excerpts from their correspondence outlining their views [see in particular pp. 53–55].

878 Kompaneysky, Nikolay Ivanovich. "Znachenie N. A. Rimskogo-Korsakova v russkoy tserkovnoy muzyke." [N. A. Rimsky-Korsakov's Significance in Russian Sacred Music.] *RMG* (1908): cols. 837–42.

Kompaneysky's conclusion is that the few liturgical works Rimsky-Korsakov did compose were of "enormous significance," indicating a new direction for subsequent composers of sacred music. Forms part of the special memorial issue of *RMG*.

879 Lisitsyn, Mikhail Aleksandrovich. *Obzor Dukhovno-Muzykal'noy literatury. 110 avtorov, okolo 1500 proizvedeniy.* [A Survey of Sacred Musical Literature. 110 authors, about 1500 works.] St. Petersburg, 1901. 315 pp.

For a description of Rimsky-Korsakov's sacred works, including *St. John of the Golden Mouth Liturgy, Our Father*, and Cherubic hymns, see pp. 268–70. Lisitsyn comments on their simplicity and directness, observing that the settings of the Obikhod chants are notable for their strict liturgical contrapuntal style and are attractive both musically and artistically.

880 Metallov, Vasily Mikhaylovich. *Ocherk istorii Pravoslavnogo Tserkovnogo peniya v Rossii.* [Outline of the History of Orthodox Church Chant in Russia.] Moscow: Tipografiya G. Lissnera i A. Geshelya, 1900. 154 pp.

Contains a short section on the characteristic features of Rimsky-Korsakov's sacred music.

881 Morosan, Vladimir. *Choral Performance in Pre-Revolutionary Russia.* Ann Arbor, Michigan: UMI Research Press, 1986. 398 pp. ISBN-10: 0835717135. ISBN-13: 978-0835717137.

Bibliography: Musical Works 171

For Balakirev's and Rimsky-Korsakov's work in the Imperial Chapel, see pp. 96–97 and 168–69. Lists the total number of the composer's small sacred works as 40, p. 93, and notes that he also preferred the sound of women's and men's voices to that of boys, p. 157.

882 ——, ed. *Monuments of Russian Sacred Music*, III: *Nikolai Rimsky-Korsakov. Polnoye sobraniye duhovno-muzïkal'nïh proizvedeniy.* [Nikolay Rimsky-Korsakov. The Complete Collection of Sacred Musical Works.], with intro. by Marina Rakhmanova. Madison, CT: Musica Russica, 1999. xli, 356 pp. ISBN: 0962946095. ISBN-13: 978-0962946097.

Preceded by an authoritative introduction entitled "The Sacred Choral Works of Nikolai Rimsky-Korsakov" by Marina Rakhmanova, translated by Vl. Morosan, the volume, which includes *a cappella* works for 4-8 voices and unison chants, is divided into four sections containing three collections:

Collection 1: Sacred Musical Compositions used at the Imperial Court.
Collection 2: Sacred Musical Chant Arrangements.
Rimsky-Korsakov's setting of "We Praise Thee, O God" for double chorus.
Collection 3: Sacred Musical Compositions and Arrangements.

The three appendices contain "Critical Notes," "The Unison Chants used by Rimsky-Korsakov," and "Notes on the RUSSICA TM Transliteration System." Excellent translations of all relevant materials, including the texts of the sacred works, are provided throughout. Rimsky-Korsakov's complete sacred choral works have been recorded on CD by the Moscow sacred music ensemble "Blagovest" under the direction of Galina Kol'tsova, released on the German label Cantica/Duophon, No. 03013/2 [p. xxxi, note].

883 Preobrazhensky, Antonin Viktorovich. *Kul'tovaya muzyka v Rossii.* [Religious Music in Russia.] Leningrad: Academia, 1924. 123 pp.

For an examination of the work of Balakirev and Rimsky-Korsakov in the Imperial Chapel, including a discussion of Rimsky-Korsakov's sacred music and his method of approach in harmonizing Russian chant, see Chapter XVIII, pp. 107–11.

884 Rakhmanova, Marina Pavlovna. "Duhovnaya muzyka." [Religious Music.] *MA* (2) (1994): 51–63. ISSN: 0869-4516.

A discussion of Rimsky-Korsakov's sacred compositions, his arrangements of religious music, and his work with the Imperial Court Choir, written by a leading Russian specialist, including a number of letters.

885 Vasil'ev, Vladimir. "Dirizhërsko-khorovoe obrazovanie v Rossii kontsa XIX i nachala XX vekov." [Choral-Conducting Training in Russia in the Late 19th and early 20th centuries.] MA dissertation, Pedagogy, Leningrad: Leningradskaya Gosudarstvennaya Konservatoriya, 1981. 22 pp.

In the summary of the thesis, the author describes teaching at the former Imperial Chapel and the part played by Rimsky-Korsakov and his compositions.

886   Zolotarëv, Vasily Andreevich. "Nikolay Andreevich Rimsky-Korsakov v Pevcheskoy kapelle. Iz vospominaniy uchenika." [Nikolay Andreevich Rimsky-Korsakov in the Choral Chapel. A Pupil's Recollections.] *SM* 9 (1948): 52–56.

Zolotarëv's reminiscences of his time as a pupil at the Imperial Chapel, written from memory many years later. Compares Balakirev's and Rimsky-Korsakov's methods, and describes the evolution of the Chapel School Orchestra from a small string body to a larger ensemble, including a reproduction of a program of a concert in 1889 in which Zolotarëv participated as a violinist. Gives details of vocal training in which there was complete uniformity of voices, producing an organ-like sonority. Rimsky-Korsakov often used the orchestra as a vehicle to try out new compositions.

CHORAL WORKS: SECULAR

887   Derzhanovsky, V. "K ispolneniyu prelyudii-kantaty 'Iz Gomera'." [On the Performance of the Prelude-Cantata *From Homer.*] *Muzyka* 28 (1911): 602–03.

Signed "Vl. D.," this is an account of the choral work *From Homer,* accompanied by the text.

888   M. "Novye sochineniya Rimskogo-Korsakova. 'Svitezyanka'." [New Works by Rimsky-Korsakov. *Svitezyanka.*] *RMG* 10 (1898): cols. 908–09.

A critical review of the work which the writer describes as "being written only for himself, with exceptional facility, over a cup of tea, by way of a rest from other more serious labours."

889   Seaman, Gerald. "Slavonic Nationalism from Dvořák to the Soviets." In A. Jacobs, ed. *Choral Music. A Symposium.* London: Pelican, 1963: 286–304. Second edition, 1979. ISBN-10: 0140205330. ISBN-13: 978-0140205336.

Includes a brief discussion of his four cantatas and unaccompanied choruses.

890   Skaftymova, Lyudmila Aleksandrovna. *Vokal'no-simfonicheskoe tvorchestvo S. V. Rakhmaninova i russkaya kantata nachala XX veka.* [The Vocal-Symphonic Works of S. V. Rakhmaninov and the Russian Cantata at the Beginning of the 20th Century.] PhD dissertation, Gosudarstvennaya Konservatoriya imeni Rimskogo-Korsakova, Sankt-Peterburg [State Conservatory named after Rimsky-Korsakov, St. Petersburg], 1998.

An analysis of the cantatas of Rakhmaninov compared with other Russian cantatas of the period, including Rimsky-Korsakov's *Iz Gomera* [From Homer] and *Svitezyanka.*

Bibliography: Musical Works 173

VOCAL WORKS

891   Abraham, Gerald. "Rimsky-Korsakov's Songs." *Monthly Musical Record.* 74 (1944): 51–57. Reprinted: *Slavonic and Romantic Music.* London: Faber & Faber, 1968: Chapter XIII, 202–13. Reprinted: London: Faber & Faber, 2013. ISBN-10: 0571302807. ISBN-13: 978-0571302802.

Abraham considers that approximately a dozen of Rimsky-Korsakov's 80 songs are of significance. The writing of his songs falls into three widely separated groups: some two dozen early songs, a few composed c. 1882, and a large number in 1897–98. While the early songs have a warmth and vitality, most of the later songs show a more cerebral approach. Outstanding are the songs "Plenivshis' rozoy, solovey" [Enslaved by the Rose, the Nightingale], Op. 2, No. 2 ("interesting as the earliest of the composer's essays in the pseudo-oriental") and the "Kolybel'naya pesnya" [Cradle Song], Op. 2, No. 3, used later in the second version of *The Maid of Pskov.* Also highly rated are "Na Kholmakh Gruzii" [On the Hills of Georgia], Op. 3, No. 4, and "Nochevala tuchka zolotaya" [The Golden Cloud has Slept], Op. 3, No. 3. Of the remaining songs, those of his middle period are considered technically faultless but lacking in imagination, while only a few of the 1897–98 group rise above the mediocre. Abraham illustrates technical details by means of music examples, drawing comparisons with Tchaikovsky's settings of identical texts.

892   ——. "Russia." In Denis Stevens, ed. *A History of Song.* London: Hutchinson, 1960: 338–75. Reprinted: *Slavonic and Romantic Music.* London: Faber & Faber, 1968: 202–11; 2013. ISBN-10: 0571302807. ISBN-13: 978-0571302802.

For a discussion of Rimsky-Korsakov's songs, a condensed version of the survey in *The Monthly Musical Record* 74 (1944): 51–57, see pp. 358–61.

893   Berry, C. "Vocal Duets by Nineteenth-Century Russian Composers." *Music Review* 45 (1) (1984): 4–5.

A short discussion of Rimsky-Korsakov's vocal duets Op. 47, Nos. 1 and 2, and Op. 52, Nos. 1 and 2, written in the period 1897–98, the former reflecting his interest in Russian folk song, the latter "his absorption of Western forms and techniques."

894   Famintsyn, Aleksandr Sergeevich. "Novye russkie romansy." [New Russian Songs.] *Muzykal'ny Sezon* (5 February 1870).

A discussion of Rimsky-Korsakov as a vocal composer.

895   Kuznetsov, Konstantin Alekseevich. "N. Rimsky-Korsakov. Polnoe sobranie sochineniy. Tom 45. Romansy. Muzgiz, 1946." [N. Rimsky-Korsakov. Complete Collection of Works. Vol. 45. Songs. Muzgiz, 1946.] *SM* 6 (1948): 103–04.

A criticism of Vol. 45 of the composer's *Complete Works* (Rimsky-Korsakov's Songs), together with a general discussion of the manuscript sources, variants, and his approach towards vocal composition.

896   Kyui, Tsezar A. [Cui, César]. *Russky romans. Ocherk ego razvitiya.* [The Russian Romance. An Outline of its Development.] St. Petersburg, N. F. Findeyzen, 1896. 211 pp.

For a discussion of Rimsky-Korsakov's songs, see pp. 136–52. Cui praises Rimsky-Korsakov's meticulous, fastidious approach in the setting of text, the accuracy of verbal stresses, the avoidance of word repetition and the employment of attractive harmonies. He notes the composer's rather cold, passionless approach and the lack of gratifying melodic lines. Cui suggests that the best songs are those of a descriptive nature, "landscapes in sound," and he comments that Rimsky-Korsakov responds well to verses of outstanding poets such as Pushkin and Lermontov.

897   M. "Novye sochineniya Rimskogo-Korsakova. ('U morya,' 'Anchara,' 'Prorok')." [New Works by Rimsky-Korsakov. ("By the Sea," "The Upas Tree," "The Prophet").] *RMG* 11 (1898): 1009–12.

A review of some of the stylistic features of Rimsky-Korsakov's songs.

898   ——. "Novye sochineniya Rimskogo-Korsakova. 4 romansa dlya tenora, Op. 55; 2 romansa dlya soprano, Op. 56. Izdanie M. P. Belyaeva v Leyptsige." [New Works by Rimsky-Korsakov. 4 Songs for Tenor, Op. 55; 2 Songs for Soprano, Op. 56. Published M. P. Belaieff, Leipzig.] *RMG* 21–22 (1899): cols. 607–09.

A review of Rimsky-Korsakov's Op. 55 and 56 with observations on their structure and relationship of words to music.

899   Maggid, Sofiya Davidovna. "Stilisticheskie osobennosti romansov N. A. Rimskogo-Korsakova." [Stylistic Peculiarities of N. A. Rimsky-Korsakov's Romances.] In B. V. Asaf'ev. *Russky romans.* [The Russian Romance.] Moscow-Leningrad: Academia, 1930: 147–67.

Following a short account of Rimsky-Korsakov's songs, pointing out that they were written at irregular intervals, Maggid examines the romances under four main headings: "Musical fabric" (rhythmic organization, modal elements, tetrachordal structure, characteristic intervals, etc.), "Oriental romances," "Landscape and coloring in Rimsky-Korsakov's romances," and "Lyrical-meditative romances." While noting that many of the songs are repressed in nature, Maggid observes that the most singable melodies often have an instrumental rather than a vocal character.

900   Vasina-Grossman, Vera Andreevna. *Russky klassichesky romans XIX veka.* [The Russian Classical Romance of the 19th Century.] Moscow: Izd. Akad. Nauk SSR, 1956. 352 pp. Review: *SM* 7 (July 1957): 145–48.

Bibliography: Musical Works 175

For Rimsky-Korsakov's songs, together with nine music examples, see pp. 228–52. Vasina-Grossman examines the songs chronologically, noting their relationship with other works of the period. Circumstances of composition are described, and the chapter has many extracts from Rimsky-Korsakov's writings and those of contemporary scholars.

901 ——. "Polska poezja w piesni rosyjskiej." [Polish Poetry in Russian Song.] In Z. Lissa, ed. *Polsko-rosyjskie miscellanea muzyczne.* [Polish-Russian Music Miscellanea.] Kraków: Polskie Wyd. Muz., 1967.

Includes discussion of some of the composer's songs based on Polish texts of Mickiewicz.

RIMSKY-KORSAKOV: EDITOR

902 Tiersot, Julien. "Russian Composers as Described by Themselves." *MQ* 7 (3) (1921): 376–98.

A discussion of music in Russia in the second half of the nineteenth century as seen primarily through the eyes of Rimsky-Korsakov and related in his *Chronicle*. Discusses the part played by the composer in editing and completing his colleagues' works. Includes discussion of the last years of his life.

Borodin

903 Abraham, Gerald. "The History of 'Prince Igor'." In No. 284: 147–168.

Includes discussion of Rimsky-Korsakov's work in completing and editing the opera.

904 Belyaev, Viktor Mikhaylovich. *Aleksandr Konstantinovich Glazunov. Materialy k ego biografii. Tom 1-y. Zhizn'.* [Glazunov. Materials for his Biography. Vol. 1. Life.] Peterburg: Gosudarstvennaya Filarmoniya, 1922. 150 pp.

For excerpts from Rimsky-Korsakov's letters to M. P. Belyaev, written in 1888, which deal with the publication of Borodin's *Prince Igor,* completed by Glazunov and Rimsky-Korsakov and published on 30 October of that year, see pp. 125–28.

905 Bobéth, Marek. "Borodin und seine Oper 'Fürst Igor': Geschichte – Analyse – Konsequenzen." PhD dissertation, Musicology, Freie University, 1979. 223 pp. Published: Wiesenfelden: Bernd Katzbichler, 1982. ISBN-10: 3873970481. ISBN-13: 978-3873970489. Reviews: Alfred Clayton. *Die Musikforschung* 38 (3) (1985): 232. ISSN: 0027-4801. Detlef Gojowy. *Musica* (Germany) 39 (2) (1985): 199. ISSN: 0027-4518. Michael Stegemann. *Neue Zeitschrift für Musik* 145 (9) (1984): 52.

This examination of Borodin's *Prince Igor* attempts to assess the part played by Rimsky-Korsakov and Glazunov in its composition.

906 Bulycheva, Anna Valentinovna. "*Knyaz' Igor'* Borodina i Rimsky-Korsakov." [Borodin's and Rimsky-Korsakov's *Prince Igor*.] *Opera musicologica: Nauchny zhurnal Sankt-Peterburgskoy konservatorii* [Opera Musicologica: Scientific Journal of the St. Petersburg Conservatory] 4 (6) (2010): 70. ISSN: 2075-4078.

A description of the work undertaken by the author in restoring Borodin's original version of the opera *Knyaz' Igor'*, postulating the argument that Borodin's opera was all but complete when Rimsky-Korsakov and Glazunov set about the task of editing it.

907 Domokos, Zsuzsanna. "Monológ vagy ária: Igor herceg áriájának korábbi változata Borogyin operájában." [Monologue or Aria: The First Version of Prince Igor's Aria in Borodin's Opera.] *Magyar zene: zenetudományi folyóirat* 34 (3) (1993): 299–332. ISSN: 0025-0384.

An edition of the little-known first version of Prince Igor's aria in Act II of Borodin's eponymous opera, based on the MS copy in RNB, including discussion of the editorial role of Rimsky-Korsakov.

908 Gribanova, Anastasiya Petrovna. "Iz istorii Vtorogo kvarteta A. P. Borodina." [On the History of A. P. Borodin's Second Quartet.] In V. M. Vasil'eva, comp. *N. A. Rimsky-Korsakov i russkaya khudozhestvennaya kul'tura. Materialy nauchnoy konferentsii. Vechasha-Lyubensk.* [N. A. Rimsky-Korsakov and Russian Artistic Culture. Materials from a Scientific Conference. Vechasha-Lyubensk.] Pskov, 2008.

An examination of Rimsky-Korsakov's arrangement for violin and orchestra of Borodin's Nocturne from the String Quartet No. 2.

909 Lloyd-Jones, David. "Towards a Scholarly Edition of Borodin's Symphonies." *Soundings* VI (1977): 81–87.

It was previously considered that Rimsky-Korsakov and Glazunov were responsible for the editing of both Borodin's First and Second Symphonies. It now seems clear that Borodin prepared the score of the First Symphony himself and that Rimsky-Korsakov's alterations to the score of the Second Symphony were of a minor nature.

910 Montes, Roberto. "El principe Igor de Alexander Borodin." *Melómano: La revista de música clásica* 13 (137) (December 2008): 26. ISSN: 1136-4939.

An article written in Spanish describing the history of Borodin's opera *Prince Igor* and its completion by Rimsky-Korsakov and Glazunov.

Dargomyzhsky

911 Abraham, Gerald. "The Stone Guest." In No. 283: 68–86.

Mentions Rimsky-Korsakov's work in editing Dargomyzhsky's opera *The Stone Guest*.

912 Ratser, Evgeny Yakovlevich. "Zagadki *Kamennogo gostya*." [The Riddles of *The Stone Guest*.] *SM* 52 (6) (1988): 86. ISSN: 0131-6818.

A critical examination of the additions and alterations made to Dargomyzhsky's score *Kamenny gost'* [The Stone Guest] by Rimsky-Korsakov, the orchestral score of which was published in 1870.

Glinka

913 Guseynova, Zivar Mahmudovna. "N. A. Rimsky-Korsakov i A. K. Glazunov – redaktory *Zhizni za tsarya*." [N. A. Rimsky-Korsakov and A. K. Glazunov – Editors of *A Life for the Tsar*.] In V. M. Vasil'eva, comp. *N. A. Rimsky-Korsakov i russkaya khudozhestvennaya kul'tura. Materialy nauchnoy konferentsii. Vechasha-Lyubensk.* [N. A. Rimsky-Korsakov and Russian Artistic Culture. Materials from a Scientific Conference. Vechasha-Lyubensk.] Pskov, 2008.

An examination of Rimsky-Korsakov's and Glazunov's remarks and corrections made during the course of their editing of Glinka's manuscripts, in particular Glinka's *Zhizn' za tsarya* [A Life for the Tsar].

Musorgsky

914 Akulov, Evgeny F. and Pokrovsky, Boris Aleksandrovich. *Tri Borisa: Sravnitel'ny muzykal'no-dramatichesky analiz partitur opery Boris Godunov Musorgskogo, Rimskogo-Korsakova, Shostakovicha.* [Three Borises: A Musical-Dramatic Analysis of the Scores of the Opera *Boris Godunov* as edited by Musorgsky, Rimsky-Korsakov, and Shostakovich.] Russian Federation, 1997.

A musical-dramatic analysis comparing three versions of Musorgsky's *Boris Godunov*: Musorgsky's own, and those of Rimsky-Korsakov and Shostakovich.

915 Calvocoressi, Michael Dimitri. *Modest Mussorgsky. His Life and Works.* London: Rockliff, 1956. xix, 322 pp.

Among the many references to Rimsky-Korsakov and his compositions, of particular importance is Chapter XV, which discusses the part played by Rimsky-Korsakov in editing Musorgsky's works. The bibliographical references to articles in European periodicals should be noted.

916 Gozenpud, Abram Akimovich "V bor'be za nasledie Musorgskogo." [In the Struggle for Musorgsky's Legacy.] *SM* 3 (1956): 88–93.

On the question of Rimsky-Korsakov as an editor of Musorgsky's works, describing problems with censorship and bureaucracy in his efforts to have the works performed.

178   *Nikolay Andreevich Rimsky-Korsakov: A Research and Information Guide*

917   Keldysh, Yu. and Yakovlev, V., eds. *M. P. Musorgsky. K pyatidesyatiletiyu so dnya smerti 1881-1931. Stat'i i materialy.* [M. P. Musorgsky. On the Fiftieth Anniversary of his Death 1881-1931. Articles and Materials.] Moscow: Muzgiz, 1932. 350 pp.

        Includes references to Rimsky-Korsakov's editing of various Musorgsky scores, and the difference in outlook between the two composers.

918   Kunin, Iosif Filippovich. "Rimsky-Korsakov i Musorgsky." [Rimsky-Korsakov and Musorgsky.] *MZ* 5 (1969): 4–5.

        A discussion of Rimsky-Korsakov's role in editing and completing Musorgsky's work and their joint achievement.

919   Mooser, Robert-Aloys. "Rimsky-Korsakof contra Moussorgsky." *Schweizerische Musikzeitung* 101 (1961): 28–33.

        Using the Soviet edition of Yastrebtsëv's *Memoirs of Rimsky-Korsakov*, Mooser highlights the essentially antipathetical natures of Rimsky-Korsakov and Musorgsky, suggesting that their different esthetic outlooks could only lead to incompatability and that Musorgsky's harmonic innovations were beyond Rimsky-Korsakov's grasp.

920   Petrovsky, Evgeny M. "Vozobnovlenny *Boris* (fragmenty)." [*Boris* Revived (Fragments).] *MA* (2) (1994): 66–70. ISSN: 0869-4516.

        A discussion of the differences between Musorgsky's *Boris Godunov* in its original version and its re-orchestration by Rimsky-Korsakov on the occasion of a revival performance of the opera at the St. Petersburg Mariinsky Theater, together with observations taken from *RMG* 47, 49, 50, 51, 52 (1904).

921   Redlich, Hans F. "Modest Moussorgsky redivivus." *Anbruch* 11 (1929): 70–78.

        Redlich suggests that Rimsky-Korsakov often lessened the impact of Musorgsky's harmonies when editing his music, illustrated by comparative examples taken from Musorgsky's original versions, published by Pavel Lamm, and the same works as edited by Rimsky-Korsakov.

922   Teterina, Nadezhda Ivanovna. "V redaktsii Rimskogo-Korsakova." [Rimsky-Korsakov's Editing.] *MA* (2) (1994): 64. ISSN: 0869-4516.

        An analysis of Rimsky-Korsakov's work in editing and orchestrating Musorgsky's opera *Boris Godunov*.

923   Tyulin, Yury Nikolaevich, ed. *Voprosy opernoy dramaturgii. Sbornik statey.* [Questions of Operatic Dramaturgy. A Collection of Articles.] Moscow: Muzyka, 1975. 315 pp.

        Two articles by N. Ostapenko and Yu. Tyulin concerning Rimsky-Korsakov as an editor of Musorgsky's work, with many other references to Rimsky-Korsakov.

Bibliography: Musical Works 179

924 Asaf'ev, Boris Vladimirovich [pseud. Glebov, Igor']. *K vosstanovleniem 'Borisa Godunova' Musorgskogo. Sbornik statey.* [On the Restoration of Musorgsky's *Boris Godunov*. Collection of Articles.] Moscow: Muzykal'ny Sektor, 1928. 72 pp.

Includes references to Rimsky-Korsakov's revision of the score of Musorgsky's opera *Boris Godunov*.

925 ———. "'Boris Godunov' i ego 'redaktsii' v svete sotsialogicheskoy problemy. (K vykhodu v svet polnogo klavira 'Borisa Godunova' Musorgskogo)." [*Boris Godunov* and its "Editing" in the Light of a Sociological Problem. (On the Appearance of the Complete Vocal Score of Musorgsky's *Boris Godunov*).] *Muzyka i revolyutsiya* 7–8 (1928): 6–13.

A discussion of the fact that music reflects the current thinking of the times and that Rimsky-Korsakov, in editing *Boris Godunov*, was a victim of contemporary tastes, which thus prevented him from understanding Musorgsky's intentions.

926 Braudo, E. M. and Rimsky-Korsakov, A. N. *"Boris Godunov" Musorgskogo.* [Musorgsky's *Boris Godunov*.] Moscow: Izd. Kino-pechat', 1927. 47 pp. Review: M. Ivanov-Boretsky. *Muzykal'noe obozrenie* 1–2 (1927): 238–39.

In his article "N. A. Rimsky-Korsakov as editor of Musorgsky's Boris Godunov," pp. 34–41, the author (Andrey Nikolaevich Rimsky-Korsakov) endeavors to elucidate his father's editorial policy and attitude towards the original work.

927 Engel', Yuly Dmitrievich. "'Boris Godunov' M. P. Musorgskogo." [M. P. Musorgsky's *Boris Godunov*.] In No. 313: 41–46.

First published in *Russkie Vedomosti* 280 (10 December 1898), this contains observations on Rimsky-Korsakov's work as an editor of *Boris Godunov*.

928 Fulle, Gerlinde. *Modest Mussorgskijs Boris Godunow: Geschichte und Werk, Fassungen und Theaterpraxis.* Wiesbaden: Breitkopf & Härtel, 1974. 357 pp. ISBN-10: 3765100781. ISBN-13: 978-3765100789.

Discusses all five versions of *Boris Godunov*: Musorgsky's versions of 1869 and 1874, Rimsky-Korsakov's adaptations of 1896 and 1904, and Shostakovich's re-orchestration of 1940.

929 Godet, Robert. "Les deux Boris." In *La Révue musicale Année* 3 (April 1922): 1–17.

An account of Musorgsky's and Rimsky-Korsakov's versions of the opera *Boris Godunov*, with comparative music examples.

930 ——. *En merge de "Boris Godounof". Notes sur les documents iconographiques de l'édition Chester*. Vols. 1–2. Librarie Félix Alcan, Londres: J. & W. Chester, 1926. 551 pp.

Contained within pp. 513–41 of the final chapter "La découverte de Moussorgsky. Les deux Boris" are comparative music examples showing Musorgsky's original and its revision by Rimsky-Korsakov. Includes many other references in this extensive study.

931 Jacobs, A. "Will the real 'Boris Godunov' please stand up?" *Opera* 22 (May 1971): 388–96.

A discussion of Musorgsky's opera and its revision by Rimsky-Korsakov, noting some of the differences and utilizing comparative music examples.

932 Lloyd-Jones, David, ed. *Modest Mussorgsky: Boris Godunov: opera in four acts with a prologue, the complete original texts of Mussorgsky's 'initial' (1869) and 'definitive' (1872) versions with additional variants and fragments.* 2 Vols. London: Oxford University Press, 1975. Digitized: 2010. ISBN-10: 0193376997. ISBN-13: 978-0193376991.

Based on the existing vocal score and performing materials edited by Paul Lamm and published by OUP in 1928, this edition is essential for any study of Rimsky-Korsakov's work as an editor. For a discussion of Rimsky-Korsakov's versions of the opera, see pp. 13–15 of the *Critical Commentary and Appendices*.

933 Nagy, Ferenc. "És a Borisz kié?" [And to Whom does Boris Belong?] *Muzsika* XXI, (1978): 29–35.

A comparison of the original version of Musorgsky's *Boris Godunov* with Rimsky-Korsakov's revised one, noting salient differences.

934 Nilsson, Kurt. *Die Rimskij-Korssakoffsche Bearbeitung des "Boris Godunoff" von Mussorgskij als Objekt der vergleichenden Musikwissenschaft.* Münster i. W.: H. Buschmann, Abt. Helios-Verlag, 1937. 47 pp. (Universitas-Archiv. Bd. 76). Digitized: 2010.

A comparison of the two versions of Musorgsky's opera and the manner in which they reflect the contrasting personalities of the two composers. A complex musicological study, utilizing linear approaches. Numerous comparative music examples.

935 Oldani, Robert William, Jr. "New Perspectives on Musorgsky's 'Boris Godunov'." PhD dissertation, University of Michigan, 1978.

A detailed discussion of Musorgsky's and Rimsky-Korsakov's revisions.

936 ——. "Editions of Boris Godunov." In No. 1265: 179–214.

A detailed discussion of the various editions of the opera, including material on Rimsky-Korsakov's work as editor.

Bibliography: Musical Works

937   Rudakovskaya, E. "M. M. Ippolitov-Ivanov o redaktsii 'Boris Godunova'."
       [M. M. Ippolitov-Ivanov on the Editing of *Boris Godunov.*] *SM* 12 (1959):
       59–62.

       Discusses Rimsky-Korsakov's editing of Musorgsky's *Boris Godunov*, in the
       form of a commentary and correspondence between M. M. Ippolitov-Ivanov,
       A. K. Glazunov, and A. M. Pazovsky.

938   Schandert, Manfred. "Das Problem der originalen Instrumentation des Boris
       Godunow von M. P. Mussorgski." PhD dissertation, University of Hamburg,
       1979. *Schriftenreihe zur Musik* 15. Hamburg: Wagner, 1979. iv, 195 pp. ISBN-
       10: 3921029651. ISBN-13: 978-3921029657.

       A discussion of the various versions of the opera.

939   Smoje, Dujka. "L'authenticité en tant que valeur esthétique en musique." *Les
       cahiers de la Société Québécoise de Recherche en Musique* III (1–2) (September
       1999): 77. ISSN: 1480-1132.

       Entitled "Authenticity as aesthetic value in music," the article discusses
       esthetic inauthenticity in the work of different composers, as, for example,
       in Rimsky-Korsakov's editing of Modest Musorgsky's opera *Boris Godunov*.

940   Taruskin, Richard. "Musorgsky vs. Musorgsky: The Versions of *Boris
       Godunov.*" In *19th Century Music* VIII (2) (1984): 91–118; (3) (1984): 245–72.

       A major article on the various editions of the opera, extensively illustrated
       and documented.

941   Veprik, Aleksandr Moiseevich. "Tri orkestrovye redaktsii 'Borisa Godunova'."
       [Three Orchestral Editions of *Boris Godunov.*] *SM* 7 (1959): 80–87.

       Part of an unfinished book. In this article Veprik compares the three editions
       of the opera by Musorgsky, Rimsky-Korsakov and Shostakovich, discussing
       Rimsky-Korsakov's alterations to the harmony and melody as seen in the
       opening of the Prologue. His conclusion is that Shostakovich's version, which
       changes nothing of the original harmonies but strengthens the orchestration,
       is closest to an understanding of Musorgsky's artistic intentions.

942   Volkov, Solomon. *Testimony. The Memoirs of Dmitri Shostakovich as related
       to and edited by Solomon Volkov.* Trans. Antonia W. Bouis. London: Hamish
       Hamilton, 1979. 238 pp. Reprinted: London: Faber & Faber, 2005. 272 pp.
       ISBN-10: 0571227929. ISBN-13: 978-0571227921.

       For a commentary on aspects of the various editions of Musorgsky's
       Boris Godunov, see pp. 175–82. Rimsky-Korsakov is referred to on several
       occasions in this work, among the points discussed being the possibility
       that Tchaikovsky's existence inhibited Rimsky-Korsakov's composing [see pp.
       48–50].

943   Wolfurt, Kurt von. "Das Problem Mussorgskij-Rimskij-Korsakoff. Ein
       Vergleich zwischen dem Original-klavierauszug von Mussorgskij's 'Boris

Godunoff' und Rimskij-Korsakoff's Bearbeitung." *Die Musik* XVII Jahrgang. Zweiter Halbjahrsband: 481–91.

Takes the form of a comparison between Musorgsky's original vocal score of *Boris Godunov* and Rimsky-Korsakov's arrangement, with numerous music examples.

944   Baroni, Mario. "*Chovanshina.*" *Convegno Internazionale Musorgskij.* Milan: Teatro alla Scala, 1981: 26.

Includes a discussion of revisions of *Khovanshchina* by Rimsky-Korsakov and Shostakovich.

945   Findeyzen, Nikolay Fëdorovich. "Redaktsiya Rimskogo-Korsakova 'Khovanshchiny' Musorgskogo." [Rimsky-Korsakov's Editing of Musorgsky's *Khovanshchina.*] *RMG* 10 (1911): cols. 260–66.

Observing that the "Persian Dance" from *Khovanshchina* was orchestrated during Musorgsky's lifetime, Findeyzen considers that Rimsky-Korsakov's orchestration of the opera is commendable and that the material selected to make a performable score shows understanding of his colleague's intentions.

946   Gurevich, V. "Orkestrovaya dramaturgiya 'Khovanshchiny' v redaktsii Rimskogo-Korsakova." [The Orchestral Dramaturgy of *Khovanshchina* in Rimsky-Korsakov's Version.] In No. 923.

947   Karatygin, Vyacheslav Gavrilovich. "'Khovanshchina' i eë avtory: Rimsky-Korsakov i drugie." [*Khovanshchina* and its Authors: Rimsky-Korsakov and Others.] *EIT* VII (1911).

A discussion of the history of the opera *Khovanshchina* and Rimsky-Korsakov's editorial role.

948   Norris, Geoffrey. "An Opera Restored: Rimsky-Korsakov, Shostakovich and the Khovansky Business." *MT* 123 (October 1982): 672–75.

An illuminating discussion of *Khovanshchina*, its revisions, and completions by Rimsky-Korsakov and Shostakovich. The author considers that Shostakovich's score most closely approaches Musorgsky's original intentions.

949   Threlfall, Robert. "The Stravinsky version of 'Khovanshchina'." *Studies in Music* 15 (1981): 106–15.

Rimsky-Korsakov's version of *Khovanshchina* was used by Stravinsky as the basis for his own edition of the work when it was staged by Sergey Dyagilev [Serge Diaghilev] in 1913. The article contains information on the nature of Rimsky-Korsakov's revisions.

950   Montgomery, Alan Gene. "An analytical comparison of the Composer's original and the Rimsky-Korsakov edition of Mussorgsky's 'Night on the Bare Mountain'." Bloomington: Indiana University, 1971. 233 pp.

Bibliography: Musical Works 183

An unpublished Master's dissertation comparing Musorgsky's original version published by Muzgiz, Moscow, the version contained in *The Fair of Sorochinsk*, edited by Paul Lamm, and Rimsky-Korsakov's edition. Effective use is made of comparative music examples.

951 Reilly, Edward R. "The first extant version of 'Night on the Bare Mountain'." In No. 1265: 135–62.

Includes a section entitled: "Rimsky-Korsakov's Orchestral Adaptation."

952 Worbs, Hans Christoph. *Modest P. Mussorgsky in Selbst-zeugnissen und Bilddokumenten.* Reinbek bei Hamburg: Rowohlt, 1976. 151 pp.

Contains a comparative evaluation of the original version of Musorgsky's *Night on the Bald Mountain* and Rimsky-Korsakov's arrangement.

953 Musorgskij, Modest. *Bilder einer Ausstellung/Kartinki s vystavki/Pictures at an Exhibition (1874).* Christoph Hellmundt, ed. Leipzig: Peters, 1976. 41 pp.

A new edition based on autograph materials, which differs from the version edited by Rimsky-Korsakov.

954 Garden, Edward J. C. "Three Nights on Bare Mountain." *MT* 129 (1745) (July 1988): 333. ISSN: 0027-4666.

A comparison of the three versions of Modest Musorgsky's *Ivanova noch' na Lysoy gore* [St. John's Night on Bare Mountain], noting the changes made to the score by Rimsky-Korsakov when editing the work.

955 Lochrie, Daniel W. *A Critical Evaluation of the Current Performance Versions of Musorgsky's Night on Bald Mountain. Based on the History and Content of Musorgsky's Original Extant Versions.* DMA dissertation, Columbus: Ohio State University, 1992. Ann Arbor, Michigan: UMI, 1993.

An examination of the two completed versions of Musorgsky's *Ivanova noch' na Lysoy gore* [St. John's Night on Bald Mountain] consisting of an early orchestral tone poem and an extensively revised piano-vocal score (both extant), together with discussion of the editorial role of Rimsky-Korsakov.

4

Bibliography: General

ESTHETIC CREDO, IDEOLOGICAL INTERPRETATIONS

956 Abraham, Gerald. "Some Psychological Peculiarities of Russian Creative Artists." In *On Russian Music*. London: William Reeves, 1939: 243–54 [see No. 284].

In this discussion of Rimsky-Korsakov and his psychological profile [see pp. 248-51], Abraham sees him as a rationalist, with an inclination to pantheistic ideology.

957 Alshwang, Arnol'd Aleksandrovich. "N. A. Rimsky-Korsakov." *Voks Bulletin* [published by USSR Society for Cultural Relations with Foreign Countries] 3–4 (1942): 78–83.

Rimsky-Korsakov as seen in the Soviet ideological interpretation of the period. An account of his work, stressing the "democratic" elements and his indebtedness to Russian folk song.

958 Anonymous. "Govoryat klassiki." [The Classics Speak.] *SM* 1 (1948): 29–52.

Arising from the Decree of the Communist Party Central Committee on Muradeli's opera *Velikaya druzhba* [The Great Friendship] in 1948 and General Zhdanov's address, this unsigned article (emanating from the highest authorities) is a selection of writings on music by Glinka, Odoevsky, Dargomyzhsky, Serov, Balakirev, Borodin, Musorgsky, Rimsky-Korsakov, Stasov, Tchaikovsky, Taneev, and Larosh. The excerpts by Rimsky-Korsakov occur on pp. 40–45 and are taken from his *Chronicle* [see No. 210], *Musical Articles and Notes* [see No. 211], and various letters, a recurring theme being the value of folk song as a source of compositional material.

184

Bibliography: General

959 Anonymous. "Russkie klassiki o narodnosti." [The Russian Classicists on Populism.] *SM* 12 (1952): 13–23.

A discussion of *narodnost'* [populism] occupied an important place in Soviet musical esthetics. This article contains four quotations from Rimsky-Korsakov [see p. 21], for example, "In my best music I aim at picturesqueness and the portrayal of the life of the people."

960 Anonymous. "Russkie klassiki o realizme." [The Russian Classics on Realism.] *SM* 2 (1953): 22–33.

This article on Soviet music esthetics contains numerous references to Rimsky-Korsakov, having special emphasis on his personal statements with regard to the Russian musical classicists [see p. 32]. An ideological interpretation of Rimsky-Korsakov's compositions.

961 Asaf'ev, Boris Vladimirovich [pseud. Glebov, Igor']. "Slukh Glinki." [Glinka's Hearing.] In No. 1256: Vol. I, 289–328.

Though primarily concerned with a discussion of Glinka, this article contains observations by Rimsky-Korsakov on the nature of sound, the processes of hearing, and aural training.

962 ——. "Nikolay Andreevich Rimsky-Korsakov. K stoletiyu so dnya rozhdeniya." [Nikolay Andreevich Rimsky-Korsakov. On the Centenary of his Birth.] *Vestnik Akademii Nauk SSSR* 6 (1944): 4–10. Reprinted: No. 1256: Vol. III, 229–34.

Discusses Rimsky-Korsakov's esthetic credo, the varied sources of his inspiration, and the different means by which he embodies these ideas in his music.

963 Cone, Edward T. "Stravinsky at the Tomb of Rimsky-Korsakov." In *Hearing and Knowing Music: The Unpublished Essays of Edward T. Cone*. Princeton University Press, 2009. ISBN-10: 0691140111. ISBN-13: 978-0691140117.

Describes the manner in which Rimsky-Korsakov derived much of his knowledge of orchestration from the writings of Berlioz, passing this information on to his pupil Stravinsky, who, in turn, developed his own highly individual idiom.

964 Eberlein, Dorothee. *Russische Musikanschauung um 1900 von 9 russischen Komponisten, dargestellt aus Briefen, Selbstzeugnissen, Erinnerungen und Kritiken*. Regensburg: Gustav Bosse Verlag, 1978. 207 pp. ISBN-10: 3764921366. ISBN-13: 978-3764921361.

The section "Nikolaj-A. Rimskij-Korsakov" contains three references to the composer:

"Abgrenzung Balakirev-Beljaev-Kreis. (Problem des Dilettantismus. Künstlerische Krisis um 1890)": 25–28.

"Die Rangfolge der Künste." (Opernlibretti und Pantheismus. Über musikalischen Symbolismus. Das Schöne. Die Phantastik. Tonalitäten als Farben- und Gefühlträger): 30–38.

"Rimskij-Korsakov über Musik und Musiker." (Glinka, Dargomysskij, Musorgskij, Čajkovskij, italienische und französische Opernmusik, R. Strauss, Wagner, Debussy, Skrjabin, Wiener Klassik, Barockmusik, Folklore und National-schulen): 39–46.

As the title of the work suggests, this is a skilful compilation of writings and observations about Rimsky-Korsakov. The bibliographical sources are diverse.

965   Fedorovtsev, S. "Nekotorye voprosy soderzhaniya i formy v estetike N. A. Rimskogo-Korsakova." [Some Questions of Content and Form in Rimsky-Korsakov's Esthetics.] In V. K. Skatershchikov and S. Kh. Rappaport, comps. *Esteticheskie ocherki*. [Essays on Esthetics.] Moscow, 1963.

An ideological article discussing Rimsky-Korsakov's esthetic outlook.

966   Ferman, Valentin Eduardovich. "Opernye vozzreniya Rimskogo-Korsakova." [Rimsky-Korsakov's Views on Opera.] In V. E. Ferman. *Operny teatr. Stat'i i issledovaniya*. [The Opera Theater. Articles and Research.] Moscow, 1961.

Valentin Ferman (1895–1948), initially trained for the law, wrote on many aspects of music, especially opera. A selection of his writings was published in 1961.

967   Friedlander, Maryla. "Unpublished Letters of Nikolas Rimsky-Korsakoff. Correspondence of the Composer of Coq D'Or." *Opera* (5 March 1945): 9–13.

Excerpts from six of Rimsky-Korsakov's letters (1864–1906). The first, dated 18 January 1864, concerning *Tannhäuser* is to Balakirev from Annapolis, Maryland (United States), where Rimsky-Korsakov stopped during his world cruise on the clipper ship "Almaz." The second (undated) is to Ippolitov-Ivanov, who was contemplating leaving Moscow, where he was conductor of the Moscow Private Opera, to go to Kiev. The third (19 August 1894) and fourth (8 June 1899), both to V. V. Stasov, are concerned mainly with *Sadko* and a discussion of Glinka's phrase: "I am almost convinced that one can unite the western fugue with the individualities of our own music by the ties of a legitimate union." Letter five (23 June 1902) concerns the production of *The Snow Maiden* and the possibility of presenting *Kashchey the Immortal* and *May Night* as a double bill. The last letter (undated) speaks enthusiastically of Wagner's *Meistersinger*, although regretting "its excessive length and repetitions."

968   Frolov, Sergei Vladimirovich. "N. Rimsky-Korsakov i 'peterburgsky tekst russkoy literatury'." [N. Rimsky-Korsakov and the "Petersburg Text of Russian Literature."] *MA* (1) (2009): 88–92. ISSN: 0869-4516.

Bibliography: General

A discussion of the structure and imagery of what is termed the "St. Petersburg text," a literary-cultural phenomenon which sees St. Petersburg as being the focus and inspiration of a host of literary and musical compositions from the nineteenth century to the present day, noting the extent to which Rimsky-Korsakov's works form a part, including some of the composer's thoughts about religion [see p. 92].

969   Galeev, Bulat Mahmudovich. "Tsvetnoy slukh: Chudo ili yudo?" [Color Hearing: Miracle or Deception?] *Chelovek: illyustrirovanny naucho-populyarny zhurnal* 4 (2000): 135. ISSN: 0236-2007.

An examination of the phenomenon of synesthesia, or color-hearing, as found in the works of Skryabin, Rimsky-Korsakov, and Messiaen.

970   Gozenpud, Abram Akimovich. "N. A. Rimsky-Korsakov (Po neopublikovannym dokumentam)." [N. A. Rimsky-Korsakov (From Unpublished Documents).] *SM* 2 (1950): 58–67.

Written during the last years of the Stalinist era and adopting an extreme pro-Russian stance, this article consists of carefully selected extracts from hitherto unpublished letters by Rimsky-Korsakov to his parents and documents relating to Yastrebtsëv, taken from the Rimsky-Korsakov Archive in RNB, SPBGATI, and SPGK. These are concerned with his youth, voyage around the world, and visit to London and the United States, together with his attitude towards contemporary affairs as described in unpublished parts of Yastrebtsëv's reminiscences. Includes material on Rimsky-Korsakov's negative attitude towards Mahler, Richard Strauss, and other contemporary composers, and his views on musical composition. Gozenpud states that Rimsky-Korsakov said of Stravinsky in 1907 that "he addicted himself too zealously to modernism."

971   ——. *Russky Sovetsky operny teatr (1917-1941)*. [The Russian Soviet Operatic Theater (1917-1941).] Leningrad: Muzgiz, 1963. 440 pp.

Although no specific chapter is devoted to Rimsky-Korsakov, there are many references to the composer and accounts of new interpretations of his operas staged during the Soviet period [see pp. 177–87].

972   Istel, Edgar. "Rimsky-Korsakov, the Oriental Wizard." Trans. T. Baker, *MQ* 15 (3) (1929): 388–414.

A discussion of the composer and his creative development, paying particular attention to the exotic elements in his works. Valuable for its insight into Rimsky-Korsakov's imaginative powers, orchestration, and association of keys with specific subjects and emotions.

973   Karasev, Pavel Alekseevich. "Besedy s N. A. Rimskim-Korsakovym." [Chats with N. A. Rimsky-Korsakov.] *RMG* 49 (1908): cols. 1112–22.

A series of conversations held in 1900 covering a variety of topics, including Wagner, philosophy, folk song, opera, sacred music, and Musorgsky.

974   Kremlëv, Yuly Anatol'evich. "Deyateli Moguchey kuchki – A. P. Borodin, N. A. Rimsky-Korsakov, M. A. Balakirev, M. P. Musorgsky." [The Members of the Mighty Handful – A. P. Borodin, N. A. Rimsky-Korsakov, M. A. Balakirev, M. P. Musorgsky.] In Y. A. Kremlëv. *Russkaya mysl' o muzyke. Ocherki istorii russkoy muzykal'noy kritiki i estetiki v XIX veke.* [Russian Thought on Music. Essays on the History of Russian Musical Criticism and Esthetics in the 19th Century.] Vol. II, 1861–80. Leningrad: Muzgiz, 1958: 248–96.

A substantial article highlighting the esthetic outlook of the members of the *Moguchaya Kuchka,* with extracts from reviews, letters, and other literary materials, reflecting the ideological turmoil of the 1860s and Rimsky-Korsakov's work as seen through the eyes of his contemporaries.

975   ——. "M. A. Balakirev. A. P. Borodin. N. A. Rimsky-Korsakov." In Yu. A. Kremlëv. *Russkaya mysl' o muzyke. Ocherki istorii russkoy muzykal'noy kritiki i estetiki v XIX veke.* [Russian Thought on Music. Essays on the History of Russian Musical Criticism and Esthetics in the 19th Century.] Vol. III, 1881–94. Leningrad: Muzgiz, 1960: 189–216.

A philosophical esthetic examination of Rimsky-Korsakov and his ideas as manifest in his compositions and literary writings of the period 1881–94. In Rimsky-Korsakov "the fundamental, philosophical, gnosiological questions of music esthetics are solved half-heartedly, with more or less significant inclinations towards idealism," p. 216.

976   ——. *Estetika prirody v tvorchestve N. A. Rimskogo-Korsakova.* [The Esthetic of Nature in the Work of N. A. Rimsky-Korsakov.] Moscow: Muzgiz, 1962. 109 pp.

Discusses the part played by descriptive scene painting in Rimsky-Korsakov's work, as well as the general role of nature.

977   ——. *Natsional'nye cherty russkoy muzyki.* [National Features of Russian Music.] Leningrad: Muzyka, 1968. 120 pp.

This ideological study of *narodnost'* [populism] in Russian music comprises four chapters, with an introduction and a conclusion, and includes several sections on Rimsky-Korsakov, principally pp. 44–47 and 74–79. There is no index.

978   Lapshin, Ivan Ivanovich. *Khudozhestvennoe tvorchestvo.* [Artistic Creativity.] Petrograd: Tsentral'noe Kooperativnoe izd. Mysl', 1923.

Contains two chapters on the composer, "Rimsky-Korsakov's musical lyricism," pp. 270–82, being a discussion of the lyrical element in his work, especially in his operas and songs, and "Philosophical motives in

Bibliography: General

Rimsky-Korsakov's work," pp. 283–303, a general examination of his esthetic and religious beliefs. Both contain references to pantheistic elements.

979 Lapshin, Ivan Ivanovich, and Rakhmanova, Marina Pavlovna. "Filosofskie motivy v tvorchestve Rimskogo-Korsakova." [Philosophical Motives in the Work of Rimsky-Korsakov.] *MA* (2) (1994): 3–7. ISSN: 0869-4516.

A discussion of the part played by literary-philosophical ideas in the work of Rimsky-Korsakov.

980 Livanova, Tamara Nikolaevna. "K sporam o muzykal'nom nasledii." [By Way of Discussion about Musical Heritage.] *SM* 10 (1950): 9–20.

A politico-critical article on Russian music of the nineteenth and early twentieth centuries, discussing ideological trends, highlighting the "democratic" and "realist" elements found in Rimsky-Korsakov's work as opposed to certain negative features in some other composers.

981 Maine, Basil. "Rimsky re-interpreted." *Musical Opinion* 57 (February 1934): 409.

An article questioning the validity of interpreting the composer's operas in a political manner.

982 Montagu-Nathan, Montagu. "The Story of Russian Music. VIII – Rimsky-Korsakof." *The Music Student* (April 1917): 261–63.

An article discussing the composer's statement that "art is in substance an enchanting and intoxicating untruth," together with some observations on his thoughts on religion.

983 Ogolevets, Aleksey Stepanovich, comp. *Materialy i dokumenty po istorii russkoy realisticheskoy muzykal'noy estetiki. Khrestomatiya. Klassiki russkoy muzyki i muzykal'noy kritiki ob iskusstve.* [Materials and Documents on the History of Russian Realist Musical Esthetics. An Anthology. Classics of Russian Music and of Musical Criticism about Art.] Vol. I, Moscow: Muzgiz, 1954; Vol. II, 1956.

The contents are as follows:

Volume I: Two articles by Serov:
Rimsky-Korsakov's *Serbian Fantasy*: 505.
Rimsky-Korsakov's *Sadko*: 505–08.

Volume II, Chapter V:
A short introductory article: 529–44.
Extracts from Rimsky-Korsakov's *Chronicle*: 545–628.
Two articles by Rimsky-Korsakov:

i. Wagner and Dargomyzhsky. The Joint Production of Two Arts or Musical Drama: 629–40.
ii. *The Snow Maiden* – A Tale of Spring: 641–57.

A selection of Rimsky-Korsakov's letters: 658–67.

984 Orlov, Genrikh Aleksandrovich. "N. A. Rimsky-Korsakov na poroge XX veka. Puti iskaniy." [N. A. Rimsky-Korsakov on the Threshold of the XX Century. Strivings.] In *Voprosy teorii i estetiki muzyki.* [Questions of Musical Theory and Esthetics.] A. I. Klimovitsky, ed. Vol. 14. Leningrad: Muzyka, 1975: 3–30.

An examination of Rimsky-Korsakov's ideological evolution, especially as seen in the last three decades of his life. With a discussion of some of his unfulfilled operatic projects, including a biblical opera on the subject of Saul and David. Orlov sees the composer, however, as a confirmed atheist.

985 Orlova, Elena Mikhaylovna. "Mysli N. A. Rimskogo-Korsakova ob analize muzykal'nykh proizvedeniy." [N. A. Rimsky-Korsakov's Thoughts on the Analysis of Musical Works.] In No. 1435: 107–18.

An article on Rimsky-Korsakov's musical-esthetic views as revealed in analyses of his compositions in his *Chronicle* and in his thematic survey of *The Snow Maiden*, originally published in *RMG* in 1908. Rimsky-Korsakov saw music as "an art of poetic thought" and Orlova pays special attention to an examination of his terminology used in the classification of harmony and melody.

986 Rakhmanova, Marina Pavlovna. "Poslednie gody." [The Last Years.] *MA* (2) (1994): 75–89. ISSN: 0869-4516.

An excellently documented examination of Rimsky-Korsakov's creative activities during the years 1890–1900, including features of his style, the performance of his operas by prominent artists, and his spiritual affinity with the work of Viktor Vasnetsov and Mikhail Aleksandrovich Vrubel'.

987 ———. "Vstuplenie." [Introduction.] *MA* (2) (1994): 41–43. ISSN: 0869-4516.

A discussion of Rimsky-Korsakov's esthetic credo, compared with that of Musorgsky, and the part played by it in his creative evolution, noting that very few major studies of Rimsky-Korsakov have been made by non-Russian scholars.

988 ———. "Tvorchestvo N. A. Rimskogo-Korsakova: Opyt sovremennogo osmysleniya." [The Work of N. A. Rimsky-Korsakov: An Attempt at Current Understanding.] PhD dissertation, Gosudarstvenny Institut Iskusstvoznaniya, Moscow, 1997.

A dissertation providing a contemporary analysis of Rimsky-Korsakov's spiritual, philosophical, esthetic, and theoretical legacy.

989 Rimsky-Korsakov, Andrey Nikolaevich. "Rol' uchёby i samokritiki v tvorchestve N. A. Rimskogo-Korsakova." [The Role of Training and Self-criticism in N. A. Rimsky-Korsakov's Work.] *SM* 10 (1934): 22–27.

Bibliography: General 191

A short article describing Rimsky-Korsakov's persistent struggle for musical improvement and his passion for revision, as seen in *Antar* (four versions), *The Maid of Pskov* (three versions), "Sadko" (three versions), the First Symphony (two versions), *Overture on Russian Themes* (two versions), and the Third Symphony.

990   Rimsky-Korsakov, Vladimir Nikolaevich. "Nemnogo yumora." [A Little Humour.] *SM* 6 (1958): 81–84.

Rimsky-Korsakov had a keen sense of humor, liked to play with words, devise funny verses, write witty letters, and send musical missives to his friends, all of which are described in this short article. Also included is a photograph of a musical letter to Bel'sky, preserved in the St. Petersburg State Conservatory [SPGK], and a sketch by Shalyapin [Chaliapin].

991   Ryzhkin, Iosif Yakovlevich. *Russkoe klassicheskoe muzykoznanie v bor'be protiv formalizma.* [Russian Classical Musicology in the Struggle against Formalism.] Moscow-Leningrad: Muzgiz, 1951. 152 pp.

An ideological discussion of Russian music, including quotations from writers and critics to show that the most "progressive" composers reflect actuality in their work. There is no specific discussion of Rimsky-Korsakov in this book, although excerpts from his *Chronicle* [see No. 210] and *Musical Articles and Notes* (1869–1907) [see No. 211] are included.

992   Sabaneev, Leonid Leonidovich. "The Relation between Sound and Colour." Trans. S. W. Pring. *ML* X (1929): 266–77.

An article discussing a subject which was of particular interest to Russian composers such as Rimsky-Korsakov and Skryabin.

993   Sarriugarte Gómez, Íñigo. "La fusión pintura, música y danza: La apuesta de Sergei Diaguilev." *Música y educación: Revista internacional de pedagogía musical* 22 (1:77) (2009): 41. ISSN: 0214-4786.

Entitled "The Fusion of Painting, Music, and Dance: The Challenge of Sergei Diaghilev," this article, written in Spanish, discusses how Russian performers such as Shalyapin [Chaliapin], and the composers Musorgsky, Rimsky-Korsakov, Borodin, and Rakhmaninov, all contributed to the success of the Ballets Russes.

994   Savel'eva, Irina. "Tema kosmosa v tvorchestve russkikh kompozitorov serebryannogo veka." [The Theme of the Cosmos in the Work of Russian Composers of the Silver Age.] In *Voprosy estetiki v muzykal'nom obrazovanii.* [Questions of Esthetics in Music Education.] Russian Federation, 2002.

A discussion of elements of religious mystery and liturgy found in the works of Rimsky-Korsakov and other Russian composers of the late nineteenth century.

995 Stepanova, Elena Viktorovna. "Nabroski kamerno-instrumental'nykh sochineniy v zapisnoy knizhke N. A. Rimskogo-Korsakova." [Sketches of Chamber Instrumental Compositions in a Notebook of N. A. Rimsky-Korsakov.] *Musicus* 2 (April–June 2012): 25. ISSN: 2072-0262.

An article published in *Musicus*, the journal of the St. Petersburg Conservatory, describing sketches of several chamber instrumental works contained in a notebook belonging to Rimsky-Korsakov, analysis of which provides insight into the composer's creative process.

996 Yastrebtsëv, Vasily Vasil'evich. "O tsvetnom zvukosozertsanie N. A. Rimskogo-Korsakova." [N. A. Rimsky-Korsakov's Contemplation of Colour with Sound.] *RMG* 39–40 (1908): cols. 842–45.

Printed in the special memorial volume of *RMG*, this discusses Rimsky-Korsakov's association of color with specific keys and chords.

997 ——. "Koe-chto o slukhovykh zabluzhdeniyakh i kompozitorskoy glukhote." [Something about Auditory Delusions and Composer Deafness.] *RMG* (1909): cols. 545–54.

In this article, published in the special Rimsky-Korsakov commemorative issue of *RMG*, Yastrebtsëv describes how the composer was concerned with the question of "auditory delusion." Yastrebtsëv reproduces an essay by Rimsky-Korsakov on the subject, as well as reports of conversations, which highlight some aspects of the composer's esthetic credo. Discusses the impact of sound and intervals as affecting personal taste.

ARCHIVES AND MUSEUMS: RESOURCES

998 Anonymous. "Pamyati N. A. Rimskogo-Korsakova." [In Memory of N. A. Rimsky -Korsakov.] *SM* 5 (1948): 74.

An account of an exhibition of Rimsky-Korsakov's life and work held in 1948 to mark the 40th anniversary of the composer's death, using materials from MMKG, GTTMB, the music library of the former Union of Soviet Composers, and other sources, including designs for Rimsky-Korsakov's stage work by Korovin, Golovin, Vasnetsov, and Fedorovsky.

999 Anonymous. "Imeny Rimskogo-Korsakova." [Named after Rimsky-Korsakov.] *SM* 3 (1962): 155.

A short description of the founding of the *Gosudarstvenny memorial'ny dom-myzey N. A. Rimskogo-Korsakova* [State Memorial House Museum of N. A. Rimsky-Korsakov] in 1944 in Tikhvin, near St. Petersburg. Together with preserving artifacts and other materials connected with the birth place of the composer, the museum is used for educational purposes, including exhibitions, lectures, and concerts.

Bibliography: General

1000 Anonymous. "Novosti tikhvinskogo muzeya." [News of the Tikhvin Museum.] *SM* 11 (1964): 158–59.

An account of the *Gosudarstvenny memorial'ny dom-myzey N. A. Rimskogo-Korsakova* [State Memorial House Museum of N. A. Rimsky-Korsakov] at Tikhvin, describing developments in the course of its first 20 years' existence. New acquisitions included a piano, personal effects, and an annual competition. Rimsky-Korsakov's son, Vladimir Nikolaevich, presented the museum with a lamp formerly owned by the composer, used for the piano music stand.

1001 Anonymous. "Leningrad: A Rimsky-Korsakov Museum." *Opera* 20 (5) (1969): 394.

A brief mention of the opening of a museum in an apartment, now known as the *Memorial'ny muzey-kvartira N. A. Rimskogo-Korsakova* [Rimsky-Korsakov Memorial Apartment Museum, St. Petersburg], where the composer lived from 1893. Rimsky-Korsakov's 84-year old daughter Nadezhda and his 88-year old son, Vladimir, assisted in setting up the apartment, which is now a branch of the St. Petersburg State Museum.

1002 Chirkova, Larisa. "Dom na Zagorodnom." [House in the Zagorodny.] *MA* (2) (1994): 30–32. ISSN: 0869-4516.

A discussion of the Rimsky-Korsakov Memorial Apartment Museum in the Zagorodny Prospekt, formerly Rimsky-Korsakov's home in St. Petersburg, in which the composer resided for 15 years.

1003 Golubovsky, I. V., ed. *Muzykal'ny Leningrad – 1917-1957.* [Musical Leningrad – 1917-1957.] Leningrad: Muzgiz, 1958. 527 pp.

An informative volume about the musical life of Leningrad, containing a description of the Rimsky-Korsakov family archive in SPBGATI, pp. 405–10, and what is now the *Gosudarstvenny memorial'ny dom-myzey N. A. Rimskogo-Korsakova* [State Memorial House Museum of N. A. Rimsky-Korsakov], Tikhvin, pp. 410–11.

1004 Gozenpud, Abram Akimovich. "Zapisnye knizhki Rimskogo-Korsakova." [Rimsky-Korsakov's Notebooks.] In A. A. Gozenpud. *Izbrannye stat'i.* [Selected Articles.] Leningrad-Moscow: Sovetsky Kompozitor, 1941: 174–239.

This article is a sequel to the publication in 1938 of A. N. Rimsky-Korsakov's *Musical Treasures of the MS Section of the State Public Library* [see No. 1019]. The MS Section of the RNB has 10 notebooks, one of them containing exercises in harmony. They consist of small interlaced music books of approximately 100 pages in length, each of which has four music staves. Another two belong to Rimsky-Korsakov's family. Gozenpud discusses 11 books containing material on the operas *Mlada*, *Sadko*, *The Tsar's Bride*, *The Tale of Tsar Saltan*, *Kashchey the Immortal*, *Servilia*, *Pan Voevoda*, *The Legend of the Invisible City of Kitezh*, and *The Golden Cockerel*, together with sketches

194   *Nikolay Andreevich Rimsky-Korsakov: A Research and Information Guide*

for the uncompleted operas *The Barber of Baghdad, Sten'ka Razin, Dobrynya Nikitich, Nausicaä, The Tale of the Fisherman and the Fish, Earth and Sky,* and *Il'ya Muromets.* Gozenpud considers, however, that not all Rimsky-Korsakov's notebooks have come down to us. The last section is concerned with the unfinished opera *Sten'ka Razin.*

1005   Kiselëv, Vasily Aleksandrovich. *Avtografy N.A. Rimskogo-Korsakova v fondakh Gosudarstvennogo Tsentral'nogo Muzeya Muzykal'noy Kul'tury imeni M. I. Glinki. Katalog-spravochnik.* [Autographs of N. A. Rimsky-Korsakov in the Fonds of the State Central Museum of Musical Culture named after M. I. Glinka. Catalog-Handbook.] Moscow: Gos. Tsen. Muzey Muz. Kul't. im. M. I. Glinki, 1958. 65 pp.

This gives details of 45 autographs, 176 letters to 33 correspondents, 49 various autographs, and 42 dedicatory inscriptions of Rimsky-Korsakov preserved in MMKG. Each entry is meticulously described and there are biographical notes on those persons referred to in the text.

1006   Komitet po chestvovaniyu pamyati N. A. Rimskogo-Korsakova. [Committee Honouring the Memory of N. A. Rimsky-Korsakov.] *N. A. Rimsky-Korsakov i ego epokha. Kratky putevoditel' po vystavke v Russkom Muzee. Zelëny zal.* [N. A. Rimsky-Korsakov and his Epoch. Short Guide to the Exhibition in the Russian Museum. Green Hall.] Leningrad: Russky Muzey, 1933. 20 pp.

This book is part of the elaborate celebrations marking the 25th anniversary of the composer's death. The exhibition, devised to illustrate progressively the various political stages of Russian cultural development as interpreted in terms of Marxist-Leninist ideology and held in the Green Hall of the Russian Museum, opened on the date of the composer's death (8 [21] June, 1908).

Of the six sections forming the Exhibition, Section 1 was largely devoted to opera, it being pointed out that Rimsky-Korsakov's operas (and those of other composers arranged by him) constituted more than half of the regular Russian operatic repertoire. Also in this section were materials relating to the singers Zabela-Vrubel' and Ershov, portraits, personal effects of the composer, Rimsky-Korsakov's ancestors, Tikhvin and its historical associations, family albums, and matters relating to the composer's father (a mason exiled by Nicholas I and obliged to live without a pension).

Sections 2–6 contained materials relating to the 1860s–1900s, consisting of autographs, quotations, programs, scores, articles, books, photos, and portraits of the *Moguchaya Kuchka* [Mighty Handful], portraits of the composer's wife and sister-in-law, his favorite places of work, and matters relating to the 1905 Revolution. A special place was given to descriptions of performances of his operas abroad – *The Golden Cockerel* as staged by Sergey Dyagilev [Serge Diaghilev] in Paris and London, *The Tale of Tsar Saltan* in Milan and Rio de Janeiro, *The Snow Maiden* in London (1933), and *The Legend of the Invisible City of Kitezh* in London and Barcelona. There was a display of proposed but unfinished projects, including scenarios and libretti of Shakespeare's *The Tempest*, Byron's *Earth and Sky, Nausicaä* (from The Odyssey), *Saul and David* (from the Bible), *The Barber of Baghdad*, and *Sten'ka Razin*. Other materials included a short article by V. Shkafer and a list of concerts, operas, and lectures given from 13 May to 21 June.

1007 Krasovsky, Yu. and Chernikov, N. "Materialy i dokumenty o russkikh muzykantakh, khranyashchiesya v TSGLA." [Materials and Documents about Russian Musicians preserved in the Central State Archive of Literature of the SSR.] *SM* 8 (1953): 45–48.

A short account of some of the musical materials preserved in the Central State Archive of Literature of the SSR, including those relating to Rimsky-Korsakov—MS sketches of scenes from the operas *Sadko* and *Christmas Eve*, and 180 letters by him addressed to musicians, theatrical figures, and publishers, together with details of the archives of the former St. Petersburg and Moscow theaters.

1008 Krupeychenko, I. P. and Balyasov, N. K. *Tikhvin. Prezhde i teper'.* [Tikhvin. Past and Present.] Leningrad: Lenizdat, 1970. 120 pp.

Contains materials on the composer's place of birth, together with information on Rimsky-Korsakov and his forebears [see pp. 24–28].

1009 Kutateladze, Larisa Mikhaylovna, ed. "Iz pisem N. A. Rimskogo-Korsakova k synu." [From N. A. Rimsky-Korsakov's Letters to His Son.] *SM* 2 (1964): 52–62.

Preceded by an article describing some of the contents of the Rimsky-Korsakov family archive at the Leningrad Institute of Theater, Music and Cinema, founded in 1944, this states that the fond of the composer himself contains MSS and over 800 letters to his parents, wife, and children. The fond of his son, Nikolay Andreevich (1878–1940), contains letters with more than 600 correspondents. The 11 letters reproduced cover the period 3 [15] October 1899 to 19 July 1905 and are all to his son. They are full of details of Rimsky-Korsakov's life, not only on musical and political matters, but that the cuckoo has started cuckooing and that the grass has been cut!

1010 L. "Dom v Tikhvine v kotorom N. A. Rimsky-Korsakov rodilsya." [The House in Tikhvin where N. A. Rimsky-Korsakov was Born.] *RMG* 51 (1900): cols. 1282–84.

An informative discussion of some of the prevailing influences on the composer during his childhood in Tikhvin, with a picture of the house.

1011 Mikhaylova, A. N. "Arkhiv Rimskogo-Korsakova." [The Rimsky-Korsakov Archive.] *Ogonëk* 7 (1944): 10.

A discussion of the contents of an important source of information relating to Rimsky-Korsakov.

1012 Mordvinov, I. P. "Berednikovsky arkhiv. Pis'ma A. P. Rimskogo-Korsakova. 1827-1853." [Berednikov Archive. Letters of A. P. Rimsky-Korsakov. 1827-1853.] *Russky arkhiv*, Kn. 2, Vyp. 5 [Book 2, Issue 5] (1916): 21.

Contains materials about the composer's father.

1013 Obraztsova, I. M., et al. *N. A. Rimsky-Korsakov na Pskovshchine*. [N. A. Rimsky-Korsakov and the Pskov Region.] Leningrad: Lenizdat, 1981. 87 pp.

This volume examines areas of Pskov which Rimsky-Korsakov knew and which were a source of inspiration. Utilizes materials from family documents and albums from the archives of SPBGATI and RNB. Illustrated with photographs from the former Leningrad Theater Museum, many of them published for the first time. No documentation.

1014 Ossovsky, Aleksandr Vyacheslavovich. "Khudozhestvennoe nasledstvo N. A. Rimskogo-Korsakova." [N. A. Rimsky-Korsakov's Artistic Legacy.] *Muzykal'ny Truzhenik* 21 (1908): 6–9.

A description of literary and musical MSS found after his death.

1015 Petrov, Nikolay Aleksandrovich. *Dom-muzey N. A. Rimskogo-Korsakova v Tikhvine. Kratky ocherk-putevoditel'*. [The House Museum of N. A. Rimsky-Korsakov in Tikhvin. A Short Guide.] Leningrad: Muzyka, 1969. 56 pp.

Consists of seven chapters:

i.   History of the House and the Museum.
ii. The Occupants of the House in the 1840s and 1850s.
iii. To Be a Sailor or a Composer?
iv. Tikhvin in Rimsky-Korsakov's Music.
v.   The Composer's Creative Path (according to Exhibitions in the Museum's Rooms).
vi. The Children's Room on the Mezzanine Floor and the Memorial Garden.
vii. In the Work Rooms and Outside the Museum.

Illustrated with photographs and other materials, it is prefaced by a brief history of Tikhvin. The establishment of a Dobrovol'noe obshchestvo druzey Doma-muzeya N. A. Rimskogo-Korsakova [Voluntary Society of Friends of the House Museum of N. A. Rimsky-Korsakov] at Tikhvin in 1962 is described on p. 55.

1016 Petrovskaya, Ira Fëdorovna. *Istochnikovedenie istorii russkoy muzykal'noy kul'tury XVIII – nachala XX veka*. [Source Study of the History of Russian Musical Culture of the Eighteenth to Early Twentieth Century.] Moscow: Muzgiz, 1983: 67–69.

For important sources of material for research, see pp. 67–69. Pointing out that the eight volumes of the *Complete Collection of Compositions. Literary Works and Correspondence* by Rimsky-Korsakov [see No. 282] so far published cover only a small part of the total number of existing letters, the author enumerates the contents of Vols. V, VI, VII, and VIII, noting that various letters to his wife were published in the two-volume study: *Musical Legacy. Rimsky-Korsakov. Research. Materials. Letters.* [see No. 1204]. Some letters to his son, Andrey Nikolaevich, were published in *SM* 6 (1958) [see No. 258]. The book *N. A. Rimsky-Korsakov. Collection of Documents* [see No. 1527] contains letters to a large number of correspondents, including Andreev, Bessel', Zimin, Mamontov, Safonov, Cui, and Cheshikhin. Letters to Ostrovsky are published in the volume *A. N. Ostrovsky and Russian Composers. Letters* [see No. 453].

The largest source of materials is to be found in the Rimsky-Korsakov Archive, RNB, containing thousands of letters relating to the composer, both by himself and by other correspondents, together with autobiographical materials, and matters relating to different stages of his musical life. The N. A. and A. N. Rimsky-Korsakov Archive at the SPBGATI, established in 1944, contains extensive material relating to the Rimsky-Korsakov family over several generations, together with archival materials concerning his friends. The voluminous correspondence between the composer and his son, Andrey, which provides insight into Rimsky-Korsakov's opinions on contemporary music, current personalities, and events, is held in RNB and MMKG. Other repositories are the archive of his son, Andrey Nikolaevich, various family archives, particularly that of the Purgol'd family (Leningrad Institute of Theater, Music and Cinematography), the Bel'sky Archive, and that of Yastrebtsëv, whose personal diaries of the composer contain a wealth of material, much of which was not included in his *Reminiscences* [see No. 1422]. Part of a diary kept by N. N. Purgol'd [who later became Rimsky-Korsakov's wife], for the period 1871–72, was published in *SM* [see No. 1174].

1017   Polevaya, Marina. *Rimsky-Korsakov v Peterburge.* [Rimsky-Korsakov in St. Petersburg.] Leningrad: Lenizdat, 1989.

Rimsky-Korsakov spent most of his life in St. Petersburg, many of his operas being performed in the Imperial Theaters. Together with accounts of places with which he was closely associated, in particular the St. Petersburg Conservatory, the book includes a description of his apartment in Zagorodny Prospekt, which is now a museum.

1018   Reynaud, Alain. "Année croisée France-Russie 2010: L'appartement-musée Rimski-Korsakov." *Lélio: La lettre de l'AnHB* (24) (October 2010): 39. ISSN: 1760-9127.

Published by the Association nationale Hector Berlioz [AnHB] as part of the Crossover Year *France-Russia 2010*, the article discusses the Rimsky-Korsakov Memorial Apartment Museum, formerly Rimsky-Korsakov's residence, in St. Petersburg, together with an account of his life there.

1019 Rimsky-Korsakov, Andrey Nikolaevich, ed. *Muzykal'nye sokrovishcha rukopisnogo otdeleniya Gosudarstvennoy Publichnoy Biblioteki imeni M. E. Saltykova-Shchedrina (obzor muzykal'nykh rukopisnykh fondov)*. [Musical Treasures of the MS Section of the State Public Library named after Saltykov-Shchedrin (Survey of the Music MS Fonds).] Leningrad: Izd. Gos. Pub. Biblioteki, 1938. 111 pp.

For a description of the Rimsky-Korsakov Archive, of which the first curator was Rimsky-Korsakov's widow, Nadezhda Nikolaevna Rimskaya-Korsakova, until she was succeeded on her death in 1919 by her son Andrey, see pp. 59–72. Consisting of MSS ranging from finished works to rough sketches, the archive contains the following:

i. Considerable materials relating to the three versions of *The Maid of Pskov*, on which Rimsky-Korsakov worked over a period of 25 years.

ii. A large selection of information on the operas *The Snow Maiden*, *Sadko*, *Christmas Eve*, *The Tale of Tsar Saltan*, *Kashchey the Immortal*, and *The Golden Cockerel*.

iii. A substantial collection of materials on the orchestral and chamber works.

iv. Sketches for various unfinished projects, including *Sten'ka Razin*, *Nausicaä* (from Homer), *Earth and Sky* (after Byron), and *The Tale of the Fisherman and the Fish* (after Pushkin).

v. Materials on Rimsky-Korsakov's arrangements of works by Musorgsky, Borodin, and Acts II and III of Dargomyzhsky's *The Stone Guest* in its second orchestral version.

vi. Materials for work on his manuals of orchestration and harmony, exercises in counterpoint and fugue, autographs, fragments from a diary, articles on music, and a large collection of letters to Glazunov, Petrovsky, Kruglikov, Zabela-Vrubel', Bel'sky, Rimsky-Korsakov's parents, Findeyzen (39 letters), V. V. Stasov (42 letters), and others.

vii. Musical MSS of different Russian composers connected with Rimsky-Korsakov, including Azanchevsky, Artsybushev, Balakirev, Glazunov, Gussakovsky, S. M. and F. M. Ippolitov-Ivanov, Cui, Dargomyzhsky, and Igor Stravinsky.

viii. More than 1,000 letters to Rimsky-Korsakov from different correspondents both in Russia and abroad, written in Russian and other languages, including George Bainton (Coventry), F. G. Gleason (Chicago), Franz Liszt (Rome), von Sternberg (Philadelphia), and J. Tiersot (Paris), to mention only a few.

ix. Various official letters.

x. A collection of papers belonging to Bel'sky, with whom Rimsky-Korsakov cooperated in writing the libretti of *The Tale of Tsar Saltan*, *The Legend of the Invisible City of Kitezh*, *The Golden Cockerel*, and other projects, which contains many auxiliary pages, letters, and other materials.

Bibliography: General 199

xi. A collection of papers belonging to Yastrebtsëv, containing letters, reminiscences and music MSS, Rimsky-Korsakov's literary works on the teaching of music theory and practical composition, and 149 letters to Yastrebtsëv, together with a large number of letters collected by Yastrebtsëv, including ones from V. V. Stasov to Rimsky-Korsakov and his wife, and many others.

1020 Rimsky-Korsakov, Vladimir Nikolaevich. "Muzykal'no-esteticheskie printsipy 'Osnov orkestrovki' N. Rimskogo-Korsakova." [Musical Esthetic Principles of N. Rimsky-Korsakov's *Principles of Orchestration.*] *SM* 9 (1955): 56–70.

This detailed survey of a number of MSS in the Rimsky-Korsakov Archives of the SPBGATI and RNB discusses material relating to esthetics, melody, harmony, form, orchestration, and other matters, not previously included by his widow in the volume *Muzykal'nye stat'i i zametki* [Musical Articles and Notes] [see No. 211]. These include a sketch concerning his *Osnovy orkestrovki* [Principles of Orchestration] [see No. 212] entitled "Continuation of the Introduction," a MS belonging to 1904 with the heading "Manual on Contemporary Symphonic and Operatic Orchestration," and other materials.

1021 Solzhenikina, Valentina I. *Nikolay Andreevich Rimsky-Korsakov v Vechasha i Lyubenske.* [Nikolay Andreevich Rimsky-Korsakov in Vechasha and Lyubensk.] Russian Federation, 1994.

A description of the country estates of Vechasha and Lyubensk in the Pskov oblast' [province], where Rimsky-Korsakov composed several works. Museums in Vechasha and Lyubensk have now been established.

1022 Stepanova, Anna. "Tikhvinsky dom." [The House in Tikhvin.] *MA* (2) (1994): 23–29. ISSN: 0869-4516.

An account of the history of the Gosudarstvenny memorial'ny dom-myzey [State Memorial House Museum] of Nikolay Andreevich Rimsky-Korsakov when he lived in the town of Tikhvin, including such details as a picture of the church where he was christened.

1023 Tkachev, Donat Vasil'evich. "Neizvestnye sochineniya N. A. Rimskogo-Korsakova." [Unknown Works of N. A. Rimsky-Korsakov.] *Sovetskaya kul'tura* 101 (24 August 1954): 3.

A list of compositions by Rimsky-Korsakov found in the archives of the former Imperial Chapel. Six titles.

1024 Velimirović, Miloš. "Russian Autographs at Harvard." *Notes* 17 (4) (1960): 539–58.

Describes Russian materials given to the Houghton Library, Harvard University, by Bayard L. Kilgour, Jr., including a small piece of paper written in Dargomyzhsky's handwriting, containing an "Arabic" melody taken, it seems, from Khristianovich's *Esquisse historique de la musique arabe aux temps anciens*, and which was given by Dargomyzhsky to Rimsky-Korsakov, who employed it in the last movement of *Antar*. Other materials are a letter written by Rimsky-Korsakov to Lipaev, dated 3 [16] March 1908, a rough sketch of the "cradle song" in *The Golden Cockerel*, and an early sketch for his last song "Summer Night's Dream," subsequently published as Op. 56, No. 2. The autograph is dated 7 September 1898.

1025 Wright, Craig. "Rare Music Manuscripts at Harvard." *Current Musicology* 10 (1970): 25–33.

Includes mention of materials by Rimsky-Korsakov, described by Miloš Velimirović in *Notes* 17 (1960): 539–58. [See No. 1024.]

PERSONAL RELATIONSHIPS

Balakirev

1026 Balakirev, Mily Alekseevich. *Vospominaniya i pis'ma*. [Reminiscences and Letters.] E. L. Frid, ed. Leningrad: Muzgiz, 1962. 479 pp.

Consisting of letters and reminiscences, Rimsky-Korsakov is referred to frequently in this volume. See, in particular, Balakirev's correspondence with Tchaikovsky, pp. 115–203, Filippov, pp. 222–35, Bulich, pp. 237–76, and others. The index contains over a hundred references.

1027 Garden, Edward. *Balakirev. A Critical Study of his Life and Music*. London: Faber & Faber, 1967. 352 pp. ISBN-10: 0312065809. ISBN-13: 978-0312065805.

A detailed study of the musical life of the period with numerous references to Rimsky-Korsakov.

1028 Lyapunova, Anastasiya Sergeevna, ed. *M. A. Balakirev i V. V. Stasov. Perepiska*. [M. A. Balakirev and V. V. Stasov. Correspondence.] 2 Vols. Moscow: Muzyka, 1970–71. Vol. I: 487 pp., Vol. II: 422 pp. Index to both Vols. in: Vol. II.

As might be expected, there are many references to Rimsky-Korsakov and his work in these two volumes. Lyapunova's introductory essay in Vol. I discusses some of the complex relationships of the *Moguchaya Kuchka* [Mighty Handful], pp. 17–22, this being further underlined by such letters as that of Stasov to Balakirev dated 3 June 1887, Vol. II, pp. 104–05. The volumes are well indexed and annotated.

1029 Lyapunov, Sergey Mikhaylovich. "M. A. Balakirev." *EIT*. Prilozhenie [Supplement] VII. St. Petersburg (1910): 40–67; Prilozhenie VIII. St. Petersburg (1910): 31–53.

For Balakirev's relations with the other members of the *Moguchaya Kuchka* [Mighty Handful] and the way in which they gradually asserted their individuality, see Prilozhenie [Supplement] VII, pp. 52–67. Lyapunov quotes

Bibliography: General   201

Rimsky-Korsakov's severe reproach of Balakirev, but points out that Balakirev was a powerful catalyst and produced remarkable results. For a description of Balakirev's work in the Imperial Chapel and the part played by Rimsky-Korsakov, see Supplement VIII: 46–49.

Belyaev [Belaieff]

1030 Reed, David F. "Victor Ewald and the Russian Chamber Brass School." DMA dissertation, Eastman School of Music, 1979. 322 pp.

A discussion of Belyaev's Musical Gatherings which included Rimsky-Korsakov.

1031 Stasov, Vladimir Vasil'evich. *Mitrofan Petrovich Belyaev. Biografichesky ocherk.* [Mitrofan Petrovich Belyaev. A Biographical Sketch.] St. Petersburg: *Russkaya Muzykal'naya Gazeta* (1895). 55 pp. Reprinted: Moscow, 1954. 58 pp.

An account of two concerts of Russian music given at the Paris Exposition Universelle, the Palais du Trocadéro, on 22 and 29 June 1889, is found on pp. 22–26 of this short biography of the Maecenas, Mitrofan Belyaev. The concerts featured Rimsky-Korsakov's *Antar, Capriccio Espagnol,* and the Piano Concerto. Includes extracts from contemporary French reviews.

1032 Traynin, Vladimir Yakovlevich. *M. P. Belyaev i ego kruzhok. Populyarny ocherk.* [M. P. Belyaev and his Circle. A Popular Study.] Leningrad: Muzyka, 1975. 128 pp.

This "popular study" contains considerable material on Rimsky-Korsakov and his relations with the Russian publisher, Belyaev. The Appendices list the programs of the "Russian Symphony Concerts," 1885–95, and winners of the Glinka Prizes from 1884 to 1917, which were established by Belyaev for the encouragement of Russian music, and in both of which Rimsky-Korsakov was involved as conductor, composer, and prize winner.

Borodin

1033 Borodin, Aleksandr Porfir'evich. *Pis'ma.* [Letters.] S. Dianin, ed., with commentary and notes, Vols. I–IV. Moscow-Leningrad: Muzgiz, 1927–50.

Borodin's letters contain a wealth of information on Rimsky-Korsakov and his part in the Balakirev Circle. Though no complete translation of his letters has yet appeared in English, a number of translations are available from different sources. For a translation of several letters on Rimsky-Korsakov, see G. R. Seaman. "Borodin's Letters." *MQ* 70 (4) (1984): 476–98.

1034 ——. *O muzyke i muzykantakh (iz pisem).* [On Music and Musicians (from the Letters).] V. A. Kiselëv, ed., with notes and commentary. Moscow: Muzgiz, 1958. 354 pp.

Consisting of extracts from Borodin's letters, mainly to his wife but also to friends and colleagues, this contains references to 16 works of Rimsky-Korsakov, providing an impression of Rimsky-Korsakov and his relationship to members of the *Moguchaya Kuchka* [Mighty Handful].

Debussy

1035 Ruschenburg, Peter. "Stilkritische Untersuchungen zu den Liedern Claude Debussy's." *Die Musikforschung* XX 3 (1967): 316–17.

This summary of the author's dissertation includes reference to the influence of Rimsky-Korsakov on Debussy.

1036 Schaeffner, André. "Debussy et ses rapports avec la musique russe." In *Musique Russe. Etudes réunies par Pierre Souvtchinsky.* Tome premier. Paris: Presses Universitaires de France, 1953: 95–138.

Schaeffner points out that Debussy was familiar with a number of Rimsky-Korsakov's works, which he heard performed in Russia and abroad, concluding that certain elements could well have been assimilated by him.

Dyagilev [Diaghilev]

1037 Nest'ev, Izrail Vladimirovich. "Sergey Dyagilev – russky muzykant." [Sergey Diaghilev – Russian Musician.] *SM* 10 (1978): 111–26.

A general article on Diaghilev, including details of his association with Rimsky-Korsakov, with extracts from his correspondence.

Glazunov

1038 Ganina, Mariya Alekseevna. "N. A. Rimsky-Korsakov i A. K. Glazunov." [N. A. Rimsky-Korsakov and A. K. Glazunov.] In No. 1435: 135–57.

Divided into eight sections, this traces the relationship between Rimsky-Korsakov and Glazunov from 1879. Includes a discussion of their editorial work, musical connections, pedagogical links, concert activity, the Belyaev Circle, and other factors.

1039 Glezer, Raisa Vladimirovna, ed. "Pis'ma A. K. Glazunova k S. N. Kruglikovu." [A. K. Glazunov's Letters to S. N. Kruglikov.] *SM* 2–3 (1946): 108–20; 4 (1946): 61–71.

These letters, written by Glazunov to Kruglikov between 1882 and 1908, mention Rimsky-Korsakov, with observations on his new works and their reception. Includes a critical account of the first performance of *Scheherazade* (letter 11, dated 2 November 1888). Also described are Rimsky-Korsakov's

Bibliography: General 203

Belgian concerts and those organized by Belyaev at the Paris All-World Exposition in 1889. Glezer gives an informative introduction.

1040 Kurtsman, Alisa. *A. K. Glazunov.* Moscow: Muzyka, 1977. 126 pp.

Includes discussion of Glazunov's association with Rimsky-Korsakov.

Glinka

1041 Fedorovtsev, S. "O tvorcheskikh svyazyakh Rimskogo-Korsakova s Glinkoy." [On Rimsky-Korsakov's Creative Links with Glinka.] In *Pamyati Glinki. 1857-1957. Issledovaniya i materialy.* [In Memory of Glinka. 1857-1957. Research and Materials.] Moscow: Izd. Akad. Nauk, 1958: 349–62.

An article highlighting the manner in which Rimsky-Korsakov's music and thought were influenced by Glinka's compositions and methods.

1042 Garden, Edward. "Classic and Romantic in Russian Music." *ML* 50 (1) (1969): 153–57.

An examination of Rimsky-Korsakov's stylistic development and his relationship with contemporary Russian musicians. The author sees Rimsky-Korsakov as a link between Glinka and Stravinsky in the fusing of the Classical and Romantic in Russian music.

1043 Kremlëv, Yuly Anatol'evich. "Bessmertnye traditsii Glinki." [The Immortal Traditions of Glinka.] *SM* 5 (1954): 49–56.

The author sees similarities between women's roles in Rimsky-Korsakov's operas and those of Glinka, and parallels in scoring and certain features of instrumentation, considering that both had an interest in the "Orient" and Spain, the same clarity of sound, clean part-writing, and share a common elegance and harmonic strength.

1044 Rimsky-Korsakov, Vladimir Nikolaevich. "Shkola zhizni." [School of Life.] *SM* 6 (1954): 57–61.

A short article highlighting Rimsky-Korsakov's admiration for Glinka's music and the extent to which this influenced his composition.

Liszt

1045 Abraham, Gerald. "Liszt's Influence on the 'Mighty Handful'." In No. 284: 81–90. ISBN-13: 978-0571307272.

Discusses the influence of such works as Liszt's *Mephisto Waltz, Ce qu'on entend sur la montagne, Hunnenschlacht, Totentanz, Der nächtliche Zug,* the *Faust Symphony* on Rimsky-Korsakov and other Russian composers.

1046 Kiselëv, Vasily Aleksandrovich. *Frants List i ego otnoshenie k russkomu iskusstvu.* [Franz Liszt and His Attitude Towards Russian Art.] Moscow: Muzykal'ny Sektor, 1929. 47 pp.

For a discussion of Liszt and Rimsky-Korsakov, including comments on Liszt, on Rimsky-Korsakov's folk song collection, and the collective *Paraphrases*, to which he also contributed, see pp. 24–30. Rimsky-Korsakov's Piano Concerto was dedicated to Liszt, whose influence is apparent in a number of structural features.

1047 Suttoni, Charles. "Liszt and Louise de Mercy-Argenteau." *JALS* 34 (July–December 1993). ISSN: 0147-4413.

A discussion of Liszt's friendship with the Countess Louise de Mercy-Argenteau (1837–90) and the part she played in helping to promote the music of the *Moguchaya Kuchka* [Mighty Handful], including that of Rimsky-Korsakov.

Lyadov

1048 Eberlein, Dorothee. "Anatolij Ljadow (1855-1914): Leben. Werk. Musikanschauung." PhD dissertation, Musicology, University of Köln, 1978.

Includes materials on Rimsky-Korsakov.

1049 Mikhaylov, Mikhail Kesarevich. "N. A. Rimsky-Korsakov i A. K. Lyadov." [N. A. Rimsky-Korsakov and A. K. Lyadov.] In No. 1435: 158–69.

Of all Rimsky-Korsakov's pupils, none were closer to him than Glazunov and Lyadov. This article traces the development of the relationship between Lyadov and his teacher, including details of Rimsky-Korsakov's apparent bewilderment over Lyadov's slow productivity. Rimsky-Korsakov held Lyadov in high esteem as a teacher and conductor and throughout his life they maintained a lively correspondence.

1050 ——. "Iz neopublikovannykh i maloizvestnykh materialov." [From Unpublished and Little-Known Materials.] *SM* 8 (1980): 116–23.

Concerned primarily with Lyadov, this article includes materials from Rimsky-Korsakov's incomplete memoirs.

Musorgsky

1051 Kunin, Iosif Filippovich. "Rimsky-Korsakov i Musorgsky." [Rimsky-Korsakov and Musorgsky.] *MZ* 5 (1969): 4.

Contains observations on the relationship between the two composers.

1052 Leyda, Jay and Bertensson, Sergei, eds. and trans. *The Musorgsky Reader. A Life of Modeste Petrovich Musorgsky in Letters and Documents.* New York: Norton, 1947. xxiii, 474 pp. Reprint: New York: Da Capo Press, 1970.

Contains more than a dozen letters by Rimsky-Korsakov, and many references to Rimsky-Korsakov and his works.

Bibliography: General

1053 *Atti del Covegno Internazionale Musorgskij.* Milano: Teatro alla Scala, 1981. 340 pp.

Proceedings of the international conference on Musorgsky held in 1981, containing many references to Rimsky-Korsakov, including papers by Baroni, Lloyd-Jones, Oldani, and others.

1054 Musorgsky, Modest Petrovich. *Pis'ma. Biograficheskie materialy i dokumenty.* [Letters, Biographical Materials and Documents.] A. A. Orlova and M. S. Pekelis, eds. Moscow: Muzyka, 1971. 400 pp.

Rimsky-Korsakov and Musorgsky were particularly close during 1867–72 as may be seen by their correspondence. Though relations cooled towards 1874, Rimsky-Korsakov conducted and orchestrated several of Musorgsky's works and performed them in 1874, 1879, and 1880. This volume provides information on Rimsky-Korsakov's creative aims and highlights facets of his personality.

1055 ——. *Pis'ma.* [Letters.] Moscow: Muzyka, 1981. 359 pp.

Includes Musorgsky's extensive correspondence with Rimsky-Korsakov.

1056 Rimskaya-Korsakova, Nadezhda Nikolaevna. "Neizdannye pis'ma M. P. Musorgskogo k N. A. Rimskomu-Korsakovu." [M. P. Musorgsky's Unpublished Letters to N. A. Rimsky-Korsakov.] *RMG* 13–14 (1909): cols. 353–58; 16 (1909): cols. 417–23; 17 (1909): cols. 449–43; 18–19 (1909): cols. 485–87.

Communicated and annotated by Rimsky-Korsakov's widow, and preceded by a short introductory note by Findeyzen, the editor of *RMG*, this consists of nine letters from Musorgsky to Rimsky-Korsakov, written during the period 1869–76, expressing Musorgsky's opinions about various works of Rimsky-Korsakov [*Antar,* "Sadko"].

1057 Tyumenev, I. F. "Posledny put' Musorgskogo. (Iz dnevnika)." [Musorgsky's Last Moments. (From a Diary).] *SM* 7 (1959).

Extracts from a diary kept by Tyumenev, a pupil of Rimsky-Korsakov, including brief reference to the part played by Rimsky-Korsakov in Musorgsky's obsequies.

Pushkin

1058 Asaf'ev, Boris Vladimirovich [pseud. Glebov, Igor']. "Pushkin v russkoy muzyke." [Pushkin in Russian Music.] *SM* 6 (1949): 7–13. Reprinted: No. 1256: Vol. IV, 144–53.

A eulogistic article on Pushkin, describing how Rimsky-Korsakov drew inspiration from him when composing *The Tale of Tsar Saltan, Mozart and Salieri,* and *The Golden Cockerel.* Asaf'ev highlights the links between the verbal brilliance of poet and composer.

1059 Braudo, Evgeny Maksimovich. "Pushkin v russkoy muzyke." [Pushkin in Russian Music.] *Teatral'naya dekada* 5 (135) (1937): 7–8.

Discusses Rimsky-Korsakov's links with Pushkin.

1060 Lapshin, Ivan Ivanovich. "Pushkin i russkie kompozitory." [Pushkin and Russian Composers.] In V. Ossovsky, ed. *Orfey* [Orpheus], Book I. Petrograd: Gosudarstvennaya Filarmoniya, 1922: 62–79.

First published in the program of a symphony concert "In Memory of Pushkin," given by the Petrograd Philharmonic on 12 February 1922, this wide-ranging philosophico-esthetic article underlines Rimsky-Korsakov's indebtedness to Pushkin and the effect Pushkin's work had on those composers who utilized his themes.

1061 Vasina, Vera Andreevna. "Lirika Pushkina v puti russkogo romansa." [Pushkin's Lyric Poetry in the Course of the Russian *Romance*.] *SM* 7 (1949): 7–13.

A brief discussion of Pushkin's influence on the development of chamber song in Russian music, including various settings of Pushkin's poems by Rimsky-Korsakov.

1062 Yakovlev, Vasily Vasil'evich. "Pushkin i russky operny teatr (Musorgsky i Rimsky-Korsakov)." [Pushkin and the Russian Opera Theater (Musorgsky and Rimsky-Korsakov).] *SM* 6 (1937): 42–54.

Includes a discussion of *Mozart and Salieri, The Tale of Tsar Saltan*, and *The Golden Cockerel*, showing that three completely different works of Pushkin evoked varied responses from Rimsky-Korsakov [see No. 897].

1063 ——. *Pushkin i Rimsky-Korsakov*. [Pushkin and Rimsky-Korsakov.] Review by Semën Isaakovich Korev. *SM* 8 (1950): 102–03.

Korev's review contains some critical observations about Yakovlev's book, questioning some of the author's judgements.

1064 ——. *Pushkin i muzyka*. [Pushkin and Music.] (1949). Second edition, Moscow: Muzgiz, 1957. 264 pp.

Includes a chapter "Pushkin and Rimsky-Korsakov," pp. 180–208, which discusses briefly his songs to Pushkin's texts, followed by the operas *Mozart and Salieri, The Tale of Tsar Saltan*, and *The Golden Cockerel*.

Rakhmaninov

1065 Bertensson, S. and Leyda, J. *Sergei Rachmaninoff. A Lifetime in Music*. London: Allen & Unwin, 1965. 446 pp. ISBN-10: 0253214211. ISBN-13: 978-0253214218.

Rakhmaninov conducted the première of a number of Rimsky-Korsakov's works and expressed his opinion on the composer on several occasions. This

Bibliography: General 207

volume contains material on the relationship between the two musicians as seen in letters, reminiscences, and other sources.

1066 Konenkov, S. "Vospominaniya o Rakhmaninove." [Reminiscences of Rakhmaninov.] *SM* 4 (1953): 64–66.

Contains observations on Rimsky-Korsakov, stressing his roots in Russian soil.

1067 Palmieri, Robert. *Sergei Vasil'evich Rachmaninoff. A Guide to Research.* New York and London: Garland Publishing, 1985. ISBN-10: 0824089960. ISBN-13: 978-0824089962.

Contains references to Rimsky-Korsakov. A piano arrangement of "The Flight of the Bumble Bee" played a prominent part in Rakhmaninov's concert programs as an encore.

Rubinstein

1068 Barenboym, Lev Aronovich. *Nikolay Grigor'evich Rubinshteyn. Istoriya zhizni i deyatel'nosti.* [Nikolay Grigor'evich Rubinshteyn. History of Life and Work.] Moscow: Muzyka, 1982. 277 pp.

Includes references to Rimsky-Korsakov and a section entitled "Rubinshteyn and Rimsky-Korsakov (prior to the Paris Concerts)," pp. 170–72.

1069 Petrov, I., ed. *Russian Symphonic Music*, Vol. III. Muzïka/Collets. Review: Edward Garden. *MT* 2 (1987): 91.

A review, noting the influence of Anton Rubinstein's Musical Picture *Ivan IV the Terrible* on Rimsky-Korsakov.

Skryabin [Scriabin]

1070 Rimskaya-Korsakova, Nadezhda Nikolaevna. "N. A. Rimsky-Korsakov i A. N. Skryabin." [N. A. Rimsky-Korsakov and A. N. Skryabin.] *SM* 5 (1950): 67–69. German trans. N. N. Rimskaya-Korsakova. "Rimskij-Korssakow und Skrjabin." *Osterreichische Musikzeitschrift* (October–November, 1950): 221–24.

A short account by Rimsky-Korsakov's widow, written in 1915, about the relationship of the two composers. Rimsky-Korsakov had a somewhat curious regard for Skryabin, though he saw deficiencies in his later works. A few corrections have been made by V. N. Rimsky-Korsakov.

1071 Verdi, Luigi. "Kandinskij e Skrjabin: Realtà e utopia nella Russia pre-rivoluzionaria." Italy: Akademos musica, 1996. 176 pp. ISBN-10: 8870961516. ISBN-13: 978-8870961515.

Entitled "Kandinsky and Scriabin: Reality and Utopia in Pre-revolutionary Russia," this discusses the work of Aleksandr Skryabin and Vasily Kandinsky

208   *Nikolay Andreevich Rimsky-Korsakov: A Research and Information Guide*

in the period 1895–1925 and their attitude towards synesthesia, including letters to Skryabin written by Rimsky-Korsakov.

Spendiarov

1072   Tigranov, Georgy Grigor'evich. *A. Spendiarov. Po materialam pisem i vospominaniy.* [A. Spendiarov. Based on Materials from Letters and Reminiscences.] Erevan: Aypetrat, 1953. 190 pp. Second edition, Moscow: Muzgiz, 1959. 330 pp.

An account of Spendiarov's relationship with Rimsky-Korsakov, with whom he studied from 1896 to 1900, is discussed on pp. 36–45 of the second edition. Tigranov considers Spendiarov to be indebted to Rimsky-Korsakov, who paid much attention to the treatment of folk elements as well as their harmonization and orchestration. Spendiarov's *Kontsertnaya uvertyura* [Concert Overture] Op. 4, published by Bessel' (1900), is dedicated to Rimsky-Korsakov, as is also the *Traurnaya prelyudiya* [Funeral Prelude] Op. 20 (1908), written in his memory.

1073   ——. "N. A. Rimsky-Korsakov i A. A. Spendiarov." [Rimsky-Korsakov and Spendiarov.] In No. 1435: 170–79.

Rimsky-Korsakov's relations with the Armenian composer, Spendiarov.

Stasov

1074   Blinova, M. P. and Rimsky-Korsakov, V. N., eds. "Pis'ma V. V. Stasova k S. N. Kruglikovu (1881-1906)." [V. V. Stasov's letters to S. N. Kruglikov (1881-1906).] *SM* 8 (1949): 56–64; 9 (1949): 48–51; 10 (1949): 73–74; 11 (1949): 78–85; 12 (1949): 94–100.

The references to Rimsky-Korsakov show how he was regarded by his friends and colleagues. Balakirev's and Rimsky-Korsakov's work at the Imperial Chapel is discussed in *SM* 8, pp. 56–64.

1075   Karenin, Vladimir [pseud. Stasova, Varvara Dmitrievna]. *Vladimir Stasov. Ocherk ego zhizni i deyatel'nosti.* [Vladimir Stasov. Outline of His Life and Work.] Vols. I–II. Leningrad: Mysl', 1927. 727 pp.

Contains many references to Rimsky-Korsakov, pp. 423–31 being concerned with his relationship with Stasov and the St. Petersburg ambience.

1076   Livanova, Tamara Nikolaevna. "Stasov v sotrudnichestve s Borodinym i Rimskim-Korsakovym." [Stasov in Collaboration with Borodin and Rimsky-Korsakov.] In T. N. Livanova. *Stasov i russkaya klassicheskaya opera.* [Stasov and Russian Classical Opera.] Moscow: Muzgiz, 1957: 265–354.

Bibliography: General 209

For an account of Rimsky-Korsakov's indebtedness to V. V. Stasov, who championed his cause through his writings and suggested subjects for compositions, including the scenario for the opera *Sadko,* see pp. 265–354.

1077 Olkhovsky, Yuri. *Vladimir Stasov and Russian National Culture.* Ann Arbor, Michigan: UMI Research Press, 1983. 195 pp. ISBN-10: 0835714128. ISBN-13: 978-0835714129.

For an account of Stasov's and Rimsky-Korsakov's relationship, including Stasov's ambivalent attitudes, see pp. 74–77.

1078 Jonas, Florence, trans. *Stasov, Vladimir Vasil'evich. "Selected Essays on Music."* Intro. by Gerald Abraham. London: Barrie and Rockliff, 1968; London: Cresset Press, 1968. New York: Frederick A. Praeger, 1968. London: Barrie & Jenkins, 1969. 202 pp. ISBN-10: 0214160394. ISBN-13: 978-0214160394. Reprinted: Da Capo Press 1980. ISBN-10: 0306760339. ISBN-13: 978-0306760334.

Numerous references to Rimsky-Korsakov, including a discussion on pp. 105–07, showing the kind of support the composer received from the critic, Stasov.

1079 Yankovsky, Moisey Osipovich. "Stasov i Rimsky-Korsakov." [Stasov and Rimsky-Korsakov.] In No. 1204: Vol. I, 337–403.

Describes the interaction between the two personalities, particular mention being made of Stasov's encouragement of the composition of *Sadko, The Tale of Tsar Saltan,* and *Scheherazade.*

Stravinsky, Igor' Fëdorovich

1080 Asaf'ev, Boris Vladimirovich [pseud. Glebov, Igor']. *Kniga o Stravinskom.* [A Book about Stravinsky.] Leningrad: Triton, 1929. Second edition, Moscow, 1977. English trans. Richard F. French, intro. by Robert Craft. Ann Arbor, Michigan: UMI Research Press, 1982. 325 pp. ISBN-10: 0835713202. ISBN-13: 978-0835713207.

Discusses Stravinsky's indebtedness to Rimsky-Korsakov as seen in his early works.

1081 Druskin, Mikhail Semënovich. *Igor' Stravinsky. Lichnost'. Tvorchestvo. Vzglyady.* [Igor Stravinsky. Personality. Work. Opinions.] Leningrad-Moscow: Sovetsky Kompozitor, 1974. 221 pp.

Contains references to Rimsky-Korsakov, including Stravinsky's work with the composer in the last years of his life. For a discussion of the extent of Stravinsky's indebtedness to his teacher, see pp. 42–44.

1082 Smirnov, Valery Vasil'evich. *Tvorcheskoe formirovanie I. F. Stravinskogo.* [I. F. Stravinsky's Creative Formulation.] Leningrad: Muzyka, 1970. 151 pp.

Discusses the influences on Stravinsky's early life, his indebtedness to Rimsky-Korsakov for certain harmonic and melodic materials, the influence of *Kashchey the Immortal*, and other factors. [See pp. 42–43, 45–50, 91–94, 104–06, 117–19, 126–48, 141–47.]

1083 Stravinsky, Igor Fëdorovich. *An Autobiography*. New York: Simon & Schuster, 1936. Reprinted: New York: W. W. Norton, 1998; 2013. 192 pp. ISBN-10: 0393318567. ISBN-13: 978-0393318562.

Published originally in Paris in 1935–36 as *Chroniques de ma vie*, the numerous references to Rimsky-Korsakov are only part of the many to be found in the total corpus of Stravinsky literature, embracing such works as his *Poetique musicale sous forme de six leçons* of 1942 and the numerous conversations with Robert Craft.

1084 Taruskin, Richard. "Russian Folk Melodies in 'The Rite of Spring'." *JAMS* 33 (3) (1980): 501–43. ISSN: 0003-0139.

The author notes Stravinsky's indebtedness to Rimsky-Korsakov, observing that whereas Rimsky-Korsakov tended to employ folk motives as thematic material, his pupil used them in a more subtle and complex manner which became an integral part of his musical style.

1085 Vershinina, Inna. *Rannie balety Stravinskogo. Zhar'-ptitsa, Petrushka, Vesna svyashchënnaya*. [Stravinsky's Early Ballets. *Firebird, Petrushka, Rite of Spring*.] Moscow: Nauka, 1967. 223 pp.

Includes a discussion of Stravinsky's links with Rimsky-Korsakov and his school, and the latter's influence on his work.

Taneev

1086 Bernandt, Grigory Borisovich. *S. I. Taneev*. Moscow-Leningrad: Muzgiz, 1950. 378 pp.

For a discussion of Taneev's opinions regarding some of Rimsky-Korsakov's works, see pp. 164–70. While approving of *Sadko* and *Kashchey the Immortal*, he was less enthusiastic about *The Tale of Tsar Saltan*. He commended Rimsky-Korsakov's *Principles of Orchestration* and expressed his admiration for the composer, dedicating to him his First String Quintet, Op. 14, in the third movement of which he quotes fragments from *Sadko*.

1087 Taneev, Sergey Ivanovich. *Materialy i dokumenty. Tom I. Perepiska i vospominaniya*. [Materials and Documents. Vol. I. Correspondence and Reminiscences.] B. V. Asaf'ev, ed. Moscow: Izd. Akad. Nauk SSSR, 1962. 255 pp.

Contains Taneev's correspondence with Rimsky-Korsakov and his wife.

Bibliography: General 211

Tchaikovsky [Chaykovsky]

1088 Chaykovsky [Tchaikovsky], Pëtr Il'ich. *Perepiska s N. F. fon Mekk.* [Correspondence with N. F. von Meck.], V. A. Zhdanov and N. T. Zhegin, eds., Vol. III. 1882–1900. Moscow: Academia, 1936. 683 pp.

Contains numerous references to Rimsky-Korsakov, including a letter dated 26 December 1888 in which Tchaikovsky speaks of the high regard in which he holds Rimsky-Korsakov and members of the *Moguchaya Kuchka* [Mighty Handful], pp. 560–61. In a letter dated 27 October 1885, Tchaikovsky mentions hearing a performance of *The Snow Maiden*, but makes no comment except that it was "very decently performed."

1089 ———. "Beseda s Chaykovskim v noyabre 1892 g v Peterburge." [A Conversation with Tchaikovsky in November 1892 in Petersburg.] In V. V. Yakovlev, ed. *P. I. Chaykovsky. Muzykal'no-kriticheskie stat'i.* [P. I. Tchaikovsky. Musical-Critical Articles.] Moscow: Muzgiz, 1953: 367–73; 421–22.

Tchaikovsky speaks of his high regard for Rimsky-Korsakov, pp. 372–73, pointing out similarities in their musical aims and achievements.

1090 ———. *Pis'ma k blizkim. Izbrannoe* [Letters to Relatives. Selections], V. A. Zhdanov, ed., with commentary. Moscow: Muzgiz, 1955. XV, 671 pp.

For references to Rimsky-Korsakov, see Index, p. 650.

1091 Garden, Edward. "The Influence of Balakirev on Tchaikovsky." *Proceedings of the Royal Musical Association* CVII (1981): 86–100.

This discussion of Tchaikovsky's association with Balakirev and his Circle, including Rimsky-Korsakov, concludes that Tchaikovsky's music is no more "Westernised" than that of Balakirev or Rimsky-Korsakov.

1092 G. B. [Bernandt, Grigory.] "Zabytoe intervyu s P. I. Chaykovskim." [A Forgotten Interview with Tchaikovsky.] *SM* 7 (1949): 59–61.

Includes several references to Rimsky-Korsakov, in which Tchaikovsky asserts that he and Rimsky often had common aims.

1093 Keeton, A. E. "Nikolai Andreyevitch Rimsky-Korsakov." *Contemporary Review* 89 (1906): 539–48.

Despite occasional factual inaccuracies, the author draws parallels between Rimsky-Korsakov and Tchaikovsky, and with the marine painter Ivan K. Ayvazovsky. He concludes with a plea that Russian songs should be sung in their original language.

1094 Stein, Richard. *Tschaikowskij.* Stuttgart, Berlin und Leipzig: Deutsche Verlags-Anstalt, 1927. 508 pp.

For Rimsky-Korsakov, see pp. 51–53. Includes comments on Rimsky-Korsakov by Tchaikovsky and observations on his general significance.

Wagner

1095 Gozenpud, Abram Akimovich. "Rikhard Vagner i russkaya kul'tura." [Richard Wagner and Russian Culture.] *SM* 4 (1983): 78–87; 5 (1983): 84–90.

For Wagner's influence on Rimsky-Korsakov, see pp. 85–87.

1096 Gunst, Evgeny Ottovich. "Rimsky-Korsakov o Vagnere." [Rimsky-Korsakov on Wagner.] *Maski* 5 (1912–13).

An examination of Rimsky-Korsakov's attitude towards Wagner's music.

1097 Korzhukin, Ivan Alekseevich. *N. Rimsky-Korsakov i Rikhard Vagner.* [N. Rimsky-Korsakov and Richard Wagner.] Berlin: O. Stolberg, 1920. 46 pp.

An article showing some of the parallels and differences between the two operatic composers and the extent to which both drew their inspiration from their national heritage. Expresses the idea that emerging Russia should create a Rimsky-Korsakov theater just as Germany had its Bayreuth.

1098 Malecka, Teresa. "Rimski-Korsakow a dramat muzyczny Wagnera." [Rimsky-Korsakov and Wagner's Music Drama.] *Muzyka* XIX 1 (1974): 69–74.

A discussion of Wagner's influence on Rimsky-Korsakov and the Russian composer's attitude towards him as reflected in literary writings and correspondence.

1099 Rimsky-Korsakov, Nikolay Andreevich. "Vagner i Dargomyzhsky. Sovokupnoe proizvedenie dvukh iskusstv ili muzykal'naya drama." [Wagner and Dargomyzhsky. A Combined Work of Two Arts or Music Drama.] *SM* 3 (1933): 136–43.

First published in the volume: N. A. Rimsky-Korsakov. *Musical Articles and Notes (1869-1907)* [see No. 211], this article is identical to the original apart from an unsigned editorial introduction. Rimsky-Korsakov examines Wagner's contribution from various angles (rhythm, use of leitmotifs, coordination of the vocal line with orchestra, orchestration, tempo, harmony, the system of endless melody) and many other factors such as Wagner's avoidance of folk song. Rimsky-Korsakov, despite some reservations, sees Wagner as "a creator of wonderful, poetic scenes, the creator of moments of beautiful descriptive music, which are scattered throughout his musical-dramatic works: therein lies his main strength" [see p. 143].

1100 Yastrebtsëv, Vasily Vasil'evich. "Rimsky-Korsakov o Vagnere (po lichnym vospominaniyami)." [Rimsky-Korsakov on Wagner (from Personal Reminiscences).] *SM* 5 (1933): 122–25.

Bibliography: General

This article, originally published in the paper *Russkie vedomosti* 130 (8 June 1911), concerns Rimsky-Korsakov's opinions on Wagner, and forms a complement to his own article "Wagner and Dargomyzhsky" [see Nos. 211 and 1099]. While Rimsky-Korsakov liked Wagner's "Waldweben" [Forest Murmurs], he disliked the "Siegfried Idyll" and the Funeral March from the *Götterdämmerung*. Of the operas, he enjoyed most *Die Walküre, Siegfried, Tristan*, and *Die Meistersinger*, although, while admiring many of Wagner's orchestral innovations, he found him lacking in rhythm. The article contains some substantial comments by Rimsky-Korsakov on *Tristan* and *Siegfried*, in which he compares his own musical qualities with those of Wagner and their creative aims.

Miscellaneous

1101   Abbasov, Ashraf Dzhalal ogly. "Ob Uzeire Gadzhibekove." [Uzeir Gadzhibekov.] *SM* 8 (1977): 40–43.

Examines Rimsky-Korsakov's influence on Gadzhibekov and the subsequent development of Azerbaidzhan opera.

1102   Anonymous. "Russkie muzykanti i kritiki o Shopene." [Russian Musicians and Critics on Chopin.] *SM* 5 (1949): 72–76.

Discusses Rimsky-Korsakov's indebtedness to Chopin, both melodically and harmonically, with observations on Chopin and his influence on Russian music.

1103   Braudo, Evgeny Maksimovich. "Ostrovsky v muzyke." [Ostrovsky in Music.] *Teatral'naya dekada* 31 (1934): 6–7.

Discusses Rimsky-Korsakov's association with A. N. Ostrovsky.

1104   Covell, Roger. "Berlioz, Russia and the Twentieth Century." *Studies in Music* IV (1970): 40–51.

Includes a brief discussion of Berlioz's influences on Rimsky-Korsakov.

1105   Livanova, Tamara Nikolaevna. *Motsart i russkaya muzykal'naya kul'tura.* [Mozart and Russian Musical Culture.] Moscow: Muzgiz, 1956. 112 pp.

For a discussion of Rimsky-Korsakov's attitude towards Mozart, whom he venerated along with Glinka, and the manner in which Mozartian elements influenced his own music and esthetic outlook, see pp. 81–87.

1106   Lysenko, Osip Nikolaevich. "Tvorcheskie svyazi N. A. Rimskogo-Korsakova i N. V. Lysenko (po lichnym vospominaniyam)." [Creative Links Between N. A. Rimsky-Korsakov and N. V. Lysenko (from Personal Reminiscences).] In No. 1435: 185–88.

Nikolay Vital'evich Lysenko studied orchestration under Rimsky-Korsakov from 1874 to 1876. The article, written by his son, describes the friendly relations between the young Ukrainian composer and the manner in which Lysenko was able to return Rimsky-Korsakov's hospitality when on his visit to Kiev in 1897.

1107 Peppercorn, Lisa M. "Foreign influences in Villa-Lobos' music." *Ibero-Amerikanisches Archiv* III (1) (1977): 37–51.

Includes references to Rimsky-Korsakov's influence on Villa-Lobos.

1108 Rastopchina, Nataliya Markovna. "Pis'ma k N. A. Rimskomu-Korsakovu." [Letters to N. A. Rimsky-Korsakov.] *SM* 8 (1973): 89–96.

The friendship of Feliks Blumenfel'd with the composer began in the autumn of 1881 when he performed Rimsky-Korsakov's Piano Concerto, accompanied Shalyapin [Chaliapin] and other notable performers of Rimsky-Korsakov's songs, and as a conductor gave his orchestral and operatic works in which he was reckoned to have displayed greater sensitivity than Nápravník. His 12 letters to the composer cover the period 1897–1908. One letter describes performances of *Boris Godunov* and *The Snow Maiden* in Paris in 1908.

1109 Rozova, T. G. "N. A. Rimsky-Korsakov i M. M. Ippolitov-Ivanov." [N. A. Rimsky-Korsakov and M. M. Ippolitov-Ivanov.] In No. 1435: 179–84.

An account of Rimsky-Korsakov's friendship with Ippolitov-Ivanov who was his student at the St. Petersburg Conservatory from 1878 to 1882.

1110 Tyumeneva, Galina Aleksandrovna. *Gogol' i muzyka.* [Gogol and Music.] Moscow: Muzyka, 1966. 215 pp.

Rimsky-Korsakov's indebtedness to Gogol, as seen in the operas *May Night* and *Christmas Eve*, is discussed on pp. 119–47.

BIOGRAPHY

1111 A. K-y. "K 35-letnemu yubileyu N. A. Rimskogo-Korsakova." [On the 35th Jubilee of N. A. Rimsky-Korsakov.] *RMG* 51 (1900): cols. 1259–61.

A tribute to the composer, recalling his first compositions in 1865 and referring to him as the senior figure of contemporary Russian music. With a facsimile of his musical handwriting and a poem.

1112 Abraham, Gerald. *Rimsky-Korsakov. A Short Biography.* London: Duckworth, 1945. 142 pp. Reprinted: New York: AMS Press, 1975. ISBN-10: 0404145000. ISBN-13: 978-0404145002.

Relies heavily on the composer's *Chronicle.* Contains list of compositions.

Bibliography: General 215

1113 Anonymous. "Our Portrait of Rimsky-Korsakov." *Musical Standard* 19 (1903): 339.

A short, contemporary biographical sketch with a list of the composer's chief works until that date.

1114 Anonymous. "Pamyati Nikolaya Andreevicha Rimskogo-Korsakova." [In Memory of Nikolay Andreevich Rimsky-Korsakov.] *RMG* 24–25 (1908): cols. 529–32.

A nationalistic article opining the loss of a great Russian composer, "a mighty singer of Russian folk antiquity."

1115 Anonymous. "K konchine N. A. Rimskogo-Korsakova." [On the Death of N. A. Rimsky-Korsakov.] *RMG* 24–25 (1908): cols. 533–34; 26–27 (1908): cols. 565–66; 30–31 (1908): col. 626; 32–33 (1908): cols. 656–58.

A series of articles in memory of the composer, including details of his last rites. One account [see *RMG* Nos. 26–27, col. 566], expresses Glazunov's hypothesis that Rimsky-Korsakov's death was hastened by the arrival of two letters, one announcing that the censor had refused permission for the performance of *The Golden Cockerel*, the other from the Society of French Composers declining his application for membership, thus preventing him from receiving fees from productions of his operas in France. No. 32–33, cols. 656–58, gives details of unfinished projects, including the operas *Tragediya synov chelovecheskikh* [The Tragedy of Human Sons] based on Byron's *Heaven and Earth*, for which he made a number of sketches, *Sten'ka Razin*, and *Skazka o rybake i rybke* [The Tale of the Fisherman and the Fish].

1116 Asaf'ev, Boris Vladimirovich [pseud. Glebov, Igor']. "N. A. Rimsky-Korsakov." In No. 296: 40–48.

First published as a supplement to a program of a concert given by the Petrograd Philharmonic in 1919, Asaf'ev discusses the composer's self-discipline, unremitting labor, determination, pedagogical work, esthetic attitudes, together with a brief outline of his life.

1117 ——. "Geniy russkoy muzyki." [A Genius of Russian Music.] *MZ* 5 (1969): 1.

A reprint of an article written in 1944, published in a special issue of the journal marking the composer's 125th anniversary.

1118 ——. *Nikolay Andreevich Rimsky-Korsakov (1844-1944)*. Moscow-Leningrad: Muzgiz, 1944. 91 pp. Reprinted: No. 1256: Vol. III, 171–224. Reviews: *Ogonëk* 12–13 (1944): 12; *Oktyabr'* 1–2 (1944): 172–73.

Rather than a critical biography, this is an extended essay on the composer, comprising four untitled sections and a conclusion. Clearly influenced by the ideology of the period, it stresses the importance of folk culture as a creative source of inspiration.

1119 Barsowa, L. "Rimski-Korsakow, verehrt und gemalt." *Kunst und Literatur* 33 (2) (1985): 282–86.

A eulogistic article about Rimsky-Korsakov, noting his outstanding gifts.

1120 Braudo, Evgeny Maksimovich. "Rimsky-Korsakov." In *Malaya sovetskaya entsiklopediya.* [Small Soviet Encyclopedia.] Vol. 7. Moscow, 1930: cols. 346–47.

A concise, informative article about Rimsky-Korsakov.

1121 ——. "Nikolay Andreevich Rimsky-Korsakov, 1844-1908." *Sovetskaya nauka* 2 (1938): 136–44.

A descriptive account of Rimsky-Korsakov and his musical achievements.

1122 Brook, Donald. *Six Great Russian Composers.* London: Rockliff, 1946. 193 pp. Reprinted: Stratford, NH: Ayer, 1970. ISBN-10: 0836980387. ISBN-13: 978-0836980387.

Includes a chapter on the composer, pp. 137–71, together with several good quality illustrations.

1123 Brown, David. *Tchaikovsky: A Biographical and Cultural Study,* 4 Vols. New York: Norton, 1978–91: Vol. 1: "The Early Years" (1840-1874), 1978. 348 pp. ISBN-10: 0393075354. ISBN-13: 978-0393075359. Vol. 2: "The Crisis Years" (1874-1878), 1982–83. 312 pp. ISBN-10: 0393017079. ISBN-13: 978-0393017076. Vol. 3: "The Years of Wandering" (1878-1885), 1986. 336 pp. ISBN-10: 0393336042. ISBN-13: 978-0393336047. Vol. 4: "The Final Years" (1885-1893), 1991–92. 527 pp. ISBN-10: 0393030997. ISBN-13: 978-0393030990.

Both Tchaikovsky and Rimsky-Korsakov, apart from having produced books on music theory, in some respects held similar esthetic views, often exchanging letters, evidence of which is seen in the many references to Rimsky-Korsakov found in this substantial study.

1124 Brown, David. *Tchaikovsky: The Man and His Music.* New York: Pegasus Books (2007). 512 pp. ISBN-10: 1933648309. ISBN-13: 978-1933648309.

A condensed version of No. 1123, containing references to Rimsky-Korsakov.

1125 Burian, Karel Vladimir. *N. A. Rimskij-Korsakov.* Praha, 1949.

A factual account of Rimsky-Korsakov and his work, written in Czech.

1126 Calvocoressi, M. D. and Abraham, G. *Masters of Russian Music.* London: Duckworth, 1936. 511 pp.

In the ninth section of this work, Abraham discusses Rimsky-Korsakov [see pp. 335–423]. This takes the form of a detailed biography, describing the circumstances of composition of his principal works and his relationship with members of the Balakirev Circle. Based largely on the composer's

Bibliography: General 217

Chronicle of My Musical Life [see No. 210], the article is not concerned with musical analysis and there is no precise documentation.

1127 Cendrars, Blaise. *Rimsky-Korsakov et la nouvelle musique russe.* Paris, 1913.

Though listed in O. B. Stepanov's bibliography [see No. 1195] this book was never published. Some corrected proofs are preserved in the Bibliothèque Doucet, Paris [see Jean-Marc Debenedetti. *Blaise Cendrars.* Paris: Editions Henri Veyrier, 1985: 211].

1128 Dolzhansky, Aleksandr Naumovich. *N. A. Rimsky-Korsakov (1844-1908).* Arkhangel'sk, 1938.

An early publication by Dolzhansky, better known as a specialist on Shostakovich.

1129 Drozdov, Anatoly Nikolaevich. *Nikolay Andreevich Rimsky-Korsakov. (Zhizneopisanie i muzykal'naya kharakteristika).* [Nikolay Andreevich Rimsky-Korsakov. (Account of His Life and Characteristics of His Music).] Moscow, 1929.

After studying at the St. Petersburg Law School and at the Sorbonne, Paris, Drozdov taught at St. Petersburg Conservatory (1916–17) and as a professor at Moscow Conservatory (1920–24). His study of Rimsky-Korsakov reflects his cultured background.

1130 E. P. "Prelyudia." [Prelude.] *RMG* 39–40 (1908): cols. 801–03.

A short tribute to the composer in the special memorial issue of *RMG* entitled "In Memory of Rimsky-Korsakov."

1131 Feuer, Mária. *Rimszkij-Korszakov.* Budapest: Zeneműkiadó, 1966.

One of the few books about Rimsky-Korsakov to be published in the Hungarian language.

1132 Findeyzen, Nikolay Fёdorovich. *Nikolay Andreevich Rimsky-Korsakov. Ocherk ego muzykal'noy deyatel'nosti.* [Nikolay Andreevich Rimsky-Korsakov. An Outline of his Music.] St. Petersburg-Moscow: V. Bessel', 1908. 96 pp.

Findeyzen states in his foreword that this work was intended to fill a gap, since, apart from two newspaper articles by V. V. Stasov and P. Trifonov on Rimsky-Korsakov, no general outline of the composer had hitherto been published. Using the materials by Stasov and Trifonov, together with personal reminiscences, various individual studies, Glazunov's reminiscences, Borodin's and Tchaikovsky's letters and other materials, Findeyzen divides his book into seven chapters which describe the principal events of the composer's life. Findeyzen's approach is essentially a factual one in which he displays his customary perception. He lists Rimsky-Korsakov's compositions published by Bessel', together with various arrangements.

1133 N.F. [Findeyzen, Nikolay]. "N. A. Rimsky-Korsakov. Fakty ego zhizni – proizvedeniya. (Biograficheskaya khronologiya)." [N. A. Rimsky-Korsakov. Facts of his Life – Works. (A Biographical Chronology).] *RMG* 39–40 (1908): cols. 818–26.

A chronology of the composer's life, noting dates of compositions and other relevant details, published in the special issue of the journal marking the composer's death. Some of the information needs to be corrected in light of modern research.

1134 ——. "Cherez polgoda." [Half a Year Later.] *RMG* 49 (1908): cols. 1105–12.

An account of the various tributes and musical activities undertaken in Russia in the first six months following the composer's death, and suggestions as to what might be done, such as the erection of a memorial or a museum in his name, or a provisional theater devoted to the performance of his operas.

1135 ——, ed. "Pamyati N. A. Rimskogo-Korsakova k godovshchine dnya ego konchiny (8 iyunya 1908 g.)." [In Memory of Rimsky-Korsakov on the Anniversary of his Death (8 [21] June 1908).] *RMG* 22/23 (1909).

A special issue of the journal *RMG* devoted to Rimsky-Korsakov.

1136 García Morillo, Roberto. *Rimsky-Korsakov.* Buenos Aires: Ricordi Americana, 1945. 205 pp.

A volume in the "Musicos celebres" series, this consists of a life of the composer, pp. 9–100, followed by an examination of his symphonic, vocal, and theatrical compositions. Also discusses his theoretical works.

1137 Golemba, A. *N. A. Rimsky-Korsakov. Zhizn' i tvorchestvo. (Besedy po istorii muzyki).* [N. A. Rimsky-Korsakov. Life and Work. (Discussions about Music History).] Moscow: Vsesoyuz. dom. nar. tvorchestva im. N. K. Krupskoy, 1940.

1138 Gozenpud, Abram Akimovich. *Rimsky-Korsakov.* Leningrad, 1955.

As an associate of the former State Scientific Research Institute of Theater, Music and Cinematography, Leningrad, Gozenpud had access to many materials on Rimsky-Korsakov, this being reflected in this publication.

1139 Hill, E. B. "Nicolas Rimsky-Korsakoff." *The Etude* 25 (1907): 508.

An account of the composer by a contemporary American writer. Though critical of some of Rimsky-Korsakov's work, such as some songs and piano pieces, he notes his "brilliant, skillfully instrumented and imaginative orchestral pieces," along with some of their performances abroad, i.e., *Antar* at Magdeburg in 1881 under Arthur Nikisch, *May Night* in Frankfurt on 3 May 1900, and *The Tsar's Bride* in Prague on 4 December 1902.

1140 Hofmann, Rostislav-Michel. *Rimski-Korsakov; sa vie, son oeuvre.* Paris: Flammarion, 1958. 236 pp.

Bibliography: General

This descriptive biography of the composer is intended primarily for the non-specialist. There is a list of works and records up to 1958, but no footnotes or illustrations.

1141 ——. *La Vie des Grands Musiciens Russes.* Paris: Editions du Sud, 1965. 287 pp.

The section entitled "Rimski-Korsakov ou la vie dans...une lanterne magique," pp. 121–40, consists of 14 paragraphs, each on some facet of the composer's work or personality. There is also a biographical impression "La portrait de Rimski par sa fille Sophie," p. 138. There is no precise documentation or bibliography.

1142 Il'insky, Aleksandr Aleksandrovich. *Biografii kompozitorov s IV-XX vek s portretami.* [Biographies of Composers from the 4th-20th Centuries with Portraits.] Moscow: K. A. Durnovo, 1904.

Il'insky's account of the composer, pp. 566–71, is set out chronologically and presents the main facts of his life, along with a summary of his achievement in the final paragraph.

1143 Kandinsky, Aleksey Ivanovich. "N. A. Rimsky-Korsakov." In E. L. Frid, ed. *Russkaya muzykal'naya literatura* [Russian Musical Literature], Vol. III. Leningrad: Muzgiz, 1959: 3–179. Second edition rev. Leningrad, 1967.

Divided into four main sections, this discusses Rimsky-Korsakov's life and work, selected operas, *Scheherazade*, and several songs. Approved by The Ministry of Culture as a textbook in secondary music schools, it is illustrated with 128 music examples. A few footnotes, two illustrations, but no bibliography.

1144 Karatygin, Vyacheslav Gavrilovich. "Rimsky-Korsakov." *EIT*, Vyp. 1 [Issue 1] (1909): 39–76.

An important and fundamental article, this consists of a long introduction, discussing the general characteristics of Rimsky-Korsakov's music as opposed to that of other members of the Nationalist school, followed by a detailed biographical account of his life and forebears. Emphasis is placed on his association with the Belyaev Circle, which group Karatygin considers to have had a profound influence both on Rimsky-Korsakov and on Russian music in general. Including much information on his compositions and professional life, the article is concluded by a list of the composer's musical, theoretical, and critical works.

1145 ——. "Pamyati N. A. Rimskogo-Korsakova (k 10-letiyu so dnya ego smerti)." [In Memory of N. A. Rimsky-Korsakov (on the 10th Anniversary of the Day of His Death.] *Nash Vek* 98 (9 June 1918). Reprinted: A. Rimsky-Korsakov, V. Shishtarëv, and P. Gruber, eds. *V. G. Karatygin. Zhizn'. Deyatel'nost'. Stat'i i materialy.* [V. G. Karatygin. Life. Work. Articles and Materials.]

Leningrad: Academia, 1927. Reprinted: V. G. Karatygin. *Izbrannye stat'i.* [Selected Articles.] Moscow-Leningrad: Muzyka, 1965: 240–47.

The first of several projected articles about Rimsky-Korsakov and his work, of which only one was completed. Among the matters discussed are the individuality of his music, its national roots, and the manner in which it differs from the music of Wagner.

1146   Kashkin, Nikolay Dmitrievich. "N. A. Rimsky-Korsakov; ego deyatel'nost' i znachenie." [N. A. Rimsky-Korsakov; His Work and Significance.] *Moskovsky Ezhenedel'nik* 37 (20 September 1908): 34–53. Reprinted: N. D. Kashkin. *Stat'i o russkoy muzyke i muzykantakh.* [Articles on Russian Music and Musicians.] Moscow: Muzgiz, 1953: 45–67.

An account of the composer's life and work, stressing his importance in the history of Russian music. Rimsky-Korsakov is seen as an exponent of Russian artistic realism, full of optimism and joy of life.

1147   Keldysh, Yury Vsevolodovich. *Istoriya russkoy muzyki.* [History of Russian Music.] Vol. II. Moscow-Leningrad: Muzgiz, 1947. 389 pp.

A discussion of Rimsky-Korsakov's work can be found in Chapter 8, pp. 215–93, this being divided into six major sections:

i.   The composer placed in his historical context as the founder of a new school of composition, his work being examined from the point of view of significant features of style.

ii. Rimsky-Korsakov's early years, his association with Balakirev and the *Moguchaya Kuchka* [Mighty Handful], and his first compositions.

iii. A survey of Rimsky-Korsakov's first significant operas *May Night* and *The Snow Maiden.*

iv. Rimsky-Korsakov's compositions of the 1880s: *Scheherazade,* the *Capriccio Espagnol,* and the operas *Christmas Eve* and *Sadko.*

v.   Rimsky-Korsakov's quest for new forms of expression and the operas *The Tsar's Bride* and *The Tale of Tsar Saltan.*

vi. An examination of Rimsky-Korsakov's last operas and the composer's attitude to the events of 1905.

There is no mention of Rimsky-Korsakov's sacred works. Ideologically Keldysh sees Rimsky-Korsakov as a brilliant composer, strongly motivated by the principles of realism and *narodnost'* [populism].

1148   Klein, John W. Nicholas. "Rimsky-Korsakov: 1844-1908. A Centennial Appreciation." *Musical Opinion* 67 (March 1944): 185–86; (April 1944): 217–18.

Contains observations on the composer's strengths and weaknesses, noting the reasons for his actions as an editor, particularly of *Boris Godunov.* An informative and well-balanced vignette.

Bibliography: General

1149 Kruglikov, Semën Nikolaevich. "N. A. Rimsky-Korsakov." *Artist* 11 (1890): 53–57.

An early biographical article on the composer, enumerating cardinal events in his life.

1150 Kryukov, Andrey Nikolaevich. *"Moguchaya Kuchka." Stranitsy istorii peterburgskogo kruzhka muzykantov.* [The "Mighty Handful." Pages from the History of the Petersburg Circle of Musicians.] Leningrad: Lenizdat, 1977. 272 pp.

An account of the development of the Balakirev Circle, with a list of residences occupied by Rimsky-Korsakov and details of those still existing today. There are many illustrations, some of them little known and rarely encountered in other Russian publications.

1151 Kriúkov, Román. "El viaje de Rimski-Kórsakov al Brasil." *Amér. Latina* IV (1974): 92–102.

A discussion of the composer's four-month stay in Brazil, documented by extracts from his correspondence.

1152 Kunin, Iosif Filippovich. *Rimsky-Korsakov.* Moscow: Molodaya gvardiya, 1964. 240 pp.

Divided into 19 chapters, this contains the essential details of Rimsky-Korsakov's life and work, providing a good insight into his character. Kunin stresses in particular the composer's inner qualities and his personal warmth (a view not necessarily shared by some other biographers).

1153 ——. *N. A. Rimsky-Korsakov. Zhizn' i tvorchestvo v vospominaniyakh, pis'makh i kriticheskikh otzyvakh.* [N. A. Rimsky-Korsakov. Life and Work in Reminiscences, Letters and Critical Reviews.] Moscow: Sovetsky Kompozitor, 1974. 274 pp.

Divided into three parts, the first concerned with the composer's early life up to the composition of *The Maid of Pskov,* the second up to 1897, and the third the final period of his creative life, Kunin draws extensively from the periodical literature of the time, utilizing extracts from Kashkin, Cui, Engel', and others. Though relying in its main outlines on A. N. Rimsky-Korsakov's 5-volume study [see No. 1180] and on Rimsky-Korsakov's own *Chronicle* [see No. 210], Kunin assembles an interesting set of materials. Though lacking an index, the book contains a List of Sources, a brief survey of books and articles on the composer, and 16 photographs.

1154 ——. *Nikolay Andreevich Rimsky-Korsakov.* Moscow: Muzyka, 1979. 128 pp. Second edition. Moscow, 1983. 132 pp.

A well-produced biographical account of the composer and his works, intended for the general reader. The real value of the book, however, lies in its many illustrations and photographs, several of which are in color. The selection of illustrations is unusual and the quality of reproduction much higher than customary. Includes a number of photographs of Tikhvin and the State Memorial House Museum of N. A. Rimsky-Korsakov. There is no index.

1155   ——. *Nikolai Rimski-Korsakow.* Trans. E. Kuhn. Berlin: Verlag Neue Musik, 1981. 217 pp. Review: *Musik und Gesellschaft* 33 (April 1983): 250–51.

1156   Kuznetsov, Konstantin Alekseevich. "Rimsky-Korsakov." In *Etyudy o muzyke.* [Studies on Music.] Odessa: Omfalos, 1919: 43–52.

Pointing out that Rimsky-Korsakov, like Glinka, Skryabin, and Rakhmaninov, was of noble descent, Kuznetsov notes the influence of Tikhvin on his development and the manner in which Rimsky-Korsakov was susceptible to his different environments, as seen in his voyage around the world and his work as a teacher at the Imperial Chapel. Among the points discussed are his indebtedness to Glinka, his obligations to Berlioz, Liszt, and Wagner, his work as an editor of compositions by Glinka, Dargomyzhsky, Borodin, and Musorgsky, characteristic stylistic features, and the qualities of his orchestration, together with comparisons between Rimsky-Korsakov and Tchaikovsky.

1157   Lapshin, Ivan Ivanovich. *N. A. Rimsky-Korsakov i ego znachenie v istorii russkoy muzyki.* [N. A. Rimsky-Korsakov and His Significance in the History of Russian Music.] Prague: Russkaya Uchënaya Akademiya, 1945. 109 pp.

This short critical biography consists of 15 sections:

i.   Biography.
ii. Works.
iii. Melos.
iv. Tempo, rhythm, measure.
v.   Polyphony.
vi. Harmony.
vii. Orchestration.
viii. Sound-painting.
ix. World of poetic images.
x.   Comic element: humour, grotesquerie and satire.
xi. Operatic styles.
xii. Symphonic and chamber ensemble.
xiii. Romances.
xiv. Church chants.
xv. The influence of Rimsky-Korsakov in the history of Russian music.

A perceptive account of Rimsky-Korsakov and his work, full of well-substantiated observations. The last chapter discusses his influence on other composers.

Bibliography: General 223

1158 ——. *Ruská hudba. Profily skladatelu. Z rustiny prelozila Zofie Pohorecká.* [Russian Music. Portraits of Composers. Trans. from the Russian by Zofie Pohorecká.] Praha: Vydavatelství za svobodu, 1947. 522 pp.

Written originally in Russian and translated into Czech by Zofie Pohorecká, there are many references to Rimsky-Korsakov throughout this history of Russian music, the principal section being Chapter 11, pp. 282–396, consisting of 15 headings, covering comedy, humor, grotesqueries and satire, sacred music, and poetic imagery.

1159 Lipaev, Ivan Vasil'evich. "Iz Moskvy. Rimsko-Korsakovskie dni." [From Moscow. Rimsky-Korsakov Days.] *RMG* 2 (1901): cols. 56–58.

A vivid description of the reception given to Rimsky-Korsakov in Moscow during the celebrations marking his 35 years as a composer.

1160 ——. "N. A. Rimsky-Korsakov. Ocherk muzykal'noy deyatel'nosti." [N. A. Rimsky -Korsakov. An Outline of his Musical Work.] *Muzykal'ny Truzhenik* 1, 4, 10, 12–13, 16–17 (1908).

An account of Rimsky-Korsakov, written on the occasion of his death.

1161 Lissa, Zofia. *Historia muzyki rosyjskiej.* [History of Russian Music.] Cracow: Polskie Wydawnictwo muzyczne, 1955. 504 pp.

Included in Chapter XVI, "Nikolaj Rimski-Korsakow," pp. 313–37, are brief examinations of *The Snow Maiden, Sadko, The Tsar's Bride, The Tale of Tsar Saltan,* and *The Golden Cockerel,* together with some orchestral works, songs, and a discussion of Rimsky-Korsakov's chief stylistic traits.

1162 Lunacharsky, Anatoly Vasil'evich. "N. A. Rimsky-Korsakov (Muzykal'no kriticheskaya fantaziya. K 25-letiyu so dnya smerti)." [N. A. Rimsky-Korsakov (A Musical-Critical Fantasy. To Mark the 25th Anniversary of the Day of His Death).] In A. V. Lunacharsky. *V mire muzyki.* [In the World of Music.] Moscow: Sovetsky kompozitor, 1971: 413–23.

1163 MacKenzie, David. "Rimskii-Korsakov, Nikolai Andreevich (1844-1908)." In Joseph L. Wieczynski, ed. *The Modern Encyclopedia of Russian and Soviet History,* Vol. 31. Gulf Breeze, Florida: Academic International Press, 1983: 101–06. ISBN-10: 0875690645. ISBN-13: 978-0875690643.

A well-informed critical biographical account of the composer and his work.

1164 Markévitch, Igor. *Rimsky-Korsakov.* In *Maîtres de la musique ancienne et moderne* 16. Paris: Les Editions Rieder, 1934. 87 pp. Review: *ML* XVI (iii) (1935): 248.

Possibly the most valuable aspect of this work is its 40 illustrations, containing some of the best known photographs associated with Rimsky-Korsakov, together with a few lesser known ones. Divided into nine untitled sections, the content is primarily biographical with little serious discussion of the music. Sparse footnotes and no bibliography.

1165 Montagu-Nathan, Montagu. *Rimsky-Korsakof.* London: Constable, 1916. 124 pp.

This volume is of interest as one of the earliest critical biographies of the composer in the English language. Preceded by a short introduction, it consists of three main sections: "Career," "Rimsky-Korsakof as Operatic Composer," and "Instrumental and Vocal Compositions." Contains synopses of 15 operas and the programs of the orchestral works *Antar* and *Scheherazade.* There are no music examples or bibliography.

1166 ——. "Musician and Midshipman: An account of the correspondence between Balakirev and Rimsky-Korsakov." *MT* 96 (1955): 357–60.

An article on the correspondence between Balakirev and Rimsky-Korsakov, 1862–64, the period of the latter's three-year cruise on the Russian clipper ship "Almaz" [Diamond], and his visits to England, Denmark, Germany, the United States, and Brazil.

1167 Oldani, Robert William. "Rimsky-Korsakov, Nikolai." In John Merriman and Jay Winter, eds. *The Scribner Library of Modern Europe 1789-1914: Encyclopaedia of the Age of Industry and Empire.* Vol. 4. Detroit: Charles Scribner, 2006: 1999–2000. ISBN-10: 0684313596. ISBN-13: 978-0684313597.

A succinct, well-informed account providing details of Rimsky-Korsakov, his life, work, stylistic characteristics, his role as a teacher and editor, and his place in the history of Russian music.

1168 Orlova, Elena Mikhaylovna. *B. V. Asaf'ev. Put' issledovatelya i publitsista.* [B. V. Asaf'ev. Researcher and Publicist.] Leningrad: Muzyka, 1964. 461 pp.

Chapter XVI, pp. 349–54, contains an examination of articles on Rimsky-Korsakov written by Asaf'ev in the 1940s: "Nikolay Andreevich Rimsky-Korsakov. (1844-1944)" [see No. 1118], "A brilliant Russian musical talent," [see No. 1117], and "The music of Rimsky-Korsakov in the context of folk-poetical Slavic culture and mythology" [see No. 1229]. Orlova sees these articles as breaking new ground in Soviet musicology in Rimsky-Korsakov studies.

1169 Ossovsky, Aleksandr Vyacheslavovich. "N. A. Rimsky-Korsakov: Nekrolog." [N. A. Rimsky-Korsakov: Obituary.] *Slovo* 479 (1908). Reprinted: *MA* (2) (1994): 162–63. ISSN: 0869-4516.

An obituary of Rimsky-Korsakov by A. V. Ossovsky (1871–1957), a professor at the St. Petersburg Conservatory and a pupil of the composer.

1170 ——. *N. A. Rimsky-Korsakov.* Petrograd: Muzyka, 1922.

Bibliography: General 225

Ossovsky studied under Rimsky-Korsakov over the period 1896–1902, participating in the musical gatherings known as the "Musical Wednesdays" held in the composer's apartment, where he met members of the Belyaev Circle. His writings about the composer are authoritative, the information drawn from first-hand experience.

1171 ——. "N. A. Rimsky-Korsakov i russkaya kul'tura." [N. A. Rimsky-Korsakov and Russian Culture.] In *Sovetskaya Muzyka. Vtoroy sbornik statey.* [Soviet Music. Second Volume of Articles.] Moscow: Muzgiz, 1944: 67–68.

A panegyric on Rimsky-Korsakov, emphasizing the composer's indebtedness to Russian culture.

1172 Pekelis, Mikhail Samoylovich, ed. *Istoriya russkoy muzyki.* [History of Russian Music.] Vol. II. Moscow-Leningrad: Muzgiz, 1940. 455 pp.

Devoted to Rimsky-Korsakov, Chapter XX, pp. 265–333, is divided into five sections: "Creative Path," "Bases of Musical Style," "Operas," "Symphonic Works," and "Romances." Pekelis' general erudition and musical discernment are evident throughout this article, good use being made of relevant music examples illustrating leitmotifs and certain harmonic idiosyncrasies. The comparative lack of emphasis on ideology and the stressing of the influences of Western-European music were certainly some of the factors causing this history to be withdrawn and replaced by that of Keldysh.

1173 Polyanovsky, Georgij Aleksandrowitsch. *N. A. Rimskij-Korssakow.* Potsdam: E. Stichnote, 1948. 31 pp.

A short general account of the composer's life and works.

1174 Purgol'd, Nadezhda Nikolaevna. "Vyderzhki iz dnevnika, 1871-72." [Excerpts from a Diary, 1871-72.] *SM* 5 (1957): 134–38.

Excerpts from a diary kept by Nadezhda Nikolaevna Purgol'd, who became Rimsky-Korsakov's wife in 1872.

1175 Pushanov, V. A. *N. A. Rimsky-Korsakov (1844-1908).* Leningrad, 1928.

1176 Racek, Jan. *Ruská hudba. Od nejstarsích dob az po Velkou ríjnovou revoluci.* [Russian Music. From Recent Times up to the Great Patriotic Revolution.] Praz: Státní nakladatelství krásné literatury, hudby a umení, 1953.

For an account of Rimsky-Korsakov and his work, pointing out that one of his father's ancestors, Václav Zigmontovic Korsak, was a Czech, see pp. 93–102. Includes a short account of his operas and symphonic music, with a brief bibliography of materials on the composer in the Czech language.

1177 Ratskaya, Tsetsiliya Samoylovna. *N. A. Rimsky-Korsakov.* Moscow: Muzgiz, 1953. 138 pp. Second edition, rev. Moscow: Muzyka, 1977 [see No. 1178].

This 21-chapter survey is an official interpretation of the composer's work from the ideological viewpoint of the time. The illustrations include some unusual (and most competent) drawings by Rimsky-Korsakov as a child.

1178 ——. *N. A. Rimsky-Korsakov.* Second edition, rev. Moscow: Muzyka, 1977. 112 pp.

A short popular biographical account, describing Rimsky-Korsakov's work as a teacher, his most important compositions, and his participation in the Revolution of 1905. Intended for music lovers. Illustrations include a portrait by Repin.

1179 Rimsky-Korsakov, A., Shishtarëv, V., and Gruber, P., eds. *V. G. Karatygin. Zhizn'. Deyatel'nost'. Stat'i i materialy.* [V. G. Karatygin. Life. Work. Articles and Materials.] Leningrad: Academia, 1927. 263 pp.

Contains many references to Rimsky-Korsakov, including Karatygin's article "In Memory of Rimsky-Korsakov," pp. 174–80, first published in the journal *Nash Vek* 98 (1918). This article covers a wide range of issues, including the composer's constant searching for ideal melodic rendering of his texts.

1180 Rimsky-Korsakov, Andrey Nikolaevich. *N. A. Rimsky-Korsakov. Zhizn' i tvorchestvo.* [N. A. Rimsky-Korsakov. Life and Work.] Vols. I–V. Moscow: Ogiz-Muzgiz, 1933–46.

Andrey Nikolaevich Rimsky-Korsakov's biography of his father is a fundamental work for the study of the composer. Conceived originally as a 6-volume edition, its completion was prevented by the author's death in 1940, although from surviving papers it is known that its contents were to include a creative portrait of the composer, a collection of reference and other materials, a list of pupils, a survey of the performance and propagation of his works outside Russia both during and after his lifetime, and an alphabetical index to all six volumes. Nevertheless, Andrey Nikolaevich managed to realize most of his intentions, Vol. I appearing in 1933, Vol. II in 1935, Vol. III in 1936, Vol. IV in 1937, and Vol. V in 1946.

Vols. I–III are continuous in that they contain a total of five chapters spanning the period from Rimsky-Korsakov's birth up to the 1890s. Vol. IV, however, is divided into 12 chapters, commencing with the renewal of his compositional activity in 1894, including a detailed examination of such works as *Christmas Eve*, the new edition of *Boris Godunov*, the operas *Sadko*, *Mozart and Salieri*, and *The Tale of Tsar Saltan*, various songs, and a discussion of S. N. Kruglikov, Savva Mamontov, and A. N. Molas's Sunday gatherings, and other matters.

Vol. V, publication of which was prevented by the outbreak of the Second World War, completes the biography of the composer, comprising five chapters, culminating in *The Golden Cockerel*, together with a description of the composer's last days. Especially valuable are the extracts from writings of contemporary critics such as Kashkin and Kruglikov, excerpts from letters, the chronological tables, and the many illustrations, all of which have provided, and continue to provide, an invaluable source of material for Rimsky-Korsakov scholarship.

Bibliography: General

1181 Rimsky-Korsakov, Vladimir Nikolaevich. "Iz vospominaniy i materialov semeynogo arkhiva." [From Reminiscences and Materials in the Family Archive.] In No. 1204: Vol. 11, 113–76.

This article is divided into four sections:

i. "The House at Tikhvin and its Occupants" (biographical materials on the Rimsky-Korsakov family, including a reproduction of the family calendar showing a note of Rimsky-Korsakov's birth, childhood sketches, and handwriting): 113–28.
ii. "In the Naval Cadet Corps" (Rimsky-Korsakov's response to a new environment): 129–51.
iii. "From Recollections of Father" (reminiscences of the composer and home life by Rimsky-Korsakov's children, taken from a MS in SPBGATI): 151–62.
iv. "A faithful Life-Companion (Nadezhda Nikolaevna Rimskaya-Korsakova)" (an account of Rimsky-Korsakov's wife, stressing her musical gifts): 162–76.

1182 ——. "Tikhvinskaya uchitel'nitsa muzyki (publikatsiya V. Rimskogo-Korsakova)." [A Tikhvin Music-teacher (Publication by V. Rimsky-Korsakov).] *SM* 6 (1958): 63–65.

A short article about Ol'ga Feliksovna Feyl', Rimsky-Korsakov's third music teacher in Tikhvin. Part of a series of articles in a volume of *SM* marking the 50th anniversary of the composer's death.

1183 Rosenfeld, Paul. "Rimski-Korsakov." *Canadian Journal of Music* 5 (2) (1918): 26, 30. Reprinted: P. Rosenfeld. "Rimsky-Korsakoff." In *Musical Portraits*. New York, 1920: 159–68.

A portrait of Rimsky-Korsakov stressing his ingenuousness, for example, "The music of Rimski-Korsakov is like one of the books, full of gay pictures, which are given to children."

1184 Sabaneev, Leonid Leonidovich. "Rimsky-Korsakov, Nikolay Andreevich." In *Entsiklopedichesky slovar' Russkogo bibliograficheskogo instituta Granat*. Vol. 36, Part II. Moscow, 1933: cols. 530–36.

An article on the composer and his music, noting his indebtedness to Berlioz, Liszt, and Wagner, and underlining the importance of his work as editor and writer.

1185 Schmitz, Eugen. *Das mächtige Häuflein: (Modest Mussorgskij, Nicolai Rimskij-Korssakow, Alex. Borodin, César Cui, und Mili Balakirew.)* In the series *Musikbücherei für Jedermann*, Nr. 4. Leipzig: VEB Breitkopf u. Härtel, 1955. 72 pp.

A popular outline of the work of the *Maguchaya Kuchka* [Mighty Handful].

1186 Slonimsky, Sergei. "Die lebendige moderne Kunst Rimski-Korsakows." *Kunst und Literatur* XVII (12) (1969): 1307–16. Trans. from *SM* 3 (1969): 34–41.

A general discussion of Rimsky-Korsakov by an important contemporary Soviet composer, highlighting his significance, stylistic qualities, place in Russian music, folk roots, and the essentially positive outlook of his work: "Aber vor allem anderen hohes Vertrauen in die Musik und optimistischen Glauben an ihre unbegrenzten Horizonte." Slonimsky considers that the ingenuity of Rimsky-Korsakov's tonal and rhythmic elements influenced Debussy, Ravel, and Bartók.

1187 Solovtsov, Anatoly Aleksandrovich. *N. A. Rimsky-Korsakov.* Moscow: Muzgiz, 1948. 217 pp. Third edition, 1958.

Divided into 18 sections, this examines Rimsky-Korsakov's principal compositions in their historical sequence, with analyses. *Narodnost'* [populism] is seen as a fundamental quality of his general style.

1188 ———. *N. A. Rimsky-Korsakov. Kratky ocherk zhizni i tvorchestva.* [N. A. Rimsky-Korsakov. A Brief Outline of Life and Work.] Third edition, rev. Moscow: Muzgiz, 1958. 216 pp.

A general biographical account for the non-specialist, this is divided into seven sections. Containing neither music examples nor footnotes, it is notable primarily for its unusually extensive bibliography, pp. 209–16.

1189 ———. *Rimsky-Korsakov. Nauchno-populyarny ocherk.* [Rimsky-Korsakov. A Popular Scientific Outline.] Moscow: Muzgiz, 1960. 312 pp.

A book intended for music lovers. Divided into nine sections, it provides a chronological account of the composer's work.

1190 ———. *Zhizn' i tvorchestvo N. A. Rimskogo-Korsakova.* [The Life and Work of N. A. Rimsky-Korsakov.] Moscow: Muzyka, 1964. 688 pp. Second edition, Moscow: Muzyka, 1969. Review: Christoph Rüger. *Beiträge zur Musikwissenschaft* X (1–2) (1968): 97–99.

This volume in the series "Classics of World Musical Culture" is Solovtsov's major work on Rimsky-Korsakov. Divided into 17 chapters with descriptive headings, it combines a biographical and analytical approach, utilizing a diverse body of critical, epistolary, and autobiographical materials. The book is concluded by a brief chronology of his life and works, a list of his compositions, index of names, and an eight-page bibliography. There are 228 music examples and numerous illustrations.

1191 ———. *Zhizn' i tvorchestvo N. A. Rimskogo-Korsakova.* [The Life and Work of N. A. Rimsky-Korsakov.] Moscow: Muzyka, 1969. 669 pp.

Includes analysis of his operas and orchestral works and the manner in which they reflected current esthetic-ideological tendencies.

Bibliography: General 229

1192 ——. *Nikolay Andreevich Rimsky-Korsakov. Ocherk zhizni i tvorchestva.* [Nikolay Andreevich Rimsky-Korsakov. An Essay on His Life and Work.] Third edition, rev. Moscow: Muzgiz, 1984. 400 pp.

This monograph on Rimsky-Korsakov, containing 17 chapters and a conclusion, presents the basic facts of the composer's life and work, a list of compositions, literary works, and an index of names. The bibliography, pp. 391–93, includes references to a number of pre-revolutionary publications.

1193 Stasov, Vladimir Vasil'evich. *Stat'i o Rimskom-Korsakove* [Articles on Rimsky-Korsakov], V. A. Kiselëv, ed., with intro. and notes. In the series *Russian Classical Musical Criticism.* Moscow: Muzgiz, 1953. 91 pp.

Preceded by an introduction, this work by Stasov, with annotations by Kiselëv, is a collection of eulogistic monographs on Rimsky-Korsakov, consisting of:

i. Nikolay Andreevich Rimsky-Korsakov.
ii. Address on the Jubilee of Rimsky-Korsakov.
iii. Rimsky-Korsakov's Baton.
iv. An incredibly funny musical Fault-Finder.
v. A fragment from [Stasov's] *Art of the Nineteenth Century.*
vi. The Russian Music Society and Rimsky-Korsakov.
vii. Speech in Honour of Rimsky-Korsakov on 27 March 1905.

1194 ——. "Nikolay Andreevich Rimsky-Korsakov." *Severny Vestnik* (December 1890): 175–200. Reprinted: V. V. Stasov. *Stat'i o muzyke. V pyati vypuskakh* [Articles on Music. In Five Issues], Vl. Protopopov, ed., Vol. IV. Moscow: Muzgiz, 1978: 174–97.

This article is of historical importance in that it is one of the first major monographs to be written about the composer, and one which served as a foundation for subsequent research.

1195 Stepanov, O. B. "Rimsky-Korsakov, Nikolay Andreevich." In Yu. V. Keldysh, ed. *Muzykal'naya entsiklopediya* [Musical Encyclopedia] Vol. 4. Moscow: Sovetskaya entsiklopediya, 1978: cols. 631–52.

An important article on the composer and his work, with a bibliography of over 300 entries.

1196 Stromenger, Karol. *Nikolaj Rimski-Korsakow.* Wroclaw: Czytelnik, 1950. 54 pp.

A short biographical account of the composer, consisting of an introduction, five chapters, and notes.

1197 Trifonov, Porfiry Alekseevich. "N. A. Rimsky-Korsakov." *Vestnik Evropy* V–VI (1891).

An early biographical account of the composer and his work, written by a pupil.

230   *Nikolay Andreevich Rimsky-Korsakov: A Research and Information Guide*

1198   Troeger, G. *Mussorgskij und Rimskij-Korssakoff. – Ein Vergleich ihrer Personlichkeiten und künstlerische Ziele.* Breslau: Priebatsch's Buchhandlung, 1941. 180 pp.

1199   Tsendrovsky, Vladimir Mikhaylovich. "125 let so dnya rozhdeniya N. A. Rimskogo-Korsakova." [125 Years from the Birth of N. A. Rimsky-Korsakov.] *SM* 3 (1969).

A general discussion of Rimsky-Korsakov, containing observations written by Vladimir Tsendrovsky, a specialist on music theory.

1200   Tumanina, Nadezhda Vasil'evna, ed. *Istoriya russkoy muzyki.* [History of Russian Music.] Vol. II. Moscow: Muzgiz, 1958. 422 pp.

Chapter VII of this official *History of Russian Music*, pp. 183–284, commences with an introduction placing the composer in his historical and ideological context, followed by an account of his life, together with an examination of his operas (regarded as his highest achievement), orchestral music, folk song collections, and songs. Generously illustrated with music examples, attention is drawn to Rimsky-Korsakov's role as teacher and communicator.

1201   V. V. [V. G. Val'ter?] "Pamyati N. A. Rimskogo-Korsakova." [In Memory of N. A. Rimsky-Korsakov.] *Russkaya Starina* 136 (October–December 1908): 303–28.

A substantial account of Rimsky-Korsakov and his work on the occasion of his death.

1202   Val'ter, Viktor Grigor'evich. "Nikolay Andreevich Rimsky-Korsakov. Nekrolog." [Nikolay Andreevich Rimsky-Korsakov. Obituary.] *Sovremenny Mir* 7, Part 2 (1908): 122–24.

A short obituary notice by Val'ter, containing sentiments characteristic of a much later period, for example, "The main strength of Nikolay Andreevich's operatic work was in the depiction of the life and daily existence of the folk masses, and in the reproduction of the world of nature which N. A. limned for the most part in triumphal, even sometimes menacing choruses."

1203   Vaynkop, Yulian Yakovlevich. *N. A. Rimsky-Korsakov. Kratky ocherk zhizni i tvorchestva. K 25-letiyu so dnya smerti.* [N. A. Rimsky-Korsakov. A Short Essay on His Life and Work. To Mark the 25th Anniversary of the Day of His Death.] Leningrad, 1933.

A pupil of Boris Asaf'ev, this work is the precursor of his later study of Rimsky-Korsakov published in 1944.

1204   Yankovsky, Moisey Osipovich, ed. *Muzykal'noe nasledstvo. Rimsky-Korsakov. Issledovaniya. Materialy. Pis'ma. (V dvukh tomakh).* [Musical Legacy. Rimsky-Korsakov. Research. Materials. Letters. (In Two Volumes).] Vol. I. Moscow: Izd. Akad. Nauk SSSR, 1953. 416 pp. Vol. II. *Publikatsii i vospominaniya.*

Bibliography: General 231

[Publications and Reminiscences.] Moscow: Izd. Akad. Nauk. SSSR, 1954. 368 pp.

These two volumes, compiled by a board of editors under the chairmanship of Yankovsky, contain an important collection of articles on Rimsky-Korsakov. The first volume is preceded by an editorial introduction establishing Rimsky-Korsakov's ideological position as a "realist-composer" and explaining the aims of the publication.

1205 Yastrebtsëv, Vasily Vasil'evich. "N. A. Rimsky-Korsakov." *RMG* 51 (1900): cols. 1261–69.

A short biographical account of the composer and his importance in the history of Russian music.

1206 ——. *Nikolay Andreevich Rimsky-Korsakov. Ocherk ego zhizni i deyatel'nosti. Polny spisok sochineniy. S prilozheniem portreta i faksimile.* [Nikolay Andreevich Rimsky-Korsakov. Outline of His Life and Work. Complete List of Compositions. With a Supplement of a Portrait and Facsimile.] Moscow: P. Yurgenson, 1908. 29 pp.

Consisting of an introductory obituary note, pp. 7–18 consist of a short biography of the composer, providing information on his own compositions and his editorial work on those of other composers. Yastrebtsëv pays special attention to the use of modal elements, Rimsky-Korsakov's employment of an artificial scale made up of tone, semitone, tone, semitone, and his use of unusual time signatures, all of which he illustrates. The remainder of the book [pp. 19–26] comprises a list of Rimsky-Korsakov's compositions, with an appendix giving dates of operatic premières.

1207 Zetlin, Michael. "The Youth of Rimsky-Korsakov." Trans. Catharine Butakov. *Russian Review* 5 (1945): 89–101. Reprinted in No. 1330: English edition.

CONDUCTING

1208 Gurevich, Evgeniya L'vovna. "Vlastelin konservatorii." [The Master of the Conservatory.] *MA* (3) (2002): 164. ISSN: 0869-4516.

A detailed examination of the work of the conductor, pianist, and teacher Vasily Il'ich Safonov (1852–1918), using archival materials preserved in RGALI, including correspondence with Rimsky-Korsakov.

1209 Karatygin, Vyacheslav Gavrilovich. "Kuper kak dirizhër teatral'ny." [Cooper as a Theater Conductor.] *Zhizn' iskusstva* 14 (1923).

An article on the conductor, Emil Cooper [see No. 1212].

1210 Rozanov, Aleksandr Semënovich. *Muzykal'ny Pavlovsk.* [Musical Pavlovsk.] Leningrad: Muzyka, 1978. 168 pp.

A well-illustrated volume describing the musical life of Pavlovsk, and the concerts given at the "Pavlovsky vokzal" [Pavlovsk Vauxhall]. For a discussion about the conductor Galkin, to whom Rimsky-Korsakov and his colleagues dedicated "Variations on a Russian Theme" [see No. 42], see pp. 96–102. Photograph of Galkin, but no index.

1211   Stasov. Vladimir Vasil'evich. "Dirizhërskaya palochka Rimskogo-Korsakova." [Rimsky-Korsakov's Baton.] *Novosti i Birzhevaya Gazeta* 332 (1896). In No. 1193. Reprinted: Vl. Protopopov, ed. *V. V. Stasov. Stat'i o muzyke. V pyati vypuskakh.* [V. V. Stasov. Articles on Music. In Five Issues.] Vol. Va. Moscow: Muzgiz, 1979.

An account of two performances of *Boris Godunov*, conducted by Rimsky-Korsakov.

1212   Yudin, Gavriil Yakovlevich. "Emil' Kuper." [Emil Cooper.] *SM* 3 (1979): 86–96.

An article about the work of Emil' Al'bertovich Kuper [Emil Cooper], a prominent Russian conductor, under whose baton the première of Rimsky-Korsakov's opera *The Golden Cockerel* was given at Zimin's Opera Theater, Moscow, in 1909.

RIMSKY-KORSAKOV'S FAMILY

1213   Findeyzen, Nikolay Fëdorovich. "Nad. Nik. Rimskaya-Korsakova." [Nadezhda Nikolaevna Rimskaya-Korsakova.] *RMG* 39–40 (1908): cols. 827–29.

A short article on the composer's widow, published in the special memorial issue of the *RMG*.

1214   Kopytova, Galina Viktorovna. "Svidetel'stvo o rozhdenii i kreshenii N. A. Rimskogo-Korsakova." [Evidence of the Birth and Christening of N. A. Rimsky-Korsakov.] In V. M. Vasil'eva, comp. *N. A. Rimsky-Korsakov i russkaya khudozhestvennaya kul'tura. Materialy nauchnoy konferentsii. Vechasha-Lyubensk.* [N. A. Rimsky-Korsakov and Russian Artistic Culture. Materials from a Scientific Conference. Vechasha-Lyubensk.] Pskov, 2008.

A description and analysis of Rimsky-Korsakov's birth and baptismal certificates, together with information about the composer's parents.

1215   Mel'nikov, Vladimir. "Pamyatnik." [Memorial.] *MA* (2) (1994): 164–69. ISSN: 0869-4516.

A discussion of the relationship between the painter Nikolay Rerih (1874–1947) and Rimsky-Korsakov and his family. The composer's tombstone was based on a drawing by Rerih.

1216   Rimskaya-Korsakova, Nadezhda Nikolaevna.

Bibliography: General 233

A character sketch by Nadezhda Nikolaevna Rimskaya-Korsakova, the composer's wife, of their daughter, Sof'ya Vasil'evna Rimskaya-Korsakova, is to be found in No. 1204.

1217 Rimskaya-Korsakova, Tat'yana Vladimirovna. "Rodoslovnaya." [Genealogy.] *MA* (2) (1994): 9–23. ISSN: 0869-4516.

A long and detailed discussion of the genealogy of the Rimsky-Korsakov family, illustrated with rare portraits tracing the history of the family back to the fourteenth century.

1218 ——. *Detstvo i yunost' N. A. Rimskogo-Korsakova. Iz semeynoy perepiski.* [The Childhood and Youth of N. A. Rimsky-Korsakov. From Family Correspondence.] St. Petersburg: Izdatel'stvo "Kompozitor" ["Composer" Publishing House] (1995). 278 pp. Second edition, enl.: Rimskaya-Korsakova, T. V. and Metelitsa, Natal'ya. *N.A. Rimsky-Korsakov: iz semeynoy perepiski: po knigam Tat'iany Vladimirovny Rimskoy-Korsakovoy "Detstvo i yunost' N. A. Rimskogo-Korsakova," "N. A. Rimsky-Korsakov v sem'e."* [N. A. Rimsky-Korsakov: From Family Correspondence: Based on the Books by Tat'yana Vladimirovna Rimskaya-Korsakova "The Childhood and Youth of N. A. Rimsky-Korsakov," "N. A. Rimsky-Korsakov in the Family."] St. Petersburg: Kompozitor, 2008. English trans. forthcoming, 2014.

Based on letters contained in the family archive, this valuable work provides new information relating to the chronicle of the life of the composer, particularly the years spent on the clipper ship *Almaz* [Diamond]. Written by Rimsky-Korsakov's granddaughter, Tat'yana Vladimirovna Rimskaya-Korsakova, who lived in St. Petersburg, the book provides much interesting information not only about the Rimsky-Korsakov family, which traces its genealogy from the fourteenth century, but also about the little-known years of his early life up to 1865. Published with the support of the Ministry of Culture of the Russian Federation, it is made up of 15 chapters. The book is illustrated with many photographs, including family portraits, the composer's birth certificate, a group of Russian sailors at Niagara Falls, a facsimile of the composer's elegant handwriting, and a map showing the route of the *Almaz* from Kronshtadt to Montevideo.

1219 Rimsky-Korsakov, Andrey Nikolaevich. "Tikhvinsky zatvornik, ego predki i sem'ya. Detskie i yunosheskie gody N. A. Rimskogo-Korsakova." [The Tikhvin Hermit, His Forebears and Family. Rimsky-Korsakov's Childhood Years and Adolescence.] In *Muzykal'naya Letopis'.* [Musical Chronicle.] Sbornik [Vol.] I. Petrograd: Mysl', 1922: 5–60. Reprinted, abridged, in No. 1180: Vol. I.

1220 Rimsky-Korsakov, Vladimir Nikolaevich. "Iz semeynoy perepiski." [From Family Correspondence.] *SM* 3 (1969): 72–76.

A discussion of the relationship between Rimsky-Korsakov and his future wife, showing the gradual development of their feelings, illustrated by extracts from their correspondence during 1871.

1221 Yastrebtsëv, Vasily Vasil'evich. "Materialy dlya biografii N. A. Rimskogo-Korsakova." [Materials for a Biography of N. A. Rimsky-Korsakov.] *RMG* 39–40 (1908): cols. 816–18.

An account of the composer's forebears from 1390 and a genealogical table from the beginning of the eighteenth century.

RIMSKY-KORSAKOV AND FILM

1222 Abramova, A. and Roshal', G. *Rimsky-Korsakov: Kinostsenariy.* [Rimsky-Korsakov: a Film Script.] Moscow: Goskinoizdat, 1952. 96 pp.

A film script, highlighting events from Rimsky-Korsakov's musical life and his relationship with Glazunov, Lyadov, Stasov, and others. Includes the 1905 Revolution, his resignation from the Conservatory, and his dealings with the administration. Musical excerpts from his works; reflects the ideological tendencies of the 1950s.

1223 Bertz-Dostal, Helga. *Oper im Fernsehen. Grundlagenforschung im Rahmen des Forschungsprogramms des Instituts für Theater-wissenschaft an der Universität Wien.* Herausgegeben mit Förderung der Gesellschaft für Musiktheater. Vol. II. Wien, 1971.

For the titles of five of Rimsky-Korsakov's operas given on Soviet and Czech television during the period examined, namely *Boyarynya Vera Sheloga, Kashchey the Immortal, Mozart and Salieri, The Tale of Tsar Saltan,* and *The Tsar's Bride,* see Vol. II, Nos. 1162–67, pp. 841–42.

1224 Medvedev, Aleksandr Viktorovich. "Obraz kompozitora (Rimskogo-Korsakova) na ekrane." [Image of the Composer (Rimsky-Korsakov) on the Screen.] *SM* 3 (1953): 83–90.

Discusses three films about Glinka, Musorgsky, and Rimsky-Korsakov. That concerning Rimsky-Korsakov covers the latter part of his life (i.e., 1894–1908). The scenario is rated at a lower level than that of the other two and is said to be superficial, with insufficient awareness of the composer's social significance.

1225 Payne, Anthony. "Wide-screen Rimsky." *Music and Musicians* (15 March 1967): 32–33.

A discussion of the Soviet film *Sadko.* Filmed in Sov-color, the quiet shades of blue and green were ideally suited for the representation of the underwater

Bibliography: General 235

scenes in the submarine kingdom of the Morskoy Tsar' [The King of the Sea].

1226 Pomerantseva, E. "Bylina, opera, fil'm." *Iskusstvo kino* 2 (1953): 48–61.

Concerns the film of the opera *Sadko.*

1227 Troitskaya, G. *Opernaya klassika na ekrane.* [Opera Classics on the Screen.] *SM* 8 (1982): 82.

An account of the film of *Mozart and Salieri* made in the early 1960s.

FOLK SONG

1228 Abraham, Gerald. "The Folk-Song Element." In *Studies in Russian Music.* London: William Reeves, n.d. [1935]: 43–67. Reprinted: 2011 [see No. 283].

A commentary on the attitude of various Russian composers towards Russian folk song. Abraham considers that Rimsky-Korsakov's creative faculty was never permeated by the folk idiom to the same degree as Musorgsky and that his whole approach to folk music was artificial.

1229 Asaf'ev, Boris Vladimirovich [pseud. Glebov, Igor']. "Muzyka Rimskogo-Korsakova v aspekte narodno-poeticheskoy slavyanskoy kul'tury i mifologii." [Rimsky-Korsakov's Music in the Context of Folk-Poetical Slavic Culture and Mythology.] *SM* 7 (1946): 67–79.

Forming part of a cycle "Russian Music and Slavdom," *SM* 5–6 (1946), this is a study of some of the Slavic elements in Rimsky-Korsakov's work.

1230 ——. "O russkoy prirode i russkoy muzyke." [On Russian Nature and Russian Music.] *SM* 5 (1948): 29–39. Reprinted: No. 1256: Vol. IV, 84–97.

Written in 1944, this is a lyrical article on the relationship between Russian composers and folk music. Rimsky-Korsakov is seen as a master of sound painting, with outstanding examples being found in operas such as *The Snow Maiden, Christmas Eve, Sadko,* and others.

1231 Bachinskaya, Nina Mikhaylovna. *Narodnye pesni v tvorchestve russkikh kompozitorov.* [Folk Songs in the Work of Russian Composers.] Evgeny Gippius, ed. Moscow: Muzgiz, 1962. 202 pp.

Edited by Evgeny Gippius, a leading authority on Russian folk music, this volume lists the names of folk songs Rimsky-Korsakov employed in various operatic and orchestral works, giving precise details of where to find such songs and the melodies themselves. Provides information on the specific folk song collections from which the original tunes were taken (if not written down by the composer himself), together with details of modern reprints.

1232 Belza, Igor' Fëdorovich. *Iz istorii russko-pol'skikh muzykal'nykh svyazey.* [From the History of Russian-Polish Musical Links.] Moscow: Muzgiz, 1955. 63 pp.

Belza draws attention to the fact that Rimsky-Korsakov's mother used to sing Polish melodies to him as a child (see pp. 42–44), as a result of which Rimsky-Korsakov retained an affection for Polish music all his life. Among his works are several songs and the choral work *Svitezyanka*, written to words of Mickiewicz, the opera *Pan Voevoda*, and a Mazurka for violin and small orchestra, based on Polish themes remembered from his childhhood. The harmonic and melodic influence of Chopin is also underlined.

1233 Biryukov, V. A. *45 russkikh narodnykh pesen (iz sbornika N. A. Rimskogo-Korsakova). Polozhennykh na tri odnorodnykh golosa i prisposoblennykh dlya uchebnykh zavedeniy V. A. Biryukovym.* [45 Russian Folk Songs (from N. A. Rimsky-Korsakov's Collection). Arranged for Three Voices of the Same Kind and Adapted for Use in Teaching Establishments by V. A. Biryukov.] St. Petersburg-Moscow: Bessel', n.d. [c.1912].

Rimsky-Korsakov's folk song collection served an important educational purpose and Biryukov's volume is a good illustration of the type of arrangement freqently chosen.

1234 Evseev, Sergey Vasil'evich. *Rimsky-Korsakov i russkaya narodnaya pesnya.* [Rimsky-Korsakov and Russian Folk Song.] V. M. Tsendrovsky, ed. Moscow: Myzyka, 1970. 175 pp.

This combines two works by the folklore specialist S. V. Evseev (1894–1956), written in 1945. The first, entitled "Russian Folk Songs as Treated by Rimsky-Korsakov," pp. 7–115, looks at Rimsky-Korsakov's many arrangements of Russian folk song as seen in his folk song collections and choral works, and the extent to which he was influenced by his predecessors. The second article is entitled "Russian Folk Song Features in Rimsky-Korsakov's Musical Language," pp. 116–72. An introductory note is provided by Tsendrovsky, pp. 3–6.

1235 Gordeeva, Evgeniya Mikhaylovna, comp. *Kompozitory moguchey kuchki o narodnoy muzyke.* [The Composers of the "Mighty Handful" on Folk Music.] Moscow: Muzgiz, 1957. 247 pp.

Consists of extracts from articles and memoir literature relating to folk song, with half of the 129 entries by Rimsky-Korsakov. Illustrated with numerous music examples, there are several appendices giving names of works and persons referred to, titles of folk songs, individual compositions, and a list of folk songs and dances mentioned in the text.

1236 ——. "Folklornye istochniki 'Antara' i 'Ispanskogo kaprichchio'." [The Folk Sources of *Antar* and the *Spanish Caprice*.] *SM* 6 (1958): 33–41.

A discussion of the folk elements in *Antar* and *Spanish Caprice*. Part of a series of articles in a volume of *SM* marking the 50th anniversary of the composer's death.

Bibliography: General

1237 Gozenpud, Abram Akimovich. "Lysenko i Moguchaya kuchka." [Lysenko and the "Mighty Handful."] *SM* 12 (1952): 62–67.

An account of the relationship between the Ukrainian composer Lysenko and the Russian Five, noting the use of Ukrainian elements in Rimsky-Korsakov's music. Lysenko also performed a number of his works. Materials from this article were used again in No. 1238.

1238 ——. *N. V. Lysenko i russkaya muzykal'naya kul'tura.* [Lysenko and Russian Musical Culture.] Moscow: Muzgiz, 1954. 153p.

Lysenko was Rimsky-Korsakov's personal friend, having studied under him at the St. Petersburg Conservatory. Rimsky-Korsakov wrote down several Ukrainian folk songs from him, one of which he used in his unfinished "Ukrainian Fantaziya" [see pp. 7–9 and 35–39].

1239 Kaufman, Leonid Sergeevich. "Poltavskaya nakhodka." [A Find in Poltava.] *SM* 11 (1966): 59–66.

Following the discovery in Poltava of two folk songs arranged for unaccompanied male voices by Musorgsky, the author notes that the melodies are based on two of the folk songs written down by Rimsky-Korsakov on his hearing the singing of T. I. Filippov, and which were published in the 1882 collection. Part of Kaufman's discussion is concerned with Filippov's work as a folk song collector and the role played by Rimsky-Korsakov.

1240 Kulapina, Ol'ga Ivanovna. "Osobennosti garmonizatsii russkikh narodnykh pesen v tvorchestve otechestvennykh kompozitorov-klassikov." [Peculiarities of the Harmonization of Russian Folk Songs in the Work of Russian Classical Composers.] In *Peterburgskaya konservatoriya v mirovom muzykal'nom protsesse, 1862-2002: Materialy mezhnarodnoy muzykal'noy nauchnoy sessii, posvyashchënnoy 140-letiyu Konservatorii.* [The St. Petersburg Conservatory in the World Musical Process, 1862-2002: Materials of an International Musical Scientific Session, Dedicated to the 140th Anniversary of the Conservatory.] St. Petersburg, 2002.

An examination of the stylistic features of arrangements of Russian folk songs by Rimsky-Korsakov and others.

1241 Malecka, Theresa. "Ludowosc w Sadko i Bajce o carze Saltanie Rimskiego-Korsakowa." [Folk Music Elements in Rimsky-Korsakov's *Sadko* and *The Tale of Tsar Saltan.*] *Muzyka* XIX 4 (1974): 32–43.

An article by Theresa Malecka, a distinguished Polish scholar and specialist in Russian music.

1242 Maslov, Aleksandr Leont'evich. "Russkaya narodnaya pesnya v proizvedeniyakh Rimskogo-Korsakova." [Russian Folk Song in the Works of Rimsky-Korsakov.] *Muzyka i Zhizn'* 6 (1909).

Aleksandr Maslov (1877–1914) was a folklorist who, in 1901, took part in various folk song expeditions. From 1908 to 1912 he was publisher and editor of the journal *Muzyka i zhizn'* [Music and Life].

1243 Obram, Vera Alekseevna. "Rimsky-Korsakov i narodnaya pesnya." [Rimsky-Korsakov and Folk Song.] In No. 1204: Vol. I, 252–84.

A well-illustrated commentary on Rimsky-Korsakov's use of folk songs in his music, with comparative examples showing similarities between authentic melodies and his own tunes written in the folk idiom.

1244 Panoff, Peter. "Der nationale Stil N. A. Rimsky-Korsakows." *Archiv für Musikwissenschaft Jahrg.* 8 (1926): 78–117.

A discussion of the various national elements in Rimsky-Korsakov's music. Illustrated with numerous music examples.

1245 Prokhorov, Yakov Vasil'evich. "Elementy narodnosti v tvorchestve N. A. Rimskogo-Korsakova." [Elements of *Narodnost'* in the Work of N. A. Rimsky-Korsakov.] *RMG* 26–27 (1913): cols. 46–52.

A discussion of the part played by *narodnost'* [populism] and folk elements in the composer's work.

1246 Ryazanov, Pëtr Borisovich. "O sootnoshenii pedagogicheskikh vozzreniy i kompozitsionno-tekhnicheskikh resursov N. A. Rimskogo-Korsakova." [On the Relationship Between N. A. Rimsky-Korsakov's Pedagogical Views and Compositional-Technical Resources.] In No. 1435: 119–32.

An essay on characteristic features of Rimsky-Korsakov's style, prepared for publication by the ethnomusicologist F. A. Rubtsov, paying special attention to the influence of folk elements in his melodies, part-writing, and harmony.

1247 Stepantsevich, Kaleriya Iosifovna. "O nekotorykh zhanrakh russkoy narodnoy pesni v operakh Rimskogo-Korsakova i ikh roli v muzykal'noy dramaturgii." [Of Some Genres of Russian Folk Song in Rimsky-Korsakov's Operas and Their Roles in the Musical Dramaturgy.] In *Nauchno-metodicheskie zapiski Belorusskoy Konservatorii* [Scientific-Methodical Transactions of the Belorus Conservatory], Vyp. 1 [Issue 1]. Minsk, 1958.

1248 Tsukkerman, Viktor Abramovich. *"Kamarinskaya" Glinki i eë traditsii v russkoy muzyke.* [Glinka's *Kamarinskaya* and its Traditions in Russian Music.] Moscow: Muzgiz, 1957. 497 pp.

There are numerous references to Rimsky-Korsakov throughout this study of the folk melodies used in Glinka's orchestral fantasy *Kamarinskaya*. For a commentary on Rimsky-Korsakov's *Serbian Fantasy* and *Concert Fantasy on Russian Themes for Violin and Orchestra*, see pp. 403–06. Discussion of his procedure for the writing of variations, as seen in the orchestral *Skazka* and the operas *The Maid of Pskov*, *Sadko* and *The Tale of Tsar Saltan*, is found on pp. 446–52. No index.

Bibliography: General 239

1249 ——. "Rimsky-Korsakov i narodnaya pesnya." [Rimsky-Korsakov and Folk Song.] *SM* 10–11 (1938): 104–27. Reprinted: *Muzykal'no-teoreticheskie ocherki i etyudy* [Musical-Theoretical Essays and Studies], Vol. I. Moscow: Sovetsky Kompozitor, 1970: 311–50.

Examines Rimsky-Korsakov's attitude towards folk song and the manner in which it influenced his creative thinking in the devising of themes in the folk idiom and the construction of idiomatic accompaniments and harmonizations.

1250 Yankovsky, Moisey Osipovich. "Bylinye istoki opery 'Sadko' N. A. Rimskogo-Korsakova." [The Byliny Sources of N. A. Rimsky-Korsakov's Opera *Sadko.*] In *Uchënye zapiski.* [Scientific Notes.] A. N. Sokhor, ed., Vol. II. Leningrad: Gos. Nauchno-issledovatel'sky Institut Teatr, Muzyki i Kinematografii, 1958: 319–52.

This article discusses the sources of Rimsky-Korsakov's opera *Sadko* under three headings:

i.   "The *Byliny* about Sadko the Merchant, the Rich One." [An examination of some of the *byliny* variants.]
ii. "The historical basis of the *bylina.*" [A brief survey of aspects of Novgorod and Kiev and their customs.]
iii. "The folk-poetical sources and ideological concept of the opera." [Rimsky-Korsakov's own understanding of the material and his method of approach.]

GENERAL

1251 Abraham, Gerald. *Slavonic and Romantic Music.* London: Faber & Faber, 1968. 360 pp. Reprinted: 2013. ISBN-10: 0571302807. ISBN-13: 978-0571302802.

Two of the 29 articles in this volume concern Rimsky-Korsakov and are entitled: "Rimsky-Korsakov as Self-Critic," pp. 195–201, and "Rimsky-Korsakov's Songs," pp. 202–11, written in 1963 and 1944, respectively.

1252 ——, ed. "Romanticism (1830-1890)." *The New Oxford History of Music.* Vol. IX. Oxford and New York: Oxford University Press, 1974. ISBN: 0193163101.

For a discussion of the music of Rimsky-Korsakov, see pp. 444–50, 506–09, and 710–12.

1253 ——. *Essays on Russian and East European Music.* Oxford: Clarendon Press, 1985. 193 pp. Reprinted: London: Faber & Faber, 2011. 204 pp. ISBN-10: 0571276741. ISBN-13: 978-0571276745.

Includes reprints of previously published articles: "Russian Song," "*Pskovityanka*: The original version of Rimsky-Korsakov's first opera," "Satire and symbolism in *The Golden Cockerel*," and "Arab melodies in Rimsky-Korsakov and Borodin."

1254 Allorge, Henri. Sonnet: "Rimsky-Korsakof." *RMG* 7 (1907): cols. 215–16.

A French sonnet taken from a book of verse entitled *Le Clavier des harmonies* by Henri Allorge [see Contents].

1255 Asaf'ev, Boris Vladimirovich [pseud. Glebov, Igor']. *Izbrannye stat'i o russkoy muzyke.* [Selected Articles on Russian Music.] Moscow: Muzgiz, 1952: Vol. l, 80 pp; Vol. 2, 78 pp. Review: *SM* 1 (1953): 104–05.

These contain many materials on Rimsky-Korsakov.

1256 ——. *Izbrannye trudy.* [Selected Works.] 5 Vols. Moscow: Izd. Akad. Nauk SSSR, 1952–57.

An important source of materials on Rimsky-Korsakov.

1257 Bakst, James. *A History of Russian-Soviet Music.* New York: Dodd, Mead, 1962; 1966. 406 pp. Reprinted: Westport, CT: Greenwood Press, 1977. ISBN-10: 0837194229. ISBN-13: 978-0837194226.

For information on Rimsky-Korsakov, see Chapter 12, pp. 137–61. Following a brief outline of the composer and his aims and achievements, the subject matter (not the musical content) of the operas *Sadko* and *The Snow Maiden* is discussed, succeeded by brief notes on the composer's symphonic style. Much of Bakst's factual information is indebted to Pekelis' History and, ideologically, to that of Keldysh [see Nos. 1147 and 1172].

1258 Barsova, Lyudmila Grigor'evna. "Muzykal'ny fanatik Vasily Yastrebtsëv." [Vasily Yastrebtsëv: Music Fanatic.] *Neva: Ezhemesyachny literaturny zhurnal* [Neva: Monthly literary Journal] (7) (1997): 219. ISSN: 0130-741X.

An article concerning Vasily Yastrebtsëv, Rimsky-Korsakov's biographer.

1259 Baruttseva, Era-Sofya Surenovna. "Iskusstvo memuarista." [The Art of a Memoir Writer.] *SM* 48 (9) (September 1984): 64. ISSN: 0131-6818.

A survey of Boris Vladimirovich Asaf'ev's autobiographical *Mysli i dumy* [Thoughts and Reflections], including references to Rimsky-Korsakov.

1260 Baur, Steven. "Ravel's 'Russian' Period: Octatonicism in His Early Works, 1893-1908." *JAMS* 52 (3) (1999): 531. ISSN: 0003-0139.

An examination of the use of the octatonic scale as an alternative to diatonic practice in the work of composers such as Franz Liszt, Rimsky-Korsakov, Igor Stravinsky, and Maurice Ravel.

1261 Berezovsky, V. V. *Russkaya muzyka: Kritiko-istorichesky ocherk natsional'noy muzykal'noy shkoly v eya predstavitelyakh.* [Russian Music: A Critico-Historical Outline of the National Music School in its Representatives.] St. Petersburg: Yu. N. Erklikh, 1898. 524 pp.

Bibliography: General *241*

In this account of Rimsky-Korsakov, Chapter IV, pp. 168–239, Berezovsky adopts a chronological approach, including outlines of the plots of the chief operas into the general text. There is no real analysis of the music, although the author's observations are sometimes of interest.

1262 Bessel', Vasily Vasil'evich. *Kratky ocherk muzyki v Rossii.* [Short Outline of Music in Russia.] St. Petersburg-Moscow: V. Bessel', 1905. 48 pp.

A brief survey of Rimsky-Korsakov and his operas by Vasily Bessel', one of the leading pre-revolutionary Russian publishers, is to be found on pp. 26–29, together with a discussion of his orchestral works on pp. 39–40.

1263 Braudo, Evgeny Maksimovich. *Szhaty ocherk istorii muzyki (s mnogochislennymi notnymi primerami i tekstovymi illyustratsiyami).* [A Concise History of Music (With Many Music Examples and Illustrations to the Text).] Moscow: Muzykal'ny sektor, 1928. 366 pp. Second edition, corr. and enl. Moscow: Muzgiz, 1935. 464 pp.

Although only three pages of this general history of Western music are devoted to Rimsky-Korsakov and his achievements, Braudo succeeds in condensing a considerable amount of information into a modest space. Noting Rimsky-Korsakov's remarkable productivity, Braudo stresses his many-sided skills as a fastidious composer, teacher, editor, conductor, writer, and historiographer. While acknowledging his use of folk materials, Rimsky-Korsakov, he feels, was too much an establishment figure to involve himself with political activism, although an element of social satire is evident in his final works.

1264 Brody, Elaine. "The Russians in Paris (1889-1914)." In Malcolm Hamrick Brown, ed. *Russian and Soviet Music. Essays for Boris Schwarz.* Ann Arbor, Michigan: UMI Research Press, 1984: 157–83. ISBN-10: 0835715450. ISBN-13: 978-0835715454.

Makes reference to a number of articles on Russian composers, including Rimsky-Korsakov, in the French press of the period, as well as details of the reception of Russian music in France.

1265 Brown, Malcolm Hamrick, ed. *Musorgsky. In Memoriam, 1881-1981.* Ann Arbor, Michigan: UMI Research Press, 1982. 337 pp. ISBN-13: 978-0835712958.

An important volume for its insight into the musical life of the period. Rimsky-Korsakov is mentioned frequently throughout the work.

1266 Bullock, Philip Ross. *Rosa Newmarch and Russian Music in Late Nineteenth and Early Twentieth-Century England. RMA Monographs 18.* Farnham: Ashgate, 2009. ix, 195 pp. ISBN-10: 075466662X. ISBN-13: 978-0754666622.

Rosa Newmarch (1857–1940) did much to draw attention to Russian culture, particularly Russian music, visiting Russia and meeting Rimsky-Korsakov and others, whose work she described in English journals and articles for

242 Nikolay Andreevich Rimsky-Korsakov: A Research and Information Guide

Grove's Dictionary of Music and Musicians. Her personal reminiscences of Rimsky-Korsakov were published in the *Monthly Musical Record* 38 (452) (August 1908): 172–73.

1267 Calvocoressi, Michel Dimitri. *A Survey of Russian Music*. Middlesex, England: Penguin Books, 1944. Reprinted: Westport, CT: Greenwood Press, 1975. ISBN-10: 078129567X. ISBN-13: 978-0781295673.

Based on a series of lectures delivered by Calvocoressi while Cramb Lecturer at Glasgow University in 1935, Chapter IX, pp. 60–65, describes Rimsky-Korsakov's personality as "a complex, disconcerting mixture of contrasting and, indeed, conflicting elements," and notes that his striving for academic perfection in his work often led to a loss of spontaneity. In Calvocoressi's opinion, the composer's best works were his early (mainly orchestral) compositions, his later works being more synthetic and academic in style. The author questions Rimsky-Korsakov's originality, and considers his chief fascination to lie in his coruscating color schemes, his "skill in manipulating and contrasting the elements he uses" and, above all, in "a certain verve."

1268 Cooper, M. du P. "Rimsky-Korsakoff." *Oxford Outlook* 11 (1931): 201–08; 12 (1931): 30–41.

A thought-provoking account of the composer, the Russian cultural milieu, and notable features of his strengths and weaknesses. The author notes Rimsky-Korsakov's inability to write convincing "love music," a certain lack of human emotion, which enveloped him "in a world of beautiful, cold, highly-coloured glass...," together with a fascination for the "passionless fairy world, of beings half sub-human, half super-human." While noting that Rimsky-Korsakov's music, written to express human emotions, is "simple, unambiguous, and verging always on the commonplace," the author notes that this "holiday from humanity seems to have given him strength." Of *The Golden Cockerel* he comments on the predominance of the clarinet, detecting its prevalence in every possible capacity, lyric, comic, orgiastic. Rimsky-Korsakov, he feels, was no great musical thinker, nor one who makes great emotional or intellectual demands. Rather, he is a composer of "charming and exquisitely written" music, without which there would possibly have been no *Firebird* or *Petrushka*.

1269 Cui, César. *La Musique en Russie*. Paris: G. Fischbacher, 1880. 174 pp.

Divided into four sections: "Musique vocale," "Musique instrumentale," "Moyens d'exécution," and "Critique musicale," this includes a 9-page description of Rimsky-Korsakov's *The Maid of Pskov*, pp. 80–88. Although Cui notes his weakness as a melodic writer and his tendency towards repetition, his final assessment of the opera is of a work "un peu pâle" and "peu monotone," but with "très hautes qualités musicales," p. 87. Short notes

Bibliography: General 243

on Rimsky-Korsakov's *romances* are found on p. 124 and, on his orchestral music ("Sadko" and *Antar*), on pp. 129–30.

1270 Eberlein, Dorothee. *Der Musikverlag M. P. Belaieff: Eine Stiftung wird Musikgeschichte, 1885-1985.* Leipzig: Belaieff, 1985. 32 pp. ISBN-10: 3870540044. ISBN-13: 978-3870540043.

Entitled "The Music Publishing House of M. P. Belaieff: A Foundation Becomes Music History, 1885-1985," this describes the work of the Maecenas and promoter of Russian music, Mitrofan Petrovich Belyaev (1836–1903), whose Belaieff-Stiftung continues to this day. His relations with Rimsky-Korsakov were particularly close.

1271 Enberg, Brita. *Rimsky-Korsakov och den "ungryska" musikerkretsen, en rapsodisk överblick.* Stockholm: Lindfors, 1948. 182 pp.

Divided into ten chapters, with a music supplement of principal themes from his works (primarily operas), this volume includes comments from Scandinavian publications, especially the *Svenska Dagbladet.* Some of the 19 illustrations are unusual.

1272 Engel', Yuly Dmitrievich. "Muzyka v Rossii posle 60-kh godov." [Music in Russia after the 60s.] In *Istoriya Rossii v XIX veke.* [History of Russia in the 19th Century.] Vol. VII. St. Petersburg, 1903.

A critical assessment of the composer is found on pp. 258–61, in which Engel' notes that Rimsky-Korsakov, although aware of contemporary trends in music, never gave way to extremes, and thus could produce examples of musical modernism ("decadence") without being decadent, could be impressionistic without being precious, and employ symbolism without being pretentious. The author considers that although Rimsky-Korsakov's music contains no great élan ("pod'ëmov"), it is characterized by a Hellenic, Apollonian quality, full of positive life-asserting forces.

1273 Famintsyn, Aleksandr Sergeevich. "Vnutrennie novosti. Peterburgskaya khronika." [Home News. Petersburg Chronicle.] *Golos* 343 (12 December 1867).

The critic Aleksandr Famintsyn did not believe that the future of Russian music lay in the development of folk material and *narodnost'* [populism]. While praising Rimsky-Korsakov's orchestration and undoubted gifts, as manifest in the musical *bylina* "Sadko," Famintsyn expresses the hope that the young composer will rid himself of dilettantism and follow his true artistic path along Classical lines.

1274 Fardel, Max Durand. *Trois des cinq; Moussorgsky, Rimsky-Korsakov, Borodine.* Nice (?): Edition des Iles de Lérins, 1942. 35 pp.

A short descriptive and comparative account of Rimsky-Korsakov's work from a French viewpoint.

1275 Figes, Orlando. *Natasha's Dance. A Cultural History of Russia.* London: Penguin Books, 2002. xxxiii, 729. ISBN-10: 0312421958. ISBN-13: 978-0312421953.

This discerning and comprehensive study of Russian culture covering the period circa 1700–1950 devotes considerable attention to music, in particular the works of the Russian Nationalists, including an examination of selected operas by Rimsky-Korsakov.

1276 Findeyzen, Nikolay Fëdorovich. *Ocherk razvitiya russkoy (svetskoy) muzyki v 19om veke.* [Outline of the Development of Russian (Secular) Music in the 19th Century.] St. Petersburg, 1906. 68 pp.

Findeyzen devotes pp. 54–58 to a discussion of Rimsky-Korsakov, noting the composer's self-discipline and meticulous approach towards his work. His symphonic skills, the folk element, use of reminiscence motives, and his melodic gifts are all examined.

1277 Frolova-Walker, Marina. "Rimsky-Korsakov. Russian family of musicians. (1) Nikolay Andreyevich Rimsky-Korsakov." In Stanley Sadie, ed. *The New Grove Dictionary of Music and Musicians,* Second edition, Vol. 21. London: Macmillan, 2001: 400–23. Second edition. New York: Oxford University Press, 2001; 2004. ISBN-10: 0195170679. ISBN-13: 978-0195170672.

An extensive article on Rimsky-Korsakov, his life and work, giving details of his compositions, together with a bibliography.

1278 Gavazzeni, Gianandrea. *Musorgskij e la Musica Russa dell'800.* Firenze: G. C. Sansoni, 1943. 315 pp.

For a discussion of Rimsky-Korsakov's personality, his esthetic credo, compositional technique, and place in the history of Russian music, being regarded as a link between the Russian National School and Stravinsky, see Chapter IX, pp. 277–307.

1279 Genika, Rostislav Vladimirovich. *Ocherki istorii muzyki. Tom II. Istoriya russkoy muzyki.* [Outlines of Music History. Vol. II. History of Russian Music.] St. Petersburg: Russkaya Muzykal'naya Gazeta, 1912. 156 pp.

Containing some observations on the composer and his creative ideals (pp. 96–112), skillful use is made of relevant excerpts from his writings and those of other composers and critics.

1280 Goddard, Scott. "Rimsky-Korsakov i angliyskaya muzyka." [Rimsky-Korsakov and English Music.] *Britansky soyuznik* 12. Moscow, 1944: 8.

The *Britansky soyuznik* [British Ally] was published from 1942 to 1948 by the British Embassy, Moscow, its content being subject to close scrutiny by the Soviet authorities.

1281 Gofman [Hofmann], R. "Rimsky-Korsakov v Parizhe." [Rimsky-Korsakov in Paris.] *SM* 6 (1958): 48–55.

Bibliography: General 245

A translation of a French article by Rostislav-Michel Hofmann, describing performances of Rimsky-Korsakov's works in Paris. Part of a series of articles in a volume of *SM* marking the 50th anniversary of the composer's death.

1282 Gordeeva, Evgeniya Mikhaylovna. *Moguchaya Kuchka.* [The Mighty Handful.] Second edition, enl. Moscow: Muzyka, 1966. 325 pp.

Despite the irritating format of this book (imprecise chapter headings, no index), considerable information on Rimsky-Korsakov, together with materials on sources and other details, can be obtained. For a chronology listing the chief events of the composer's life see pp. 302–19.

1283 Griffiths, Steven A. K. "A Critical Study of the Music of Rimsky-Korsakov, 1844-1890." PhD Thesis, Musicology. Sheffield University, England. 436 pp. Listed in Cecil Adkins and Alis Dickinson, eds. *Doctoral Dissertations in Musicology.* American Musicological Society, 1984: 276. Published as *A Critical Study of the Music of Rimsky-Korsakov, 1844-1890.* In Outstanding Dissertations from British Universities. New York: Garland, 1989. 432 pp. ISBN-10: 0824001974. ISBN-13: 978-0824001971.

Includes discussion of the four Rimsky-Korsakov operas written prior to 1890, namely *The Maid of Pskov, May Night, The Snow Maiden,* and *Mlada.*

1284 Haine, Malou. "Paris à l'heure musicale russe: Rôle des expositions universelles de 1867 à 1900." *Musique, images, instruments: Revue française d'organologie et d'iconographie musicale* 13 (2012): 15. ISSN: 1264-7020.

Although France's first experience of Russian music occurred in the 1840s, it was as a result of the concerts of foreign music organized as part of the Expositions Universelles from 1867 to 1900 that brought the music of such composers as Rimsky-Korsakov to public notice.

1285 Hofmann, Rostislav-Michel. *La Musique en Russie des origines à nos jours.* Paris: Société française de diffusion musicale et artistique, 1956. 351 pp.

An account of Rimsky-Korsakov and his work is to be found on pp. 173–200 of this concise history of Russian and Soviet music. Written in conversational style, punctuated with frequent quotations, Hofmann relates the composition of various works to events in the composer's personal life, together with observations on his musical style and his contribution to Russian music. Meager documentation.

1286 Ivanov, Mikhail Mikhaylovich. *Istoriya muzykal'nogo razvitiya Rossii. V 2-kh tomakh.* [History of the Musical Development of Russia. In 2 Volumes.] Vol. II. St. Petersburg: A. S. Suvorin, 1912. 448 pp

Ivanov is described in most Soviet music histories and encyclopedias as "reactionary," since, together with a number of other writers, he was critical of the "Mighty Handful" and their achievements. Far from ignoring Rimsky-Korsakov, however, a substantial section of Chapter XVIII, pp. 132–62, discusses his operas, although only pp. 221–22 cover his orchestral works. Other sections are concerned with his songs, pp. 271–72, his folk song collection, pp. 340–42, and his various literary writings, pp. 388–89. Ivanov was a severe critic whose opinions merit attention.

1287   Ivanov-Ekhvet, Aleksey Ivanovich. "Svyazuyushchie niti vremën." [Threads Connecting the Times.] *SM* 50 (1) (1986): 94. ISSN: 0131-6818.

Discusses the interaction of the composers known as the *Moguchaya Kuchka* [Mighty Handful], of which Rimsky-Korsakov was a member, with St. Petersburg and Russian society, including their relationship with representatives of the revolutionary movement.

1288   Jaffé, Daniel, and Woronoff, Jon. *Historical Dictionary of Russian Music*. In *Historical Dictionaries of Literature and the Arts*. Lanham, MD: Scarecrow Press, 2012. xxxviii, 417 pp. ISBN-10: 0810853116. ISBN-13: 978-0810853119.

A comprehensive, clearly written dictionary of Russian music from the earliest times, including materials on Rimsky-Korsakov.

1289   Kashkin, Nikolay Dmitrievich. *Ocherk istorii russkoy muzyki.* [An Outline of the History of Russian Music.] Moscow-Leningrad: Yurgenson, 1908. 223 pp.

For a discussion of the composer and his music, particularly his operas, see pp. 153–63 of Chapter XII, entitled "Rimsky-Korsakov and his School." Kashkin notes the composer's weaknesses as well as his strengths.

1290   Keldysh, Yury Vsevolodovich. *Ocherki i issledovaniya po istorii russkoy muzyki.* [Essays and Research on the History of Russian Music.] Moscow: Sovetsky Kompozitor, 1978. 511 pp.

There are many references to Rimsky-Korsakov throughout this collection of essays by Keldysh, in particular in the sections "Glazunov," pp. 199–345, "Russian Opera in the Period 1907-1917," pp. 365–433, and "Musical Polemics in the Years Preceding the October Revolution," pp. 434–85.

1291   Kochetov, Nikolay Razumnikovich. *Ocherk istorii muzyki.* [An Outline of the History of Music.] Fourth edition, reprint of Third Edition, corr. and enl. Moscow: Muzykal'ny Sektor, 1929. 213 pp.

For a critical assessment of the composer and his work, see pp. 150–54. Kochetov notes the harmonic qualities of Rimsky-Korsakov's music, his orchestral skills, his preference for national themes, and the similarities of his music to that of Wagner.

1292   Krestan, Michael. *Das russische Glockengeläute und sein Einfluss auf die Kunstmusik Russlands im 19. und 20. Jahrhundert. Diskordanzen* 9. PhD dissertation, Universität Hildesheim. Published: Hildesheim, New York: Georg Olms, 2001. 338 pp. ISBN-10: 3487115549. ISBN-13: 978-3487115542.

Bibliography: General 247

A discussion of bell ringing in the Russian Orthodox Church ritual and its influence on Russian art music of the nineteenth and twentieth centuries, with special reference to the work of Musorgsky, Rimsky-Korsakov, and Rakhmaninov.

1293 Kruglikov, Semën Nikolaevich. "Dva russkikh kontserta na Parizhskoy vystavke." [Two Russian Concerts at the Paris Exhibition.] *Artist* 1 (1889): 92–101.

Contains details of accounts in various Parisian papers (*Le progres artistique, Le Ménestrel, Le monde artiste, L'art musical, Le monde musical, Le soir, Figaro, Paris, La patrie, Le moniteur universel, La France nouvelle, Gil Blas, Le télégraphe, La republique française, La liberté, Le monde illustré*), with particular attention paid to the music of Rimsky-Korsakov.

1294 Kyui, Tsezar' Antonovich [Cui, César]. *Izbrannye stat'i*. [Selected articles.] I. L. Gusin, ed. and comp. Leningrad: Muzgiz, 1952. lxviii, 692 pp.

Apart from many references to Rimsky-Korsakov in this large collection of articles by Cui covering the period 1864–1917, a dozen or so are specifically concerned with performances of Rimsky-Korsakov's compositions. These include an account of *The Maid of Pskov* from the *Sanktpeterburgskie Vedomosti* (St Petersburg Gazette) in January 1873, and a review of the opera *Sadko* published in the *Novosti i Birzhevaya Gazeta* in March 1898. Cui was a notoriously biased critic who held strong personal convictions. His writings, therefore, often provide a different viewpoint and, like those of Famintsyn, Ivanov, and Larosh, represent another facet of Russian musical criticism. Gusin's edition is rich in notes and extensively indexed. The individual monographs, and other important articles by Cui on Rimsky-Korsakov, are listed separately in the present volume, Vol. I. of Cui's *Musical Critical Articles* being published in Petrograd in 1918.

1295 Larosh [Laroche], German Avgustovich. *Izbrannye stat'i. IV: Simfonicheskaya i kamerno-instrumental'naya muzyka*. [Selected Articles. IV: Symphonic and Instrumental Chamber Music.] Abram Gozenpud, ed. Leningrad: Muzyka, 1977.

Includes materials on Rimsky-Korsakov, written by a leading nineteenth-century Russian critic.

1296 Laux, Carl August. *Die Musik in Russland und in der Sowetunion...Mit 165 Notenbeispielen und 98 Abbildungen*. Berlin: Henschelverlag, 1958. 463 pp.

For a discussion of Rimsky-Korsakov, his life and works, with particular reference to his operas, see pp. 136–62. Includes a short chronology, observations on the composer's significance as a musician and teacher, and a selected bibliography of books and articles in German, noting that a film of the opera *May Night* was made in the USSR circa 1950.

248   *Nikolay Andreevich Rimsky-Korsakov: A Research and Information Guide*

1297 Leonard, Richard Anthony. *A History of Russian Music.* London: Jarrolds, 1956. 395 pp. New edition: Westport, CT: Greenwood Press, 1977. 414 pp. ISBN-10: 0837196582. ISBN-13: 978-0837196589.

Information concerning Rimsky-Korsakov in this history of Russian music is to be found in Chapter VIII, pp. 144–72. Adopting a chronological approach, Leonard makes a general survey of the composer's music, using several quotations from Rimsky-Korsakov's *Chronicle of My Musical Life.* There are no music examples, the work clearly being intended for the non-specialist.

1298 Livanova, Tamara Nikolaevna. "B. V. Asaf'ev – issledovatel'russkoy muzykal'noy klassiki." [B. V. Asaf'ev – Researcher into Russian Classical Music.] In *Pamyati akademika Borisa Vladimirovicha Asaf'eva.* [In Memory of Academician Boris Vladimirovich Asaf'ev.] Moscow: Akad. nauk SSSR, 1951: 35–54.

For details of Asaf'ev's writings on Rimsky-Korsakov, see pp. 46–48.

1299 Maes, Francis. *A History of Russian Music. From Kamarinskaya to Babi-Yar.* Trans. Arnold J. Pomerans and Erica Pomerans. Berkeley, Los Angeles, London: University of California Press, 2002. xiv, 427 pp. ISBN-10: 0520218159. ISBN-13: 978-0520218154.

Written originally in Dutch, Maes' history provides a comprehensive and perceptive survey of Russian musical nationalism in the nineteenth century with many references to Rimsky-Korsakov, in particular Chapter 8, "A Musical Conscience: Rimsky-Korsakov and the Belyaev Circle."

1300 Marco, Guy. *Opera: A Research and Information Guide.* First edition. New York: Garland, 1984. Second rev. edition. New York: Routledge, 2001. xx, 632 pp. ISBN-10: 0815335164. ISBN-13: 978-0815335160. Review: T. Kaufman. *The Opera Quarterly* 18 (3) Summer, 2002: 457–459. ISSN: 0736-0053.

An excellent guide to opera, pp. 295–97 being devoted to publications regarding Rimsky-Korsakov.

1301 Melnikas, Leonidas. "Maximilian Steinberg: Irony of Fate." *Lietuvos muzikologija/Lithuanian musicology* 11 (2010): 121. ISSN: 1392-9313.

A discussion of the work of the teacher and composer Maksimilian Oseevich Shteynberg (1883–1946), who was born and raised in Vilnius. During his time in St. Petersburg, Shteynberg was a pupil of Rimsky-Korsakov, whose daughter, Nadezhda, he married in the summer of 1908. Stravinsky, who was a fellow student at the time, celebrated the event by dedicating to the young couple his *Feu d'artifice.* As executor of the late composer's estate, in 1913 Shteynberg completed and published Rimsky-Korsakov's *Osnovy orkestrovki* [Principles of Orchestration] and edited several of his operas for posthumous publication, as well as preparing several orchestral suites such as that from

Bibliography: General 249

The Golden Cockerel, which enjoyed great success. Among Shteynberg's pupils were Stasys Šimkus, Juozas Tallat-Kelpša, and Juozas Žilevičius.

1302 Morov, Aleksey. *Russkaya lira.* [The Russian Lyre.] Moscow: Sovetskaya Rossiya, 1971. 285 pp.

Includes discussion of the composer and his works.

1303 Neff, Lyle K. "Rimsky-Korsakov, Nikolay Andreevich." In Allan Ho and Dmitry Feofanov, Editors-in-Chief. *Biographical Dictionary of Russian/Soviet Composers.* New York, Westport, CT, London: Greenwood Press, 1989: 442– 45. ISBN-10: 0313244855. ISBN-13: 978-0313244858.

A short critical biographical article about the composer, including a list of Rimsky-Korsakov's pupils both inside and outside the St. Petersburg Conservatory. The *Biographical Dictionary* also contains short monographs on Nadezhda Nikolaevna Rimskaya-Korsakova, the composer's wife, and Georgy Mikhailovich Rimsky-Korsakov, the composer's grandson, renowned for his work on quarter-tone music and as inventor of the *emiriton*, an electronic musical instrument.

1304 Nemtsov, Jascha. "Lazar' Saminskij." In *Komponisten der Gegenwart: Loseblatt-Lexikon.* Nachlieferung, XVII. München, 1999.

A discussion of the life and work of Lazare Saminsky (1882–1959), conductor, musicologist, and teacher, who was born in Ukraine. While studying mathematics and philosophy at the St. Petersburg University (1906–09), he also took lessons in composition with Rimsky-Korsakov. As a result of Rimsky-Korsakov's support for his interest in Jewish studies, in particular folk music, in 1908 Saminsky subsequently founded the St. Petersburg Society for Jewish Folk Music. From 1911 to 1918 he worked in Tbilisi, teaching at the People's Conservatory. After moving abroad in 1919, in 1920 he settled in New York, where he became co-founder and chairman of the American League of Composers, being renowned as a conductor. In 1925 he became director of New York's largest synagogue, the Temple Emanu-El.

1305 Neuer, Adam. "Rimski-Korsakow." In Elżbieta Dziębowska, ed. *Encyklopedia Muzyczna PWM.* Kraków: Polskie Wydawnictwo Muzyczne SA, 2004: 404– 37. ISBN-10: 8322401124. ISBN-13: 978-8322401125.

A substantial article in Polish discussing Rimsky-Korsakov and his work, illustrated with attractive drawings and well-chosen photographs. The list of works is very well set out, the bibliography being of particular interest in that it includes a number of publications in Polish.

1306 Ossovsky, Aleksandr Vyacheslavovich. *Mirovoe znachenie russkoy klassicheskoy muzyki.* [The World Significance of Russian Classical Music.] Leningrad: Vses. obsh. po rspr. politich. i nauchn. znaniy Len. otd., 1948. 28 pp.

A stenogram of a public lecture read in Leningrad in 1948, pp. 19–21, containing extracts from Rimsky-Korsakov's letters to Ossovsky.

1307   Pavlov-Arbenin, Andrey Borisovich. "K 100-letiyu so dnya rozhdeniya B. V. Asaf'eva. Igor' Glebov: *Muzyka moey rodiny.*" [On the 100th Anniversary of the Birth of B. V. Asaf'ev. Igor' Glebov: *Music of My Motherland.*] *SM* 48 (4) (1984): 87. ISSN: 0131-6818.

Consists of unpublished fragments entitled *Muzyka moey rodiny* [Music of My Motherland] written by Boris Asaf'ev under the pseudonym Igor' Glebov, including his views on Rimsky-Korsakov.

1308   Pestalozza, Luigi. *La scuola nazionale russa.* Milano: Ricordi, 1958. 238 pp.

For a general account of the composer and his work, see pp. 79–107. No Russian language sources are listed in the bibliography.

1309   Plantinga, Leon. *Romantic Music. A History of Musical Style in Nineteenth Century Europe.* New York and London: W. W. Norton, 1985. 544 pp. ISBN-10: 0393951960. ISBN-13: 978-0393951967.

References to Rimsky-Korsakov are to be found on pp. 379–83.

1310   Pougin, Arthur. *A Short History of Russian Music.* Trans. Lawrence Haward. New York: Brentane's, 1915. 332 pp. Reprinted: Nabu Press, 2010. 360 pp. ISBN-10: 117801004X. ISBN-13: 978-1178010046.

First published in Paris in 1904 under the title *Essai Historique sur la Musique en Russie*, pp. 248–68 are devoted to a discussion of Rimsky-Korsakov and his work. Although dealing mainly with his operas, Pougin also examines orchestral pieces such as *Antar, Scheherazade*, the *Capriccio espagnol*, and the *Russian Easter Festival Overture*, as well as looking briefly at his piano compositions, the piano concerto (which he rates highly), and a few vocal works. Pougin's History is one of the earliest major works on Russian music and much of his information was sent to him by correspondents in Russia.

1311   Rapatskaya, Lyudmila Aleksandrovna. *Istoriya russkoy muzyki ot drevney Rusi do "serebryannogo veka." Uchebnik dlya studentov pedagogicheskikh vysshikh uchebnikh zavedeniy.* [History of Russian Music from Ancient Russia up to the "Silver Age." A Textbook for Students of Pedagogical Higher Educational Establishments.] Moscow: VLADOS, 2001. 384 pp. ISBN-10: 5691005340. ISBN-13: 978-5691005343.

This textbook is of particular interest, being one of the first works to be written in the post-Soviet period covering the history of music in Russia from antiquity to 1913. Chapter 15, "The Poetisation of Russian Folk Life," is devoted to Rimsky-Korsakov [see pp. 215–45].

1312   Redepenning, Dorothea. "Rimskij-Korsakov." In Ludwig Finscher, ed. *MGG,* Second edition: Personenteil 14. Bärenreiter: Kassel, 2005. Cols. 138–65. ISBN-10: 3476410099. ISBN-13: 978-3476410092.

Bibliography: General 251

A discerning account of Rimsky-Korsakov's life and work, with extensive factual information on his compositions, including instrumental music, operas, and other genres, together with discussion of his work as a teacher, writer, and editor. The bibliography is comprehensive.

1313 Ridenour, Robert C. *Nationalism, Modernism, and Personal Rivalry in Nineteenth-Century Russian Music.* Malcolm Hamrick Brown, ed. Ann Arbor, Michigan: UMI Research Press, 1981. 258 pp. ISBN-10: 0835711625. ISBN-13: 978-0835711623.

Originating from a Doctoral Dissertation, Indiana University, 1977, this work provides an insight into the conflicting personalities and ideologies prevalent in Russia from circa 1859 to the mid-1870s. Rimsky-Korsakov's role in the Balakirev Circle, his appointment as a teacher at the St. Petersburg Conservatory, his relationship with other musicians of the day, his first compositions, and other matters are all discussed.

1314 Rimsky-Korsakov, Andrey Nikolaevich. "Muzykal'no-istoricheskaya perspektiva proyasnyaetsya. Ob otnoshenii k naslediyu N. A. Rimskogo-Korsakova." [A Musical-Historical Perspective Clarified. On the Attitude Towards Rimsky-Korsakov's Legacy.] *SM* 3 (1933): 126.

1315 Sabaneev, Leonid Leonidovich. *Istoriya russkoy muzyki.* [History of Russian Music.] Moscow: Rabotnik Prosveshcheniya, 1924. 87 pp. German version: Ssabanejew, L. *Geschichte der russischen Musik.* Für deutsche Leser bearbeitet mit einem Vorwort und einem Nachtrag versehen von O. von Riesemann. Leipzig, 1926. 214 pp. Reprinted: Olms Verlag, 1982. ISBN-10: 3487072696. ISBN-13: 978-3487072692.

An account of Rimsky-Korsakov is found on pp. 65–68. After enumerating various sources of his style, including a short discussion of the influence of Berlioz, Liszt, and Wagner, as well as that of Glinka and Russian folk melody, Sabaneev notes the composer's skill in portraying natural forces, but considers that lyricism and individual pathos are basically alien to his disposition. This is not a discussion of Rimsky-Korsakov's individual works but rather an analytical overview of features of the composer's musical style and psychological make-up.

1316 Seaman, Gerald. "Rimskij-Korsakov, Nikolaj Andreevič." Trans. Cesare Dopino. In Alberto Basso, ed. *Dizionario Enciclopedico Universale della Musica e dei Musicisti*, Vol. 6. Turin: UTET, 1988. 357–63. ISBN-10: 8802041660. ISBN-13: 978-8802041667.

A comprehensive biographical article, translated into Italian by Cesare Dopino, discussing the principal elements of Rimsky-Korsakov's work, including an extensive bibliography.

1317 Seaman, Gerald. *Nikolai Andreevich Rimsky-Korsakov: A Guide to Research.* *First edition:* New York and London: Garland, 1988. ISBN-10: 0824084667. ISBN-13: 978-0824084660. Reviews: R. Guenther. *Notes: Quarterly Journal of the Music Library Association* 48 (2) 1991: 491. ISSN. 0027-4380. E. Garden. *ML* LXXI (2) 1990: 268–70. ISSN: 0027-4224.

A detailed examination of the work of Rimsky-Korsakov as composer and writer, consisting of 1,305 annotated entries, providing insight into his place in the cultural life of Russia at the time and his ideological significance during the Soviet period, including a wide range of international bibliographical materials, together with indexes of authors, titles, and topics.

1318 Seroff, Victor I. *The Mighty Five. The Cradle of Russian National Music.* New York: Allen, Towne & Heath, 1948. 280 pp. Reprinted: New York: Books for Libraries Press, 1970. ISBN-10: 0836954831. ISBN-13: 978-0836954838.

A general account of "The Five," with numerous references to Rimsky-Korsakov, written in a conversational style.

1319 Shabshaevich, Elena Markovna. "O muzyke na Vserossiyskoy khudozhestvenno-promyshlennoy vystavke 1882 v Moskve." [On Music at the 1882 All-Russian Art-Industrial Exhibition in Moscow.] *MA* (4) (2009): 147. ISSN: 0869-4516.

An examination of the part played by music in the All-Russian Art and Industry Exhibition of 1882 held in Moscow, including concerts given by the Russian Music Society with the participation of Rimsky-Korsakov.

1320 Shaverdyan, Aleksandr Isaakovich. *Izbrannye stat'i.* [Selected Articles.] Moscow: Sovetsky Kompozitor, 1958.

Contains two articles:

i. "Kniga o Rimskom-Korsakove" [A Book about Rimsky-Korsakov]: 365–72. Concerned with the completion of Vol. IV of A. N. Rimsky-Korsakov's study *N. A. Rimsky-Korsakov. Life and Work* [see No. 1180].
ii. "Velikaya tragediya (k 30-letiyu so dnya smerti N. A. Rimskogo-Korsakova)" [A Great Tragedy (to Mark the 30th Anniversary of Rimsky-Korsakov's Death)]: 373–78. A brief survey of the composer's life and his place in Russian music.

1321 Shebalin. B., Shaporin, Yu., Obukhova, N., and Stepanova, E. "Venok Rimskomu-Korsakovu." [A Garland for Rimsky-Korsakov.] *SM* 6 (1958): 7–14.

A series of tributes to Rimsky-Korsakov marking the 50th anniversary of his death.

1322 Sorokina, E. *Istoriya russkoy muzyki.* [History of Russian Music.] 3 Vols. Russian Federation: Muzyka, 2009. ISBN-10: 5714008618. ISBN-13: 978-5714008610.

Bibliography: General 253

A history of Russian music providing biographical information on leading composers, including Rimsky-Korsakov.

1323   Soubies, Albert. *Histoire de la Musique en Russie*. Paris: Alcide Picard et Kaan, Editeurs, 1898. Paris: Société Française d'Editions d'Art, L. Henry May, 1898. 303 pp. Reprinted: United States: Nabu Press, 2010. 310 pp. ISBN-10: 1178114848. ISBN-13: 978-1178114843. Reprinted: United States: Hardpress Publishing, 2013. 314 pp. ISBN-10: 1314053833. ISBN-13: 978-1314053838.

The main section on Rimsky-Korsakov in this early history of Russian music is to be found in Chapter IX, "La 'Nouvelle Ecole'," pp. 168–79. Written during the composer's lifetime, Soubies discusses briefly *The Maid of Pskov, May Night, The Snow Maiden, Mlada, Christmas Eve,* and *Sadko,* and refers to some orchestral and instrumental works. Valuable on account of its pictorial illustrations, the chapter concludes with a few remarks on Mme. Rimsky-Korsakov's musical talents, among her compositions being a piano sonata and an orchestral fantasy *La Nuit de la Saint-Jean* based on the story by Gogol.

1324   Stasov, Vladimir Vasil'evich. "Nasha muzyka za poslednye 25 let." [Our Music over the Last 25 Years.] *Vestnik Evropy* 10 (1883). Reprinted: V. V. Stasov. *Izbrannye sochineniya v trëkh tomakh. Zhivopis'. Skul'ptura. Muzyka.* [Selected Works in Three Volumes. Painting. Sculpture. Music.] Moscow: Iskusstvo, 1952: Vol. II, 522–68. English trans.: V. V. Stasov, *Selected Essays on Music.* Intro. by Gerald Abraham. Trans. Florence Jonas. London: Barrie & Rockcliff, 1968: 66–116. ISBN-10: 0214160394. ISBN-13: 978-0214160394.

Forming the fourth section of the monograph "Twenty-Five Years of Russian Art," this article deals with the development of Russian music from Glinka to Rimsky-Korsakov and his contemporaries.

1325   ——. *Stat'i o muzyke. V pyati vypuskakh.* [Articles on Music. In Five Volumes.] Vl. Protopopov, ed. Vols. I–V. Moscow: Muzgiz, 1974–80.

This comprehensive collection of Stasov's musical writings contains most of his articles on Rimsky-Korsakov. The contents include:

i.   Slavyansky kontsert g-na Balakireva. [Mr. Balakirev's Slavonic Concert.]: II, 110.
ii.   Nasha muzyka. [Our Music.]: III, 143.
iii. Nikolay Andreevich Rimsky-Korsakov: IV, 174.
iv.   Adres N. A. Rimskomu-Korsakovu. [An Address to N. A. Rimsky-Korsakov.]: IV, 206.
v.   Rech' na chestvovanii N. A. Rimskogo-Korsakova. [Speech in Honour of N. A. Rimsky-Korsakov.]: Va, 117.
vi.   Mitrofan Petrovich Belyaev: Va, 117.
vii. Dirizhërskaya palochka Rimskogo-Korsakova. [Rimsky-Korsakov's Baton.]: Va, 178.

viii. Radost' bezmernaya. [An Immense Joy.]: Va, 200.
ix. Rech' na chestvovanii N. A. Rimskogo-Korsakova. [Speech in Honour of N. A. Rimsky-Korsakov.]: Va, 249.
x. Rech' na chestvovanii N. A. Rimskogo-Korsakova 27 marta (9 aprelya) 1905 goda. [Speech in Honour of N. A. Rimsky-Korsakov on 27 March (9 April) 1905.]: Va, 350.
xi. Russkoe muzykal'noe obshchestvo i Rimsky-Korsakov. [The Russian Music Society and Rimsky-Korsakov.]: Va, 348.

1326   Swan, Alfred J. *Russian Music and Its Sources in Chant and Folk-Song.* London: John Baker, 1973. 234 pp. ISBN-10: 0212984217. ISBN-13: 978-0212984213.

Rimsky-Korsakov figures prominently throughout this study. See, in particular, Chapter 6, "Moussorgsky and Rimsky-Korsakov, 1868-1881," pp. 91–104.

1327   Taruskin, Richard. "Realism as Preached and Practiced: The Russian Opera Dialogue." *MQ* 56 (3) (1970): 431–54.

This article, although not primarily concerned with Rimsky-Korsakov, provides an insight into the esthetico-philosophical background of the period and the quest for realism in Russian opera. Contains long quotations from Chernyshevsky, Cui, and V. V. Stasov.

1328   ——. *Stravinsky and the Russian Traditions: A Biography of the Works through Mavra.* 2 Vols. University of California Press, 1996. ISBN-10: 0520070992; ISBN-13: 978-0520070998.

The references to the work of Rimsky-Korsakov contained in this voluminous work, in particular the operas, are too many to be listed separately. The influence of Rimsky-Korsakov on the young Stravinsky, the impact of the innovative musical language of *Kashchey the Immortal*, octatonicism, Rimsky-Korsakov's *Principles of Orchestration*, Stravinsky's first compositions written under his teacher's tutelage, the musical gatherings at the distinguished composer's home, are only a fraction of the subjects discussed in this impressive discourse which provides a picture not only of Stravinsky's creative evolution, but also a panoramic view of a musical world in which Rimsky-Korsakov played a leading role.

1329   ——. *On Russian Music.* University of California Press, 2009: 407. ISBN-10: 0520249798. ISBN-13: 978-0520249790.

Preceded by an informative introduction entitled "Taking it Personally," this is a compendium of 36 well-researched articles on differing aspects of music, including reprints of several monographs on Rimsky-Korsakov, references to whom are found throughout the book.

1330   Tsetlin (Zetlin), Mikhail Osipovich. *Pyatero i drugie.* [The Five and Others.] New York: *Novy zhurnal*, 1944. 398 pp. English edition: Zetlin, M. *The*

Five: The Evolution of the Russian School of Music. George Panin, trans. and ed. New York: International Universities Press, 1959. Reprinted, facsimile edition: Westport, CT: Greenwood Press, 1976. 344 pp. ISBN-10: 0837167973. ISBN-13: 978-0837167978.

This falls into three main sections and 18 chapters, Chapter VI, entitled "Prelestnoe detya" [A Charming Child], being a light-hearted description of Rimsky-Korsakov's youth. No footnotes, music examples, or bibliography.

1331   Zorina, Angelina. *Moguchaya kuchka.* [The Mighty Handful.] Leningrad: Muzyka, 1973. 95 pp.

Includes a discussion of the composer.

LITERARY WORKS

1332   Berkov, Viktor Osipovich. *Uchebnik garmonii Rimskogo-Korsakova. (Znachenie, teoreticheskie osnovy, metodika). Ocherk.* [Rimsky-Korsakov's Manual of Harmony. (Significance, Theoretical Bases, Methods). An Essay.] Moscow: Muzgiz, 1953. 72 pp.

Commences with a brief discussion of the two textbooks on harmony by Tchaikovsky and Rimsky-Korsakov, produced in 1871 and 1884, respectively. Rimsky-Korsakov's manual, discussed from a wide range of viewpoints, is seen as a work of immense significance in the training of young musicians, and a milestone in Russian musical pedagogy. Contents are as follows:

1.   Introduction: 3–12.
2.   On the History of the Work's Composition: 12–22.
3.   Features of the Textbook's Format. Practical Tasks for Students: 22–30.
4.   Questions of Mode and Function: 31–39.
5.   Questions of Harmony and Form, Modulation, Sequence: 39–46.
6.   Rimsky-Korsakov's Manual on Individual Characteristics of Harmony, Plagal Cadences, Harmonic Variation: 46–49.
7.   Clarification of Some Questions of Chromaticism in Rimsky-Korsakov's Manual: 49–54.
8.   Rimsky-Korsakov's Esthetic Views as Reflected in His Textbook: 60–67.
9.   Conclusion: 67–68.
10. Appendix.

1333   Findeyzen, Nikolay Fëdorovich. "Avtobiografiya Nikolaya Rimskogo-Korsakova." [Rimsky-Korsakov's Autobiography.] *RMG* 16 (1909). Reprinted: *MA* (2) (1994): 163. ISSN: 0869-4516.

Nikolay Findeyzen (1868–1928) was one of the greatest Russian musicologists prior to the Revolution. The article published here is his review of the first edition of Rimsky-Korsakov's *Letopis' moey muzykal'noy zhizni* [Chronicle of My Musical Life] as it appeared in *RMG* No. 16 (1909).

1334 Lischke, André, trans. and annotator. *Nikolaï Rimski-Korsakov. Chronique de ma vie musicale.* Paris: Fayard, 2008 [see No. 210]. ISBN-10: 2213635463. ISBN-13: 978-2213635460.

1335 McQuere, Gordon D. *Russian Theoretical Thought in Music.* Ann Arbor, Michigan: UMI Research Press, 1983. 394 pp. Reprinted: New York: University of Rochester Press, 2009. 404 pp. ISBN-10: 1580463193. ISBN-13: 978-1580463195.

For a discussion of Rimsky-Korsakov's *Practical Manual of Harmony,* see pp. 22–27.

1336 Messwarb, Katja. "Instrumentationslehre des 19. Jahrhunderts." PhD dissertation, Johann Wolfgang Goethe-Universität, Frankfurt am Main. In *Europäische Hochschulschriften.* XXXVI: *Musikwissenschaft* 171. Frankfurt am Main: Peter Lang, 1997. ISSN: 0721-3611.

While Berlioz's *Grand traité d'instrumentation et d'orchestration modernes* is still of fundamental importance in the teaching of orchestration, nevertheless Rimsky-Korsakov's *Osnovy orkestrovki* [Principles of Orchestration] is also of significance in its discussion of the development of orchestration, especially brass instruments, in the latter part of the nineteenth century.

1337 Miller, Larisa Alekseevna. "Ranny uchebnik instrumentovki N. A. Rimskogo-Korsakova: Neizvestny avtograf 1870-kh godov." [An Early Textbook on Orchestration by N. A. Rimsky-Korsakov: An Unknown Autograph of the 1870s.] In V. M. Vasil'eva, comp. *N. A. Rimsky-Korsakov i russkaya khudozhestvennaya kul'tura. Materialy nauchnoy konferentsii. Vechasha-Lyubensk.* [N. A. Rimsky-Korsakov and Russian Artistic Culture. Materials from a Scientific Conference. Vechasha-Lyubensk.] Pskov, 2008.

A discussion of Rimsky-Korsakov's work on his textbook on orchestration and its place in his creative biography.

1338 Neff, Lyle K., trans. "A Documentary Glance at Tchaikovsky and Rimsky-Korsakov as Music Theorists." In Leslie Kearney, ed. *Tchaikovsky and His World.* Princeton University Press, 1998: 333–54. ISBN-10: 0691004307. ISBN-13: 978-0691004303.

An examination of writings on music theory by Tchaikovsky and Rimsky-Korsakov, including translations of Tchaikovsky's prefatory remarks to his *Rukovodstvo k praktichskomu izucheniyu garmonii* [Guide to the Practical Study of Harmony] and Rimsky-Korsakov's "Razbor 'Snegurochki'" [Analysis of *The Snow Maiden*].

1339 Protopopov, Vladimir Vasil'evich. "Ob uchebnike garmonii Rimskogo-Korsakova." [On Rimsky-Korsakov's Manual of Harmony.] *SM* 6 (1958): 56–57.

Bibliography: General

A short discussion of some of the characteristic features of Rimsky-Korsakov's textbook on harmony. Part of a series of articles in *SM* marking the 50th anniversary of the composer's death.

1340 Rimskaya-Korsakova, Nadezhda Nikolaevna, ed. "Die musikalischen Aufsätze und Notate Rimsky-Korsakows: Vorwort zur russischen Erstausgabe (1910 [sic])." In *Studia slavica musicologica* 16: *Nikolai Rimsky-Korsakow. Kleinere musiktheoretische Schriften und Fragmente. Texte zur Musikgeschichte, Musikpädagogik und Musikästhetik.* Berlin: Ernst Kuhn, 2004. ISBN-10: 392886467X. ISBN-13: 978-3928864671.

A translation into German of the introductory article to the Russian first edition of Rimsky-Korsakov's *Muzykal'nye stat'i i zametki* [Musical Articles and Notes] edited by N. Rimskaya-Korsakova, St. Petersburg: M. Stasyulevich, 1911 [see No. 211].

1341 Rimsky-Korsakov, Nikolay Andreevich. *Praktichesky uchebnik Garmonii. Sostavil N. Rimsky-Korsakov. 12-e izdanie ispravlennoe i dopolnennoe pod redaktsiey I. I. Vitolya i M. O. Shteynberga.* [Practical Manual of Harmony. Compiled by N. Rimsky-Korsakov. 12th Edition, corr. and enl. I. I. Vitols and M. O. Shteynberg, eds.] Petrograd: M. P. Belyaev, 1918. x, 148.

Rimsky-Korsakov states in his introduction to the First Edition (1884–1885), reprinted in this volume: "In compiling this manual, I have endeavoured in the first place to make it as concise as possible; secondly, to adapt it to the progress [prokhozhdenie] of harmony as established at the present time in the St. Petersburg Conservatory, Court Chapel and other schools of music; thirdly to adapt it as far as possible for self-instruction. I have furnished it with a significant number of harmonic examples and exercises. The fulfilment by a student of these tasks must go jointly with the composing of similar tasks or examples of his own composition." Also included is the Introduction to the Third Edition, in which, apart from additional exercises, are a number of chorales. Translated into many languages, this work has continued to be of significance and has been constantly reprinted. For further details, see *Literary Works* Vol. IV. [See also Nos. 196 and 282.]

1342 ——. "Epidemiya dirizhërstva." [The Epidemic of Conducting.] In Nos. 200 and 211; German trans. No. 1343. Reprinted: E. S. Vlasova and E. G. Sorokina, eds. *Nasledie: Russkaya muzyka – mirovaya kul'tura.* [Heritage: Russian Music – World Culture.] I. Research Center, Moscow Conservatory, 2009. ISBN-13: 978-5895982303.

Rimsky-Korsakov's views on conductors and conducting, in particular during a period when a number of new conductors appeared in Russia in the 1890s.

1343 Rimsky-Korsakow, Nikolai. "Eine Epidemie des Dirigierens." In *Studia slavica musicologica* 16: *Nikolai Rimsky-Korsakow. Kleinere musiktheoretische Schriften und Fragmente. Texte zur Musikgeschichte, Musikpädagogik und Musikästhetik.*

Berlin: Ernst Kuhn, 2004 [see No. 1342]. ISBN-10: 392886467X. ISBN-13: 978-3928864671.

1344 Rimsky-Korsakow, Nikolai, Schmidt, Hans, Štejnberg, Maksimilian Oseevič, and Vītols, Jāzeps. "Praktisches Lehrbuch der Harmonie." In *Studia slavica musicologica* 16: *Nikolai Rimsky-Korsakow. Kleinere musiktheoretische Schriften und Fragmente. Texte zur Musikgeschichte, Musikpädagogik und Musikästhetik.* Berlin: Ernst Kuhn, 2004. ISBN-10: 392886467X. ISBN-13: 978-3928864671.

A complete facsimile of N. A. Rimsky-Korsakov's *Uchebnik garmonii.* [Manual of Harmony.] Leipzig: M. P. Belaieff, 1913.

1345 Rimsky-Korsakow, Nikolai. "Über Verirrungen des musikalischen Hörens (1901): Fragment." In *Studia slavica musicologica* 16: *Nikolai Rimsky-Korsakow. Kleinere musiktheoretische Schriften und Fragmente. Texte zur Musikgeschichte, Musikpädagogik und Musikästhetik.* Berlin: Ernst Kuhn, 2004. ISBN-10: 392886467X. ISBN-13: 978-3928864671.

A German translation of N. A. Rimsky-Korsakov's short work on the perception of music, originally published in N. N. Rimskaya-Korsakova, ed. *N. A. Rimskij-Korsakov. Muzykal'nye stat'i i zametki (1869-1907).* [N. A. Rimsky-Korsakov. Musical Articles and Notes (1869–1907).] St. Petersburg: M. Stasyulevich, 1911 [see No. 211].

1346 ——. "Wagner und Dargomyshki: Das Gesamtwerk zweier Künste oder das Musikdrama Fragment." In *Studia slavica musicologica* 16: *Nikolai Rimsky-Korsakow. Kleinere musiktheoretische Schriften und Fragmente. Texte zur Musikgeschichte, Musikpädagogik und Musikästhetik.* Berlin: Ernst Kuhn, 2004 [see Nos. 211 and 282]. ISBN-10: 392886467X. ISBN-13: 978-3928864671.

A German translation of an article by Rimsky-Korsakov discussing the music dramas of Wagner and Dargomyzhsky, noting the desire of both to break away from traditional opera and to achieve operatic reform.

1347 ——. "An alle Besucher des Marientheaters, welche die Oper als ein musikalisches Kunstwerk schätzen." In *Studia slavica musicologica* 16: *Nikolai Rimsky-Korsakow. Kleinere musiktheoretische Schriften und Fragmente. Texte zur Musikgeschichte, Musikpädagogik und Musikästhetik.* Berlin: Ernst Kuhn, 2004 [see Nos. 211 and 282]. ISBN-10: 392886467X. ISBN-13: 978-3928864671.

A German translation of an article by Rimsky-Korsakov surveying the status of opera in Western Europe and Russia, having special reference to the repertoire of the Mariinsky Theater in St. Petersburg.

1348 Ripanti, Luca, trans. *Rimskij-Korsakov, Nikolaj Andreevič. Principi de orchestrazione.* Milan: Rugginenti editore, 1992. 179 pp. [see No. 212]. ISBN-10: 8876650733. ISBN-13: 978-8876650734.

1349 Ryzhin, Iosif Yakovlevich. "Traditsionnaya shkola teorii muzyka." [The Traditional School of Music Theory.] *SM* 3 (1933): 74–98.

Bibliography: General

For a discussion of Tchaikovsky's and Rimsky-Korsakov's harmony manuals, see pp. 85–90. With comparative music examples.

1350   Tyulin, Yury Nikolaevich. "Ob istoricheskom znachenii uchebnika garmonii N. A. Rimskogo-Korsakova." [On the Historical Significance of Rimsky-Korsakov's Manual of Harmony.] In No. 1435: 81–93.

Pointing out that in 1956 Rimsky-Korsakov's *Manual of Harmony* had already reached its nineteenth edition and been translated into many languages, Tyulin describes the circumstances of its composition and the reasons for its popularity. Of special interest are Tchaikovsky's penciled notes on the first edition of 1884, which was sent to Tchaikovsky for comment before the work was published in 1885 in its revised form, the form in which it is today.

1351   Findeyzen, Nikolay Fëdorovich. "Avtobiografiya Rimskogo-Korsakova." [Rimsky-Korsakov's Autobiography.] *RMG* 16 (1909): cols. 429–31; 17 (1909): cols. 456–58; 20–21 (1909): cols. 523–26.

A sympathetic review of Rimsky-Korsakov's *Chronicle of My Musical Life. 1844-1906* [see No. 210], edited by his widow, written soon after its appearance, pointing out that its publication caused much more of a stir in musical circles than did Glinka's memoirs or the publications of Modest Tchaikovsky. Findeyzen stresses the book's value as a historical document and the insight it gives into the "new Russian school" and the composer.

1352   Korabel'nikova, L. "Uroki 'Letopisi'." [Lessons from the "Chronicle."] *SM* 8 (1981): 90–93.

A discussion of the eighth edition of Rimsky-Korsakov's *Chronicle of My Musical Life. 1844-1906* [see No. 210], commenting on its significance and its relevance to the modern period, and noting the manner in which it differs from previous editions.

1353   Kunin, Iosif Filippovich. "Odna lish' pravda." [One Truth Alone.] *SM* 3 (1969): 63–72.

A discussion of Rimsky-Korsakov's *Chronicle of My Musical Life. 1844-1906* [see No. 210], as a historical document, examining both the reaction to the work when it was first published and Rimsky-Korsakov's own judgements on contemporary critics and composers.

1354   Norris, Geoffrey. "My Musical Life by Rimsky-Korsakov." *MT* 116 (May 1975): 446.

A review of the translation by Judah A. Joffe of the fourth and fifth editions of the Russian version of Rimsky-Korsakov's *Chronicle of My Musical Life. 1844-1906* [see No. 210].

1355   Dziebowska, Elżbieta. "Instrumentacja w nauce kompozycuk w XIX wieku." [Instrumentation in the Teaching of Composition in the 19th Century.] *Muzyka* XX 1 (1976): 13–33.

Includes a discussion of Rimsky-Korsakov.

1356 Kandinsky, Aleksey Ivanovich. "Novoe izdanie 'Osnov orkestrovki' Rimskogo-Korsakova." [A New Edition of Rimsky-Korsakov's *Principles of Orchestration.*] *SM* 5 (1960).

An article reviewing the publication of the third edition of Rimsky-Korsakov's *Principles of Orchestration,* published as *Literary Works* Vol. III [see No. 282]. Kandinsky notes that the new edition contains a number of changes to the original music examples integrated into the text, and new appendices have been added, which, though valuable, are not necessarily appropriate to an academic publication. The editor, too, has not always presented material in a chronological manner and is unsystematic.

1357 Kurdyumov, Yu. V. "Posmertny trud N. A. Rimskogo-Korsakova." [A Posthumous Work by N. A. Rimsky-Korsakov.] *RMG* 26–27 (1913): cols. 582–86.

A discussion of Rimsky-Korsakov's *Principles of Orchestration,* ed. Maksimilian Shteynberg [see Nos. 212 and 282].

1358 Trambitsky, Viktor Nikolaevich. "Trud istoricheskogo znacheniya." [A Work of Historical Importance.] SM 3 (1969): 42–44.

A discussion of Rimsky-Korsakov's *Principles of Orchestration* [see Nos. 212 and 282], his reasons for writing it, and its significance compared with other treatises on instrumentation, for example, that of Berlioz.

1359 Veprik, Aleksandr Moiseevich. *Traktovka instrumentov orkestra.* [Treatment of the Instruments of the Orchestra.] Moscow-Leningrad, 1948. 309 pp.

Consisting of three chapters: "The Bi-functionality of Timbre," "Rimsky-Korsakov and Wagner," and "On the Development of an Orchestral Whole," the author discusses some of the composer's orchestral practices as outlined in his *Principles of Orchestration* [see Nos. 212 and 282] and his other works. Illustrated with many music examples, but no index.

1360 Gnesin, Mikhail Fabianovich. "Muzykal'no-nauchnye trudy Rimskogo-Korsakova." [Rimsky-Korsakov's Musical-Scientific Works.] *Muzyka* 133 (1913).

1361 Lischké, André. "Les leitmotive de Snégoourotchka analysés par Rimsky-Korsakov." *Revue de Musicologie* LXV 1 (1979): 51–75.

Discusses Rimsky-Korsakov's analysis of *The Snow Maiden* [see No. 208], of which he completed only the first part, followed by the article in French translation. Summary in English, p. 100.

1362 Livanova, Tamara Nikolaevna. *Kriticheskaya deyatel'nost' russkikh kompozitorov-klassikov.* [Critical Work of Russian-Classical Composers.]

Bibliography: General 261

Moscow-Leningrad: Muzgiz, 1950. 101 pp. Review: E. Dobrynina and Yu. Korev. *SM* 9 (1951): 101–05.

For an account of Rimsky-Korsakov's critical writings in the *Sanktpeterburgskie Vedomosti* [St. Petersburg Gazette] [see Nos. 192 and 193] and other publications, see pp. 75–99. Includes discussion of his attitude towards Russian music, Wagner, and esthetic considerations.

1363 Muir, Stephen. "'About as Wild and Barbaric As Well Could Be Imagined...': The Critical Reception of Rimsky-Korsakov in Nineteenth-Century England." *ML* 93 (4) (2012): 513. ISSN: 0027-4224.

Rimsky-Korsakov was the most frequently performed Russian composer in England at the end of the nineteenth century after Tchaikovsky and Anton Rubinstein. However, whereas there was widespread support for Tchaikovsky's music, that of Rimsky-Korsakov was attacked from many sides. The article examines the attitude towards Russian music then prevailing in England at the time, this being beneficial to the writings of Rosa Newmarch and others.

1364 Rimsky-Korsakow, Nikolai. "*William Ratcliff:* Eine Oper in drei Akten von César Cui." In *Studia slavica musicologica* 16: *Nikolai Rimsky-Korsakow. Kleinere musiktheoretische Schriften und Fragmente. Texte zur Musikgeschichte, Musikpädagogik und Musikästhetik.* Berlin: Ernst Kuhn, 2004. ISBN-10: 392886467X. ISBN-13: 978-3928864671.

A German translation of a review by Rimsky-Korsakov of César Cui's opera *Vil'yam Ratklif* [William Ratcliffe], first published in the *Sanktpetersburgskie vedomosti* (21 February 1869) [see No. 211].

1365 Tyuneev, Boris Dmitrievich. "Muzykal'nye stat'i Rimskogo-Korsakova." [Rimsky-Korsakov's Articles on Music.] *RMG* 24–25 (1911): 521–27.

Discusses Rimsky-Korsakov's *Musical Articles and Notes (1869-1907)*, N. Rimskaya-Korsakova, ed. St. Petersburg: M. Stasyulevich, 1911 [see No. 211].

1366 Yankovsky, Moisey Osipovich. "N. A. Rimsky-Korsakov. Nabroski dnevnika." [N. A. Rimsky-Korsakov. Drafts of a Diary.] In No. 1204: Vol. II, 7–18.

The existence of a diary relating to the last years of the composer's life has been known for some time. The diary preserved in the Manuscript Section of RNB contains the composer's thoughts on Bach and Berlioz, questions of orchestration, and on aspects of contemporary music, including that of Debussy and Stravinsky.

MEMOIRS

1367 Anonymous. "Iz memuarov M. M. Ippolitova-Ivanova." [From M. M. Ippolitov-Ivanov's Memoirs.] *SM* 3 (1933): 147–5̂0.

A personal account of Ippolitov-Ivanov's time as a composition student under Rimsky-Korsakov at the St. Petersburg Conservatory, where he graduated in 1882.

1368 Asaf'ev, Boris Vladimirovich [pseud. Glebov, Igor']. "N. A. Rimsky-Korsakov v vospominaniyakh V. V. Yastrebtsëva." [N. A. Rimsky-Korsakov as Remembered in Yastrebtsëv's Reminiscences.] *Melos* [Petrograd], Kniga [Book] 2 (1918).

A critique by Boris Asaf'ev of Yastrebtsëv's Reminiscences.

1369 ——. "Vstrechi i razdum'ya." [Meetings and Reflections.] *SM* 8 (1954): 42–52; 11 (1954): 35–42; 1 (1955): 49–58.

Written in an anecdotal style, the first article describes Asaf'ev's meeting with Rimsky-Korsakov and the impression the composer made upon the young musician and future musicologist. The second article is largely concerned with a description of Rimsky-Korsakov's sister-in-law, Aleksandra Nikolaevna Molas (*née* Purgol'd), a singer, who, having been given a number of manuscripts by Musorgsky, was indignant at her brother-in-law's "corrections." The third article contains descriptions of the composer and the manner in which the artists Repin and Valentin Serov captured facets of his personality in their portraits.

1370 Bronfin, E. F., ed. "Iz vospominaniy A. V. Ossovskogo." [From A. V. Ossovsky's Reminiscences.] In No. 1435: 189–96.

Ossovsky studied harmony and counterpoint with Rimsky-Korsakov from 1896 to 1898 and knew him in several capacities. His recollections give an insight into the composer's mind and personality, although they differ from those published later by Ossovsky in 1968.

1371 Brounoff, Platon. "Rimsky-Korsakoff as I knew Him." *The Musical World* 3 (Boston, 1903): 76–78.

Brounoff, who studied under Rimsky-Korsakov for six years, gives an account of the composer's work and his use of national elements, together with anecdotes. Describing Rimsky-Korsakov's appearance, his musical tastes, his personality, behavior, and the timbre of his singing voice ("which resembled the sound of a mill-saw"), he acknowledges the service which Rimsky-Korsakov provided for Russian music in the editing and completion of his friends' works, for which he refused any remuneration.

1372 Chaliapin, F. I. [Shalyapin, Fëdor Ivanovich.] *Chaliapin – An Autobiography as told to Maxim Gorky*. New York: Stein & Day, 1967. 320 pp. Reprint: London: Columbus Books, 1968; 1988. ISBN-10: 0862873967. ISBN-13: 978-0862873967.

Makes frequent mention of Rimsky-Korsakov and his work.

Bibliography: General 263

1373 Cherepnin, Nikolay Nikolaevich. *Vospominaniya muzykanta.* [A Musician's Reminiscences.] Leningrad: Muzyka, 1976. 128 pp.

The reminiscences of Cherepnin, one of Rimsky-Korsakov's students at the St. Petersburg Conservatory from 1895 to 1898, contain a wealth of anecdotal information about the composer and Russian musical life of the period. Well documented but no index.

1374 Dmitrieva-Mey, Tat'yana Pavlovna. "Iz vospominaniy B. V. Asaf'eva." [From B. V. Asaf'ev's Reminiscences.] In No. 1435: 209–17.

Asaf'ev, a student at the St. Petersburg Conservatory from 1906 to 1910, studied instrumentation with the composer for two years. This article differs from his previous account of his meeting with Rimsky-Korsakov [see *SM* 8 (1954): 42–52] in that it includes details of his experiences in the composer's orchestral class.

1375 Durylin, Sergey Nikolaevich. "Iz teatral'nykh vospominaniy." [From Theatrical Reminiscences.] In No. 1204: Vol. II, 319–33.

A discussion of some of the Moscow performers of Rimsky-Korsakov's operas, including Zabela-Vrubel', Sekar-Rozhansky, Sobinov, Chaliapin, and others.

1376 Fortunato, Sofiya Vladimirovna. "Vospominaniya o vstrechakh s N. A. Rimskim-Korsakovym." [Recollections of Meetings with N. A. Rimsky-Korsakov.] *RMG* 22–23 (1909): cols. 554–61. Reprinted: *MA* (2) (1994): 60–62. ISSN: 0869-4516.

Written by Sof'ya Fortunato, daughter of the music critic Vladimir Stasov, these recollections of meetings with Rimsky-Korsakov from the mid-1860s, including those at the dachas in Pargolovo and Yalta, are rich in detail and observations regarding the composer, his circle, his work, and his vocal accomplishments. The original article formed part of the special edition of the *RMG* published on the first anniversary of his death.

1377 Galkauskas, Konstantin Mikhaylovich. "Vospominaniya ob uchitele." [Reminiscences of My Teacher.] In No. 1407: 60–68.

An account of a student's life at the St. Petersburg Conservatory (1903–08), during which time Galkauskas studied under Rimsky-Korsakov, Glazunov, and Lyadov. Written in an anecdotal style, it stresses Rimsky-Korsakov's attitude and personal kindness towards his students.

1378 Glazunov, Anatoly Konstantinovich. "Vospominaniya o N. A. Rimskom-Korsakove." [Reminiscences of N. A. Rimsky-Korsakov.] In *Muzykal'ny Truzhenik* 10–11 (1909). Reprinted: *SM* 9 (1954): 70–74. Reprinted: A. K. Glazunov. *Pis'ma, stat'i, vospominaniya. Izbrannoe.* [Letters, Articles, Reminiscences. Selections.] Moscow: Muzgiz, 1958: 439–51.

One of a number of articles written to mark the 25th anniversary of Rimsky-Korsakov's death, this is a sympathetic account of Glazunov's recollections of the composer, whom he first met in 1879 and from whom he took lessons in 1880. Apart from painting a vivid picture of Rimsky-Korsakov's personality and tastes (he loved nature and astronomy), Glazunov describes his work with him in completing Borodin's *Prince Igor*, and the many different undertakings of Rimsky-Korsakov, as composer, conductor, inspector, and teacher. He comments on his perfect pitch, his perceptive remarks at rehearsals, and also the fact (as Borodin also noted) that he always seemed to conduct better at rehearsals than at the live performance, which factor he attributed to his natural shyness and modesty. Other subjects discussed include Rimsky-Korsakov's problems over censorship (especially *The Maid of Pskov* and *Christmas Eve*), his dismissal from the conservatory, and his last days.

1379   ——. "O N. A. Rimskom-Korsakove." [On N. A. Rimsky-Korsakov.] In *Glazunov. Muzykal'noe nasledie.* [Glazunov. Musical legacy.] Vol. II. Leningrad: Muzgiz, 1960: 146–56.

One of two articles written by Glazunov to mark the 25th anniversary of the composer's death. Originally in French, it was translated into Russian by the composer's widow. Taking the form of an autobiographical account, it describes Glazunov's lessons with Rimsky-Korsakov, the advice he received, the concerts given at the Exposition Universelle in 1889 (which included *Antar*, the Piano Concerto, and the *Capriccio espagnol*), and the observation that Rimsky-Korsakov's French was not very good. Includes a short biographical sketch. Elsewhere Glazunov discusses Rimsky-Korsakov's work as an editor of Musorgsky's and Borodin's compositions, in which he defends Rimsky-Korsakov's version of *Boris Godunov*, pointing out that although Musorgsky was an excellent pianist, he was not a skilled orchestrator. He also stresses the fact that Rimsky-Korsakov asked for no payment for his labors over *Boris Godunov*, *Khovanshchina*, and *Prince Igor*, and refused all author's rights for performance in Russia. [See also No. 1420.]

1380   Gnesin, Mikhail Fabianovich. "N. A. Rimsky-Korsakov – pedagog i chelovek (iz lichnikh vospominaniy)." [N. A. Rimsky-Korsakov – Teacher and Human Being (from Personal Reminiscences).] In *Sovetskaya Muzyka. Trety sbornik statey.* [Soviet Music. Third Volume of Articles.] Moscow, 1945: 67–78. Also in No. 1381.

Gnesin's personal recollections of his former teacher

1381   ——. *Mysli i vospominaniya o N. A. Rimskom-Korsakove.* [Thoughts and Reminiscences about N. A. Rimsky-Korsakov.] D. V. Zhitomirsky, ed. Moscow: Muzgiz, 1956. 336 pp. Review: A. Solovtsov. *SM* 1 (1957): 139–45.

This volume, by one of Rimsky-Korsakov's pupils, contains a wealth of material relating to different aspects of the composer's work. Illustrated

Bibliography: General 265

with music examples, photographs of music manuscripts, programs, and personalia, it consists of an introduction and forewords by the editor and the author, followed by six chapters and three appendices:

Introduction (Formation of Rimsky-Korsakov's Personality, Searching for Ideas, Creative Evolution).
On Epic Symphonism.
The Opera-Bylina *Sadko.*
Kashchey the Immortal.
The Golden Cockerel.
Rimsky-Korsakov's Relationship with His Pupils. [First appeared in *Muzyka i revolyutsiya* 7–8 (1928).]
Some Reminiscences from People Close to Rimsky-Korsakov. [Glazunov, Lyadov, Nadezhda Ivanovna Zabela-Vrubel'.]

Appendices:

i.   Documents and Articles about the Revolutionary Movement in the St. Petersburg Conservatory, 1905.
ii. Glazunov's Letters to Yu. L. Landau (Veysberg).
iii. A Letter by Glazunov to V. F. Pavlovksy.

1382   Gol'denveyzer, Aleksandr Borisovich. *O muzykal'nom iskusstve.* [On the Art of Music.] D. D. Blagoy, ed. and comp. Moscow: Muzyka, 1975. 416 pp.

Of main interest in this volume is the chapter "Vospominaniya o N. A. Rimskom-Korsakove" [Reminiscences of N. A. Rimsky-Korsakov], pp. 168–71, covering the period 1897–99.

1383   Gretchaninoff, Alexandre. *My Life.* Intro. and trans. Nicolas Slonimsky. New York: Coleman-Ross, 1952.

Gretchaninoff became a student of Rimsky-Korsakov at the St. Petersburg Conservatory in 1890. For numerous references to their relationship, see pp. 35–54. No index.

1384   Ippolitov-Ivanov, Mikhail Mikhaylovich. *50 let russkoy muzyki v moikh vospominaniyakh.* [50 Years of Russian Music in My Recollections.] Moscow: Muzgiz, 1934: 129–31.

Ippolitov-Ivanov was one of Rimsky-Korsakov's pupils and was present at the première of *The Maid of Pskov.* Noting the impression Rimsky-Korsakov made on young people, he points out that, whereas Rimsky-Korsakov created a whole school of successors, Tchaikovsky left behind few followers. After drawing further comparisons between the two composers, Ippolitov-Ivanov recounts that Rimsky-Korsakov demanded that his students knew by heart the main themes of all Beethoven's and Schumann's symphonies, Liszt's symphonic poems, and major works in general. He made his students write down complex harmonies by ear and short pieces such as scherzos and minuets. Classes were small, the five members in Ippolitov-Ivanov's class being Arensky, Kazachenko, Antipov, N. Sokolov, and himself. An absorbing and informative account.

1385 Mal'ko, Nikolay Andreevich. "Vospominaniya o Rimskom-Korsakove." [Reminiscences of Rimsky-Korsakov.] *SM* 8 (1958).

Nikolay Mal'ko (1883–1961) was one of Rimsky-Korsakov's last composition students at the St. Petersburg Conservatory, from where he graduated in 1909.

1386 Morozova, Margarita Kirillovna. "Iz vospominaniy." [From Reminiscences.] *MZ* 5 (1969): 3. Reprinted: *MA* (2) (1994): 79. ISSN: 0869-4516.

A vivid eye-witness account of Rimsky-Korsakov conducting two of the Grand Opéra concerts organized by Dyagilev [Diaghilev] in Paris in 1907. Also includes a description of his attendance at musical evenings at Skryabin's home and how, in 1907, he saw a performance of Strauss's *Salome* at the Théâtre du Châtelet in Paris.

1387 Newmarch, Rosa. "Rimsky-Korsakov. Personal Reminiscences." *Monthly Musical Record* 38 (452) (1908): 172–73.

An account of Rosa Newmarch's meetings with the composer, full of sympathetic description and rich in picturesque detail.

1388 Nikol'skaya, L. B., ed. "Vospominaniya M. O. Shteynberga." [M. O. Shteynberg's Reminiscences.] In No. 1435: 196–209.

Maksimilian Shteynberg was Rimsky-Korsakov's student from 1902 to 1908 and later became his son-in-law. As a teacher at the St. Petersburg Conservatory, Shteynberg adhered closely to Rimsky-Korsakov's pedagogical methods, his memoirs being full of details of student life as well as descriptions of a more personal nature. These memoirs differ from those in the volume by G. G. Tigranov, *The Leningrad Conservatory in Reminiscences 1862-1962*, Leningrad: Muzgiz, 1962 [see No. 1407].

1389 Ossovsky, Aleksandr Vyacheslavovich. *Vospominaniya. Issledovaniya.* [Reminiscences. Research.] Leningrad: Muzyka, 1968. 450 pp.

Contains two articles on Rimsky-Korsakov: "Reminiscences," pp. 25–48, and "Rimsky-Korsakov – Thinker and Artist," pp. 275–341. Ossovsky's memoirs cover the period 1896–1908, during part of which he was the composer's student. Written in a conversational style, Ossovsky describes the composer's personality, pointing out the two sides of his character. On the one hand there is the serious, introspective, reserved rationalist, on the other a warm-hearted rather shy lyricist. The second article is concerned with the composer's esthetic outlook as manifest in his literary and musical compositions.

1390 Pokhitonov, Daniil Il'ich. *Iz proshlogo russkoy opery.* [From the Past of Russian Opera.] S. S. Danilov, ed., with introductory article. Leningrad: Vserossiyskoe Teatral'noe Obshchestvo, 1949: 27–64.

Encapsulated within pp. 27–56 is a witty description of Pokhitonov's entry into the St. Petersburg Conservatory, with an account of his preliminary audition and life as a student, pp. 57–64 describing his relationship with the composer. Rimsky-Korsakov did not like to waste time, was always punctual, and expected the same self-discipline from his pupils. The article includes details of the composer's personality, teaching methods, and impulsiveness, together with a description of the first performance of *The Legend of the Invisible City of Kitezh* and a brief account of his funeral.

1391 Prokof'ev, Sergey Sergeevich. "Yunye gody." [Youthful Years.] In No. 1407: 60–68.

In this article, Prokofiev describes his studies at the St. Petersburg Conservatory, his audition and interview, and his work with Rimsky-Korsakov. Prokofiev's own ideas came into conflict with those of his teacher, as a result of which he was given the assessment: "capable but immature."

1392 ——. *Avtobiografiya.* [Autobiography.] M. G. Kozlova, ed. Moscow: Sovetsky Kompozitor, 1973. 704 pp.

Important for Prokofiev's reminiscences of his teacher and for the many observations on Rimsky-Korsakov's compositions.

1393 Rimsky-Korsakov, Mikhail Nikolaevich. "Iz vospominaniy ob ottse." [From Reminiscences of My Father.] *Ogonëk* 14–15 (1944): 12.

1394 Rimsky-Korsakov, Vladimir Nikolaevich. "Iz vospominaniy." [From My Reminiscences.] *Literatura i iskusstvo* 12, 116 (18 March 1944).

A sympathetic and informative account of the composer's life at Tikhvin, his working habits, his perfect pitch, his concern over the timbre of each orchestral instrument, and his systematic organization (which could well have left its mark on Stravinsky).

1395 ——. "Iz vospominaniy ob ottse." [From Recollections of my Father.] *Ogonëk* 26 (1958): 17.

1396 Rimsky-Korsakov, Mikhail Nikolaevich, and Kopytova, Galina Viktorovna. "Vospominaniya i zamechniya o zhizni Nikolaya Rimskogo-Korsakova i ego sem'i." [Reminiscences and Remarks on the Life of Nikolay Rimsky-Korsakov and His Family.] *MA* (2) (1994): 33–40. ISSN: 0869-4516.

The first chapter of the reminiscences of the composer's eldest son, Mikhail Nikolaevich Rimsky-Korsakov, covering the period 1873–83, including a sketch by Shalyapin and humorous verses written by Rimsky-Korsakov circa 1852.

1397 Rizemann, Oskar fon. "Iz vospominaniy, zapisannyh Oskarom fon Risemannom." [From Recollections, Written Down by Oscar von Riesemann.] *MA* (2) (1994): 81. ISSN: 0869-4516.

Rakhmaninov's recollections of Rimsky-Korsakov as recounted by Oscar von Riesemann.

1398 Sandulenko, A. "The Korsakoff Wednesday." Trans. and arr. Alfred J. Swan. *Chesterian* 15 (July–August, 1934): 165–68.

A reference to the musical gatherings Rimsky-Korsakov liked to hold in his apartment in St. Petersburg on Wednesday evenings.

1399 Shalyapin, Fëdor Ivanovich. *Stranitsy iz moey zhizni (Avtobiografiya).* [Pages from My Life (Autobiography).] Leningrad: Priboy, 1926. 220 pp. Republished: Perm, 1961. 240 pp. English trans. entitled: *Pages from My Life.* London, 1927.

Chaliapin's Autobiography gives a good insight into stage productions of the period. For an account of his first brief meeting with Rimsky-Korsakov, see p. 186. Pages 203–05 discuss the performance of *The Maid of Pskov,* in which Chaliapin took the part of Ivan the Terrible, describing how he studied the various portraits of Ivan by Shvarts, Repin, Vasnetsov, and the sculptor Antokol'sky. For Rimsky-Korsakov's productions in general, see pp. 211–19. No index.

1400 ——. *Maska i dusha. Moi sorok let na teatrakh.* [Mask and Soul. My Forty Years in the Theater.] Parizh: Sovremennyaya zapiski, 1932. 357 pp. English trans. *Man and Mask. Forty Years in the Life of a Singer.* London, 1932.

The memoirs of one of Russia's greatest singers, full of anecdotes and interesting details.

1401 Shestakova, Lyudmila Ivanovna. "Iz neizdannykh vospominaniy o novoy russkoy shkole." [From Unpublished Reminiscences about the New Russian School.] *RMG* 51–52 (1913): cols. 1179–86.

Written in 1889, cols. 1184–86 are concerned specifically with Rimsky-Korsakov, whom Lyudmila Shestakova describes as a person "honourable, distinguished and tactful to the highest degree, with a passionately loving nature, despite his external coldness." The last part of the article describes his unselfish work in completing his friends' compositions.

1402 Shteynberg, Maksimilian Oseevich. "Vospominaniya o N. A. Rimskom-Korsakove i A. K. Glazunove." [Recollections of N. A. Rimsky-Korsakov and A. K. Glazunov.] In No. 1407: 40–49.

Shteynberg first met Rimsky-Korsakov at the St Petersburg Conservatory in Spring 1903. He describes the impression Rimsky-Korsakov made on the students, the types of melody given to them for harmonization, instruction in fugue, and the manner in which the students would be taken to rehearsals to hear important musical works.

1403 Sokolov, Nikolay Aleksandrovich. "Vospominaniya o N. A. Rimskom-Korsakove." [Reminiscences of N. A. Rimsky-Korsakov.] *RMG* 39–40 (1908): cols. 829–36; 41 (1908): cols. 867–73. Reprinted: *MA* 2 (1994): 52–55.

Sokolov first made the acquaintance of Rimsky-Korsakov in 1878 as a student of the St. Petersburg Conservatory. In this article, he presents a first-hand account of his experiences and feelings as a pupil in Rimsky-Korsakov's class, discussing the composer's psychology of teaching and describing his work at the Imperial Chapel. Facsimile of the composer's handwriting.

1404 Strasser, W. "Personal observations on Rimsky-Korsakoff." *The Etude* 51 (October 1933): 661, 705.

A short account of the writer's association with the composer, whom he assisted with arrangements, together with details of the composer's work habits and methods of composition. With an excellent engraving of the composer at his desk.

1405 Tartakov, Georgy Ioakimovich. "Vydayushchy russky pevets." [An Outstanding Russian Singer.] *SM* 2 (1977): 84–89.

The memoirs of Ioakim Tartakov (1860–1923), a singer, recalling his connections with Rimsky-Korsakov and performances in Odessa, Kiev, and St. Petersburg.

1406 Ter-Gevondyan, Anushavan Grigor'evich. "Nezabyvaemaya pora." [An Unforgettable Time.] In No. 1407: 49–58.

An account by a student at the St. Petersburg Conservatory, who first met Rimsky-Korsakov in 1907 and entered the Conservatory in 1908. Brief details of the composer and his personality.

1407 Tigranov, Georgy Grigor'evich, ed. *Leningradskaya konservatoriya v vospominaniyakh 1862-1962.* [The Leningrad Conservatory in Reminiscences 1862-1962.] Leningrad: Muzgiz, 1962. 415 pp.

This compendium, produced to mark the centenary of the founding of the Leningrad Conservatory, contains personal accounts of Rimsky-Korsakov by former pupils: Gnesin, pp. 17–32, Zolotarëv, pp. 32–37, Galkauskas, pp. 37–40, Shteynberg, pp. 40–49, Ter-Gevondyan, pp. 49–58, and Prokofiev, pp. 60–68.

1408 Tynson, Khel'ga Leopol'dovna. "Vospominaniya Marta Saara." [Recollections of Mart Saar.] In No. 1435: 225–28.

The Estonian, Mart Saar, studied at the St. Petersburg Conservatory in Rimsky-Korsakov's counterpoint and practical composition class from 1902 to 1904. His reminiscences, written originally in Estonian, were published in the Tallin paper *Serp i molot* [Sickle and Hammer] in 1948.

1409 Van'kovich-Gnesina, Mikhail Fabianovich. "Vyskazyvaniya N. A. Rimskogo-Korsakova. Iz zapisnoy knizhki M. F. Gnesina." [Sayings of N. A. Rimsky-Korsakov. From M. F. Gnesin's Notebook.] *MZ* 2 (1958): 21–22.

A collection of Rimsky-Korsakov's comments and remarks gathered by his pupil Gnesin over the period 1902–08. The sayings are divided into two groups: those of a political nature, and those on music in general.

1410 Vasilenko, Sergey Nikiforovich. *Stranitsy vospominaniy.* [Pages of Reminiscences.] Moscow-Leningrad: Muzgiz, 1948. 188 pp.

Vasilenko's reminiscences of Rimsky-Korsakov are found on pp. 50–57, together with a description of Vasilenko's own *Legend of the Invisible City of Kitezh* performed before the senior composer in 1902. No index.

1411 ———. "Moi vospominaniya o dirizhërakh." [My Recollections of Conductors.] *SM* 1 (1949): 92–97.

This survey of some pre-revolutionary Russian conductors contains some notes on Rimsky-Korsakov as a conductor and the reason why he tended to conduct mainly his own works. Vasilenko notes his authority, excellent hearing, clear directions, and love of a rich full sound.

1412 ———. *Vospominaniya.* [Reminiscences.] Tamara Livanova, ed. Moscow: Sovetsky Kompozitor, 1979. 376 pp.

Includes discussion of Vasilenko's meetings with Rimsky-Korsakov.

1413 Vasilenko, Sergey Nikiforovich, and Livanova, Tamara Nikolaevna. "Iz vospominaniy." [From Recollections.] *MA* (2) (1994): 100–02. ISSN: 0869-4516.

Recollections of S. N. Vasilenko (1872–1956), describing meetings and creative contacts with Rimsky-Korsakov, including observations on his conducting. Vasilenko's student opera-cantata *Skazanie o grade velikom Kitezhe i tikhom ozere Svetoyar* [Legend of the Great City of Kitezh and the Quiet Lake Svetoyar], Op. 5 (1903), which was performed by the Moscow Private Russian Opera, predates Rimsky-Korsakov's opera *The Legend of the Invisible City of Kitezh.*

1414 Veysberg, Yuliya Lazarevna. "Iz vospominaniy muzykanta o 1905 g." [From a Musician's Reminiscences of the Year 1905.] *Iskusstvo trudyashchimsya* 3 (1926): 5–7.

On a performance of *Kashchey the Immortal.*

1415 Vitmer, A. N. "Pamyati N. A. Rimskogo-Korsakova. (Vospominaniya A. N. Vitmera)." [In Memory of N. A. Rimsky-Korsakov. (Reminiscences of A. N. Vitmer).] *Niva* 12 (1912): 417–21.

A description of Tikhvin, mentioning that it was noted for its miraculous icon of the Virgin Mary, which made it a place of pilgrimage for the whole of North Russia. Contains information on the Rimsky-Korsakov family, the composer's parents, and his brother Voin.

1416 ———. "Rodina N. A. Rimskogo-Korsakova." [N. A. Rimsky-Korsakov's Homeland.] *RMG* 36–37 (1912): cols. 739–43.

A reproduction of Vitmer's article as it appeared in the journal *Niva* 12.

Bibliography: General

1417 Vitols [Vītoliņš], Yakob Yanovich. "Iz vospominaniy Yazepa Vitola." [From Jāzeps Vītols' Reminiscences.] In No. 1435: 217–25.

Jāzeps Vītols was a student in Rimsky-Korsakov's class of instrumentation and practical composition at the St. Petersburg Conservatory from 1883 to 1886. These autobiographical excerpts, describing his association with his teacher and life at the Conservatory, 1881–1908, are taken from his unpublished memoirs *Manas dz è ves atmiņs* [Reminiscences of My Life], written in Latvian in 1936–42.

1418 ——. *Vospominaniya, stat'i, pis'ma.* [Reminiscences, Articles, Letters.] Leningrad: Muzyka (1969). 336 pp.

Rimsky-Korsakov is frequently mentioned in this volume. Vitols was a student at the St. Petersburg Conservatory and a pupil of the composer. Particular attention is drawn to pp. 30–40, his article on *The Tsar's Bride*, pp. 154–57, and *The Legend of the Invisible City of Kitezh*, pp.198–201. *From Homer* is mentioned on p. 185. No index.

1419 Yankovsky, Moisey Osipovich. "I. F. Tyumenev. Vospominaniya o N. A. Rimskom-Korsakove." [I. F. Tyumenev. Recollections of N. A. Rimsky-Korsakov.] In No. 1204: Vol. II, 17–247.

Tyumenev (1855–1927) kept a diary of his life, in which are included reminiscences of Rimsky-Korsakov. Two copies are known to exist, one being preserved in the Rimsky-Korsakov Archive of SPBGATI, the other, containing 10 diaries, unpublished letters of Rimsky-Korsakov, and other materials, in the I. F. Tyumenev Archive of RNB. Extracts from these materials have been used in the formulation of Yankovsky's article, which covers the period 1875–1905. Full of detail, Tyumenev's observations add further light on Rimsky-Korsakov's life and work, especially the operas *The Tsar's Bride* and *Pan Voevoda*, for which he was the librettist.

1420 ——, ed. *Glazunov. Muzykal'noe nasledie. Issledovaniya, materialy, publikatsii, pis'ma. V dvukh tomakh.* [Glazunov. Musical Heritage. Research, Materials, Publications, Letters. In Two Volumes.] Vol. I. Leningrad: Muzgiz, 1959; Vol. II. Leningrad: Muzgiz, 1960.

Volume II of this collection of materials contains two articles on Rimsky-Korsakov:

i. "O N. A. Rimskom-Korsakove" [About N. A. Rimsky-Korsakov]: 146–56. Consists of personal recollections of Rimsky-Korsakov, written by Glazunov on the occasion of the 25th anniversary of his former teacher's death.

ii. A publication of 129 letters, pp. 157–269, exchanged between Glazunov and Rimsky-Korsakov, of which 41 are by the latter. Though some of the letters are very brief, they contain much detail, including the reasons why Rimsky-Korsakov had no desire to receive an honorary degree from either Oxford or Cambridge (Letter 19), considering such honors inappropriate for composers.

1421 Yastrebtsëv, Vasily Vasil'evich. *Moi vospominaniya o Nikolae Andreeviche Rimskom-Korsakove.* [My Reminiscences of Nikolay Andreevich Rimsky-Korsakov.] Parts I–II, Petrograd. 1917.

Yastrebtsëv's first collection of reminiscences only covered the period to March 1895 and did not include the letters which were published in the later edition of 1959–60.

1422 ——. *Nikolay Andreevich Rimsky-Korsakov. Vospominaniya V. V. Yastrebtsëva.* [Nikolay Andreevich Rimsky-Korsakov. Reminiscences of Yastrebtsëv.] A. V. Ossovsky, ed. 2 Vols. Leningrad: Muzgiz, 1959–60. Vol. I: 527 pp., Vol. II: 634 pp.

Yastrebtsëv's reminiscences first appeared in 1917 when two volumes covering the period 1890–95 were published in Petrograd. A two-volume abbreviated edition, covering the periods 1886–97 and 1898–1908, but with the omission of letters and other materials, appeared in 1959–60. Yastrebtsëv was truly a Russian Boswell, his diary of his almost daily meetings with the composer providing a unique insight into Rimsky-Korsakov's life, his home environment, his compositions, their rehearsal and performance, and his creative plans. Yastrebtsëv's observations also reflect the European cultural scene. A *sine qua non* for any study of the composer. Comprehensive index.

1423 ——. *Reminiscences of Rimsky-Korsakov.* Trans. and abridged, Florence Jonas. New York: Columbia University Press, 1985. 578 pp. [A condensed translation of No. 1422, reducing nearly 1000 pages by half.] ISBN-10: 023105260X. ISBN-13: 978-0231052603. Reviews: Gojowy, Detlef. "Reminiscences of Rimsky-Korsakov." *Die Musikforschung* 40 (3) (1987): 284. ISSN: 0027-4801. Waters, Edward N. "Reminiscences of Rimsky-Korsakov." *JALS* 21 (January–June 1987): 85. ISSN: 0147-4413.

As Florence Jonas points out in the translator's note, often entire entries have been abridged and excised, this signifying that even where whole paragraphs have been included, words, numbers, and other data may have been omitted, without any indication of this fact. While the translation is informative and entertaining, therefore, caution must be exercised in employing the material, and consultation of the original Russian text is essential should precise quotation be required. Contains a Foreword by Gerald Abraham, Notes, a List of Rimsky-Korsakov's works (not in the 1959–60 edition), and an index.

1424 Zolotarëv, Vasily Andreevich. "O moikh uchitelyakh, druz'yakh i tovarishchakh." [About my Teachers, Friends and Comrades.] In No. 1407: 49–58.

Bibliography: General 273

A discussion of life at the St. Petersburg Conservatory, the nature of Rimsky-Korsakov's teaching and his conduct of classes, and the types of work recommended for study, for example, the fugues of Bach, Tchaikovsky's Fourth Symphony, etc. A sequel to his earlier article describing life in the Imperial Chapel [see No. 886].

MILITARY BANDS

1425 Butir, Leonid Mironovič. "Nikolai Rimsky-Korsakov's Unknown Text about [the] Clarinet." *The Clarinet* 31 (3) (June 2004): 88. ISSN: 0361-5553.

A comprehensive discussion of Rimsky-Korsakov's attitude towards the clarinet, an instrument which he himself played, including an examination of sketches, manuscripts, and prints preserved in RNB.

1426 Nozdurnov, Boris Mitrofanovich. "Rimsky-Korsakov – inspektor voennykh orkestrov." [Rimsky-Korsakov – Inspector of Military Orchestras.] *SM* 6 (1958): 58–62.

A short discussion of Rimsky-Korsakov's work as an inspector of military orchestras and of his successful achievements. Part of a series of articles in a volume of *SM* marking the 50th anniversary of the composer's death.

1427 Lipaev, Ivan Vasil'evich. "Rimsky-Korsakov kak voenny kapel'meyster." [Rimsky-Korsakov as a Military Bandmaster.] *Muzykal'ny Truzhenik* 7 (1910).

1428 Stoffel, Lawrence, F. "Russian and Western Influences on Nicholai Rimsky-Korsakov as Inspector of Naval Bands." In *Blas- und Bläsermusik: Beziehungen zur Öffentlichkeit im 19. und 20. Jahrhundert – Die Bedeutung für Bildung, Kultur, Politik und Militär.* Mainz: Kongressbericht, 1996. Reprinted: *Alta Musica* 20. Tutzing: H. Schneider, 1998: 31–47. ISBN-10: 3795209420. ISBN-13: 978-3795209421.

A discussion of Rimsky-Korsakov's role as Inspector of Naval Bands from 1873 to 1884, a period about which little is known.

MUSIC EDUCATION

1429 Aleksandrova, Vera Nikolaevna. "Zametka N. A. Rimskogo-Korsakova o prepodovanii kompozitsii." [N. A. Rimsky-Korsakov's Note on the Teaching of Composition.] In No. 1435: 246–48.

A copy of Rimsky-Korsakov's note, preserved in RGALI, is given here in a new more accurate translation than that employed by Kiselëv in his publication: *N. A. Rimsky-Korsakov. Collection of Documents* [see No. 1527].

274   *Nikolay Andreevich Rimsky-Korsakov: A Research and Information Guide*

1430   Anonymous. "Nachalo raboty N. A. Rimskogo-Korsakova v konservatorii." [The Beginning of N. A. Rimsky-Korsakov's Work in the Conservatory.] *SM* 9 (1951): 110–11.

A short article on the circumstances of Rimsky-Korsakov's appointment as a professor at the St. Petersburg Conservatory in 1871 and the reaction to this.

1431   Bel'sky, Rafail. "Vospominanie o vozniknovenii Obshchestva Muzykal'nykh Sobraniy v Peterburge." [Recollections of the Rise of the Society for Musical Gatherings in St. Petersburg.] *MA* (2) (1994): 144. ISSN: 0869-4516.

An account written by a former member of the Obshchestva Muzykal'nykh Sobraniy [Society for Musical Gatherings], a student organization founded in St. Petersburg in 1889 by enthusiasts for Rimsky-Korsakov's music, which they helped to propagandize.

1432   Choi, Seung-Ho. "Igor Stravinsky's Early Period of Establishing Musical Language." *Seoyang eum'aghag* [Journal of the Musicological Society of Korea] 21 (2009): 153. ISSN: 1598-9224.

This paper examines the development of Igor Stravinsky's musical language over the period preceding composition of *Le sacre du printemps* written in 1913, including the part played by Rimsky-Korsakov in instructing him in the art of orchestration.

1433   Druskin, Mikhail. *Igor' Stravinsky – lichnost', tvorchestvo, vzglyady.* [Igor Stravinsky – Personality, Creativity, Views.] Moscow: Sovetsky Kompozitor, 1979. Trans. Martin Cooper. *Igor Stravinsky. His Personality, Works and Views.* Cambridge: Cambridge University Press, 1983. 194 pp. ISBN-10: 0521245907. ISBN-13: 978-0521245906.

Contains several references to Rimsky-Korsakov, including those pertaining to his influence on the young Stravinsky, pp. 29–30, 36–37.

1434   Ganina, Mariya Alekseevna. "Neizdannaya zapiska N. A. Rimskogo-Korsakova 1905 goda." [An Unpublished Note by N. A. Rimsky-Korsakov of 1905.] In No. 1435: 249–51.

A letter written to the Arts Council of the St. Petersburg Conservatory on 28 February 1905, preserved in SPGK, in which Rimsky-Korsakov expresses his views on the role of the Conservatory in the troubled times of the 1905 Revolution.

1435   Ginzburg, Semën L'vovich, ed. *N. A. Rimsky-Korsakov i muzykal'noe obrazovanie. Stat'i i materialy.* [N. A. Rimsky-Korsakov and Music Education. Articles and Materials.] Leningrad: Muzgiz. 1959. 327 pp.

A fundamental volume for any study of Rimsky-Korsakov, this consists of four major sections and an appendix:

Bibliography: General

i. "Rimsky-Korsakov's pedagogical views and work." (Eight articles by Mikhaylov, Ginzburg, Ostrovsky, Zorin, Tyulin, Dmitriev, Orlova, and Ryazanov.)

ii. "Rimsky-Korsakov in his relations with his students." (Five articles by Ganina, Mikhaylov, Tigranov, Rozova, and Lysenko.)

iii. "Recollections of Rimsky-Korsakov by his pupils." (Memoirs by Ossovsky, Shteynberg, Asaf'ev, Jāzeps Vītols, and Mart Saar.)

iv. Materials on Rimsky-Korsakov's work in the St. Petersburg Conservatory.

Appendix: A bibliography of 800 entries concerning Rimsky-Korsakov (1917–57), comp. S. M. Vil'sker. Illustrations. [For a description of each of these entries, locate the author through the index.]

1436 ——. "N. A. Rimsky-Korsakov i podgotovka deyateley natsional'nykh muzykal'nykh kul'tur narodov SSSR." [N. A. Rimsky-Korsakov and the Preparation of Workers of the National Music Cultures of the USSR.] In No. 1435: 46–57.

Discusses the achievements of some of Rimsky-Korsakov's non-Russian pupils, for example, the Ukrainians Lysenko, Kazachenko, Davidovsky, and Akimenko, the Latvians Andrey Yurlyan and Jāzeps Vītols, the Estonians Artur Kapp and Mart Saar, the Lithuanian Konstantin Galkauskas, and the Caucasians Spendiarov and Meliton Balanchivadze. Stresses Rimsky-Korsakov's interest in the music of other nationalities and his encouragement of his students' talents.

1437 Gnesin, Mikhail Fabianovich. "N. A. Rimsky-Korsakov v obshchenii so svoimi uchenikami." [N. A. Rimsky-Korsakov's Relationship with His Pupils.] *Muzyka i revolyutsiya* 7–8 (1928): 13–18. With changes, in Gnesin, M. F. *Mysli i vospominaniya o N. A. Rimskom-Korsakove.* [Thoughts and Reminiscences about N. A. Rimsky-Korsakov.] Moscow: 1956.

1438 ——. "Muzykal'no-pedagogicheskie vozzreniya Rimskogo-Korsakova." [Rimsky-Korsakov's Musical-Pedagogical Opinions.] *SM* 10 (1934): 28–33.

Discusses the position of musical education in Russia in the second half of the nineteenth century as seen by Rimsky-Korsakov, the ways in which he considered that musical education should serve a wide public, together with a discussion by Gnesin of the relevance of such ideas to contemporary Soviet music education.

1439 Joseph, Charles M. "Stravinsky's piano scherzo (1902) in perspective: a new starting point." *MQ* 67 (1) (1981): 82–93.

Includes discussion of the composer's influence on the young Stravinsky.

1440 ——. *Stravinsky and the Piano.* Ann Arbor, Michigan: UMI Research Press, 1983. 304 pp. ISBN-10: 0835714268. ISBN-13: 978-0835714266.

Contains a number of references to Stravinsky's indebtedness to Rimsky-Korsakov.

1441 Khoprova, Tat'yana Aleksandrova. "Spisok uchenikov N. A. Rimskogo-Korsakova v peterburgskoy konservatorii." [List of N. A. Rimsky-Korsakov's Pupils in the St. Petersburg Conservatory.] In No. 1435: 258–70.

Rimsky-Korsakov taught at the St. Petersburg Conservatory for 37 years. Using mainly examination books preserved in TSGIA SPB, Khoprova has assembled a list of some 230 students who passed through his hands. The examination books reveal that from 1873 to 1876 he taught special instrumentation and practical composition. In 1886, following a reorganization of the Conservatory curriculum, he taught a 5-year course on the theory of composition, which included harmony, counterpoint, fugue, and practical composition. In 1906, he again taught only practical composition and special instrumentation.

1442 Konstantinova, Marianna Aleksandrovna. "N. A. Rimsky-Korsakov – direktor Besplatnoy muzykal'noy shkoly (po arkhivnym dokumentam)." [N. A. Rimsky-Korsakov – Director of the Free Music School (Based on Archival Materials).] *Muzykovedenie* [Musicology] (3) (2007): 32. ISSN: 2072-9979.

Utilizing archival materials preserved in Russian libraries, this gives an account of the work of Rimsky-Korsakov as an administrator and teacher during the period from 1874 to 1881 when he served as director of the Besplatnaya muzykal'naya shkola [Free Music School], an institution providing free tuition, set up originally as a rival to the St. Petersburg Conservatory.

1443 Levenson, Boris. "How Rimsky-Korsakoff taught." *The Etude* 46 (March 1928): 197–198.

A first-hand account of the composer's teaching methods, including a vivid picture of Rimsky-Korsakov himself, by a pupil of 1902.

1444 Livanova, Tamara Nikolaevna. *Pedagogicheskaya deyatel'nost' russkikh kompozitorov-klassikov.* [The Pedagogical Work of Russian Classical Composers.] Moscow-Leningrad: Muzgiz, 1951. 110 pp. Review: E. Dobrynina and Yu. Korev, SM 9 (1951): 101–05.

For an account of Rimsky-Korsakov and his activities as a teacher in the St. Petersburg Conservatory, where he taught from 1871 to 1908, see pp. 43–73. There is also discussion of his work as Inspector of Naval Bands, his links with the Free Music School and the Imperial Chapel, and his ideas on music education as set out in two articles published posthumously. Includes comments on his academic textbooks.

1445 Lokshin, Daniil L'vovich. *Vydayushchiesya russkie khory i ikh dirizhëry. Kratkie ocherki.* [Outstanding Russian Choruses and Their Conductors. Short Essays.] Moscow: Muzgiz, 1953. 132 pp.

Two articles discussing Rimsky-Korsakov, the first, pp. 16–32, being concerned with his work as assistant to Balakirev at the Imperial Chapel. Following the introduction by Bortnyansky and Glinka of educational classes at the chapel, Balakirev and Rimsky-Korsakov instituted instructions in orchestral playing and choral training. Rimsky-Korsakov's *Podrobnaya Programa regentskogo klassa Pridvornoy kapelly* [Detailed Program of the Choral Class of the Imperial Chapel] has served as a foundation for much subsequent teaching. Among the subjects taught were elementary music theory (with strong emphasis on aural training), piano, violin, and cello playing. The second article, pp. 55–64, is concerned with Rimsky-Korsakov's work as Head of the Free Music School and his encouragement of choral music by means of performance of excerpts from Bach's *St. Matthew Passion*, the *Mass in B Minor*, Kyries by Palestrina, and choruses from Handel. During his time at the Free Music School, Rimsky-Korsakov wrote a number of choral works, for example, *6 Choruses a cappella*, Op.16; *4 Variations and a Fughetta on the Theme of a Russian Folk Song*, Op. 14, all of which were performed at the school concerts.

1446   ——. *Leningradskaya Gosudarstvennaya Akademicheskaya Kapella imeni M. I. Glinki.* [The Leningrad State Academic Chapel named after M. I. Glinka.] Moscow: Muzgiz, 1955. 37 pp.

For an account of the development of Russia's oldest choir, discussing the part played by Rimsky-Korsakov as a teacher during the period 1883–93, see pp. 17–24. There is no index or bibliography.

1447   Makurenkova, Elena Petrovna. "Pedagogicheskaya sistema N. A. Rimskogo-Korsakova." [N. A. Rimsky-Korsakov's Pedagogical System.] *Muzykal'noe prosveshchenie: Obshcherossiysky informatsionno-analitichesky zhurnal* [Music Education: An All-Russian Information-Analytical Journal] (3) (2008): 17.

A survey of the development of music education in Russia, specifically among the nobility in the nineteenth century, together with the role of the conservatories in forming the foundation for professional music education as exemplified by such teachers as Rimsky-Korsakov.

1448   Mikhaylov, Mikhail Kesarevich. "N. A. Rimsky-Korsakov – vospitatel' kompozitorov." [N. A. Rimsky-Korsakov – Composers' Teacher.] In No. 1435: 13–45.

Taking as the basis of his discussion Rimsky-Korsakov's two articles: "On Musical Education," written in 1892, and "Project for the Reform of the Program of Theory, Music and Practical Composition in the Conservatory" (1901), both published in 1911, this takes the form of a long and detailed survey of Rimsky-Korsakov's philosophy of music education and his method of teaching as experienced and recorded by his pupils.

1449 Móricz, Klára. "The Confines of Judaism and the Illusiveness of Universality in Ernest Bloch's *Avodath Hakodesh* (Sacred Service)." In *Repercussions* V (1–2) (Spring–Fall 1996): 184–241.

A discussion of the Jewish national movement in music, with special reference to the part played by the Obshchestvo Evreyskoy Narodnoy Muzyki [Society of Jewish Folk Music] founded in St. Petersburg in 1908 by students of Rimsky-Korsakov.

1450 Muzalevsky, Vladimir Il'ich. *Stareyshy russky khor. K 225-letiyu Leningradskoy gosudarstvennoy akademicheskoy kapelly.* [The Oldest Russian Choir. To Mark the 225th Anniversary of the Leningrad State Academic Chorus.] Leningrad-Moscow: Iskusstvo, 1938. 375 pp.

For a brief discussion of some of Rimsky-Korsakov's work in the Imperial Chapel, where he organized classes and arranged concerts, see pp. 32–34.

1451 Myasoedov, Andrey. "Traditsii Chaykovskogo v prepodavanii garmonii." [Tchaikovsky's Traditions in Teaching Harmony.] PhD dissertation, Theory, Moscow Conservatory, 1974. 147 pp.

Discusses Rimsky-Korsakov's and Tchaikovsky's methods of teaching harmony.

1452 Ostrovsky, Aron L'vovich. "Vzglyady N. A. Rimskogo-Korsakova na obrazovanie muzykantov-ispolniteley." [N. A. Rimsky-Korsakov's Views on the Education of Musician-Performers.] In No. 1435: 58–70.

Although Rimsky-Korsakov never taught performers (apart from encountering them in his orchestral class), he was concerned with the question of how they should best be prepared, and was against any kind of "assembly-line" production. This article discusses the composer's views on this subject, stressing the need for good aural training, strong theoretical bases, and the general expansion of musical sensitivity.

1453 Ploumpidīs, Giōrgos P. "Η μουσική εκπαίδευση στη Ρωσία." [Music Education in Russia.] *Mousikologia: Periodikī ekdosī mousikīs theōrias kai praxīs* (18) (2003): 48. ISSN: 1012-0203.

An article in Greek surveying the historical development of music education in Russia, beginning with the activities of Peter the Great in the early eighteenth century, and describing the founding of the St. Petersburg Conservatory in 1862 and the part played by such teachers as Rimsky-Korsakov.

1454 Semenov-Tyan-Shansky, Veniamin, and Rakhmanova, Marina Pavlovna. "O muzykal'nom kruzhke Shtrupa N. M." [On the Musical Circle of N. M. Shtrup.] MA (2) (1994): 140–43. ISSN: 0869-4516.

Recollections of a participant in the Obshchestvo Muzykal'nyh Sobraniy [Society of Musical Gatherings] in St. Petersburg, a society founded in 1889

Bibliography: General 279

by students attracted to the music of Rimsky-Korsakov. The article was written in 1936.

1455 Shelkova, N. V. "Rol' Rimskogo-Korsakova kak organizatora podgotovki v peterburgskoy konservatorii muzykantov dlya voenno-morskogo flota." [Rimsky-Korsakov's Role as an Organiser of the Preparation of Musicians in the St. Petersburg Conservatory for the Military-Naval Fleet.] In No. 1435: 252–57.

Rimsky-Korsakov was still a Naval Lieutenant when first appointed a professor at the St. Petersburg Conservatory in 1871. This article discusses the manner in which he attempted to maintain links between the teaching at the Conservatory and the requirements of the naval bands.

1456 Slonimsky, Sergey Mikhaylovich. "Balakirev – pedagog." [Balakirev – Teacher.] *SM* (3) (March 1990): 7–12. ISSN: 0131-6818.

An examination of Balakirev's role as a teacher and his method of teaching, among his composition students being Rimsky-Korsakov.

1457 Vul'fius, Pavel Aleksandrovich. "Programmy N. A. Rimskogo-Korsakova po teorii i istorii muzyki." [N. A. Rimsky-Korsakov's Programs on the Theory and History of Music.] In No. 1435: 231–45.

A discussion of three unpublished documents by the composer preserved in the Leningrad archives, all relating to the teaching of music theory and music history. The documents are entitled: "Program of a Course of Special Theory" [TSGIA SPB], "Program of Classes of Compulsory Theory" [TSGIA SPB], and "Music Theory and History" [RNB]. Of these, the last is the most extensive.

1458 Weisser, Albert, ed. "Lazare Saminsky's Years in Russia and Palestine: Excerpts from an Unpublished Autobiography." *Musica Judaica* II (1) (1977–78): 1–20.

Includes information on his time at the St. Petersburg Conservatory as a pupil of Rimsky-Korsakov.

1459 Zarin' [Zarins], Marger Ottovich. "My – ego vnuki i pravnuki." [We Are His Grandchildren and Great-Grandchildren.] *SM* 3 (1969): 87–88.

A short article on Latvian music, showing the manner in which it has been influenced by Rimsky-Korsakov through his pupil Jāzeps Vītols.

1460 Zorina, Angelina Petrovna. "Voprosy muzykal'noy pedagogiki v perepiske N. A. Rimskogo-Korsakova s S. N. Kruglikovym." [Questions of Musical Pedagogics in the Correspondence between N. A. Rimsky-Korsakov and S. N. Kruglikov.] In No. 1435: 71–80.

The composer's correspondence with the Moscow critic Semën Nikolaevich Kruglikov consists of over 500 letters, of which 280 were written by Rimsky-Korsakov. Apart from an extensive discussion on questions of music education, particular attention is paid in this correspondence to his manual on harmony, the progress and development of which were witnessed by Kruglikov, and who also encouraged him to write a manual on orchestration.

MUSICAL STYLE

1461 Abraham, Gerald. "The Essence of Russian Music." In No. 283: 1–20.

An enumeration of some stylistic features of Russian music, with a discussion of some of Rimsky-Korsakov's harmonic and contrapuntal procedures.

1462 ——. "The Whole-Tone Scale in Russian Music." In No. 284: 62–71.

A general discussion of the use of the whole-tone scale, with special reference to *Scheherazade*.

1463 ——. "Oriental Elements in Russian Music." In No. 284: 72–80.

Includes discussion of the composer's artifical scale of alternating tones and semitones.

1464 ——. "The Evolution of Russian Harmony." In No. 284: 255–74.

On Russian harmony in general, with some references to Rimsky-Korsakov.

1465 Aleksandrova, E. L., comp. *N. A. Rimsky-Korsakov. Cherty stilya. Sbornik statey.* [N. A. Rimsky-Korsakov. Features of Style. Collection of Articles.] St. Petersburg Conservatory, 1995. 233 pp.

1466 Brazhnik, Larisa Vladimirovna. "Angemitonnaya melodika v operakh N. A. Rimskogo-Korsakova." [Anhemitonic Melody in the Operas of N. A. Rimsky-Korsakov.] *Muzyka: Iskusstvo, nauka, praktika.* [Music: Art, Science, Practical Work.] (1) (2012): 27. ISSN: 2226-3330.

An examination of the part played by anhemitonic melodies in Rimsky-Korsakov's operas, noting that these are not a major factor in the composer's musical oeuvre, but are used in his operas for specific effects.

1467 Budrin, B. "Nekotorye voprosy garmonicheskogo yazyka Rimskogo-Korsakova v operakh pervoy poloviny 90kh godov." [Some Questions about Rimsky-Korsakov's Harmonic Language in the Operas of the First Half of the 1890s.] In *Trudy kafedry teorii muzyki Moskovskoy konservatorii* [Transactions of the Department of Music Theory of Moscow Conservatory], Vyp. 1 [Issue 1]. Moscow: Muzgiz, 1960: 143–218.

A searching discussion of the composer's employment of chromatic harmony in the operas *Mlada*, *Christmas Eve*, and *Sadko*.

1468 DeVoto, Mark. "The Russian Submediant in the Nineteenth Century." *Current Musicology* (59) (1995): 48–76. ISSN: 0011-3735.

A discussion of the use of modal harmony in nineteenth-century Russian music, including an examination of harmonic elements in the music of Rimsky-Korsakov.

Bibliography: General

1469 Drukt, Aleksandr. "O natural'no-ladovoy garmonii kuchkistov." [On the Natural-Mode Harmony of the Mighty Handful.] *SM* 50 (9) (September 1986): 103–06. ISSN: 0131-6818.

An examination of the natural-mode harmony in the musical output of Rimsky-Korsakov, Borodin, and Musorgsky.

1470 E. P. "Primechanie k biografii." [Note to a Biography.] *RMG* 51 (1900): cols. 1276–82.

A survey of the composer's musical style, its colorfulness, and simplicity.

1471 Goryachikh, Vladimir Vladimirovich. "Iz nablyudeniy nad tvorcheskim metodom N. A. Rimskogo-Korsakova." [Observations on the Creative Method of N. A. Rimsky-Korsakov.] *Musicus* 4 (13) (October–December 2008): 15. ISSN: 2072-0262.

Published in *Musicus*, the journal of the St. Petersburg Conservatory, this is an examination of the compositional principles of Rimsky-Korsakov and their role in his creative evolution.

1472 Grigor'ev, Stepan Stepanovich. "Mnogogolosnye melodii i obosoblennye garmonicheskie sloi v muzyke Rimskogo-Korsakova." [Polyphonic Melodies and Isolated Harmonic Layers in the Music of Rimsky-Korsakov.] In *Trudy kafedry teorii muzyki Moskovskoy konservatorii* [Transactions of the Department of Music Theory of Moscow Conservatory], Vyp. 1 [Issue 1]. Moscow: Muzgiz, 1960: 112–42.

An examination of polyphonic elements in Rimsky-Korsakov's operas, with special attention to *The Legend of the Invisible City of Kitezh*, including modal elements, folk polyphony, and harmony.

1473 ——. *O melodike Rimskogo-Korsakova.* [On Rimsky-Korsakov's Melody.] Moscow: Muzgiz, 1961. 183 pp.

Preceded by a discussion of other Soviet works concerned with the question of Rimsky-Korsakov's melody, Grigor'ev sees the purpose of his book as "an analysis of the basic principles of the formation and structure of different melodic types, belonging to the one concrete musical style." The element of melody in Rimsky-Korsakov's music is examined from a wide range of viewpoints and is subjected to close structural analysis.

1474 Gui, Vittorio. "L'anima slava nella musica moderna." In *Russia: Revista di litteratura, storia e filosofia*. Diretta da Ettore Lo Gatto. Anno I. Marzo, 1922: No. VI, 144–46, "Nicola Rimskij Korsakof."

A perceptive article in which Gui notes the psychological content of some of Rimsky-Korsakov's work, relating it to contemporary influences.

1475 Gut, Serge. "L'échelle à double seconde augmentée: Origines et utilisation dans la musique occidentale." *Musurgia: Analyse et pratique musicales* 7 (2) (2000): 41–60. ISSN: 1257-7537.

Entitled "The Scale with Two Augmented Seconds: Origins and Usage in Occidental Music," this French study examines two types of scales with two augmented seconds, noting the fact that double harmonic scales are found in the music of such composers as Glinka and Rimsky-Korsakov.

1476 Jackson, Larisa Petrushkevich. "Modulation and Tonal Space in the Practical Manual of Harmony: Rimsky-Korsakov's Harmonic Theory and Its Historical Antecedents." PhD dissertation, New York: Columbia University, 1996. UMI: 9631765. ML: 410 R52 J33 1996g.

A commentary on the concept of modulation and the relationship of keys in Rimsky-Korsakov's *Uchebnik garmonii* [Manual of Harmony]. In addition to providing information about the musical life of St. Petersburg and the circumstances surrounding the work's composition, reference is also made to Rimsky-Korsakov's awareness of German theoretical thought.

1477 Jankélévitch, Vladimir. *La rhapsodie; verve et improvisation musicale*. Paris: Flammarion, 1955: 251 pp.

For an account of Rimsky-Korsakov, seen as a master craftsman in the art of sound painting, see pp. 56–149. The various chapters, full of complex imagery, have evocative titles such as "Le livre d'images," "L'est et le sud," "La mer," "La terre," "Le ciel et la nuit," "De l'aube A midi," and "Le soleil et le printemps," all of which are concerned with different facets of the composer's art, whether operatic or symphonic.

1478 Kahan, Sylvia. "'Rien de la tonalité usuelle': Edmond de Polignac and the Octatonic Scale in Nineteenth-Century France." *19th-Century Music* 29 (2) (2005): 97–120. ISSN: 0148-2076.

A discussion of the history of the octatonic scale and its structure, and the manner in which it was employed by Prince Edmond de Polignac and Rimsky-Korsakov.

1479 Kholopova, Valentina Nikolaevna. *Voprosy ritma v tvorchestve kompozitorov pervoy poloviny XX veka*. [Questions of Rhythm in the Work of Composers of the First Half of the 20th Century.] Moscow: Muzyka, 1971. 304 pp. German trans. Detlef Gojowy, *Die Musikforschung* XXVII (4) (1974): 435–46.

For a commentary on the rhythmic features of Rimsky-Korsakov's music, showing parallels to analogous instances in Stravinsky's music, see pp. 228–34.

1480 Kuhn, Ernst, Lapschin, Iwan, Korsuchin, Iwan, and Ossowski, Alexander. *Nikolai Rimsky-Korsakow: Zugänge zu Leben und Werk: Monographien. Schriften. Tagebücher. Verzeichnisse*. (Musik konkret. Quellentexte und Abhandlungen zur russischen Musik des 19. und 20. Jahrhunderts, 12). Berlin: Ernst Kuhn (2000). ISBN-10: 3928864157. ISBN-13: 978-3928864152.

Entitled *Nikolay Rimsky-Korsakov: Approaches to His Life and Work: Monographs. Writings, Diaries. Catalogues*, this volume includes factual information about the

Bibliography: General 283

composer and his work, including details of notable recent performances of his operas.

1481 Kunguris, Georgius. "U istokov novogrecheskoy kompozitorskoy shkoly: Tvorchestvo Manolisa Kalomirisa i traditsii N. A. Rimskogo-Korsakova." [At the Root of the New Greek School of Composition: The Creativity of Manōlīs Kalomoirīs and the Traditions of N. A. Rimsky-Korsakov.] In *MA* (3) (2010): 171. ISSN: 0869-4516.

A discussion of the manner in which the ideas of Rimsky-Korsakov have influenced the work of Manōlīs Kalomoirīs, the founder of the modern Greek school of composition.

1482 Kushnarëv, Khristofor Stepanovich. *O polifonii. Sbornik statey.* [On Polyphony. A Collection of Articles.] Yu. Tyulin and I. Pustyl'nik, eds. Moscow: Muzyka, 1971. 136 pp.

Includes discussion of contrapuntal elements in Rimsky-Korsakov's work.

1483 Longyear, Rey M. and Covington, Kate R. "Tonic Major, Mediant Major: A Variant in 19th-century Sonata Form." *Studies in Music from the University of Western Ontario* 10 (1985): 105. ISSN: 0703-3052.

Includes discussion of Rimsky-Korsakov's approach to the question of sonata form and the use of the mediant major.

1484 Morrison, Simon. "The Semiotics of Symmetry, or Rimsky-Korsakov's Operatic History Lesson." *Cambridge Opera Journal* 13 (3) (2001): 261. ISSN: 0954-5867. Reprinted: Michael C. Tusa, ed. *National Traditions in Nineteenth-Century Opera,* Vol. II: *Central and Eastern Europe.* Farnham: Ashgate, 2010. ISBN-10: 0754629066. ISBN-13: 978-0754629061.

A discussion of Rimsky-Korsakov's creative processes, treatment of time and space relationships, and his interest in national and exotic subject matters manifest in such operas as *Sadko.*

1485 Mutli, Andrey Fëdorovich. *O modulyatsii. (K voprosu o razvitii ucheniya N.A.Rimskogo-Korsakova o srodstve tonal'nostey).* [On Modulation. (On the Question of the Development of Rimsky-Korsakov's Teaching on the Relationship of Tonalities).] Moscow-Leningrad: Muzgiz, 1948. 56 pp.

Using Rimsky-Korsakov's *Manual of Harmony* as a basis, the author discusses the composer's approach towards tonality, key relationships, and modulation. The book is divided into two chapters with six sub-sections.

1486 Myuller, Teodor, ed. and comp. *Voprosy teorii muzyki.* [Problems of Music Theory.] Vyp. 3 [Issue 3]. Moscow: Muzyka, 1975. 375 pp.

Among the references to Rimsky-Korsakov and his work, of particular note is the analytical discussion by V. Rukavishnikov of the composer's system of key relationship.

1487 Perret, Carine. "Le romantisme ravélien, un héritage choisi." *Musurgia: Analyse et pratique musicales* 13 (2) (2006): 17–32. ISSN: 1257-7537.

While Ravel's music belongs to the Romantic stylistic heritage, his work also reveals extraneous influences such as those of Edgar Allan Poe and Rimsky-Korsakov.

1488 Puzey, N. M. "Zametki o garmonii N. A. Rimskogo-Korsakova." [Notes on N. A. Rimsky-Korsakov's Harmony.] In *Nauchno-metodicheskie zapiski Ural'skoy Konservatorii.* [Scientific-Methodical Transactions of the Urals Conservatory.] Vyp. II [Issue II]. Sverdlovsk, 1959.

1489 Skrebkova, Ol'ga Leonidovna. "O nekotorykh priëmakh garmonicheskogo var'irovaniya v tvorchestve Rimskogo-Korsakova." [Of Some of the Means of Harmonic Variation in the Work of Rimsky-Korsakov.] In Yu. V. Keldysh, ed. *Voprosy muzykoznaniya. Sbornik statey.* [Questions of Musicology. A Collection of Articles.] Vol. III. Moscow: Muzgiz, 1960: 539–64.

This copiously illustrated article discusses some of the ways in which Rimsky-Korsakov develops his material by means of ingenious variation and chromatic coloring of the basic harmonies, which in some cases is carried to such lengths that it creates a feeling of polytonality. The music examples are selected from the operas and folk song arrangements. While continuing Glinka's principle of "changing background" technique, whereby the melody remains unchanged but the accompaniment and harmony are varied, Rimsky-Korsakov took the process still further, his contribution to Russian music in this respect being considerable.

1490 Street, Donald. "The Modes of Limited Transposition." *MT* 117 (October 1976): 819–23.

The seven modes of limited transposition delineated by Messiaen are not the only ones possible and they are not purely a twentieth-century phenomenon. Examples of their use can be found in the work of many nineteenth-century composers, including Rimsky-Korsakov. The scale of alternating semitones and tones (Messiaen's Mode 2) is found in the orchestral "Sadko," other instances being in the Symphonic Suite "Antar" and the operas *The Maid of Pskov, Christmas Eve, The Tale of Tsar Saltan, Kashchey the Immortal, Pan Voevoda, The Legend of the Invisible City of Kitezh,* and, in particular, *Mlada* and *Sadko.* A combination of two transpositions of Mode 2 may be seen also in *Mlada,* while an example of a six-note mode may be found in *The Golden Cockerel* (Act I, cues 91–92). The author also observes that Mode 1 (the whole-tone scale) occurs frequently in Rimsky-Korsakov's operas.

1491 Taruskin, Richard. "Chernomor to Kashchei: Harmonic Sorcery; or Stravinsky's 'Angle'." *JAMS* 38 (1) (1985): 72–142.

Taking the "octatonic scale" (i.e., a scale consisting of steps of alternating tones and semitones) as his starting point, Taruskin notes its employment in

Bibliography: General 285

the work of European composers such as Schubert and Liszt, and subsequently in that of the Russian composers Rimsky-Korsakov and his pupil, Stravinsky. Informative and well documented.

1492 ——. *"Chez Pétrouchka*: Harmony and Tonality *chez* Stravinsky." *19th-Century Music* 10 (3) (Spring 1987): 265–86. ISSN: 0148-2076. Reprinted: Kerman, Joseph, ed. *Music at the Turn of the Century: A 19th Century Music Reader.* Berkeley: University of California, 1990: 71–92. ISBN-10: 0520068556. ISBN-13: 978-0520068551.

A discussion of the second tableau of Stravinsky's *Petrushka* from the point of view of harmony and tonality and the employment of the octatonic scale, comparing it with works of Rimsky-Korsakov and Maksimilian Shteynberg.

1493 ——. "Catching up with Rimsky-Korsakov." *Music Theory Spectrum* 33 (2) University of California Press, Journals and Digital Publishing, 2011: 169–85. See Oxford Journals. Humanities: *Music Theory Spectrum*, 2014: Archives. ISSN: 0195-6167. *eISSN:* 1533-8339.

An article primarily concerned with the element of octatonicism and the part it plays in the music of both Stravinsky and Rimsky-Korsakov, Arthur Berger's article "Problems of Pitch Organization in Stravinsky" being used as a starting point.

1494 Trevitt, John. "The role of the diminished seventh and related phenomena in the development of harmonic dissension from Beethoven to Messiaen, with special reference to Claude Debussy." PhD dissertation, University of East Anglia, 1975.

Includes discussion of Rimsky-Korsakov's scale of alternating tones and semitones.

1495 Tsukkerman, Viktor Abramovich. "O vyrazitel'nosti garmonii Rimskogo-Korsakova." [On Rimsky-Korsakov's Harmonic Expressiveness.] In *SM* 10 (1956): 59–64; 11 (1956): 57–67.

An examination of Rimsky-Korsakov's harmonic techniques, illustrated with music examples from his works. The influence of Chopinesque harmonies on his composition is also stressed.

1496 Tyut'manov, Il'ya Fëdorovich. "Nekotorye osobennosti lado-garmonicheskogo stilya N. A. Rimskogo-Korsakova. (Vvodnaya glava kandidatskoy dissertatsii)." [Some Peculiarities of N. A. Rimsky-Korsakov's Modal-Harmonic Style. (Introductory Chapter of a *Kandidat* Thesis).] In *Nauchno-metodicheskie zapiski Saratovskoy Konservatorii.* [Scientific-Methodical Transactions of the Saratov Conservatory.] Saratov, 1957: 39–64.

1497 ——. "Gamma ton-polutona..." [The Tone-Semitone Scale...] In *Nauchno-metodicheskie zapiski Saratovskoy Konservatorii.* [Scientific-Methodical Transactions of the Saratov Conservatory.] Saratov, 1959.

An analysis of octatonic elements in the music of Rimsky-Korsakov.

1498 Blagodatov, Georgy Ivanovich. *Istoriya simfonicheskogo orkestra.* [History of the Symphony Orchestra.] Leningrad: Muzyka, 1969. 312 pp.

For observations on Rimsky-Korsakov's orchestration as seen in his symphonic and operatic music, see pp. 227–35. Harmony, polyphony, timbre, and good part-writing are seen as some of the important elements in producing a euphonious score.

1499 Dmitriev, A N. "Razvitie vzglyadov N. A. Rimskogo-Korsakova na kurs orkestrovki." [The Development of N. A. Rimsky-Korsakov's Opinions on the Orchestration Course.] In No. 1435: 94–106.

Observing that much of Rimsky-Korsakov's adult life was spent in teaching orchestration and compiling a textbook on it, the author traces the development of the composer's ideas on orchestration, which he eventually saw as having both a technological and a musical-esthetic significance. Dmitriev notes that Rimsky-Korsakov was the first Russian musician to undertake a large-scale investigation of the art of orchestration, and points out the merits of the latest (third edition) of the work under his editorship.

1500 Tsukkerman, Viktor Abramovich. "Tembr i faktura." [Timbre and Scoring.] *SM* 3 (1969): 45–52; 5 (1969): 97–103.

A short monograph of Rimsky-Korsakov's orchestration and mixing of tone colors, including the relationship between timbre and scoring, and the manner in which he obtains his distinctive sound effects.

1501 Vanovskaya, Irina Nikolaevna. "Teoriya i praktika muzykal'noy kompozitsii: Reformatorskie idei N. A. Rimskogo-Korsakova." [Theory and Practice of Music Composition: Reformist Ideas of N. A. Rimsky-Korsakov.] *Observatoriya kul'tury* [Observatory of Culture] I (4) (July–August 2012): 100. ISSN: 2072-3156.

A review of Rimsky-Korsakov's ideas on theory and the practice of music composition, which were influential in the development of conservatory education in Russia.

1502 Vitachek, Faby Evgenevich. *Ocherki po iskusstvu orkestrovki XIX veka.* [Essays on the Art of Orchestration in the 19th Century.] Moscow: Muzyka, 1978. 151 pp.

Includes discussion of Rimsky-Korsakov's orchestral style.

1503 Asaf'ev, Boris Vladimirovich [pseud. Glebov, Igor']. "Geniy russkoy muzyki." [A Genius of Russian Music.] In No. 1256: Vol. III, 225–28. Reprinted: *MZ* 5 (1969): 1.

A short article published originally in 1944, paying special attention to the "Russian-ness" of Rimsky-Korsakov's compositions and noting the

Bibliography: General 287

manner in which traditional national elements influence his musical style psychologically.

1504 ——. "O chuzhikh stranakh i lyudyakh." [Of Strange Lands and People.] *SM* 12 (1953): 39–46. Reprinted: No. 1256: Vol. IV, 122–43.

A general discussion of exotic elements in Russian music, including brief observations on *Antar, Scheherazade,* and *The Golden Cockerel.*

1505 Belyaev, Viktor Mikhaylovich. "O 'skhodstve' i 'tozhdestve' u Bakha i Rimskogo-Korsakova. Otvet B. Sabaneevu." [On the "Similarity" and "Identity" of Bach and Rimsky-Korsakov. An Answer to B. Sabaneev.] *Muzyka* 181 (1914) [see No. 1508].

1506 Lapshin, Ivan Ivanovich. *Rimsky-Korsakov. Dva ocherka.* [Rimsky-Korsakov. Two Essays.] Petrograd: Gos. filarmoniya, 1922.

Contains two articles:

i. "Filosofskie motivy v tvorchestve Rimskogo-Korsakova." [Philosophical Motives in Rimsky-Korsakov's Work.]: 5–46.
ii. "Muzykal'naya lirika Rimskogo-Korsakova." [Rimsky-Korsakov's Musical Lyricism]: 49–74.

1507 Rimsky-Korsakov, Vladimir Nikolaevich. "Priroda v tvorchestve Rimskogo-Korsakova." [Nature in the Work of Rimsky-Korsakov.] *MZ* 5 (1969): 1–2.

A commentary on some of the outstanding "nature pictures" in Rimsky-Korsakov's music, presented in an article written by his youngest son for a special number of the journal, commemorating Rimsky-Korsakov's 125th anniversary.

1508 Sabaneev, Boris Leonidovich. "O 'skhodstve' i 'tozhdestve' u Bakha i Rimskogo-Korsakova." [On the "Similarity" and "Identity" of Bach and Rimsky-Korsakov.] *Muzyka* 180 (1914) [see No. 1505].

1509 Tsendrovsky, Vladimir Mikhaylovich. "Sonatnaya forma v uvertyurakh k dramaticheskim operam Rimskogo-Korsakova." [Sonata Form in the Overtures to Rimsky-Korsakov's Dramatic Operas.] In V. Protopopov, ed. *Voprosy muzykal'noy formy.* [Problems of Musical Form.] Moscow: Muzyka, 1972.

An examination of theoretical elements in Rimsky-Korsakov's works.

1510 Tsukkerman, Viktor Abramovich. *Muzykal'no-teoreticheskie ocherki i etyudy. O muzykal'noy rechi N. A. Rimskogo-Korsakova.* [Musical-Theoretical Essays and Studies. On the Musical Language of N. A. Rimsky-Korsakov.] Vol. 2. Moscow: Sovetsky Kompozitor, 1975. 464 pp.

Volume 2 of this collection of essays is divided into five sections:

i. Rimsky-Korsakov's esthetic positions in questions of musical language.
ii. The complex of the dissonant diatonic.

iii. Several questions of harmony.
iv. Some principles regarding the structure of form.
v. Timbre and scoring in Rimsky-Korsakov's orchestration.

Illustrated with 225 music examples, Tsukkerman stresses Rimsky-Korsakov's contribution to Russian music and the novel elements of his style, though points out that the pursuit of logic in his composition did not always have satisfactory results. An important study.

1511 ——. "O nekotorykh chertakh stilya Rimskogo-Korsakova: Ocherk pervy." [Some Stylistic Features of Rimsky-Korsakov: Essay I.] *SM* 6 (1958): 15–23.

A discussion of Rimsky-Korsakov's attitude towards Russian folk song and an examination of some of the ways in which he treats it in his compositions.

1512 Van den Toorn, Pieter C. "To the Editor." *Music Theory Spectrum: The Journal of the Society for Music Theory* 34 (1) (Spring 2012): 151. See Oxford Journals. Humanities: *Music Theory Spectrum*, 2014: Archives. ISSN: 0195-6167.

A discussion of the response from Richard Taruskin to respondents of his essay "Catching up with Rimsky-Korsakov."

PORTRAITS

1513 Binevich, Evgeny. "Rimsky-Korsakov v risunkakh sovremennikov." [Rimsky-Korsakov in Drawings by Contemporaries.] *SM* 6 (1978): 97–100.

Consists of seven sketches of the composer (mostly good-natured) by contemporary caricaturists in such journals as *Teatr i iskusstvo*, *Peterburgskaya zhizn'*, *Strekoza*, and others, most of which are concerned with the events of 1905. A full-size portrait of Rimsky-Korsakov was painted by Repin in 1893. A portrait and a drawing by V. A. Serov in 1898 and 1908, respectively, are preserved in the Tret'yakov Gallery. A photograph of a painting by E. Vizol' (1908) in the Leningrad Russky Muzey [Russian Museum] is reproduced in *SM* 3 (1969): 49. A bust of the composer, numerous photographs, and a portrait are contained in the Dom-muzey [House-Museum] in Tikhvin. For a picture of the monument on his tomb, see *Muzyka* 80 (1912): 508. For an engraving of the composer by Strasser, see *The Etude* 51 (October 1933): 661. A sculpture was made by Antokol'sky.

RESOURCE MATERIALS

1514 Abraham, Gerald. "Rimsky-Korsakov, Nikolay Andreyevich." In Stanley Sadie, ed. *The New Grove Dictionary of Music and Musicians*, Vol. 16. London: Macmillan, 1980: 27–41. ISBN-10: 0333231112. ISBN-13: 978-0333231111.

Bibliography: General   289

A major article on the composer and his work, with list of compositions and selected bibliography.

1515 ——. "Nikolay Rimsky-Korsakov." In Stanley Sadie, ed. *The New Grove. Russian Masters*, Vol. 2: Rimsky-Korsakov, Skryabin, Rakhmaninov, Prokofiev, Shostakovich. London: Macmillan, 1986: 1–47. ISBN-10: 0333402383. ISBN-13: 978-0333402382.

Primarily a reprint of the article in *The New Grove Dictionary* with some additional bibliographical material.

1516 Anonymous. *Russkaya Muzykal'naya Gazeta. Ukazatel' statey za 10 let (1894-1903 gg.).* [*Russian Musical Gazette.* Index of Articles for 10 years (1894-1903).] Published as a supplement to *RMG* 52 (1903): cols. 1–72.

For details of the second decade, see No. 1263.

1517 Anonymous. *Sistematichesky ukazatel' soderzhaniya "Russkoy Muzykal'noy Gazety" za vtoroe desyatiletie (1904-1913).* [Systematic Index of the Contents of the *Russian Musical Gazette* for the Second Decade (1904-1913).] S. G. Kondr, ed. St. Petersburg: Russkaya Muzykal'naya Gazeta, 1914 [?].

1518 Bernandt, Grigory Borisovich. *Slovar' oper vpervye postavlennykh ili izdannykh v dorevolyutsionnoy Rossii i v SSSR, 1736-1959.* [Dictionary of Operas First Performed or Published in Pre-Revolutionary Russia and the USSR, 1736-1959.] Moscow: Sovetsky Kompozitor, 1962. 554 pp.

This volume gives details of each of Rimsky-Korsakov's operas as to number of acts, librettist, dates of composition, cast, première, and names of company, conductor, designers, and cast, together with materials on other notable performances in Russia and abroad.

1519 Bernandt, G. B. and Yampol'sky, I. M. *Kto pisal o muzyke. Bio-bibliografichesky slovar' muzykal'nykh kritikov i lits, pisavshikh o muzyke v dorevolyutsionnoy Rossii i SSSR.* [Who Wrote about Music. Bio-Bibliographical Dictionary of Musical Criticisms and Persons, Writing on Music in Pre-Revolutionary Russia and the USSR.] Vols. I–III. Moscow: Sovetsky Kompozitor, 1971–89.

For a list of some of Rimsky-Korsakov's writings and those of his family, see Vol. III, 20–23.

1520 Bystrova, M. *N. A. Rimsky-Korsakov. 1844-1908. Ukazatel' literatury.* [N. A. Rimsky-Korsakov. 1844-1908. Index of Literature.] Leningrad, 1968. 12 pp.

A useful bibliographical resource.

1521 Card Catalogue of the Music Library of the St. Petersburg State Conservatory (Rimsky-Korsakov). Monuments in Microfilm Publishing. New York: Norman Ross, 2002: Microfiche, in Russian.

The catalog of the music library of the Gosudarstvennaya Konservatoriya imeni N. A. Rimskogo-Korsakova in St. Petersburg is arranged into three sections: books on music, musical scores, and manuscripts.

1522 Dan'ko, L. G. and Skvirskaya, T. Z., eds. and comps. *Peterburgsky muzykal'ny arkhiv. Sbornik statey i materialov. Vypusk 1.* [St. Petersburg Musical Archive. Collection of Articles and Materials. Issue 1.] St. Petersburg: Kanon, 1997. 168 pp. ISBN-10: 5874990224. ISBN-13: 978-5874990220.

A description of the musical manuscripts held in the Scientific Library of the Manuscript Department of the St. Petersburg Conservatory, providing details of the 48 autographs of works by Rimsky-Korsakov, including full scores of the operas *May Night* and *Pan Voevoda*, together with excerpts from the operas *The Maid of Pskov, Christmas Eve, The Tsar's Bride, The Legend of the Invisible City of Kitezh, Sadko, The Golden Cockerel,* and other works.

1523 Findeyzen, Nikolay Fëdorovich. *Ocherk deyatel'nosti S.-Peterburgskago otdeleniya Imperatorskago Russkago Muzykal'nago Obshchestva (1859-1909).* [Outline of the Work of the St. Petersburg Branch of the Imperial Russian Music Society (1859-1909).] St. Petersburg: Tipografiya Glavnago Upravleniya Udelov, 1909. 231 pp.

This reference work enables one to see the frequency with which Rimsky-Korsakov's orchestral, vocal, and chamber works were performed at concerts of the St. Petersburg Branch of the Imperial Russian Music Society during the 50-year period 1859–1909. For his symphonic and choral music, see p. 65; his songs and chamber music, see p. 112.

1524 Gaub, Albrecht. "Internationales Kolloquium der handschriftliche Nachlass von Nikolaj Andreevič Rimskij-Korsakov." *Die Musikforschung* 57 (3) (July–September 2004): 276. ISSN: 0027-4801.

A discussion of Rimsky-Korsakov's manuscript legacy held at an international conference in St. Petersburg on 17–18 March 2004.

1525 Glushchenko, Georgy Semënovich. *N. D. Kashkin.* Moscow: Muzyka, 1974. 326 pp.

This survey of the critic Kashkin's life and work contains a number of references to Rimsky-Korsakov. It gives a list of principal reviews but has no index.

1526 Grimsted, Patricia Kennedy. *Archives and Manuscript Repositories in the USSR: Moscow and Leningrad (Columbia University. Studies of the Russian Institute).* New Jersey: Princeton University Press, 1972. 468 pp. ISBN-10: 0691051496. ISBN-13: 978-0691051499.

Includes a description of the Glinka State Central Museum of Musical Culture [now MMKG], containing the Rimsky-Korsakov Archive, the personal archive of the composer in the *Gosudarstvennaya publichnaya*

Bibliography: General 291

biblioteka imeni Saltykova-Shchedrina, Leningrad [now RNB], the separate Rimsky-Korsakov Museum and Archive in the *Gosudarstvenny nauchno-issledovatel'sky institut teatra, muzyki i kinematografii, Leningrad* [now SPBGATI], the manuscript holdings of the Library of the *Leningradskaya gosudarstvennaya Konservatoriya imeni N. A. Rimskogo-Korsakova* [now SPGK], and mention of the Gosudarstvenny memorial'ny dom-myzey [State Memorial House Museum] of N. A. Rimsky-Korsakov in Tikhvin.

Following the breakup of the Soviet Union, Patricia Grimsted has since published a further work entitled *Archives of Russia: a Directory and Bibliographic Guide to Holdings in Moscow and St. Petersburg. 2 Vols.* Ed. Patricia Kennedy Grimsted. Comp. by Patricia Kennedy Grimsted, Lada Vladimirovna Repulo, and Irina Vladimirovna Tunkina, with an intro. by Vladimir Petrovich Kozlov. English Edition Armonk, NY: M. E. Sharpe, 2000.

1527   Kiselëv, Vasily Aleksandrovich, ed. *N. A. Rimsky-Korsakov. Sbornik dokumentov.* [N. A. Rimsky-Korsakov. Collection of Documents.] Moscow-Leningrad: Muzgiz, 1951. 290 pp.

This reference work falls into three main sections:

i.   Survey of Rimsky-Korsakov's music manuscripts: 9–40.
ii.   Rimsky-Korsakov's letters: 41–202.
iii. Miscellaneous documents: 203–271.

The second section contains letters to 20 people, including Cui, Mamontov, the Yurgensons, Cheshikhin, and others. The last section provides information on the composer's work as an adjudicator at the Russian Music Society's competitions, of his work as a government inspector, the St. Petersburg Conservatory, the Imperial Theaters, censorship, contracts, and domestic matters. There is an index of names, works mentioned in the text, and list of illustrations.

1528   Koltypina, G. B. *Bibliografiya muzykal'noy bibliografii. Annotirovanny perechen' ukazateley literatury, izdannoy na russkom yazyke.* [Bibliography of Music Bibliography. An Annotated List of Indexes of Literature, Published in the Russian Language.] Moscow: Gos. Ord. Lenina Biblioteka SSSR imeni V. I. Lenina, 1963.

For bibliographical materials regarding Rimsky-Korsakov, see pp. 164–68 (Nos. 939–67).

1529   Kremlëv, Yuly Anatol'evich. *Leningradskaya Gosudarstvennaya Konservatoriya. 1862-1937.* [The Leningrad State Conservatory. 1862-1937.] Moscow: Muzgiz, 1938. 179 pp.

For a list of articles relating to Rimsky-Korsakov's dismissal from the Conservatory in 1905, see pp. 173–74.

292   *Nikolay Andreevich Rimsky-Korsakov: A Research and Information Guide*

1530   Livanova, Tamara Nikolaevna, ed. *Muzykal'naya bibliografiya russkoy periodicheskoy pechati XIX veka.* [Musical Bibliography of the Russian Periodical Press of the 19th Century.] VI (1): 1871–1880. Moscow: Sovetsky kompozitor, 1974; VI (2), 1976; VI (3), 1979; VI (4), 1979.

The first volume of this immense undertaking by Tamara Livanova, which covers the period 1801–25, was published in 1960. Since the publication of the first issue a further ten volumes have appeared, of which entries pertaining to Rimsky-Korsakov are found in the volumes relating to the 1870s [see, in particular, Issue 6, Part 1, pp. 284–87]. Whether further volumes covering the remainder of the nineteenth century will yet appear is not known.

1531   Moldon, David. *A Bibliography of Russian Composers.* London, Sydney and Toronto: White Lion Publishers, 1976. xviii, 364 pp. ISBN: 0728401010. ISBN-13: 978-0728401013.

For Rimsky-Korsakov and his works, see Nos. 1320–1419, pp. 149–60, of this guide on writings on Russian music in the English language.

1532   Muir, Stephen. "Bibliografiya angliyskikh i amerikanskikh issledovaniy o N. A. Rimskom-Korsakove." [Bibliography of English and American Studies on N. A. Rimsky-Korsakov.] In N. V. Gradoboeva and F. E. Purtov, eds. *Voprosy muzykal'nogo istochnikovedeniya i bibliografii: Sbornik nauchnykh statey.* [Problems of Music Source Study: Collection of Scientific Articles.] St. Petersburg: Academic Library of the St. Petersburg Conservatory, 2001. pp. 102–10.

A survey of scholarly publications on Rimsky-Korsakov in English in the 1990s.

1533   Nekrasova, Elena Vladimirovna. "The History, Collections and Activities of the Music Research Library of the St. Petersburg Rimsky-Korsakov State Conservatoire." *Fontes Artis Musicae* 53 (3): *Russian Music Libraries* (July–September 2006): 130–36. ISSN: 0015-6191.

An account of the history of the St. Petersburg Conservatory and its library founded in 1862. The foundation of the library was the music collection of the St. Petersburg branch of the Imperial Russian Music Society. The library contains a number of materials relating to Russian composers, including scores, autographs, photographs, unpublished correspondence, and memoir literature.

1534   Orlov, Georgy Pavlovich. *Muzykal'naya literatura. Bibliografichesky ukazatel' knizhnoy i zhurnal'noy literatury o muzyke na russkom yazyke.* [Musical Literature. A Bibliographical Index of Literature on Music in Books and Journals in the Russian Language.] Leningrad: izd. Filarmonii, 1935. 293 pp.

A valuable research guide.

1535   Orlova, A. A. and Rimsky-Korsakov, V. N., eds. *Stranitsy zhizni N. A. Rimskogo-Korsakova. Letopis' zhizni i tvorchestva.* [Pages from N. A.

Bibliography: General 293

Rimsky-Korsakov's Life. Chronicle of Life and Work.] 4 Vols. Leningrad: Muzyka, 1969–73.

This meticulously documented 4-volume chronology gives an extraordinarily detailed account of the composer from a few months before his birth until his death, the first entry being 25 October 1843. Annotations are included in each entry and the whole tetralogy is illustrated with photographs, other factual materials, and substantial extracts from his correspondence. An essential research tool for any study of the composer.

1536   Orlova, Aleksandra Anatol'evna. "Khronika ego zhizni." [A Chronicle of His Life.] *SM* 3 (1969): 72–76.

A discussion of the work *Stranitsy zhizni N. A. Rimskogo-Korsakova. Letopis' zhizni i tvorchestva.* [Pages from N. A. Rimsky-Korsakov's Life. Chronicle of Life and Work.] conducted between A. A. Orlova and V. N. Rimsky-Korsakov following the publication of the first of the proposed four volumes. Orlova explains the aims of the tetralogy, its contents, and the reasons for producing it. Discusses some of the influences on the future composer, especially that of his elder brother, Voin Andreevich, as well as describing the general family ambience and Rimsky-Korsakov's intellectual development.

1537   Popova, Tat'yana Vasil'evna. *Nikolay Andreevich Rimsky-Korsakov. Kratky rekomendatel'ny ukazatel'.* [Nikolay Andreevich Rimsky-Korsakov. A Short Recommended Index.] Moscow: Gos. Biblioteka SSSR. imeni V. I. Lenina, 1955. 70 pp.

A listing of Rimsky-Korsakov's most important musical works, his music (with quotations from other Russian musicians), dates of his life and work, 41 titles of books and articles written in the period 1933–54, with comments, advice for a librarian, and list of records recommended for illustrating a talk on the composer.

1538   Rakhmanova, Marina Pavlovna. "Nemetskie knigi o russkoy muzyke." [German Books on Russian Music.] *MA* (2) (2000): 135–39. ISSN: 0869-4516.

A discussion of scholarly studies and documents on the works of Russian composers, including some materials on Rimsky-Korsakov.

1539   Savelova, Z. and Livanova, T. "Ukazatel' literatury o N. A. Rimskom-Korsakove (na russkom yazyke)." [Index of Literature on N. A. Rimsky-Korsakov (in the Russian Language).] *SM* 3 (1933): 188–94.

A bibliography of over 260 materials relating to the composer, including many articles written in pre-revolutionary periodicals. Over a fifth are taken from the *Russkaya Muzykal'naya Gazeta* [Russian Musical Gazette]. The entries are divided into specific genres: the composer's works, correspondence, memoir literature, biographical material, and compositions.

294   *Nikolay Andreevich Rimsky-Korsakov: A Research and Information Guide*

1540   Skvirskaya, Tamara Zakirovna. "N. A. Rimsky-Korsakov v zerkale svoikh rukopisey." [N. A. Rimsky-Korsakov in the Mirror of His Own Manuscripts.] *Musicus* 4 (13) (October–December 2008): 25. ISSN: 2072-0262.

   Musicus, the journal of the St. Petersburg Conservatory, contains a wealth of articles on music, including, as in this instance, a discussion of manuscripts of Rimsky-Korsakov preserved in archives in St. Petersburg, Moscow, and other cities.

1541   ——. "Avtografy N. A. Rimskogo-Korsakova v otdele rukopisey biblioteki Peterburgskoy konservatorii." [N. A. Rimsky-Korsakov's Autographs in the Manuscript Department of the St. Petersburg Conservatory.] In V. M. Vasil'eva, comp. *N. A. Rimsky-Korsakov i russkaya khudozhestvennaya kul'tura. Materialy nauchnoy konferentsii. Vechasha-Lyubensk.* [N. A. Rimsky-Korsakov and Russian Artistic Culture. Materials from a Scientific Conference. Vechasha-Lyubensk.] Pskov, 2008.

   A description of over 300 manuscripts of Rimsky-Korsakov preserved in the library collection of the St. Petersburg Conservatory.

1542   Thompson, Pamela. "Russian Music Libraries." *Fontes artis musicae* 53 (3) (July–September 2006). ISSN: 0015-6191.

   An invaluable publication containing a wealth of information on Russian music libraries, with many materials relevant to Rimsky-Korsakov.

1543   Vil'sker, S. M., comp. "Bibliografiya N. A. Rimskogo-Korsakova. 1917-1957." [Bibliography of N. A. Rimsky-Korsakov. 1917-1957.] In No. 1435: 273–319.

   A bibliography of 800 entries relating to Rimsky-Korsakov, covering half a century from 1917 to 1957. Divided into two sections, the first part deals with the composer's literary works and correspondence (see Entries 1–35), while the second part consists of books and articles referring to him. Containing a number of bibliographical rarities and many of the most important works written about the composer and his creative achievement, this bibliography is a foundation stone for any research on the composer. The bibliography is concerned only with Soviet publications in the Russian language.

1544   Yastrebtsëv, Vasily Vasil'evich. "Spisok proizvedeniy N. A. Rimskogo-Korsakova." [List of N. A. Rimsky-Korsakov's Works.] *RMG* 51 (1900): cols. 1270–76.

   A list of compositions set out in order of opus number, works without opus number, and operas.

1545   Startsev, Ivan Ivanovich. *Sovetskaya literatura o muzyke 1918-1947. Bibliografichesky ukazatel' knig.* [Soviet Literature about Music 1918-1947. Bibliographical Index of Books.] Moscow: Sovetsky Kompozitor, 1963. 294 pp.

   A useful research guide including materials on Rimsky-Korsakov.

Bibliography: General

1546 Uspenskaya, S. L. *Literatura o muzyke 1948-1953. Bibliografichesky ukazatel'*. [Literature about Music 1948-1953. Bibliographical Index.] Moscow: Izd. Vsesoyuznoy Knizhnoy Palaty, 1955. 344 pp.

1547 ——. *Literatura o muzyke 1954-1956. Bibliografichesky ukazatel'*. [Literature about Music 1954-1956. Bibliographical Index.] Moscow: Izd. Vsesoyuznoy Knizhnoy Palaty, 1958.

1548 Uspenskaya, S. and Yagolim, B. S., eds. *Sovetskaya literatura o muzyke. Bibliografichesky ukazatel' za 1957 god*. [Soviet Literature about Music. Bibliographical Index for 1957.] Moscow: Sovetsky Kompozitor, 1959. 182 pp.

1549 Uspenskaya, S. and Koltypina, G. B., eds. *Sovetskaya literatura o muzyke 1958-1959. Bibliografichesky ukazatel'*. [Soviet Literature about Music 1958-1959. Bibliographical Index.] Moscow: Sovetsky Kompozitor, 1963. 182 pp.

1550 Uspenskaya, S., et al., eds. *Sovetskaya literatura o muzyke 1960-1962*. [Soviet Literature on Music 1960-1962.] Moscow: Sovetsky Kompozitor, 1967. 512 pp.

Sof'ya L'vovna Uspenskaya was an assiduous and indefatigable bibliographer. As can be seen from the following Nos. 1552, 1553, and 1554, her cooperation with the bibliographers Boris Savel'evich Yagolim, A. Kolbanovskaya, and Galina Borisovna Koltypina led to the production of a series of extremely valuable collections of bibliographical materials, which, together with those of Tamara Livanova [see Nos. 340 and 1530], provide a foundation for any research into Russian music, especially Rimsky-Korsakov.

1551 Kolbanovskaya, A. and Yagolim, B. S., eds. *Sovetskaya literatura o muzyke. Bibliografichesky ukazatel' knig, zhurnal'nykh statey i retsenziy za 1963-1965 gg*. [Soviet Literature on Music. Bibliographical Index of Books, Magazine Articles and Reviews for 1963-1965.] Moscow: Sovetsky Kompozitor, 1971. 526 pp.

1552 Yagolim, B. S. and Koltypina, G. B., eds. *Sovetskaya literatura o muzyke. Bibliografichesky ukazatel' knig, zhurnal'nykh statey i retsenziy 1966-1967 gg*. (Soviet Literature on Music. Bibliographical Index of Books, Magazine Articles and Reviews for 1966-1967.] Moscow: Sovetsky Kompozitor,1974. 491 pp.

1553 Koltypina, G. B. and Pavlova, N. G., eds. *Sovetskaya literatura o muzyke. Bibliografichesky ukazatel' knig, zhurnal'nykh statey i retsenziy za 1968-1970 gg*. [Soviet Literature on Music. Bibliographical Index of Books, Magazines, Articles and Reviews for 1968-1970.] Part I. Moscow: Sovetsky Kompozitor, 1979. 335 pp.

REVOLUTION OF 1905

1554 Anonymous. "Zametki. Konservatorsky konflikt." [Notes. The Conflict at the Conservatory.] *RMG* 15 (1905): 433–40.

On Rimsky-Korsakov's dismissal.

1555   Dreyden, Simon. *Muzyka-Revolyutsii*. [Music of the Revolution.] Second edition. Moscow: Sovetsky Kompozitor, 1970. 607 pp.

Includes discussion of Rimsky-Korsakov's involvement in the 1905 Revolution and the part played by his music in the years preceding and following 1917.

1556   Drozdov, Anatoly Nikolaevich. "1905 god v Leningradskoy Konservatorii. Vospominaniya uchastnika sobytiy." [The Year 1905 in the Leningrad Conservatory. Recollections of a Participant in the Events.] *Muzyka i Revolyutsiya* 1 (1926): 6–14; 2 (1926): 10–17.

This highly-charged article on the manner in which Rimsky-Korsakov and the St. Petersburg Conservatory became involved in the 1905 Revolution falls into seven sections of which the fourth, "Spektakl'-manifestatsiya 'Koshchey Bessmertny' i uvol'nenie N. A. Rimskogo-Korsakova" [The Performance-Demonstration *Kashchey the Immortal* and N. A. Rimsky-Korsakov's Dismissal] is a first-hand account of the première of the opera and the way in which it was politically interpreted.

1557   ——. "Vam burya vorota otkryla." [A Storm Opened the Gates for You.] *Sovetskoe iskusstvo* (20 June 1938): 31.

Recollections of Rimsky-Korsakov and the student movement of 1905.

1558   E. P. "Razvyazka konservatorskoy komedii." [The Outcome of the Conservatory Comedy.] *RMG* 50 (1905): cols. 1214–17.

The final chapter in the saga of Rimsky-Korsakov's dismissal, with his reinstatement in the Conservatory and the institution's autonomy.

1559   Engel', Yuly Dmitrievich. "N. A. Rimsky-Korsakov i Peterburgskaya Konservatoriya." [N. A. Rimsky-Korsakov and the St. Petersburg Conservatory.] Reprinted: No. 313: 145–47.

First published in *Russkie Vedomosti* 80 (24 March 1905), this gives the immediate reaction to the news of Rimsky-Korsakov's dismissal from the St. Petersburg Conservatory. For other accounts (not reprinted in *Glazami sovremennika*) see *Russkie Vedomosti* Nos. 85, 88, 89, 91, 93, 95.

1560   Findeyzen, Nikolay Fëdorovich. "Uvolnenie Rimskogo-Korsakova iz Spb. Konservatorii." [Rimsky-Korsakov's Dismissal from the St. Petersburg Conservatory.] *RMG* 14 (1905): cols. 401–13.

A factual article describing Rimsky-Korsakov's dismissal, demonstrations, his open letters, expressions of support, the Conservatory's explanations of its actions, and the ensuing events, with extensive quotation from relevant materials.

1561   Glazunov, Aleksandr Konstantinovich. "A. Glazunov v dni revolyutsii 1905-1907 gg. (Iz neopublikovannykh pisem kompozitora)." [A. Glazunov

Bibliography: General   297

During the Days of the Revolution 1905-1907. (From the Composer's Unpublished Letters).] *SM* 4 (1955): 21–30.

1562   Kolomiytsov, Viktor Pavlovich. *Stat'i i pis'ma.* [Articles and Letters.] E. V. Tomashevskaya, ed. Leningrad: Muzyka, 1971. 224 pp.

Viktor Kolomiytsov (1868–1936) was a prolific writer on music and translator of 40 opera libretti (including nine by Wagner) and more than 2,000 song texts. The main reference to Rimsky-Korsakov and his work is an article entitled: "A Resumé of the Rimsky-Korsakov Affair," pp. 14–16. Originally published in the paper *Rus'* on 15 [28] April 1905, this examines the composer's dismissal from the Conservatory from a moral and legal point of view. Also contains a letter from the composer to Kolomiytsov, p. 163.

1563   Kompaneysky, Nikolay Ivanovich. "Otkrytoe pis'mo N. A. Rimskomu-Korsakovu." [Open Letter to N. A. Rimsky-Korsakov.] *RMG* 14 (1905): cols. 413–14.

A letter supporting Rimsky-Korsakov after his dismissal, stressing the power of his secular and sacred music.

1564   Markov, Nikolay Ivanovich. "N. A. Rimsky-Korsakov i revolyutsiya 1905 g." [N. A. Rimsky-Korsakov and the Revolution of 1905.] *Literaturny Sovremennik* 7 (1933): 143–53.

1565   Open Letter. "K uvol'neniyu N. A. Rimskogo-Korsakova." [On N. A. Rimsky-Korsakov's Dismissal.] *Russkie Vedomosti* 87 (31 March 1905).

Following the publication in No. 85 of the *Russkie Vedomosti* of an Open Letter to the Administrative Board of the Imperial Russian Music Society, No. 87 contains another letter from Moscow musicians expressing indignation at the composer's peremptory dismissal.

1566   Sargeant, Lynn M. *Harmony and Discord: Music and the Transformation of Russian Cultural Life.* Oxford: Oxford University Press, 2011. 368 pp. ISBN-10: 0199735263. ISBN-13: 978-0199735266.

A well-researched study of Russian cultural life in the nineteenth century and the part played by the Russian Music Society, including discussion of Rimsky-Korsakov's political views and his role in the 1905 Revolution which resulted in his dismissal and subsequent reinstatement.

1567   Telyakovsky, Vladimir Arkad'evich. *Imperatorskie teatry i 1905 god.* [The Imperial Theaters and the Year 1905.] E. M. Kuznetsov, ed. Leningrad: Academia, 1926. 178 pp.

For references to Rimsky-Korsakov and his operas, see pp. 13, 68, and 146.

1568   Yankovsky, Moisey Osipovich. *Rimsky-Korsakov i Revolyutsiya 1905 goda.* [Rimsky-Korsakov and the 1905 Revolution.] Moscow-Leningrad: Muzgiz, 1950. 131 pp. Review: *SM* 8 (1951): 105–07.

An examination of Rimsky-Korsakov's attitude towards the revolutionary currents of the period and the manner in which his own political beliefs are seen in his last compositions, particularly the opera *The Golden Cockerel*. With special reference to his dismissal from the Conservatory and the consequent events.

RIMSKY-KORSAKOV AND THE SOVIET REPUBLICS

1569 Zhiganov, Nazib Gayazovich. "I segodnya on novator." [And Today He is an Innovator.] *SM* 3 (1969): 86–87.

A general article on Rimsky-Korsakov's music and its significance for the Soviet Union, including the manner in which his operas have served as a catalyst for composition in the Soviet Republics.

Index of Rimsky-Korsakov's Musical Works

Operas

B

Barber of Baghdad, The, 7, 745, 1004, 1006.
Boyarynya Vera Sheloga. A Musical-dramatic
  prologue to L. Mey's drama "The Maid
  of Pskov," Op. 54, 10, 32, 331, 361, 386,
  557–60, 1223.

E

Earth and Sky, 18, 271, 746, 1004, 1006, 1019.

G

Golden Cockerel, The. A Dramatised Fairy Tale.
  Opera in 3 acts, 19, 51, 271, 282–83,
  287, 296, 302, 307, 310, 312–13,
  323–24, 330, 333, 337–38, 354, 357–59,
  361–62, 369, 400, 475, 697–744,
  748–49, 758, 768, 773, 1004, 1006,
  1019, 1024, 1058, 1062, 1064, 1115,
  1161, 1180, 1212, 1253, 1268, 1301,
  1381, 1490, 1504, 1522, 1568.

K

Kashchey the Immortal. An Autumn Fairy Tale.
  Opera in 1 act, 14, 240, 249, 285–86,
  296, 307, 310, 313, 330, 333, 337, 357,
  364, 377, 473, 622–39, 748, 751, 768,
  770, 790, 967, 1004, 1019, 1082, 1086,
  1223, 1328, 1381, 1414, 1490, 1556.

L

Legend of the Invisible City of Kitezh and the
  Maiden Fevroniya. Opera in 4 acts, 16,
  53, 249, 251, 271, 290, 295, 305, 307,
  309, 322–23, 330, 333, 348, 357, 359,
372, 377, 633, 648–96, 748–49, 759–61,
763, 782, 1004, 1006, 1019, 1390, 1410,
1413, 1418, 1472, 1490, 1522.

M

Maid of Pskov, The, Op. 4, 1, 10, 32, 134, 218,
  283, 295–96, 299–300, 310, 322, 325,
  333, 339, 347, 357–58, 369, 378–410,
  421, 581, 748, 751, 762, 774, 779,
  781–82, 891, 989, 1019, 1153, 1248,
  1269, 1283, 1294, 1323, 1378, 1384,
  1399, 1490, 1522.
May Night. An opera in three acts after the story
  by Gogol, 3, 282–83, 286, 290, 296,
  309, 312, 325, 333, 336, 338, 344, 349,
  355, 357, 361–62, 364, 366, 415–30,
  458, 568, 782, 785, 787–88, 796, 967,
  1110, 1139, 1147, 1283, 1296, 1323,
  1522.
Mlada. Ballet-opera in 4 acts (collective work),
  2, 284, 411–13.
Mlada. A magical opera-ballet in 4 acts, 5, 41,
  284, 290, 296, 324–25, 332–33, 357,
  414, 471–81, 1004, 1283, 1323, 1467,
  1490.
Mozart and Salieri. Dramatic scenes from A. S.
  Pushkin, Op. 48, 9, 108, 290, 310, 331,
  333, 357, 364, 509, 535–56, 781–82,
  1058, 1062, 1064, 1180, 1223, 1227.

N

Night Before Christmas, The. A Christmas tale
  after the story by N. V. Gogol. Opera in
  4 acts, 6, 283, 286, 290, 296, 310, 324,
  333, 344, 349–50, 358, 415, 482–94,
  748, 762–63, 788, 1007, 1019, 1110,
  1147, 1180, 1230, 1323, 1378, 1467,
  1490, 1522.

299

300 *Indexes*

P

Pan Voevoda. Opera in 4 acts, 15, 46, 56, 207, 286, 294, 304, 307, 333, 342, 355, 359, 640–47, 748, 1004, 1232, 1419, 1490, 1522.

S

Sadko. Opera-bylina in seven scenes, 8, 28, 64, 222, 277, 283, 286, 295–96, 300, 309, 312, 324, 332–33, 336, 339, 349, 354, 357, 359, 364–65, 495–534, 664, 748–49, 762–63, 768, 770, 772, 779, 782, 795, 967, 983, 989, 1004, 1007, 1019, 1076, 1079, 1086, 1147, 1161, 1180, 1225–26, 1230, 1241, 1248, 1250, 1257, 1294, 1323, 1381, 1467, 1484, 1490, 1522.
Servilia. Opera in 5 acts, 13, 282, 290, 307, 333, 358, 614–21, 641, 762–63, 1004.
Snow Maiden, The (Spring Fairy Tale). Subject borrowed from Ostrovsky's eponymous play. Opera in 4 acts with a prologue, 4, 29, 208, 211, 241, 252, 282–83, 285, 290, 294, 296, 300, 309, 324–26, 333, 336–37, 339, 349, 357, 360, 364, 369, 375, 431–70, 748, 759, 762, 767, 785–88, 795, 967, 983, 985, 1006, 1019, 1088, 1108, 1147, 1161, 1230, 1257, 1283, 1323, 1338, 1361.

T

Tale of Tsar Saltan, The. Opera in 4 acts with a prologue, 12, 43, 240, 252, 271, 286, 296, 309, 315, 324, 326, 333, 336, 354–55, 357, 364, 591–613, 725, 748–49, 759, 768, 795–96, 1004, 1006, 1019, 1058, 1062, 1064, 1079, 1086, 1147, 1161, 1180, 1223, 1241, 1248, 1490.
Tsar's Bride, The. Opera in 4 acts. Content borrowed from the drama by L. Mey, 11, 252, 283, 286, 309, 331, 333, 338, 344, 349, 356–57, 359, 361–62, 364, 366, 369, 496, 561–90, 641, 748, 766, 768, 770, 795–96, 1004, 1139, 1147, 1161, 1223, 1418, 1419, 1522.

Other Operatic Projects

D

Dobrynya Nitkitich, 20.

I

Il'ya Muromets, 22.

N

Nausicaä, 21, 271, 1004, 1006, 1019.

S

Saul and David, 24, 984, 1006.
Sten'ka Razin, 17, 271, 754, 1004, 1006, 1019, 1115.

T

Tale of the Fisherman and the Fish, The, sketch for unfinished opera, 1004, 1019, 1115.
Tempest, The, 23, 1006.

Works for Orchestra

A

"Antar." Symphonic Suite, Op. 9, 30, 826–33.

C

Capriccio espagnol, Op. 34, 36, 808, 839–42, 1031, 1147, 1310, 1379.
Concert Fantasia on Russian Themes, Op. 33, 55, 864.
Concerto for piano and orch., Op. 30, 54, 856–63.

D

Dubinushka. Russian Song, Op. 62, 48, 218.

F

Fantasia on Serbian Themes, Op. 6, 27, 82, 810, 815–19.

Indexes 301

G

Golden Cockerel, The. Intro. and Wedding Procession, Suite, 51, 855.

J

Joyous Festival. Easter Overture on Themes, Op. 36, 39, 810, 853–84.

L

Legend of the Invisible City of Kitezh. Suite from the Opera, 53.
Little-Russian Fantasia, 37, 843.

M

Mazurka on Polish Folk Themes for violin and orchestra, 56.
Mlada. Suite from the Opera, 44.
Musical Pictures from The Tale of Tsar Saltan. Suite for Orchestra, Op. 57, 43.
Neapolitan Song, Op. 63, 50.

N

Night Before Christmas, The. Suite from the Opera, 45.
Night on Mount Triglav (Third Act of Opera-ballet Mlada), 41, 808.

O

On the Tomb. Prelude, Op. 61, 47.
Overture and Entr'actes to "The Maid of Pskov", 32.
Overture on Russian Themes, Op. 28, 26, 100, 799, 820, 989.

P

Pan Voevoda. Suite from the Opera, Op. 59, 46.

S

"Sadko." A Musical Picture, Op. 5, 28, 299, 350, 800, 806, 810, 821–25, 1056, 1269, 1273, 1490.
Scheherazade. Symphonic Suite, Op. 35, 38, 753, 804, 808, 810, 844–52, 1039, 1079, 1143, 1147, 1165, 1310, 1462, 1504.
Serenade for cello and orch., Op. 37, 57, 71.
Sinfonietta, Op. 31, 34, 64.
Skazka [A Fairy Tale], Op. 29, 33, 99, 296, 596, 800, 804, 806, 810, 838, 1248.
Sketch of a Scherzo for a Fourth Symphony, 35.
Snow Maiden, The. Suite from the Opera, 40.
Symphony No. 1, Op. 1, 25, 195, 799, 810–14, 909, 989.
Symphony No. 2: see *"Antar." Symphonic Suite*, Op. 9.
Symphony in B minor, 29.
Symphony No. 3, Op. 32, 31, 834–37.

T

Tale of the Fisherman and the Fish, The, 52.
Theme and Fourth Variation from "Variations on a Russian Theme," 42, 1210.
Zdravitsa [Toast to A. K. Glazunov], 49.

Solo Instrument and Wind Orchestra

C

Concerto for clarinet, 60.
Concerto for trombone, 58.

V

Variations for oboe, 59.

Chamber Music

A

Allegro from the Collection "The Fridays" for string quartet, 75.

C

Canzonetta and Tarantella for two clarinets, 70.

F

Four Variations on a Chorale for string quartet, 65.

302 *Indexes*

K

Khorovod from the String Quartet "Name-day," 67.

N

Nocturne for four horns, 68.

Q

Quintet for piano and wind instruments, 63.

S

Serenade for cello and piano, Op. 37, 57, 71.
Sextet for two violins, two violas and two cellos, 62, 866–68.
String Quartet in F major, Op. 12, 61, 865.
String Quartet in G major, 73.
String Quartet on Russian Themes. Fugue "In the Monastery", 64, 97.
String Quartet on the Theme B-la-F. First movement, 66, 101.

T

Theme and Fourth Variation from "Variations on a Russian Theme" for string quartet, 74.
Trio for piano, violin and cello, 72, 869.
Two Duets for two horns, 69.

Piano Music

A

Allegretto in C major, 105.
Allegro in D minor, 77.
At the Grave. Prelude, Op. 61, 111.

C

Capriccio espagnol. Capriccio on Spanish Themes, Op. 34, 102.

D

Dubinushka. Russian Song, 112.

F

Fantasia on Serbian Themes, Op. 6, 82.
Finale from Joke-quadrille, 104.

Four-Part Fugue, C major, 83.
Fugue: "In the Monastery," 64, 97.
Funeral March in D minor, 80.

I

Impromptu, Novelette, Scherzino, Etude, Op. 11, 93.
Intermezzo-fughetta, G minor, 108.

L

Little Song (in the Dorian Mode), 110.

M

Musical Letter to Lyadov, 96.

N

Neapolitan Song, Op. 63, 50, 113.
Nocturne in B-flat minor, 79.

O

Overture, incomplete, 76.
Overture on Russian Themes, Op. 28, 100.

P

Paraphrases. 24 variations and 15 pieces on an unchanged well-known theme, 95.
Prelude-Impromptu, Mazurka, Op. 38, 107.
Prelude in G major, 106.

S

Scheherazade. Symphonic Suite, Op. 35, 103.
Scherzo in C minor for Piano Duet, 81.
Six Fugues, Op. 17, 90.
Six Variations on the Theme B-A-C-H for Piano, Op. 10, 94.
Skazka [A Fairy Tale], Op. 29, 99.
String Quartet on the Theme B-la-F. First movement, 66, 101.

T

Three Four-Part Fugues, C major, E and G minor, 89.
Three Fughettas on Russian Themes, G, D and G minor, 88.

Indexes 303

Three Three-Part Fugues, E and A major, D minor, 85.
Three-Part Fugue, D major, 86.
Three-Part Fugue, G minor, 92.
Three-Part Fugue. Variant of the preceding fugue, D major, 87.
Two Three-Part Fugues, G and F major, 84.

V

Variations on a Russian Theme, 78.
Variations on a Russian Theme taken from Abramychev's Folk Song Collection, 109.
Variations on a Theme by Misha, 98.

W

Waltz, Song and Fugue, Op. 15, 91.

Choral Music: Sacred

C

Collection of Sacred-Musical Arrangements, Op. 22b, 116.
Collection of Sacred-Musical Compositions and Arrangements, 117.
Collection of Sacred-Musical Works, including 8 numbers from the "Liturgy of St. John Chrysostom", Op. 22, 115.

W

We Praise Thee, O God, 114, 882.

Choral Music: Secular

F

Fifteen Russian Folk Songs, Op. 19, 123.
Four Three-Part Choruses, Op. 23, 124.
Four Variations and Fughetta on the theme "Nadoeli nochi", Op. 14, 119.

I

Iz Gomera [From Homer]. Prelude-cantata, Op. 60, 130, 887, 890, 1418.

P

Poem about Aleksey, Man of God, Op. 20, 122.

R

Robbers' Song, "Rise, rise, thou red sun," 127.

S

Six Choruses, Op. 16, 120.
Slava [Glory]. "Under the Dish" Song, Op. 21, 125.
Song of the Prophet Oleg, Op. 58, 129.
Svitezyanka [Switezianka]. Cantata, Op. 44, 128, 888, 890, 1232.

T

Two Choruses for children's voices, 126.
Two Choruses, Op. 18, 121.
Two Three-part Women's Choruses, Op. 13, 118.

Vocal Works

B

Butterfly, 131.
By the Sea, Op. 46, 150.

C

Come Out to Me, Signora, 132.

D

Dragonflies. Trio for women's voices, Op. 53, 156.

F

Five Songs, Op. 51, 154.
Four Songs, Op. 2, 134.
Four Songs, Op. 3, 136.
Four Songs, Op. 4, 137.
Four Songs, Op. 7, 138.
Four Songs, Op. 26, 141.
Four Songs, Op. 27, 142.
Four Songs, Op. 39, 143.

Four Songs, Op. 40, 144.
Four Songs, Op. 41, 145.
Four Songs, Op. 42, 146.
Four Songs, Op. 50, 153.
Four Songs, Op. 55, 157.

I

In Spring, Op. 43, 147.
In the Blood Burns the Fire of Desire, 133.

S

Six Songs, Op. 8, 139.

T

The Poet, 149.
To the Poet, Op. 45, 148.
Two Duets, Op. 47, 151.
Two Duets, Op. 52, 155.
Two Songs, Op. 25, 140.
Two Songs, Op. 49, 152.
Two Songs, Op. 56, 158.

Y

You Will Soon Forget Me, 135.

Folk Song Collections

C

Collection of Russian Folk Songs, Op. 24, 159.

F

40 Folk Songs, collected by T. I. Filippov, harmonised by N. A. Rimsky-Korsakov], 88, 123, 160.

Arrangements, Orchestrations, and Revisions

Borodin

M

Mlada (collective work). Finale to Act IV orch., 164.

P

Prince Igor, Opera, 161, 903–07, 910, 1378–79.

S

Songs: "The Sleeping Princess" and "The Sea" orch., 165.
String Quartet No. 2. Nocturne arr., 162, 908.
Symphonies Nos. 1 and 2, 163.

Cui

W

William Ratcliff, Opera, 166.

Dargomyzhsky

R

Rogdana, Opera, 168.

T

The Stone Guest, Opera, 167, 285, 911–12, 1019.

Glinka

A

A Life for the Tsar, Opera, 170.

R

Ruslan and Lyudmila, Opera, 169.

W

Works arr. and ed. by Rimsky-Korsakov: *Jota aragonesa, Finsky zaliv* [Gulf of Finland], *Kamarinskaya, Prince Kholmsky, Souvenir d'une Nuit d'Eté à Madrid, Valse-Fantaisie*, and others, 171.

Handel

S

Samson, Oratorio, 172.

Indexes

Musorgsky

B

Boris Godunov, Opera, 177, 203, 249, 914, 920, 922, 924–43, 1148, 1180, 1379.

D

Destruction of Sennacherib, The, Opera, 173.

K

Khovanshchina, Opera, 174, 194, 944–49, 1379.

M

Marriage, The, Opera, 178.

S

Songs and Dances of Death, 180.
Songs: "Hopak," "Gathering Mushrooms," "Peasant Lullaby," "With Nurse," "Night," "The Field-Marshall," 179.
Sorochintsy Fair, Opera, 176.

V

Various orchestral and choral works, songs, etc., 175.

Schubert

G

Grand March in A Minor, 181.

Schumann

C

Carnaval, Op. 9, 182.

Arrangements for Military Band (1873–83)

B

Beethoven: Overture to *Egmont*, 183.

G

Glinka: *A Life for the Tsar*: Finale, 184.

M

Meyer, L. de: *Marche marocaine*: Berlioz's version, 185.
Mendelssohn: *Incidental Music to A Midsummer Night's Dream*: Nocturne and Wedding March, 186.
Meyerbeer: *Robert le Diable*: Isabela's Aria, 187.
Meyerbeer: *Les Huguenots*: Conspiracy Scene, 188.
Meyerbeer: *Le Prophète*: Coronation March, 189.

S

Schubert: March in B-Flat Minor, 190.

W

Wagner: Prelude to *Lohengrin*, 191.

Index of Rimsky-Korsakov's Literary Works

Literary Works

C

Chronicle of My Musical Life, 76, 210, 282, 294, 664, 1126, 1297, 1333, 1351–54.

M

Manual of Harmony, Parts 1–2, 196, 282, 1332, 1335, 1339, 1341, 1344, 1350, 1476, 1485.
Musical Articles and Notes (1869–1907). With an introductory article by M. F. Gnesin. Edited by N. Rimskaya-Korsakova, 211, 958, 991, 1020, 1099, 1340, 1365.

P

Principles of Orchestration. With Examples in Score from his Own Works, 211, 212, 282, 1020, 1086, 1301, 1328, 1336, 1356–59.

Articles and Reviews

E

"Excerpt from a Planned Work on the Art of Music," 201, 211, 282.
"Excerpt from the Intro. to 'Esthetics of the Art of Music'," 202, 211, 282.

F

"From a Diary," 209, 211, 282.

M

"My First Symphony," 195, 282.

N

"N. A. Rimsky-Korsakov on his Own Works," 213.

O

"On Auditory Delusions," 205, 211, 282.
"On Music Education," 198, 211, 282.

T

"The Epidemic of Conducting," 200, 211, 282, 1342–43.
"*The People of Nizhny-Novgorod.* Opera by Nápravník," 192, 211, 282.
"*The Snow Maiden* – A Spring Fairy Tale (Thematic Analysis)," 208, 211, 282, 462, 468.
"Three Verse Impromptus by Rimsky-Korsakov," 207.
"To Listeners and Connoisseurs of Opera as a Musical Art-Work," 204, 211, 282.

V

"Various Thoughts to Remember," 206, 282.

W

"Wagner and Dargomyzhsky," 199, 211, 282, 983, 1099, 1100, 1346.
"*William Ratcliff*, Opera in 3 Acts by Mr. Cui," 193, 211, 282, 1364.

Forewords

F

Foreword to Musorgsky's *Boris Godunov*, 203.
Foreword to orch. score of Musorgsky's *St. John's Night on Bald Mountain*, 197.
Foreword to vocal score of Musorgsky's *Khovanshchina*, 194.

Indexes

Correspondence

A

A Letter to Yan Batka (1955), 256.
A. N. Ostrovsky and N. A. Rimsky-Korsakov (Letters) (1937), 241.
An unknown letter to S. V. Smolensky (1977), 272.

C

Correspondence with A. I. Ziloti (1963), 264.
Correspondence with A. K. Glazunov (1960), 260.
Correspondence with An. K. Lyadov (1916), 231.
Correspondence with B. Kalensky (1955), 255.
Correspondence with Lyudmila Shestakova (2009), 279.
Correspondence with M. A. Balakirev (1913–17), 229.
Correspondence with M. A. Balakirev (1915–17), 233.
Correspondence with M. M. Ippolitov-Ivanov (1933), 240.
Correspondence with M. P. Belyaev (1933), 238.
Correspondence with M. P. Musorgsky (1913), 226.
Correspondence with M. P. Musorgsky (1932), 237.
Correspondence with P. I. Tchaikovsky (1945), 245.
Correspondence with S. I. Taneev (1952), 250.
Correspondence with S. N. Kruglikov (1951), 248.
Correspondence with V. I. Bel'sky (1976), 271.
Correspondence with V. V. Stasov (1910), 220.
Correspondence with V. V. Stasov (1910), 221.
Correspondence with V. V. Stasov a propos "Sadko" (1910–11), 222.

E

Excerpts from unpublished correspondence of Rimsky-Korsakov preserved in the Belyaev Archive (2008), 278.
Extensive correspondence between Rimsky-Korsakov and his brother Voin Andreevich (1994), 276.

F

Five unpublished letters to Michel Delin while in Paris (1955) 254.
From the letters of Igor Stravinsky to Rimsky-Korsakov's family (1992), 274.
From the letters of N. M. Shtrup (1994), 277.

I

In the tracks of an unknown letter by N. A. Rimsky-Korsakov (1971), 269.

L

Letter of N. A. Rimsky-Korsakov to the Editorial Board of *RMG* (1899), 214.
Letter to A. G. Chesnokov (1964), 267.
Letter to A. N. Rimsky-Korsakov (1913), 224.
Letter to A. N. Vinogradsky (1962), 262.
Letter to A. V. Ossovsky (1944), 244.
Letter to M. I. Delin (Ashkenazi) (1965), 268.
Letter to N. N. Ikonnikov (1961), 261.
Letter to V. I. Suk (1933), 239.
Letters from Rimsky-Korsakov to his son Andrey, von Bülow, Sheyn and Ossovsky (1958), 258.
Letters of Rimsky-Korsakov and V. S. Kalinnikov to S. N. Kruglikov (1910), 219.
Letters of Rimsky-Korsakov preserved in the Vilna Archives (1980), 273.
Letters of Rimsky-Korsakov to his son Andrey (1964), 266.
Letters of V. I. and A. K. Bel'sky (1994), 275.
Letters to A. P. Borodin and V. V. Yastrebtsëv (1909), 217.
Letters to C. A. Cui (1911), 223.
Letters to E. Petrovsky (1952), 249.
Letters to Fëdor Stravinsky (1972), 270.
Letters to L. I. Shestakova (1916), 232.
Letters to M. A. Vrubel' (1963), 265.
Letters to N. F. Findeyzen (1924), 235.
Letters to V. I. Suk (1922), 234.
Letters to V. I. Suk (1926), 236.
Letters to V. V. Vasil'ev (1939), 243.
Letters to V. V. Yastrebtsëv (1914), 230.

O

"On the Simplified Score" (1907), 215.

R

Rimsky-Korsakov's letter regarding Cui's opera *Andzhelo* (1954), 253.

S

Selected letters to N. N. Rimskaya-Korsakova (1954), 252, 1180, 1204.
Six letters from Rimsky-Korsakov to Borodin (1960), 259.
Six letters from Rimsky-Korsakov to Cui (1955), 257.
Six letters from Rimsky-Korsakov to Kruglikov and Belanovsky (1948), 247.

T

Two letters to A. P. Borodin (1879), 216.
Two unpublished letters to S. I. Taneev (1947), 246.
Three letters to V. V. Yastrebtsëv (1906), 218.

U

Unknown letters of V. A. Telyakovsky and Rimsky-Korsakov (1953), 251.

Unpublished correspondence with Musorgsky (1913) 228.
Unpublished letter to B. L. Levenson (1905), 263.
Unpublished letter to V. V. Yastrebtsëv (1913), 225.
Unpublished letters to N. F. Findeyzen (1913), 227.
Unpublished letters to S. I. Taneev (1937), 242.

Other References

C

Complete Collection of Compositions. Literary Works and Correspondence, Vols. I-VIII, 282; see also 192–93, 195–96, 198–202, 204–06, 208–10, 212, 446, 462, 653, 1016, 1341, 1346–47, 1356–59.

N

N. A. Rimsky-Korsakov. Life and Work. Vols. I–V, 280; see also 1180, 1320.

M

Musical Legacy. Rimsky-Korsakov. Research. Materials. Letters, 281; see also 252, 1016, 1204.

Index of Authors, Editors, Compilers, Translators, and Librettists

A

A. K-y., 1111.

Abbasov, Ashraf Dzhalal ogly, 1101.

Abel, Jörg Michael, 798.

Abraham, Gerald, 283–85, 378–79, 411, 415, 431, 471, 495–97, 561, 591, 648, 697–98, 799, 826, 844–45, 891–92, 903, 911, 956, 1045, 1078, 1112, 1126, 1228, 1251–53, 1324, 1423, 1461–64, 1514–15.

Abramova, A., 1222.

Agate, E., 212.

Akulov, Evgeny F., 914.

Aleksandrov, A., 472.

Aleksandrova, E. L., 1465.

Aleksandrova, Vera Nikolaevna, 1429.

Alekseev, Aleksandr Dmitrievich, 870.

Alekseevsky, N., 279, 416.

Allorge, Henri, 1254.

Alshwang, Arnol'd Aleksandrovich, 957.

An. Kup., 640.

Angert, G. A., 748.

Arenzon, Evgenij, 288–89.

Asaf'ev, Boris Vladimirovich [pseud. Glebov, Igor'], 290–96, 381–82, 418–19, 435–39, 473–75, 482, 501–03, 536, 563–66, 594–97, 624–25, 650–52, 700–03, 760–61, 899, 924–25, 961–62, 1058, 1080, 1087, 1116–18, 1168, 1229–30, 1255–56, 1259, 1298, 1307, 1368–69, 1374, 1435, 1503–04; Other, 1203.

Ashkinazi, Mikhail Osipovich, 383.

B

B.-B., 626.

B. M-g., 627.

Bachinskaya, N. M.: see Vladykina-Bachinskaya, N. M.

Bagirova, Liana Mashallaevna, 297–98.

Bakanova, Lyudmila, 440.

Baker, T., 972.

Bakst, James, 1257.

Bakulin, V., 567.

Balakirev, Mily Alekseevich, Author, 416, 958; Composer, 88, 119, 123, 134, 169–70, 856, 858, 1027, 1091, 1126, 1147, 1150, 1313; Conductor, 25–28, 54; Correspondence, 229, 233, 238, 282, 299, 967, 974–75, 1026, 1028, 1033, 1166; Other, 30, 136, 139, 283–84, 347, 819, 881, 883, 886, 964, 1019, 1029, 1074, 1325, 1445, 1456.

Balyasov, N. K., 1008.

Barenboym, Lev Aronovich, 1068.

Barnes, Christopher, 771.

Baroni, Mario, 944, 1053.

Barsova, Lyudmila Grigor'evna, 790–92, 1119, 1258.

Barsowa, L.: see Barsova, L. G.

Bellaigue, Camille, 441.

Bel'sky, Rafail, 749, 1431.

Bel'sky, Vladimir Ivanovich, Archive, 129, 1016; Librettist, 8, 12, 16–17, 19, 666–67, 698, 734, 738, 746–47, 749, 1019; Correspondence, 271, 275, 990; Other, 145, 157.

Bely, P., 442.

Belyaev, Viktor Mikhaylovich, 568, 871, 904, 1505.

Belza, Igor' Fëdorovich, 255–56, 537, 770, 1232.

Bemol', 569.

Benua, A., 704.

Berezovsky, V. V., 1261.

Berkov, Viktor Osipovich, 287, 300, 705, 1332.

310 Indexes

Bernandt, Grigory Borisovich, 725, 823, 1086, 1092, 1518–19.
Bernstein, N. D., 653.
Berry, C., 893.
Bertensson, Sergei, 1052, 1065.
Bertz-Dostal, Helga, 1223.
Beskin, Em., 706.
Binevich, Evgeny, 1513.
Biryukov, V. A., 1233.
Blagodatov, Georgy Ivanovich, 1498.
Blagoy, D. D., 1382.
Blinova, M. P., 1074.
Blumberg, Georges, 210
Bogdanov-Berezovsky, Valerian Mikhaylovich, 762, 788.
Bogdany, Wanda, 273.
Borodin, Aleksandr Porfir'evich, Author, 827; Composer, 2, 66, 75, 95, 161–65, 282–84, 412, 652, 826, 872, 903–10, 958, 1019, 1156, 1253, 1274, 1378–79, 1469; Correspondence, 216–17, 259, 282, 1033–34, 1132; Other, 27, 39, 136, 974–75, 993, 1076, 1185.
Borovsky, Victor, 707, 776.
Bouis, Antonia W., 942.
Bozina, Ol'ga Arkad'evna, 628.
Braudo, Evgeny Maksimovich, 538, 926, 1059, 1103, 1120, 1263.
Brazhnik, Larisa Vladimirovna, 1466.
Brill, Nicholas P., 874.
Brody, Elaine, 1264.
Bronfin, E. F., 1370.
Bronsky, P., 750.
Brook, Donald, 1122.
Brounoff, Platon, 1371.
Brown, Clive, 644.
Brown, David, 1123–24.
Brown, Malcolm Hamrick, 406, 1264–65, 1313.
Budrin, B., 1467.
Bugoslavsky, Sergey Alekseevich, 654.
Bullock, Philip Ross, 1266.
Bulycheva, Anna Valentinovna, 906.
Burian, Karel Vladimir, 1125.
Butakov, Catharine, 1207.
Butir, Leonid Mironovič, 1425.
Bystrova, M., 1520.

C

C. M., 384.

Calvocoressi, Michael Dimitri, 301, 915, 1126, 1267.
Cendrars, Blaise, 1127.
Chaliapin, Fyodor: see Shalyapin, F. I.
Chaykovsky, Pëtr Il'ich: see Tchaikovsky, P. I.
Chemodanov, Sergey, 504.
Chernikov, N., 1007.
Chernov, Konstantin Nikolaevich, 282, 800, 846.
Cheshikhin, Vsevolod Evgrafovich, 281, 304, 751, 1016, 1527.
Chirkova, Larisa, 1002.
Choi, Seung-Ho, 1432.
Churova, Marina Abramovna, 385.
Cone, Edward T., 963.
Cooper, David, 644.
Cooper, Martin du P., 305–06, 1268, 1433.
Covell, Roger, 1104,
Covington, Kate R., 1483.
Cowgill, Rachel, 644.
Cui, César [Kyui, Tsezar' Antonovich], Author, 257, 396, 416, 422–23, 456, 515, 546, 558, 811, 817, 820–21, 829, 835, 840, 848, 853, 857, 864, 896, 1269, 1294; Composer, 2, 95, 107, 137, 166, 193, 223, 253, 257, 281–82, 345, 412, 552, 799, 872, 1016, 1019, 1153, 1185, 1327, 1364, 1527; Other, 30, 134, 137.
Cunningham, Thomas Thurston, 570.

D

Danilevich, Lev Vasil'evich, 307.
Dan'ko, L. G., 1522.
Derzhanovsky, V., 887.
DeVoto, Mark, 1468.
Dianin, Sergey Aleksandrovich, 148, 259, 1033.
Dietz, Max, 614, 621.
Dmitriev, A. N., 282, 1435, 1499.
Dmitrieva-Mey, Tat'yana Pavlovna, 1374.
Dobrynina, E., 708, 1362, 1444.
Dolinskaya, Elena Borisovna, 709.
Dolzhansky, Aleksandr Naumovich, 1128.
Domokos, Zsuzsanna, 907.
Donald, Paul, 847.
Dopino, Cesare, 1316.
Dreyden, Simon, 1555.
Drozdov, Anatoly Nikolaevich, 1129, 1556.
Drukt, Aleksandr, 1469.

Indexes

Druskin, Mikhail Semënovich, 308, 1081, 1433.
Durylin, Sergey Nikolaevich, 539, 571, 711, 1375.
Dziebowska, Elżbieta, 1355.

E

Earl of Harewood, George Henry Hubert Lascelles, 311.
Eberlein, Dorothee, 964, 1048, 1270.
Edmunds, Catherine J., 752.
Eeckhout, Antoon, 801.
"Efgro," 557.
Engel', Yuly Dmitrievich, 312–13, 386, 420, 445, 483, 505, 540–41, 572, 598–99, 629, 641, 656, 713, 716, 927, 1153, 1272, 1559.
Entelis, L. A., 753.
E. P-sky, 655.
E. P., 443, 1130, 1470, 1558.
Es., 444, 712.
Everett, William A., 717.
Evg. G-s.: see Gippius, E. V.
Eyges, Iosif, 802.

F

Fahlbusch, Lothar, 210.
Famintsyn, Aleksandr Sergeevich, 894, 1273, 1294.
Farizova, N., 506.
Favia-Artsay, Aida, 764.
Feinberg, Saul, 855.
Ferman, Valentin Eduardovich, 314, 484, 966.
Figes, Orlando, 1275.
Filippov, T. I., 88, 123, 160, 1026, 1239.
Filippov, V., 241, 453.
Findeyzen, Nikolay Fëdorovich, Author, 388, 446, 476, 615, 642, 718, 945, 1056, 1132, 1133, 1213, 1276, 1333, 1351, 1523, 1560; Correspondence, 227, 235, 1019; Other, 8, 896.
Finkel'shteyn, Z., 421.
Frangopulo, M. Kh., 753.
Frelikh, O., 315.
French, Richard F., 1080.
Frolov, Sergei Vladimirovich, 968.
Frolova-Walker, Marina, 616, 1277.

Fukac, J., 389.
Fulle, Gerlinde, 928.

G

G. N-ov., 602.
Galeev, Bulat Mahmudovich, 969.
Galkauskas, Konstantin Mikhaylovich, 1377, 1407, 1436.
Ganina, Mariya Alekseevna, 1038, 1434–35.
García Morillo, Roberto, 1136.
Garden, Edward, J. C., 856, 954, 1027, 1042, 1069, 1091, 1317.
Gardner, I. A. [Johann von], 875.
Gaub, Albrecht, 412–13, 1524.
Gavazzeni, Gianandrea, 1278.
Gaydamovich, Tat'yana Alekseevna, 869.
Genika, Rostislav Vladimirovich, 1279.
Getteman, H., 447.
Geylig, M., 316.
Gilse van der Pals, N. van, 301, 317, 607.
Gilyarovskaya, N., 318.
Ginzburg, Semën L'vovich, 1435.
Gippius, Evgeny Vladimirovich, 657, 719, 1231.
Glazunov, Aleksandr Konstantinovich, Archive, 69–70; Author, 1132, 1378–79, 1420, 1561; Composer, 42, 51, 66–67, 74–75, 104, 109, 161, 163, 170, 284, 904–06, 909–10, 913, 937, 1019, 1290; Conductor, 28, 128; Correspondence, 38, 260, 282, 937, 1019, 1039, 1381, 1420, 1561; Other, 33, 49, 142, 155, 282, 1019, 1038, 1040, 1049, 1115, 1222, 1290, 1377, 1381, 1402.
Glebov, Igor' [pseud.]: see Asaf'ev, B. V.
Glezer, Raisa Vladimirovna, 1039.
Glushchenko, Georgy Semënovich, 1525.
Gnesin, Mikhail Fabianovich, 68, 211, 630, 794, 803, 1360, 1380, 1407, 1409, 1437–38.
Goddard, Scott, 1280.
Godet, Robert, 929.
Gofman, R.: see Hofmann, R.
Gojowy, Detlef, 905, 1423, 1479.
Gol'denveyzer, Aleksandr Borisovich, 1382.
Golemba, A., 1137.
Golubovsky, I. V., 1003.
Gordeeva, Evgeniya Mikhaylovna, 375, 804, 1235, 1282.

312

Gorodetskaya, Zinaida Izrailevna, 300, 390.

Goryachikh, Vladimir Vladimirovich, 1471.

Gozenpud, Abram Akimovich, 319, 321, 323, 391, 745, 754, 777, 916, 970, 1004, 1095, 1138, 1237, 1295.

Grachev, Panteleymon Vladimirovich, 324.

Greenwalt, Terence Lee, 805.

Gretchaninoff, Alexandre, 1383.

Gribanova, Anastasiya Petrovna, 908.

Gribble, Lyubomira Parpulobova, 658.

Griffiths, Steven, A. K., 325, 1283.

Grigor'ev, Stepan Stepanovich, 1472–73.

Grimsted, Patricia Kennedy, 1526.

Grosheva, Elena Andreeva, 308, 326, 603, 643, 759, 778.

Grushke, N., 617.

Gryunfel'd, Nil's Edgarovich, 659.

Gui, Vittorio, 1474.

Gulyants, E. I., 604.

Gunst, Evgeny Ottovich, 1096.

Gurevich, Evgeniya L'vovna, 1208.

Gurevich, L. Ya., 328.

Gurevich, V., 946.

Guseynova, Zivar Mahmudovna, 542, 913.

Gusin, I. L., 253, 257, 1294.

Gut, Serge, 1475.

H

Haas, David, 296.

Hadland, F. A., 543.

Haine, Malou, 1284.

Halbe, Gregory A., 448.

Hale, Philip, 839.

Halpérine, M-me P.: see Halpérine-Kaminsky, E.

Halpérine-Kaminsky, E., 210, 433, 443.

Hapgood, Elizabeth Reynolds, 366.

Haward, Lawrence, 1310.

Hellmundt, Christoph, 953.

Hill, E. B., 1139.

Hofmann, Rostislav-Michel, 329, 1140, 1281, 1285.

Humiston, William H., 720.

I

Il'in, Igor' Pavlovich, 507.

Il'insky, Aleksandr Aleksandrovich, 1142.

Ippolitov-Ivanov, Mikhail Mikhaylovich, Author, 937, 1367, 1384; Composer, 1019; Correspondence, 240, 282, 967; Other, 11, 14, 364, 1109.

Istel, Edgar, 972.

Ivanov, Mikhail Mikhaylovich, 485, 493, 1286, 1294.

J

Jackson, Larisa Petrushkevich, 1476.

Jacobs, A., 889, 931.

Jaffé, Daniel, 1288.

Jankélévitch, Vladimir, 1477.

Joffe, Judah A., 210, 1354.

Jonas, Florence, 1078, 1324, 1423.

Joseph, Charles M., 1439.

K

Kabalevsky, Dmitry Borisovich, 330, 376, 663, 669.

Kahan, Sylvia, 1478.

Kandinsky, Aleksey Ivanovich, 282, 331–34, 392–93, 449, 508–09, 721, 806, 876, 1143, 1356.

Karasev, Pavel Alekseevich, 661, 973.

Karatygin, Vyacheslav Gavrilovich, 450, 722, 947, 1144–45, 1179, 1209.

Karenin, Vladimir [pseud. Stasova, Varvara Dmitrievna], 1075.

Kashintsev, Dmitry Aleksandrovich [pseud. Uglov, Anton], 589.

Kashkin, Nikolay Dimitrievich, 154, 364, 394, 486, 510, 574-75, 622, 662, 1146, 1153, 1180, 1289, 1525.

Katonova, Natal'ya Yur'evna, 619.

Kaufman, Leonid Sergeevich, 1239.

Kaufman, T., 1300.

Kazansky, Sergey Pavlovich, 451.

Keeton, A. E., 1093.

Keldysh, Yury Vsevolodovich, 663, 669, 673, 677-78, 723, 917, 1147, 1172, 1195, 1257, 1290, 1489.

Kenigsberg, Alla Konstantinovna, 335, 664.

Kerman, Joseph, 1492.

Kershner, L., 665.

Kharissov, Ildar, 544.

Kharkeevich, Irina, 269.

Indexes

Khessin, Aleksandr Borisovich, 512.
Kholopova, Valentina Nikolaevna, 1479.
Khoprova, Tat'yana Aleksandrovna, 336, 685–86, 747, 1441.
Khubov, Georgy Nikitich, 513, 818, 824–25.
Kiselëv, Vasily Aleksandrovich, 241–42, 299, 452–53, 514, 1005, 1034, 1046, 1193, 1429, 1527.
Klein, John W. Nicholas, 1148.
Kloiber, Rudolf, 807.
Kobbé, Gustav, 311.
Kochetov, Nikolay Razumnikovich, 622, 1291.
Kolbanovskaya, A., 1550–01.
Kolomiytsov, Viktor Pavlovich, 1562.
Kolosova, E., 241, 453.
Koltypina, Galina Borisovna, 1528, 1549, 1550, 1552–53.
Komarnitskaya, Ol'ga Vissarionovna, 337, 666–67.
Kompaneysky, Nikolay Ivanovich, 878, 1563.
Konen, V., 806.
Konenkov, S., 1066.
Konopleva, I. A., 282.
Konstantinova, Marianna Aleksandrovna, 1442.
Koposova-Derzhanovskaya, Ekaterina Vasil'evna, 793.
Kopytova, Galina Viktorovna, 274, 276, 1214, 1396.
Korabel'nikova, Lyudmila Zinov'evna, 254, 1352.
Korableva, A., 668.
Koren, Marija, 816.
Korev, Semën Isaakovich, 1063.
Korev, Yury, 1362, 1444.
Korzhukin, Ivan Alekseevich, 1097, 1480.
Krasovsky, Yury, 1007.
Kremlëv, Yuly Anatol'evich, 974–75, 1043, 1529.
Krestan, Michael, 1292.
Kristi, G., 338.
Kruglikov, Semën Nikolaevich, 33, 141, 154, 219, 247–48, 282, 339, 364, 395, 454, 622, 631, 1019, 1039, 1074, 1149, 1180, 1293, 1460.
Krupeychenko, I. P., 1008.
Krylov, Viktor, 2, 5, 413.
Kryukov, Andrey Nikolaevich, 1150.
Kudryumov, Yu. V., 545.

Kuhn, Ernst, Author, 1155, 1480; Publisher, 412, 463–65, 798, 813, 1340, 1343–47, 1364, 1480.
Kukharsky, Vasily Fedos'evich, 669–70.
Kulakovsky, Lev Vladimirovich, 300, 455.
Kulapina, Ol'ga Ivanovna, 1240.
Kunguris, Georgius, 1481.
Kunin, Iosif Filippovich, 247, 282, 313, 918, 1051, 1152–53, 1353.
Kurdyumov, Yu. V., 1357.
Kurkov, Nikolay Vasil'evich, 773.
Kurtsman, Alisa, 1040.
Kushnarëv, Khristofor Stepanovich, 1482.
Kustodiev, B., 576.
Kutateladze, Larisa Mikhaylovna, 270, 458, 1009.
Kuznetsov, E. M., 1567.
Kuznetsov, Konstantin Alekseevich, 895, 1156.
Kyui, Tsezar' Antonovich: see Cui, C.

L

Laloy, Louis, 653.
Lapin, V., 671.
Lapshin, Ivan Ivanovich, 978–79, 1060, 1157, 1480, 1506.
Larosh, German [Herman] Avgustovich, 397, 424, 488, 493, 547, 830–31, 865, 958, 1294–95.
Lascelles, George Henry Hubert: see Earl of Harewood.
Laux, Carl August, 1296.
Leonard, Richard Anthony, 1297.
Lepel, Felix von, 849.
Levenson, Boris, 1443.
Levenson, Osip Yakovlevich, 282, 822
Levik, Boris Veniaminovich, 548.
Levik, Sergey Yur'evich, 765.
Leyda, Jay, 1052, 1065.
Lifar, Serge, 254.
Lipaev, Ivan Vasil'evich, 281, 516, 549, 559, 577, 605, 618, 1024, 1159, 1427.
Lischke, André, 210, 1334.
Lisitsyn, Mikhail Aleksandrovich, 879.
Lissa, Zofia, 901, 1161.
Livanova, Tamara Nikolaevna, 339, 980, 1076, 1105, 1298, 1362, 1412–13, 1444, 1530, 1539, 1550.
Lochrie, Daniel W., 955.

314 Indexes

"Loge," 808.
Lokshin, Daniil L'vovich, 1445.
Longyear, Rey M., 837, 1483.
Lunacharsky, Anatoly Vasil'evich, 550, 606, 672, 725, 734, 1162.
L'vov, Mikhail L'vovich, 766, 768, 785.
L'vov, Pavel Rubimovich, 726.
Lyapunov, Sergey Mikhaylovich, 229, 233, 1029.
Lyapunova, Anastasiya Sergeevna, 282, 1028.
Lysenko, Osip Nikolaevich, 1106.
Lyubimov, A., 673.
Lyutsh, Vs., 425, 578, 632.

M

MacKenzie, David, 1163.
McQuere, Gordon D., 1335.
Maes, Francis, 1299.
Maggid, Sofiya Davidovna, 899.
Maine, Basil, 981.
Maksimov, Evgeny Ivanovich, 872.
Makurenkova, Elena Petrovna, 1447.
Mal'ko, Nikolay Andreevich, 1385.
Malecka, Teresa, 633, 1098, 1241.
Malkov, Nikolay Petrovich, 341, 426.
Marchenkov, Vladimir Leonidovich, 517.
Marco, Guy, 1300.
Markov, Nikolay Ivanovich, 1564.
Martens, Frederick H., 727.
Martín Bermúdez, Santiago, 399.
Martynov, Ivan Ivanovich, 518.
Maslennikova, Irina Ivanovna, 767.
Maslov, Aleksandr Leont'evich, 1242.
Mason, Daniel Gregory, 850.
Medvedev, Aleksandr Viktorovich, 1224.
Melnikas, Leonidas, 1301.
Messwarb, Katja, 1336.
Metallov, Vasily Mikhaylovich, 880.
Mey, Lev Aleksandrovich, Librettist, 1, 10–11, 13, 32, 128, 410, 583, 586, 619; Song Texts, 134, 138–39, 151; Translator, 138, 146.
Migay, Sergey Ivanovich, 786.
Mikhaylov, Mikhail Kesarevich, 134, 136–37, 140, 1049–50, 1435, 1448.
Mikhaylova, A. N., 1011.
Miller, Larisa Alekseevna, 1337.
Mokul'sky, Stefan Stefanovich, 457.

Moldon, David, 1531.
Molzinsky, Vladimir Vladimirovich, 674.
Montagu-Nathan, Montagu, 551, 607, 720, 728–29, 982, 1165.
Montes, Roberto, 910.
Mooser, Robert-Aloys, 919.
Mörchen, Roland, 489.
Mordvinov, I. P., 1012.
Morgan, Edward, 765.
Móricz, Klára, 1449.
Morosan, Vladimir, 881–82.
Morov, Aleksey, 1302.
Morozova, Margarita Kirillovna, 1386.
Morrison, Simon Alexander, 675, 1484.
Muir, Stephen, 342, 519, 619, 644, 1363, 1532.
Mutli, Andrey Fëdorovich, 1485.
Muzalevsky, Vladimir Il'ich, 579, 1450.
Myasoedov, Andrey, 1451.
Myers, Gregory, 490.
Myuller, Teodor, 1486.

N

Nagy, Ferenc, 933.
Nectoux, Jean-Michel, 851.
Neef, Sigrid, 343.
Neff, Lyle Kevin, 344–45, 1303, 1338.
Nekrasova, Elena Vladimirovna, 1533.
Nemtsov, Jascha, 1304.
Nest'ev, Izrail Vladimirovich, 520, 1037.
Neuer, Adam, 1305.
Newman, Ernest, 400.
Newmarch, Rosa, 346–47, 720, 1266, 1363, 1387.
Nikol'skaya, L. B., 1388.
Nikulin, L., 268.
Nilsson, Kurt, 934.
Norris, Geoffrey, 948, 1354.
Norris, Jeremy P., 858–59.
Nozdurnov, Boris Mitrofanovich, 1426.

O

O'Riordan, C. L., 459.
Obram, Vera Alekseevna, 843, 1243.
Obraztsova, I. M., 1013.
Obukhova, Nadezhda Andreevna, 756, 770, 1321.
Odoevsky, Vladimir Fëdorovich, 823, 958.

Indexes 315

Ogolevets, Aleksey Stepanovich, 484, 818, 983.
Okser, S., 608.
Oldani, Robert William, 935, 1053, 1167.
Olkhovsky, Yuri, 1077.
Orlov, Genrikh Aleksandrovich, 676, 860, 984.
Orlov, Georgy Pavlovich, 1534.
Orlova, Aleksandra Anatol'evna, 271, 1054, 1435, 1535–36.
Orlova, Elena Mikhaylovna, 293, 985, 1168.
Osipova, Liya, 794
Ossovsky, Aleksandr Vyacheslavovich, 210, 244, 258, 282, 1014, 1169–70, 1306, 1370, 1389, 1422, 1435.
Ossovsky, V., 538, 1060.
Ostrovsky, Aron L'vovich, 1435, 1452.
Ostrovsky, Aleksandr Nikolaevich, 4, 241, 443, 448, 452–53, 460, 1016, 1103, 1480.
Ozeretskovskaya, I., 609.

P

Palmer, Christopher, 581.
Palmieri, Robert, 1067.
Panin, George, 1330.
Pankratova, V. A., 755.
Panoff, Peter, 1244.
Pashenko, Mikhail V., 678.
Pashkalov, V., 248.
Pavlov-Arbenin, Andrey Borisovich, 1307.
Pavlova, N. G., 1553.
Payne, Anthony, 1225.
Peattie, Antony, 311.
Pekelis, Mikhail Samoylovich, 552, 668, 1054, 1172, 1257.
Peppercorn, Lisa M., 1107.
Perret, Carine, 1487.
Pestalozza, Luigi, 1308.
Petrov, I., 1069.
Petrov, Nikolay Aleksandrovich, 1015.
Petrovskaya, Ira Fëdorovna, 1016.
Petrovsky, Evgeny Maksimovich, 14, 249, 491, 522, 635, 655, 679, 920, 1019.
Plantinga, Leon, 1309.
Ploumpidīs, Giōrgos P., 1453.
Pokhitonov, Daniil Il'ich, 1390.
Pokrovsky, Boris Aleksandrovich, 348, 680, 914.
Polevaya, Marina, 1017.
Polyakova, Lyudmila Viktorovna, 401, 755.

Polyanovsky, Georgy Aleksandrovich, 758, 769, 1173.
Pomerans, Arnold J., 1299.
Pomerans, Erica, 1299.
Pomerantseva, E., 1226.
Popov, Sergey Sergeevich, 349.
Popova, Tat'yana Vasil'evna, 1537.
Pougin, Arthur, 350, 1310.
Preobrazhensky, Antonin Viktorovich, 883.
Pring, S. W., 363, 992.
Prokhorov, Yakov Vasil'evich, 282, 1245.
Prokhorova, I., 461.
Prokof'ev, Grigory Petrovich, 477, 610, 731.
Prokof'ev [Prokofiev], Sergey Sergeevich, Author, 1391–92, 1407; Composer, 581, 855, 1515.
Prokop'eva, Ekaterina, 634.
Protopopov, Vladimir Vasil'evich, 282, 287, 300, 351, 705, 733, 1194, 1211, 1325, 1339, 1509.
P-sky, E.: see Petrovsky, E. M.
Purgol'd, Nadezhda Nikolaevna: see Rimskaya-Korsakova, N. I.
Pushanov, V. A., 1175.
Pushkin, Aleksandr Sergeevich, Author, *A Fairy Tale*, 33; *Fisherman and the Fish*, 52, 1019; *Golden Cockerel*, 19, 698, 709, 726, 734, 738, 1058, 1062, 1064; *Mozart and Salieri*, 9, 537–39, 552, 556, 1058, 1062, 1064; *Song of the Prophet Oleg*, 129; *Tale of Tsar Saltan*, 12, 734, 1058, 1062, 1064; Vocal Settings, 120, 124, 133, 136–39, 141–42, 146, 148–49, 152, 154, 157, 179, 896, 1061, 1064; Other, 404, 603, 752, 1059–60, 1063, 1064.
Puzey, N. M., 1488.

Q

Quraishi, Ibrahim, 681.

R

Raaben, Lev Nikolaevich, 264, 867.
Rabeneck, Nicolai, 354.
Racek, Jan, 1176.
Rachmaninov, Sergey Vasil'evich: see Rakhmaninov, S. V.

Rakhmaninov [Rachmaninov], Sergey
Vasil'evich, Author, 355, 1066, 1397;
Composer, 355, 364, 552, 876, 890, 993,
1292, 1515; Conductor, 294, 355, 364,
514, 727, 1065, 1067; Correspondence,
355; Other, 1156.
Rakhmanova, Marina Pavlovna, 277, 282, 478,
635, 682, 882, 884, 979, 986–88, 1454,
1538.
Rapatskaya, Lyudmila Aleksandrovna, 1311.
Rappaport, S. Kh., 965.
Rappaport, Viktor Romanovich, 523, 734.
Rastopchina, Nataliya Markovna, 1108.
Ratser, Evgeny Yakovlevich, 356, 912.
Ratskaya, Tsetsiliya Samoylovna, 1177.
Redepenning, Dorothea, 357, 1312.
Redlich, Hans F., 921.
Reed, David F., 1030.
Reilly, Edward R., 735, 951.
Remezov, Ivan Ivanovich, 239, 358.
Reynaud, Alain, 1018.
Ridenour, Robert C., 1313.
Riesemann, Oskar von, 210, 809, 1315, 1397.
Rimsky-Korsakov, Andrey Nikolaevich, 224,
252, 280, 736, 926, 989, 1004, 1016,
1019, 1145, 1153, 1179–80, 1219, 1314,
1320.
Rimsky-Korsakov, Mikhail [Misha]
Nikolaevich, Correspondence, 275;
Author, 1393, 1396; Other, 98, 146.
Rimsky-Korsakov, Nikolay Andreevich,
463–65, 813, 1340–47, 1364.
Rimsky-Korsakov, Vladimir Nikolaevich,
Author, 210, 282, 479, 990, 1020, 1044,
1074, 1181–82, 1220, 1394, 1507, 1535,
Other, 72, 1070, 1536.
Rimskaya-Korsakova [née Purgol'd],
Nadezhda Ivanovna, Author, 210–11,
1056, 1070, 1216, 1340, 1345, 1365;
Correspondence, 252, 274, 282; Diary
[Purgol'd], 1016, 1174; Curator, 1019;
Dedications, 3, 91, 120, 139, 141–43,
154; Other, 1181, 1213, 1303.
Rimskaya-Korsakova, Tat'yana Vladimirovna,
1217–18.
Rimsky-Korsakow, Nikolai: see Rimsky-
Korsakov, Nikolay Andreevich.
Ripanti, Luca, 212, 1348.
Ritter, William, 466.

Roberge, Marc-André, 524.
Rosenfeld, Paul, 1183.
Roshal', G., 1222.
"Rostislav" [pseud.]: see Tolstoy, F. M.
Rozanov, Aleksandr Semënovich, 1210.
Rozhdestvenskaya, Natal'ya Petrovna, 775.
Rozova, T. G., 1109, 1435.
Ruch'evskaya, Ekaterina Aleksandrovna, 360.
Rudakovskaya, E., 937.
Rumyantsev, Pavel Ivanovich, 361–362, 366.
Ruschenburg, Peter, 1035.
Ryazanov, Pëtr Borisovich, 1246, 1435.
Ryzhkin, Iosif Yakovlevich, 991.

S

Sabaneev, Boris Leonidovich, 1508.
Sabaneev, Leonid Leonidovich, 363, 992, 1184,
1315, 1505.
Sabinina, Marina Dmitrievna, 467.
Saminsky, Lazare, 1304, 1458.
Sánchez, Ramón Sobrino, 841.
Sandulenko, A., 1398.
Sargeant, Lynn M., 1566.
Sarriugarte Gómez, Íñigo, 993.
Savel'eva, Irina, 994.
Savelova, Z., 1539.
Schaeffner, André, 1036.
Schandert, Manfred, 938.
Schloezer, Boris de, 210, 683.
Schmitz, Eugen, 1185.
Schuster-Craig, John, 737.
Seaman, Gerald R., 889, 1033, 1316–17.
Semenov-Tyan-Shansky, Veniamin, 1454.
Senilov, Vladimir Alekseevich, 636.
Serebryakova, Lyubov' Alekseevna, 684–86.
Seroff [Serov], Victor I., 1318.
Serov, Aleksandr Nikolaevich, Author, 506,
818, 824–25, 958, 983; Composer, 799.
Serova, Valentina Semënovna, 480.
Shabshaevich, Elena Markovna, 1319.
Shakhov, Vadim Viktorovich, 814.
Shalyapin, Fëdor Ivanovich [Chaliapin,
Fyodor], Author, 990, 1372, 1396,
1399; Singer, 9, 313, 347–48, 539–40,
756, 762, 776–82, 993, 1108, 1375.
Shaporin, Yu., 1321.
Shaverdyan, Aleksandr Isaakovich, 526, 1320.
Shebalin, B., 1321.

Indexes   317

Shelkov, N. V., 282.
Shelkova, N. V., 1455.
Shestakova, Lyudmila Ivanovna, Author, 1401;
    Correspondence, 210, 232, 279, 282;
    Other, 134, 148.
Shkafer, Vasily Petrovich, 364, 783, 1006.
Shlifshteyn, Semën Isaakovich, 404, 866.
Shpiller, Natal'ya Dmitrievna, 527, 784.
Shteynberg, A.
Shteynberg [Steinberg], Maksimilian
    Oseevich, Author, 196, 212, 247, 282,
    553, 866, 1301, 1341, 1357, 1388, 1402,
    1407, 1435; Composer, 18, 51, 72, 142,
    274, 869, 1301, 1492; Correspondence,
    282; Other, 10, 59.
Shtrup, Nikolay Martynovich, 8, 145, 277,
    427, 1454.
Shumskaya, N., 528.
Skaftymova, Lyudmila Aleksandrovna, 890.
Skatershchikov, V. K., 965.
Skrebkova, Ol'ga Leonidovna, 1489.
Skrynnikova, Ol'ga Anatol'evna, 738.
Skvirskaya, Tamara Zakirovna, 1522,
    1540–41.
Sletov, V., 772.
Slonimsky, Nicholas, 428, 1383.
Slonimsky, Sergey [Sergei] Mikhaylovich,
    1186, 1456.
Smirnov, Mstislav Anatol'evich,
    861–62, 873.
Smirnov, Valery Vasil'evich, 1082.
Smoje, Dujka, 939.
Sobolevskaya, Ol'ga, 582.
Sokolov, Nikolay Aleksandrovich, Author,
    1403; Composer, 42, 74–75, 104, 109,
    145; Other, 1384.
Sokolov, O., 405.
Sokolova, T., 375.
Sollertinsky, Ivan Ivanovich, 529.
Solov'ëv, Nikolay Feopemptovich, 645.
Solovtsov, Anatoly Aleksandrovich, 365, 462,
    468, 583, 810, 1187, 1190, 1381.
Solzhenikina, Valentina I., 1021.
Somov, Vladimir Aleksandrovich, 278.
Sorokina, E. G., 1322, 1342.
Soubies, Albert, 1323.
Stahl, Erik, 842.
Stanislavski, C., 366.
Stark, E. A., 757, 789.

Startsev, Ivan Ivanovich, 1545.
Stasov, D. V., 282
Stasov, Vladimir Vasil'evich, Author, 1, 8, 347,
    416, 506, 779, 819, 958, 1031, 1132,
    1193–94, 1211, 1324–35, 1327, 1376;
    Correspondence, 220-22, 282, 500,
    967, 1019, 1028, 1074; Relationship
    with Rimsky-Korsakov, 1075–79, 1222;
    Other, 140, 152, 159, 282.
Stasova, Varvara Dmitrievna [pseud.]: see
    Karenin, Vl.
Steane, John, 780.
Stein, Richard, 1094.
Steinberg, Maksimilian Oseevich: see
    Shteynberg, M. O.
Stepanov, L.
Stepanov, O. B., 1195.
Stepanova, Anna, 1022.
Stepanova, Elena Viktorovna, 995, 1321.
Stepantsevich, Kaleriya Iosifovna, 1247.
Stoffel, Lawrence, F., 1428.
Strasser, W., 1404.
Stravinsky, Fëdor Ignat'evich,
    Correspondence, 270; Singer, 4–6,
    757, 762, 788–89; Other, 152.
Stravinsky, Igor' Fëdorovich, Author, 1083;
    Composer, 531, 855, 949, 963, 970,
    1019, 1042, 1080–85, 1260, 1278, 1301,
    1328, 1366, 1394, 1432–33, 1439–40,
    1479, 1491–93; Correspondence, 274;
    Other, 4–6, 125, 329, 788.
Street, Donald, 1490.
Strel'nikov, Nikolay Mikhaylovich, 584,
    739, 863.
Stromenger, Karol, 1196.
Suttoni, Charles, 1047.
Swan, Alfred J., 1326, 1398.

T

Taneev, Sergey Ivanovich, Author, 1086–87;
    Composer, 958; Correspondence, 242,
    246, 250, 282; Other, 128.
Tartakov, Georgy Ioakimovich, 1405.
Taruskin, Richard, 367–68, 406–07, 414, 429,
    469, 481, 492, 530, 554–55, 585–86,
    611, 620, 637, 646, 687–88, 740, 837,
    940, 1084, 1327–29, 1491, 1512.
Taylor, Philip, 493.

Tchaikovsky, Pyotr Ilyich [Chaykovsky, Pëtr Il'ich], Author, 815, 834, 1088–89, 1123–24, 1332, 1338, 1349–50; Composer, 139, 283–84, 293, 312, 314, 334, 460, 484, 493, 652, 787, 856, 877, 891, 942, 958, 1090–94, 1156, 1363, 1424; Correspondence, 245, 251, 282, 1026, 1132; Other, 339, 869, 1384, 1451.

Telyakovsky, Vladimir Arkad'evich, 251, 1567.

Ter-Gevondyan, Anushavan Grigor'evich, 1406–07.

Teroganyan, M. I., 587.

Teterina, Nadezhda Ivanovna, 922.

Thompson, Pamela, 1542.

Threlfall, Robert, 949.

Tideböhl, Ellen von, 470, 689, 741–42.

Tiersot, Julien, 902, 1019.

Tigranov, Georgy Grigor'evich, 674, 1072, 1388, 1407, 1435.

Tkachev, Donat Vasil'evich, 1023.

Tolstoy, Count Aleksey Konstantinovich, 142–43, 145, 147, 150, 156.

Tolstoy, Feofil Matveevich [pseud. "Rostislav"], 832.

Tolstoy, Lev Nikolaevich, 305.

Toorn, Pieter C., Van den, 531, 1512.

Tovey, Sir Donald Francis, 838.

Trambitsky, Viktor Nikolaevich, 1358.

Traynin, Vladimir Yakovlevich, 1032.

Trevitt, John, 1494.

Trifonov, Porfiry Alekseevich, 1132, 1197.

Troeger, G., 1198.

Troitskaya, G., 1227.

Tsendrovsky, Vladimir Mikhaylovich, 287, 369, 371, 638, 1199, 1234, 1509.

Tsetlin (Zetlin), Mikhail Osipovich, 1207, 1330.

Tsuker, Anatoly Moiseevich, 556.

Tsukkerman, Viktor Abramovich, 300, 372, 532, 1248, 1495, 1500, 1510.

Tsvetkova, Anastasiya Nikolaevna, 746–47.

Tsypin, G. M., 755.

Tumanina, Nadezhda Vasil'evna, 1200.

Tumanov, Alexander, 771.

Tynson, Khel'ga Leopol'dovna, 1408.

Tyulin, Yury Nikolaevich, 567, 923, 1350, 1435, 1482.

Tyumenev, Il'ya Fëdorovich, Correspondence, 282; Diary, 1057, 1419; Librettist, 11, 15; Other, 157.

Tyumeneva, Galina Aleksandrovna, 1110.

Tyuneev, Boris Dmitrievich, 1365.

Tyut'manov, Il'ya Fëdorovich, 1496.

U

Uglov, Anton [pseud.]: see Kashintsev, D. A.

Uspenskaya, Sof'ya L'vovna, 1546, 1548–50.

Uvarova, I., 370, 373, 421, 533.

V

V-va, O., 494.

V. and M., 690.

V. M-y., 534.

V. V. [V. G. Val'ter?]: see Val'ter, Viktor Grigor'evich.

Vakhromeev, V., 272.

Val'ter, Viktor Grigor'evich, 691, 1201–02.

Van den Toorn, Pieter C.: see Toorn, Pieter C., Van den.

Van'kovich, G., 238.

Van'kovich-Gnesina, Mikhail Fabianovich, 1409.

Vanovskaya, Irina Nikolaevna, 833, 1501.

Vasil'ev, Vladimir, 885.

Vasil'ev, V. V., 282.

Vasil'eva, V. M., 278, 413, 908, 913, 1214, 1337, 1541.

Vasilenko, Sergey Nikiforovich, 1410–13.

Vasina, V. A.: see Vasina-Grossman, V. A.

Vasina-Grossman, Vera Andreevna, 900, 1061.

Vaynkop, Yulian Yakovlevich, 1203.

Velichko, Artem Tagievich, 430, 692.

Velimirović, Miloš, 263, 1024–25.

Veprik, Aleksandr Moiseevich, 941, 1359.

Vershinina, Inna, 1085.

Veynberg, Y. L., 281.

Vikhanskaya, Anna Moiseevna, 408, 560.

Vil'sker, S. M., 1435, 1543.

Vitachek, Faby Evgenevich, 1502.

Vitmer, A. N., 1415–16.

Vitols, I. I. [Vitols, Y. Y.?], 1341.

Vitols [Vītoliņš], Yakob Yanovich, Author, 590, 693, 1417–18; Composer, 42, 74, 104, 109.

Indexes 319

Vitols, Yazep [Vītols, Jāzeps]: see Vitols [Vītoliņš], Y. Y.

Vladimirov, V., 608.

Vladykina-Bachinskaya, Nina Mikhaylovna, 787, 1231.

Vlasova, E. S., 1342.

Volkov, Solomon, 942.

Vuillermoz, E., 852.

Vul'fius, Pavel Aleksandrovich, 1457.

W

Walker, Robert Matthew, 612.

Weaver, W., 409.

Weir, Justin, 743.

Weisser, Albert, 1458.

Werck, Isabelle, 854.

Wieczynski, Joseph L., 1163.

Wittig, Peter, 694.

Wolfurt, Kurt von, 943.

Worbs, Hans Christoph, 952.

Woronoff, Jon, 1288.

Wright, Craig, 1025.

Y

Yagolim, Boris Savel'evich, 1548, 1550–52.

Yakovlev, Vasily Vasil'evich, 374–75, 453, 815, 834, 917, 1062–63, 1089.

Yampol'sky, I. M., 1519.

Yankovsky, Moisey Osipovich, 252, 281, 781, 795, 1079, 1204, 1250, 1366, 1419, 1568.

Yarustovsky, Boris Mikhaylovich, 268, 376–77.

Yastrebtsëv, Vasily Vasil'evich, Archive, 6, 1016, 1019; Author, 8, 410, 613, 639, 919, 970, 996–97, 1019, 1100, 1205–06, 1221, 1258, 1368, 1421–22, 1544; Correspondence, 217–18, 225, 230; Other, 146.

Yazovitskaya, E. E., 282.

Yudin, Gavriil Yakovlevich, 282, 1212.

Z

Zarin' [Zarins], Marger Ottovich, 1459.

Zataevich, Aleksandr Viktorovich, 621, 647, 696.

Zetel, I., 695.

Zetlin, Michael: see Tsetlin (Zetlin), M. O.

Zhiganov, Nazib Gayazovich, 1569.

Zhilyaev, Nikolay Sergeevich, 744.

Zlatogorova, Bronislava Yakovlevna, 797.

Zolotarëv, Vasily Andreevich, 886, 1407, 1422.

Zorina, Angelina Petrovna, 282, 1331, 1460.

Index of Composers and Conductors

A

Abramychev, Nikolay Ivanovich, Archive, 105, Composer, 109.
Al'tani, Ippolit Karlovich, Conductor, 10.
Antipov, Konstantin Afanas'evich, 1384.
Arensky, Anton Stepanovich, 282, 1384.
Artsybushev [Artcibouscheff], Nikolay Vasil'evich, 34, 42, 74, 107, 282, 1019.

B

Balakirev, Mily Alekseevich, Author, 299, 416, 974–75, 1026; Balakirev Circle, 347, 964, 974, 1033, 1091, 1126, 1147, 1150, 1313; Composer, 28, 30, 88, 119, 123, 134, 136, 139, 169–70, 283–84, 856, 858, 958, 975, 1019, 1027, 1456; Conductor, 25–28, 54, 282, 819, 1325; Correspondence, 229, 233, 282, 299, 967, 1028, 1166; Imperial Chapel, 881, 883, 886, 1029, 1074, 1445; Other, 238, 282.
Balanchivadze, Meliton Antonovich, 1436.
Bartók, Béla, 1186.
Beethoven, Ludwig van, 125, 183, 830, 1384, 1494.
Berlioz, Hector, 185, 575, 830, 963, 1018, 1104, 1156, 1184, 1315, 1336, 1358, 1366.
Blumenfel'd, Feliks Mikhaylovich, Composer, 74, 109, 144, 146, 150, Conductor, 13, 16, 1108.
Blumenfel'd, Sigizmund Mikhaylovich, 146, 150.
Borodin, Aleksandr Porfir'evich, Author, 827; Balakirev Circle, 1033; Composer, 2, 27, 39, 66, 75, 95, 136, 161–65, 282–84, 412, 652, 826, 872, 903–10, 958, 975, 993, 1019, 1076, 1156, 1253, 1274, 1378–79, 1469; Correspondence, 216–17, 259, 282, 1132; Moguchaya Kuchka [Mighty Handful], 974, 1034, 1185.

Bortnyansky, Dmitry Stepanovich, 1445.

C

Chaykovsky, Pëtr Il'ich: see Tchaikovsky, P. I.
Cherepnin [Tcherepnin], Nikolay Nikolaevich, 282, 1373.
Chopin, Fryderyk Franciszek [Frédéric François], 15, 1102, 1232, 1495.
Cooper, Emil, Conductor, 19, 313, 602, 657, 1209, 1212.
Cui, César [Kyui, Tsezar' Antonovich], Author, 257, 396, 416, 422–23, 456, 515, 546, 558, 811, 817, 820–21, 829, 835, 840, 848, 853, 857, 864, 896, 1269, 1294; Composer, 2, 30, 95, 107, 137, 166, 193, 223, 253, 257, 281–82, 345, 412, 552, 799, 872, 1016, 1019, 1153, 1185, 1327, 1364, 1527.

D

Dargomyzhsky, Aleksandr Sergeevich, 167–68, 199, 211, 314, 510, 535, 552, 554, 799, 911–12, 958, 983, 1019, 1024, 1099–1100, 1156, 1346.
David, Félicien, 799.
Debussy, Claude, 965, 1035–36, 1186, 1366, 1494.
Dorati, Antal, Conductor, 710.

E

Esposito, Eugenio, Conductor, 8.
Eval'd, Viktor Vladimirovich, 74.

G

Glazunov, Aleksandr Konstantinovich, Archive, 69–70; Author, 1132, 1378–79, 1381, 1420, 1561; Composer, 33, 42, 49, 51, 66–67, 74–75, 104, 109, 142, 155,

Indexes

161, 163, 170, 284, 904–06, 909–10, 913, 937, 1019, 1038, 1040, 1049, 1115, 1222, 1290, 1377, 1402; Conductor, 28, 128; Correspondence, 38, 260, 282, 937, 1019, 1039, 1381, 1420, 1561.
Glinka, Mikhail Ivanovich, 59, 169–71, 184, 282–84, 314, 324, 329, 334, 360, 652, 717, 799, 805, 813, 842, 877, 913, 958, 961, 964, 967, 1005, 1041–44, 1105, 1156, 1224, 1248, 1315, 1324, 1351, 1445–46, 1475, 1489, 1526; Prizes, 1032.
Grechaninov, Aleksandr Tikhonovich, 282.

H

Handel, George Frideric, 172, 1445.

I

Ippolitov-Ivanov, Mikhail Mikhaylovich, Author, 937, 1367, 1384; Composer, 364, 1019, 1109; Conductor, 11, 12, 14, 364; Correspondence, 240, 282, 937, 967.

K

Kabalevsky, Dmitry Borisovich, Author, 330, 376, 663, 669.
Kalafati, Vasily Pavlovich, 41, 282.
Kalinnikov, Vasily Sergeevich, 219.
Kapp, Artur, 1436.
Kyui, Tsezar' Antonovich: see Cui, César.

L

Liszt, Franz, 54, 95, 488, 653, 737, 799, 830, 872, 1019, 1045–47, 1156, 1184, 1260, 1315, 1384, 1491.
Lyadov, Anatoly Konstantinovich, 32, 42, 66–67, 74–75, 86, 94–96, 104, 109, 144, 151, 169–70, 207, 231, 282, 812, 872, 1048–50, 1222, 1377, 1381.
Lysenko, Nikolay Vital'evich, 1106, 1237–38, 1435–36.

M

Mendelssohn, Felix, 186, 822.
Meyerbeer, Giacomo, 187–89.

Mozart, Wolfgang Amadeus, 537, 1105.
Musorgsky, Modest Petrovich, Composer, 1, 2, 30, 39, 125, 134, 138, 173–80, 194, 197, 203, 279, 314, 334, 404, 412, 914–55, 958, 973, 987, 993, 1019, 1051, 1053, 1057, 1062, 1156, 1224, 1228, 1239, 1265, 1292, 1369, 1379, 1469; Correspondence, 226, 228, 237, 282, 1052, 1054–56; Moguchaya Kuchka [Mighty Handful], 974.
Myaskovsky, Nikolay Yakovlevich, 866.

N

Nápravník, Eduard Franzevich, Author, 458; Composer, 192; Conductor, 1, 3–6, 416, 464, 1108.

P

Palestrina, Giovani Pierluigi da, 1445.
Prokof'ev [Prokofiev], Sergey Sergeevich, Author, 1391–92, 1407; Composer, 581, 855, 1515.

R

Rachmaninov, Sergey Vasil'evich: see Rakhmaninov, S. V.
Rakhmaninov [Rachmaninov], Sergey Vasil'evich, Author, 355, 1066, 1397; Composer, 355, 364, 552, 876, 890, 993, 1156, 1292, 1515; Conductor, 294, 355, 364, 514, 727, 1065, 1067; Correspondence, 355.
Ravel, Maurice, 1186, 1260, 1487.
Rubinstein [Rubinshteyn], Anton Grigor'evich, 64, 787, 822, 1069, 1363.
Rubinstein [Rubinshteyn], Nikolay [Nicolas] Grigor'evich, Composer, 64, 1068; Conductor, 350; Correspondence, 299.

S

Saminsky, Lazar' [Lazare] Semënovich, Conductor, 1304, 1458.
Schubert, Franz, 181, 190, 1491.
Schumann, Robert, 182, 813, 1384.
Serov, Aleksandr Nikolaevich, Author, 506, 818, 824–25, 958, 983; Composer, 799.

Shcherbachëv, Nikolay Vladimirovich, 95.
Shostakovich, Dmitry Dmitrievich, Composer, 855, 914, 928, 941, 944, 948, 1128, 1515; Memoirs, 942.
Shteynberg, Maksimilian Oseevich, Archive, 10, 59; Author, 196, 212, 247, 282, 553, 866, 1301, 1341, 1357, 1388, 1402, 1407, 1435; Composer, 18, 51, 72, 142, 274, 869, 1301, 1492; Correspondence, 282.
Skryabin [Scriabin], Aleksandr Nikolaevich, 1071.
Sokolov, Nikolay Aleksandrovich, Author, 1403; Composer, 42, 74–75, 104, 109, 145, 1384.
Spendiarov, Aleksandr Afanas'evich, 282, 1072–73, 1043.
Strauss, Richard, 426, 718, 964, 970, 1386.
Stravinsky, Igor' Fëdorovich, Author, 1083; Composer, 4–6, 125, 329, 531, 855, 949, 963, 970, 1019, 1042, 1080–85, 1260, 1278, 1301, 1328, 1366, 1394, 1432–33, 1439–40, 1479, 1491–93; Correspondence, 274.
Suk, Vyacheslav Ivanovich, Conductor, 15, 294, 313, 359, 514; Correspondence, 234, 236, 239.

T

Taneev, Sergey Ivanovich, Author, 1086–87; Composer, 128, 958; Correspondence, 242, 246, 250, 282.
Tchaikovsky, Pyotr Ilyich [Chaykovsky, Pëtr

Il'ich], Author, 815, 834, 1088–89, 1123–24, 1332, 1338, 1349–50; Composer, 139, 283–84, 293, 312, 314, 334, 339, 460, 484, 493, 652, 787, 856, 869, 877, 891, 942, 958, 1090–94, 1156, 1363, 1384, 1424, 1451; Correspondence, 245, 251, 282, 1026, 1132.
Tcherepnin, Nikolay Nikolaevich: see Cherepnin, N. N.
Truffi, Iosif, Conductor, 9.

V

Villa-Lobos, Heitor, 1107.
Vitols, I. I.: see Vitols, Yazep.
Vitols [Vītoliņš], Yakob Yanovich: see Vitols, Yazep.
Vitols, Yazep [Vītols, Jāzeps], Author, 590, 693, 1341, 1417; Composer, 42, 74, 104, 109, 1418.

W

Wagner, Richard, 191, 199, 211, 268, 360, 445, 448, 472, 478, 510, 614, 664, 682–83, 751, 763, 964, 967, 973, 983, 1095–1100, 1145, 1156, 1184, 1291, 1315, 1346, 1362, 1562.

Z

Zolotarëv, Vasily Andreevich, Author, 886, 1407, 1422.

Index of Names

A

Antokol'sky, Mark Matveyevich, 1399, 1513.
Auer, Leopol'd, 62.

B

Bainton, George, 1019.
Barsova, Valeriya Vladimirovna, 758.
Beecham, Sir Joseph, 347, 400.
Belaieff, M. P.: see Belyaev, M. P.
Bel'skaya, Agrippina K., 275.
Belyaev, Mitrofan Petrovich, Archive, 11, 278;
  Belyaev Circle, 868, 1030, 1032, 1038,
  1144, 1170, 1299; Concerts, 1032,
  1039; Correspondence, 238, 299, 904;
  Publisher, 41, 47, 66–67, 74, 898, 1031,
  1270, 1325, 1341.
Bessel', Vasily Vasil'evich, 1, 4, 10, 13–15, 25,
  30, 32, 40, 46, 85, 89–91, 107, 114, 121,
  194, 197, 203, 281, 285, 317, 383, 443,
  1016, 1072, 1132, 1233, 1262.
Bilibin, Ivan Yakovlevich, 318.
Bocharov, Mikhail Vasil'evich, 318.
Borodina, Ekaterina Sergeevna, 139.
Büttner, A., 93–95, 118–19, 124–25, 140–42.

C

Chaliapin, Fyodor, I.: see Shalyapin, Fëdor
  Ivanovich.
Chesnokov, A. G., 267.
Chuprynnikov, Mitrofan Mikhaylovich, 153.
Cui, Malvina Rafailovna: see Kyui, M. R.

D

Davydov, Karl, 62.
Derzhinskaya, Kseniya Georgievna, 756, 759.

E

Egorov, Aleksandr, 62.

Ershov, Ivan Vasil'evich, 313, 756–57, 760–63,
  765, 1006.
Eykhenval'd, Margarita Aleksandrovna
  [Eichenwald, Margaret], 764.

F

Fedorovsky, Fëdor Fëdorovich, stage designer,
  998.
Ficino, Marsilio, 517.

G

Gabel', Stanislav Ivanovich, 148.
Gleason, F. G., 1019.
Golovin, Aleksandr Yakovlevich, 318, 998.

I

Il'insky, Vladimir Nikanorovich, 141–42.
Iogansen, Avgust Reyngol'dovich, 27, 82,
  136–38.
Ivanov, Vyacheslav Ivanovich, 517.

K

Kandinsky, Vasily Vasil'evich, 1071.
Komarova, Varvara Dmitrievna, 147.
Korovin, Konstantin Alekseyevich, 364, 505,
  998.
Kuhn, Ernst, Author, 1155, 1480; Publisher,
  412, 463–65, 798, 813, 1340, 1343–47,
  1364, 1480.
Kuznetsov, Aleksandr Vasil'evich, 62.
Kyui, Malvina Rafailovna, 134.

L

Lamm, Pavel [Paul], 921, 932, 950.
Levenson, Berka Leibovich, 263.
Levik, Sergey Yur'evich, 765.
Lunacharsky, Mikhail Vasil'evich, 154.

M

Maksakova, Mariya Petrovna, 766.
Maslennikova, Irina Ivanovna, 767.
Matorin, Vladimir Anatol'evich, 318.
Mercy-Argenteau, Countess Louise de, 1047.
Molas [née Purgol'd], Aleksandra Nikolaevna, 139, 1016, 1369.
Mysovskaya, Anna Dmitrievna, 460.

N

Nezhdanova, Antonina Vasil'evna, 294, 314, 756, 762, 765, 768–69.
Nikol'sky, Fëdor Kalinovich, 1.

O

Obukhova, Nadezhda Andreevna, 756; Literary Works, 770, 1321.
Olenina-d'Alheim, Maria, 771.
Ozerov, Nikolay Nikolaevich, 772.

P

Panteleev, Maksim Petrovich, 773.
Pikkel', I., 62.
Plato, 517.
Purgol'd, Aleksandra Nikolaevna: see Molas, A. N.
Purgol'd, Fëdor Nikolaevich, 140, 1016.

R

Rahter, Daniel, 3.
Repin, Il'ya Yefimovich, 532, 1178, 1369, 1399, 1513.
Reyzen, Mark Osipovich, 774.
Rimsky-Korsakov, Georgy Mikhailovich, 1303.
Rimskaya-Korsakova, Mariya [Masha] Fëdorovna, 138.
Rimskaya-Korsakova, Sofiya [Sonya] Nikolaevna, 14, 144.
Rozhdestvenskaya, Natal'ya Petrovna, 775.
Rubinstein, Aaron, 64.

S

Samus', Vasily Maksimovich, 148.
Serov, Valentin Aleksandrovich, 364, 1369, 1513.

Shalyapin, Fëdor Ivanovich [Chaliapin, Fyodor], Author, 990, 1372, 1396, 1399; Singer, 9, 313, 347–48, 539–40, 756, 762, 776–82, 993, 1108, 1375.
Shestakova, Lyudmila Ivanovna, 148.
Shishkov, Vyacheslav Yakovlevich, 318.
Shkafer, Vasily Petrovich, 364, 783, 1006.
Shpiller, Natal'ya Dmitrievna, 527, 784.
Shtrup, Nikolay Martynovich, Author, 427; Correspondence, 277; Composer, 8, 145; Other, 1454.
Shvarts, Evgeny L'vovich, 1399.
Sobinov, Leonid Vital'evich, 294, 313, 756–57, 762, 785–87, 1375.
Solov'ëv, Konstantin Nikolaevich, 123.
Stravinsky, Fëdor Ignat'evich, 4–6, 152, 270, 757, 762, 788–89.

T

Tchaikovsky, Modest, 1351.
Telyakovsky, Vladimir Arkad'evich, 251, 1567.
Tiersot, J., 1019.

V

Vasnetsov, Viktor Mikhaylovich, 318, 364, 532, 986, 998, 1399.
Veykman, Ieronim, 62.
Vrubel', Mikhail Aleksandrovich, Artist, 318, 364, 790, 794, 986; Correspondence 265; Other, 158.

Y

Yurgenson [Jurgenson], Boris Petrovich, Correspondence, 1527; Publisher, 51.
Yurgenson [Jurgenson], Pëtr Ivanovich, Correspondence, 1527; Publisher, 19, 28, 51, 61, 123, 127, 139, 160, 281, 304, 718, 1206, 1289.

Z

Zabela [Zabela-Vrubel'], Nadezhda Ivanovna, 153, 158, 315, 339, 756, 790–96, 1006, 1019, 1375, 1381.
Zherebtsova-Evreinova, Anna Grigor'evna, 144.
Zlatogorova, Bronislava Yakovlevna, 797.

Index of N. A. Rimsky-Korsakov, Life and Creativity

Professional and Domestic Life

A

Adjudicator, 253.

C

Censorship, 358, 391.
Conductor, 1211, 1413.

E

Editorial Work, 902; Compositions by Borodin, 903–10; Dargomyzhsky, 911-12; Glinka, 913; Musorgsky, 914-55.

F

Family, 276, 1213–21, 1415.
Film, 1222–27, 1296.

I

Imperial Chapel, 886, 1403, 1445, 1450.

N

Naval Bands, 1426–28, 1444, 1455.

P

Portraits, Repin, 1513; Serov, 1513; Engraving, 1404, 1513.

R

Revolution of 1905, 1178; Dismissal from Conservatory, 1554–68.

S

Self-criticism, 799, 1251.

Sense of Humor, 257, 730, 990.
Synesthesia [color and sound], 297, 301, 969, 992, 996.

T

Teaching, 242, 1303, 1384, 1390, 1402–03, 1424, 1429–60, 1501.

W

Working Habits, 285, 296, 321, Notebooks, 1004, 1404; Creative process, 1484.

Esthetic Credo

L

Love of Nature, 218.

M

Morals and Politics, 218, 252, 307.
Musical Polemics, 1290.

N

Narodnost' [populism], 959, 977.

P

Personality, Psychological Make-up, 284–85, 290, 1267, 1378, 1389–90, 1401, 1406, 1411.
Philosophical Elements, 331, 956–97, 1327, 1389, 1506.

Musical style

A

Anhemitonic Melodies, 1466.

326　　　　　　　　　　　　　　　　　　　　　　　　　　　　　　　*Indexes*

D

Double Harmonic Scales, 1470–74, 1475.

E

Exoticism, 1498, 1504.

I

Innovation, 634.

K

Key Relationships, 1476.

L

Leitmotifs, 324, 351, 449, 405.

O

Orchestral, 371, 1499–1500, 1502.
Orchestral Innovation, 476.

R

Rhythmic Elements, 1477, 1479.

S

Scene Painting, 976, 1268–69, 1272, 1276,
　　1289, 1291, 1461–1512.
Sonata Form, 1480, 1482, 1509.

T

Theme Transformation, 400, 446.

U

Use of Contrapuntal elements, 353.

V

Variation Technique, 292, 352.

Harmony

C

Chromatic Harmony, 1464, 1495, 1467.
Clarinet, 1425.

H

Harmonic Variation, 1489.
Harmony in Late Works, 737.

M

Modal Harmony, 1468–69.
Modes of Limited Transposition, 490.

O

Octatonicism, 531, 1260, 1463, 1478,
　　1491–94, 1497.

T

Tonality, 1485–86.
Tonal Symbolism, 298.

U

Use of *Byliny* Material, 519.

W

Whole Tone Scale, 1452.

Opera

A

Apocalyptic Elements, 686.

C

Choice of Language, 344.
Comparison of Rimsky-Korsakov's and
　　Tchaikovsky's Operas, 293.
Costumes, Décor, 318.
Creative Principles, 343.

E

Elements of Fantasy, 336.

I

Ideological Content of Late Operas, 247, 296,
　　319, 330.
Ideological Significance of Operas, 406.

Indexes 327

M

Mamontov, Savva Ivanovich, Biography, 288; Correspondence, 281, 1016, 1527; Entrepreneur, 288–89, 1180; Moscow Private Russian Opera, 364, 374–75.
Mozart and Salieri, New materials, 542; London, Spectacular performance, 543.

P

Pantheistic and Christian Elements in Operas, 54, 363, 490, 636, 666–67, 674.
Philosophical Concept and Principles of Poetics, 337.
Portrayal of Women, 702.

R

Reception of Operas, in Prague, 427; in England, 1363.
Russian Operatic Realism and Folk Allegory, Relationship between, 367.

S

Sadko and the Myth of Orpheus, 517.
Socio-political Significance of Last Operas, 365.
Structural Devices, 314.
Symbolist Movement, Influence of, 675.

U

Use of Mass Scenes, 295.

Folk Music

E

Employment of Ukrainian Elements, 1237.

F

Folk Elements in *Antar* and *Spanish Caprice*, 1236.
Folk Music Elements in *Sadko* and *The Tale of Tsar Saltan*, 1241.
Folk Song Sources used in *The Snow Maiden*, 447.
Folk Sources of *Kitezh*, 671.

G

Genres of Russian Folk Song in Rimsky-Korsakov's operas, 1247.

I

Importance of Folk Song in Rimsky-Korsakov's Music, 396.
Influence of Folk Elements in Rimsky-Korsakov's Melodies, Part-writing and Harmony, 1246.
Influence of Glinka's Orchestral Fantasy *Kamarinskaya* on Rimsky-Korsakov, 1248.

N

Names of Folk Songs Employed by Rimsky-Korsakov, 1231.
National Elements in Rimsky-Korsakov's Music, 1244.

P

Psychological Influence of Traditional Elements on Rimsky-Korsakov's Musical Style, 1503.

R

Relationship between Russian Composers and Folk Music, 1230.
Rimsky-Korsakov and Polish Melodies, 1232.
Rimsky-Korsakov's Approach Towards Folk Song, 1228.
Rimsky-Korsakov's Attitude Towards Russian Folk Song, 1511.
Rimsky-Korsakov's Treatment of Russian Folk Songs, 1234.
Rimsky-Korsakov's Writings on Russian Folk Song, 1235.
Role of *Narodnost'* [Populism] and Folk Elements in the Work of Rimsky-Korsakov, 1245.
Russian Folk Song in the Works of Rimsky-Korsakov, 1242–43, 1249.

S

Slavic Elements in Rimsky-Korsakov's Work, 1229.

Sources of Rimsky-Korsakov's Opera *Sadko*, 1250.
Stylistic Features of Rimsky-Korsakov's Arrangements of Russian Folk Songs, 1240.

T

T. I. Filippov, Folk Song Collector, and Rimsky-Korsakov, 1239.

U

Ukrainian Folk Songs Provided by Lysenko, 1238.
Use of Arab Melodies in Rimsky-Korsakov's Work, 826.
Use of Folk Ritual in *May* Night, 430.

Sacred music

R

Rimsky-Korsakov's Perception of Russian Sacred Music, 252, 532, 878–79.

General

E

Employment of Old Russian Literature, 658.

F

France, 254, 1264, 1284, 1293.

I

Influence on Greek Music, 1481.

M

Marxist-Leninism, 537, 725.

P

Poland, 644, 1232.

Memoirs of Rimsky-Korsakov

A

Asaf'ev, B. V., 1374.

B

Brounoff, P., 1371.

C

Chaliapin, F. I., 1372.
Cherepnin, N. N., 1373.

D

Durylin, S. N., 1375.

F

Fortunato, S. V., 1376.

G

Galkauskas, K. M., 1377, 1407.
Glazunov, A. K., 1378–79.
Gnesin, M. F., 1380, 1407, 1409.
Gol'denveyzer, A. B., 1370, 1382.
Gretchaninoff, A., 1383.

I

Ippolitov-Ivanov, M. M., 1384.

M

Mal'ko, N. A., 1385.
Morozova, M. K., 1386.

N

Newmarch, R., 1387.

O

Ossovsky, A. V., 1389.

P

Pokhitonov, D. I., 1390.
Prokof'ev, S. S., 1391–92, 1407.

R

Riesemann, O. von, 1397.
Rimsky-Korsakov, M. N., 1393.
Rimsky-Korsakov, M. N. and Kopytova, G. V., 1396.

Indexes

329

Rimsky-Korsakov, V. N., 1394–95.

S

Sandulenko, A., 1398.
Shalyapin, F. I., 1399–1400.
Shestakova, L. I., 1401.
Shteynberg, M. O., 1388, 1402, 1407.
Sokolov, N. A., 1403.
Strasser, W., 1404.

T

Tartakov, G. I., 1405.
Ter-Gevondyan, A. G., 1406–07.

Tyumenev, I. F., 1419.

V

Vasilenko, S. N., 1410–12.
Veysberg, Yu. L., 1414.
Vitmer, A. N., 1415.
Vitols [Vītoliņš], Ya., 1417–18.

Z

Zhitomirsky, D. V., 1381.
Zolotarëv, V. A., 1407, 1424.

Subject Index

A

Archives, 1005, 1007, 1009, 1012–14, 1016, 1019–20, 1023–24, 1419–23, 1514–15, 1516–17, 1518–24, 1526–27, 1528, 1530–36, 1539–69.

B

Balakirev Circle, 347, 964, 974, 1033, 1091, 1126, 1147, 1150, 1313.
Ballets Russes, 993.
Belyaev Circle, 868, 1030, 1032, 1038, 1144, 1170, 1299; see also Belyaev, M. P.

C

Card Catalogue, Music Library, St. Petersburg State Conservatory, 1521.

F

Free Music School, Concerts, 25, 54, 210, 282, 811, 827; Other, 1442, 1444–1445.

I

Imperial Russian Music Society, Competitions, 121, 124, 1527; Concerts, 28, 30, 33–34, 129, 812, 818, 824, 827, 1319, 1523; Correspondence, 210, 282; Library, 1533; Other, 282, 1193, 1565, 1325, 1566.

M

Moguchaya Kuchka [Mighty Handful], 771, 804, 819, 861, 873, 974, 1006, 1028–29, 1034, 1045, 1047, 1088, 1147, 1150, 1185, 1235, 1237, 1282, 1286–87, 1331, 1469.
Museums, Lyubensk, 1021; Rimsky-Korsakov Memorial Apartment Museum, St. Petersburg, 1001–02, 1017–18; State Memorial House Museum, Tikhvin, 999–1000, 1003, 1010, 1015, 1022; Vechasha, 1021.